DISCOVERING
ANTHROPOLOGY

gap and of neocolonialism in maintaining it, and discusses several theories of underdevelopment. Chapter 20, Urban and Industrial Culture, explores the dominant settlement pattern of many if not most of the countries in the world today, considering how people adapt effectively to the special conditions of urban living, how industrialism affects people's lives, and what role the environmentalist movement plays in society. Chapter 21, Health, Disease, and Culture, presents the basics of medical anthropology, identifying cultural components in the recognition, categorization, and treatment of illness. It discusses the culturally prescribed actions and attitudes of practitioners and patients, the role of the social support system in healing, and pluralism in medical choices. The three chapters that make up Part Seven are unusual in an introductory anthropology text, as is Chapter 3 on cultural meanings; I believe that it is important to give expanded coverage to these areas of current interest and concern.

Part Eight, Expression in Society, is concerned with how individual impulses, aspirations, and traits are shaped and channeled by society into religious, artistic, or other forms. Chapter 22, Religion and Social Structure, looks at some of the elements of religious experience and practice and considers theories about the relationship of religion to its social context. Chapter 23, Art and Culture, explores the different roles art and artists play in different societies as well as the relationship of art to social organization and complexity. Chapter 24, Society and the Individual, examines the relationship between personality and culture, looks at the question of cultural personality, and considers several theories of personality formation and organization.

FEATURES AND LEARNING AIDS

The features and learning aids incorporated in the book are designed to support the aims and approach I have outlined here. Primary among these are the 23 essays called "Anthropologists at Work," which appear at the end of every chapter beginning with Chapter 2. These essays, which were commissioned especially for this book, provide a rich sampler of anthropological pursuits, interests, and methods. Tied

in with the chapters they follow, they allow students to hear first-hand accounts of research and field work in a variety of voices and to encounter different points of view.

A feature called "Get Involved," appearing at the end of chapters, invites students to participate in anthropology themselves through projects and exercises related to the chapter content. For example, students are asked to do a time-allocation study among a small sample of people they know; investigate an ecosystem in their area; survey the forms of nonmarket exchange that occur in their community; make a kinship chart for a variety of television families and consider what trends are reflected in their structures; and select a series of films or novels depicting the colonial experience in a particular country and analyze them for clues about colonial relationships. The "Get Involved" items include both individual and group projects.

Boxed material reinforces the student's sense of anthropology's diversity and vitality. Ranging from theoretical to anecdotal, the boxes cover topics of special interest, research findings, historical background, and personal experiences.

Many other learning aids help students organize, learn, and remember the material presented in the book. Each part begins with a brief introduction explaining how the following chapters relate to the overall field of anthropology and fit into the scheme of the book. Each chapter in turn opens with an outline to further orient the student, along with a color image capturing some aspect of the chapter material. Within the chapter, important terms appear in bold type and are defined at the bottom of the page in a comprehensive running glossary. At the ends of chapters, in addition to the "Anthropologists at Work" essays and the "Get Involved" projects, there are chapter summaries and listings of suggested readings for students, and at the end of the book there is an extensive bibliography. A gallery of maps helps students locate the areas and peoples described in the text.

SUPPLEMENTARY MATERIAL

Available with *Discovering Anthropology* is a complete package of supplementary materials to enhance both teaching and learning.

The *Instructor's Manual* includes a test bank of more than 1,000 questions, as well as topics for class discussions, a list of recommended films and their sources for use in the classroom, and transparency masters for use in teaching.

The *Study Guide,* prepared by Ester Maring of Southern Illinois University, Carbondale, contains for each of the 24 chapters learning objectives, chapter overviews and outlines, key terms and definitions, review questions (multiple-choice, fill-in, and true/false), and study questions, which may also be used as essay questions.

The *Computerized Test Bank* is a powerful, easy-to-use test generation system that provides all test items on computer disk for IBM-compatible, Apple, and Macintosh computers. Instructors can select, add, or edit questions, randomize them, and print tests appropriate for their individual classes. The system also includes a convenient "gradebook" that enables the instructor to keep detailed performance records for individual students and for the entire class; maintain student averages; graph each student's progress; and set the desired grade distribution, maximum score, and weight for every test.

ACKNOWLEDGMENTS

This book was by no means a solitary undertaking. I had help from many, many people in ways too numerous to mention. I must first thank my wife, Silêde, and my children, Sylvia and Tony, for their encouragement, for their hundreds of hours of tedious, unpaid labor, and above all for their patience when I was too busy for other things because I was working on this book.

For their help with the manuscript I owe special thanks to Steven Austin, who worked tirelessly in bringing together thousands of details for the final version; Janice Molina, who carefully reviewed the final draft; Michael Park, who reworked the chapter on evolution; Nancy Flowers, who provided constructive criticism; and Clark Baxter, who planted the seed that grew into this book.

I must give special mention to two lifelong friends and role models: Conrad Kottak, who first encouraged me to study anthropology and guided me at key

points in my career, and Douglas Rumble, who over our long friendship has served as an example of dedication to science. Encouragement and guidance have also come from Stuart Culbertson, Armando Souto Maior, and Michael Cernea; from my college professors Karl J. Weintraub and Dudley Shapere; from Marvin Harris, who gave me the theoretical perspective that has guided me throughout my career; from Charles Wagley, who introduced me to Brazil; from the late Morton Fried and Robert F. Murphy; and from Harvey Pitkin, Eliott Skinner, and Pete Vayda. I also want to thank the Wednesday group and the gang at High Noon for their fellowship and understanding.

In addition, I owe an incalculable debt to many colleagues, from whom I learned much of what is in these pages: Antonio Augusto Arantes Neto, Daniel Bates, Clifford Behrens, Celso Bianco, Stanley Brandes, the late Lucile Brockway, Diana Brown, Stephen Brush, Roberto Cardoso de Oliveira, Jean-Luc Chodkiewicz, Gentil Martins Dias, Muriel Dimen, Carol Ember, Melvin Ember, Kenneth Erickson, Bela Feldman Bianco, Kaja Finkler, Shepard Forman, Thomas Gregor, Scott Guggenheim, David Guillet, Allen Johnson, Gregory Johnson, Susan Lees, Maxine Margolis, Barbara D. Miller, George Morren, Roberto Motta, Burton Pasternak, Stuart Plattner, Sonia Ramagem, Alcida Ramos, Gustavo Lins Ribeiro, Madeline Ritter, Paul Shankman, Judith Shapiro, Ligia Simonian, Christopher Tavener, Kenneth Taylor, Xavier Totti, Dennis Werner, Klaas Woortmann, John Yellen, and John Zarur.

I am grateful to the many contributors who provided fascinating samples of their work for the "Anthropologists at Work" sections; their names appear on their essays. I also want to thank the anonymous reviewers as well as the following academic reviewers, whose ideas helped to shape the book. I deeply appreciate their advice, even though I was not always able to follow it.

Peter J. Brown, Emory University
James Calcagno, Loyola University of Chicago
Carolyn Ehardt, University of Georgia
Rick Flores, St. Cloud State University
James Green, University of Washington
Edward Jay, Californinia State University, Hayward
James Kiriazis, Youngstown State University
Holly Mathews, East Carolina University

James Mielke, University of Kansas
Keith Morton, California State University, Northridge
Michael Park, Central Connecticut State University
Rebecca Storey, University of Houston
Donald E. Tyler, University of Idaho

Finally, I am grateful to the staff of Mayfield Publishing Company, especially Janet Beatty, senior editor, for her sound judgment, unfailing encouragement, and incredible organizational ability; Kate Engelberg, developmental editor, for her ability to bring order out of confusion; Linda Toy, director of production, for her skilled management of the production process; and Loralee Windsor, copy editor, for her excellent editing. To all I offer my heartfelt thanks.

CONTENTS

▲▲▲

To Silêde, Sylvia, and Anthony
with love and devotion

Bering Strait

Arctic
Ocean

Inuit

Inuit

Inuit

Inuit

Haida

Kwakiutl

Newfoundland

Seattle
Marmes

Chippewa

Oneida
Onondaga
Seneca
Huron

Pine Ridge
(Sioux Reservation)

Muscongus Bay
Mohawk

Crow

Detroit

New York City

Shoshone

Cheyenne

Cayuga

Omaha

Three-Mile Island

Hopi

Navaho

Pueblo

Cherokee

Cibecue Apache

Atlantic
Ocean

San Juan

Pacific
Ocean

Mixtec

Teotihuacan

Tenochtitlán, Aztec Empire

Yucatan

Tepoztlan &

Tehuacan Valley

Netzahualcoyotl Izcalli

Maya

Olmec Empire
Chiapas

Caribbean Sea

Guatemala City

**Cultural and Prehistoric Sites
in North America**

Caribbean Sea

Atlantic Ocean

● Jonestown

Azuero Peninsula

● Yanomamo

Tukano ●

Galapagos
Islands

Jívaro ●

Mundurucu ●

Mekranoti-Kayapó ●

● Tapirapé

● Kanela

Shipibo ●

Nambikwara ●

● Xavante

Lima ●

● Mehinaku

Cuzco, Inca Empire ●

Machiguenga ●
Aymara

Qolla ●

● Suyá

Bom Jesus
da Lapa ●

Tiahuanaco ●

Bororo ●

● Rio de Janeiro

Pacific Ocean

● Guarani

Yahgan ●

**Cultural and Prehistoric Sites
in South America**

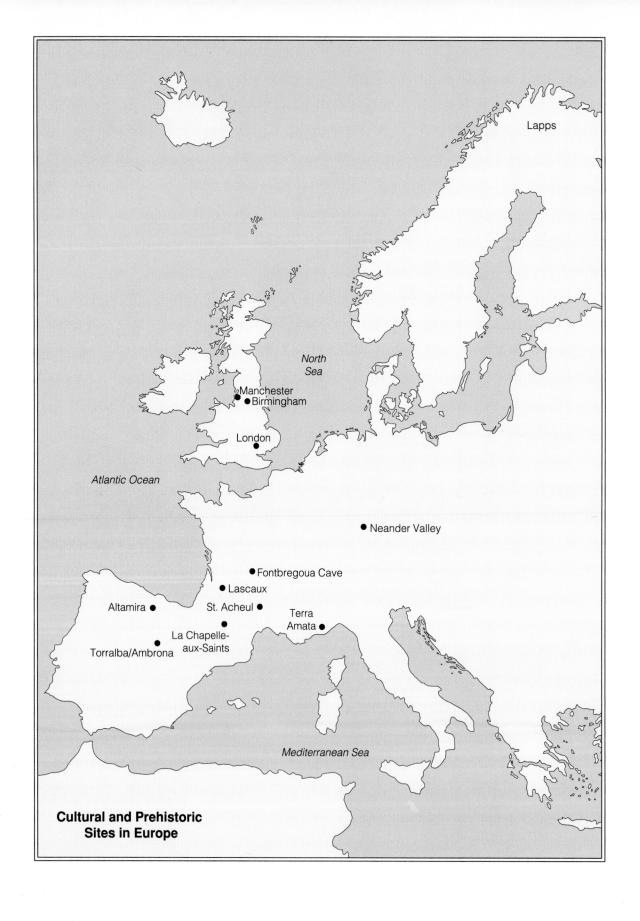

Lapps

North
Sea

Manchester
● Birmingham

London

Atlantic Ocean

● Neander Valley

● Fontbregoua Cave

● Lascaux

Altamira ●   St. Acheul ●

Terra
Amata ●

La Chapelle-
aux-Saints

Torralba/Ambrona

Mediterranean Sea

**Cultural and Prehistoric
Sites in Europe**

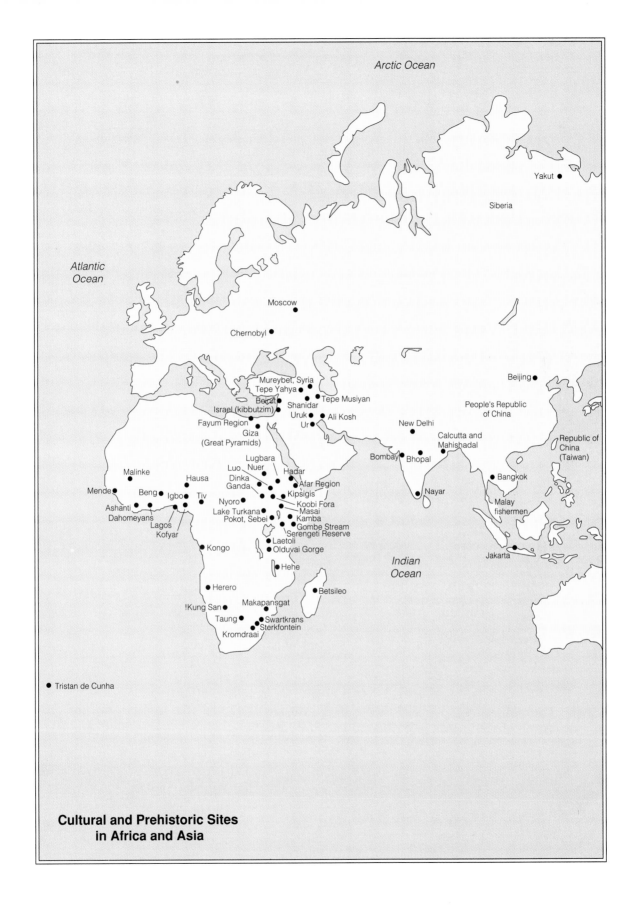

Arctic Ocean

Yakut ●

Siberia

Atlantic
Ocean

Moscow ●

Chernobyl ●

Beijing ●

Mureybet, Syria
Tepe Yahya ●
Beirut ● ● Tepe Musiyan
Shanidar ●
Israel (kibbutzim) ● Uruk ● ● Ali Kosh
Ur ●
Fayum Region ●
Giza
(Great Pyramids)

People's Republic
of China

New Delhi ●

Calcutta and
Mahishadal ●

Republic of
China
(Taiwan)

Lugbara
Luo ● Nuer
Dinka ● Hadar
Ganda ● Afar Region
Kipsigis ●
Koobi Fora
Masai
Kamba
Gombe Stream
Serengeti Reserve

Malinke ●

Hausa ●

Mende ●
Beng ● Igbo ● Tiv ●
Ashanti ●
Dahomeyans ●
Lagos ●
Kofyar ●

Nyoro ●
Lake Turkana
Pokot, Sebei

Bombay ● ● Bhopal

Bangkok ●

Malay
fishermen

Nayar ●

Kongo ●

Laetoli ●
Olduvai Gorge ●

Hehe ●

Jakarta ●

Indian
Ocean

Herero ●

Betsileo ●

Makapansgat ●

!Kung San ●
Taung ●
Swartkrans ●
Sterkfontein ●
Kromdraai ●

● Tristan de Cunha

**Cultural and Prehistoric Sites
in Africa and Asia**

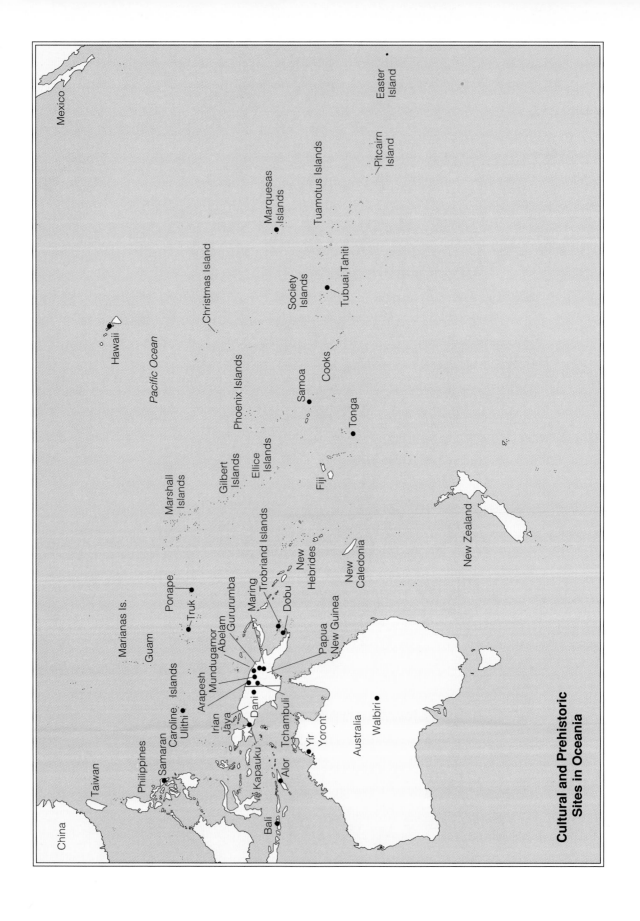

**Cultural and Prehistoric
Sites in Oceania**

China

Taiwan

Philippines

Mexico

Marianas Is.

Guam

Caroline Islands

Samaran

Ulithi

Bali

Kapauku

Alor

Irian
Jaya

Arapesh

Mundugamor

Gururumba

Abelam

Dani

Tchambuli

Yir
Yoront

Maring

Trobriand Islands

Dobu

Papua
New Guinea

Ponape

Truk

Pacific Ocean

Hawaii

Marshall
Islands

Gilbert
Islands

Ellice
Islands

Christmas Island

Phoenix Islands

Marquesas
Islands

Tuamotus Islands

Pitcairn
Island

Easter
Island

Society
Islands

Tubuai,Tahiti

Cooks

Samoa

Tonga

Fiji

New
Hebrides

New
Caledonia

New Zealand

Australia

Walbiri

DISCOVERING ANTHROPOLOGY

WHAT IS ANTHROPOLOGY?

As a student new to the field, you may be wondering exactly what anthropology is and what anthropologists do. In simple terms, anthropology may be defined as the study of humanity in all its diversity, both cultural and biological, seen against the backdrop of a universally shared human nature. It is a study with the broadest possible historical and geographical scope, embracing the behaviors and practices of humanity from prehistoric times to the present and across the entire inhabited globe.

Part One of this book offers an invitation and an orientation to anthropology. Chapter 1 shows how the various subfields of anthropology, including biological anthropology, archaeology, linguistics, ethnology, and many others, are tied together by their interest in the human species. The first chapter also presents close-up views of anthropologists doing research. (These close-ups continue throughout the book in sections called "Anthropologists at Work.") Chapter 2 focuses on anthropology as a science. It shows how anthropologists ensure the validity of their work by using scientific methods—formulating hypotheses, making observations, collecting data, and performing experiments.

One of the most lasting rewards of studying anthropology can be an expansion of your personal horizons. When we shine a bright light on the culture of a people unfamiliar to us, it often reflects back and illuminates our own culture. We find that some of our customs and habits—the way we define male and female roles, for example, or select leaders, or diagnose and treat illness—are not as universal as we would have expected. We begin to see them as "products of culture" in the same way we see the practices of the people we're studying. On the other hand, some behaviors turn out to be present in all human societies, and we realize that these are more or less biologically determined for our species.

From knowledge like this we begin to gain perspective on our own lives and society and to liberate ourselves from culture-bound views. We find that we are capable of transcending the limits of a single point of view and seeing the broader patterns of human existence. We become able to evaluate our own social and cultural traditions and perhaps even attempt to change some of them. In this sense the process of discovering anthropology can also be a journey of self-discovery. Part One of Discovering Anthropology takes you on the first steps of this journey.

This Kathakali dancer from India wears striking face paint and ornaments to create an illusion. Anthropologists study people in all their aspects—from the mundane to the extraordinary.

STUDYING PEOPLE
The Work of Anthropology

▲▲▲

he 1984 film *Raiders of the Lost Ark* gave the public a swashbuckling image of an anthropologist in the character Indiana Jones, played by Harrison Ford (Figure 1.1). Millions of moviegoers watched enthralled as Indiana outwitted and outfought villains in pursuit of an ancient relic. The film reinforced a popular view of anthropologists as fieldworkers making dramatic discoveries of lost cities and fabulous treasures at archaeological "digs." Another popular image is that of Margaret Mead (see Figure 1.1), probably the most famous anthropologist of the 20th century. Mead was often photographed among the people of New Guinea and Samoa where she did field research.

These images represent just two of the many facets of anthropology and barely hint at the diversity of the field. Anthropologists work on every continent; in cities, towns, and countryside; in hot climates and cold. To do their work anthropologists may ride camels, sleep in tents, endure loneliness and rejection in alien cultures, engage in delicate diplomacy, or learn exotic languages. Closer to home they may also spend endless hours doing painstaking work in offices and libraries, at computer terminals and drawing boards.

The common thread that ties anthropology together is a focus on the human species. Simply put, anthropology is the **holistic** study of humankind viewed across space and time. It is holistic because it embraces all of the aspects of humans that can be studied. Anthropology gives equal importance to the biological and nonbiological aspects of human existence. It is a young science, first recognized toward the end of the 19th century. It is usually considered to be a **social science**, but it has important links to the life sciences and the humanities as well. Anthropology encompasses human biology and human evolution. It

Figure 1.1 *Popular images of anthropologists: Indiana Jones, intrepid archaeologist, and Margaret Mead, famous chronicler of Samoan lifeways. The work of anthropology encompasses much more than is suggested by these images.*

is tied to the humanities by its emphasis on culture, history, meaning, and values. Its reliance on quantitative methods and physical, chemical, and biochemical measurement techniques gives it a relationship to the physical sciences. The focus that unites anthropology as a field is humankind—its past, present, and future.

Anthropologists are particularly concerned with **human variation** (Figure 1.2). The world is as complex as it is largely because of the immense differences among people. These differences can be physical, mental, social, or cultural; they can involve genetic differences, physical traits, habits, customs, attitudes, beliefs, or capabilities. Anthropology decodes these differences, seeking to understand how they came to be and why people think and act as they do. Anthropology also emphasizes basic human similarities—the continuities in form, behavior, and thought that bind human populations together across space and time. There are some universals in human affairs, but often the similarities are hard to see through a dazzling diversity of appearances. Anthropologists seek to understand both the differences and the similarities.

It is an understatement to say that the goals of anthropology are extremely ambitious. Do not get discouraged if you find there are no certain answers to some questions. For example, after years of accumulating data from thousands of sites, anthropologists still do not know precisely when humans first entered the New World.

Anthropology involves so many types of knowledge that it may seem like a "library" of disciplines (Figure 1.3). Early in the development of the discipline some anthropologists did a little of everything, but now there is a strong tendency to specialize. Anthropologists perform such tasks as excavating a prehistoric site, observing rituals in a tribal society, mapping the distribution of speech dialects, and deducing ancient disease patterns from old burials. Each of these tasks requires different skills and depends on different sources of data. To understand the forces responsible for human diversity, anthropology encompasses two broad subdisciplines: **biological** (or physical) **anthropology** and **cultural anthropology**. The kind of evidence used by anthropologists determines the subdiscipline to which they belong. Each of these is subdivided into fields; however, they are not rigid compartments, and elements of one often appear in another.

Biological anthropology is usually divided into three fields: **paleoanthropology**, human variation, and **primatology**. Cultural anthropology can be divided into **ethnology**, **archaeology**, and **anthropological linguistics**. Beyond this core of subdisciplines there are several other fields that belong to anthropology but do not fall neatly into one of these categories. For example, **medical anthropology** stands at the crossroads of anthropology and the health sciences. **Applied anthropology** also defies classification since it refers to practical, problem-solving applications of any field of anthropological knowledge. The focus of each of these subdisciplines and fields is explained in the following discussion.

---

holistic Comprehensive, covering many aspects.

social science Any of the disciplines concerned with social behavior, including anthropology, sociology, political science, history, and others.

human variation Generally, the diversity of customs, languages, and physical types found among humankind; more specifically, a branch of biological anthropology dealing with human physical differences.

biological anthropology One of the two major subdivisions of anthropology, concerned with humans as biological organisms and including paleoanthropology, human variation, and primatology.

cultural anthropology One of the two major subdivisions of anthropology, concerned with nonbiological human variation and including ethnology, archaeology, and anthropological linguistics.

paleoanthropology The branch of biological anthropology concerned with reconstructing human evolution through the study of fossils and other traces.

primatology The study of primate behavior and ecology in the field.

ethnology The subdiscipline of cultural anthropology that focuses on the comparative study of human social and cultural variation.

archaeology The subdiscipline of cultural anthropology that relies primarily on information obtained from the material traces left behind by human behavior.

anthropological linguistics The subdiscipline of cultural anthropology that studies the structure, function, and evolution of language.

medical anthropology A subdiscipline of anthropology that applies anthropological theory and method to human illness and healing.

applied anthropology The application of anthropological knowledge to practical problems, generally in social policy.

Figure 1.2 *Anthropologists study humanity in all its cultural and biological diversity. They might be interested in the religious practices of a trance dancer in Bali (left), or the foraging strategies of the !Kung San hunters of Botswana (below), or the traits sought in a leader by Algerian horsemen (bottom).*

Figure 1.3   *The subdisciplines of anthropology.*

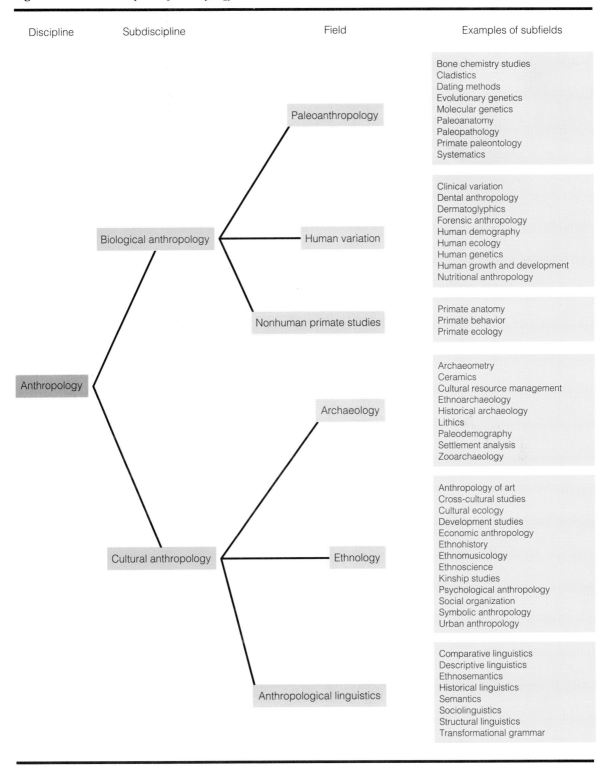

| Discipline | Subdiscipline | Field | Examples of subfields |

To give the flavor of the actual work that anthropologists do, this section includes sketches of four anthropological projects. They show the adventure in anthropology as well as the less dramatic, but necessary aspects of the discipline. When reading the sketches, do not be concerned about the details of the studies. Read them to get a sense of what an anthropologist's life is like. Pay attention to the wide variety of methods and tools that anthropologists use, and note that many common skills, as well as the ability to seize an unexpected opportunity, are important parts of being a successful anthropologist.

BIOLOGICAL ANTHROPOLOGY

Biological anthropology is the study of humans as biological organisms. It is particularly concerned with human evolution. Paleoanthropologists examine the **fossil record** for evidence about human origins. They deal primarily with the last 5 million years of biological evolution, during which the ancestors of our species first distinguished themselves from other animals. Some of their work involves locating and excavating fossil remains, but most of their time is spent in laboratories. Recently the search for human origins has moved to the molecular level. Anthropologists use **recombinant DNA** and other up-to-date techniques to trace the human lineage back in time.

Other biological anthropologists are concerned with contemporary biological variation. Often they search for clues to the same processes investigated by paleoanthropologists, only on a much shorter time scale. They examine such areas as variation in the incidence of diabetes, in skin color, and in blood types and such questions as how human populations respond to environmental changes like changes in diet. Recently, for example, biological anthropologists have been examining the skeletons of 2,000-year-old North American populations to determine the effects of the introduction of agriculture on growth and nutrition (Goodman and Armelagos 1991). Their work is complementary to other areas of human biology, including medicine, but it focuses mainly on broad evolutionary principles. This is the field of human variation and it includes **human genetics**, **paleopathology**, **human growth and development**, **dermatoglyphics**, and other subfields.

The study of nonhuman primates is sometimes differentiated as a third subdivision in biological anthropology. It focuses on the anatomy, behavior, and ecology of monkeys, apes, and other primates. In a few cases biological anthropologists use other animal species as **models** to learn about some feature of structure or behavior.

Biological Anthropologists at Work

Let's look at the moment when a team of paleoanthropologists unexpectedly makes one of the major fossil finds of the 20th century. Although the rule in anthropological research is the slow, patient accumulation of evidence, occasionally a sudden discovery can make grown people dance around like children.

The Death of a Hominid.   Picture a scene in the Hadar region of northern Ethiopia in the middle of the Great Rift Valley of Africa (Figure 1.4). Looking out from the rim of a valley you can see the Awash River flowing through a desolate set of hills almost barren of vegetation. Millions of years ago, this was a fertile, rainy land, supporting vegetation and many animal species, some now extinct. Among them were several mammals related to modern pigs and elephants. From 4 to 2.6 million years ago (MYA) a large lake gradually filled with water. Then, as the climate changed, it dried up under the intense equatorial sun, becoming first a swamp and then a barren desert crossed by a narrow river.

The area had undergone intense geological pressures. Volcanoes deposited layers of basaltic rock, and continental drift twisted the earth's crust. In one episode layers of rock and sand laid down by millennia of flooding and erosion were tilted upward, leaving them exposed like a layer cake set on edge. Thus the geologic history of the area could be "read" without researchers' having to burrow beneath the surface.

One day, more than 3 MYA, a lone female died on the lake shore. Although she was only about 28 years old, she suffered from arthritis. The cause of her death is unknown. Somehow, her small body became mired in the sandy lake bottom before it could decompose or be devoured by other animals.

The Discovery.   Over 3 million years later a joint French and American scientific team camped on the

Figure 1.4 *The Great Rift Valley of Africa, crossed by the Awash River. In this area anthropologists found the fossil known as Lucy, considered the oldest ancestor of humans as yet discovered.*

edge of the Awash River to search for fossil evidence of human evolution. The day was a scorcher: At sunrise the temperature was already over 32°C (90°F). Two North American researchers—Donald Johanson, a biological anthropologist, and Tom Gray, a paleontologist—were surveying a plot shown on their map as locality 162. As the sun rose to its zenith, the temperature climbed to 43°C (109°F) and the two scientists found little of interest. They were about to return to camp when Johanson, for no special reason, decided to return to a gully he had already inspected. Something caught his eye. He spotted a tiny piece of bone embedded in the gully wall and exposed by a recent rainfall. As Johanson stooped to examine it, he recognized a humanlike bit of arm bone.

"I can't believe it," Johanson shouted, astounded by the luck of his find. "I just can't believe it." Gray howled back, "By God, you'd better believe it!" In a few more minutes of breathless scrounging, they had found parts of a skull, parts of the backbone, ribs, half a pelvis, and a thighbone. Suddenly, under the blazing Ethiopian sun, the two sweating men hugged each other and danced around crazily as if they had just won a million-dollar lottery (Johanson and Edey 1981). What had happened was just about as unlikely as winning the lottery: They had found a nearly complete **fossil** skeleton of a very old animal in the same line as humans (Figure 1.5).

Evaluating the Find. Several weeks were to pass before they were sure. If "Lucy"—the name Johanson gave to the fossil—turned out to be a collection of bones from different individuals, the discovery might be less significant. The entire team turned to a pains-

---

fossil record The body of evidence available in the remains or other physical traces of past life forms.

recombinant DNA A technique used in anthropology to identify the degree of relationship between different organisms by artificially separating the strands of DNA from two individuals and determining the degree of correspondence.

human genetics The study of biological inheritance in humans.

paleopathology The study of disease in past populations based mainly on traces left behind in the fossil record.

human growth and development The study of physical growth patterns in humans under varying conditions.

dermatoglyphics The study of variation in fingerprints.

model In science, a representation of a phenomenon that aids in understanding how it behaves.

fossil Physical remains or traces left behind by a long-dead organism.

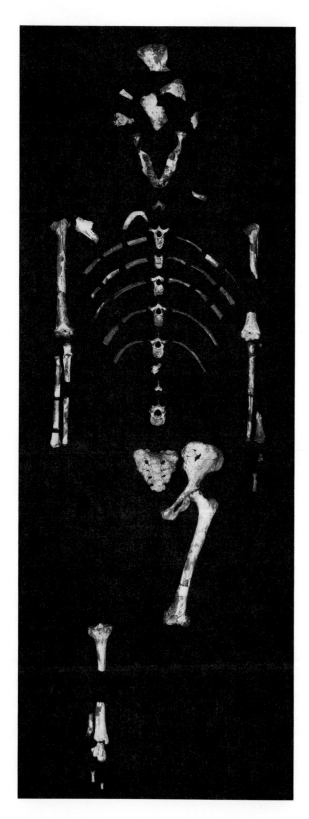

Figure 1.5   *The discovery of Lucy, the extraordinarily complete fossil skeleton of a hominid who lived over 3 million years ago, led to a rethinking of human genealogy.*

taking search of the immediate area of the find, sifting through every bit of rock and sand. Lucy turned out well: She was the most complete fossil **hominid** (a biological family consisting of humans and their bipedal ancestors) of that age ever found. Only 107 cm (3 ft, 6 in) tall, she was **bipedal** (walked upright on two legs); she was clearly not an ape (Johanson and Edey 1981).

Where did Lucy stand in human evolution? Just how old was she? Was she an ancestor of *Homo sapiens*? Was there any relationship between Lucy and other fossil hominids of similar age found elsewhere in Africa? It is not easy to get an ancient fossil, no matter how complete, to give up these secrets.

The analysis of Lucy required thousands of hours of work in Johanson's laboratory, preparing the fossil, measuring it, reconstructing missing parts, and comparing the parts of the skeleton to other comparable fossils. Some of the several fossil hominids found at Hadar had to be cleaned with a small pneumatic drill to chip away the encrusted rocks from the skull. The last stages had to be done with a dental pick. The teeth were very important because the number and arrangement of the little bumps, or **cusps**, can reveal a great deal about a fossil's closest relatives. And so the analysis proceeded, cusp by cusp, tooth by tooth, as the investigators estimated the exact size of the brain case and measured the angle of protrusion of the lower jaw and dozens of other features. Johanson invited several specialists to check over the fossils to test and extend his conclusions. One of the first specialists to examine Lucy confirmed Johanson's early conclusion: Lucy was bipedal (Box 1.1).

Perhaps the single most important determination to be made was the age of the fossil skeleton. Anthropologists subjected Lucy and the rocks above and below her skeleton to a battery of the most sophisticated dating tests known. Bones of other animals found in the adjacent rock strata—in particular, a set of pig bones—provided a means of relative dating.

The scientists used the **potassium-argon technique** to estimate the absolute age of volcanic rocks adjacent to the Lucy fossil. Radioactive potassium

BOX 1.1

Did Lucy Walk Like Groucho Marx?

While all experts agree that Lucy walked upright on two legs, a controversy has erupted over just how she walked. Some experts suggest that Lucy and her contemporary hominids walked with bent legs like Groucho Marx's exaggerated crouch-walk in films. They point out that her feet were fairly long relative to her leg bones, which would have forced her to lift her legs higher during the swing phase of walking, like trying to walk with swim fins on your feet. They also point out that Lucy's toes were curved, rather than straight like those of modern humans. Curved toes often occur among primates who need a powerful grip with their hind feet to grasp tree branches. Thus the possibility exists that Lucy and her kind spent a good deal of time in trees even though they were upright-walking animals.

Dr. Owen Lovejoy has reconstructed Lucy's pelvis and concluded that these bones are adapted to withstand the vertical stresses of walking and *not* those of climbing. Other anthropologists and anatomists, including Donald Johanson, her discoverer, agree that Lucy walked essentially like modern humans. The matter has not been settled, and it is possible that this controversy—like many others in science—will remain active until we find new evidence or a new way to approach the existing evidence. Given the pace of discovery of 3-million-year-old hominid fossils, this is likely to take some time.

Sculpture of A. afarensis, *by medical artist Michael Anderson on the basis of data from physical anthropologist Erik Trinkaus.*

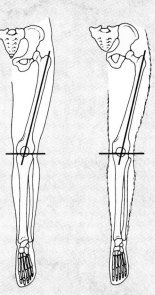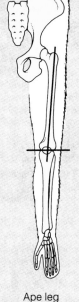

Human leg   *Afarensis* leg   Ape leg

Diagram showing different pelvic structures in humans, apes, and A. afarensis; also shown are different angles at which knee and thighbone connect, an angle critical to bipedal locomotion.

hominid A member of the family (*Hominidae*) of bipedal primates, including *Australopithecus* and *Homo*.

bipedal Standing and walking upright on two legs.

cusps The points or bumps found on the crowns of molar teeth.

potassium-argon technique An absolute dating technique based on the rate at which radioactive potassium (K_{40}) decays into argon gas; useful for dating volcanic rocks; accurate at the level of 100,000 years.

(K$_{40}$) decays at a known rate; over the course of 1.3 billion years half the K$_{40}$ trapped in rocks will turn into a rare gas called argon. Although porous bone releases argon into the environment, volcanic rock retains the gas as crystals "frozen" from the moment the lava spewed forth on the earth's surface. The rocks can be heated to release the argon. The amount of argon given off by samples of volcanic rock and the ratio of K$_{40}$ to stable potassium isotopes can be measured to within a few parts per million by an instrument called a mass spectrometer. This dating technique is indirect because it can be done only on adjacent rocks, not on the fossils themselves.

Johanson also asked a colleague to perform **fission track dating**. This technique relies on tiny tracks left by naturally decaying uranium in the zircon crystals found in volcanic stones. For another estimate, a colleague used a technique called **paleomagnetism**, which depends on the knowledge that the magnetic poles of earth reversed themselves at certain times in Earth's history. The scientists worked independently to conduct these tests. Although each technique is subject to error, the estimates converged on an age of at least 3 million years for Lucy.

Lucy's Pedigree. Perhaps the knottiest problem was Lucy's place in the human lineage. To solve it, Johanson and Tim White, a paleontologist, spent many months closeted in Johanson's laboratory measuring and remeasuring every conceivable aspect of Lucy and related Hadar fossils. They examined each tooth under magnification, observing its shape, wear pattern, size, and placement. They also assembled a large collection of casts of other African fossils for comparison with the Hadar fossils.

To give order to their work, they followed a scheme suggested in the 1950s by a British paleontologist, W. E. Le Gros Clark. Le Gros Clark proposed 11 features that distinguish human teeth from those of apes. For example, apes have long canine teeth projecting below the level of the other upper teeth (see Figure 6.8); humans do not. In this regard, and in several others, Lucy's teeth were intermediate between those of apes and humans. Lucy and other Hadar fragments appeared to be small-brained creatures (like apes) who walked upright (like people). After a long period of measurement, analysis, and sometimes bitter arguments, Johanson and White reached their conclusion. They agreed that Lucy is a hominid of the genus *Aus-*

tralopithecus of a previously unknown species that they named *afarensis*. They also agreed that Lucy was an ancestor of modern humans. (For an idea of what a living member of Lucy's family may have looked like, see Box 1.1.)

No sooner had Lucy been classified scientifically than she gained some enemies. Paleoanthropologist Mary Leakey was bitter about Johanson's use of some information about fossils that she and her late husband Louis Leakey had found in Kenya. Johanson had used the information to support arguments she did not accept. In particular, she did not agree that *Homo sapiens,* the species of modern humans, was a descendent of *Australopithecus.* Some anthropologists agreed with Leakey, but others sided with Johanson. While Johanson's book, *Lucy: The Beginnings of Humankind* (1981), has become a best-seller and Johanson is now a scientific celebrity, the controversy goes on.

CULTURAL ANTHROPOLOGY

Just as biological anthropology is concerned with physical variation in human populations, cultural anthropology is concerned with nonbiological variation. *Culture* is perhaps the single most widely used term in anthropology. A common definition of culture refers to the fine arts, painting, music, and literature. But the term **culture**, as used by anthropologists, refers to learned patterns of thought and behavior acquired by people as members of society. Sometimes we refer to a group of people itself as a "culture"—as in the statement "Ancient Greek culture was fascinated with the human body"—but it is more appropriate to say that a group "shares" a culture. Because it is so pervasive, people sometimes refer to culture as a palpable object or thing, as in the statement "The Armenian people cling to their culture."

Culture is not a thing. People do not "have" a culture the same way they have a pair of shoes or a bank account. Culture is a convenient way of describing certain capabilities and traits, but it is not a thing in itself. The only way we can observe culture is through the behavior of individuals and the objects and environmental changes they create. Some anthropologists feel that the term *culture* is overused and misleads people into thinking that culture exists as a thing, not just a convenient designation for a range of phenomena. They would discard the term and refer only to behavior, **cognitive patterns**, and other specific elements of culture.

In all higher animal species, behavior has both a learned side and an instinctive (inborn) side. Culture in humans is so important that there is hardly a single aspect of human behavior that can be considered without referring to it. Consider the biological function of eating. In many animal species biologically inherited traits (instincts and anatomy) determine which foods they eat and how they obtain them. In *Homo sapiens*, however, nearly all food-related behavior depends on culture. Most societies prescribe what can or cannot be eaten. In France, for example, horse meat is a popular delicacy; across the Channel, the English would not even consider eating horse. Thus human food preferences cannot be reduced to a simple response to biological drives, although biology certainly takes a part in cultural behavior.

There are several different fields within the subdiscipline of cultural anthropology, including ethnology, archaeology, and anthropological linguistics. These three subfields are discussed in the following sections.

Figure 1.6 *Ethnographer Napoleon Chagnon has spent years doing field work among the Yanomamo of Brazil. Here, he uses a solar-powered computer to record their creation myths.*

Ethnology

Ethnology is the comparative study of human customs and behavior. Within ethnology, subspecialties may be based on the regions of the world where investigators work or on the kinds of methods they use. The descriptive side of ethnological research is **ethnography.** Ethnographers often study societies through **participant observation.** This means going to live with the people they study and sharing their lives as much as possible. Ethnographers go "to the field" to study "natives" where they live. For many people, these words conjure up the image of traveling to a remote part of the globe and coming face-to-face with exotic folk who don't wear many clothes. But it could just as easily mean traveling to a city in North America and mingling with people who wear neckties and travel in automobiles. Ethnographers work among all types of people in every part of the world.

As they immerse themselves in the lives of the people they are studying, ethnographers observe their subjects' behavior, watching how they interact with each other and with the environment. They study communication and symbolic meanings by observing speech, art, body movement, and meaningful products such as literature, myths, paintings, and music. Ethnographic data is often gathered and stored by using still and movie cameras, tape recorders, video recorders, questionnaires, formal interviews, and time-and-motion studies (Figure 1.6). Ethnographers and

---

fission track dating An absolute dating technique based on the alignment of tiny tracks left by naturally decaying uranium in zircon crystals in volcanic stones.

paleomagnetism A dating technique based on known shifts in the polar magnetic fields over the past several million years.

culture The behavior, ideas, and institutions that are acquired by people as members of a society.

cognitive patterns Styles of organizing information peculiar to particular cultural traditions.

ethnography The description and recording of the lifeways of a people.

participant observation The study of behavior in which the observer participates directly in the social life of the group under study.

BOX 1.2

Culture Shock: U.S. Slugger in Japan

When the Atlanta Braves did not renew baseball slugger Bob Horner's contract for the 1987 season, he signed to play with the Yakult Swallows, a Japanese team perennially at the bottom of its league. His pay was an astronomical $2.4 million for one season. Horner did well with the Swallows, and he became an instant celebrity in Japan, swamped with adoring fans wherever he went. To make life easier for him, the Swallows provided Horner with a $15,000-a-month condo and a car with an English-speaking driver. His family joined him in Japan. Still, when the season was over, Horner turned down a contract for $10 million over three years. He simply couldn't adjust to living in Japan.

Reflecting on his experience, Horner observed, "Life last year was not amusing. The people were as friendly as you can be without communicating. That was the single most stressful thing—you couldn't communicate. I thought there'd be more people in the street who spoke English. . . . It wasn't any one thing that made life difficult. . . . It was a compilation of things—not understanding the language, not being able to read the street signs or menus, not being able to buy books or magazines. Coming back with a lot of mystery foods from the supermarket—it *looked* like steak or chicken, but was it steak or chicken?" (Swift 1988, 62).

It apparently did not occur to Horner to try to learn some Japanese, at least enough to ask about the foods or to read the street signs. But then Horner was in Japan to play baseball, not to study Japanese culture. Sometimes the only solution to culture shock is to go home.

Culture shock proved insurmountable for Horner.

ethnohistorians visit archives and libraries to cull ethnographic information from written documents.

Ethnographers learn to tolerate social customs that may be quite different from what they were taught. They must be flexible, diplomatic people, able to understand the viewpoints of people different from themselves. Often they find themselves in extremely unfamiliar situations, not the least of which involves sampling new foods.

Participating in a foreign culture may actually cut the ethnographer off from parts of that society. Many female ethnographers working in Latin America, for example, find that they do not have access to bars and other places where men congregate. In the Middle East, female ethnographers have been obliged to cover their heads and even their faces in deference to local custom. In some cases, female ethnographers have re-

lied on their alien status to exempt themselves from local taboos and have simply behaved in ways prohibited to local women. Male ethnographers may also be barred from participation in important aspects of social life, such as the conversations that take place in kitchens. Ethnographer Gerald Berreman (1962) describes the task of the ethnographer as a delicate job of "image management." Ethnographers must reveal enough of themselves to be accepted as fellow human beings, but they cannot present aspects of themselves that may offend or disturb their hosts, thereby jeopardizing their ability to collect accurate data.

Sometimes the strain of living in a different culture can be unbearable. **Culture shock** is the name given to the disorientation that many people feel when immersed in a foreign culture. Culture shock may involve stages of rejection, depression, loneliness, de-

Figure 1.7 *Ethnographers often venture far from home to do their field work. After this first glimpse of Xavante territory in central Brazil, Nancy Flowers was to spend over a year living in a Xavante village.*

nial, projection of one's thoughts and feelings onto others, and even physical symptoms (Box 1.2). Some people never recover from it.

Most ethnographers and other travelers do recover from culture shock. Often they move from alienation to a sense of belonging. After a long period of immersion in a foreign culture, some anthropologists begin to empathize with their hosts and to feel and think as they do. Many have experienced "reverse culture shock" upon returning home to their native society after a long stay abroad. Some ethnographers have devoted most of their careers to conveying to others the special understanding they achieved when they finally crossed the wide gulf that separates different cultures.

Other anthropologists remain skeptical that anyone can ever learn to think and feel exactly like a native. But almost no one will deny that after the painful period of culture shock is over, **fieldwork** is one of the most rewarding experiences that life can offer. For many researchers it is a major test of self-reliance to find their way in a new world. When they immerse themselves in an alien culture, they realize how de-pendent people are on shared understandings and habits in their home environment. This gives them new insights into their own cultures. For some people, a cross-cultural experience is profoundly unsettling but at the same time exhilarating.

Ethnographers at Work

In February 1976 Nancy Flowers arrived in Brazil to join a team formed to study the relationship between environment and society in four tribal societies in central Brazil. Like most cultural anthropologists, Flowers wanted to do participant observation as the basis for her doctoral dissertation. She already spoke Portuguese, and she knew Brazil from an earlier career as a photojournalist. Little in her background, however, prepared her for life among the Xavante.

The Xavante. The Xavante (pronounced Shah-von-tee) are about 6,000 people living in ten villages west of the Rio das Mortes (River of Death) in Mato Grosso State (Figure 1.7). Until quite recently, the Xavante

---

ethnohistory The study of the cultural past of a social group through reminiscences, historical records, and other sources.

culture shock Psychological stress and disorientation arising from an encounter with a society whose cultural patterns differ from one's own.

fieldwork The gathering of data through direct contact in the natural setting in which a phenomenon normally occurs.

Figure 1.8 *Apowē, the warrior chief of the Xavante.*

were largely self-sufficient. They obtained all their food by hunting, gathering, and gardening. Aside from a few shotguns and metal tools, their technology was very simple with no labor-saving machinery. In this isolated region the Xavante resisted permanent contact with Brazilian settlements by making bloody attacks against government missions sent to pacify them. They also fought among themselves. One leader, Apowē, apparently killed off an entire Xavante clan (Figure 1.8). The last major attack on Brazilians occurred in 1944 when a Xavante band led by Apowē attacked a small military detachment, killing the Brazilian commander, Pimentel Barbosa. During the 1950s, the Xavante were gradually "pacified," meaning they were settled in villages on reservations administered by the Brazilian government. On their reservations, however, there was relatively little interference from outsiders. A British ethnographer, David Maybury-Lewis, spent about a year with the Xavante during the late 1950s, sharing their life as a seminomadic group (Maybury-Lewis 1967).

Preparing for the Field.   To visit the Xavante, Flowers needed permission from the National Indian Foundation (FUNAI), the government agency responsible for Indian affairs in Brazil. Flowers spent three months in Brasília, the national capital, waiting for the papers to come through. She spent this time reading everything she could find about the Xavante. In May 1976 Flowers left Brasília on a three-day trip by pickup truck to begin participant observation with the group responsible for the 1944 attack (Box 1.3). When she arrived at the reservation, she found that only a few men and no women spoke Portuguese. FUNAI maintained a permanent agent and a health post on the large reservation, but the agent was seldom on duty and the health post lacked essential medicines. And the atmosphere was somewhat unsettled: A few months earlier the Xavante at this post had burned a settler's house and held him captive for several days in retaliation for the man's encroachment on their reservation.

Nancy Flowers's personality proved to be ideal for working with the Xavante. She spent more than a year in the village, most of the time as the only non-Xavante. The Xavante value toughness and self-reliance and often try to bully people into getting what they want. At the same time they have a sense of humor and can take "no" for an answer, particularly if it's delivered with some humor. Flowers was able to face down the Xavante men who occasionally menaced her. Her strategy was simply to remain patient, generous, and smiling and whenever she needed to say "no" to make it a firm one.

As in many fieldwork situations, the ethnographer entered into an exchange with the Xavante. In return for their tolerating her in the village, helping her obtain food, and answering her many questions, Flowers gave the Xavante tools, some medications, cloth, and other goods they wanted. After she had been in the village a few weeks, a group of men offered to build her a thatch house on the village circle for a fee. Gradually the Xavante came to accept, respect, and like Flowers. She also developed a deep appreciation for their customs and a sense of identification with them. Later in her stay a severe influenza epidemic swept the village. (Influenza is an "introduced" disease to which the Indians have little acquired resistance.) Since the post pharmacy had no medicines, Flowers walked several miles to a ranch, demanded the use of a truck, and drove 46 km (29 mi) to the nearest Brazilian settlement to buy medicine. In spite of her efforts, three Xavante died.

Flowers' research focused on the transition from seminomadic hunting and gathering to a more settled way of life that relied on cultivated food. The Xavante

BOX 1.3

First Meeting with the Xavante

Hostility turned to amazement when the Xavante saw instant photographs for the first time.

Our first moments in the village were dramatic. Flowers and I arrived in a pickup truck, dusty and tired after two days of driving on unpaved roads. After presenting our papers to the Indian agent we walked to the village a short distance away. In the center of the village we were surrounded by tall, husky men wearing shorts, dozens of yapping dogs, and a few children. We were presented to the wizened old headman, Apowẽ, who sat calmly watching the activity around him.

We began to explain that Nancy planned to stay there and conduct a study. We mentioned that we knew David Maybury-Lewis, and this brought some approving murmurs from the men. After a few min-

These notes are adapted from field notes taken by the author in 1976 on the occasion of his first visit to the Pimentel Barbosa Reservation in the company of ethnographer Nancy Flowers.

utes, we decided it would be a good moment to "break the ice." Nancy took out her Polaroid and began snapping pictures of the Xavante. I followed her, taking pictures with my 35mm camera. The men's expressions tightened, and after a few words in Xavante, they stepped toward Nancy and me in a threatening way. It seemed we had made a major blunder. I quickly found a man who spoke fluent Portuguese and began explaining that we meant no harm and that the pictures would . . . when Nancy pulled the first instant picture out of the camera and presented it to the nearest man. Suddenly the expressions that seemed so hostile turned to incredulity and fascination and finally amused smiles. The pictures communicated that we intended to collect information about the Xavante, but we also wanted to share with them.

had been cultivators as long as anyone could remember, but much of their diet came from wild food. Flowers focused on the effects of **sedentization** (settling down) on diet, health, and social life. She made careful notes about food consumed, gardens and hunting, and the growth of children. Flowers visited each of the 25 households in the village, counted the members, and weighed and measured the small children. She had to estimate ages because the Xavante do not reckon time in years. She also collected genealogical information on people sharing households.

In addition to these quantitative measurements, Flowers made extensive notes on many other aspects of village life. She observed rituals such as naming ceremonies for young women, relay races run with heavy logs, and initiation ordeals for men entering warrior status (see Figure 15.4). As a baseline for her own findings Flowers used information collected 20 years earlier by Maybury-Lewis, but such a resource is often not available because no earlier ethnographies exist.

Studying Time Allocation.　Flowers collected extensive data on how the Xavante spent their time for comparison with other groups more dependent on cultivated crops. In previous **time-allocation studies** ethnographers usually followed a few "typical" people around for several days and recorded all their activities. This method is very time-consuming, and there is no way of knowing that the activities of the selected people are typical. Furthermore, people who are followed may not behave normally.

To overcome these "sampling problems," Flowers used the technique of spot-checking activities at randomly selected times, a technique developed by anthropologist Allen Johnson (1975). Each week Flowers randomly selected 12 households in the village to visit at randomly chosen times. The randomness ensured that no individual had a greater chance of being observed than any other. On each spot check, Flowers took along a chart of household members on which she wrote down what she saw them doing the moment she arrived. For those who were absent, Flowers asked someone to report what they were doing. Upon cross-checking, these reports proved to be highly accurate.

During the year Flowers compiled nearly 5,000 separate observations of individual activities. She observed most of the 285 people in the village several times in a wide range of activities (Figure 1.9). She then classified the data by individual, household, and type of activity. For example, she coded hoeing weeds as GW (category: gardening, subcategory: weeding). Of course, any classification involves some lumping

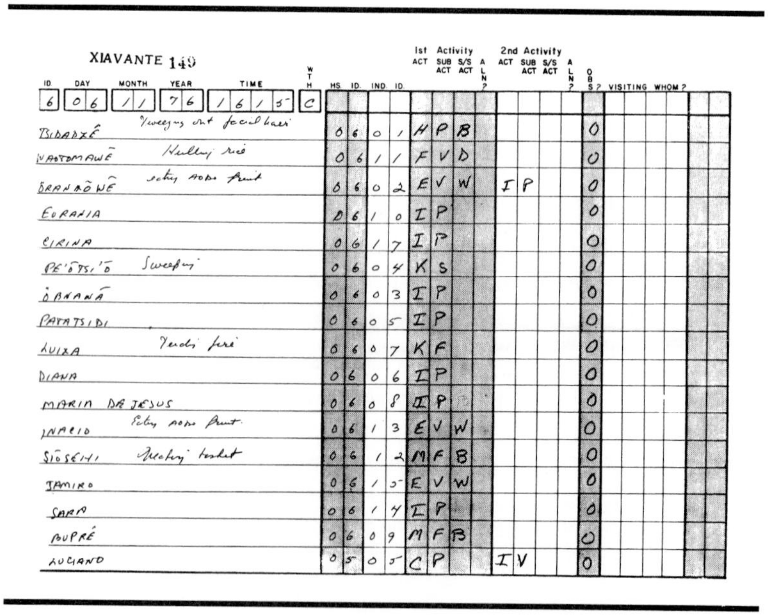

Figure 1.9　*A sample of Nancy Flowers's field notes from her time-allocation survey.*

Table 1.1 Xavante Time Allocation

Activities	Hours/Day
Hunting and fishing	.91
Gathering wild food	.32
Gardening	2.09
Tending domestic animals	.08
Market labor (e.g., wage labor)	.57
Other work (including housework and child care)	3.29
Nonwork (nonproductive activities)	6.73
Total	14.00

and splitting. For example, weeding with a hoe was not distinguished from weeding with a machete.

When Flowers returned to the United States, she began to analyze her time-allocation data. A computer can sort through thousands of records quickly and accurately, so Flowers entered each observation into the computer classified by date and time, the identity of the individual, household, and the activity code. By combining the information about individuals in a given category, such as females between ages 15 and 44 years of age, Flowers could find out what different kinds of people did with their time.

How was it possible to convert an observation made at a single moment into information about how much time people spend at activities? This conversion rests on the assumption that the number of times a group of people is observed at a given activity—say, gardening—is proportional to the amount of time they actually spend on that activity. Thus, if 20 percent of the observations show women involved in child care, we can estimate that women spend about 20 percent of their time involved in child care. This assumption allowed Flowers to construct a table showing the time allocated to different activities (Table 1.1).

Flowers's data show that the Xavante do not spend as many hours on a food quest as people do in most technologically advanced societies. Although their agriculture is not highly developed and they still rely heavily on wild food, the average adult Xavante produces an adequate amount of food in less than $3\frac{1}{2}$ hours of work per day. This amount of time is characteristic of societies that do not use their resources intensively.

Archaeology

Archaeologists have many of the same goals as ethnologists, but they use a different kind of evidence. Archaeologists study behavior through the material remains left behind by people in the everyday business of living. People create or modify many objects where they live and work. For example, the people of prehistoric Europe quarried stone and flaked it into tools, leaving behind hundreds of broken pieces of stone in their "workshops." The job of the archaeologist is to determine what kinds of activity are likely to have produced such **artifacts** (objects made by humans) and the patterns in which they occurred. Archaeologists also examine disturbances in the environment, such as faint changes in soil color that mark where house posts once stood.

Ethnoarchaeologists go beyond the boundaries of traditional archaeology by studying not just the artifacts but also the behavior patterns that produce them. By necessity they limit themselves to studying behavior in contemporary societies. Ethnoarchaeologists have made fascinating studies of pottery making, waste disposal, even courtship and marriage through examination of physical traces (Kramer 1979). Ethnoarchaeology allows archaeologists to check their inferences about behavior of peoples in the past against actual behavior patterns. **Historical archaeologists** specialize in periods of human history

---

sedentization The process of settling down by a wandering people.

time-allocation studies The study of how people use time through the construction of time budgets.

artifact An object created by human activity.

ethnoarchaeology The archaeological study of contemporary peoples focusing particularly on the behavior patterns responsible for creating physical objects and their distribution in space.

historical archaeology The archaeological study of literate societies for which historical records can be used to complement archaeological data.

for which some historical documentation is also available (Figure 1.10).

Archaeologists, like ethnologists, tend to specialize in specific kinds of societies and regions, such as early agricultural societies of Europe. Some specialize in a technique, such as pollen analysis; a topic, such as **lithics** (the analysis of stone artifacts) or **ceramics** (the analysis of pottery); a particular behavior pattern, such as **settlement patterns** (how people distribute themselves in space); or a type of **subsistence activity,** such as hunting.

Archaeologists at Work

In the movies, archaeologists always seem to search for a carved idol that will unlock the secret of a hidden tomb full of golden treasure. The truth is less glamorous: Archaeologists generally spend more time in their laboratories than at their excavations. Modern techniques of analysis make it possible for archaeologists to extract much information from the objects they find. But the cost is high in hours of painstaking examination of bits of wood, stone, bone, and pottery and microscopic flecks of pollen. Although the goal of archaeology is the same as that of ethnology—to de-

scribe and analyze human behavior and the processes of change over time—archaeological research generally covers much longer time spans and can examine social processes requiring centuries to unfold.

Organizing an Archaeological Field Expedition. Frank Hole and Kent Flannery first met as graduate students at the University of Chicago, a major center for archaeological studies of the Middle East. Flannery had previously worked with Hole in Iran and with James Neely in Mexico. The three shared an interest in the social significance of agriculture and in the archaeology of southwestern Asia (modern Iran, Syria, and Iraq; see Figure 13.5). People in this region began to shift from wild to domesticated plants and animals as food sources nearly 10,000 years ago.

The domestication of plants and animals was one of the most important events in human history—equal in importance to the industrial revolution of the 18th and 19th centuries. Until the late 1960s, the leading theory of the origins of agriculture held that familiarity fostered domestication. According to the theory, people who spent their lives hunting and gathering wild animals and plants would be most familiar with them. They would therefore be likely to be the first to domesticate those species. From this theory

Figure 1.10 *Archaeological research often extends into modern cities. Historical archaeologist Robert Schuyler and his associates dug into the past of the New England textile industry in Lowell, Mass. The parking lot in the foreground was the site of boarding houses built in the 1820s for factory workers employed by the Merrimack Manufacturing Company. To recruit labor from the predominantly agricultural population, factory owners had to provide "decent" living quarters for the young, single women who made up the bulk of the work force.*

Figure 1.11 *The barren Deh Luran Plain of Iran is dotted with mounds such as this, indicating the location of ancient settlements. The mounds grew up over millennia as new dwellings were built on the remains of old.*

came the hypothesis that domestication first occurred in areas where the wild ancestors of domestic plants and animals lived.

Hole, Flannery, and Neely had little interest in finding the earliest remains of agriculture. Neither were they looking for magnificent temples or fine buried pottery. They wrote, "We confess a little amusement at the thought that, while most Near Eastern archaeologists have dug for buildings and incidentally recovered a few seeds in the process, we dug for seeds and incidentally recovered a few fragments of buildings in the process" (Hole, Flannery, and Neely 1969, 4). The three archaeologists wanted to learn about the *process* that led to domestication.

Unlike Indiana Jones, the archaeological team made careful preparations before departing for the field. In Teheran (the capital of Iran) they had to get permission to excavate from the Department of Antiquities, a lengthy process. Most countries have laws to protect prehistoric sites from unauthorized distur-

bance. Over the centuries unscrupulous treasure hunters have looted such sites, commercializing the heritage of many nations and carelessly destroying sites that, properly excavated, could have yielded valuable information. Archaeologists must therefore be scrupulous in conforming to the laws of the countries where they excavate. With permission finally in hand, Hole, Flannery, and Neely set out in 1961 with their spouses and guides in rugged four-wheel-drive vehicles.

The Deh Luran Plain lies across the Zagros Mountains from Teheran. Nowadays it is a desolate place, inhabited mainly by sheep, goats, and their herders (Figure 1.11). It is only 530 km (330 mi) from Teheran on the map, but it takes three bone-jarring days on the ground, first on paved highways, then on dirt tracks, and finally across the trackless plain, guided only by the occasional shrines poking up from the desert sands. The intrepid archaeologists arrived and set up camp in 1961. They built crude huts out of

---

lithics   The archaeological study of stone artifacts.

ceramics   The archaeological study of artifacts manufactured from clay.

settlement patterns   The distribution of people, dwellings, and other domestic artifacts in a region.

subsistence activities   The practices involved in producing, storing, and consuming food.

Figure 1.12 *Archaeologists divided the Tepe Musiyan site into 1-m squares and sampled deposits in alternate sections at successive levels. The site yielded evidence of early plant and animal domestication.*

poles covered with reed mats and waterproofed with asphalt from nearby tar pits. Their diet was about as primitive as the accommodations. Flannery reminisces:

> Our usual meal consisted of lamb, rice, and yoghurt (all domestic) plus gazelle and wild boar (shot by local border guards). Getting our Kurdish cook to make wild boar kebab was lots of fun (Kent Flannery, personal communication).

Excavation. The first step was a survey to locate ancient sites and collect artifacts found on the surface. In the Middle East many early sites appear as low, flat mounds raised above the surrounding plain during successive generations of human habitation. Houses were built on the foundations of earlier dwellings and tons of accumulated human refuse. The larger mounds, rising as much as 50 m (163 ft) above the surrounding terrain, can be identified by their distinc-

tive shape. The smaller mounds are often found when farmers plow the land and discover pieces of pottery and other artifacts. Their survey completed, Hole, Flannery, and Neely decided to excavate a few selected sites where they felt the best information could be obtained. One mound, Tepe Musiyan, seemed promising, but it covered a daunting area of 13.5 hectares (33 acres). It was impossible to excavate the entire mound, so the investigators laid out a grid of 1-m squares like a checkerboard (Figure 1.12) and "sampled" from them.

The archaeologists recruited from the local villages 30 tough shepherds used to the searing heat of the region. They trained the men in excavation techniques, forming teams of workmen, each with a pickman, a dirt carrier, and two sievers. Each pickman worked with a sharp trowel. The workers learned to distinguish by feel the hard fill and the slightly softer material of old walls, which were indistinguishable to the eye. The pickmen scraped away the dirt in each square, in 10-cm (4-in) layers. They placed the contents of each layer in a bag and labeled it by location and level. They sifted each bag of dirt through a series of screens, each with a finer mesh than the last. Anything found in the screen that bore information—a bit of pottery, an animal bone, a stone tool—was labeled by location and level and stored away.

Even after screening, the dirt yielded valuable information. Mixed with various liquids, it produced tiny seeds that floated to the surface and were scooped up, labeled, and saved for later analysis. Specialists could determine the species of plant from which the seeds came and whether it was a wild or domesticated variety. In this **flotation analysis** Hole, Flannery, and Neely found many seeds of domesticated wheat and barley. But as they dug deeper into the site, they did not encounter the wild ancestors of these varieties as had been hypothesized.

To determine the age of the material they collected, the archaeologists used two types of techniques: **relative dating** and **absolute dating**. Relative dating establishes the age of an item in relation to other items. It reveals whether one item is older or younger than another. **Stratigraphy** is the simplest means of relative dating. Clear layers, or strata, in the earth that covers mounds represent successive habitations at that site. Usually the most recent deposits are closest to the surface, with older remains buried below them. Stratigraphy can reveal, for example, which pottery style is older than another, but not exactly how old they are. By correlating the stratigraphic information from a variety of related sites, archaeologists can work out the prehistoric **chronology** of a region. Perhaps some day archaeologists will work out the chronology of modern Western civilization by plotting the distri-bution of glass, steel, aluminum, and plastic containers of soft drinks.

To estimate absolute dates, the archaeologists used **radiocarbon dating**, one of several absolute dating techniques. They did this by measuring the proportion of an unstable isotope of carbon (known as Carbon 14 or C_{14}) found in samples of ash recovered from ancient hearths. Carbon 14 accumulates in all living organic matter (trees, for example), and it stops being absorbed when the organism dies. Because C_{14} decays at a known rate, the amount of C_{14} in relation to other isotopes yields an estimate of the absolute age of the sample (allowing for a certain margin of error).

The excavators collected pottery sherds in nearly every level of the site, representing 4,000 years of human habitation. During this time, there were many changes in decorative style. At one level, called Musiyan E, the team found 849 broken pieces of pottery. Back in the laboratory they classified them as belonging to 23 separate vessel types (shapes) and six decorative styles. They entered each sherd into the computer as a record, noting style, vessel type, location, and level. Musiyan E contained 302 pieces of a particular decorative style known as Susiana Black-on-Buff, about a third of the total. Hole computed the relative percentages of these vessel types of Susiana Black-on-Buff, comparing them to the percentages of this style and vessel type found at other sites. Some of the pottery was very similar to that found at another mound in the area called Tepe Sabz, a site where the chronology had been thoroughly worked out. Using C_{14} dating techniques on pieces of burnt wood from Tepe Sabz, archaeologists determined that the samples at one level had been burned between 4120 and 3460 B.C. Repeating the same procedure many times for

---

flotation analysis An archaeological technique in which samples from an excavation are immersed in liquids with different levels of specific gravity to identify seeds and pollen.

relative dating Archaeological techniques that determine the age of an object in relation to other objects from the same or similar sites without stipulating its actual age.

absolute dating Archaeological techniques that permit a quantitative estimate of the age of an object.

stratigraphy A dating technique based on the observable pattern of deposition in rock or soils that allows deductions to be made about the relative age of objects found in different layers.

chronology A known pattern of succession based on stylistic, technological, or other features of artifacts, used to identify phases of development within a given area.

radiocarbon dating The archaeological technique used to estimate the ages of carbonized organic remains based on the rate of decay of an isotope of the carbon atom (C_{14}).

other levels, they were able to reconstruct the chronology of occupation at Tepe Musiyan.

Findings.   Hole, Flannery, and Neely's findings were not published until several years after the excavations because of the lengthy analysis period. Ultimately a wealth of new understanding emerged from their painstaking work in both the field and the laboratory. Although they did not uncover fabulous temples or the first known example of anything, their discoveries helped tip the balance of evidence against one of the major theories of plant domestication. Their work showed that the first people to domesticate plants in the Deh Luran Plain used plants from outside the immediate area. They concluded that the origin of agriculture here could not have been based simply on familiarity with edible wild plants, because the wild ancestors of wheat and barley did not exist at the site. Instead, they proposed, domestication occurred when people transported wild plants to a new area and adapted them to their needs.

Anthropological Linguistics

The third major field of cultural anthropology is anthropological linguistics. Specialists in this field use speech and other forms of communication as their primary source of data. Speech is a cultural product, and language is a form of cultural behavior. Often anthropologists use language as a primary basis for distinguishing one people from another. The Basque people, for example, are citizens of Spain, but they have a separate social identity in Spain based on their distinctive language and social traditions.

Linguists examine language as a system of sounds that combine to form meaningful utterances. They analyze both the way sounds convey meaning and the grammatical structures that give language form (Figure 1.13). **Comparative linguistics** and **historical linguistics** examine variation and change in languages; **semantics** is the branch of linguistics that examines meanings.

APPLIED ANTHROPOLOGY

Many sciences have both theoretical and applied branches. Some psychologists, for example, practice as clinicians to help people solve personal problems; or they may work in psychological testing or personnel placement. Some sociologists teach and do research in universities, while others work as pollsters or market researchers. Anthropology also has an applied side. While most anthropologists teach or do research at the university level, a growing number

Figure 1.13 *Linguist Francesca Merlin converses with people in Highland New Guinea. Her field work involves studying the patterns of meaning in their language.*

Figure 1.14 *A member of the Argentine Forensic Anthropology Team exhumes the grave of one of the* Desaparecidos *("the disappeared ones"), killed by the Argentine military death squads between 1976 and 1979. The team was headed by well-known forensic anthropologist Clyde Snow.*

practice applied anthropology. Applied anthropology is a **policy science** that applies anthropological knowledge on behalf of government agencies, international organizations, and communities (Partridge and Eddy 1987). One example of applied anthropology is **forensic anthropology**. Forensic anthropologists apply physical anthropological and archaeological techniques to the collection and analysis of evidence in legal proceedings, especially in the identification of human remains (Figure 1.14).

---

comparative linguistics The systematic comparison of languages, based on words or other features, aimed at understanding the historical relationship among different languages.

historical linguistics The study of language development through comparative techniques.

semantics The study of meaning in language.

policy science The systematic study of public decisions, including their causes and consequences.

forensic anthropology The use of anthropological techniques to develop evidence used in the legal process, especially in the identification of human remains.

Archaeologists also apply their knowledge to **cultural resource management**, carrying out studies and excavations at construction sites to determine how best to preserve culturally significant sites, buildings, and objects. In the United States many states have an office of "state archaeologist" that is responsible for the preservation and maintenance of that state's prehistoric and historical heritage. Archaeologists and ethnologists also help plan and manage public parks, monuments, and museums, and they design and implement cultural awareness programs.

Ethnologists and anthropological linguists often work in primary and secondary education, designing or implementing programs for cultural and linguistic minorities. When governmental and international agencies consider social intervention, cultural anthropologists may be asked to analyze conditions and then recommend how the project can be carried out without infringing on the rights, sensibilities, and livelihood of the affected people. For example, large-scale development projects such as dams often displace many people. One of the greatest challenges in applied anthropology is the design of **resettlement** projects that will disrupt the lives of the displaced population as little as possible.

Many medical outreach programs employ anthropologists, especially when there are cultural differences between the providers and the recipients of the health services. An increasing number of anthropologists work for international development agencies such as the World Bank and the U.S. Agency for International Development. A growing number of anthropologists work in the private sector in management consulting, marketing, and computer software design. The skills, knowledge, and experience acquired by an anthropologist during professional training and field research are invaluable in many nonacademic settings. Nowadays more than half the anthropologists completing professional degrees (M.A. and Ph.D.) go into applied work.

Applied Anthropologists at Work

Ethnographers continually warn each other to avoid **ethnocentrism**, the familiar mindset that says "our way is the best way." **Cultural relativism**—the view that cultural practices should be addressed in terms

familiar to the people practicing them—helps researchers suspend the tendency to condemn everything different. The idea of relativism is usually extended to include noninterference. It is an elementary rule of science that accurate measurement depends on minimizing the effect of the observer on the thing being observed. If anthropologists interfere in a society under study, they will not be able to observe things accurately as they are.

Paradoxically, applied anthropologists use anthropological knowledge to direct social and cultural change. In doing so, they suspend cultural relativism by deciding that some aspects of culture *should* be changed. Consider the case of Allen Holmberg, an anthropologist from Cornell University who took a lease on a 30,000-acre hacienda (agricultural estate) high in the Peruvian Andes. Holmberg arrived in Peru in 1949 to do a study of the impact of a power dam in the vicinity of Vicos. When an avalanche destroyed the power project, Holmberg turned his attention to the hacienda. His preliminary research showed that the people of Hacienda Vicos lived under "semifeudal" conditions (Holmberg 1960). A landlord had life-and-death power over the peasants; the peasants had never known a life free from arbitrary authority, poverty, and deprivation. The *patrón* (owner) reserved the best land for himself and allotted to the peasants only rocky hillsides to grow their crops (Figure 1.15).

By a stroke of fate the previous *patrón* of Vicos went bankrupt just as Holmberg's power dam study collapsed. In a bold moment, Holmberg put in a bid on behalf of Cornell University to lease the estate from its owner. Suddenly, a professor from Ithaca, New York, became the master on a semifeudal estate.

Assessing the Problems.   The lease on Vicos granted Holmberg rights to the labor of about 380 men out of the roughly 2,000 people on the land. Under the **labor rent system**, which had been in place for hundreds of years, each able-bodied male tenant had an obligation to work three days a week for a wage of about a penny a day in exchange for the right to live on the land and grow a little food. The *patrón* had the right to require tenants to work in his houses on the hacienda and in the city; he even had the right to hire out the workers to someone else while pocketing their wages. These workers (Quechua-speaking peasants) were regarded by others as inferiors to be ordered about. Many peasants seemed to accept this status and

Figure 1.15 *Peruvian peasants sorting their potato harvest on the Vicos hacienda. As a result of the Cornell-Peru project, an experiment in applied anthropology, the peasants were able to purchase the hacienda for themselves.*

all the burdens that went with it: illiteracy, malnutrition, disease, and beatings for disobedience.

Recognizing that these features were part of Andean culture, Holmberg nevertheless made plans to change them. His goal was to introduce reforms that would allow greater freedom and autonomy for the Vicos peasants and provide more comfortable, secure lives for them. He hoped that these new ideas might spread spontaneously from Vicos to other estates and gradually throughout the Andes. This is called the **demonstration effect.** Holmberg saw from the beginning that no change would be permanent unless freely

---

cultural resource management A branch of cultural anthropology concerned with the conservation, scientific investigation, display, and educational use of environments and objects having a particular cultural significance.

resettlement The (usually) involuntary removal of entire communities from one place to another, which results in disruptions in social and economic life.

ethnocentrism A tendency to interpret or judge other cultures in terms or values belonging to the observer's culture; cultural bias.

cultural relativism The temporary suspension of judgment or culture-bound values in dealing with cultural phenomena.

labor rent system A system of landholding in which tenants pay rent to their landlords in days of agricultural labor.

demonstration effect The spontaneous diffusion and adoption of new ideas or technology based on a successful experiment in a particular locale.

adopted by the peasants themselves. He began in the role of the all-powerful, paternalistic *patrón* but with the intention of dropping that role.

Designing and Implementing Solutions.   One of Holmberg's first moves was to abolish labor rents so that peasants were free to work full-time for themselves. He decided to put all the income from the estate lands into a special fund. This fund would eventually be available for purchase of the hacienda by the peasants themselves.

Previously all the peasants of Vicos had been obliged to meet once a week to receive their work assignments from the *mayorales* (foremen). Holmberg turned this convocation into a community meeting in which peasants could express their opinions, and he transformed the *mayorales* from foremen into community leaders.

Holmberg decided to make the local school into a force for change. Previously only boys had gone to school, and most studied for only a year or two before dropping out. There simply was no incentive for children to study, and they were needed for farmwork. The facilities were abysmal and teacher absence was high. In 1952, enrollment fluctuated between 15 and 20. The Cornell program showed the peasants that learning could pay dividends. By 1956 enrollment had risen to 200 and the community had constructed its own schoolhouse and auditorium with volunteer labor.

Holmberg brought his family to live in a ramshackle adobe house on Vicos, and he taught himself to speak Quechua. He brought in agronomists, health providers, and other technical personnel to improve the potato crop yields and to raise health standards. At first the peasants were confused and suspicious. No one had ever treated them like this before. Could they trust this man? Most of the people working in Vicos were Peruvians; except for the researchers, only the project director was an American. Holmberg did all he could to avoid making his own personality an issue. He did not want to be the leader or a benevolent *patrón;* he wanted the peasants to help themselves. By sharing their lives, listening to them, and showing them new ways of doing things, Holmberg gradually succeeded. Eventually the peasants were able to purchase the hacienda for themselves.

A New Round of Problems.   Even after overcoming the suspicions of the Vicos peasants, the project still had to contend with serious problems. With each step toward autonomy and prosperity, opposition to the project grew outside the hacienda. Peasants on other estates were envious of the benefits received by the Vicos peasants. Merchants in the nearby town found they lost customers as the Vicos peasants became self-sufficient. Local intellectuals who favored revolution rather than reform denounced the project as a plot. Others accused the Americans of being communists. When one group of peasants on a nearby estate requested the use of uncultivated land for a communal enterprise, the *patrón* called in the national police. He believed that his life and property were being threatened. The police precipitated an incident with the peasants, shooting eight and killing three.

The experiment probably would have failed at many junctures had it not been for high-level political backing from influential people in the capital. As they came to understand what was happening in Vicos, many Peruvians supported it. The ideas tried first in Vicos spread to other estates in various regions. Soon peasants from Vicos were traveling to other estates to teach the methods they had learned.

Through four years of the Vicos Project, Holmberg had to play the role of diplomat, technician, arbitrator, and spokesperson. He moved from "participant observation" to what he called "participant intervention." He convinced a generation of anthropologists that anthropology was more than the passive study of culture, that it was capable of introducing cultural change. But the people of Vicos and the surrounding area paid a high price. The violence suffered by some imitators of Vicos was indirectly the result of the project. Holmberg intervened in a foreign culture and imposed a new model of social life. While he tried to involve the Vicos peasants in decisions at every point, he found that at many points he had to make decisions for the peasants. In other words, he introduced changes in a traditional paternalistic fashion.

In spite of the demonstration effect, there were few successful imitators of the Vicos project, and Vicos itself has fallen on hard times. In recent years, without the constant support of outsiders, potato production in the community has fallen sharply. Ultimately the project fell short of transforming rural life in Peru. However, it did raise the aspirations of thousands of peasants in Vicos and surrounding areas, and it yielded valuable knowledge that has been applied in later projects.

Some critics of Vicos feel that the project was poorly conceived because of its exclusive focus on the hacienda. As the project developed, it became clear that Vicos did not exist in a vacuum. The semifeudal structure of the old hacienda received support from the political and economic system of the region and the country as a whole. Although there were reform-minded people in Peru, there were many who wanted to see Vicos fail. Since the peasants had little influence over the government, merchants, and landlords, they could not force major changes, no matter how much they favored them (see Chapter 18).

Unlike Vicos, most applied anthropology projects are sponsored by government agencies. Anthropologists are generally brought in to find ways of minimizing the disruption of development projects or persuading people to accept change. Until recently, applied anthropologists have usually not been invited to participate in the design phase of major projects. As a result they are often powerless to avoid problems when they arise. Managers of development programs are beginning to understand the importance of tailoring development projects to the needs of people. There is growing recognition of the need for anthropological input to programs of social and economic change.

ANTHROPOLOGY AND OTHER DISCIPLINES

Now that we have looked at the subdisciplines within anthropology and seen the kind of work that different kinds of anthropologists do, let's look again at the links between anthropology and other fields. Most universities separate disciplines into departments, each with its own faculty, facilities, budget, and courses. To some extent these divisions are arbitrary

and have as much to do with historical events as with basic differences among the various disciplines. In the social sciences there is much overlap among the disciplines, just as there is in the physical sciences. Paleo-anthropology, for example, can be regarded as a branch of **vertebrate paleontology.** Primatologists are often found working in departments of zoology or psychology. Archaeologists sometimes teach in history departments; many linguists work in departments of language and literature. Anthropology is distinctive in uniting aspects of these disciplines into a single field with a primary focus on humankind.

Cultural anthropology, especially ethnology, is closely related to **sociology.** In fact sociology and ethnology recognize two of the same "founders," Émile Durkheim and Max Weber. Sociological training, however, does not include human biology or prehistory. One anthropologist defined the difference between sociology and anthropology by pointing out that sociologists have no museums.

Anthropology is sometimes compared to **psychology,** and there are some close similarities. Like anthropology, psychology examines behavior, considering both biological and nonbiological influences. Like anthropologists, some psychologists study social influences on values and behavior. Psychologists interest themselves particularly in learned behavior and the process of learning. They often employ experimental methods, using animal models to uncover patterns of learning and response. Unlike anthropologists, however, psychologists generally see their subjects as generic representatives of the human species. Anthropologists, by contrast, are far more concerned with features that distinguish one group of humans from another.

Links also occur between anthropology and history, political science, and economics. Anthropologists investigating social processes must sometimes delve into the past, and they often consult historical documents for data. Historians of non-Western societies, particularly in Africa, rely heavily on anthropo-

---

vertebrate paleontology The study of animals with backbones through an analysis of their remains over spans of geological time.

sociology The study of the structure and function of human society and its institutions.

psychology The study of the behavior and mental life of people and animals and the clinical application of psychological principles.

logical research. Anthropologists also study legal and political processes, how decisions get made, and how people exercise power in a variety of contexts. Anthropology has a close affinity to economics in its study of exchange systems and economizing behavior.

There are also strong links between anthropology and the humanities. The investment that many anthropologists make in learning the language, history, and culture of non-Western societies makes them experts in the literature, music, and plastic arts of such societies almost by default. But the ties run much deeper. **Interpretative anthropology** (see Chapter 3) has much in common with literary and social criticism. Some anthropologists define cultural phenomena as "text" to be read and interpreted. When anthropologists analyze fundamental thought patterns in different cultural traditions, they find themselves deep into philosophy. Philosophers, literary critics, and language specialists often look to anthropology for theoretical inspiration and for data available nowhere else.

Because anthropologists frequently study non-Western groups, people often identify anthropology with the study of "primitive" peoples. However, anthropologists do not restrict themselves to these subjects. Seeking to understand human variation in the broadest possible context, anthropologists have sought out both the commonplace and the unusual in both industrialized and nonindustrialized countries. The setting of an ethnographic study is just as likely to be a factory town, a hospital, an urban slum, or a cocktail lounge as a remote rural village. Anthropologists study people in their usual habitat, interfering as little as possible in the lives of their subjects. Thus anthropology tends to be a more "natural" science, which observes things encountered in nature, than a laboratory science with rigorous experimental controls. Increasingly, however, anthropologists bring data in from the field and manipulate it in a laboratory or with a computer.

Professional anthropologists are sometimes highly specialized, such as archaeologists who spend a lifetime deciphering ancient Mayan stone inscriptions. Their training and the very nature of the discipline lead anthropologists to cross boundaries between subdisciplines and fields. Anthropologists delve into such diverse fields as nutrition, ecology, biosystematics, artificial intelligence, astronomy, geology, chemistry,

or molecular biology when a topic under investigation leads them in that direction. This is just one of the things that makes anthropology so exciting.

This book is not targeted specifically for people planning a career in anthropology. The study of anthropology offers much more than career training. It introduces a way of looking at the world that broadens and deepens people's understanding of themselves and their environment. It can enlighten the citizen, the decision maker, and the scientist, as well as the person who simply wants to understand the world better. We go a long way toward addressing the complexity of the modern world when we begin to explore the human past and present and to understand the differences and similarities that exist within the human species. As in other scientific fields, there are wide gaps in anthropological understanding, leaving ample room for disagreement among the experts and for new discoveries in the future.

SUMMARY

- Anthropology is the holistic study of humankind, encompassing the human past and present.
- Anthropology is distinguished from the other social sciences by its holistic approach: It examines both cultural and physical aspects of human nature and attempts to understand human variation across the widest possible range of time and space.
- As a discipline, anthropology is divided into subdisciplines of biological and cultural anthropology, each of which is further divided into many subareas.
- Modern anthropological research does have much of the romance and adventure that people imagine. Anthropologists travel to remote areas and experience exotic cultures, although much research also takes place close to home, wherever that might be.
- Most modern anthropological research centers around specific goals and elaborate techniques of analysis. Each subdiscipline has specific methods for both field and laboratory. Some of these methods are quite specialized and mastered by only a few people.

- It is common for anthropological problems to require a variety of types of evidence cutting across the boundaries of disciplines and subdisciplines. Because of this increasing complexity, anthropological research increasingly requires a team effort.

GET INVOLVED

1. Visit your local anthropological museum or museum of natural history and look over the exhibits. What branches of anthropology are represented in the collection? Try to find out what kinds of collections are present in the museum in addition to the material exhibited. Where are they from? How did they get into the museum?
2. Review a sample of the press for a week or more, including newspapers, news magazines, literary reviews, and magazines of fact and opinion. You will find that a week does not go by without major anthropological issues arising in the press, even if they are not identified as such. Identify the anthropological questions arising in the news and other articles over the period you review. How do you think an anthropological approach to the subjects would differ from the approach taken by sociology, history, psychology, or other disciplines?
3. Investigate the opportunities in your area to become involved in an anthropological research project. The most common kind of opportunity is probably volunteer participation in an archaeological excavation (a "dig"). You can find such opportunities by contacting faculty at local institutions, your state archaeological agency, or your local historical society. Plan to spend a week working at the activity you select.

SUGGESTED READINGS

Miner, Horace. 1956. Body ritual among the Nacirema. *American Anthropologist* 58:503–507.*

Murray, Gerald F. 1987. The domestication of wood in Haiti: A case study in applied evolution. In *Anthropological praxis,* ed. R. Wulff and S. Fiske. Boulder, Colo.: Westview Press.*

Pastron, Allen G. 1989. Opportunities in cultural resources management. In *Applying anthropology: An introductory reader,* ed. A. Podolefsky and P. J. Brown. Mountain View, Calif.: Mayfield.*

Richardson, Miles. 1990. The myth teller. In *Cry lonesome and other accounts of the anthropologist's project.* Albany: State University of New York Press.

Snow, Clyde C., and James L. Luke. 1970. The Oklahoma City child disappearances: Forensic anthropology in the identification of skeletal remains. *Journal of Forensic Sciences* 15:125–153.*

* This selection is anthologized in *Applying Anthropology*, 2d ed., ed. A. Podolefsky and P. J. Brown (Mountain View, Calif.: Mayfield, 1992).

---

interpretative anthropology   An approach that stresses the meaningful elements of cultural behavior and their symbolic and psychological values.

Pottery styles often provide valuable clues about the age of an archaeological site. These pottery shards depict styles found over time on the Deh Luran Plain in southwestern Asia.

2

USING SCIENTIFIC METHODS
The Tools of Anthropology

▲▲▲

In Chapter 1 we mentioned that anthropology is linked to the humanities by its interest in the **interpretation** of culture, history, and values. We also noted that interpretive anthropology shares many concerns with literary and social criticism. Although it is true that anthropology is an interpretative discipline that seeks to analyze the meaning in human events, for many people in the field, anthropology is above all a **natural science**. As such, it seeks to make valid generalizations about human differences and similarities, that is, to offer scientific explanations of human customs and behavior. This chapter focuses on anthropology as a science and on some of the ideas and methods that scientists use in carrying out their work. It also looks carefully at the issue of scientific objectivity and how anthropologists can attain the same degree of objectivity as scientists in other fields. (Chapters 3 and 4 address the ways that anthropologists approach meaning.)

Scientific knowledge is distinguished from other kinds of knowledge not by its content but by the way it is acquired, that is, its methods. Because scientists follow certain rules in their investigations, the knowledge they obtain is considered more rational, objective, and reliable than other kinds of knowledge. Ideally scientific inquiry is not affected by the personal beliefs of scientists or the social environment. Most anthropologists believe, however, that knowledge cannot be "culture free." The very rules scientists follow are the product of a certain cultural tradition, and the problems they try to solve similarly grow out of our culturally based concerns. Science developed as a result of cultural changes: People became dissatisfied with supernatural explanations of events and began to demand explanations based on "natural law." Even our faith in natural science is part of a cultural tradition: Science itself is an artifact of culture.

Natural science concerns itself with the explanation of observable facts, objects, or events. While sometimes restricted to chemistry, physics, and biology, the term can refer to all the phenomena of the natural world. Scientific **explanation** is parallel to **prediction**. A prediction is a statement about the conditions under which events are likely to occur. For example, based on her knowledge of wind currents and atmospheric pressure systems, a meteorologist may predict that a cold front will pass through southeastern Canada following a snowstorm. Explanation may apply to actual events in the past or the present, to events that never occurred, or to phenomena that have not been observed.

Scientific predictions about past events are known as **retrodictions**. For example, the same scientific principles that enable me to predict the time of high tide tomorrow also allow me to retrodict the time of high tide one year ago. Archaeologists have successfully retrodicted that certain kinds of remains would be found. For example, many anthropologists felt that a complex society like the ancient Maya could not have rested on low-energy agriculture like that practiced by the modern Maya in Mexico, Belize, and Guatemala. They patiently searched until they found evidence for intensive agriculture in prehistoric Mayan society (Figure 2.1).

Knowledge accumulates in natural science by observation, classification, experimentation (or comparison), and generalization. All **scientific research** has both **deductive** and **inductive** aspects. When an investigation builds on knowledge obtained from observation of particular phenomena, it is inductive. When a study begins with general theoretical propositions, it is deductive. Young sciences tend to be inductive since they typically concern themselves more with observation and classification than with generalization. As they mature, more powerful theories arise that can account for a greater range of observations. Physics is an example of a highly mature science. Anthropology is a relatively young and therefore inductive science. That is one reason why anthropologists busy themselves with systematically collecting data.

OBSERVATION

Scientific investigations begin with **observation**, that is, collecting and recording information (data) about a phenomenon, through the senses or with instruments. Usually the phenomenon is a recurring one, such as a ceremony, the shape of the teeth on certain fossil skulls, or a particular grammatical construction. A scientist's observations must be made so that another scientist can repeat them and compare results. This is **replicability**. For example, two astronomers observing an eclipse from different vantage points must carefully note their positions to explain any differences in what they observe.

Many people believe that the physical sciences (such as chemistry and physics) are more "exact" than

Figure 2.1 *Ancient Mayan ridged fields in Belize. The existence of such fields, which allowed the Maya to practice a reliable, high-yield form of agriculture was retrodicted by anthropologists.*

interpretation Understanding based on empathy, intuition, or the analysis of meaning inherent in phenomena.

natural science A field of study in which phenomena can be observed in nature and studied scientifically.

explanation An approach to understanding that seeks to subsume particular events under general propositions verifiable by replicable empirical observation and experimentation.

prediction A statement about the likely occurrence of a future event, made on the basis of experience.

retrodiction A statement about the likely occurrence of a past event, made on the basis of experience.

scientific research Studies based on replicable operations aimed at understanding the nature and causes of observable phenomena.

deductive Pertaining to an approach that depends on reasoning from principles.

inductive Pertaining to an approach that depends on the accumulation of evidence.

observation The collecting and recording of data about a phenomenon.

replicability The possibility of repeating experiments or observations to confirm the results obtained in other experiments.

the social and life sciences. They believe that a physical observation is a fact but that there are no "social facts," because social behavior depends on individual actions and opinions. Émile Durkheim, a founder of modern social science, demonstrated a century ago that there *are* social facts and they have the same reality as the facts of physics and chemistry. Durkheim showed that suicide rates in different countries were stable, year after year, even though suicides are highly individual acts.

Of course, the facts in any field are only as good as the observations they rest on, and they are always subject to revision. Thus in physics the prevailing view once was that the earth was the center of the universe and the sun and planets revolved around it. This fact became a nonfact when better observations and some brilliant creative thinking led Copernicus to propose that the earth revolves around the sun.

Formulating a Hypothesis

Actual investigations are usually guided by hypotheses. A **hypothesis** is a provisional statement about how two or more variables are related. For example, anthropologists believe that complex societies arise only when intensive food production systems are present. In this hypothesis, intensive food production is an **independent variable**, while the rise of the state is a **dependent variable**. To put this another way, intensive food production is a **necessary condition** of a complex society.

Although they are not always clearly or precisely stated, hypotheses are present in nearly all scientific investigations. Hypotheses are necessary to guide the selection of facts (variables) that will be observed and measured. The testing of hypotheses is discussed later in this chapter.

Classification and Variables

Even with simple phenomena, you can make a very large number of observations, and no two events or cases are ever identical in every respect. Without **classification** observation would yield only a confused jumble of information. Classification is the process of selecting attributes that distinguish things as the same or different. For example, if you are studying how fast

billiard balls roll down an inclined plane, the size and mass of the balls are important attributes; their color is not. But if you are studying how well the balls reflect light, their color is important. So classification presupposes some ideas about what is important.

The scientist's ideas about what is important come from theory, which is present in every investigation, even when we are unaware of it. Let us take a simple example: Suppose that a paleoanthropologist suspects that heavily worn molar teeth on a primate fossil are the result of a diet of coarse grasses and nuts. From this point on, the investigator may classify all the teeth she observes into those reflecting this wear pattern and those that do not. The variables in this example, are *kinds of teeth* and the attribute used for classification is *degree of wear*. Depending on how accurately the investigator can measure tooth wear, the classification may rely on a simple **bivariate distribution** between worn and unworn teeth, or it may estimate tooth wear in a **continuous distribution** ranging from 0 percent to 100 percent of wear. Theory comes into the picture in the form of suppositions about the relationship between kinds of food consumed and tooth wear.

Measurement

To avoid being overwhelmed by a huge number of facts, some important, some irrelevant, scientists classify phenomena through **variables.** A variable is an attribute of a phenomenon distinguished into two or more values. For example, a pole can be short or tall. In this case the phenomenon is pole, the variable is height, and the values are short and tall. **Measurement** refers to recording information about variables. Measurement involves answering questions like "how much?" and "how large?" as well as questions like "how frequent?" or "how intense?" The variables in these cases are amount, size, frequency, and intensity. Of course scientists always attempt to measure as precisely as possible, but all measurement is limited in the degree of precision that can be obtained. As we saw in Chapter 1, archaeologists must sometimes be satisfied with the determination that one artifact is older than another one (relative dating). Physicists determine the pathway of particles to a degree of probability, not certainty. In many cases, making the measurement requires a certain interference with the thing being measured. The more precise the measurement, the greater the interference. This principle is known as the **Heisenberg uncertainty principle**, and it is as important to anthropology as it is to physics.

Anthropologists use many instruments to make measurements. For example, a paleoanthropologist may use a caliper to measure the thickness of a fossil jawbone. A primatologist may make tape recordings of monkey calls to analyze with acoustic instruments in the laboratory. Archaeologists use surveying instruments in the field. In the laboratory they use a wide array of devices, such as microscopes, mass spectrometers, even electron beams. Ethnographers use cameras, tape recorders, and questionnaires to record, classify, and store information about human culture. Nowadays nearly all anthropologists use computers for data storage, retrieval, and manipulation. In ethnography, however, the principal measurement instrument is a human being, the ethnographer.

THE PROBLEM OF BIAS

Many scientists believe they can observe phenomena without "coloring" them with their own feelings and expectations. But objectivity is not so simple. Consider two people, Calvin and Heather, meeting in a room where the temperature is 20°C (68°F). Calvin has just come in from outdoors, where the temperature is 10°C, and Heather has come from a warmer room, where the temperature is 24°C. Calvin feels warm, while Heather feels cool. The difference arises from **subjective bias,** or influences on perception that depend on the standpoint or experience of the observer.

To minimize subjective bias in measuring temperature, scientists use an instrument that is not subject to bias. A thermometer, for example, is a device in which a closed column of mercury rises and falls with the heat in the environment. The user reads temperature as a visible mark along a graduated scale. Thermometers are so calibrated and standardized that two accurate thermometers side by side will reliably give the same reading. Such unbiased instruments extend the capabilities of our senses and make our observations more reliable.

Because the primary ethnographic measuring device is the human observer, ethnography presents the most difficult problems in avoiding bias. Human observers are not standardized and calibrated like thermometers. The human measurement device interacts with the environment in complex, unpredictable ways. A large part of this complexity comes from the fact that every individual observes and interprets behavior and ideas in terms of a unique frame of reference: cultural background (Box 2.1). In India a common greeting consists of pressing the hands together just in front of one's chin, head inclined forward, eyes downcast (Figure 2.2). This same gesture in the West might be interpreted as praying. Ethnologists take particular interest in ideas and customs that people acquire as members of society. People raised in one tradition tend to regard customs and beliefs from another tradition as strange, exotic, perhaps even evil. Prejudice and ethnocentrism—a sense that one's own culture is the best and most reasonable—are based on this principle.

Such biases are normal in human society, and no one can grow up without them. Even though they are the product of a particular cultural tradition, they are

---

hypothesis A provisional statement about how two or more variables are related.

independent variable A variable taken to be a necessary condition of another.

dependent variable A variable whose value is determined by that of another.

necessary condition A particular event that always precedes another event.

classification Selection of attributes for the purpose of arranging things in categories.

bivariate distribution Distribution of scores on a variable that has two possible values (for example, black or white; worn or unworn).

continuous distribution Distribution of scores on a variable that can take any point value between two extremes (for example, test scores between 0 and 100).

variable An attribute that can have different values, such as age, gender, income, or size of household.

measurement The collecting and recording of information about the value of variables.

Heisenberg uncertainty principle A principle in science stating that the more precisely we attempt to measure certain variables, the more likely we are to interfere with the phenomenon we are attempting to measure.

subjective bias Influences on perception arising from the particular experience or point of view of the observer.

BOX 2.1

Learning to Drive in Brazil: On the Relativity of Culture

I arrived in Rio de Janeiro from New York. Nothing I had seen in New York prepared me for my first drive in Rio's traffic. I was afraid for my life. Drivers in Rio de Janeiro seemed bent on suicide or vehicular homicide. Cars whizzed by on the right and left. Drivers seemed to feel they had to fill every inch of space between their vehicles and others. I found other drivers swearing and gesticulating at me for "normal" reactions like slowing down for pedestrians. After a few nerve-shattering months, my perspective changed. I began to see the aggressive Brazilian style of driving as "normal." When I returned to New York, drivers seemed restrained to me. Brazilian friends visiting me noted how "polite" the drivers were in New York. Now I smile when I hear Americans from other regions commenting on how "savage" New York drivers are!

Figure 2.2 *Greeting or prayer? This gesture has different meanings in different cultural contexts.*

not necessarily identical from individual to individual. This is because **socialization**—the acquisition of cultural standards—consists of thousands of learning events and is not a rigorously controlled procedure. In other words, unlike calibrated scientific instruments, no two humans undergo exactly the same set of experiences.

Can we have confidence in measurements collected by such biased instruments? We would not accept reports from astronomers whose telescopes were known to have distorting lenses. Nor would we accept dates submitted by archaeologists using uncalibrated instruments. How can anthropologists be scientific if their observations depend on unscientific biases that form part of their heritage?

Types of Bias

We can think of cultural bias as a kind of distorting lens. Distortions may be introduced in various ways. There are three kinds of bias: evaluative, cognitive, and conceptual. **Evaluative bias**, or **value judgments**, enter when we judge something as good or bad in terms of our own **norms** (common cultural values). For example, most North Americans condemn a man who marries more than one woman because our traditions (and laws) prohibit having more than one spouse at a time. Inuit (Eskimos) have a deeply held taboo against the direct expression of anger by women. Ethnographer Jean L. Briggs found herself ostracized from the Arctic community she had lived with for a year after she expressed anger at white sport fishermen who had demanded the use of the

Figure 2.3 *Cultural ideas about individuality, conformity, and membership in the group are fundamentally different in Japan than they are in the United States.*

Inuit community's only serviceable canoe (Briggs 1970). Her behavior would probably not have aroused much attention in a Western community, but it was perceived as evidence of grave character defects by her adoptive Eskimo father.

Cognitive bias arises when we try to understand the meaning of words, acts, or symbols in terms of a culture different from the one in which they occurred. An American putting the tip of his index finger to his thumb to form an O is making a gesture signifying "everything is okay." The same gesture is considered obscene in Brazil, because it signifies the anus.

Conceptual bias comes from contrasting world views. In North America, for example, the individual

human being is the central focus of decisions and actions. In most Western religions, individuals are expected to choose their beliefs freely and form a personal relationship with God. Individual initiative and decision making are highly regarded in business, sports, and academics. In other societies, however, individuals recede into the background and the family, the clan, the business firm, or a broader community receives greater emphasis. A grown man in China will often consult his parents and brothers before making any important decision, and in Japan people are trained to think in terms of the group they belong to before they think of themselves (Figure 2.3). In Brazil, students often do their homework in groups.

---

socialization The process of acquiring cultural standards, also known as enculturation.

evaluative bias Bias that arises when a belief or behavior is judged as good or bad in terms of one's own cultural values.

value judgment An opinion about the value of something, such as whether it is good or bad, usually based on individual or cultural standards.

norms Shared cultural values or standards.

cognitive bias Bias that arises from differences in the meaning of words, acts, or symbols between the observer and the observed.

conceptual bias Bias arising from differences in basic world view between the observer and the observed.

They are much less concerned than North American students with getting individual credit for the work they have done. Such differences make it difficult to understand the behavior of people in other societies.

Dealing with Bias

How can we overcome these sources of bias and turn human observers into reliable instruments? There are two possible solutions. The first approach attempts to discover the source of bias and compensate for it. The second sets up rules for systematic, objective observation and carefully brackets observations likely to be distorted by cultural or individual biases. Each of these approaches has advantages and disadvantages.

Awareness and Compensation: Cultural Relativism. The late ethnologist Margaret Mead advocated the awareness and compensation approach. In 1970 she wrote that the training of an ethnographer must include

> enhanced awareness of his own culture, and his place . . . within his own culture. . . . The student who analyzes his own sociocultural position, so that he is able to think about it with disciplined detachment, will be a better-prepared recording instrument when he is asked to use his own responses as ways of recognizing, diagnosing, and analyzing the behavior of the members of a strange culture. . . . [Mead 1970, 247–248]

If ethnographers follow Mead's counsel, they can correct for their cultural biases, provided they are aware of them.

In surveying the broad spectrum of human habits, customs, and beliefs, the ethnographer will be severely tested in trying to set aside deeply ingrained cultural beliefs. Consider the case of ethnographer Charles Wagley, who did research among the Tapirapé Indians of central Brazil in 1940 (Figure 2.4). At that time, the Tapirapé had a strict rule that a woman could not have more than three living children or more than two of the same sex (Wagley 1977, 135). Wagley suggests that the Tapirapé needed to limit the size of their population to maintain a delicate ecological balance with the environment. Fathers expressed the fear that they would not be able to feed large families. They also observed food taboos that prohibited

fathers of young children from eating meat. On one occasion a woman, Chawaniuma's wife, Mikantu, who already had two boys and a girl, gave birth to a child outside the village near old garden sites.

> Almost immediately she stood up and walked back to her house to lie in the hammock. A group of women (and the author) gathered around the child who seemed to be a healthy boy. There was considerable discussion, most of which I did not understand, but I was able to express my opinion that the child should be kept. "Perhaps a family would keep the child," I remember saying. I seemed to win out at least for the moment, for the umbilical cord was cut and tied with a cotton string. . . . I did not visit the family for several days for I felt that I had intruded enough upon their personal affairs. But several days later, Chawaniuma came . . . and told me shyly that the infant had died . . . because he himself had eaten a forest fowl which is taboo to fathers of infants. But my friend and informant Champukwi said that everyone knew that Chawaniuma had buried the child at night. "He does not want more children. He does not want to stop eating venison. His wife did not want to nurse another child," Champukwi said to me. [Wagley 1977, 137–139]

Figure 2.4   *The Tapirapé of Brazil once limited family size through infanticide, a practice that conflicts with Western cultural beliefs.*

Because of his awareness of his bias, Wagley did not allow the incident to shake his acceptance of the fundamental humanity of the Tapirapé. Indeed, his book shows great empathy and understanding of the Tapirapé and their customs in spite of his disagreement with their practice of infanticide (allowing or causing a child to die). Wagley was able to compensate for his feelings of revulsion at the Tapirapé practice of infanticide.

The concept of cultural relativism aims at helping anthropologists retain their objectivity in the face of customs they do not accept. Anthropology is a scientific discipline, however, not a source of moral authority. Cultural relativism may be a useful methodological tool, but it cannot force an anthropologist to accept a custom he or she disagrees with. Wagley was able to deal with his bias because he was aware of it. He recognized his own personal and cultural bias, but he gave in to the impulse to try to save the baby—a product of his upbringing and values.

Unconscious Bias.   We can look at every interaction as a transaction in which each party has its own expectations and responses, based largely on cultural conditioning. Show a clenched fist and many spectators will perceive a threatening and angry gesture. Among African Americans, however, the same gesture could be a symbol of solidarity, stylized as a greeting. At an athletic contest a similar gesture expresses triumph and determination. Knowing the code behind the gesture allows us to react appropriately. When the pattern by which the gesture is interpreted is unconscious, however, the anthropologist cannot compensate for it.

Psychologists have long recognized that transactions may occur between people unconsciously. One unconscious psychological process is the **placebo effect**, a favorable response to a drug that has no biological basis. When doing research on the effects of a drug, scientists must administer a placebo to half the group and an active drug to the other half. This division allows experimenters to distinguish the effects of the drug itself from the effects of the testing experience. The procedure is known as **blind testing**, because the subjects do not know whether they are taking a real drug or a placebo. In **double-blind testing**, experimenters themselves do not know which subjects get which drug. This technique was found to be necessary because researchers were unconsciously communicating to patients that they were receiving placebos.

We know from this and other evidence, then, that people react to each other in complex ways. The very presence of an outside observer may lead people to change their behavior without being aware of it. How can anthropologists compensate for their unconscious biases and for their subjects' unconscious responses? No matter how much the ethnographer tries to compensate for bias, it is always possible that he or she had additional unconscious biases. Blind testing and placebos can't be used in ethnography.

Ethnographers frequently provide long prefaces about their relationship to the people in their studies to allow readers to form their own judgments about bias. This practice would be unusual in most other natural sciences, but it is equivalent to describing the equipment used in a chemistry experiment. As ethnographers participate more and more in the society under study, they improve their ability to recognize what is normal in that society. At this point, another danger arises: The ethnographers may identify so closely with the subjects that they lose the outsider's objectivity. In either case, objective understanding may be an illusion because of unconscious transactions between observers and actors.

---

placebo effect   The effect of a biologically inactive drug on the person who takes it; also known as psychological effect.

blind testing   A procedure used in the social and biomedical sciences designed to reduce subjective bias by not allowing the subject to know the particular treatment to which he or she is exposed.

double-blind testing   A procedure used in the social and biomedical sciences designed to reduce subjective bias by allowing neither the subject nor the observer to know which subjects belong to the experimental group and which belong to the control group until after the experiment is over.

Figure 2.5 *Nuer men and their cattle. A Western definition of wealth would not make sense among the Nuer, for whom cattle are prestigious objects and a medium of exchange.*

Establishing Operational Definitions. Many anthropologists feel that it is not sufficient simply to be aware of one's own cultural bias or to spend years and years living with the "natives." These anthropologists advocate the **operational definition** of the variables under study on the model provided by other sciences. That is, they believe it is necessary to state precisely the conditions for saying that any observation belongs to a class of objects. Suppose, for example, that an anthropologist wants to know how attitudes toward wealth have changed in China since the death of Chairman Mao Tse-tung. An operational definition of wealth might be "the market value in local currency of all the goods owned or exclusively controlled by an individual and members of his or her household."

This definition might be inapplicable in a society where there is no currency. Or this indicator of wealth may not correspond to the natives' conception of wealth. In some societies, such as the Nuer in East Africa, the only truly valued goods are cattle (Figure 2.5).

What good is an operational definition when definitions are arbitrary and possibly do not apply in all situations? Operational definitions are useful, precisely because they are rigid. If applied rigorously, they allow the ethnographer to determine accurately the presence or absence of a trait, minimizing the bias he or she might have toward the object. Consider the example of aggressive drivers described in Box 2.1. An operational definition of aggressive driving might be the frequency of collisions, or aggressiveness might be defined by certain kinds of answers on a sentence-completion test.

Every cultural tradition defines things in a different way, and many ideas have several shades of meaning within a single cultural tradition. It may be objected that an operational definition does not fully embody the meaning of an idea like aggression. This objection is valid, but it misses the point of operational definition. Scientific use requires that terms be sharply, not broadly, defined. Otherwise it would be impossible to test hypotheses.

Operational definitions of terms provide some protection from the conscious and unconscious biases that all ethnographers carry with them. They allow for greater precision because they exclude wide areas of meaning in human affairs to which people in their everyday lives pay close attention. People could not live their lives by defining their universe operationally. The actual world of behavior and human intentions is often purposefully ambiguous, as when the quarterback fakes a handoff in football. Operational definition is useful only in science, and even there we recognize that it restricts the meaning of terms to a range narrower than the theoretical conception of them. It is not necessary or even desirable to define operationally every term in an analysis. Operational definitions do not cover all the meanings a term can have, but they satisfy the demand for precision and clarity in science.

Emics and Etics

Anthropologists find it useful to distinguish between the outsider's and the insider's view of cultural practices and artifacts. Actor-oriented terms in ethnographic work are referred to as **emic**; observer-oriented terms are referred to as **etic** (Harris 1968). Emic observations can be made only with the aid of a native informant, because they involve distinctions or ideas that are unique parts of the actor's cultural experience. Etic observations are those made in the language of the observer, in this case, the anthropologist. This dichotomy is more easily understood through an illustration. Suppose an Indonesian ethnographer wants to study popular festivals in North America. Interviews with natives about the meaning of Christmas might elicit responses like these:

- Christmas celebrates the birth of Christ, God's only son, who died so that we might live.
- At Christmas, children hang stockings over the fireplace so that Santa Claus will come down the chimney and fill them with presents.
- Christmas is a time of peace when we rededicate ourselves to peace on earth and good will toward all.
- Christmas is a time for devotion to family.

- Christmas used to be a beautiful holiday, but now it's so commercialized that it has lost all its beauty and meaning.

Unless the Indonesian ethnographer is familiar with Christianity, the Christmas tradition, and recent American history, it would be difficult for her to evaluate these statements. There is nothing in the ethnographer's tool kit that could explain the meaning of Christmas to those who celebrate it without consulting the natives' own viewpoint. Who, for example, is this Santa Claus person? Is he available for interviews? Why does he come into the house through the chimney instead of through the door like most people? Is he a burglar?

Suppose, on the other hand, that the Indonesian wished to measure the impact of Christmas on the economy of North America. She might do this by examining the percentage of retail sales attributable to Christmas, tracing the effects of Christmas sales through the manufacturing system, the credit network, wages and employment, and so on. These are generally etic considerations, because they involve concepts in the observer's data language, independent of the actors' perception.

Emic and etic observations of culture both contribute to understanding. Many features of culture can be examined from an emic or an etic perspective or both. Neither approach is better or more important than the other. Both can be compared across cultures. The emic-etic distinction is not the same thing as "ideal" and "real," because emic things are just as real as etic ones. The important difference is the source of the information. Nor does the distinction refer to the objective-subjective distinction. The Tapirapé rule limiting family size is an example of an emic cultural item. But it is not necessarily subjective, that is, it does not vary with the vantage point of the individual Tapirapé.

Even though they are complementary, emic and etic observations must be kept separate. Emic things, like Tapirapé rules for infanticide, must be treated as artifacts of culture and investigated from the perspective of the actors themselves. Etic things are also cul-

---

operational definition The specification of the operations used to carry out a measurement.

emic Pertaining to observations made from the point of view of the cultural insider (the native).

etic Pertaining to observations made from the point of view of an outside observer.

tural products, but they can be investigated without concern for the natives' view. Tapirapé infant mortality rates are the etic data relevant to the Tapirapé practice of infanticide. It is always interesting to compare emic rules with etic behavior, because there are often divergences between the two.

EXPERIMENTATION

To be accepted, hypotheses must withstand both logical and empirical tests. Hypotheses must be logically sound. If a hypothesis contradicts itself, it must be rejected. The statement "most paupers are wealthy" is invalid because it is false on its face. Sometimes hypotheses are rejected because they are inconsistent with well-accepted laws. For instance, few scientists would care to test the hypothesis that chilled water runs uphill, because it fails to agree with what we know about water and gravity. Scientists also reject untestable hypotheses, such as "Christmas was better this year than last."

Empirical testing means checking a hypothesis against observations through experimentation. An **experiment** is any fair test of a hypothesis involving systematic comparisons. The experimenter follows rules to avoid biasing the results. When an experiment yields results in the direction indicated by a hypothesis, scientists do not claim to have *proved* their point. They prefer to say that the evidence is consistent with the hypothesis. They prefer to use the term *suggest* rather than *prove*. In science nothing is ever proven beyond all doubt.

Research Design

Whenever possible, scientists test hypotheses through **controlled experiments,** often in laboratories. Controlled experiments are artificially constructed situations in which the variables can be manipulated to make exact comparisons. The purpose of experimental controls is to determine the effect of one (independent) variable on another (dependent) variable.

A typical experiment compares two or more situations in which one variable differs. Social psychologists, for example, may perform experiments to determine how time pressure (the independent variable) affects students' performance on tests (the dependent variable). The same test can be administered to two groups of students known to have approximately equal scores. The experimental design may call for applying time pressure to one group, say, by calling out time signals and urging the students to hurry and finish. If the two groups showed no substantial difference on previous test scores, any differences on the experimental tests could be attributed to the difference in pressure applied.

In the social and medical sciences, experimental controls may be difficult or unacceptable for ethical reasons. In many cases, we do not accept the risk involved in experimenting on human beings. Changing attitudes are also leading to questions about experimenting on animals, especially higher mammals. These restrictions do not require us to abandon experimental design in the social and medical sciences. Instead, social and medical scientists use **correlations** among variables under natural conditions to find clues to the relationships between the variables.

In **naturalistic studies, statistical controls** are substituted for laboratory controls. Consider, for example, a study that seeks to determine the effect of cigarette smoking on health. Investigators can perform a natural experiment by dividing a sample population into two segments, one that has never smoked cigarettes (the **control group**) and the other that smokes cigarettes regularly (the **experimental group**). Of course, other factors also affect health, such as diet, exercise, and pollution, but they are probably equally distributed in both groups. If the sample has been correctly drawn, however, these other factors will not affect the outcome of the experiment. A positive correlation would show that the smoker group has a higher incidence of lung disease (cancer or emphysema). A negative correlation would show that the smoker population has a lower incidence of disease. If the incidence of disease is about the same in both populations, the investigator would conclude that there is no correlation, that is, the variables are not related. This is the way in which the link between cigarette smoking and lung cancer was established.

Proper **sampling** is crucial to successful experiments. Correct sampling requires that cases be drawn from the universe of possible cases in a way that does not bias the outcome. Samples must also be large enough to reduce the effect of random variation. Suppose that anthropologists find a fossil skull deformed by the weight of the soil under which it was buried. If other fossils of the same species cannot be found, the deformed skull may lead observers to draw erroneous conclusions. Another common sampling error is caused by the timing of observations. The Bororo people of Central Brazil have been reported in the anthropological literature to be nomadic hunter-gatherers even though they are a settled village people practicing agriculture. This error occurred because the ethnographers visited them during the season when the Bororo left their villages and went on extended hunting trips. A correctly drawn sample is one in which any individual case in the sampling universe has as great a chance of being selected for observation as any other. For example, in the studies of the Bororo, several observations made at random intervals throughout the year would have provided a better sample of the tribe's subsistence activities, because such activities generally follow a yearly cycle.

Experimental Design in Anthropology: The Study of *Susto*

The experimental approach in anthropology can be illustrated by a study of illness and culture in the highlands of Peru. Anthropologist Ralph Bolton studied the nature and causes of *susto,* a common medical syndrome in Latin American countries characterized by sleep disturbances, listlessness, appetite loss, apathy, fatigue, and depression (Bolton 1981). Anthropologists have debated whether *susto* is a **folk illness,**

that is, a cultural manifestation, or an organic disease with a physical basis (see Chapter 21).

To help answer this question, Bolton selected a sample of 41 adult men in a Quechua-speaking community in Peru (Figure 2.6). Bolton hypothesized that *susto* was caused by high levels of hostility. This hypothesis was inspired by psychological theories suggesting that high levels of hostility may produce psychosomatic disease symptoms. Bolton asked the men if they had ever suffered from *susto.* This was the dependent variable. He also asked the men to take a sentence-completion test as a measure of their hostility level. Bolton classified men with scores above the median score as hostile. (The **median** is the value that divides a range of scores down the middle, so that half the scores are higher and half are lower.) Bolton classified those with scores below the median as low in hostility. This was the independent variable.

As often occurs, the operational definition of a variable—in this case, hostility—may not reflect all that people commonly understand in the idea. But it is objective and replicable. Figure 2.7 shows that hostility and *susto* are positively correlated. Very few men who were low on the hostility scale had ever suffered from *susto.* More men who were high in hostility had had the disease.

There were several exceptions to the positive correlation: Some of the hostile men had not had the disease and some of the nonhostile ones had. These apparent exceptions could be due to **measurement error.** For example, some men may have concealed having had *susto.* Or there could be a **coding error.**

---

experiment   The testing of a hypothesis by making repeated observations in which a single variable is manipulated to determine its effect.

controlled experiment   An experiment in which the conditions are manipulated so the effect of variables on each other can be measured.

correlation   An observed relationship between two or more variables.

naturalistic studies   Research studies that uses statistical controls rather than laboratory controls to manipulate variables.

statistical controls   A kind of experiment in which laboratory controls are replaced by the search for significant correlations between variables.

control group   In an experiment, the group in which the experimental treatment is not applied or in which the independent variable is thought to be absent.

experimental group   In an experiment, the group in which the experimental treatment is applied or in which the independent variable is expected to have a measurable effect on the dependent variable.

sampling   In social science, the selection of part of a population for observation.

folk illness   An illness in which culturally defined symptoms play a significant part.

median   The point in a distribution at which there is an equal number of higher and lower scores.

measurement error   An error occurring when the observer mistakes the correct value of the variable.

coding error   An error occurring when the value of a variable is recorded incorrectly.

Figure 2.6   *Qolla men of Peru. Anthropologists have used the experimental method to study the medical syndrome known as* susto *in this population.*

Figure 2.7   *The relation between* susto *and hostility.*

Score on hostility scale*

		High	Low
Man has had susto	Yes	11	3
	No	8	15

*Four cases were not scorable.

For example, the scorer of the hostility test might have misconstrued some of the answers. A third kind of error, **sampling error**, could arise if the sample were too small or biased in some way. A statistical test called **Chi square** (χ^2) gives the probability that these results were caused by random error. In the distribution shown in Figure 2.7, the chance is less than 1 in 100. Most social scientists feel this probability is low enough to place confidence in the results. Is one variable the cause of the other? The correlation alone does not tell us. Hostility may or may not be the cause of *susto,* or both of these variables might be caused by a third variable. In fact, further tests showed that subjects with a history of *susto* were also likely to test positive for hypoglycemia, a metabolic disorder. Finally, the association between the variables could be due to chance, although it is unlikely in this case.

Bolton did not reach a definitive conclusion about the causes of *susto*, but he did show that both organic and culturally controlled factors may interact to cause the syndrome. This is an important finding for both medicine and anthropology.

Bolton's research shows how experimental design can be used outside the laboratory. He compared individuals to each other within a single cultural unit, but comparisons can also be made among two or more cultural units. Some examples of this type of comparison are given later in this chapter.

Bolton's work is an example of an explicit use of experimental design in anthropological research. Many other research projects are more descriptive (or inductive) than this one, and often they are not aimed directly at comparison. Many anthropologists feel it is imperative just to record cultural data before it disappears forever. They feel comparisons can be carried out later. Unfortunately, gathering data for this reason may not be useful, because, as we have noted, the definition of variables and the classification of data depend on the problem under consideration.

GENERALIZATION AND THE SEARCH FOR LAWS IN ANTHROPOLOGY

When hypotheses are confirmed repeatedly, under a variety of conditions, **generalizations** emerge about how variables are related. **Laws** are general statements that have been accepted after repeated testing. Scientists do not run about willy-nilly testing any hypothesis that comes into their heads; they usually build on a body of **theory**. A theory is a collection of hypotheses, laws, and guesses logically linked together. For example, laws about the tides can be explained in terms of

higher laws concerning the attraction exerted by heavy bodies on each other (the theory of gravity).

All laws, hypotheses, and theories are provisional. Even the most respected theory may be changed or abandoned if new information fails to support it. Recently a new experiment raised questions about Newton's theory of gravity, thought to be one of the most secure laws of nature (Pool 1988). Some scientific theories have been solidly confirmed in test after test, so their general validity is not often questioned by scientists. Such theories are influential in setting the agenda for science. However, because there are unexplored and controversial realms in every area of science, and because better measurements may bring new results to light, any theory is subject to revision.

Early Anthropological Theory

Because anthropology is a relatively young discipline and tends to be inductive, it has few widely accepted laws or generalizations. There is even disagreement about what might be a valid anthropological law. During the 19th century, the forerunners of modern anthropology tried to formulate laws to account for the development of culture. Scholars like Edward Tylor, Lewis H. Morgan, and Herbert Spencer proposed that human societies evolve in identifiable patterns, a concept known as cultural evolution. They suggested that women once dominated all societies (matriarchy). According to this theory, as societies become more developed and mature, they pass through an intermediate stage and finally become patriarchal. As evidence, they presented data concerning customs among many different societies around the world in which matriarchal and transitional customs appeared to be preserved as vestiges of past stages. For example, these early anthropologists interpreted the reckoning

---

sampling error An error occurring when a sample has been chosen that is not representative of the total population.

chi square (χ^2) A statistical test of significance that measures the likelihood that a given distribution could have been obtained by chance.

generalization A statement of general scope about the relationship of two or more variables.

law A generalization that has been accepted as true after repeated testing.

theory A network of laws, hypotheses, and guesses linked in a logical and coherent way.

of descent through the mother's line (matriliny) as evidence that a society had passed through a matriarchal stage.

There were many flaws in the methods used in the 19th century. The ideas of matriarchy and patriarchy were never defined clearly. There is little or no evidence that there ever were societies in which women ruled. A better understanding of matrilineal descent now shows that it has little to do with which gender is politically dominant. The cultural evolution concept also seems to reflect an ethnocentric bias because it assumes that male-dominated societies like those of North America and Western Europe are the most highly evolved.

The mistakes of these early anthropologists caused what may have been an overreaction. Doubt was cast not only on their conclusions but also on the value of proposing and testing generalizations. Many anthropologists, particularly followers of Franz Boas, a founder of academic anthropology in the United States, virtually abandoned comparison and generalization as goals of anthropology. They became known as **historical particularists,** and they produced highly detailed descriptive ethnographies that downgraded the importance of theory. The early anthropologists assumed that societies existing at the same time could represent different stages of evolution, in the same way that amphibians and mammals represent different stages in the evolution of animals. The historical particularists insisted that no society was more evolved than any other.

New Approaches to Anthropological Generalization

Recently some anthropologists revived the attempt to formulate developmental laws of culture. Robert Carneiro (1970) devised an evolutionary scale based on a different criterion from that used by the 19th-century evolutionists. In Carneiro's scheme the fundamental assumption is that cultural evolution is cumulative: New traits accumulate incrementally as society develops. It follows, then, that evolved societies should have a greater number of traits than less-evolved ones. Carneiro employed a method known as **scale analysis** to test this assumption. The method involves constructing a matrix on a piece of graph paper. Along the

bottom is a list of cases (different societies), and along one side is a selected set of culture traits (variables), one for each row.

The analysis is done by placing a plus sign (+) in each cell where a given variable is present in a given case. The two scales are rearranged in order of total number of traits from left to right. The vertical scale is similarly rearranged in order of frequency of occurrence from the bottom up. The result is a chart called a **scalogram** (Figure 2.8). The scalogram tells us whether traits have some necessary relationship to each other. If pluses appear all over the chart, more or less randomly, the two variables in question do not *scale*. If, however, the scale assumes a step shape, the variables scale. In a perfect scalogram the data show that each successive level on the scale depends on the previous ones. Because the scale is not perfect, it is more accurate to state that traits lower on the scale are necessary conditions for traits higher on the scale. If the scale in Figure 2.8 is a reflection of reality, it is possible to argue that markets are unlikely to appear in societies before the emergence of full-time political leaders.

Like his 19th-century predecessors, Carneiro used contemporary societies as evidence for cultural evolution. Thus most of the societies appearing along the bottom of the matrix in Figure 2.8 are societies that exist today or existed until the recent past. Carneiro recognizes that each one may have an equally long and rich historical past, but also that each one represents a stage or level of evolutionary development. The scale suggests that cultural evolution has occurred and that some societies are more evolved than others, in the particular sense defined by the scalogram. It does not tell the mechanism by which each level contributes to the emergence of the more highly ranked steps. This is a matter for detailed analysis at the ethnographic and comparative levels. For example, the scale implies a causal relationship between full-time leaders and markets but does not define the relationship.

The historical particularists attacked evolutionary generalizations by showing that they did not apply in particular cases. For example, examination of Figure 2.8 shows that markets are present among the Kofyar of Nigeria while full-time political leaders are not. Does this exception invalidate the scale? Possibly, but the great majority of the cases conform to the generalization. The exception could be the result of coding or measurement error, or it might be a genuine exception. Perhaps the inclusion of Kofyar in a larger market system resulted in the presence of markets even though the political system had not yet evolved to the point at which markets normally develop. Overall, however, about 85 percent of the traits appeared in the predicted order. Thus the evolutionary sequence suggested by this scalogram fits well, although not perfectly, in most particular cases. Anthropological generalizations, like those in most other sciences, hold true in a majority of cases but not all cases.

There are many other generalizations in anthropology, some of them well accepted, many more of them quite tentative and even suspect. We discuss several of them in later chapters. One of the great challenges of anthropology is to apply the rules of natural science to propose and test more and more generalizations in all its fields. The more generalizations we can verify, the greater will be our ability to understand humankind in the past and the present and perhaps even to predict the future.

THE ANTHROPOLOGICAL APPROACH: STUDYING CANNIBALISM

Anthropologists follow the scientific paradigm in much of their work, although, as we have seen, there are special problems involved in defining the object of study and overcoming bias in measurement. Anthropologists also follow interpretive paradigms in their work (see Chapters 3 and 4). In actual practice anthropologists frequently resort to "hybrid" strategies that include elements of scientific and interpretive paradigms. It is sometimes difficult even to set up precise definitions for things we want to study. Interpreting or explaining such phenomena is also difficult for a variety of reasons.

To see some of the difficulties anthropologists face, let us consider cannibalism, a custom that many people find revolting or "primitive." Cannibalism is a useful, if disturbing, example, because it demonstrates a number of important issues and concerns. It also shows how data from ethnography, human biology, and archaeology may be brought to bear on a topic. Let's consider first a few descriptions of cannibalism found in the anthropological literature.

Describing Cannibalism

The Yanomamo of Venezuela. Anthropologist Napoleon Chagnon first visited the Yanomamo of Venezuela in the early 1960s. He learned to speak their language and has made many follow-up visits to them. In describing the treatment of the dead, Chagnon made these observations:

> The bodies of dead adults are placed on a stack of firewood in the center of the village and burned as completely as possible. After the fire has cooled, someone sifts through the ashes and picks out unburnt bones and teeth. These are ground up into a powder by a close friend or relative of the dead person, who then stores the powder in hollow gourds. Any remaining powder is mixed with a banana soup and drunk by a gathering of mourners. [Chagnon 1983, 106]

The Huron of Canada. Anthropologist Bruce Trigger described Huron cannibalism in what is now Ontario, Canada, during the 17th century. Based on accounts by explorers such as Samuel de Champlain and Jesuit missionaries, Trigger claims that the Huron ate the flesh of their male war captives. The Huron would bring a captured enemy warrior to a village, where a family adopted him and treated him with kindness and generosity. Sometimes the family grew

---

historical particularism An anthropological approach in which the search for general developmental laws is rejected as a goal for anthropology in favor of recording the historical details of specific cultures.

scale analysis A method of analysis that seeks to array a set of cases along a scale ranging from the fewest to the most traits.

scalogram A diagram arranged to display a hierarchy of conditions such that more basic conditions appear before less basic ones.

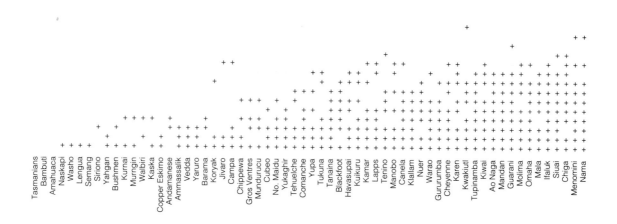

Figure 2.8 *The Carneiro scalogram of cultural evolution, which suggests that societies add culture traits in an orderly way.*

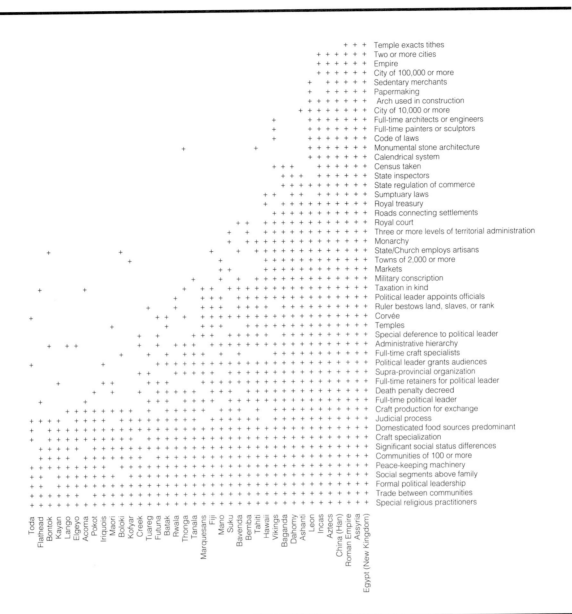

so fond of their prisoner that they decided to spare his life, but usually the kind treatment ended abruptly. Then the victim underwent a period of torture before he was finally killed. Sometimes his adoptive family joined in the torture. His body was cut up into pieces to be cooked and eaten. Some Huron seemed to have a horror of human flesh, while others seemed to enjoy it. If the prisoner had been a brave warrior, young Huron men would eat his heart in order to acquire his courage. Some tried to let the prisoner's blood run into their veins through self-inflicted cuts as a supernatural protection against being surprised by an enemy (Trigger 1969, 51).

The Aztecs of Mexico.   Probably the best-known cannibals of history are the Aztecs of Mexico, who

engaged in continual wars of conquest. (For more on the Aztecs, see Chapter 16.) Like the Huron, the Aztecs sacrificed war captives and consumed their flesh (Figure 2.9). Like the Huron, the Aztec warrior who captured an enemy considered his captive a kinsman. When Hernan Cortés captured the Aztec capital of Tenochtitlan (where Mexico City now stands) in 1521, one of the conquistadors witnessed human sacrifice and described it in his memoirs:

> The natives of this land had very large temples. . . . They had large towers with a house of worship at the top, and close to the entrance, a low stone, about knee-high, where the men or women who were to be sacrificed to their gods were thrown on their backs and of their own accord remained perfectly still. A priest then came out with a stone knife like a lance-

Figure 2.9   *That the Aztecs practiced human sacrifice and cannibalism in the 15th century is well documented, but anthropologists are still debating the meaning of such ritual sacrifice.*

head but which barely cut anything, and with this knife he opened the part where the heart is and took out the heart, without the person who was being sacrificed uttering a word. . . . Then the man or woman, having been killed in this fashion, was thrown down the steps where the body was taken and most cruelly torn to pieces, then roasted in clay ovens and eaten as a very tender delicacy; and this is the way they made sacrifices to their gods. [Aguilar 1963, 163–164]

Arriving ten years after the conquest, Father Bernardino de Sahagún, a Spanish priest, talked extensively with Aztec nobles about ritual sacrifice. Sahagún recorded such details as how the Aztecs divided up their victims' bodies. The heart was intended for the gods, a thigh was reserved for the emperor, the rest was distributed among the blood relatives of the man who had captured the enemy soldier in battle. Curiously, the captor did not himself eat his captive's flesh, saying,

"Shall I, then, eat my own flesh?" For when he took [the captive], he had said: "He is as my beloved son." [Sahagún 1951, 52–53, quoted in Berdan 1982, 115]

Does Cannibalism Exist?

Despite such evidence, anthropologist William Arens published a book in 1979 entitled *The Man-Eating Myth,* in which he argued that cannibalism does not exist. He pointed out that no group in the world today will admit it practices cannibalism, but one group often accuses another of it. After examining many reports of cannibalism, Arens found that none was fully verifiable. Arens flatly stated that the evidence for cannibalism would "not stand up in a court of law."

Arens concluded that cannibalism was a myth created by Europeans to denigrate non-Europeans and justify domination of them. The accusation of cannibalism may reflect a kind of chauvinism or ethnocen-

trism. However, Arens showed that this attitude is not confined to the West; Koreans and Chinese also accuse each other of cannibalism. And the Lugbara people of Uganda could not accept anthropologist John Middleton until they decided he was "one of those rare Europeans who did not eat African babies" (Arens 1979, 12).

The response to Arens's claim was overwhelming protest. Accounts too numerous and too consistent with each other to have been made up support the fact that cannibalism is (or was) an authentic human custom. Supporting evidence comes from the work of medical doctors, including Dr. Daniel Carlton Gajdusek, who won the Nobel Prize in Medicine in 1976. With the assistance of anthropologists Shirley Lindenbaum and Robert Glasse, Gajdusek made extensive studies of **kuru**, a brain disease afflicting members of the Fore people in Papua New Guinea (Figure 2.10). These studies showed convincingly that kuru was transmitted through the consumption of human brain tissue infected with a very slow-acting virus (Lindenbaum 1979). The Fore believe that sorcery is the cause of kuru. When this region of Papua New Guinea came under Australian rule in the 1940s, the authorities prohibited cannibalism. During this period many alleged cannibals faced trial in Australian courts. In these proceedings the evidence and testimony convinced judges that cannibalism had in fact occurred.

Further evidence of cannibalism can be found in archaeology. Dr. Paola Villa (1983) and her coworkers excavated Fontbrégoua Cave in southern France; the cave was occupied by people intermittently between 7,000 and 5,000 years ago. They herded sheep and goats and also hunted wild animals such as badger, fox, boar, and deer. Villa and her coworkers excavated 13 clusters of animal bones (both wild and domestic) from what appear to be refuse pits located in various parts of the cave. Three of these clusters contained human bones, discarded in the same fashion as the animal bones. Many of the bones had cut marks on them (Figure 2.11); several long bones had been

---

kuru   A degenerative, fatal nerve disease believed to be caused by a slow-acting virus, first described among the Fore of Papua New Guinea.

Figure 2.10 *Evidence of cannibalism among the Fore of New Guinea came from medical investigations of the brain disease kuru. Here, native curers treat a kuru victim by bleeding.*

portant point. Anthropologists must be on their guard against preconceptions and fabrications if they hope to arrive at scientifically valid conclusions.

Defining Cannibalism

How do we define cannibalism? A simple definition might be: Cannibalism is a practice in which people ingest any part of a human body. But what if people eat parts of human bodies to avoid starvation even though their culture normally forbids them to do so? This was the case when a group of young South American athletes were stranded on a snow-covered Andean peak after their plane crashed in 1972. As described in the book *Alive* by Piers Paul Read, the young men reluctantly ate the bodies of their comrades who had died in the crash. Although they consumed human flesh, most people would not call them cannibals, because cannibalism is not a normal or common occurrence in their culture.

To account for this variation, let us consider a second definition: Cannibalism is a culturally accepted practice of ingesting parts of the human body. This is a **normative** definition: It defines customs in terms of what people in society approve of. But here we run into another problem. What people approve of may be different from what they actually do. The Yanomamo, for example, seem to abhor cannibalism even though they customarily drink a soup containing pulverized human bones.

Should our definition reflect what people approve of or what they actually do? In practice the ideal definition will depend on the question the anthropologist is asking. Unlike astronomers or chemists, anthropologists deal with subjects that have their own view of themselves. As we saw earlier in this chapter, definitions in anthropology often have two aspects: things as they are understood by the people under study (emic data) and things as they are understood by the observers (etic data).

crushed as if to extract the marrow for food. By examining the cut marks under a powerful electron microscope, the archaeologists determined that the marks had been made by people using stone tools. Human bones were treated the same as animal bones; the cut marks suggest that people had systematically stripped flesh from the bones to make fillets. The investigators concluded, "We believe that cannibalism is the only satisfactory explanation for the evidence found at Fontbrégoua Cave" (1983, 436). We do not know, however, how the people who were eaten died.

The weight of evidence indicates that cannibalism has existed among human beings. While he may have been wrong on the facts, Arens's book made an im-

Explaining and Interpreting Cannibalism

Perhaps the simplest interpretation for cannibalism is that it provides needed food. Several anthropologists have evaluated the nutritional value of human flesh

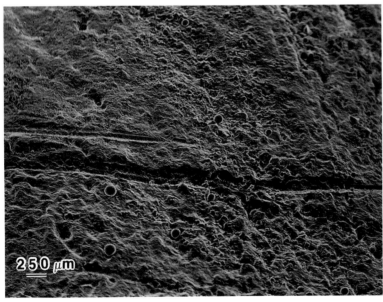

250 μm

Figure 2.11 *Human bones found in Fontbrégoua Cave in France exhibited the same kind of cut marks as the animal bones discarded with them, suggesting that cannibalism was practiced by the cave dwellers. An electron micrograph (left) of the bone shown above indicated that the cuts were made with stone tools.*

normative Relating to social standards or rules.

and its dietary significance. They concluded that raising people for slaughter like cattle would not be efficient but that human flesh could be nutritionally beneficial if a shortage of protein existed in the diet (Dornstreich and Morren 1974). Most descriptions of cannibalism, however, describe it as part of a ritual, and some investigators are careful to distinguish between *dietary cannibalism* and *ritual cannibalism*. While this distinction may be valid, we should note that flesh eaten as part of a ritual provides the same nutritional benefit as flesh eaten solely as food.

In 1977 anthropologist Michael Harner made perhaps the strongest case for dietary cannibalism. Harner suggested that Aztec cannibalism should be interpreted "as the natural and rational response to the material conditions of their existence" (132). Harner pointed out that Tenochtitlán, the Aztec capital, had a large, densely packed population lacking a reliable source of protein such as livestock, milk, or eggs. He suggested that cannibalism was a response to the depletion of wild game and that the Aztecs distributed human flesh to those most in need of protein in their diets. The ritual surrounding the custom was a means of justifying it in religious terms.

Harner's theory immediately came under attack. Some anthropologists presented evidence that protein was not in short supply in Tenochtitlán (Sahlins 1978). Others argued that the timing of sacrifices and the distribution of human flesh were not consistent with the protein scarcity argument (Ortíz de Montellano 1978, Berdan 1982). Many critics insisted that the ritual meaning of human sacrifice far outweighed any nutritional needs that it might serve (Sahlins 1978). Some critics stated that Harner had insulted the Aztecs and their Mexican descendants in his article. With the evidence presently available, the argument is difficult to resolve. Although Harner made a plausible case for dietary cannibalism among the Aztecs, his critics do not accept his evidence and have offered alternative hypotheses.

Cannibalism may also have psychological or symbolic meaning. A cannibal, partaking of the flesh of another human being, may believe he or she will acquire some of that person's traits. Cannibals who eat enemies often prefer to eat brave warriors who have distinguished themselves in battle. Ingesting the flesh of a brave adversary is a way of destroying that adversary while, at the same time, symbolically assimilating some of his courage. If we assume that cannibalism is naturally repulsive to people, the very act of eating human flesh is a display of courage.

Freudian psychology also provides some possible insight into cannibalism. In the Huron and Aztec cases, the victim is first adopted into the captor's family, only to be sacrificed and eaten later. This may be seen as a way of displacing anger from close family members to strangers by first bringing the enemy into the family and then killing and eating him. Or it could be that cannibalism satisfies the ambivalent feelings that people may have toward family members, intense love combined with hostility and rage; by consuming their bodies, the cannibal causes them to disappear while simultaneously incorporating them into his own body.

We are still far from a satisfactory general explanation of cannibalism, because we lack sufficient data to evaluate certain hypotheses. For example, in assessing the dietary explanation for Aztec cannibalism, we are aware that the Aztecs had other sources of protein; however, there is little evidence that the sources yielded enough protein to meet the nutritional needs of the population. It is difficult to analyze ritual cannibalism as well. Some explanations and interpretations fit some cases better than others. It is possible that no general explanation will cover all known types of cannibalism.

What Can We Learn from Studying Cannibalism?

Although we have not reached a comprehensive explanation of cannibalism, the example illustrates several important points about the anthropological approach. First, we can see that difficulties arise from the conflict between understanding a custom in terms of the people who practice it and in terms of a scientific community that stands apart. Second, special care must be taken to understand human traits or customs, especially if they are as controversial and emotionally charged as cannibalism. Third, the conditions that contribute to cannibalistic practices, whether they are nutritional, ecological, or psychological, are not particular to a single people but are common to humankind. Fourth, many kinds of data—ethnographic, archaeological, medical, historical—are integrated to approach a subject anthropologically. Finally, a number of possible explanations can emerge from an investigation. Some can be tested, but evidence for others may be difficult to obtain.

tration of the styles of explanation, sources of evidence, boundaries, and pitfalls in anthropological investigations. The definition of cannibalism raises questions that must be answered before explanations or interpretations can be offered. Because people themselves can define the same behavior in d.fferent ways, it is necessary to distinguish between the native definition and the observer's definition of a custom. Various kinds of evidence can be brought to bear on an anthropological question.

SUMMARY

- Anthropologists rely on different ways of knowing.
- In its scientific mode, the goal of anthropology is to produce valid generalizations about human differences and similarities. This mode of explanation is comparable to prediction.
- To explain human phenomena, anthropology relies on observation, experimentation, and generalization.
- Anthropologists use several different kinds of instruments for measurement, the most problematic of them being the human ethnographer. As measurement devices, ethnographers are not standardized or calibrated. As socialized human beings, they carry many conscious and unconscious biases. This presents a challenge to measurement in anthropology.
- Cultural relativism seeks to overcome bias by understanding each culture in its own terms. Anthropologists are urged to become aware of their biases so that they can compensate for them. But one cannot compensate for any unconsciously held biases.
- Another approach to bias is to use operational definitions. These are deliberately narrow definitions that reduce the possibility of bias.
- In spite of all the obstacles, it is possible to use experimental methods in anthropology.
- Because laboratory controls are not always possible, anthropologists often employ statistical controls. From these experiments some generalizations have emerged, but since anthropology is a young, highly inductive science, not many laws have become well established.
- The anthropology of cannibalism provides an illus-

GET INVOLVED

1. Imagine you are responsible for a program of economic change in an underdeveloped country where women are kept in virtual seclusion. They are not permitted to go out of their houses except in the company of their fathers, brothers, or husbands. They are obliged to wear clothing that covers the entire body and most of the face. Women are not permitted to work outside the home or even to touch objects that have been handled by strange men. Most of the men are fully employed in farming or commerce, and most of the people are desperately poor and suffer from poor nutrition. The only way you can see to unleash economic change is to allow women to share some of the work outside the household. At a meeting of local leaders, an elder man tells you, "You are welcome here. We look to you for new ideas. You are free to introduce any plan you like, but we must warn you, any change in the position of women in our society is absolutely unthinkable." What should you do?

2. Time-allocation studies can yield startling results. Try carrying out one yourself. Set up a list of basic time-use categories, then distribute a questionnaire to a small sample of people to ask them how much of their time they spend on each of the categories. Next, by means of random spot checks, or by use of a diary, keep tabs on how each of your sample subjects actually spends his or her time. Analyze the results, showing the difference between the subject's perception of time and how he or she actually spent time.

3. Set up a mini research project in a group or subculture close to your home that you find exotic or strange. It could be an ethnic minority, a religious group, or, perhaps, an athletic or social event you have never attended. Prepare for your research by making a list of ten things you need to find out about the group you will study. Then do your study, announcing yourself as an anthropologist (or anthropology student) to the group. When you complete your study, briefly write up your results, covering the following topics: (a) a summary of observations (following your list of ten items); (b) your reactions to what you observed; (c) the ways in which your personal subcultural background affected your reactions.

SUGGESTED READINGS

Berdan, Frances F. 1982. *The Aztecs of Central Mexico: An imperial society*. New York: Holt, Rinehart and Winston.

Bohannan, Laura. 1966. Shakespeare in the bush. *Natural History* (Aug./Sept.).*

Lett, James. 1987. *The human enterprise: A critical introduction to anthropological theory*. Boulder, Colo.: Westview Press.

Powdermaker, Hortence. 1966. *Stranger and friend*. New York: Norton.

Trager, Lillian. 1987. Living abroad: Cross-cultural training for families. *Practicing Anthropology* 9 (3): 5, 11.*

*This selection is anthologized in *Applying Anthropology*, 2d ed., A. Podolefsky and P. J. Brown (Mountain View, Calif.: Mayfield, 1992).

A Study of Lobster Fishing

James M. Acheson is a professor of anthropology at the University of Maine at Orono. In addition to his research interest in Mesoamerica, he has examined a culture much closer to his home—the lobster fishing community.

James Acheson.

In 1977 I began an intensive study of lobster fishing communities along the central coast of Maine. One phenomenon that my research associate Dr. John Bort and I noticed was that lobster traps made of wire were replacing the traditional wooden traps. Moreover, this new style of traps was being adopted in some communities but not in others. In Bremen in Muscongus Bay large numbers of lobster catchaks (the local name) were using wire traps almost exclusively, whereas in New Harbor, some 12 miles distant, virtually none of the wire traps were in use.

I asked a couple of good friends from the New Harbor area about this. They both said they were certain that there wasn't any difference in the way that wooden and wire traps fished. After all, wooden lathes and wire did the same thing, they pointed out: They covered the outside of the trap and stopped the lobsters from escaping. People who used wire traps, they said, were nothing but "damned fools," since wire traps cost more and produced no more lobsters.

This sounded sensible, particularly in view of the fact that the fishermen from Bremen did not offer any consistent reasons for using them. One fisherman said that he was using these wire traps because they fished better; but several others said they were using them because very good fishermen in their own harbor used them. That, we thought, was the secret. People were adopting the more expensive wire traps, we hypothesized, because the early adopters were high-status, influential men in the local harbor gang, and lower-status men were emulating them. The explanation, we were certain, was entirely social; economics had little to do with it.

During the fall and winter, we carried out several kinds of studies, including a long, detailed quantitative study of the factors influencing catches. We accompanied fishermen on literally dozens of fishing trips. We recorded detailed data on each trap pulled during the day, including length of all the legal-sized lobsters caught in that trap, length of trap, type of bait, depth of water, trap construction material, and so on.

When these data were coded, entered in the computer, and analyzed, we got a real surprise. Our data demonstrated beyond all reasonable doubt that wire traps did fish substantially better than the traditional wooden traps. Our hypothesis about social factors and diffusion of wire traps was clearly wrong.

I quietly showed these results to one of the first fishermen in Bremen to use wire traps. His commentary was acerbic at best. "Of course wire traps fish better," he said. "Why else do you think we would use them?" Just as quickly, he said, "You are not going to tell anyone about this are you?" In the next half hour, it became apparent that the Bremen fishermen knew very well that wire traps caught more lobsters than wooden traps and that they had been very successful in obscuring that fact with some artful misinformation, not to say outright lies. They knew that the truth would emerge eventually, but they wanted to delay that day as long as possible to maximize their catches. So far they had succeeded, and now I threatened their strategy.

I was caught in an ethical dilemma. Should I withhold scientific results and damage the informants who had helped me? I finally promised to keep the secret about the effectiveness of the wire traps until other fishermen had discovered it for themselves. It proved to be an easy promise to keep since local fishermen became convinced of the value of wire traps in a matter of months— long before I could have published the results even if I had wanted to.

This project produced a good deal of data about the factors affecting lobster catches. It also helped enlighten us about one of the more important aspects of the relationships among fishermen—namely, that they are engaged in a constant game of information management.

In broader perspective, this case underlines the fact that even good informants do not always agree on the facts; that there can be a range of opinion on vital matters even among people in the same subculture; and that people are always experimenting and learning. Those who would like to define culture as a static set of beliefs shared by everyone in the society might be advised to recall this.

PART TWO

LANGUAGE & MEANING

One of anthropology's great concerns is culture—the patterns of thinking and acting that people acquire through participation in a society, as opposed to those innate, biological capabilities they bring with them into the world. Although there are learned elements in the social lives of other animals—parents may teach their offspring how to hunt, for example, or how to respond to different kinds of calls—no other species makes use of such complex, elaborated sets of standards, traditions, ideas, values, and rules as humans do. Each new generation has to acquire this shared information if it is to survive—and if the group itself is to survive as a cultural entity.

Although all people are dependent on cultural solutions to problems of survival, different societies have developed different solutions. Some anthropologists study the more apparent differences among societies, such as their social organization or their marriage customs. Others are interested in exploring what lies under those differences—the deepest assumptions, habits of thought, and understandings of the world that give shape to different cultures. This is the realm of interpretive anthropology, and it is the subject of Chapter 3. Here we consider how anthropologists approach cultural objects, events, and ideas in ways that reveal their underlying meaning and significance for the group in which they occur. Through various approaches, such as analyzing the symbols in stories and myths or considering the words people use to describe and divide up their physical world, researchers seek a deeper understanding of diverse cultures.

The primary means by which culture and cultural meanings are shared within a group and transmitted from one generation to the next is language. Chapter 4 addresses language—the symbolic communication system of coded signs that people use to convey information and ideas—from an anthropological perspective. Anthropological linguistics focuses on such aspects of language as how it carries meaning, how it may have originated, and how it interacts with patterns of thinking and with specific social and cultural contexts. Part Two thus provides an introduction to cultural meanings, the set of ideas people in a society share about how things are to be understood, and to language, the set of signs and symbols they use to communicate meaning.

Gestures have different meanings in different cultures. These Japanese girls in Tokyo greet an American photographer with a particularly American sign.

CULTURAL MEANINGS

▲▲▲

Many questions in anthropology arise from the examination of a cultural belief or practice that seems bizarre or irrational. The example of cannibalism given in Chapter 2 illustrates this vividly. Why, anthropologists ask, do some groups engage in cannibalistic practices when so many other groups find them abhorrent? Why do the modern Maya of Chiapas, Mexico, use so much alcohol in their religious ceremonies (Figure 3.1)? What accounts for the practice, once common in India, of a widow's throwing herself onto her husband's burning funeral pyre? To explain these behaviors in terms familiar to us is often unsatisfactory. If we cannot rationalize behavior in our own terms, we may become perplexed or even angry. It seems obvious that these behaviors have to be understood according to different rules from the ones we use.

EXAMINING CULTURAL BELIEFS

Anthropologists have to try to understand what behaviors mean to the actors. The quest for meaning in anthropology is partly an attempt to learn how people from other societies rationalize their own behavior. If we cannot understand people's reasons for what they do, we can neither understand nor accept it. One of anthropology's goals is to understand why other people think and act differently.

The deepest secrets of human culture are embedded in the meanings that people attach to their experiences. To say that something has **meaning** is to say that it carries information. Meaning can be individual and personal, but anthropologists are interested in **cultural meanings**, those that are part of a tradition shared within some social group. Each social group has its own repertoire of meaningful elements combined in a distinctive way. Language is part of this repertoire, which also includes art, religion, morals, and technology.

Taking an example from our everyday lives, suppose someone asks you, "What kinds of people are there in your community?" You might answer in terms of religion (Catholics, Protestants, Jews, Muslims), politics (socialists, conservatives, liberals), professional status (professionals, workers, unemployed), family status (singles, couples, families with children, "empty nesters"), and so on. All these categories have meaningful elements, although they can be distin-

guished in other ways as well. How you answer depends not only on your community but also on how you think about it. The categories you select are most likely those that are most significant to you, reflecting the cultural traditions in which you were raised.

Meaningful things do not accumulate in a random way, like beads of different colors spilled into a bowl. Since people *learn* cultural patterns, their mental, **symbolic**, and **cognitive** aspects are especially important. The human mind organizes meaningful elements in patterns. Different anthropologists refer to these elements by various terms: **world view**, **cultural themes**, or **patterns of culture**. These patterns form the basis of cultural identity, those cues that groups use to distinguish themselves from others.

Shared cultural patterns give group members a sense of belonging. They provide a framework within which people define their relationships to each other, to nature, and to the supernatural. We gave an example of this in the last chapter in referring to individual versus group orientation. In some societies, such as Japan, individuals tend to think of themselves as only parts of a greater whole. It is small wonder that people in such societies should view the world very differently from those in individualistic societies such as the United States.

We should not assume, however, that an entire, consistent set of patterns is shared by all members of a given group. While some overlap is necessary for a group to have a sense of common identity, evidence even from small, remote, technologically simple societies suggests that individual group members may see the world differently. In complex societies there are systematic contrasts in the world views of different classes, religious sects, and other groups.

Analyzing Myth

Perhaps no area of cultural life has been so thoroughly examined for meaning as myth. **Myths** are not simply tall tales or falsehoods; they are coded messages that communicate meanings in various ways by manipulating symbols recognizable to those who tell and hear them.

Perhaps the best known myths in the Western world are those conserved in ancient Greek literature. The Oedipus myth is one familiar example. In it, Oedipus unwittingly murders his own father and marries his mother. This powerful myth has many layers of

Figure 3.1 *The modern Maya of Chiapas, Mexico, use what many North Americans would consider an excessive amount of alcohol in their religious ceremonies. To understand such unfamiliar traditions, anthropologists often try to discover what they mean to the people who practice them.*

meaning that have been explored by playwrights, philosophers, and psychologists. Another famous Greek myth tells how Prometheus stole fire from the gods and gave it to humankind, suffering eternal punishment for his trouble. This is an example of an **origin myth**, a type of myth that explains how some common feature of life came to be. The Greek myths are also a rich source of information about the structure and values of ancient Greek society. They can be

analyzed as **charters** that set down the basic beliefs underlying the social order.

Myths are typically narratives about supernatural beings or events in some unspecified period of time (sometimes called **mythic time**), involving such themes as the creation of the world or of human beings (**creation myths**), death and the afterlife, and renewal of the earth. Myths can be distinguished from **folktales** and **legends** in terms of formal differences

---

meaning Information that is carried by an object, event, or action.

cultural meaning Information that is part of a shared tradition within a social group.

symbolic Representative or suggestive of an idea or emotion other than that carried by an object itself.

cognitive Pertaining to patterns of thinking; designation for the influence of cultural patterns, which are learned by the members of a particular society, on the way people perceive and organize the world.

world view The assumptions that people in a society make regarding such matters as the purpose of human existence, the nature of reality, and the difference between good and evil.

cultural themes Principles shared by members of a society that define the limits of acceptable behavior.

patterns of culture The unique, integrated configuration of beliefs and behaviors that sets every society apart from every other society; an anthropological construct.

myths Stories that symbolically encode culturally meaningful messages; narratives, portrayed as fact, about supernatural beings or events that happened in some unspecified time in the remote past.

origin myth A story that explains how some common feature of life came into existence.

charter An origin myth that sets forth the basic beliefs underlying the social order in a particular society.

mythic time The unspecified time when a particular myth is supposed to have occurred.

creation myth A story that involves the creation of the world or human beings.

folktales Prose narratives that may be set in any time or place, are regarded as fiction, and usually have human or animal characters.

legends Narratives that are considered true by both narrator and audience, that are believed to have occurred in the historic past, and whose principle characters are humans.

BOX 3.1

What Is Culture?

Culture is a central idea for anthropology; many anthropologists build the definition of the discipline itself around this concept. The first comprehensive definition of culture in the anthropological sense was offered by Sir Edward B. Tylor, a British scholar sometimes credited with founding modern anthropology. Tylor defined culture as "that complex whole which includes knowledge, belief, art, morals, law, custom, and any other capabilities and habits acquired by man as a member of society" (1871, 1). Tylor's definition is still the most quoted definition of culture. It describes what many people refer to as social traditions. The key point is that cultural capabilities are *acquired* through participation in *society*. According to the definition, culture is learned, not innate, and closely tied to social life.

Later anthropologists distinguished between culture and society, leading to a distinction between "cultural anthropology," practiced mainly in the United States, and "social anthropology," practiced mainly in Great Britain. Generally, cultural anthropologists were concerned with traditions themselves as embodied in tools, ornaments, ceremonies, languages, and how they were passed from one society to another across space and from generation to generation through time. The social anthropologists were generally more concerned with social processes, particularly kinship and religion in non-Western societies. One British social anthropologist, A.R. Radcliffe-Brown, suggested that social anthropology was simply a form of "comparative sociology."

The distinction between social and cultural anthropology was difficult to maintain in practice. One could not study cultural artifacts such as clay pots or bark cloth without examining the social processes by which they were produced. On the other side, social anthropology never ignored custom, language, and the material paraphernalia of culture. Social anthropology maintained something of a separate position because it was wedded to functionalism in the work of Radcliffe-Brown, Bronislaw Malinowski, and others. Functionalism sought to understand social behavior in terms of the functions it plays in the maintenance of the society as a whole. Functionalists produced many interesting analyses of social process, but they had difficulty in dealing with change, such as behavior that challenges the social order.

Once the idea of culture was well established as a central concept in anthropology, anthropologists had to confront the fact that culture was not simply an object, like a suitcase, that one could carry around. They also saw that culture was dynamic and subject to change. In the early-20th-century United States, where cultural anthropology first flourished, the salient cultural fact was the arrival of millions of immigrants from many parts of the world. Each one arrived with

---

or content, but most of these comments about myth apply equally to all three forms. Myths, folktales, and legends are known as **oral literature** because they are usually transmitted by storytellers long before they are written down. Once written down, a myth may become "frozen" because the written word removes the freedom of improvisation that belongs to the storyteller (Bascom 1984).

Usually we do not know the originator of a myth, and often a myth has been told and retold so many times that it occurs in many different versions. Some stories, like that of Cinderella, are found in different versions around the world, and this striking recurrence is a major focus of the structural approach to myth and meaning in general. (We look at this model later in this chapter.) Some writers suggest that there are just a few basic themes and that all the world's literature, written and unwritten, consists of those basic stories, told over and over again.

Creating Models of Meaning

Cultural meanings consist of shared information organized in certain ways inside people's heads in a social group (Box 3.1). This information is related in complex ways to other aspects of the mind such as emotions and values. We cannot get inside people's heads to see these meanings, so we must approach them indirectly, through models we build.

special characteristics, customs, likes and dislikes, laws and norms, and kinds of speech and appearance. As fast as they arrived, the immigrants began to undergo cultural change. They learned English and assimilated American customs. The American anthropologists became fascinated with the process of change that occurs when bearers of one cultural tradition begin to borrow elements from another. They named this process acculturation. They distinguished it from enculturation, which is the process of acquiring cultural traits within a single cultural tradition.

One observation that the American cultural anthropologists made was that acculturation was an adaptive process. As new elements of culture were accepted, they frequently were adapted or reinterpreted to fit into the characteristics and needs of the adopting culture. Thus, when the Western-style homburg hat was introduced into Peru and Bolivia, it became a favored form of headgear for market women, not a men's hat as in Europe and North America. Similarly, when African religious lore mixed with Roman Catholicism among African slaves in colonial Cuba, a new religion was formed, Santería, incorporating elements of both. There seemed to be an inner dynamic or *force vital* to each cultural tradition that acted to bring borrowed elements into line with the dominant themes of the culture. Ruth Benedict named them cultural patterns in her famous book *Patterns of Culture;* Morris Opler

called them cultural themes. They and other anthropologists conceived of culture as mainly mental, rather like a template against which all forms of expression can be compared.

The American tradition placed so much emphasis on culture that the idea began to assume a life of its own. Anthropologists began to talk about culture as if it were a living, breathing thing rather than a construct or model, useful in understanding behavior. Gradually, anthropologists began to realize that they had made more of culture than they had intended. Anthropologist Edward Sapir wrote, "Cultures do not paint their fingernails—people do."

Most anthropologists today are more comfortable with the concept of culture as a cover term for ranges of phenomena. Some anthropologists understand the term quite broadly, in the tradition of Tylor, as describing anything acquired by people as part of society. Many anthropologists now recognize the existence of nonhuman animal culture, especially among primates. Some anthropologists persist in conceiving of it as a mental thing; others continue to think of culture as including behavior. Thus for some anthropologists, culture is revealed in the plan for an arrowhead in a hunter's mind, and for others, culture exists also in the act of making the arrowhead, of translating the plan into action.

A model is an approximation of something else, not an exact replica, expressed mathematically or in words. All the sciences use models. A physicist constructs a model of the behavior of light by comparing it to waves traveling through water. From Freudian psychology comes the well-known model of personality consisting of the id, the ego, and the superego. Economists construct mathematical models, equations describing idealized events, such as transactions

or "aggregate demand." Cultural anthropologists build models of the thought patterns of the people they study, by using various theories of meaning.

Meaning can be approached in a variety of ways. Each model uses its own set of ideas, techniques, and assumptions in its attempts to understand how things have meaning and how the meanings interconnect. A symbolic approach examines the symbols present in all the enactments and products of culture. A

oral literature Stories such as myths, folktales, legends, riddles, and proverbs that are transmitted by narrators before they are set down in writing.

BOX 3.2

Color Symbolism

Colors are used in nearly every cultural tradition to symbolize certain events, emotions, or ideas. Many popular festivals in the United States have color symbolism attached to them. Of course other symbols are also associated with these festivals, such as the heart and Valentine's Day, but the colors alone are sufficient to evoke thoughts of the holiday and the rest of its symbols. Here are some examples familiar to residents of the United States:

Colors	Festival or Event
Orange and black	Halloween
Red and green	Christmas
Red and pink	Valentine's Day
Red, white, and blue	Independence Day (Fourth of July)
Yellow	Remembrance of hostages or of soldiers
Green	Saint Patrick's Day or other Irish events

Like all symbols, colors have no necessary or inherent connection with the event or festival they symbolize, although some connections are apparent. At Halloween, pumpkins and death are two common themes: pumpkins are orange, and black is the color of mourning (death). At Christmas, holly boughs with green leaves and red berries are a familiar decoration. The Independence Day colors are the same as those on the U.S. flag. Along the same lines, anthropologist Edmund Leach (1970, 17) has pointed out that wherever a color is associated with danger, it is far more likely to be red than green or yellow. Perhaps this is because of the association between red and blood.

---

semiotic approach looks for a hidden grammar in a particular domain of expression or behavior, such as literature or music. **Structuralism** stresses the unconscious and hidden structures that underlie cultural meanings. The most systematic approach to meaning lies in the experimental approach to cognition known as **ethnosemantics**.

SYMBOLIC APPROACHES TO MEANING

Some cultural anthropologists take symbols as the central focus of their research. **Symbols** are observable objects that, within a given tradition, refer to ideas and emotions outside themselves. They have meaning only in a given context. Symbols appear in physical objects, such as a flag; utterances, such as "The Lord is my shepherd"; and acts, such as drinking a glass of wine at a Passover seder. Symbols may be as simple as

a particular combination of colors (Box 3.2) or as complex as the sequence of events in a Roman Catholic mass. It is no accident that rituals use many symbols, because rituals are by definition enactments of symbolic ideas (Figure 3.2).

Most symbols are ambiguous, or **multivocalic** (Victor Turner 1973). They refer simultaneously to several different ideas and are open to reinterpretation. It is precisely that openness that gives them their power. There is no such thing as a symbol with a single meaningful element.

Symbols abound in many contexts. In many Christian artworks, the cross reminds us of the crucifixion of Jesus and thus symbolizes suffering, guilt, humility, the struggle against evil, death, rebirth, and the promise of eternal life. Water and cleansing are powerful symbols used in many religious traditions. Water is found everywhere, but in religion it may have special significance, representing purity, rebirth, or oneness with God. In Jewish, Muslim, and Australian aborigine tradition, **circumcision**, the ritual cutting of the

Figure 3.2 *Traditional weddings in China and the United States. Notice the differences in colors and symbolic objects.*

foreskin of the penis, signifies purification, obedience to law, and validation of manhood.

Some anthropologists suggest that **key symbols** (Ortner 1973) stand behind many ideas and symbols within a particular cultural tradition. Certain symbols, such as the crucifix in the Christian tradition, summarize many attitudes and beliefs, giving meaning to

many other aspects of these traditions. The U.S. flag represents the 13 original colonies, the 50 states, the unity of the nation, and various interpretations of the colors, such as red for courage, white for purity, and blue for truth. The selection of colors, the same as on the British flag, reflects the historical connection between the United States and England.

---

semiotic Pertaining to an interpretive approach that looks for hidden meaning in a particular domain of expression or behavior, such as folklore, mythology, or music. Semiotics is the study of meaning in general, particularly in signs and symbols.

structuralism An approach to the study of cultural artifacts that stresses the unconscious and hidden structures that underlie cultural meanings.

ethnosemantics An experimental but systematic approach to cognition that seeks to understand the meaning of cultural categories within specific domains.

symbol An object that can be perceived by the senses and that refers to or represents ideas and emotions outside or beyond itself; it may be a word, picture, object, act, event, color, or sound.

multivocalic Ambiguous, open to multiple interpretations.

circumcision The ritual cutting of the foreskin of the penis.

key symbols Symbols that represent many ideas and values that are important to a particular cultural tradition; for example, the American flag or the cross in Christianity.

An American Tradition: Halloween

To get an idea of how an anthropologist uses a symbolic approach, let us briefly examine a popular North American folk festival from a symbolic point of view. Suppose that a visitor from China arrives in a small town in the United States in late October. Toward the end of the month, jack-o'-lanterns appear in the windows and on the doorsteps of many homes (Figure 3.3). Orange and black decorations appear in schools, stores, and many offices. The decorations feature images of witches, goblins, ghouls, ghosts, black cats, and skeletons. At the same time, colors and images reminiscent of the harvest appear, including Indian corn, gourds, and pumpkins.

Most Americans are unable to explain the history of Halloween, but some may be familiar with an old Irish legend. According to this tale, long ago in Ireland lived a stingy old soul named Jack, known for drunkenness and crafty schemes to get the best of people. His greatest triumph was when he tricked the devil himself into climbing a tree to get the best fruit. Jack trapped the devil by scratching a cross into the tree trunk, making it impossible for him to come down. Jack demanded and got the devil's promise never to claim his soul. When he died, Jack's stingy soul went straight to hell, but he was turned away because of his agreement. However, Jack was also barred from heaven because of his stinginess. Jack's ghost can still be seen in Ireland, wandering around at night, carrying a lantern made from a hollowed-out turnip (the original jack-o'-lantern), looking for a place to rest (Myers 1972).

On October 31, the Chinese visitor spots groups of children bizarrely dressed as ghosts, witches, skeletons, Frankenstein, and other monsters. Carrying sacks for their loot, they march around the neighborhood ringing doorbells and calling out "Trick or

Figure 3.3 *Halloween jack-o'-lanterns offer clues to hidden patterns of meaning in American culture.*

treat!" Every native knows this is a demand for a treat; children enforce it by roaring or making other sounds and gestures appropriate to their disguises. Adults at home prepare little gifts for the children, such as candies, fruits, perhaps a few coins. If the children get no treat at a house, they sometimes play a trick, like throwing eggs at the windows.

How could one explain Halloween to the Chinese visitor? Originally, the festival was probably brought to the United States by settlers from the British Isles. It is derived from the ancient Celtic festival for the dead, celebrated on October 31, the last day of the year in the Celtic calendar. After the British Isles became Christian, the Celtic festival evolved into All Hallows' Eve. On that night every year, people lit bonfires to encourage evil spirits such as witches and ghosts to come out and cavort for one night before being banished for All Saints (Hallows') Day on November 1, a holy day in the Christian calendar.

Halloween coincides with the end of the harvest in Europe and North America. This is normally a time to rejoice if the crops are in safely, but also a good time to reinforce the importance of sharing with others. Witches and goblins are symbols of the selfish, greedy part of each person. In a peasant farming society like the preindustrial British Isles, it might have been well to remind people of the importance of sharing. The survival of a farmer whose crops were destroyed by hailstones one year might depend on neighbors whose crops were undamaged.

Today Halloween is a true folk festival in the United States. As with other popular festivals, Halloween is identified with certain colors (see Box 3.2). It is not the official ritual of any religious group. It is practiced across a wide spectrum of the society, in cities and rural areas, among many ethnic and racial groups. Like other popular festivals, Halloween has become commercialized in recent years, but this does not reduce its authenticity. Commercialism is as much a part of American culture as Halloween.

A foreign visitor might be perplexed by the celebration of this festival in the United States. In a country whose people are proud of their rationality and pragmatism, why does a popular festival revolve around goblins and ghosts? There may be many possible answers:

• Halloween might actually be a parody of superstitions. Americans make child's play out of it to display their freedom from superstition and irrational fears.

• Halloween may simply be a way of enacting the angry feelings between adults and children that arise because parents withhold certain things from children. Children express antagonism by impersonating monsters and trying to frighten their elders. Adults, in turn, try to scare children with jack-o'-lanterns and other paraphernalia.

• Psychologically, it may be beneficial to allow children to act out their monstrous feelings without adult reprisals for one evening.

• Children, who may be frightened by things adults do, can turn the tables by trying to frighten adults for a change.

These explanations are plausible, but they are at the psychological, not the cultural, level of explanation.

Let us look again at the symbolism of Halloween. In the trick-or-treat ritual, children can show their greed for sweets and other restricted goodies by demanding them from neighbors while disguised as malicious beings. Children expect the neighbors to provide treats or else they see them as stingy and mean. Children's costumes are often reminders of the imminence of death: skeletons, ghosts, witches dressed in black, and ghouls that feed on dead bodies. The jack-o'-lantern is not just a pumpkin, as any American knows. It is a symbol of a season (autumn), of a festival (Halloween), an event (harvest), and a state of being (death). The jack-o'-lantern is a good symbol for death, because it dies when it is cut from the pumpkin vine, and it resembles a human skull when hollowed out. Halloween is full of contradictory themes: Children, just beginning life, impersonate death. Schooled in the importance of sharing, they are encouraged to be greedy and fill their sacks with restricted treats. The neighbors who give are symbolically threatened with death by the monsters who darken their doors under the ghastly glimmer of the jack-o'-lanterns.

But why, the visitor might ask, would a ritual that symbolically reinforces sharing be practiced in an urbanized, industrial, individualistic society like the United States? The answer may lie in how contemporary Americans regard giving and generosity. Many Americans remember widespread poverty from the days of the Depression in the 1930s and 1940s. Nowadays, the needy tend to be segregated, although homeless people by the thousands are becoming more visible in America's cities. Deprived people are cared for by welfare programs, not neighbors. Yet many Americans are uneasy about these institutions because they know they do not relieve poverty. Acting out a ritual of enforced generosity against a symbolic backdrop of death may be a way of symbolically displacing a central conflict in American life, that of want in the midst of plenty. **Displacement** is the use of symbols to refer indirectly to an underlying problem that is too painful (or too dangerous) to address directly. One can interpret Halloween as a somber warning that stinginess can lead to death and damnation.

What does this interpretation imply about behavior? Does Halloween make any difference in the *behavior* of Americans? Does it heighten their sensitivity to the plight of poor? Or does it lower it by reducing that concern to a set of symbolic punishments for self-

ishness and greed? Symbolic analysis alone cannot answer that question, but it raises it in such a way that permits an answer.

Symbolism in the Balinese Cockfight

Another example of a symbolic approach to behavior can be found in anthropologist Clifford Geertz's analysis of the Balinese cockfight (1972). An island state of Indonesia, Bali has centuries-old traditions that combine elements of Polynesian and Hindu beliefs. Balinese culture presents a face of harmony, balance, and equality. The people carefully disguise their emotions and present them in ritual form through dance and other means. Underneath this controlled exterior, according to Geertz, exists another reality—one of hierarchy and inequality in which only a few have power

Figure 3.4 *A symbolic approach to the Balinese cockfight suggests that it reflects and affirms the traditional social structure of Bali.*

Figure 3.5 *The acceptability of eating certain animals may reflect the symbolic meanings, such as "sacred" or "unclean," ascribed to them in different societies. This scene from a Chinese butcher shop demonstrates that one culture's "best friend" may be another culture's next meal.*

and privilege. It is also one of competition between kinship groups and local and regional factions.

All these elements appear in the cockfight, a contest that pits two roosters against each other, armed with sharp metal spurs and trained to fight to the death (Figure 3.4). The roosters symbolize their owners' masculinity and combativeness, feelings not usually displayed openly. The owners of the finest fighting cocks and their supporters make large bets on the winner, especially when the birds are relatively evenly matched and the outcome uncertain. The high stakes symbolize the uncertainty of life itself, in which arbitrary, uncontrollable forces, such as crop failures, illness, or death, can affect one's life. Poorer men who can ill afford to lose any money make many small wagers on the periphery of the fighting arena. Only men who can afford to lose some money place large bets. Thus the uncertainty of the cockfight is balanced by different levels of risk taking, according to economic status.

Even though relatively large sums may be won or lost, the bettors claim that the amounts are unimportant. Geertz notes that net winnings and losses tend to even out over the long run. Respected citizens referee the cockfights and base their decisions on a detailed rule book; no one ever disputes their rulings. Geertz suggests that the entire performance is a collective work of art presenting Balinese society in symbolic form. Participation in the cockfight, according to Geertz, has no material consequences. It is a rehearsal of the social structure of Balinese society, a kind of "deep play" for the Balinese to contemplate and savor.

The Symbolism of Food and Eating

Preparing, serving, and eating food may be filled with symbolic significance. Many peoples observe taboos or prohibitions on the kinds of foods they eat related to the symbolic significance of the food. Americans, for example, commonly eat the flesh of cattle, sheep, hogs, turkeys, chickens, and ducks; yet the idea of eating horse or dog is abhorrent. The French, on the other hand, enjoy horse meat, which is sold in special butcher shops, and the Chinese and Indonesian people sometimes eat dogs (Figure 3.5). The strong North

---

displacement The use of symbols to refer indirectly to an underlying problem that is too painful or dangerous to address directly.

American preference for beef may be viewed with horror in India, where the cow is sacred according to a Hindu doctrine called *ahimsa*.

A lively debate about food taboos continues in anthropology. Perhaps the most widespread view of food taboos is that they prevent people from eating things that may be harmful. The Jewish and Muslim taboo on eating the flesh of the pig, it is said, relates to the danger of parasites in pork. However, well-cooked pork does not present any such danger, and other people do consume it. Some anthropologists believe that food preferences and prohibitions should be understood primarily in terms of what they express symbolically. According to this view, the Jewish taboo on eating pork relates more to the classification of the pig as symbolically impure than to actual physical impurities (Douglas 1966). Other anthropologists argue that food taboos and preferences are clues to understanding the ecology and diet of people in various habitats. Anthropologist Marvin Harris suggests that the Jewish and Islamic taboo on pork is based on the difficulty of raising pigs in the arid Middle East where these religions originated (Harris 1985).

The validity of symbolic interpretations is not verifiable in the same way as the validity of scientific generalizations. Anthropologists using a symbolic approach can and should verify that the description is correct (e.g., that people use pumpkins and not pie plates for jack-o'-lanterns) and that their interpretations are internally consistent. But symbolic interpretations are not verifiable in the conventional sense; therefore they are useful chiefly in giving a sense of having looked deeply into a custom through analysis of its symbolic meanings.

Postmodernism

Recently anthropologists favoring an interpretative mode of analysis have acknowledged that their work does not meet conventional scientific standards of verification. Some of these "postmodern" anthropologists make no apologies. They feel that any attempt at objective detachment in anthropology is artificial and ultimately doomed to failure. They see anthropology as the only social science discipline capable of preserving the true humanity of the objects of their study. Their model of research is that of a literary analyst examining a "text," which is a cultural event or pattern. Their objective is not to test hypotheses within a deductive framework but to examine in depth their own sometimes deeply personal responses to encounters with people in other cultural traditions. Its proponents see the postmodern movement in anthropology as an antidote to an excessively scientific world view. It is still too early to predict how far-reaching its influence will be.

SEMIOTICS: THE STUDY OF SIGNS

Semiotics is the study of meaning in general, including noncultural meaning. Semiotic analysis is broader than symbolic analysis; it goes beyond the meanings in words and ideas and looks for meaning in gesture, dress, architecture, art—in short, in any activity at all. Semiotics grew out of linguistics, but its scope is broader than language alone. Many meanings are communicated by signs of whose existence we are only dimly aware. The codes that govern these signs are often unconscious, although they form part of social conventions in every society.

As an example let us consider the ways people use dress to communicate things about themselves. Cloth-

Figure 3.6 *Runners convey subtle but meaningful messages to each other through their clothes, shoes, and "body language."*

ing and bodily adornment has meaning beyond the need for protection and the desire to cover nakedness. Few attempts have been made to decode the complete language of dress styles. Anthropologist Jeffrey Nash (1977, 172) made one attempt, examining the wardrobe of urban runners (Figure 3.6). Nash describes a **subculture** of runners: people who share understandings through personal contacts and membership in running clubs and the activity of running. Most people going out to jog or run would deny that they pay much attention to their wardrobe: "I just throw on some old shorts." However, Nash found that runners, deliberately or not, are most attentive to nuance and detail in their outfits.

Shoes are fundamental. Runners use the logos of the major brands of running shoes (such as Nike, Puma, Tiger, Adidas, New Balance) as badges of rank and specialization. Shoe brands can set a runner apart as a "real" athlete, as opposed to the "not-so-serious" runner who wears "imitations" bought at discount stores. Some brands of shoes are thought to be best for runners who are prone to injuries, so that wearing a Karhu 2323 may communicate that the runner has a knee problem. It also says that the runner is dedicated to running in spite of the pain he or she may suffer.

Shirts are also important. Many races offer T-shirts as prizes to competitors. So wearing a T-shirt that says BAY CITY 25K, or AAU STATE CHAMPIONSHIP, proclaims that the wearer is a "serious" runner. Since races are ranked, the runner can establish his or her rank by wearing a certain T-shirt. "Serious runners" wear tank tops, even if it means wearing one over a T-shirt in cold weather to get the message across: "I am a serious runner." A shirt that reads *RUN FOR FUN* says, "I am not a serious runner."

Shorts come in many styles and colors, but "real" runners use lightweight silk or synthetic runner's shorts. Shorts and shirts alike may bear the name of a track club, which can establish the runner's prestige in the ranking of clubs. It is also impressive to wear the insignia of some faraway track club or university,

which shows that the runner has competed away from home. Hats can also bear messages. A runner in a floppy hat with the Budweiser logo on it is saying, "I'm not so dedicated that I won't take a beer in training."

Runners also take note of each other's body profiles and postures for the information they convey. Says Nash, "A person running with head down, breathing hard, moving with arms in front of the body and with fists clenched is not a runner regardless of what he or she may be wearing" (1977, 183). Runners must also know when and how to greet other runners. "Serious" runners exchange a minimal greeting consisting of a barely perceptible wave. Novices may violate the code by trying to engage in conversation someone who is training hard. Such a novice is likely to be answered with silence.

Thus clothing, body posture, and nonverbal greetings establish the boundaries between serious runners, not-so-serious runners, and nonrunners. Semiotic analysis shows that every area of human life is infused with meaning down to the minutest details. The complex, dynamic process by which meanings are created, modified, understood, and incorporated into behavior constitute an inexhaustible set of data for cultural anthropology.

STRUCTURAL ANALYSIS

Structural analysis is most closely identified with French ethnologist Claude Lévi-Strauss, who made the structural study of myth his lifelong project. Structuralism, as an intellectual style, had a major impact in both the humanities and the social sciences in such fields as literature, anthropology, and linguistics. Its basic tenet is that beneath the surface meanings and symbols in myths and other forms of expression there is another level of meaning that can be discovered by analyzing the formal arrangement of elements without reference to their inherent meaning.

---

subculture   A group that shares cultural characteristics with a larger, dominant society but also has a set of shared meanings that distinguish it from the larger society.

Lévi-Strauss examined many myths, especially the oral traditions of the North and South American Indians. He concluded that much of their oral literature can be reduced to a few basic stories; the rest are all incomplete versions of a basic outline. The underlying structure of a myth can be discovered by comparing all available versions. Lévi-Strauss extracted basic units of meaning, which he called **mythemes.** He suggested that while the symbolic elements varied from one version to another, the formal relationship between these elements remained the same in all the versions. This pattern is the true underlying meaning of the myth.

The Story of Cinderella

Let us illustrate the structural approach with the story of Cinderella, known to generations of children in many parts of the world (Figure 3.7). Some people might object that Cinderella is not a true myth, just a folktale, but this distinction is of little importance for structural analysis. Folklorists from Europe to the Orient have amassed over 500 versions of this story. Travellers apparently carried many of these stories from one part of the world to another, while some versions may have appeared independently. Lévi-Strauss points out that the Native American story of Ash Boy is structurally very similar to Cinderella, but it is unlikely to have been borrowed from Europe. In

Ash Boy many of the elements are inverted: While Cinderella is a pretty girl, Ash Boy is an ugly boy; Cinderella is unloved, Ash Boy is in love with a beautiful girl; Cinderella is transformed into a princess, Ash Boy is stripped of his ugliness.

Let us examine some variants of the story. The constants in the story are Cinderella's humiliation by relatives, her later transformation, and the love of the prince. Considerable variation abounds in the details of the different versions, however. In some versions Cinderella's stepsisters abuse her; in others her natural sisters abuse her. In some versions Cinderella's difficulties arise from her refusal to marry her own brother. In many versions Cinderella gets help not from a fairy godmother but from the spirit of her own dead mother at whose grave she prays. In a popular European version the heroine Kari Woodengown is helped by a fine bull she has befriended. In many versions the stepsisters cut off their toes and heels in an effort to squeeze their feet into the glass slipper, and in others they have their eyes plucked out by vengeful birds just as Cinderella marries the prince.

Literally dozens of symbols adorn this story, but a structural analysis reveals some basic mythemes. In virtually every version Cinderella gets into conflict with relatives who either mistreat her or love her improperly. The mytheme, in Lévi-Strauss's terms, is improper love, the over- or undervaluing of family ties. Another mytheme is found in Cinderella's reliance on animals as a source of support and compan-

Figure 3.7 *Structural analysis suggests that Cinderella is a universal tale conveying important information about the proper role of human beings in relation to both nature and culture.*

ionship. This element reflects closeness to nature. Cinderella's honesty and goodness are eventually rewarded when she is transformed into a beauty who wins the hand of the prince, a love that is correct and good.

Lévi-Strauss notes that Cinderella passes from darkness to light. The ashes (or cinders) on the hearth where she sleeps (darkness) symbolize Cinderella's degradation (in Kari Woodengown, she lives in a pigsty, with the same symbolic effect). Ashes, Lévi-Strauss notes, are significant because they are the product of combustion: Burning wood gives off heat and light and leaves ashes. Cinderella reverses this order when she is transformed into a fair maiden, dressed in a shimmering gown (light). The blinding or other mutilation of the wicked stepsisters plunges them into darkness, complementing Cinderella's movement toward light. The sisters' attempt at deception through self-mutilation complements Cinderella's simple honesty and wisdom.

Implications of Structural Analysis

Lévi-Strauss interprets Cinderella as a mediator, moving from being despised to being loved, from darkness to light, from animals to humans, falsity to truth, and poverty to wealth. Polarities, or oppositions, like these are the basic elements of all myths, according to Lévi-Strauss. According to structuralist theory, these elements need not all be present in any given version of the myth, but the relationship between them must be constant. Beneath all the relationships, according to Lévi-Strauss, lies a contradiction between nature and culture. Humans constantly struggle with the tension between their animal nature and the **superorganic** constructions of human culture. This struggle is reflected over and over in oral literature.

The underlying structures of myths are preserved by the storytellers recounting them, who have no contact with each other and are unaware of these structures, because myths rest on the basic structure of human thought. Structural analysis rests on symbolic analysis. For example, the notions of darkness and light in the analysis of Cinderella are based on symbolic interpretations of the elements of fire, ashes, blindness, and sight. Structural oppositions between these symbols are part of a model created by the analyst. As we saw, symbolic interpretations may be untestable. Critics point out that structuralists take great liberties with the evidence by interpreting symbols to fit them into the nature versus culture scheme. Structuralists have also been criticized for creating "frozen" models that do not account for the historical development of institutions over time but treat them as if they had emerged fully developed.

COGNITION AND ETHNOSEMANTICS

Symbolic and structural approaches to meaning have limits. Interpretations of symbols are based mainly on intuition and logic; there is no scientific way of verifying one person's interpretation of a symbol. Structural analysis depends on the selection and symbolic interpretation of structural elements, and this often appears to be highly intuitive if not arbitrary. The object of study in symbolic and structural studies is usually the cultural artifact, a myth, category of food, popular festival, or ritual act. In our concern for the object we may lose sight of the human authors of these artifacts. Who are these people? How do they think about these artifacts? Do our analyses apply to everyone? For instance, if our analysis of Halloween has any validity, does it apply to all Americans? Or just some?

During the 1950s some anthropologists trained in linguistic methods became concerned about the lack of rigor in these approaches to meaning. Instead of symbols these ethnosemanticists focused on **cognition**, the process of knowing things and organizing knowledge. Although psychologists also study cognition, it is important to distinguish the anthropological approach to cognition from the psychological. The

---

mythemes Basic units of meaning that can be extracted from myths; discovered by comparing different versions of the same story for the formal relationships between symbols.

superorganic Pertaining to cultural phenomena in contrast to natural and individual phenomena.

cognition The process of knowing things and organizing knowledge.

Figure 3.8   *Shoshone classification of birds.*

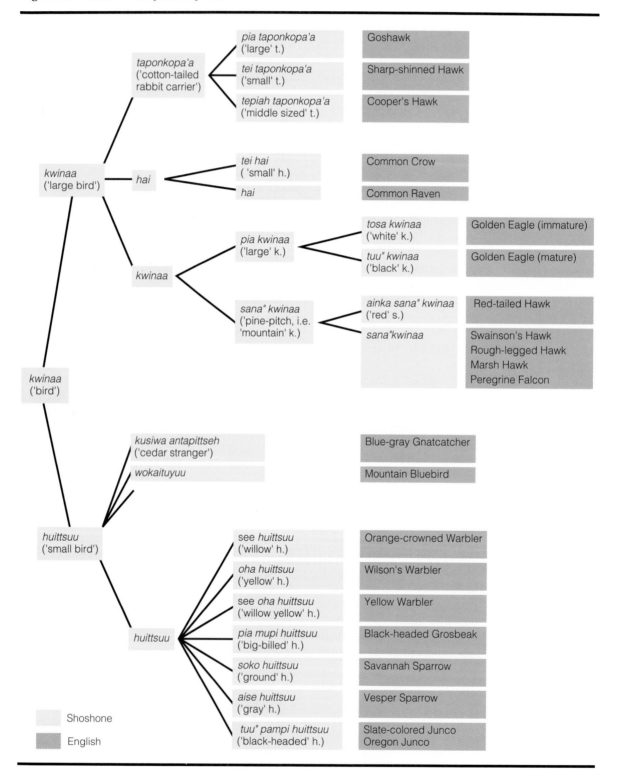

anthropologist focuses primarily on how information is organized within different cultural traditions, whereas the psychologist focuses more generically on human cognition.

In every cultural tradition people use categories to acquire, recall, and sort information. Ethnosemanticists attempt to isolate **cognitive domains.** Domains are areas of knowledge that people see as having limits. Some examples from American culture are baseball, biology, art history, and soap operas. Each of these domains contains a set of objects thought of as sharing meaningful elements. Domains can overlap, as in the case of sports and popular heroes.

Ethnosemanticists have found that there are systematic differences in how different people mentally organize and think about things. The principal objective of ethnosemantics is to learn how people organize experience, that is, to discover their rules of cognition. Knowing the rules of cognition provides a precise way of understanding meanings. As an example, let us consider some terminology used by the Shoshone, a native people of the American West. The Shoshone have a term, *kwinaa,* which refers to a domain that American English speakers call "birds" (Hage and Miller 1976). The Shoshone divide *kwinaa* into "large birds" (*kwinaa*) and "small birds" (*huittsuu*). Notice that the same word, *kwinaa,* occurs at different **levels of contrast**, with different meanings. That is, the term stands for a class of things at one level and to a specific member of that class at another level. An example of this in English is the word *family,* which, at one level, stands for an extended kin group and at another level, for the nuclear family.

Does this mean that the Shoshone cannot distinguish between large and small birds? No. They do so in the same way English speakers can distinguish between nuclear and extended families, even while using the same term for both, that is, from the context. *Kwinaa* appears at several levels of contrast standing for "bird," "large bird," and in compound forms, for several kinds of eagle, falcon, and hawk (Hage and Miller 1976, 481; Figure 3.8). In other words, the Shoshone lump together several bird species that Western ornithologists distinguish. This does not mean the Shoshone are unable to recognize the differences among species. In some cases, in fact, the Shoshone make even finer distinctions than those made by Western scientists. What it does mean is that the Shoshone "carve up" reality differently. They use different categories from those of Western ornithologists to organize what they know.

By comparing the object to which people refer (the referent) and the terms they use, ethnosemanticists isolate the different components of meaning, a technique known as **componential analysis.** In the case of the Shoshone, birds of different sizes and colors are distinguished by the vocabulary and the context. By learning how other people cognize (perceive and order) the world, the ethnosemanticist discovers what it takes to think like a member of another culture. Knowing that might permit the ethnographer to enter the world of meanings in another culture, like learning to speak a new language, and perhaps even learn how to behave appropriately in that culture.

Ethnosemantic Methods

Ethnosemanticists begin by identifying a cognitive domain for investigation. Domains exist in the minds of informants, not in the objects themselves, so this initial step involves informal probes of informants to discover what the cognitive boundaries are around a different topic. As an example let us consider how an ethnosemanticist would attempt to learn about rock music, an area of knowledge that constitutes a domain in the minds of many teenagers and young adults. It is marked off from other domains by terminological boundaries that distinguish it from others such as ballads, folk music, classical music, jazz, and so on.

Once the boundaries of the domain are known, the investigator begins to construct questions designed to reveal the implicit classifications in the way people

---

cognitive domains   Areas of knowledge that people see as having limits; objects in the same domain are seen as sharing meaningful elements.

levels of contrast   In ethnosemantics, the various contexts in which a term is used within a cognitive domain and that influences its meaning.

componential analysis   The analysis of meaning by examining elements or components.

talk about things. Many questions must be constructed and put to informants with tedious repetition. For example, the investigator might go through a list of particular songs with an informant, asking about each one, "What kind of music is X?" In each question, the investigator will substitute a song title, such as the Rolling Stones' "Sympathy for the Devil," the Beatles' "Hey Jude," or Madonna's "Material Girl."

Eventually categories begin to emerge within the domain, such as "progressive," "hard rock," "punk rock," "skinhead rock," "acid rock," "heavy metal," "fifties rock," "sixties rock," "rock 'n' roll," "reggae," "rap," "new wave." The investigator might test for equivalence by asking questions like, "Is punk rock the same as hard rock?" The next step is to identify inclusive categories, such as, "Heavy metal is a kind of hard rock." Finally the investigator may try to identify the elements of meaning or **components** that differentiate categories from each other. Some informants might say, for example, that rock is heavily amplified, while folk music relies more on acoustical instruments.

In some instances the investigator will conclude that the distinctions between categories are blurred; some folk musicians use electronic guitars and synthesizers yet are still considered folk singers. At the conclusion of the study the investigator will have identified a significant cultural domain, some of its internal divisions, and the elements of meaning that distinguish things from each other. The investigator might even be able to walk into a record store and converse knowledgeably about rock songs without ever having heard one.

There are countless other domains that can be investigated with similar techniques. For example, such knowledge could be extremely useful in designing a new public health program for a population in Ethiopia, where people believe that all diseases are either of the blood or of the digestive system.

Because it is so time-consuming, ethnosemantics is rarely done with many informants. This leads to a major criticism: How can we know if the information is typical if it was obtained from only a few informants? It is also possible that people from the same background cognize the world in different ways. For example, some people say punk is a kind of hard rock, others disagree, and still others are unsure. Even more

troublesome is the question of what these componential charts actually mean. Are they "maps" or "grammars" that reveal how people really think about things? Or are they simply convenient ways of organizing information for anthropologists? Still another troubling question is, granting that we know something about how people think, what does componential analysis tell us about how people will behave? As one skeptic put it, is componential analysis "God's truth" or "hocus-pocus?" (Burling 1964).

One test of this question is to ask whether the approach really allows us to "think like natives." Let's return to the rock music example. Could an anthropologist from another society, having completed a thorough componential analysis, select records that would satisfy a room full of teenage rock fans? On hearing a new rock song, could the anthropologist reliably classify it in the same way as a native informant? It is unlikely. The technique is not **generative**, that is, it does not allow one to generate responses, because it is static. Componential analysis shows a pattern of thought about a given set of objects, but it does not tell us much about how the informant reacts to unfamiliar situations. Even if the approach were generative, it would tell us little about real cognition, because thought and perception go far beyond classification.

The closer ethnosemanticists look at cognition, the harder it becomes to understand how people think about things in real-life situations. All meanings are context-specific, yet it would be impossible to take into account every possible context. Cognition is so complex, and its relation to behavior is so difficult to measure, that the work is necessarily slow and tedious.

Improving on Ethnosemantics: Disease Categories

Some of these problems were addressed by anthropologist Roy D'Andrade (1976), who used ethnosemantic methods to study how Americans experience and understand disease. Remember that he was approaching disease not from a medical point of view but from the point of view of ethnosemantics. His purpose was to determine the important components of meaning

---

BOX 3.3

Statements about Disease in an Ethnosemantic Study of American Students

| Sentences | Disease Terms |

Sentences

* You can catch _____ from other people.

* _____ comes from being emotionally upset.

* _____ runs in the family.

* You never really get over _____.

* Feeling generally run-down is a sign of

  _____.

* _____ brings on fever.

* _____ is a sign of old age.

Disease Terms

Appendicitis	Influenza	Dental cavities
Chicken pox	Psychosis	Poison ivy
Epilepsy		

The sentences and terms shown above were collected by Roy D'Andrade (1976) from a group of middle-class American college students. D'Andrade started with a list of 50 sentences, from which he culled 30 that showed the highest agreement among the informants and displayed the greatest contrast among the different diseases. Only some of each are shown here as examples.

Source: D'Andrade 1976.

---

about disease for a number of ordinary Americans. Presumably the way people organize disease in their heads correlates with their behavior when people are sick. It might affect, for example, whether they call an ambulance when they see a sick person instead of taking the person to the hospital on public transportation. D'Andrade's study focused on the organization of information on disease in his informants' heads.

D'Andrade began by taping a long series of interviews about illness with ten college students of middle-class American backgrounds. From these interviews, he culled the names of 30 frequently mentioned diseases, including appendicitis, chicken pox, and epilepsy. He also compiled 30 typical statements about disease (Box 3.3). He used these sentences as **frames** in which disease names could be inserted. The sentences represented modes of thinking about disease; the disease terms were primary disease categories.

D'Andrade then constructed a huge questionnaire of 900 items on which every disease name was placed in every different sentence frame. The respondents were asked to agree or disagree with each resulting sentence, for example, "You can catch epilepsy from other people." Naturally, many sentences, such as, "Your skin breaks out with dental cavities," did not make sense to the students. However, the investigator cannot prejudge the informant's response, even if he thinks he already knows how people cognize a disease.

D'Andrade next conducted a statistical analysis of the hundreds of answers to determine which clusters of meaning belong together. For example, if most of the students agreed with the statement that, "You can catch chicken pox from other people," and also that, "You can catch influenza from other people," D'Andrade could conclude that chicken pox and influenza share some common features of meaning. If, however, most of the students accept, "Feeling gener-

---

components Elements of meaning in a language that differentiate one class of objects from another.

generative Pertaining to a model that would permit anthropologists to predict how people would categorize new information or make sense of new situations.

frames In ethnosemantics, sentences that are constructed to learn whether terms have shared meanings.

ally run down is a sign of influenza," but reject the statement, "Feeling generally run down is a sign of chicken pox," he could not assign these two diseases to a common "cluster" of meaning.

Medical practitioners distinguish disease according to "defining features," generally the causes and symptoms with which the diseases are associated. A doctor, for example, defines cancer in terms of the growth patterns of certain cells in the body. D'Andrade expected that his informants would also distinguish different illnesses in terms of defining features. Instead he found that "what [nonmedical] people know about cancer is not what defines a cell as cancerous, but rather that having cancer is often fatal and painful" (1976, 177). The analysis suggested that informants thought about illness along two major dimensions: contagion ("you can catch it from someone") and seriousness ("you can die from it"). Thus there is a major divergence between the biomedical and the popular ethnosemantic conception of disease.

D'Andrade carried the analysis still further, with a sophisticated logical and statistical analysis. D'Andrade went beyond earlier work in ethnosemantics. By using statistical analysis and several different informants, he overcame the problem of the atypical informant. He succeeded in extending his model of disease perception to yield accurate predictions of how people would respond to questions he had not yet asked.

More recently anthropologists have applied similar techniques to the study of other behavior, in some cases with more than academic significance. In one study, for example, anthropologist Willett Kempton (1987) showed that many Americans conceive of the operation of their home thermostats in a different way from the engineers who design such devices. This cognitive difference has a significant impact on the use of home heating and consequently on national energy consumption. These advanced techniques of ethnosemantics promise to yield generative models of cognition through the application of rigorous quantitative techniques and exhaustive measurement. These studies are especially intriguing because many investigators believe the key to understanding culture is inside people's minds and the meanings they attach to things. Cognitive studies, using multiple informants and sophisticated statistical techniques, have emerged as the best-grounded, most verifiable approach to meaning.

SUMMARY

- Studies of meaning will continue to be an important part of anthropology since they are essential to the fundamental goal of the discipline: understanding human differences and similarities.
- Symbols are signs that occur in a particular context and acquire meaning by suggesting a relationship between ideas beyond themselves.
- Symbolic anthropology is distinguished by its attention to the meaning embedded in cultural artifacts, ritual acts, and other cultural events. It is a very satisfying approach to culture because it suggests connections between elements that otherwise may seem entirely arbitrary, such as the pumpkin and death in the Halloween tradition.
- Symbolic analysis depends on intuitive understandings and is not verifiable in the conventional scientific sense.
- Semiotic analysis is broader than symbolic analysis. It examines any kind of behavior (verbal or nonverbal), dress styles, art forms, and so on for their information content.
- There is no single technique associated with semiotics; it borrows ideas from linguistics and other disciplines.
- Structuralism involves extracting elements of myth, social organization, or other aspects of culture and manipulating them to create highly abstract formal models. These intricate models are intriguing and appear to reveal hidden relationships within and across different cultural traditions that may tell us something about the structure of human thought.
- Structural analysis has been criticized because it depends on symbolic interpretation, which is not verifiable in the conventional sense. It has also been criticized for ignoring the historical and developmental aspects of cultural phenomena.
- The scientific paradigm discussed in Chapter 2 is most clearly seen in ethnosemantics. This work requires a heroic devotion to detail and long hours spent with informants trying to understand relatively limited cultural domains.
- Early work in ethnosemantics was limited to one or a few informants and serious questions were raised about its significance for entire social groups and

its connection to behavior. Recently more grounded approaches to ethnosemantics promise answers to those problems.

GET INVOLVED

1. Select a myth or folktale from a source such as *Grimm's Fairy Tales* and do a structural analysis of it. You can also carry out structural analyses on movies, paintings, and other expressive forms. For example, pick a set of gangster movies such as the *Godfather* series, *Goodfellas,* and *Married to the Mob* and examine the opposition between raw and cooked food, kin and nonkin, violence and peacefulness. What are the hidden messages in these oppositions? What characters or features mediate between these opposites?
2. Pick a cognitive domain unfamiliar to you but familiar to some friends and acquaintances and explore its structure and boundaries by formulating a set of questions. Interview your informants about the domain. Compare the way informants with different backgrounds understand this domain.
3. Write an article for your campus newspaper presenting a symbolic analysis of local rituals (homecoming, fraternity rush, freshman hazing, graduation, a football game) as though you were reporting for a foreign (or extraterrestrial) newspaper and trying to explain these rituals to people who had never participated in them.

SUGGESTED READINGS

Douglas, Mary. 1966. *Purity and danger: An analysis of the concepts of pollution and taboo.* New York: Praeger.

Geertz, Clifford. 1972. Deep play: Notes on the Balinese cockfight. *Daedalus* 101:1–37.

Hall, Edward T. 1959. Space speaks: How different cultures use space. In *The silent language.* New York: Doubleday.[*]

Kottak, Conrad Philip. 1985. Swimming in cross-cultural currents. *Natural History* 94 (5).[*]

Lévi-Strauss, Claude. 1976. The story of Asdiwal. In *Structural anthropology,* trans. M. Layton, vol. 2. Chicago: University of Chicago Press.

[*]This selection is anthologized in *Applying anthropology,* 2d ed., ed. A. Podolefsky and P. J. Brown (Mountain View, Calif.: Mayfield, 1991).

Language as Social Semiotic:
Linguistic Anthropology Fieldwork among
the Xavante Indians of Brazil

Laura Graham is an assistant professor of anthropology at the University of Iowa. Over the past ten years, she has made several trips to central Brazil to study the relationship between language and culture among the Xavante.

Laura Graham working with an assistant.

The Xavante are an indigenous group numbering some 6,000 individuals, who speak a Gê language, one of the major linguistic families of lowland South America. My objective was to study the ways in which the Xavante exploit the rich semiotic potential of language. I wanted to discover how they use language to communicate not only referential statements (propositions about the world) but also significant socially interpretable information about such things as the speaker, the listener, and the relationship between them; the situation; or even how an utterance is to be interpreted or evaluated. How, I wondered, do the Xavante use language for social purposes? How does it work to create and maintain patterns of social organization?

To discover the social meanings of language use among the Xavante I began by doing an "ethnography of speaking." At the same time that I was learning to speak Xavante, I was also paying attention to patterns of language use in different contexts. I took my tape recorder everywhere and recorded speech in an array of situations, for example, families working in their gardens, collecting and fishing trips with men and women, the men's council, and the bachelors' hut. I also recorded everyday speech when I was in the home. I recorded women and men speaking and children playing language games, reciting little ditties. I was recording "sound images" with my tape recorder as well as visual ones with my camera.

Taking instances of naturally occurring discourse as my starting point for analysis and working with assistants, I then began the process of interpreting how the Xavante use language to perform multiple social functions. This process involved a dialectic between what my informants could tell me about language and language use and the patterns that were actually appearing in the recordings. I used a special technique in these assisted sessions. This involved using two tape recorders: one to play back the contextually situated discourse; the other to record my informants' explanations and their responses to questions of language use as we listened to the in-context recordings. In this way I could record my assistants' translations and explanations of what was happening with the language of the in-context recordings, as well their responses to elicited sentences.

This dual tape recorder method enabled me to identify discrepancies between what my assistants told me was correct and what people actually said in natural speech. For example, when translating an elder's dream narrative, my assistant Lino Sereʔubudzi consistently translated two distinct words as "he" (*te* and *date*). Was this discrepancy a mistake, or were these perhaps socially significant alternatives?

My queries were met with frustrated answers; Lino insisted that both forms were correct but could not explain their difference. How could I understand the presence of the two forms? Might the use of one or the other make a socially meaningful difference that Lino was simply not accustomed to putting into words?

I was stumped by Lino's translations. How mysterious to have two distinct pronouns for the masculine third person singular. One afternoon, in attempting to explain this discrepancy to me, Lino happened to give me an example in which he quoted himself speaking to his father. He used a form that contrasted with the one I was accustomed to. This was the key to unraveling this mysterious puzzle. Lino's example tipped me off to the fact that people use different pronoun forms depending on the social relationship between speaker and addressee (the person to whom an individual is talking) or between a speaker and

Xavante men dancing in their village. A semiotic approach to the Xavante language revealed information about how they order their social world.

the referent (the person about whom she or he is talking).

From then on I began to ask him how he would speak to other people, and eventually I was able to determine that the Xavante use certain pronoun forms to talk to and about particular kin and affines. For example, to say, "They [my parents] aren't looking," you say:

date madö2ö ö di.

But to say, "They [my uncles] aren't looking," you say:

tete madö2ö ö di.

In these two examples the underlining highlights the different pronoun forms. Lino and I discovered that the Xavante have what is known as a system of honorifics, an elaborate way of formally marking social relations through speech, which, in Xavante, is done through contrasting sets of pronouns and person-marking devices. Of course, once I became aware of these forms I heard them being used everywhere.

What are Xavante speakers doing when they use these? The answer is that they are establishing two things with the pronoun forms they select in their speech.

1. By using an honorific form the speaker shows that she or he is an adult. Since being an adult is not only biologically determined but also socially defined, there must be signs that point out who is an adult and who is not. Among the Xavante the use of honorific pronouns are one way of making this distinction. When a boy completes his initiation, or when a girl has her first baby, he or she marks this change in status by using socially salient pronouns in speech to and about certain kin and affines. Since only socially defined adults employ honorific forms, use of these forms signals a speaker's adult social status.
2. The markers point out the relationships between people. Since social relationships are not given, and can't be taken for granted, signs must exist so that people

can apprehend them. These pronouns (or person-making forms) show, in the context of daily life, who is significant to whom and in what way. They make the social relationships palpable by giving them a material form.

The method I used enabled me to discover how the Xavante exploit the rich semiotic potential of language. I found that through the complex social signals of speech people constantly tell others something about themselves (whether or not they are adults) and indicate their position in a kinship network to others who know how to read the signs of language use. By observing and recording discourse in-context and by eliciting my assistants' reflections on that usage, I was able to gain access to entirely different sorts of data from those that are typically available through traditional linguistic methods in a society where individuals are not accustomed to talking about the semiotic properties of their language.

Ideograms, such as these characters on a Korean temple bell, convey language through symbols in contrast to the alphabet most North Americans use daily to convey meaning.

4

LANGUAGE

▲▲▲

anguage is found in every human society and is a central feature of human culture. Like other features of culture, language is socially acquired. At the same time, there are aspects of language that show it to have a biological basis in the genetic endowment of all human beings. The study of language reveals a central paradox: People are born with the basic equipment necessary to speak and understand speech, but no one is born knowing how to use a specific language. That ability must be learned.

Language can be defined as a symbolic communication system that uses coded signs to convey ideas and information. In spoken languages, the signs are patterns of sound and silence. In other languages, the signs may be visual. Although many people feel that language is a uniquely human capability, some scientists challenge this idea. Many animal species communicate symbolically (Figure 4.1). For example, whales and porpoises emit calls underwater, and many land animals such as monkeys vocalize to transmit information. Stickleback fish change color to show that they are sexually receptive. Beavers slap the water with their tails to warn other beavers of danger. Bee dancing communicates to other bees the direction and distance from the hive to sources of nectar. All these forms of communication have features in common with human language.

Some people think that human language is distinctive because it consists of much more than messages. It also has **grammar**—the arrangement of elements that a language uses to convey meaning. However, grammar is not unique to human languages. Bee dancing, for example, has a grammar in which the symbolic elements—the number of turns, the frequency and intensity of tail wagging, and the direction the dancing bee faces—communicate the location of the nectar. The order and combination of these elements give the message its meaning.

Perhaps a better indicator of the uniqueness of human language is its freedom from context. Many nonhuman communication systems are tied to a specific context. A gibbon, for example, can signal "danger," but it cannot indicate the kind of danger. A bee can show the type and location of flowers but not the location of the beekeeper. A beaver can slap the water when danger is present, but it cannot use this message to describe past or future dangers. Human language can be used to communicate things about the past or the future, about inner or outer states, about observable things or things merely imagined. Language is arbitrary in that the words have no necessary connection to what they stand for.

The most powerful aspect of human language is that it can generate an unlimited number of messages by combining a limited number of elements in differ-

Figure 4.1 *Communication among bottle-nosed dolphins is the subject of Project Circe, conducted at Marine World/Africa USA. Led by Dr. Diana Reiss, researchers are studying the dolphins' ability to control certain aspects of their environment by pressing symbols on an underwater keyboard. Although dolphins do communicate symbolically, their communication system differs significantly from human language.*

ent ways. The average human language has between 20 and 50 basic units of sound, yet from these it can create tens of thousands of meaningful words and an unlimited number of meaningful messages. The human brain is like a computer that can create and decode elaborate messages different from any message ever heard before. Language is the richest and most powerful system of communication and information retrieval known.

Language is a medium of communication with links to both biology and culture. It serves social functions, reflecting and perhaps sustaining social roles. The study of language is the subject of **linguistics**, one of the most advanced areas of anthropology in theory and method. Anthropological linguistics uses sophisticated methods linked with advances in neuroscience to probe the intricacies of human language and thought. It is related to the study of meaning in general, although it is more specialized.

THE ORIGIN AND EVOLUTION OF LANGUAGE

When and how did humans (or their ancestors) begin to use language? This question has inspired hundreds of books and articles. Many people have speculated, but no one has much evidence to go on. The reason for this lack of concrete evidence lies in a central feature of human speech: "rapid fading" (Hockett 1960). As soon as a person utters a phrase, it disappears. Unlike other forms of behavior speech does not leave behind any observable residue; it cannot be recovered archaeologically. Other languages, such as sign language, are also rapid fading. Writing, a system for recording speech in a medium (stone, paper, or clay), began fairly recently in human history (Box 4.1).

How old is human language? To find out, researchers have taken various lines of investigation and have arrived at different conclusions. Some investigators focus on the development of the brain, trying to determine when human ancestors acquired the ability to form, transmit, receive, decode, and store linguistic messages. Neandertals, for example, who lived about 100,000 years ago, had brains equal in size to those of modern humans. Investigators have determined that Broca's area, a part of the brain that is important in speech production and recognition, was well developed in Neandertal brains (Tobias 1983, Falk 1975). Archaeological studies also suggest that Neandertals probably had complex belief systems, including belief in an afterlife, compatible with a complex language (see Chapters 7, 23).

Other scientists look for clues to the origin of language by studying the vocal apparatus of chimpanzees and other close relatives of humans. Some investigators have concluded that apes are incapable of humanlike speech because they cannot make the various speech sounds humans can make. From this they infer that our earliest human ancestors 4 to 6 MYA had no language. One study (Lieberman and Crelin 1971) even suggests that Neandertals may have lacked the anatomical equipment to produce modern human speech sounds.

A related line of investigation focuses on comparing the **neurological capabilities** required for speech and those required for other activities, such as tool making and artistic expression. Unlike speech, tools and art objects leave traces that allow us to study their development. Perhaps the earliest stone tools, dating from about 1.5 MYA, reflect abilities comparable to those required for rudimentary human language (see Chapter 10). On the other hand, some writers suggest that the development of artistic abilities, as seen in cave art and stone tools, shows that neurological capacity for complex languages emerged only 35,000 years ago (Eldredge and Tattersall 1982, 158–159; Simons 1989; see Chapter 23). This is a minority view, however, that does not agree with the leading theories of the origin of human capacities.

Some researchers relate the origin of language to social life. Like other members of the primate order,

---

language A symbolic communication system that uses coded signs to convey ideas and information.

grammar The arrangement of elements that a language uses to convey meaning.

linguistics The study of spoken forms of human communication.

neurological capabilities The physiological capacity of humans to perform certain activities, such as speak or make tools.

humans are intensely social animals. Social life often involves close cooperation and coordination of activities, and therefore it would favor the rise of language to facilitate cooperation. The earliest evidence for social behavior dates to about 2 MYA, from sites in Olduvai Gorge, Tanzania, in East Africa, where the distribution of bones and stone tools suggests that the ancestors of *Homo* brought food to a central place for butchering and sharing. This interpretation has been challenged, however (see Chapter 6). Better evidence for such cooperation comes from sites that date from about 1 MYA. If social cooperation is evidence for language, we may conclude that language ability was present among our human ancestors a million or more years ago.

Most theories about language origins focus on speech, yet it is possible to have language without speech. Could speechless languages have existed among humans or their ancestors before speech? Many primates produce vocalizations that communicate information but are not speech. Perhaps the earliest human languages did not rely as heavily on speech as modern languages do; however, the major design features of human language are based on speech and hearing, not on gestures or other signaling systems. Even American Sign Language (AMESLAN), the gestural sign language used by people who are hearing impaired, is based on speech. There is no evidence that the human communication system evolved from an earlier nonverbal system.

BOX 4.1

Language and Writing

People often confuse writing with language. Writing is not language, only a way of recording it. The letters used to record any language should not be confused with the sounds a speaker makes when speaking. The letters are **graphs**, and their design and function differ from one language to another. In English, Greek, Arabic, Turkish, and other *alphabetic* writing systems, the letters spell out words in bits of sound. In Chinese graphemes, each element or character stands for an idea or picture of the word or idea, so they may be called *ideograms*. Ideograms are symbols that depict graphically the thing or idea that they stand for. Consider, for example, the international sign used to warn drivers that the road ahead has sharp curves.

Alphabetic writing seems to be much more efficient because we can construct any word in the language by using a limited number of graphs; in English it's 26, plus punctuation marks. A complete set of ideograms in Chinese runs into the thousands, making it a formidable task to become literate in Chinese. Why then have societies using ideograms clung to them for so long, especially now that alphabetical writing systems have been devised for them? Fosco Maraini (1979) suggests that in some ways ideograms are superior to alphabetic writing. In China, where there are dozens of different languages and mutually unintelligible dialects, ideograms are a unifying force. People who cannot understand each other's speech can understand each other's writing. More important, Maraini says,

Ideograms function like traffic signs. . . . Ideograms are direct symbols of reality of experience: they hug the world. . . . The alphabet is simpler to learn but, as a symbol of symbols, it is far removed from experience and hence "opaque." It is also cumbersome because it requires a continuous coding and decoding from sound to sign and vice versa. Moreover it is rigidly tied to the limitations of the spoken language. . . . Ideograms are difficult to learn but they transmit information directly, transparently, like instant flashes and . . . may transcend the barriers of the spoken language. [1979, 584–585]

This traffic sign uses an ideogram to warn drivers of curves on the road ahead.

Figure 4.2 *Following the Norman conquest, commemorated here in the famous Bayeux Tapestry, the English language was transformed by the absorption of thousands of French words.*

Languages themselves yield little evidence about the origin of language. For a time some investigators sought the origin of language in **onomatopoeia**, the imitation of natural sounds by words like "buzz," "click," "whoosh," and "slosh." But no such connection can be found for most words. Most words are arbitrary symbols that can signify one or more things. Their meaning depends on the linguistic and social context and not on a connection with the objects they signify. Thus different terms—*glass* (English), *verre* (French), *tasa* (Spanish), and *copo* (Portuguese)—can all signify the same object. There is no evidence that onomatopoeia stands at the roots of all language.

What is the origin of language? Since there are no traces of early languages, or "protolanguages," available for examination, there is no evidence that bears directly on the problem. The only physical traces are some indications of brain development. Perhaps the most promising approach to the origin of language today lies in the study of language development, that is, the process by which a child learns to speak. As discussed below, the developmental process of language acquisition follows regular rules, which, at a very abstract level, are the same in every language. In these rules may be hidden some of the secrets of language origins.

Processes of Language Change

Even if the origins of language are hidden in the distant past of human existence, it is certain that languages themselves are dynamic systems that continually change and evolve. English, for example, has a long history of change, beginning with Old English, a Germanic dialect spoken on the British isles in the first millennium. Up to 85 percent of the words in Middle English, the precursor of modern English, are of French origin.

Most processes of language change are linked to social and political processes, such as migrations, conquests, contact, trade, and technological change. Some changes are directly traceable to social changes, for example, the introduction of **loan words** to a language by conquerors. After the Norman invasion of Britain in the year 1066 (Figure 4.2), thousands of

---

graphs The physical signs, such as an alphabet used to record a language. These may be alphabetic or ideogrammatic.

onomatopoeia The linguistic imitation of natural sounds, reflected in English words like *buzz, click,* and *splash.*

loan words Words that are introduced from one language to another.

Table 4.1 English Words of Anglo-Saxon and French Origin

Anglo-Saxon Origin	French Origin
thing	object
build	construct
want	desire
sad	desolate
big	immense
pretty	beautiful

French loan words entered English and have since been completely absorbed into English. Words like *imagination, nationality,* and *conceive* are all derived from French. Over 900 years later, there is still a curious distinction between words of French and Anglo-Saxon origin. Consider the list of near synonyms shown in Table 4.1. These pairs, though close in meaning, are not completely interchangeable in speech. English speakers usually find the French-derived form is used more in formal or "elegant" contexts than the Anglo-Saxon form. This difference may be a relic of status differences between the Anglo-Saxons and their French conquerors.

One of the most disturbing aspects of change to many people is the borrowing of items from other languages. Some people feel that loans affect the "purity" of the language. Spanish speakers decry the mixture of English expressions in the Puerto Rican dialect, sometimes called "Spanglish." The French government has passed laws forbidding the use of loan words from English on radio and television such as *le weekend, le drugstore, le waterproof* (raincoat), and *le whiskey.* Some familiar loan words in English include *laissez faire, ex post facto, blitzkrieg, sayonara, noblesse oblige, amigo,* and *pasta.* Those who hope to deter the "barbarization" of language through such borrowing might just as well try to hold back the tides. All languages are affected by other languages; no language stops changing until all its speakers die off.

Language Family Trees

Like biological species, languages diverge through time with the accumulation of various kinds of changes (Lewin 1988). Languages change slowly,

often conserving features of the earlier languages from which they descend. This allows historical linguists to trace the relations between "parent" and "daughter" languages even when the intervening phases have disappeared. Historical linguists can even reconstruct dead parent languages. Linguists establish **language family trees** by comparing different languages to each other. Many aspects can be compared, such as syntax, inflected forms, and vocabulary. The most common approach is to compare "standard" vocabularies of words that refer to common, universal things, such as parts of the body, family members, and so on.

Consider the words shown in Table 4.2. Even though the sample is small, it demonstrates strong similarities among the four languages. Each similar form is a **correspondence.** There are at least three possible explanations for a correspondence. One is that the forms could be similar by sheer chance. But the more correspondences found in a large sample of words, the less likely it is that they are due to chance. Another explanation is that the words could be loan words from another language. Finally the two languages could be "genetically" related either as parent-daughter or as "siblings." Languages that are geneti-

Table 4.2 Word Comparison in Four Germanic Languages

English	Swedish	Dutch	German
blood	blod	bloed	Blut
hand	hand	hand	Hand
father	fader	vader	Vater
sister	syster	zuster	Schwester
hail	hagel	hagel	Hagel
hut	hydda	hut	Hütte
death	dod	dood	Tod
birch	Bjork	berk	Birke
wind	vind	wind	Wind
door	dorr	deur	Tür

Note: The words are rendered in the alphabet of each country, not phonetically. This makes the table somewhat misleading, because the same graphemes have different values in different languages. The German *w* and *v*, for example, are pronounced as the English *v* and *f* respectively. If the words were rendered phonetically, even greater similarities would be seen.

Source: Elgin 1979, 206.

Table 4.3 Reconstruction of Proto-Algonquin

Fox	Cree	Menomini	Ojibwa	Gloss	Proto-Central Algonquin
pematesiwa	pimatisiw	pematesew	pimatisi	"he lives"	*pematisiwa
posiwa	posiw	posew	posi	"he embarks"	*posiwa
newapamawa	niwapamaw	newapamaw	niwapama	"I look at him"	*newapamawa
wapanwi	wapan	wapan	wapan	"it dawned"	*wapanwi
niyawi	niyaw	neyaw	niyaw	"my body"	*niyawi
kenosiwa	kinosiw	kenosew	kinosi	"he is long"	*kenosiwa

*Reconstructed forms are conventionally marked with an asterisk.

Note: Although the sample of phrases is small, the correspondences are clear. The main differences seem to lie in the vowels and in the ending of the phrases. The Fox vowel *i* is always *e* in Menomini. Fox phrases are generally the longest. At this point, the question is, Were the endings found in Fox added or had they been lost in Ojibwa? The answer is not obvious. The assumption made for this reconstruction is that the longer forms are older and that the endings were dropped in the daughter languages.

Source: Gleason 1961.

cally related (see Table 4.2) show repeated sound correspondences and a regular pattern of difference, such as vowel shifts. A loan word here and there, borrowed to fill a particular semantic hole, is not evidence of a genetic relationship.

After compiling evidence for a genetic relationship among languages, linguists can reconstruct a **protolanguage.** Reconstruction depends on the assumption that the changes in the divergent daughter language are regular and uniform (Table 4.3). It is difficult to know exactly how an extinct language sounded. The test of a reconstructed language is whether it helps to show the systematic similarities among the various languages descended from it.

An Italian traveller to India in the 16th century found that Hindu scholars used an ancient language (Sanskrit) that was no longer used in ordinary speech, like Latin and Greek in Europe. He noted certain similarities to Italian. For example, the Sanskrit word

for god, *deva,* resembled the Italian *dio.* The word for snake, *sarpa,* was like the Italian *serpe.* The Sanskrit numbers *sapta, ashta, nava* were also like the Italian *sette, otto, nove.* As Europeans became more familiar with Sanskrit and other modern languages of India, scholars began to search for connections between the languages of India, Europe, and the lands in between.

These discoveries eventually led to the reconstruction of **Proto-Indo-European,** an extinct language spoken some 5,000 years ago by illiterate, sedentary farmers in what today is Poland, Czechoslovakia, Hungary, and Romania. This language was ancestral to many of the existing languages of Europe and Asia (Figure 4.3). The Romance languages (French, Italian, Spanish, Catalan, Portuguese, and Romanian), the Germanic languages (English, Dutch, German, Danish, Swedish, and Norwegian), the Slavic languages (Russian, Ukrainian, Byelorussian, Czech, Slovak,

language family tree A model used in historical linguistics to portray temporal relationships of divergence from parent to daughter languages.

correspondence In comparative linguistics, a formal similarity of words. Correspondence may be attributed to chance, borrowing, or "family" relationship.

protolanguage An extinct parent language that is reconstructed by assuming that the changes in the divergent daughter languages are regular and uniform.

Proto-Indo-European A reconstructed, extinct language spoken about 5,000 years ago. It is the parent of many of the languages currently spoken in Europe and Asia.

Figure 4.3 *The branches and subbranches of the Indo-European language family tree.*

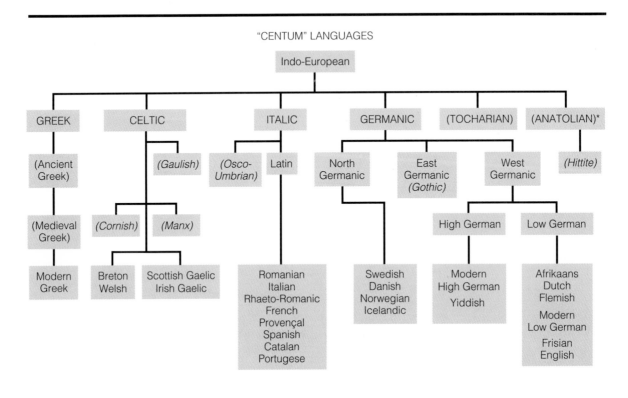

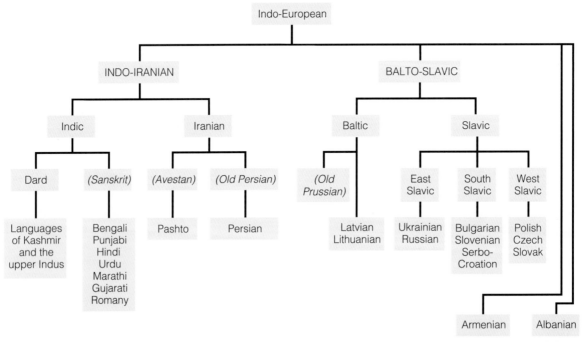

Polish, Slovene, Serbo-Croatian, and Bulgarian), and several languages of the Indian subcontinent (including Hindi and Urdu) are all languages of the Indo-European family.

The branches and subbranches on language family trees like that shown in Figure 4.3 give an exaggerated impression of sharp breaks between languages. Language change is gradual, and transitional forms often exist between the extreme differences that form dialects and, eventually, separate languages. In fact it is sometimes difficult to determine when a speech community ceases to speak a dialect and begins to speak a separate language. The usual criterion is **mutual intelligibility,** but even this is not simple to apply. Spanish and Portuguese, for example, are two Romance languages generally thought to be distinct languages. Most Portuguese speakers have no trouble understanding Spanish, but Spanish speakers often cannot understand Portuguese. There is cross-intelligibility, but it is not symmetrical.

Linguists have developed a technique, **lexicostatistics,** for determining the point of divergence between two related languages. The technique is based on the assumption that languages change at relatively steady rates. In some cases we can check such estimates by examining historical records of written languages that diverged fairly recently, such as Spanish and Portuguese. However, in the case of very old languages or unwritten languages, lexicostatistics is one of the few methods of determining the ages of languages. Recently a few scientists have begun to compare the evidence from human genetics with linguistic evidence. In a few areas they have been able to test estimates of the age of linguistic divergence with similar estimates of genetic divergence.

Linguistics is just at the threshold of understanding linguistic change. We know that languages are dynamic and change at fairly constant rates, but we don't really know what drives that change or why languages change in one direction and not another. The areas of **psycholinguistics** and **sociolinguistics** are just beginning to open up new vistas in these fascinating areas of study.

ANALYZING LANGUAGE

Languages are based on complex patterns or rules. Paradoxically, most people can speak perfectly well without knowing the rules. Consider the following two utterances:

1. These angrily basket between go extra.
2. This medical birthday flies underwater monuments.

Any English speaker, even an illiterate, can tell that both sentences are nonsensical. But there is an important difference between them. Sentence 1 is just a "word salad," while sentence 2 is recognizable as an English sentence. Even without studying grammar in school, we "feel" that the second one obeys the rules. One test of this would be to substitute other words that are the same **parts of speech** (nouns, adjectives, and so on) for some of the words in sentence 2, forming, for example,

3. This talented woman flies jet planes.

Any fluent speaker can tell when a sentence obeys the rules, regardless of whether it makes literal sense. The poet (and mathematician) Lewis Carroll knew that when he wrote "Jabberwocky" in 1872:

'Twas brillig, and the slithy toves
Did gyre and gimbol in the wabe;
All mimsy were the borogoves,
And the mome raths outgrabe,

---

mutual intelligibility A broad criterion of cross-intelligibility established by linguists to distinguish between dialects and languages. If people from two distinct speech communities can understand each other, they speak different dialects; if they cannot understand each other, they speak different languages.

lexicostatistics A statistical technique used to determine the general time of divergence from parent to daughter language.

psycholinguistics The study of the interrelationship between psychological and linguistic behavior.

sociolinguistics The study of language use in a specific social context, including the physical setting, participants, message communicated, form, channel, and so on.

part of speech A linguistic form class, such as a noun or a verb, or a particular kind of function word, such as a preposition or adjective.

Although the poem is nonsense, Carroll was careful to observe the rules of English grammar, such as agreement between subject and verb. Thus he did *not* write,

All mimsy *was* the borogoves,

Since *s* forms the plural in English, Carroll made sure he used the plural verb *were* with his nonsense plural term *borogoves.*

Unconscious Patterning

The quality that English speakers can "feel" is that of **grammaticality**, or conformity to a rule. A well-formed expression is one that does not violate a native speaker's sense of grammaticality. Like other cultural rules, the sense is unconscious. People make well-formed sentences without being consciously aware of these rules. This **unconscious patterning** of language can be observed in children's speech. Language learning takes place long before children begin school and study formal grammar. Consider the child who says,

Mommy bringed home the bacon.

The child has unconsciously learned that the past tense in English is formed by adding *ed* to the **stem**, as in *start + ed*, forming *started,* and has applied it to the irregular verb *bring.* Such errors arise from **hyperconsistency**, in which the speaker logically extends a rule to a case where it does not apply. People who have no notion of grammatical rules learn and apply such rules unconsciously. A child does not just learn and remember each correct form. In fact careful observation of children shows that children do *not* learn language by simply imitating others. Instead, language is based on general patterns that appear in a fixed developmental sequence.

Prescriptive versus Descriptive Grammars

If children already know grammar before they go to school, why must they study grammar? The prescriptive grammar taught in schools is not necessarily that used in actual speech. **Prescriptive grammars** are idealized versions of correct usage defined by a group of specialists trying to standardize speech. Prescriptive grammars are normative in that they focus on how one *ought* to speak, not on how people actually do speak. They may serve social functions, but they often require adherence to standards that are not typical in any **speech community.** A speech community is a group of people who share common patterns of speech and expression. A population may speak a single language but be divided into many different speech communities.

Descriptive linguistics approaches languages as people actually use them in natural speech. For example, most English teachers do not accept the contraction *ain't* for *am not,* but *ain't* is very common in the everyday speech of many American speech communities. And the subjunctive case in English has largely disappeared from everyday speech; however, grammar books still teach it. Linguists are generally more interested in the structure of language as people speak it.

Immediate Constituent Linguistics

In the 20th century, there have been two major approaches to understanding the rules of a language. One group of linguists considers language to consist of **speech acts,** or, more simply, things people say. This approach is known as the **immediate constituent** (IC) approach. The other approach, known as **transformational grammar** (or generative grammar) looks at language as something people know. According to this view, speech acts are merely outward signs of what they know; they are not language itself. Each approach has a distinctive method and offers particular insights into language. The difference between the two approaches reflects an important debate in the history of behavioral science.

IC linguists define spoken language as an ordered system of sound and silence used to communicate meaning. They treat language as a system of interconnected parts. In IC linguistics the speech sound is the basic unit of spoken language.

Phonology.   Most speech sounds are produced by air passing from the lungs across the vocal cords, through the **glottis**, mouth, teeth, and lips (Figure 4.4). There are hundreds of possible sounds, each created by a particular position of the mouth, lips, tongue, glottis,

Figure 4.4 *A human being can produce a wider variety of speech sounds than an animal like the chimpanzee because of the lower position of the vocal chords in relation to other parts of the vocal apparatus.*

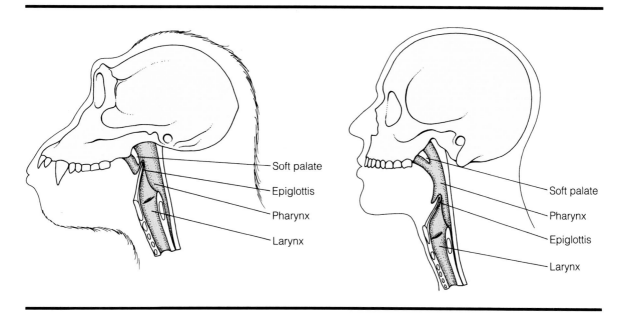

and vocal cords. When the vocal cords vibrate, speech sounds are **voiced**; when they do not, they are voiceless. The column of air from the lungs may be partially or completely blocked to produce **consonants**, or it may be open to produce **vowels**. Each language uses a distinctive set of sounds to form utterances. The "clicks" heard in some African languages, for example, are produced by closing the front and back of the oral passage, drawing the tongue downward to produce a vacuum, then releasing it.

grammaticality The determination by a native speaker that some utterance "feels" as if it conforms to the principles of grammar of that native language.

unconscious patterning The process by which people use grammatical principles that govern their own language use without being consciously aware of them.

stem A morpheme to which an affix can be added.

hyperconsistency The extension of a grammatical rule to an irregular case in which it does not apply.

prescriptive grammar An idealized version of correct usage defined by a group of specialists attempting to standardize speech.

speech community A group of people who share common patterns of speech and expression.

descriptive linguistics The branch of linguistics that studies the structure of language at a particular time, excluding historical or comparative data, as characterized by its own unique phonemes, morphemes, and syntax.

speech acts What people actually say, in contrast to what they know about the grammatical rules of their language.

immediate constituent (IC) An approach to the study of language that focuses on individual speech acts.

transformational grammar A grammar that generates sentences, assigns structural descriptions to these sentences, and relates their deep structures and meanings to the surface structures and sounds; also known as generative grammar.

glottis The opening between the vocal chords in the larynx.

voiced Speech sound uttered with vibration of the vocal chords.

consonant A phone produced by constricting the airstream in the vocal tract (glottis, mouth, teeth, and lips).

vowel A phone produced without blockage of the airstream in the vocal tract.

BOX 4.2

Phonetic Transcriptions

Linguists developed the International Phonetic Alphabet (IPA) because conventional alphabets are too limited to cover the range of phonetic variation in any language. For example, in the English alphabet the letter *a* stands for several different sounds, as in the words *ape, man,* and *bald.* The letter *e* has different sounds in the words *heel, tell,* and *the.* And *gh* may be pronounced like *f,* as in *tough,* or may be silent, as in *dough.* Consider the following spelling of the word *fish:*

> ghoti
>
> *gh* as in tough
>
> *o* as in women
>
> *ti* as in nation
>
> . . . hence, *fish*

IPA can be used to **transcribe** any language into a standardized form. In IPA each symbol stands for a separate phone, with modifications for unusual speech sounds. Tone languages, for example, require special symbols indicating the pitch overlaid on other sounds. Although the phonetic alphabet is complex and unfamiliar, it is a more precise guide to pronunciation than standard **orthography** (writing). This can be seen in the following English verse, transcribed phonetically on the left (phonetic transcription are denoted by brackets) and in standard orthography on the right.

[ðə reyn it reyniΘ an ðə jəst, ən Hlsow an ðəənjəst felə. bət čiyfliy an ðə jəst, bikəz ðə ənjəst stiylz ðəjəsts əmbrelə]	The rain it rains on the just, and also on the unjust fella, but chiefly on the just, because the unjust steals the just's umbrella.

Source: Gleason 1961.

Linguists need a **data language** to describe accurately the speech sounds occurring in any language. They devised an **International Phonetic Alphabet (IPA)** for that purpose, using letters and other symbols to stand for each sound (Box 4.2).

The system of sounds used in a language is the subject of **phonology**. A **phone** is any distinguishable speech sound, such as the eff sound in the word *phone.* Phones can be grouped into **phonemes,** the smallest units of sound important for distinguishing meanings (Table 4.4). A phonemic alphabet is just big enough to write all the words occurring in a language. Most dialects of English, for example, can be written down with about 46 phonemes. Every language has its own phonemic system.

A set of related phones that do not contrast with each other but occur in predictable ways are **allophones** of a phoneme. The idea of allophones becomes clear when we compare different languages. For example, in Spanish, [b] and [v] are allophones of a single phoneme. This explains why some Spanish speakers using English seem to confuse forms like *very* and *bury.* Mandarin Chinese treats [l] and [r] as allophones of a single phoneme. A Chinese speaker may hear *rice* and *lice* as the same word. English, on the other hand, does not distinguish nasalized from nonnasalized vowels. American English speakers may have difficulty understanding languages where nasalization marks off separate phonemes. For exam-

Table 4.4   The Constituents of Language in the IC Approach

Unit	Area of Study
Utterances [Words]*	Syntax
Morphemes Morphs	Morphology
Phonemes Phones	Phonology

*This term is in brackets because not all languages have units that can be defined as words.

Subject	English	German	French	Spanish
1st person singular	eat	esse	mange	como
2d person singular	eat	issest	manges	comes
3d person singular	eats	isst	mange	come
1st person plural	eat	essen	mangeons	comemos
2d person plural	eat	essest	mangez	coméis
3d person plural	eat	essen	mangent	comen

Table 4.5 The Verb *to eat* in Four Different European Languages

ple, a speaker who ignores this distinction in Brazil is likely to get a stick (*pau*) when he asks for bread (*pāhu*).

Morphology. **Morphs** are units (usually groups of phonemes) that carry meaning; **morphemes** are the minimum units of meaning that combine into words and sentences. (Phonemes set up contrast between meaningful elements, but they carry no meaning themselves.) **Unbound morphs** are morphs that have meaning all by themselves, while **bound morphs** can occur only in combination with other morphs, such as the *cran* in *cranberry*. An **affix** is a bound morph that modifies the meaning of the morph (or stem) with which it is combined. A morpheme may have two or more **allomorphs** that mean the same thing but sound different. The English plural, for example, is a **suffix** with three allomorphs.

s as in *cats* [kæts]

z as in *dogs* [dawgz]

z as in *horses* [hors əz]

There are exceptions, such as the plural forms of *man, sheep,* and *goose.*

Languages vary in how important affixes are. **Inflected languages** use affixes to express different tenses, numbers, aspects, or cases of a stem. Consider the array of forms of the verb *to eat* in the four European languages shown in Table 4.5. English verbs are the least inflected of the four languages. It is possible to determine the identity and number of the subject from the verb phrase only if the personal pronoun is included.

Syntax. Syntax is the level of organization in language concerned with the arrangements of mor-

transcribe In anthropological linguistics, to record speech in a written form.

orthography A commonly accepted system of spelling.

data language An accurate, systematic description of sounds used in languages around the world, such as the International Phonetic Alphabet (IPA).

International Phonetic Alphabet (IPA) A data language or compilation of linguistic phones that occur universally.

phonology The study of a language's system of sounds.

phone A discriminable speech sound.

phoneme The minimum range of sounds that serve to distinguish meaningful units from each other.

allophones A set of related phones that do not contrast with each other; that is, when interchanged, they do not change the meaning of a word.

morph Any phoneme or sequence of phonemes that bears meaning.

morpheme The minimal unit of meaning in a language.

unbound morph A morpheme that can meaningfully occur alone.

bound morph A morpheme that cannot meaningfully occur alone.

affix A bound morpheme that is attached to a stem.

allomorphs Morphemes that have the same meaning and occur in the same position but are phonemically different.

suffix An affix added to the end of a stem.

inflected language A language that uses affixes to express tense, number, aspect, cases, and so on.

phemes into meaningful sentences. The task of syntactic analysis is to understand how these units combine to create understandable utterances. Let us forget, for a moment, the English syntax we already know and see how a linguist goes about it. Read the following English sentence.

```
1     2     3   4   5   6 7 8     9       10
```
They quickly found the girl's hat at the president's house.

It is possible that each of the ten words has a unique grammatical function in the sentence. Or perhaps they can be grouped into a smaller number of functional classes. One test of this would be to see whether substituting other words for groups of words would change the basic structure of the sentence. The linguist focuses not on the meaning of the sentence but on its structure.

- We could treat items 3 through 5 as a single unit. This is not very satisfying because the word *girl's* clearly modifies something outside this block, namely 6 (*hat*).
- We could treat 4 through 6 as a single unit. We could replace it with the single term *it* without changing the structure or basic meaning of the expression.
- We could substitute a single word such as *there* for items 7 through 10, suggesting that together these words form a single unit.
- Item 3 stands alone, communicating the basic action of the sentence. If we substitute another verb, such as *burned,* the meaning changes but the structure remains the same.

The IC approach has been very successful in describing different languages. It also provides a guide to the learning of language. However, some linguists criticize IC linguistics for lacking a theory of how people acquire language.

Behaviorism and IC Linguistics. IC linguistics is highly behavioristic. **Behaviorism** is the name of a psychological theory that focuses primarily on "external," observable aspects of behavior. A behaviorist ignores processes that cannot be directly observed. Behaviorists often do experiments with animals, showing how rats or pigeons learn behavior under various kinds of stimulation.

B. F. Skinner, a founder of behavioral psychology, wrote a book called *Verbal Behavior* (1957) setting forth and defending this point of view. Skinner suggested that people acquire language the same way they learn other behavior. In his view, when people are born, their minds are like blank sheets ready to be written on. Individuals acquire language from experience, mainly by imitating older people and being corrected by them. Skinner explains language acquisition as a process of **operant conditioning**. The learner is rewarded for well-formed utterances and punished in some way for ill-formed utterances. Punishment could be a sharp look from an adult or the mocking laugh of an older child at a mistake.

According to the behaviorist view, language capability is part of a genetic human ability to acquire complex behavior. Skinner's position has been sharply attacked by some linguists who claim there is little evidence for operant conditioning in language learning. As we have already noted, some investigators have studied nonhuman primates to determine whether they are capable of learning to communicate through a symbolic language in a human fashion. These investigators seek to determine whether species other than humans can be trained to use language (see Chapter 9). If it is possible, the behaviorist position would be strengthened.

Transformational Grammar

In 1957 linguist Noam Chomsky began a series of criticisms of the IC approach. He argued that IC is capable of *describing* a language well but cannot explain how language works, that is, how meaning is expressed in sounds that we make. He criticized IC linguistics for its excessive dependence on a single level of analysis, the performance of language or speech acts. Beneath this level, Chomsky argued, there must be a level of competence, the underlying ability to create or generate messages and to decode or understand them. Nongenerative approaches, like IC, cannot account for how speakers actually create messages. Nor can they explain how people can recognize an utterance as grammatical. Rather than looking at speech and analyzing it as a hierarchy of phonemes, morphemes, and syntax, which he called the **surface structure** of language, Chomsky proposed that investigators look for the rules of grammar at the level of competence, or **deep structure**. These structures relate to the functioning of the mind itself. Chomsky suggested that people have an inborn grammatical ability; what they learn is not language but how to speak. Chomsky's position is linked with philosophical **rationalism**; it suggests that people have some knowledge independent of experience.

As an example, let us consider a sentence with two possible meanings:

Frightening kids should be against the law.

This could be taken to mean: (1) It should be illegal to frighten kids, or (2) kids who are frightening should be outlawed. There is a single surface sentence, but at the level of deep structure, it is two different sentences.

Now, let us consider two sentences that differ in surface structure but that are the same at the deeper level:

1. Professor Miller taught the class.
2. The class was taught by Professor Miller.

The basic meaning of these two sentences is the same, even though they are superficially different. IC linguistics, with its focus on the speech act, must treat these as two different sentences. How can two sentences that are phonetically and syntactically so different have virtually identical meanings? Perhaps the most important shortcoming of the IC approach is that it is not generative; it cannot account for the un-

limited creativity of language to create new messages.

Chomsky was interested in understanding the generative ability of language to function at a deep level. He wanted to find the rules, which he called "rules of transformation," that turned "mind sentences" into actual speech acts. His generative approach looks for the kernel of meaning in sentences. Consider this example.

1. A woman played the clarinet.

If it were transformed into

2. Clarinet a played woman the.

the reader would protest immediately. The core idea of this sentence lies in three words: woman, played, clarinet. The rest is just window dressing, you might say. Chomsky wanted to write some rules that would generate such sentences as "A woman played the clarinet," and perhaps also "The clarinet was played by a woman," and "A woman was playing the clarinet," but not the "word salad" of sentence 2.

Chomsky made the startling claim that all languages have a common deep structure. Chomsky believes there is a language organ in the brain responsible for the universal features of human language. In addition, he suggests that a linguist who knows the deep structure and transformational rules of a language can generate an unlimited number of permissible sentences in a language and none of the impermissible ones. Since the rules of transformation can be written in purely logical form, they can be programmed into computers. Theoretically a computer could be programmed to translate from one language

---

behaviorism A psychological theory that focuses on observable aspects of behavior, stressing operant conditioning as the primary means of learning or modifying behavior.

operant conditioning A process of learning that involves rewarding "correct" behavior and punishing "incorrect" behavior.

surface structure In Chomsky's view of transformational grammar, the components of an actually observed sentence: phonemes, morphemes, and syntax.

deep structure In Chomsky's view of transformational grammar, the abstract structure that underlies a sentence and that contains all that is necessary to analyze syntactically and interpret the sentence.

rationalism The philosophical position that people gain knowledge through reason or intellect rather than through experience.

into another. The computer would have an extensive dictionary and a program capable of "recognizing" syntactic structures.

Chomsky led a team of investigators in an effort to develop "machine translation." While Chomsky himself did not succeed in building a translating machine, other investigators have made some progress. One of the chief problems that machine translation must overcome is the dependence of language on context. Consider a series of simple English statements used in everyday speech and this point will become clear (Table 4.6). A machine programmed to translate from English into another language would have to contain a vast amount of information besides the purely syntactic and **lexical** (vocabulary) features of language. Languages establish their meaning in a rich symbolic and metaphoric context.

Transformational grammarians have been criticized for excessive dependence on their competence as native speakers. Often they use their own language— usually English—to test their formulas against their own intuitive sense of grammaticality. This raises a well-known problem in scientific validation: observer bias. If the investigators use their intuition as native speakers to test a hypothesis, their desire to see their hypotheses validated could affect their judgment.

The transformational approach shares the same philosophical background as structuralism (see Chapter 3). Structuralism and generative grammar both posit invisible structures that underlie surface images. They see these structures as more real and permanent than the shifting flux of events and messages. Yet, by their very definition, these structures cannot be observed directly. Still, the idea that there is some kind of inborn logic machine that stands behind and gives order to all the apparent variety in systems of human expression is very compelling. The question of how well generative grammar or structuralism has succeeded in identifying the basic units and structural transformations of meaning continues to be asked.

LANGUAGE AND SOCIETY

Language is embedded in social life. Communication, which is the foundation of social life, occurs largely through the medium of language. Language is also the form in which the collective knowledge or heritage of a society is created, transmitted, and stored. How a people use language is part of any cultural tradition. Sociolinguistics is the branch of linguistics and ethnology that studies language in its social context.

Languages are highly variable even within a single society. Although language depends on shared grammatical principles, morphemes, and phonemes, there still is individual and social variation. In complex societies speech is one of the primary means for classifying people (Box 4.3). As Professor Higgins says in *My Fair Lady* (Loewe and Lerner 1956),

> An Englishman's way of speaking
> Absolutely classifies him,
> The moment he opens his mouth,
> He makes some other Englishman despise him.

Table 4.6   English Phrases and Their Metaphoric Context

Phrase	Metaphoric Context	Approximate Meaning
I really struck out.	Baseball	"I failed."
I'll go out on a limb.	Tree climbing	"I'll take a risk."
She buys your argument.	Marketplace	"She accepts your reasons."
He's a real knockout.	Boxing	"He's very attractive."
She took the bull by the horns.	Rodeo	"She confronted the situation."
Why are you so blue?	Colors	"Why are you so sad?"
Let's get down to brass tacks.	Upholstery	"Let's get down to the basics."

BOX 4.3

Linguistic Markers of Status

Language differences often serve as markers of social status. William Labov, a sociolinguist, wanted to learn how systematic those differences were. He chose as a natural laboratory three department stores in New York City, ranked on the "price and fashion scale" from near the bottom to near the top: Klein's, Macy's, and Saks Fifth Avenue. Saks, located in a high-fashion shopping district, specializes in expensive lines of clothing and other merchandise. Macy's is a large, popular department store catering to a middle-income clientele. Klein's (now out of business) sold less expensive merchandise and was near poorer neighborhoods. In each store Labov asked several dozen sales clerks for directions to a department he knew was on the fourth floor. He recorded the answers in phonetic alphabet.

Labov found differences in the sales clerks' pronunciation of the *r*s in *fourth floor*. Some pronounced the *r* as in the standard English pronunciation of *roll*. Other employees used certain vowels or left out the *r* altogether in the same place in the words. For many, the response "fourth floor," sounded like "fought flaw." Labov correlated these differences with the stores' prestige and price range (Table). The distribution reflects differences in social ranking between working class, middle class, and upper class that most New Yorkers recognize. Intentionally or not, Saks recruited employees whose speech would be like that of their customers. On the other hand, the employees may have adapted their speech to the high-prestige environment of the store.

The Distribution of *r* in Three New York City Department Stores

Store	Price Range	Percentage of Clerks Pronouncing *r*
Klein's	low	20
Macy's	medium	51
Saks	high	62

Source: Labov 1972.

Dialects

Different speech styles within the same language are called **dialects.** Dialects often mark social cleavages, such as ethnic group, region, class, and educational level. A dialect may have such a sharp profile that people give it a name. In the United States, we speak of a southern "drawl," a midwestern "twang," a "down East accent," and "Brooklynese." Dialect differences also involve vocabulary, syntax, and perhaps even an "inner logic." During the 1988 presidential campaign, some people made an issue of candidate George Bush's dialect. Born in New England, Bush made Texas his official residence. Some Texans delighted in pointing out that his dialect was that of an easterner. One commentator stated archly, "In Texas, we never use *summer* as a verb."

In many societies there is a belief that certain dialects are more beautiful, more expressive, more correct, and more logical. A persistent folk belief among educated people in many countries is that their elite dialect is clearer, more elegant, and more scientific than other dialects. One common belief is that **standard dialects,** such as Castillian Spanish or Parisian French, are superior to other dialects. This linguistic form of ethnocentrism is called **glottocentrism.**

---

lexical Related to the vocabulary of a language rather than its grammar.

dialect A variety of a language shared by a particular group or regional population.

standard dialect The particular dialect of a language adopted as the model of correct usage in education, government, commerce, and mass communication.

glottocentrism The belief that one speech variety of a language is superior to others.

Why is one dialect of a language considered better and more correct? Some people claim that standard dialects are more logical, orderly, and precise than the so-called substandard dialects. Prescriptive grammars generally reflect ideal speech patterns among elite groups in a society. The elite usually have more wealth, political influence, and formal education. These same people, often clustered in a particular region of the country, form a speech community and set the standards in formal education. Standard dialects—those taught in schools—generally reflect the language patterns of elite groups in particular regions such as Northeastern United States, Oxford (England), Paris (France), Castille (Spain), and Rome (Italy).

Dialects such as Black English (a common speech pattern among African Americans), the speech of some Mexican Americans, Cockney, and Quebequois French are often thought of as substandard. Generally not used by teachers in schools, these dialects rarely occur in literature (except in certain low-status characters such as servants and slaves). Such dialects are often ridiculed by speakers of other dialects. It is no accident that these are the dialects of people occupying low status in society. The stigmatization of certain dialects, along with the idealization of others, reflects and reinforces social ranking within societies. It allows people to identify their position in relation to others and to adjust their behavior in accordance with their perception. The distribution of dialects often reflects the distribution of power in a society.

Linguistic "Deprivation"

In the United States a common example of a stigmatized dialect is Black English. Some educators believe that the language of urban African Americans is deficient, the result of "verbal deprivation." Educators who teach in inner-city schools may hear their students use expressions like "he go," "they mine," and "me got." They sometimes believe that the children who use such expressions were not exposed to well-formed sentences and consequently did not develop "normal" language skills. Thus they conclude that inner-city children are unable to express logical relations such as time (tense), number, possession, and comparison.

William Labov made extensive comparisons of standard English with Black English spoken in Philadelphia and New York City. He analyzed the speech patterns of inner-city youths and determined that they are not linguistically deprived at all. Labov found that these children grew up hearing many well-formed sentences. They were just as able to express logical relations as speakers of standard English.

Black English speakers, for example, often omit the **copula**, a "being" verb form that joins the subject and predicate. The expression, "he is" may be contracted to "he," as in "He dead." Leaving the copula out is a regular feature in standard Russian, Hungarian, and Arabic. But no one suggests those languages are illogical or that their speakers are deprived. Most English speakers can recognize the parallel between standard English forms and Black English. In other words, there is no loss of information in the nonstandard form.

If Black English has a developed grammar, is no less logical than standard English, and can express complex ideas, why is it regarded as inferior? As with other nonstandard dialects, the reasons have more to do with social structure than with the structure of language. Schools and other institutions train people to identify a particular dialect as correct.

Multilingualism and Code Switching

North Americans have a reputation for not learning foreign languages. But in fact millions of Americans are bilingual or multilingual. This number includes millions of Latinos, many immigrants from Europe and Asia, and people who have learned a second language out of interest, necessity, or ethnic pride. Many people grow up in a situation where they hear two different languages or two dialects of a language, one at home, the other at work or school. Some people become adept at switching back and forth between two languages or dialects. This is known as **code switching.** Code switching can often be used to achieve social goals, whether consciously or not.

Language may play an important political role. Sometimes powerful groups attempt to eliminate local languages and dialects to standardize the language across an entire nation. The Inca conquerors in ancient Peru did just that, wiping dozens of other languages off the map. The totalitarian government of Francisco Franco in Spain tried unsuccessfully to eliminate the regional Basque and Catalan languages as a way of strengthening the power of the central state. Franco prohibited the use of Basque and Catalan in public and on signs and billboards. Using these languages became a symbol of resistance to Franco's authority. In other cases the government may try to establish one or more "official languages." The government of India has attempted several times to declare Hindi a national language, setting off riots in some non-Hindi-speaking areas.

In some situations members of a minority speech community fight to keep their language. The French speakers of Quebec have made French the primary language of the province and demand that it be used in all state documents, road signs, and so forth. The people of the Moldavian Socialist Republic recently reinstated their language as the official language of the land to the dismay of the Kremlin and the many Russian speakers who live in Moldavia. Paraguay is officially a bilingual country whose people speak both Spanish and Guarani (an indigenous language). Paraguayans prefer Spanish in the formal arena of government and Guarani in the intimacy of the home. They feel that Guarani is a better language for poetry, and keeping it alive is a matter of national pride (Rubin 1968).

Multilingualism prevails in some situations. In the Vaupés River basin in South America live tribal peoples whose marriage customs require a person to marry a member of a different language group (Sorensen 1971). People grow up learning both their mother's and their father's languages. Since the parents are also multilingual, it is common for an individual in the Vaupés to be fluent in four or five unrelated tongues.

Dialects of a language may be quite persistent even in the face of deliberate attempts to suppress them. Many people believe that nonstandard dialects tend to die out when people come into contact with schools and the electronic media. This is not necessarily true.

Even though standard English is the predominant dialect on American radio and television, for example, the media have not erased the regional and ethnic dialects found in the United States.

Language and Culture Change

As cultural change takes place and people encounter new experiences and ideas, languages change, too. The most familiar kind of change is the elaboration of vocabulary to cover new ideas. Every English speaker is familiar with this process. In recent years, as computers have literally become household items, a number of technical terms and expressions have gained increasing currency. Terms like *RAM, ROM, byte, software,* and *diskette* have become familiar to millions of people. Not only have new words been added to our vocabulary, but also familiar words have acquired new meanings and grammatical functions. A mouse, for example, is not necessarily a small rodent but a hand-held device that rolls along the table top to position the cursor on a computer screen.

Cultural factors have an important influence on language. Some anthropologists and linguists believe the opposite also occurs. They suggest that the language we use exerts an influence on thought and behavior patterns. Various linguists have suggested this theory, but it is most closely identified with Benjamin Lee Whorf and Edward Sapir and is known as the Sapir-Whorf hypothesis. Whorf, an executive who became an amateur anthropologist, sometimes drew on his experience in the insurance business. He pointed out that workers were very careful around things called "gasoline drums" because they believed them to be dangerous. They tended to be careless around things called "empty gasoline drums." The "empty" drums, however, are far more dangerous because the vapor residues that may remain are more explosive than gasoline itself. According to Whorf, it is the language used to describe the situation that lulls the workers into careless inattention. Whorf studied Hopi, a North American native language, and sug-

---

copula Any part of the verb *to be* used as the main verb in the predicate of a clause.

code switching Changing back and forth between two or more language varieties.

gested that, because of its treatment of time and space, Hopi might be a better language than English for discussing theories in modern physics (Whorf 1936).

Communicating Without Words

In every society, people have ways of communicating without the use of audible signals. Communication can also take place through visual and tactile channels. Even silence can communicate. Anthropologist

Keith Basso studied the western Apache on a reservation in Arizona. Many aspects of communication were surprising. Basso observed that the Apache do not introduce strangers to each other; they may spend days in each other's presence before speaking. There are several other situations in which the Apache consider silence, rather than talk, appropriate. One such situation occurs when children return home after an absence. When Apache children come home from boarding school, their parents meet them at a trading post. Rather than excited talk, there is silence. Chil-

Figure 4.5   *Body language often conveys meaning as dramatically as words can. The tension of a close basketball game can be seen in these players' intensely focused attention, clasped hands, and suspended movements.*

dren and their parents may not exchange a word for 15 minutes. When someone speaks, at last, it is the child; the parents may wait for hours. Basso requested an explanation from his Apache informant, who replied,

> some of them learn to want to be whitemen, so they come back and try to act that way. But we are still Apaches! So we don't know them anymore, and it is like we never knew them. It is hard to talk to them when they are like that. [Basso 1973, 77]

Analyzing situations in which the Apache remain silent, Basso concluded that silence is an Apache response to a situation in which the status of the principal actors is ambiguous. People don't know what to expect from each other, so they remain silent. Thus silence is a response to uncertainty in social relations. The "silent treatment" given to children returning home from school can be read as: "You have been among the white people. Are you still an Apache, or do you think you have become white?"

Another important medium for communication is "body language." **Body language** can operate alongside verbal language, sometimes adding critical dimensions (Figure 4.5). Americans, for example, know not to take seriously statements accompanied by a wink of the eye. Gestures involving the face, hands, legs, torso, and body posture can also stand alone. In North America, rolling the eyes upward, for example, expresses disbelief, exasperation, or mild disgust. Both hands clapped over the cheeks, often indicates dismay.

Some aspects of body language may be universal. Several investigators suggest that the primate order as a whole employs the smile (corners of the mouth upturned) to signify pleasure, acceptance, and good humor. Other kinds of body language have meanings specific to the context. Greeks say "no" by jerking the head back in a gesture resembling the nod in the United States.

Not only specific gestures but also such matters as "zones of communication" are culturally prescribed.

Most North Americans and northern Europeans are comfortable talking at a distance of about 4 feet. Latin Americans prefer a much closer zone, around 2 feet, that permits frequent touching. This can create misunderstandings. One Latin American amuses himself at parties by standing very close to British and American guests. Their "personal space" is violated and they may back around an entire room as they unconsciously strive to maintain a "proper" communication zone.

As we saw in Chapter 3, there are many nonverbal forms of expression, including dress, food, and dance, that are rich in symbolic meaning. Some anthropologists, interested in the semiotics of nonverbal behavior, have referred to the language of the body, of food, of hairstyles, and so on. But the syntax of such languages does not begin to approach the complexity of verbal languages. Natural selection seems to have favored the vocal-auditory channel as the primary means for communicating the complicated things people have on their minds.

AN OPEN QUESTION: ARE ALL LANGUAGES EQUALLY DEVELOPED?

Until the early 20th century, many educated people believed that certain languages, such as English, French, and classical Latin and Greek, were more evolved than other languages, especially those spoken by people who lacked writing. This idea was based on certain measures of complexity and assumptions about the ability of languages to convey complex thoughts. Beginning in the 1920s, this notion came under attack by anthropological linguists imbued with the notion of cultural relativism. They suggested that all contemporary languages are equally developed. They pointed out that some languages spoken by technologically simple peoples were highly inflected and syntactically complex. In the past two decades, however, some investigators have suggested again that

---

body language The use of the body to communicate meaning.

languages differ in degree of evolution, although they do not measure language evolution in terms of degree of inflection.

Claims about the superiority of one language or dialect over others are rooted in social differences, as we saw earlier in this chapter. No language has been shown to be logically superior or more precise than any other, which is not to say that a particular language may not be more apt for dealing with certain ideas. Each speech community develops a language adequate to express the ideas and experiences it considers significant. If the Apache language lacks an expression signifying the square root of a number, it is not an inferior language; it simply developed in a context where this concept was not necessary.

Nearly all languages preserve some elements from the past (such as the English pronouns *thee, thou,* and *ye*). But the existence of such **archaic forms** does not mean that a language is less evolved than others. If sheer complexity were an accurate measure of a language's development, languages like Old English and Latin would be considered more developed than the less-inflected modern languages descended from them.

Color Terminology

There is some evidence for the view that not all languages are equally developed. A striking example emerged in a study by anthropologists Brent Berlin and Paul Kay (1969). Berlin and Kay were interested in how different peoples refer to colors. They examined color terminologies in a number of different languages by showing a standard color chart (similar to the ones in paint stores) to people who speak different languages. They reduced the color terms to the most basic ones recognized in the language. For example, English speakers who identify crimson, scarlet, cranberry, cherry, blood red, and so on generally agree that these hues are all different shades of the same basic color that they call red. Berlin and Kay found that all languages have a minimum of 2 and a maximum of 11 basic color terms: *white, black, red, green, yellow, blue, brown, purple, pink, orange,* and *gray*. Color terms are not randomly distributed, however. Berlin and Kay found that languages having only three basic color terms always have the same three: white,

black, and red. If there are four terms, the fourth will be green or yellow. In other words, color terms appear in languages in a fixed order depending on the total number of terms used, as follows:

1. All languages contain terms for white and black.
2. If a language contains three terms, it contains a term for red.
3. If a language contains four terms, it contains a term for either green or yellow (but not both).
4. If a language contains five terms, it contains terms for both green and yellow.
5. If a language contains six terms, it contains a term for blue.
6. If a language contains seven terms, it contains a term for brown.
7. If a language contains eight or more terms, it contains a term for purple, pink, orange, grey, or some combination of these.

Berlin and Kay distinguished seven different stages of language development, depending on the number of basic color terms identified in the language. For the most part, technologically advanced societies have more color terms and recognize more different points of the color spectrum than less technologically sophisticated societies. These findings run counter to the relativistic notion that all languages are equally developed. In addition, they further suggest that languages evolve in a fixed and orderly sequence from simple to complex.

Creole, Pidgin, and Child Languages

Further evidence comes from recent studies done on **creole** languages. These are languages arising out of close contact between two speech communities. This kind of contact was frequent during the expansion of European colonialism to the New World. From the 16th to the 19th century, Africans were transported in large numbers as slaves to work in plantations and mines. The earliest stage in the development of a creole is the appearance of a pidgin language. **Pidgin** languages have limited vocabulary and syntax and are minimal communication systems for people who must interact. They make use of forms from each parent language but rarely incorporate any of the more complex syntactic devices, such as inflection, affixes, and the like. After a generation or two, children who grow up hearing pidgin may begin to develop a creole language.

Over the years, linguists viewed creole languages as linguistic oddities, inferior hybrids. As descriptions of creoles accumulated, however, some scholars noticed that many creoles were similar to each other in both morphology and syntactic structure. Some scholars suggested that the similarity was due to a common **substrate** language from which all creoles were derived, perhaps Portuguese. Portuguese navigators did establish colonies on every continent during the 16th century, but this theory has been discredited. No single language could have been the substrate of all creoles.

A dramatically new approach to the creole convergence came from Hawaii. Toward the end of the last century, migrants from many lands converged on Hawaii to work on the enlarged sugar plantations. Within a short period Chinese, Filipino, Japanese, Korean, Portuguese, Puerto Rican, and Anglo-American migrants joined the native Hawaiians, and a pidgin based on an English substrate emerged. Linguist Derek Bickerton (1983) interviewed people who migrated to Hawaii during that period and spoke pidgin.

In Bickerton's words, Hawaiian pidgin was a "linguistic free-for-all." Yet within a single generation the children of the migrants developed a fully formed, consistent, and uniform creole language. How was this possible, especially given the fact that many creole speakers conserved their parent's native languages as well? Hawaiian Creole was not a homogenized form of English with some features acquired "cafeteria style" from Japanese, Chinese, Spanish, and so on. In fact it differed in important respects from all its substrate languages.

Bickerton compared Hawaiian Creole to other creole languages. He found that "creole languages throughout the world display the same uniformity and even the same grammatical structures that are observed in Hawaii." One common trait is the use of a "particle" to denote the tense. "I stay go" in Hawaiian creole is glossed (interpreted) as a present participle, "I am going." Other particles produce the effect of the past, conditional, and future tenses in English. A comparison to Haitian Creole and Sranan, an English-based creole from the South American coast, shows almost identical patterns of tense formation, even though the specific forms are different. Similarly the distinction of singular, plural, and neutral number markers occurs in all other creole languages.

Bickerton made the startling suggestion that these syntactical correspondences are genetically based; that is, the similarity between unrelated creoles derives from a universal, inborn way of acquiring language. Bickerton views creoles not simply as mixed languages but as the key to the biological basis for language acquisition. To support these assertions, Bickerton compared several utterances collected from very young English-speaking children to creoles with an English substrate. Some of the parallels are remarkable (Table 4.7). Bickerton's results are still controversial, and many linguists do not accept his theory.

We have already mentioned Chomsky's suggestion that there is an innate grammar behind all human languages. But he allowed for a variety of grammatical patterns from which the developing child "chooses" depending on the language he or she was exposed to. Bickerton took Chomsky's ideas a step further by proposing that there are also universal patterns in surface structure. The patterns are visible in the early development of language skills. A psycholinguist specializing in child language has even suggested there is a universal "basic child grammar" (Slobin 1982). Only

---

archaic forms Elements from the past that continue to be used, though rarely, in the present.

creole A language arising from close contact between two speech communities.

pidgin A simplified language representing the earliest stage in the development of a creole. Pidgin languages have a limited vocabulary and syntax and are minimal communication systems for people who must interact.

substrate A hypothesized language from which another is derived.

Table 4.7   Child Language and English Creoles Compared

Child Language	English Creoles
Where I can put it?	Where I can put om? (Hawaii)
I go full Angela bucket.	I go full Angela bucket. (Guyana)
Lookit a boy play ball.	Luku one boy a play ball. (Jamaica)
Nobody don't like me.	Nobody no like me. (Guyana)
I no like do that.	I no like do that. (Hawaii)
Johnny big more than me.	Johnny big more than me. (Jamaica)
Let Daddy get pen write it.	Make Daddy get pen write am. (Guyana)
I more better than Johnny.	I more better than Johnny. (Hawaii)

Note: The phrases in the left-hand column were collected from actual speech of children between two and four years of age. Those on the right were collected by linguists in various creole languages. In these examples it may be significant that verbs appear only in their uninflected form or are omitted entirely, as in "Johnny big more than me."

Source: D. Bickerton 1983, 122.

as children grow older does their speech differentiate into specific linguistic patterns.

Most linguists believe that no language is inherently harder to learn than any other. But Bickerton suggests that the more similar a language is to a creole base, the easier it is to learn, and vice versa. His theory also suggests that some languages may be more "mature" than others. Creoles are like "child languages." It is noteworthy that this theory, like Berlin and Kay's findings on color terminology, questions basic relativistic principles about language. They suggest that not all languages are equally developed.

SUMMARY

- Language is a central aspect of human culture. It is the richest and most powerful system of communication and information retrieval known.
- Like other aspects of culture, language is learned, arbitrary, and symbolic. At the same time, there are aspects of language that reveal its biological basis and that are shaped by the design of the human brain.
- Human language is extraordinary because it provides a means for communicating complex thoughts about the past, present, future, possible, and impossible.
- Every human society has a language; some have more than one. In complex societies, differences in language reflect and reinforce the social differences. Glottocentrism is a kind of ethnocentrism that defines and maintains boundaries between groups.
- There is no evidence that any language is more complex or expressive than any other. However, there is evidence that languages differ in the extent to which they encode particular aspects of experience, such as colors.
- Writing systems encode language as ideograms or alphabetically. They extend the storage and transmission capabilities of language.
- Linguistics is one of the most advanced areas of anthropology in theory and method. The study of language has branched into sophisticated computer methods linked with advances in neuroscience. Language studies provide an avenue into the human brain and insights into how we think.

- There are two major approaches to language, one reflecting a behaviorist approach, the other reflecting a rationalist approach.
- The behaviorist approach, called Immediate Constituent (IC) linguistics, sees language as a communication system consisting of patterns of sounds and silence, learned entirely after birth. IC linguists approach language through a hierarchy of fragments, beginning with the units of speech sounds and building up to complete utterances.
- The rationalist approach, called transformational grammar, stresses an inborn competence and universal underlying structures of the brain. Actual expression (or performance) is only the observable aspect of competence.
- The transformational grammar approach seeks to write rules that allow valid sentences, and only valid sentences, to be derived from deep structural ideas.
- Languages change all the time. Languages have internal processes of change that are not related to particular external causes. These are the cumulative effects of trends in pronunciation, syntax, and grammar.
- Most ideas about "pure" languages are misguided because all existing languages can be shown to have been influenced by others. Creole languages arise from crude pidgin languages, the result of recent language contact. They may provide insight into the nature of language acquisition itself.
- The family trees of languages can be reconstructed, and even "dead" languages can be reconstructed with some accuracy.
- Body language is a form of nonverbal communication in which meaning is conveyed through gestures, posture, and other conscious and unconscious signals.
- For decades, the dominant trend in anthropological linguistics was relativistic. All languages were viewed as equal in their ability to express the thoughts of their speakers and equal in complexity. Recent findings challenge this view. Color terminology and possibly other cognitive domains increase in complexity as the social system grows more complex. Creole languages, once thought to be transitional but fully developed languages, are viewed by some investigators as analogous to "child language," reflecting the early stages of language acquisition.

GET INVOLVED

1. Select a language other than your own and analyze the way in which the structure of the language itself conveys meaning. Consider concepts such as time, agency, silence, mood, conditionality, contingency, and voice. You may need to enlist the help of a native speaker of that language who is also familiar with your language.
2. Record at least ten minutes of the speech of a nonnative English speaker or the speaker of a nonstandard dialect. A good way to do this might be to volunteer to tutor someone who needs help with his or her English. Collect at least a dozen examples of incorrect speech as measured against standard English. Analyze each error to determine whether it is (1) idiosyncratic, (2) related to the speaker's native language, or (3) governed by a particular rule. Consider how best to respond to errors of this sort.
3. Photograph or videotape a sequence of some nonverbal mode of communication and present it in a coherent fashion to people who are not familiar with it. For example, record and analyze the dress codes for all the people at a racetrack, or gestures at an auction, or facial expressions and "body language" on a television show like *Saturday Night Live* or *Wheel of Fortune*. A good forum for your presentation might be the international students' center on your campus.
4. Follow someone who regularly moves between two or more subcultures, such as a recent immigrant who lives with his or her family and works or goes to school in a different cultural setting. Collect examples of code switching and try to examine what might lead to each example. You might do this while serving as a "big brother" or "big sister" to a young immigrant in your area.

SUGGESTED READINGS

Basso, Keith. 1970. "To give up on words": Silence in Apache culture. In *Language and social context,* ed. Pier Paolo Giglioli. New York: Penguin Books.

Gal, Susan. 1987. Code-switching and consciousness in the European periphery. *American Ethnologist* 14:637–654.

Joans, Barbara. 1984. Problems in Pocatello: A study in linguistic misunderstanding. *Practicing Anthropology* 6(314): 6, 8.*

Lieberman, Philip. 1975. *On the origins of language: An introduction to the evolution of human speech.* New York: Macmillan.

Witherspoon, Gary. 1980. Language in culture and culture in language. *International Journal of American Linguistics* 46:1–15.

---

* This selection is anthologized in *Applying Anthropology,* 2d ed., ed. A. Podolefsky and P. J. Brown (Mountain View, Calif.: Mayfield, 1992).

ANTHROPOLOGISTS AT WORK

Studying Language

Author of Aspects of Language and Culture, *Carol Eastman has been doing fieldwork on language and culture in East Africa and Southeast Alaska since the 1960s. Eastman chairs the anthropology department at the University of Washington and also serves as an adjunct professor in the departments of Linguistics and Women Studies.*

I work on the northwest coast of North America with the remaining speakers of the Haida language. Haida interests linguists because it is considered an isolate, that is, unrelated to any other known language. Interested in establishing Haida's genetic affiliation, graduate student Paul Aoki and I conducted summer fieldwork in 1971 in Hydaburg on Prince of Wales Island.

Reachable only by boat or small plane from Ketchikan, Hydaburg had no road connecting it to its neighbors. We arrived in an old World War II propeller plane, buffeted about by downdrafts. Below us we glimpsed the remains of similar craft that had never made their destination.

Once we began working, town elders provided data for us that resulted in a description of phonetic segments in the local Kaigani dialect. We discovered that Hydaburg and Seattle formed a social network and that some Haida speakers lived in Seattle. This meant that back at the University of Washington I could continue to work with Haida and involve other students in the work.

In the mid-1970s Betty Edwards and I returned to Hydaburg to work on syntax. Betty wrote her Ph.D. dissertation on this work, and she and I went on to publish papers on topics such as agreement, subordination, negation, and pragmatic particles in an effort to describe the Kaigani dia-

Carol Eastman examines ts'iihlanjaao *(devil's club) before learning how to use its root to make medicinal tea.*

lect fully so that it could be compared to dialects spoken at Masset and Skidegate on the Queen Charlotte Islands off the west coast of Canada.

While working on Haida, I came to realize that I was gaining some acceptance in the Haida community due to my ability to talk appropriately to Haida culture bearers in English as well as in Haida. Entries in my field journal reveal an increasingly appropriate use of local terms. This *cultural language,* acquired as a by-product of being in the community to do formal linguistic analysis, amounted to a social rather than a linguistic dialect. This led me to write about the process of becoming communicatively competent in the Haida speech community.

To be able to talk as a community member, I had to express expected attitudes, use expected topics, and control community vocabulary. This meant knowing the *culturally loaded* (locally important) Haida words,

which are used instead of English equivalents, such as *k'ao* (herring eggs), *ts'iihlanjaao* (devil's club; a plant whose root is used for a medicinal tea), *taa'wun* (king salmon), *taay* (cohoe salmon), and so on. Certain topics would spark conversation more than others. In the 1970s, discussion was common about the impact of a road to be built linking the town to others on the island and the advantages of fishing "down inside" over working for "the cannery." A topic *radiates* expected attitudes, so that, for example, fishing "down inside" meant using seines instead of traps, more fish for the townspeople, Haida-owned boats, and a general sense of pride and self-respect. "The cannery" evoked opposite and negative values. By knowing how to use the *group talk* of the people of the Hydaburg speech community, I gradually began to acquire Haida social identity (as opposed to ethnic identity).

The ongoing work on Haida language and culture has also yielded stretches of Haida narrative speech longer than the sentences (stories, reminiscences, and so on) that Betty Edwards and I collected, analyzed, and translated with the help of Haida consultant Lillian Pettviel. These *gyaehlingaay* (stories), illustrated by noted artist Duane Pasco, were published in 1991 by Burke Museum Publications. We present the narratives in a practical orthography so that Haida speakers will be able to read them in Haida as well as in English.

The multifaceted study of language as an aspect of culture is as varied as the study of politics, economics, or kinship. But language is the only way we have to find out about, understand, and participate fully in the social systems of another culture.

PART THREE

EVOLUTION & ORIGINS

Although humans are preeminently cultural beings, dependent on learned behavior and acquired knowledge for survival, they are also biological creatures, subject to the same laws and forces as other animals. Classified by biologists as primates, they share many physiological and behavioral characteristics with other primates; in fact, they differ from chimpanzees in only 1 percent of their genetic material! Many anthropologists are interested in this fact not so much for what it says about the present-day relationship between apes and humans as for what it suggests about their common ancestry. Somewhere in the remote past, between 8 and 14 million years ago, an animal existed from whom modern-day apes and humans both descended. Over the course of millennia some of these animals—the apelike ancestors of humans—evolved into creatures who could respond creatively to the problems they encountered in the physical world. Today, human beings are the most widespread and successful species on earth, manipulating the environment to their advantage—and often to the disadvantage of other species—everywhere they go.

This is the subject of biological anthropology—where the human species came from, where it is now and how it got here, and where it may be headed. Part Three of this book explores some of the many facets of this broad area of inquiry. Chapter 5 sets forth the principles of evolution, including natural selection and genetic inheritance, to which all living creatures are subject. Chapter 6 looks at the evolution of Homo sapiens in terms of the principles that explain the evolution of other species, focusing particularly on the primate order as it has evolved over millions of years. This chapter also discusses the first upright, two-legged—but small-brained—creatures to emerge on earth, called Australopithecines, as well as what may have been the first members of our own genus, Homo. Chapter 7 traces human evolution, including stone tool technology and new patterns of food getting, from Homo erectus to modern Homo sapiens. Chapter 8 looks at how natural selection and other evolutionary processes are still operating on the human species today, producing great diversity and other, as yet unknown, effects. Together, these chapters provide a basis for understanding people as the most curious, creative, and adaptable animals on earth.

This group of fossils from England contains some of the earliest known multicellular organisms, including brachiopods and crinoids. They date to 500 to 435 MYA.

5

EVOLUTION AND GENETICS

▲▲▲

n Chapter 2 we discussed *theory* as a set of interrelated ideas, hypotheses, and principles that organize and explain certain phenomena. In biology—and in biological anthropology—many phenomena are understood in terms of the theory of evolution. The search for human origins and the many aspects of the study of contemporary humanity are conducted within the framework of this set of ideas. This chapter sets forth the main principles of the theory of evolution, particularly as it relates to our own species.

THE THEORY OF EVOLUTION

Very few theories have so dramatically changed the course of science as the theory of evolution. In 1859, when Charles Darwin proposed a reasonable and cohesive explanation for evolutionary change, science took a bold step forward. Darwin's idea about evolution and the processes that bring it about created a legacy of scientific progress that continues to this day. His basic idea became a way of thinking about the universe and the place of human beings in it that has become part of Western culture. We usually refer to it as "Darwin's theory of evolution."

There are several misconceptions linked with this phrase, however. Darwin was not alone in developing the theory of evolution we now accept. Darwin (1809–1882) was a British gentleman of independent means who decided early in life to devote himself to science. By the time he had sailed around the world as the ship's naturalist on the *H.M.S. Beagle,* he was already well known in scientific circles. But another naturalist, Alfred Russell Wallace (1823–1913), simultaneously arrived at an explanation for evolution that coincided with the basic idea that eventually appeared in Darwin's *On the Origin of Species.* The two men had hit upon virtually identical hypotheses, and, of course, both based their idea on the work of many other scientists. If Darwin had not published his famous book in 1859, Wallace or someone else would have eventually articulated the idea. The theory might be known today as "Wallacism." One might say that, in the mid-19th century, evolution was an idea whose time had come.

A second misconception arises from the word *theory.* In common usage a theory may be synonymous with a guess, a hunch, or a hypothesis. But, as explained in Chapter 2, in science *theory* refers to a coherent set of interrelated ideas that coordinate the relationship among a set of variables. Darwin's theory is

---

BOX 5.1

Evolution versus Creation

Is evolutionary theory in conflict with religion? Some religious expressions teach that all knowledge comes only from the revealed word of God, and this may put religious beliefs in conflict with scientific knowledge. Recently a few Christian groups in the United States have mounted challenges to the way biology is taught in the schools. They claim that evolution is "just a theory" and that it should be presented along with a rival theory they call "creation science."

Creation science is based on a literal interpretation of the book of Genesis. It takes a highly skeptical view of the theory of evolution and the evidence that supports it. Creationists believe that the world and all the biological species in it were divinely created only a few thousand years ago and have changed little since.

The political pressure from these groups is so great that some states have adopted legislation requiring creation science to be presented in public schools whenever evolution is taught. In case after case, however, the courts have found such requirements unconstitutional. Creation science, they have ruled, is clearly a religious, not a scientific, doctrine.

The courts, of course, have not forbidden belief in creationism or prohibited the schools from discussing it. They simply have prohibited legislatures from requiring that schools teach creationism as science. There is no necessary quarrel between religion and Darwinian evolution. Many scientists who base their work on evolutionary theory are devoutly religious and accept the teachings of the Bible. Many of them feel that their scientific activities are perfectly compatible with their religious beliefs. They do not, however, accept a literal biblical chronology for the creation of the world and all the things in it.

so well supported that it can be considered a fact, although, like any scientific idea, it is always subject to revision or even replacement.

The theory of evolution today is not just Darwin's; it is a synthesis of ideas, including Darwin's and those of many of his contemporaries and successors. Darwin contributed the fundamental idea of natural selection as the basic process of evolution, but his idea lacked virtually all that we now understand about **genetics**, a vital part of modern evolutionary theory. Nonetheless, it was Darwin who, by offering the first comprehensive explanation of biological change through time, gave us the basis for our current, well-established understanding of evolution.

Views on Biological Change Before Darwin

Long before Darwin, biologists had developed the idea of the biological **species**. A species is a population of organisms that share similar structure and behavior and are capable of mating and producing fertile offspring. Biologists recognize each species as being in a state of **adaptation**, that is, equipped for survival under the circumstances of the environment in which it lives. As an example, consider what might happen to a giraffe, an animal well suited to grazing from trees, if it were moved to a treeless plain. Each species occupies a distinctive ecological **niche**, a set of environmental conditions with which the species normally comes in contact. The niche includes a wide range of features, such as the availability of food, natural cover for hiding from predators, nesting space, daily and seasonal variations, and the presence of other species.

Until the 19th century in Europe, the predominant view was that species were fixed and unchanging through time. This view derives from a literal interpretation of the biblical book of Genesis. A contemporary version of this view is called **creationism** (Box 5.1). Discoveries in geology, however, made it clear that the earth and life forms on it had undergone change over time. Preserved in ancient rocks were the remains of plants and animals that no longer existed or were physically distinct from their living counterparts (Figure 5.1). As geologists read the **fossil** record, it began to appear that some ancient species were ancestors of modern species and that, over the entire sweep of geological time, species were related to one another on a giant, complex family tree.

Based on this evidence, scientists sought to understand how organisms, which tend to reproduce faithful copies of themselves, could change and give rise to new species. One early answer came from Jean Baptiste de Lamarck (1744–1829), a French biologist. In 1809 he published an evolutionary tree showing how all the major families of animals, from microorganisms to humans, were related. He also proposed a theory to explain how species changed over time.

Lamarck said species were adapted to their environments and were able to change in direct response to environmental change, which the geological record shows is constantly occurring. According to his idea, organisms were able to bring about new features through repeated adaptive use. By continually stretching to reach leaves in tall trees, for example, giraffes gradually developed longer limbs and necks, which they could then transmit to their offspring. Because this process produced change as needed, Lamarck thought no organisms ever became extinct; they just changed.

Called the inheritance of acquired characteristics and today known as Lamarckism, this idea was not hard to refute. People acquainted with plant and animal breeding knew which sorts of traits organisms could acquire and which ones were inherited. They realized that nature did not outfit organisms with the

---

genetics   The study of the mechanism of inheritance and the physical results of that mechanism.

species   A population of organisms sharing similar structure and behavior and able to mate and produce fertile offspring.

adaptation   Adjustment of an organism to a specific set of environmental circumstances.

niche   A set of environmental conditions to which an organism has adapted and that the organism needs to survive and reproduce.

creationism   The theological belief that the world was created in the recent past by God as described in the biblical book of Genesis and that biological and geological change has been very limited since that time.

fossil   Remains or traces of any ancient organism.

Figure 5.1 *The 19th-century view of creation was challenged by the discovery of ancient, fossilized plants and animals. These fossil crinoids, found in Kansas and dating to 100 MYA, belong to the phylum Echinodermata but are clearly different from modern echinoderms such as starfish and sea urchins.*

ability simply to acquire traits when needed or to transmit acquired traits to their offspring, no matter how beneficial. For example, tricks learned by a dog could not be inherited by its pups, and rats whose tails were cut off still gave birth to rats with tails. Evolutionary change, therefore, is not a *direct* result of environmental change. Thus there was enough evidence even in Lamarck's time to discredit his idea. But Lamarck did help set the stage for Darwin by stressing the importance of adaptation and by proposing a unified and complete theory of evolutionary change.

Another influence on Darwin's thinking was the work of Charles Lyell, the founder of modern geology. Lyell (1797–1875), an English gentleman like Darwin, spent much of his time studying rocks and earth formations. His studies convinced him that the earth could not possibly be only 6,000 years old and unchanging as was popularly believed at the time. Lyell showed that many features of the earth's crust, such as valleys, mountains, and various rock formations and types, were formed by slow processes driven by wind,

water, pressure, freezing, and heat. He also noted the presence of plant and animal fossils in relation to geological features. For example, marine fossils found in rock far from the sea showed that the earth's surface had undergone major changes that required not thousands but millions of years. Allowing enough time for these slow processes to occur meant that the earth was far older than previous estimates. Lyell also reasoned that these processes must be similar to processes observable today. He called this assumption **uniformitarianism.** It suggests that understanding the present is the key to understanding the past and that natural, observable processes are the bases for natural phenomena.

Darwin also drew on the insights of Thomas Malthus (1766–1834), the founder of modern demography. Malthus suggested that populations had a natural tendency to increase faster than their food supply and that a struggle existed over resources. From this, Darwin concluded that a struggle for existence occurred within each species, favoring the survival of those individuals to which nature, through natural variation, had granted the most advantageous characteristics. These individuals would reproduce themselves more successfully than others of the species, thus passing on the traits that made them successful.

The Darwinian Idea: Natural Selection

Darwin identified the two major aspects of evolution as reproduction and variation. On the one hand, organisms can faithfully reproduce themselves generation after generation; on the other hand, there is variation within a species. Some cows produce more milk than others; some trees grow taller; some birds have more brilliant plumage. It is this intraspecific variation, Darwin suggested, that leads to differential success in the struggle for existence.

Darwin drew a parallel between this process and the selection of specific traits practiced by plant and animal breeders. For example, dairy cattle are bred to give more milk by careful control over mating. Breeders allow the "good milkers" to reproduce, assuming that their offspring will tend to inherit the trait. Breeding dogs to be better sheepherders, or fruit trees to resist disease, works the same way. Breeders select specialized varieties to fit their needs.

Darwin suggested that a similar process of "selection" is at work in nature, only it is not a conscious or deliberate process (Box 5.2). He called this process **natural selection** (in contrast to the **artificial selection** practiced by breeders). Through a process that depends on the luck of natural variation, adaptive traits tend to accumulate over time in a species, and poorly adapted traits tend to disappear. Thus natural selection acts to maintain a species' reproductive success, or **fitness,** and may even allow a species to change with the surrounding environmental conditions (unless they change too rapidly or drastically, in which case the outcome is **extinction**). As Darwin put it, "there is a struggle for existence leading to the preservation of profitable deviations of structure or instinct" (Darwin 1859, 426).

The term *struggle for existence* does not refer to a direct struggle between organisms, as is implied by social philosopher Herbert Spencer's phrase "survival of the fittest." There is a more subtle contest—for food, space, mates, nesting places, health, and so on—in which the winners are more successful in transmitting their design to offspring. *Fitness* refers not to the ability to do battle or survive a long time but to the ability to reproduce successfully. Any variation within a species could be subject to selection. Traits that promote reproductive success are said to undergo **positive selection,** or are "selected for," while traits that are detrimental suffer **negative selection,** or are "selected against."

The advantage a trait gives an individual is always relative to a specific environment, as in the example of the giraffe on a treeless plain. Traits advantageous in one environment may be disadvantageous or neutral in another. What's adaptive for a species at one point in time may not be adaptive under changed environmental conditions; a formerly neutral trait may prove adaptive later on, as in the example of the peppered moth in the next section. Adaptive advantages come wrapped in different packages.

Adaptation: The Case of the Peppered Moth. Evolutionary change in the common peppered moth provides an example of adaptation through natural selection. The peppered moth is a favorite food for birds in English forests. It has a degree of protection from these predators because of its adaptive coloration; its wings and body closely match lichen-covered

---

uniformitarianism   The belief that the same processes of biological and geological change that are in evidence today also characterized the past.

natural selection   Evolution based on the relative reproductive success of individuals within a species, dependent on the ability of individuals to adapt to their environment.

artificial selection   Evolution as a result of human manipulation of the breeding of a species.

fitness   The ability of an organism to pass along its genes to future generations.

extinction   Dying out; the result of the inability of a species to adapt to a changing environment.

positive selection   The evolutionary process in which the environment favors the fitness of organisms carrying certain alleles.

negative selection   The evolutionary process in which the fitness of organisms carrying certain alleles is lower due to some feature of the environment.

BOX 5.2
Mother Nature's Intentions

One of the most important ideas in science is that we do not need to think in terms of intentions or purposes to understand natural phenomena. Thinking of everything that happens as the result of some intention or final purpose is **teleology**. A great deal of everyday speech is teleological. Consider the following sentence. "The purpose of the kangaroo's pouch is to carry around the baby kangaroos." It sounds like common sense, but now consider, "The purpose of ears is to hold up hats." This statement is clearly absurd. Ears have been adorning people's heads for much longer than hats, so we can easily dismiss the statement as a silly, "just-so" story.

Now it is true that female kangaroos and other marsupials carry their young around in pouches. But it would be an error to think the pouches were put there for that purpose. Darwinian theory was more successful than Lamarckian theory because it did not assume that changes take place simply to fill needs. Evolutionary theory suggests that the marsupial pouch developed out of some other organ. It was selected because it contributed to the fitness of the species from which marsupials descended. It was not designed for the purpose of nurturing and caring for the young. Still, it is remarkable how nature fits organisms to the environment as if by some grand design.

A recent study of insect wings provides insight about the question of nature's design. Everyone knows that insects use wings to fly. But did wings evolve for the purpose of flying? Evolutionary theory has been at a loss to explain the evolution of wings because intermediate forms (creatures who have rudimentary wings but are incapable of flight) would not have enjoyed any selective advantage. During the 1970s, some evolutionary biologists suggested that the first rudimentary insect wings may have been selected because they were helpful in thermal (heat) regulation. Wings could either dissipate excess heat or absorb heat from the sun. Only after wings had evolved could selection for flight begin.

In 1984 biologists Joel Kingsolver and M.A.R. Koehl tested this hypothesis. Assuming that proto-wings absorbed heat to warm the body, they tested the ability of wings of different sizes to absorb and conduct heat. Using mathematical models, Kingsolver and Koehl showed that proto-wings too small for flying could have played a significant role in temperature regulation. The mystery of the evolution of insect flight was explained, without resort to teleology.

Scientists do not ask about Mother Nature's intentions, because scientific evidence cannot be brought to bear on this question. Science does not deny that nature has a "purpose," only that such purposes can be discovered scientifically.

tree bark, making it hard to spot (Figure 5.2). A dark variety of the same moth, called the melanic form, was once rare, no doubt because it was more visible to the moth-eating birds. The dark variety was selected against.

When the industrial revolution came to England more than a century and a half ago, soot from factory chimneys killed the lichens and blackened the tree trunks. English butterfly collectors began to notice that in many parts of the country the typical peppered moth declined in frequency while the melanic form became increasingly common.

In the 1950s H. B. D. Kettlewell, a physician and amateur butterfly collector, conducted a series of experiments comparing peppered moths in highly polluted forests near Birmingham with moths in a relatively unpolluted forest in Dorset. He raised hundreds of moths of both varieties from caterpillars, marked them for later identification, and released some in each forest. Near industrial Birmingham the survival rate of the melanic moth was more than twice that of the light moth. In Dorset, where there was little industry, the trees were lighter in color and lichens still thrived, the lighter variety survived at nearly twice the rate of the melanic variety. By patiently observing the moths from a hidden location, Kettlewell determined that birds feeding on moths could locate the standouts much more easily than the camouflaged ones.

Kettlewell's experiments illustrate natural selection on a small scale and make clear a very important point: Environmental change does not *cause* adaptation as Lamarck proposed. Just as an animal breeder cannot breed a purple cow or a winged dog, selection in nature acts only on traits that have occurred spon-

Figure 5.2 *Where trees are light in color, the light form of the peppered moth has a selective advantage over the melanic form (left). Where trees are blackened by soot, the melanic form has the advantage (right). As pollution increased in England, the melanic peppered moth became more common.*

taneously by chance. Natural selection acts *opportunistically* on variation *already present* in a population.

Adaptive traits can occur at many levels of complexity. The adaptive trait may be a simple anatomical adaptation such as the color of the peppered moth, or it may involve overall structure and organization, such as the emergence of terrestrial animals from water-dwelling ones, or the appearance of the first upright-walking primate, the ancestor of modern humans. Adaptation may even take the form of *potential*

changes, such as the ability of the human body to respond to high altitudes by increasing the production of red blood cells for carrying oxygen.

Adaptations may also be behavioral. For most organisms adaptive behaviors are inborn, no different from anatomical features. For example, the peppered moths land on surfaces against which they are camouflaged. Baby calves are born able to walk, moo, suckle, and follow their mothers; no learning is necessary. But for some creatures some adaptive behaviors may be

---

teleology The philosophical doctrine that everything that happens has an intention or purpose.

learned. For example, some chimpanzees have learned to "fish" for termites by inserting twigs and blades of grass into nest openings and drawing out the clinging insects (see Chapter 9, Figure 9.8). Humans rely on learned behavior to adapt not only to the natural environment but also to the cultural environment. But even here there is an innate component: the structure of the brain that permits learning and reasoning.

Extinction: When Adaptation Fails.   The flip side of adaptation is extinction. Extinction occurs when a population has no variation that will enable it to survive and reproduce when the environment changes. The geological record is littered with the fossils of extinct species. Many of these died out leaving no descendants. Others died out after giving rise to new species that continue to live and reproduce. It was commonly believed that dinosaurs became extinct about 65 million years ago, leaving no descendants, but many paleontologists now think that modern birds are in fact living descendants of the dinosaurs.

Extinction occurs when, after some environmental change, none of the variants within a species have the traits necessary to adapt to the new conditions. Evolutionary biologists have recently become more receptive to the idea that some major extinctions resulted from abrupt environmental changes, even sudden catastrophes. One such event may have brought about the sudden disappearance of the dinosaurs and a large number of other forms. The cause may have been the collision of a large meteorite or comet with the earth, which sent up enormous clouds of dust and ash. The subsequent blocking of sunlight and cooling of the earth's climate caused the extinction of plant forms, which in turn caused the extinction of other species further up the food chain. The evidence for this lies in a thin layer of iridium-rich rock deposited 65 million years ago and found in many parts of the world. The element iridium is abundant in meteorites. The recognition that sudden, massive, unpredictable events could have changed the course of evolution is an important departure from earlier Darwinian thought, which suggested that all evolutionary change was fairly smooth and gradual.

The Origin of Species

Besides variation within species, Darwin also recognized the incredible diversity among different species of living things. Millions of species of animals and

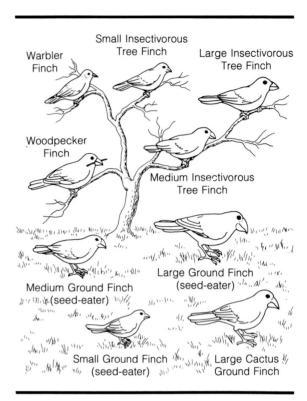

Figure 5.3 *Darwin's finches. When the ancestors of these birds reached the Galapagos Islands, they underwent an adaptive radiation, filling several available niches. The different beak forms of the descendant species reflect these niches.*

plants inhabit the earth; mammals alone comprise some 4,000 living species. Darwin concluded that the variation within species acted on by natural selection also leads to the rise of new species in two ways. For one, natural selection brings about "the accumulation of innumerable slight variations, each good for the individual possessor" (Darwin 1859, 426). In other words, the continual operation of natural selection will eventually change a single species to such an extent that it evolves into a new species. This is called **microevolution.**

In addition, new species arise when separate populations of the same species become **reproductively isolated.** This is known as **macroevolution.** If, for example, the melanic form of the peppered moth were to cease interbreeding with other moths of that species, the two varieties might eventually become new, separate species. This could happen if additional changes took place in their environment. Suppose, for example, English forests were located in patches so widely separated that interbreeding of moths between them was impossible. If the separate populations slowly became differently adapted to their specific niches they might eventually become so distinct that mating and reproduction would be impossible even if the populations were reunited. They would be, in other words, separate species. **Speciation**, the evolution of new species, is thus an outgrowth of natural selection, reproductive isolation, separate environments, and, of course, time.

When a species' environment so changes that a whole new range of niches becomes available, **adaptive radiation**—the occupation of several new ecological niches—may take place. One situation in which this occurs is when members of a species arrive in a habitat with many unfilled niches. Darwin documented such a case on the remote Galapagos Islands in the Pacific (Figure 5.3). Seed-eating finches migrated from mainland South America and, over many years, colonized the Galapagos. Over time the finches expanded into many different niches and gradually evolved into at least 13 separate species, differentiated by such traits as size and beaks specialized for eating various foods.

We now understand that species may arise more abruptly than Darwin had imagined. According to this contemporary view, called **punctuated equilibrium**, natural selection, rather than being the creative, driving force behind speciation, is a conservative process that acts mainly to *maintain* a species' adaptation, largely through negative selection. The species remains relatively unchanged and is said to be in "equilibrium." This equilibrium, however, may be "punctuated" by sudden change from within the species. Individuals with dramatically different traits may arise as part of natural variation. Most such variation would be maladaptive, but on occasion some new and very different set of traits may be beneficial and give a new species a "head start." This mode of speciation seems to fit better with what we observe in the fossil record

and the mechanism of inheritance, and a growing number of scientists believe that punctuated equilibrium, not Darwin's gradualistic model, is the basic form of evolution.

INHERITANCE

Darwin's great scientific contribution was his discovery of the relationship between reproduction, variation, and the environment. The remarkable thing is that he understood these relations without understanding the mechanisms of inheritance or the source of variation.

Unraveling the mechanism of inheritance was the contribution of Gregor Mendel (1822–1884), an Austrian monk who wanted to understand how organisms inherit traits across generations. The prevailing view in Mendel's time was that each offspring represented a blending of traits, half from each parent. The son of a plant breeder, Mendel knew the role of pollen in fertilizing plants. He also knew that many plants have both male and female organs and are capable of either cross-fertilization or self-fertilization. Peas, for example, have certain variable traits such as seed color and form, but Mendel suspected that each of these traits was inherited not by blending but through a separate unit of inheritance. In other words, inheritance was "particulate."

Mendel's Crosses

For his most famous experiments Mendel used the common peas that grew in the monastery garden. The plants he chose were all true-breeding for each of seven traits; that is, the plants could be bred again and again without any change in those traits as long as they fertilized only themselves. Each of the seven traits took two possible forms (Table 5.1; Figure 5.4).

---

microevolution The accumulation of small adaptive changes in particular local populations.

reproductive isolation The separation of two populations of the same species such that they no longer interbreed.

macroevolution The evolution of new species from existing species.

speciation The rise of new biological species from existing species.

adaptive radiation Adaptation of populations within a species to new ecological niches and the consequent diversification, increase, and spread of the species.

punctuated equilibrium The theory that evolution occurs discontinuously with relatively long periods of stability punctuated by short periods of relatively rapid change.

Table 5.1   The Seven Traits Selected by Mendel for His Pea Experiments

Trait	Two Possible Forms (Alleles)	
Form of the ripe seed	round	wrinkled
Seed color	yellow	green
Color of seed coat	white	gray
Form of ripe seed pods	inflated	constricted
Color of unripe seed pods	green	yellow
Position of flowers	axial (along stem)	terminal (end of stem)
Length of stem	tall	short

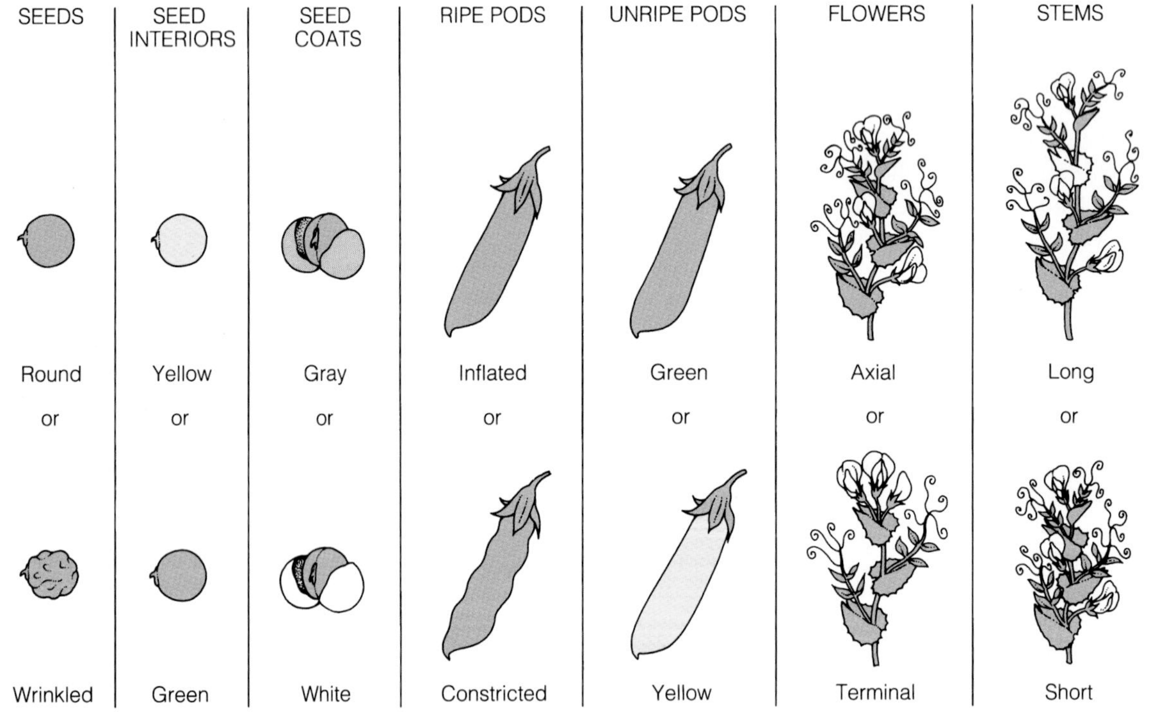

Figure 5.4   *Mendel's pioneering observations of the pea plant were based on a comparison of these seven easily identifiable traits.*

SEEDS	SEED INTERIORS	SEED COATS	RIPE PODS	UNRIPE PODS	FLOWERS	STEMS
Round	Yellow	Gray	Inflated	Green	Axial	Long
or	or	or	or	or	or	or
Wrinkled	Green	White	Constricted	Yellow	Terminal	Short

Table 5.2   Results of Mendel's Crosses

Generation	Gray (%)	White (%)
Parent generation (F0)	50	50
First cross (F1)	100	0
Second cross (F2)	75	25
Third cross, etc. (F3 . . . F_n)	75	25

Mendel's experimental design was to cross plants with contrasting traits: round seeds and wrinkled seeds, gray seed coats and white seed coats, and so on. The hybrid results of his first cross (called the F1 generation) showed only *one* of the parental traits. For example, when he crossed plants having gray seed coats with plants having white seed coats, all the offspring had gray seed coats. Where were the white-seed-coated plants, and why weren't some a blend of gray and white? Apparently the F1 generation carried the unit for white seed coats, but no individual in that generation *expressed* it. But when Mendel allowed the F1 generation to self-pollinate, he found that about a quarter of the next generation (F2) had white seed coats and the rest had gray (Table 5.2). In all later crosses (F3, F4, . . .), roughly the same ratio remained.

Mendel concluded that the "factors" that determine the expression of a trait come in pairs, each organism possessing two factors for each trait. In the formation of the cells of reproduction (**gametes**), the members of these pairs separate ("segregate" in Mendel's terminology), and each offspring receives one factor from each parent to make up its pair.

The factors for a specific trait may also come in different varieties. We now call these **alleles**. An individual may have two identical alleles, a condition called **homozygous**, or two different alleles, called **heterozygous.**

Moreover, Mendel accounted for hidden variation by concluding that the factor varieties may have different influences on the expression of the trait in the organism. In modern terminology, some alleles are **dominant** and some are **recessive.** For example, if a pea plant has two alleles for gray seed coats, its seeds are, obviously, gray. But if the plant is a heterozygote, with one gray allele and one white allele, its seed coats are gray, because the allele for that color is dominant and overrides the action of the allele for white coats. It must be noted that dominance and recessiveness have nothing to do with the adaptive value of the trait for which they code.

Trait dominance can best be demonstrated with a Punnett square, using lowercase letters for recessive alleles and uppercase for dominant. The example in Figure 5.5 shows the allele combinations (**genotype**) and the resultant physical expression (**phenotype**) in offspring of Mendel's various crosses. Note how the allele pairs of the parents segregate and are recombined at fertilization. This is now known as **recombination** and is a major source of variation within a species.

Mendel's factors are now called **genes**, and they are arranged in long strands called **chromosomes** in the nuclei of cells. The chromosomes come in pairs, carrying the pairs of genes at specific locations called **loci** (singular, **locus**), a term that is now preferred by some to *gene*. Different species have different numbers of chromosomes; humans have 23 pairs, or 46 chromosomes (Figure 5.6).

We now understand how the chromosomes and their loci behave in order to produce gametes with only one copy of each locus. When body cells divide, the chromosomes make copies of themselves so that each new cell has the full complement of chromosomes and loci. This process is called **mitosis.** When

gamete Sex cell; in females, an egg, and in males, a sperm.

allele A variant of a genetic locus. Different alleles for the same trait (e.g., eye color) carry different information for the phenotype (brown eyes, blue eyes, green eyes).

homozygous Having identical alleles in a gene pair for the same trait.

heterozygous Having different alleles in a gene pair for the same trait.

dominant Of a pair of alleles, the one that is expressed phenotypically in the heterozygous condition.

recessive Of a pair of alleles, the one that is not phenotypically expressed in the heterozygous condition.

genotype The underlying units (alleles) that determine genetic inheritance.

phenotype The physical traits that are expressed in an organism as a result of interaction between the genetic code and the environment.

recombination The shuffling of genetic material due to the process of sexual reproduction.

gene The portion of the DNA molecule that codes for a specific trait.

chromosome A structure in the nucleus of a cell that carries genetic information.

locus (plural, **loci**) The position on a strand of DNA that codes for a particular trait. *Locus* is currently preferred to *gene*.

mitosis The process of cell body division that produces exact copies of the original cell.

Figure 5.5 *Punnett squares showing relationship of genotype (allele combinations) and phenotype (physical expression) in Mendel's crosses.*

Generation	Genotypes	Phenotypes
F0	AA (gray)	aa (white)
F1	a a A Aa Aa A Aa Aa	100% Gray 0% White
F2	A a A AA Aa a Aa aa	75% Gray 25% White
F3	AA Aa aA aa AA AA Aa AA Aa Aa Aa Aa AA Aa aA aA aa aA aa aa aA aa aA aa	75% Gray 25% White

Figure 5.6 *A complete set of human chromosomes. The 23 pairs contain all of this man's genetic information.*

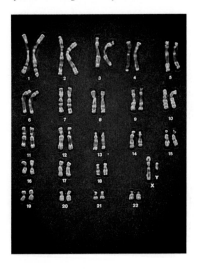

gametes divide, however, the chromosomes do not make copies of themselves in the final cell division, so each reproductive cell has only one of each chromosome pair and therefore only one of each pair of loci. This special process of cell division is called **meiosis** (Figure 5.7).

Gene Expression

Unlike the genes for the seven pea plant characteristics that Mendel observed, most genes in most organisms are not in a one-to-one relationship with their phenotypic expression. Most phenotypes are the outcome of the *interaction between genotype and environ-*

ment. Suppose, for example, that a female child is born to parents of above-average height and that she has inherited their genotypes for stature. If, however, she is malnourished or sickly in childhood, she might not reach her full genetic potential for height. Her phenotype—her appearance—reflects the influence of the environment on her genotype—her genetic endowment.

Or consider the case of diabetes mellitus, a genetic disease resulting in insufficient production or use of insulin, which affects sugar metabolism. The onset and severity of symptoms in diabetics vary considerably because of environmental influences not yet completely understood. Other genes, like the genes for blood type, are not affected by external influence, and

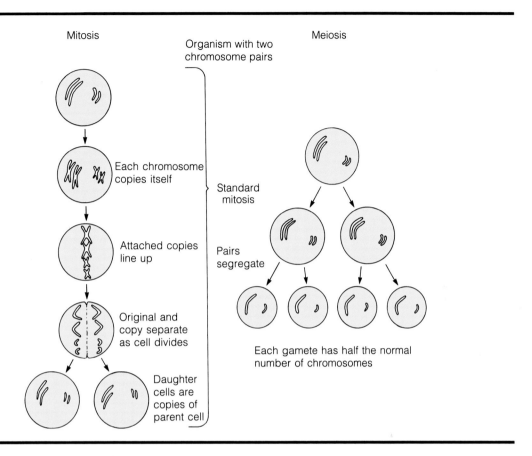

Mitosis

Meiosis

Organism with two
chromosome pairs

Each chromosome
copies itself

Standard
mitosis

Attached copies
line up

Pairs
segregate

Original and
copy separate
as cell divides

Each gamete has half the normal
number of chromosomes

Daughter
cells are
copies of
parent cell

Figure 5.7   *Body cells replicate by mitosis, a process that results in two genetically identical new cells, each with 23 pairs of chromosomes (left). Egg and sperm
cells replicate by meiosis, producing cells that are genetically different from the
original cell and that contain 23 single chromosomes (right). Meiosis ensures that
when fertilization occurs, the new individual has a total of 46 chromosomes, half
from each parent.*

so their phenotypes come in a small number of discrete expressions.

This difference in phenotypic expression is partly a
result of the fact that different phenotypes are coded
for by different numbers of genes. Traits controlled by
a single gene are said to be **monogenic.** They are usually simple traits not influenced by environmental fac-

tors. Others, such as stature, are controlled by many
genes **(polygenic),** so their expressions make up a
continuum rather than a small number of discrete
appearances.

Moreover, most genes do not have alleles with simple dominance, as do the pea plant traits that Mendel
observed. For example, the gene for flower color in

meiosis   The process of cell division by
which gametes are produced, each with
half the normal number of chromosomes
for that species.

monogenic   In reference to phenotypic
traits, controlled by only one locus or
gene.

polygenic   In reference to phenotypic
traits, controlled by more than one locus
or gene.

snapdragons displays **codominance**. Red snapdragons occur only when the plant is homozygous for red, and white flowers appear only when the plant is homozygous for white. Heterozygotes have pink flowers.

In many sexually reproducing species the chromosomes carrying the genes for sexual characteristics do not operate like the other matched pairs of chromosomes. Human females do have a pair of chromosomes, called the X chromosomes, that carry genes for sexual traits as well as many other phenotypic features. Males, however, have just one X chromosome, inherited from their mothers, and one Y chromosome, passed down from their fathers (see Figure 5.6). The Y chromosome loci are different from those on the X chromosome. Thus males may express a gene on their X chromosome, even if it is a recessive. A male carrying a recessive allele for color blindness on the X chromosome, for example, will invariably be color blind because there is no corresponding normal allele on his Y chromosome. As a result, color blindness is 23 times as common in men as in women. The same phenomenon explains the greater frequency of hemophilia in men, because the gene for the clotting agent in blood is on the X chromosome. Such traits are said to be X-linked. Traits on the Y chromosome are said to be Y-linked, and the general term for this phenomenon is **sex-linked**.

It is important to remember that selection does not operate directly on genes; it operates on their expression, that is, on the phenotype. Many alleles are deleterious (disadvantageous) when expressed because they reduce fitness in a given environment. If dominant, such alleles tend to be eliminated over time along with their carriers. But recessive deleterious alleles may be maintained in a population, expressed

Figure 5.8 *The structure of DNA can be represented as two twisting strands connected by ladderlike bars, as shown in the schematic diagram on the left and the computer model on the right.*

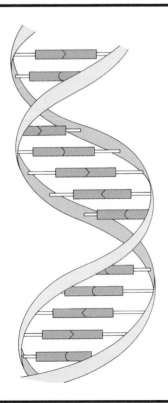
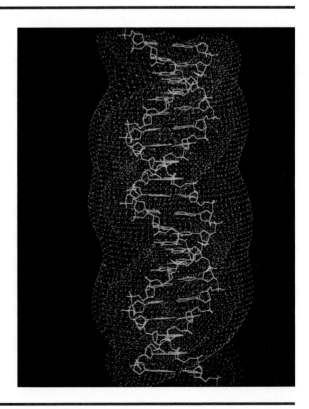

only in homozygous individuals or when sex-linked. Thus they persist despite their disadvantageous results.

The Role of DNA in Inheritance

Mendel discovered the gene and built a powerful model of the mechanism of inheritance through genetic recombination, but he knew nothing about how genes code for or transmit information. Scientists have known since 1869 that the nucleus of a cell is rich in **nucleic acid**, but its role in heredity was unclear. Later work showed that the nucleic acid molecules are like chains whose links consist of alternating phosphates and sugars. The sugar (deoxyribose) paired with a phosphate is bonded to one of four bases: adenine, thymine, cytosine, or guanine (A, T, C, G). The sugar, phosphate, and base together form a **nucleotide**, which, when joined to other nucleotides in a long chain, is known as **deoxyribonucleic acid** or **DNA.** Biologists James D. Watson and Francis Crick discovered the structure of DNA in 1953, a discovery for which they received the Nobel Prize. Based on an X-ray photograph of the molecule, Watson and Crick depicted DNA as a ladder with rails made of phosphates and sugars and rungs composed of bonded pairs of the four bases. The entire ladder is twisted into a helical shape, the famous "double helix" model (Figure 5.8).

DNA molecules form a kind of alphabet in which genetic messages are written. Each base bonds with a specific complement—A with T and G with C (Figure 5.9). In groups of three the complementary base pairs form the three-letter words of the genetic code. Each word codes for a specific **amino acid.** Amino acids, in turn, make up **proteins,** the building blocks of cells and of the chemicals that perform the cells' functions. For example, the amino acid phenylalanine is specified by the DNA codes AAA or AAG. (Many amino acids are coded for by more than one word, a redundancy that reduces the possibility of error).

The process of reading the DNA code begins when the spiraled nucleotides split apart at the bond on the "rung." As the two chains pull apart, each base of the code strand (the other strand is structural) forms a new bond with a free complementary base. The mechanism can be compared to a simple "secret code" where each letter in the code stands for a specific letter in the actual message.

The new "mirror image" strand (with uracil, U, replacing T) is called **messenger RNA** or mRNA **(ribonucleic acid).** The mRNA reads off the DNA information by forming its complementary strand, then carries it off to the cytoplasm, the portion of the cell outside the nucleus. There the message is translated, via **transfer RNA** (or tRNA), into a specific chain of amino acids that make up a protein. The secret of DNA lies in its ability to copy itself and transmit information through RNA out of the nucleus into the cell where the various functions of life take place.

Mutation as a Source of Variation

Recombination is an important source of variation for evolution. It is not creative, however, because it only shuffles the alleles already present. There must be

---

cododominance The sharing of influence by alleles on the phenotypic expression of a trait in the heterozygotic condition. For example, in snapdragons, the gene for color (red allele or white allele) in the heterozygotic condition results in a pink phenotype.

sex-linked Pertaining to a trait coded by a gene located on a sex chromosome.

nucleic acid A type of acid found in the nucleus of all living cells, commonly modeled as a chain of alternating "links" of sugars (deoxyribose) and phosphates.

nucleotide In nucleic acid, a compound formed by the bonding of a sugar (deoxyribose), a phosphate, and a base (adenine, guanine, thymine, or cytosine).

deoxyribonucleic acid (DNA) A compound formed by the joining of a long strand of nucleotides carrying the coded information for all life functions.

amino acid The chief component of proteins; amino acids are the building blocks of all life.

proteins Large molecules that are the main constituents of cells and that carry out cellular functions.

messenger RNA (ribonucleic acid) A nucleic acid that carries DNA information from the nucleus to the cytoplasm of a cell, where it processes amino acids into proteins. It differs from DNA only in its sugar component, which is ribose instead of deoxyribose.

transfer RNA (ribonucleic acid) Nucleic acid that brings amino acids together to form a protein.

Figure 5.9   *The DNA code consists of links between specific bases. Adenine links with thymine, and guanine links with cytosine.*

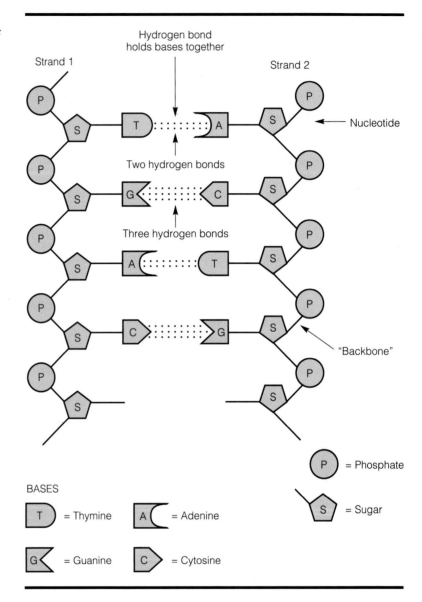

some primary source for these different alleles and for still newer alleles. This source is **mutation**.

Both the information contained in the genes and the process whereby that information produces proteins are, as you have seen, very complex. Although the accuracy of the process is very high, errors do occur. A mutation is defined as an error in the genetic mechanism. Mutations arise from various sources, ranging from structural mistakes during the complex processes of translation to the effects of radiation and

various chemicals. It is important to remember, though, that there is no connection between the adaptive requirements of the organism and the specific mutations that occur. Mutations are random; they take place at varying rates, and the time, place, and nature of a mutation are unpredictable.

Suppose, for example, that a population of animals occupied an environment where the climate suddenly shifted from wet to dry. There is no biological mechanism that could cause a mutation to, say, improve

Figure 5.10 *The woman on the left exhibits the piebald trait, which is inherited through a dominant gene. Because it does not affect reproductive fitness when it is expressed, the gene is selectively neutral and will be maintained in a population unless it is affected by chance events.*

water storage in the animals. If, however, the population by chance includes individuals with greater water storage ability, they might be selected for. Such a modification would already have occurred in the population as a result of a mutation and would have been retained simply because it was not deleterious. Given the randomness of mutation, the appearance of a beneficial modification must be viewed as a lucky accident.

Most mutations are probably deleterious because they constitute errors in a complex design. In human reproduction, errors in genetic transmission often end in fetal death. In other cases the individuals survive but are impaired to varying degrees. One example in humans is **albinism,** a recessive allele expressed as a pigment deficiency in the skin and hair causing hypersensitivity to sunlight. An example of a **benign mutation** is the **piebald trait,** a dominant trait expressed as a patch of white hair growing in the middle

of the scalp (Figure 5.10). This trait has little or no effect on its carrier's ability to survive and reproduce and is therefore maintained in a population.

Mutations that are selectively beneficial are rare, but they are vital to the process of evolution. They introduce new variation into a population, which may mean the difference between survival and extinction as environmental conditions change. Mutations with extensive phenotypic effects, called "macromutations," are responsible for the fairly sudden, major changes that mark punctuated equilibrium.

A mutation may be retained in a population even if it is deleterious. An example among humans is a disease called **phenylketonuria** or **PKU.** PKU occurs in individuals homozygous for a defective gene that fails to produce the enzyme that converts the amino acid phenylalanine into another amino acid. Excessive phenylalanine can cause mental retardation. About

mutation An alteration in the genetic code itself and the traits controlled by the code. Mutations occur randomly, but their frequency is also affected by environmental changes.

albinism A pigment deficiency in the skin and hair, resulting in hypersensitivity to the sun. The recessive allele responsible for this trait is the result of a genetic mutation.

benign mutation A trait that has little or no effect on its carrier's ability to survive and reproduce.

piebald trait A dominant trait that is expressed as a patch of white hair growing in the middle of the scalp. It is the result of a benign mutation.

phenylketonuria (PKU) A trait that appears in individuals homozygous for a defective gene that makes them incapable of converting the amino acid phenylalanine into another amino acid. It can cause mental retardation.

one baby in 10,000 has PKU. Routine screening of newborn infants can detect excessive phenylalanine in the blood, and treatment focusing on a special diet can reduce the problem of retardation. Before this screening was possible, homozygotes for this allele probably did not reproduce. Heterozygotes, who carry but do not express the allele, maintain it in the population, as does the recurrence of the mutation, which adds new carriers to the gene pool. In addition, since the disease can be diagnosed and treated, the negative selective pressure on PKU has diminished. Fitness is always relative to the environment.

Mutations provide the variation, the raw material, of evolution and therefore of life's diversity. Our modern understanding of the molecular basis of the genetic code has given us further understanding of biology and a greater ability to provide for the common good. Molecular genetics, for example, provides a tool for estimating how closely related different species are by specifically locating and counting the number of mutations that have taken place since the species diverged. It has already become possible to reprogram organisms to produce organic compounds. A common bacterium has been genetically "engineered" to produce insulin and other hormones needed by humans. Even the possibility of correcting genetic defects through "gene splicing" has come closer to reality. Recently, medicine has begun the first human trials of "gene therapy," introducing genetically engineered cells into the body to carry out functions that the individual is congenitally incapable of.

OTHER MECHANISMS OF EVOLUTION

The focus of this chapter—and, indeed, the major mechanism of evolution—is natural selection, the process by which spontaneously occurring changes provide opportunities for or impose constraints on the reproductive success of organisms. But the Darwinian idea was limited originally because no one at the time understood how inheritance worked or what produced variations. The basic laws of genetics were being discovered by Mendel during Darwin's time, but Mendel's work was unknown to the public and to most scientists. Today, with the unraveling of the genetic code, we know that evolutionary change is more complex than Darwin thought.

Since genes contain the design information for biological traits, we can define biological evolution as *genetic change through time*. Changes occurring within the life spans of individual organisms are not evolutionary. Neither are changes that are not transmitted to the next generation. Changes that are transmitted must be carried by genes, so anything that changes genes and their distributions within species must, by definition, be a mechanism of evolution.

In this sense, natural selection is a process of evolution that changes the frequency with which a certain allele appears in a population. Mechanisms other than natural selection are generally known as non-Darwinian processes. The other processes that bring about changes in allele frequencies are mutation, gene flow, and genetic drift. Mutations, discussed in the previous section, are chemical or physical alterations in the genetic code itself and thus in the traits controlled by that code (Box 5.3).

Gene flow occurs when genes from one population are introduced into another as a result of migration or some other factor that breaches reproductive isolation. This changes the frequencies of the alleles in the receiving population in a way unrelated to the adaptive significance of the traits of either population. In other words, flow is non-Darwinian. (Of course, this can only occur *within* a species.) Gene flow has probably been a factor in human populations since the first *Homo sapiens* appeared, because human populations have never been completely isolated from each other for long periods. With the massive movements of populations that have occurred since the 15th century, such as the movement of Europeans and Africans into the New World, gene flow has greatly increased.

Genetic drift consists of a number of processes. One form of drift is the **bottleneck effect,** where by chance a small number of individuals contribute disproportionately large numbers of offspring to the next generation. This may occur when the breeding population is reduced to a small size by social isolation, epidemic, warfare, shipwreck, or some other cause.

The bottleneck effect seems to have been responsible for the high incidence of *retinitis pigmentosa,* a hereditary eye disease leading to blindness, in the population of Tristan da Cunha, a remote island in the South Atlantic. All the islanders descend from a single family and a few shipwrecked sailors that settled the island in 1817. This population had expanded from a few dozen to 264 in 1961, when the entire population was evacuated because of a volcanic eruption. When the islanders reached England, four of them were di-

---

BOX 5.3

The Consequences of Genetic Errors

Unlike human language, the genetic code is very unforgiving. Most people can understand messages even with garbled pronunciation or misspelled words. But a single error in a chain of 438 characters can mean a painful condition, even death.

Consider **hemoglobin**, for example, a protein found in red blood cells. It is responsible for transporting oxygen to body tissue and returning to the lungs laden with carbon dioxide for discharge. The hemoglobin molecule consists of two long protein chains, one of which has a sequence of 146 amino acids. The DNA molecule that specifies this hemoglobin chain thus has 438 nucleotides in a specific order. The specification for the sixth amino acid on the second chain, glutamic acid, can be expressed as the DNA word *CTC*. If a mutation at this locus changes the thymine base into adenine (or *CAC*), the resulting specification is changed: Valine will be specified in that place instead of thymine. The result of this small change is an abnormal hemoglobin, which lowers the capacity of the blood cell to transport oxygen. This condition, known as **sickle-cell anemia**, affects many people in tropical Africa and the Mediterranean area as well as many African Americans (see Chapter 7).

In August 1989 newspapers around the world announced that three teams of scientists had simultaneously found the gene that causes **cystic fibrosis**, a disease that strikes one child out of every 2,000 born in the United States. In persons with this disease, only one of 1,480 amino acids is missing in the protein coded by the responsible gene, yet this slight mutation disrupts the normal functioning of the lungs, sweat glands, and pancreas. Children who are born with this disease require very special care and most die before their 30th year. Discovery of the gene that causes this condition will make it possible to diagnose it in an unborn fetus and may eventually lead to an effective therapy (Marx 1989).

---

agnosed with *retinitis pigmentosa,* a rate far higher than could be found in any large population. Evidently one of the founders of Tristan da Cunha was a carrier of the recessive allele for the disease.

A second form of drift is the **founder effect.** This occurs when a small portion of a population establishes (founds) a new population. The gene frequencies of the founding group are most likely not representative of the whole original group, so the new population is, in fact, a brand new genetic entity and all the descendants will inherit their genes (or at least a large portion of them) from the small sample present in the founders. The Hutterites, a religious isolate of the western United States and Canada, now number about 30,000, but nearly all are descendants of 300 who immigrated to the New World in the late 19th century, of whom only 90 bore children. Thus, the Hutterites of North America constitute a unique and rather homogeneous genetic population. (Figure 5.11).

A final form of drift occurs because parental generations never pass on their full complement of alleles to the next generation. An individual who is heterozygotus for some gene may simply never contrib-

---

gene flow The exchange of genes between populations.

genetic drift A source of evolutionary change that is random and not due to environmental adaptation. It includes such processes as the founder effect, the bottleneck effect, and the chance failure of a parental generation to pass on the full complement of its genome.

bottleneck effect The chance and disproportionately large contribution of only a small number of individuals to the gene pool of the next generation.

hemoglobin Protein on red blood cells that carries oxygen to the tissues of the body.

founder effect The result when a portion of a population splits off and founds a new population that has a different gene pool from the original.

sickle-cell anemia A genetically induced condition common in tropical Africa and the Mediterranean area that causes abnormal hemoglobin and results in the collapse of red blood cells and the inability of these cells to carry oxygen to the body tissue. Its negative effect on fitness is balanced by its positive effect on malaria victims.

cystic fibrosis A genetically induced condition that impairs the functioning of the lungs, sweat glands, and pancreas.

Figure 5.11 *The Hutterites of Canada and the northern United States are distinctive both culturally and genetically. They live communally, share property, and eat together in community dining halls. As long as they marry within the group, they will maintain their cultural identity and genetic homogeneity.*

ute one of the alleles to his offspring; if he is the only person who possesses that allele, then it would be completely lost to the population. It all depends on which sperm fertilizes which egg, and this is a matter of chance.

It is easy to see why drift would have a greater effect on smaller and more isolated populations. Consider, for example, a small population living in a remote mountain valley. Suppose that some family within the population possesses an unusual allele. If the members of that family themselves have larger families than the rest of the population, *for reasons that have nothing to do with that allele,* that family will have a major genetic effect on future generations. But this will occur only if the population is so small that the effect is not overshadowed by the contributions of a large number of other families.

NATURAL SELECTION IN MODERN HUMAN POPULATIONS

Natural selection occurs in humans just as it does in other species. Lethal genes arise as a result of mutations, for example, and are not inherited because the carrier does not survive when the gene is expressed. Embryologists have estimated that about 30 percent of spontaneous abortions (miscarriages) result from le-

thal genes. About 3 percent of the babies born alive in the United States (about 100,000 each year) have genetic disorders. Modern medicine has enabled many of these people to live to child-bearing age and to reproduce, thus passing on their genes to future generations. Does this kind of intervention create a problem for the human species?

Certainly deleterious alleles can be maintained in a population if they do not affect reproduction. Diabetes mellitus, for example, is often not expressed until after the carrier has passed his or her reproductive years. Thus the genes causing diabetes may be maintained. Indeed there are carriers of genetic disorders in any population. Each person carries an average of four or five recessive alleles that would be lethal if inherited from both parents. This is why matings between close relatives, who are more likely to have inherited the same genes, have a greater-than-average potential for producing offspring with genetic defects.

In some instances deleterious alleles are selected and maintained in certain populations because they provide some advantage that counterbalances their disadvantage. This phenomenon is known as a **balanced polymorphism.** A well-known example of a balanced polymorphism in humans is sickle-cell anemia. Individuals who are heterozygous for the sickle-cell gene may have nonlethal cases of the anemia; they are also more resistant to malaria. In areas of endemic malaria the sickle-cell allele produces a benefit that balances its deleterious effects, and so it tends to be maintained. Sickle-cell anemia is described in more detail in Box 5.3.

Many people are concerned about the fact that modern medicine can reduce or eliminate the deleterious effects of some genetic disorders. Hemophilia, for example, can be controlled by providing transfusions and supplementing the blood-clotting factor that hemophiliacs lack. People afflicted with PKU are treated with a diet low in phenylalanine. Albinos protect themselves from overexposure to the sun. Diabetics take insulin to replace the enzyme their bodies cannot produce. Individuals born with congenital diseases live considerably longer than they would have just a few years ago, and they are often able to reproduce. People who are concerned about this feel that medicine is interfering with natural selection and that a reservoir of defective genes is building up in the species. This view requires some clarification.

It is important to recall how selection takes place. Selection acts on phenotypes, and phenotypes are the results of interactions between genotypes and the environment. Traits present a selective advantage or disadvantage only in relation to a particular set of environmental circumstances. For example, now that medical information, proper diet, and insulin are available, the diabetic genotype no longer causes as great a reduction in fitness. Diabetes, though by no means as small a problem as, say, nearsightedness, is changing from a deleterious trait to a selectively neutral one. As the environment changes, the relationship of genotypes to it also changes. This is a normal process in evolution. The major difference today is that humans intervene in the environment, making it less hostile to carriers of certain genes.

On the other hand, some changes in our cultural environment may have created new selective pressures that are *more* hostile to certain genotypes. The most sweeping environmental changes of recent years have been urbanization and industrialization. Urban life creates stress with its noise, pollution, crowding, and insecurity caused by high levels of competition and crime. There is evidence that people vary in their abilities to deal psychologically and physically with such stress, and those with greater capacity may have greater fitness in urban settings.

Industrial expansion has introduced innumerable chemical compounds into the environment, and many are health hazards. Many of these compounds, such as acetone, asbestos, benzine, dioxin, and enriched plutonium, are carcinogens (causes of cancer). Industrialism is so recent and the rate of introduction so rapid that there has scarcely been time to gauge the evolutionary effects of new substances and forms of radiation. There is evidence, however, that cancer is increasing as a cause of death compared to other diseases. Certain kinds of cancer are on the rise, in part due to culturally induced changes in the selective environment.

Individuals vary in their susceptibility to cancer when exposed to certain chemical compounds, and this variability has a genetic component. In recent years nearly 60 major corporations in the United States have considered adopting genetic testing of their employees to screen out the people most sensitive to these compounds. Geneticists have already prepared a list of eight genetic traits that influence the risk of sickness in their carriers (Rowley 1984). This proposal raises many ethical questions, which are currently being debated in industrial and labor circles.

It seems likely that social and environmental stress, toxic compounds, and radiation apply new selective pressures on human populations. New patterns of mortality (death rate) and morbidity (disease rate) reflect these pressures. The effect of such pressures on fitness is not yet well understood, but it is clear that natural selection continues to operate on our species.

SUMMARY

- Two major phenomena define the scope of evolutionary theory: reproduction and variation.
- Natural selection is that process of nature in which beneficial traits, and thus the genes that produce

---

balanced polymorphism The selection and maintenance of a trait in a certain population because of some advantage conferred by the heterozygous condition.

them, are opportunistically selected by differential fitness and, ultimately, reproductive success.

- All organisms have DNA in their cells. This complex molecule is capable of repeating a genetic message and carrying it from one cell generation to another and from a parent to an offspring.
- These transfers of information occur with a high degree of accuracy, thereby ensuring the stability and continuity of the species. But variations appear as the messages are recombined in sexual reproduction and as the content of the messages changes through mutation.
- Mutations are usually deleterious, even lethal. Such mutations may be maintained in a population if they are formed as recessive alleles. Occasionally a mutant gene occurs that is selectively neutral. Such genes represent a pool of variability that may prove advantageous in the event of significant environmental change.
- Natural selection and human evolution have not ceased, even though changes in the environment caused by humans have reduced or eliminated the selection against certain genes.
- Many recent developments, especially those arising from industrialization and urbanization, have introduced new selective pressures to which current and future generations will be obliged to respond. The evolutionary significance of these changes has yet to unfold.

GET INVOLVED

1. Learn more about the creation vs. evolution controversy. Read statements by both sides, such as *The Monkey Business* by Niles Eldredge and *Evolution: The Fossils Say No!* by Duane Gish. There is also a journal, *Creation/Evolution,* that contains articles in support of the scientific view. Examine some middle and high school biology texts and see how well they cover evolution or how much they have been influenced by creationists. Talk with biology teachers and members of the clergy about the issue.

2. Understanding artificial selection helps in grasping the concepts of genetic variation and natural selection. Study the breeding techniques that have produced a familiar animal or plant. Interview a breeder or farmer and see actual results of selective breeding and the variation behind it.

3. See the nature of inheritance in action by tracing the transmission of a genetic trait within your family. Use the anthropological form for depicting kinship shown later in this book and draw your family tree including as many relatives as you can. Then choose a genetic characteristic and indicate the phenotype for these individuals where possible. You can use such things as blood type, any unusual trait characteristic of your family, or some simple and observable feature. Many are listed in France and Horn's *Lab Manual and Workbook for Physical Anthropology.* Given this data, see if you can discern the mode of inheritance of the trait: dominant or recessive, monogenic or polygenic.

4. To better appreciate the concept of biological adaptation, study the ecology of your area. Use general ecology texts, popular works such as David Attenborough's *The Living Planet,* and nature guides to the flora and fauna of your region. Visit a museum that uses dioramas to depict natural settings. Best of all, do some hiking armed with your nature guides and learn your area first hand.

SUGGESTED READINGS

Gould, Stephen J. 1983. What if anything is a zebra? In *Hen's teeth and horse's toes.* New York: Norton.

Katz, S. H., ed. 1975. *Biological Anthropology: Readings from Scientific American.* San Francisco: W. H. Freeman.

Lewin, Roger. 1984. DNA reveals surprises in human family tree. *Science* 226:1179–1182.

——. 1982. *Thread of life: The Smithsonian looks at evolution.* Washington, D.C.: Smithsonian Books.

Root-Bernstein, Robert, and Donald L. McEachern. 1982. Teaching theories: The evolution-creation controversy. *The American Biology Teacher* (October).

Zihlman, Adrienne L. 1982. *The human evolution coloring book.* New York: Barnes and Noble.

Studying the Genetic Basis of Arthritis

Kenneth Turner is an assistant professor of anthropology at the University of Alabama. Since 1985 he has been conducting research on the biological consequences of the arrival of Europeans in what is now the southeastern United States. Although his focus has been on the Creek Confederacy, some of this work has been on specific diseases such as rheumatoid arthritis, discussed below.

Kenneth Turner

My interests are basic human osteology, paleopathology, and forensic osteology. I chose a career in physical anthropology because I felt that my satisfaction with life would depend on how well I might manage, even in a small way, to improve the condition of the human species. One way toward that goal is to produce new knowledge about basic human biology.

Industrialization has promoted some diseases by increasing crowding and pollution. Some authorities suggest rheumatoid arthritis is a disease of the industrial age. Rheumatoid arthritis was first described in 1800 in France and was seen mostly among industrialized populations. It had never been found in skeletons of people who died before 1800. These patterns implied that some industrial pollutant might cause the disease. Some researchers attempted to identify that pollutant, hoping its eradication would eliminate the disease.

In 1988 two colleagues and I discovered rheumatoid arthritis in six people who lived about 4,000 years ago in what is now northern Alabama. Prehistoric rheumatoid arthritis has been recognized subsequently within a limited eastern North American area; it was not found outside this area until after Europeans began colonizing North America. The discovery of rheumatoid arthritis in

these prehistoric populations demonstrates that it is not an industrial age disease. We are now searching for causes of rheumatoid arthritis among things held in common by all prehistoric and living populations afflicted with this disease, particularly things that were moved from North America to Europe on sailing ships after 1500.

It has been hypothesized that rheumatoid arthritis is produced by one or more harmful genes. Indeed, most of its victims have inherited a specific human leukocyte antigen; yet the disease occurs in only one-tenth of humans with that antigen. Our discoveries indicate that before 1500 rheumatoid arthritis was found only in North America. If it is produced entirely by the action of one or more genes, it must have entered European populations through gene flow from Native American populations. Gene flow in that direction was too slight to produce the numbers of Europeans with rheumatoid arthritis, so we can rule out the possibility that it is an inherited disease.

Still, the linkage of rheumatoid arthritis to that inherited antigen may be evidence of a genetically based disease involving incomplete penetrance. Just as in some forms of diabetes, individuals may inherit a

genetic susceptibility to rheumatoid arthritis but develop the disease only if they encounter certain external environmental factors. We think these external factors occurred only in eastern North America in prehistoric times, even though people with genetic susceptibility to rheumatoid arthritis were always distributed worldwide. We are investigating the archaeology of eastern North America and the history of colonial trade. We suspect a virus or other infectious organism, perhaps transmitted by insects associated with animals.

You may wonder why rheumatoid arthritis has not been removed or made more rare by natural selection, since it apparently has some genetic basis. Although usually associated with adults past reproductive age, it actually occurs among all age groups. When all afflicted individuals are considered, rheumatoid arthritis slightly reduces reproductive success. However, under our scenario, it began spreading from eastern North America less than 15 generations ago. Given the relatively slow pace available for selection against rheumatoid arthritis, these are far too few generations for evolution to remove the disease. There is thus no reason to propose for rheumatoid arthritis a mechanism similar to the one that maintains sickle-cell anemia.

In our research we refer to several areas of knowledge: rheumatology, paleopathology, osteology, archaeology, population genetics, and history. This multifaceted approach typifies anthropology. To me, it is one aspect of anthropology that makes it challenging and enjoyable. Of course it is also fulfilling to know that by developing new knowledge about humans you may help improve the human condition.

Orangutans, such as this one from Sumatra, Indonesia, are not as closely related to humans as chimpanzees and gorillas. Orangutans diverged from the line that gave rise to chimpanzees, gorillas, and humans at least 12 MYA.

6

PRIMATES AND EARLY HOMINIDS

▲▲▲

Where do we come from? For many of us this is the most captivating question asked by anthropology, because it is tied up with our basic identity as human beings. Until recently, the secrets of human origins revealed themselves one by one in the slow, painstaking search for the fossil remains of our human ancestors and their evolutionary cousins. Recently the pace of discovery in paleoanthropology has increased thanks to new techniques for finding, dating, and interpreting fossils and to the use of powerful methods in molecular biology of tracing the human lineage. The challenge is to explain the evolution of *Homo sapiens* in terms of the principles and processes that explain the evolution of other species, as described in Chapter 5. In this chapter we examine the place that the evolutionary ancestors of humans occupy in relationship to other animals. In particular we examine the place of humans as part of the primate order.

Table 6.1 Classification of Humans

Taxonomic Category	Group Including Humans	Characteristics	Members
Kingdom	Animals	Multicellular, locomotion, nervous systems, sense organs, ingestion of food.	Animals (as opposed to single celled organisms, fungi, and plants)
Phylum	Chordata	Dorsal nervous system and notochord for support. One subphylum, Vertebrata, has an internal skeleton with segmented backbone and bilateral symmetry.	Jawless fishes, cartilagenous fishes, bony fishes, amphibians, reptiles, birds, mammals
Class	Mammals	Warm-blooded, hair, live birth, mammary glands, complex brains, care of young.	Whales, porpoises, seals, bats, hoofed animals, rodents, rabbits, carnivores, primates
Order	Primates	Tree-dwelling, grasping hands and feet, visually oriented, large, complex brains, long period of infant dependency.	Prosimians, monkeys, apes, humans
Suborder	Anthropoids	Active during the day, socially oriented, intelligent.	New World and Old World monkeys, apes, humans
Superfamily	Hominoids	Tailless, relatively large, well developed shoulders and arms, some bipedal ability.	Gibbons, siamangs, orangutans, gorillas, chimpanzees, humans
Family	Hominids	Habitually bipedal.	Humans, fossil and modern
Genus	*Homo*	Very large and complex brains, dexterous hands, tool making, advanced capacity for culture.	Several species of humans including *habilis, erectus,* and *sapiens*
Species	*Sapiens*	Brain size from 1000 to 2000 cubic centimeters, complex cultural systems.	Modern humans

TAXONOMY AND EVOLUTION

Taxonomies are classifications in which things of any kind are categorized according to their degrees of similarity and arranged in order of increasing inclusiveness. Table 6.1 shows the most commonly used **taxa** in biology and the corresponding classification for our species.

In the West biological taxonomy was originally intended to order, by physical appearance, the results of divine creation. Since the mid-19th century, however, the guiding principal for taxonomy has been Darwinian theory. This leads us to postulate that the similarities and differences in anatomy, neurological structures, physiology, DNA, and other traits among organisms reflect the order of their descent from common ancestors. Taxonomies based on the order of descent are known as **phyletic**, reflecting the history of development of a species, or **phylogeny.**

Approaches to Classification

Evolution is divergent, constantly producing new branches as adaptive radiation takes place. A diagram of evolutionary change shows branches budding from stems, which join larger branches signifying common ancestry (Figure 6.1). Scientists cannot directly observe the actual process of branching or divergence. What the evolutionary biologist sees is a thicket of different species, as if looking at a tree from above, without seeing the branches, limbs, and trunks that connect them all together.

Establishing phyletic relationships depends on the idea that if two forms resemble each other in appearance, they are related. There are important exceptions to this principle, however. Similarities among organisms may be of two different kinds: **homologies** and **analogies.** Homologies occur when two organisms share traits inherited from common ancestors (sometimes called **ancestral traits**). Analogies occur when two distantly related forms (for example, sharks and porpoises) come to resemble each other because they face analogous adaptive situations (sometimes called **convergent evolution**). Despite their similarities sharks and porpoises are not descended from a recent common ancestor (Figure 6.2).

In sorting out the relationships among different organisms, modern evolutionists take one of two basic approaches. Proponents of the first approach, known as **numerical taxonomy**, construct relationships on a basis of physical similarity, considering each identifiable trait as a separate piece of evidence and weighing it equally with all other traits in comparing forms to one another.

The second major approach to evolutionary relationships is **cladistics.** All the species sharing a common ancestor are a **clade.** As species evolve and adapt to available ecological niches, their structure and behavior change. Thus ancestral traits—those inherited

---

taxonomy A classification in which things are categorized according to their degrees of similarity, arranged in order of increasing inclusiveness.

taxon (plural, **taxa**) A position within a taxonomy.

phyletic Pertaining to the history of development of a species.

phylogeny The history of development of a species.

homology A similarity between organisms of different species due to descent from a common ancestor; distinguished from analogy.

analogy A similarity between organisms of different species due to adaptation to similar environmental conditions; distinguished from homology.

ancestral traits Traits that may give rise to similarities among organisms due to a shared ancestry (also called homologies).

convergent evolution Resemblance between two species due to adaptation to similar environments rather than common ancestry.

numerical taxonomy A taxonomy that constructs relationships on the basis of physical similarity, considering each identifiable trait as a separate piece of evidence and weighing it equally with all other traits in comparing forms to one another.

cladistics Taxonomy based on derived traits rather than physical similarities.

clade All the species sharing a common ancestor.

Figure 6.1 *A time line of primate evolution, showing the divergence of different species from common ancestors. Question marks indicate points at which there is insufficient data to establish evolutionary connections.*

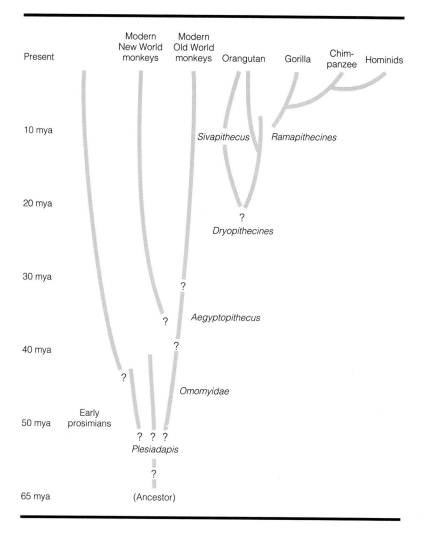

Figure 6.2 *A case of convergent evolution. The similarities between sharks and porpoises are the result of their adaptation to the same environment rather than an indication of a close evolutionary relationship.*

from some distant common ancestor—may be changed or even lost depending on the particular selective conditions. For example, the common ancestor of all land vertebrates had five toes, but now the presence or absence of five toes is mixed throughout many forms of this large group. The fact that salamanders and humans have five toes and horses do not does not tell us much about the evolutionary relationships among these species (Gould 1983). Humans are more closely related to horses than to salamanders despite the differences in their feet.

In contrast to ancestral traits, which may be misleading, **derived traits** are shared only by members of a clade and so provide evidence for immediate and true common ancestry. Derived traits reflect relatively recent adaptations that affected the ancestors of a particular group of species and no other species. As S. J. Gould (1983) points out, for example, all mammals have hair and no other organism does. Similarly, humans and chimpanzees share chromosomal similarities possessed by no other creature, and so our two species make up a clade, regardless of whether chimpanzees appear to be more similar to orangutans.

Cladistics seeks to establish evolutionary relationships purely on the basis of derived traits, unlike numerical taxonomy, which considers both derived and ancestral traits equally. Derived traits are the most reliable clues to the actual relatedness of species and hence to the sequence of evolutionary events.

Collecting and Interpreting Evidence on Human Evolution

Until recently the principal source of information on human evolution was the fossil record, the actual physical remains of human teeth and bones. Since the 1950s, however, a host of new techniques for understanding and reconstructing hominid phylogeny has become available.

The Fossil Record.   The best and most reliable data we have on the evolution of species comes from the fossil record. This consists of the fossilized remains of hard parts of animals and the stone tools and other artifacts created by cultural animals. Bone is an organic material that normally decomposes over time, although usually more slowly than soft tissue. Fossils lying on the surface, exposed to water and air, seldom last very long. For a piece of bone to survive thousands or millions of years, it has to be buried or closed off in a cave to reduce exposure. Even then the original bone is normally replaced by minerals present in the soil or rock surrounding it. Ideally this process preserves the original shape of the bone. Fossil hominids greater than 1 million years of age are found, but rarely.

Of all the parts of the skeleton, teeth are the hardest and generally the best preserved. Some fossil species are known only by their teeth, which can be identified by their shape and the pattern of little bumps, or cusps, on their grinding surfaces. The information yielded by teeth goes beyond the taxonomic identification of the animal. Teeth may provide clues about diet through microscopic analysis of tooth wear, which can reveal the texture and kind of food consumed by the species. Teeth also yield information on diet through **enamel hypoplasias**, or anomalies in the deposition of enamel layers. These anomalies correspond to periods of dietary or other stress in the individual.

Crania, or skulls, are perhaps the most important pieces of fossil evidence in the study of human evolution. They are relatively massive pieces of bone that tend to survive better than long bones. Crania can yield a wealth of information about the brain, vision, sense of smell, diet and food habits, and many other aspects of the animals to which they belonged. The size of the brain case (the interior volume measured in cubic centimeters, or cc) is an important clue to the stage of development of the brain. The relative size of the attachments for the chewing muscles is a good indicator of the use to which the jaws and teeth were

---

derived traits   Traits that are shared only by members of the same clade and that provide evidence for direct common ancestry.

enamel hypoplasias   Anomalies in the deposition of layers of tooth enamel that correspond to periods of dietary or other stress.

cranium (plural, **crania**)   Skull.

put. A massive jaw with evidence of large jaw muscles may reflect the capacity to crush and grind tough seeds. Of particular importance is the length of the snout. Over the course of primate evolution, and continuing on into hominid evolution, the snout has tended to become shorter, reflecting a reduction of the importance of the sense of smell.

The pelvic bones are invaluable in determining the sex of the owner, since females typically have flared pelvises consistent with their child-bearing role. The pelvis is also a clue to the stature of an animal, whether upright or **pronograde** (parallel to the ground). Long bones, such as the femur, tibia, ulna, or radius, are less commonly found, but they are important clues to the means of locomotion, whether **arboreal** (in the trees) or **terrestrial** (on the ground), **bipedal** (two-legged) or **quadrupedal** (four-legged).

Dating Techniques. We have already had a glimpse of dating techniques in our discussion of the analysis of the Lucy fossil (Chapter 1). Accurately estimating the date of a fossil is a major challenge to paleoanthropology and archaeology. Relative dating of fossil materials by stratigraphy and **faunal analysis** is still a mainstay of paleoanthropology, although it is valid only when great care is taken in collecting the fossils at the site. Just because a fossil is found in a specific location or stratigraphic layer is not proof positive that it was deposited at the same time as the surrounding material. The action of scavengers, burrowing animals, water, and even geological events such as volcanoes, earthquakes, folding, and faulting can cause a fossil to shift into a position inconsistent with the actual period of deposition. Many archaeologists and paleoanthropologists now specialize in **taphonomy**,

---

BOX 6.1

The Piltdown Hoax

One of the best-known events in modern paleoanthropology was the discovery of a forgery. This was the famous Piltdown man, found in a gravel pit in Sussex, England, in 1910. This "fossil" was actually a human cranium deposited near the jaw of an orangutan, which had been artificially dyed to make it look very old. Piltdown man was accepted as authentic by many investigators, possibly because its large brain case seemed to confirm the importance of intelligence in human evolution and, just possibly, because it was found in England. Piltdown allowed scientists to believe what many intuitively felt was true: Human evolution began with the evolution of a large brain, followed by other human traits. We now know this was not the true sequence of events. The earliest hominids had brains scarcely larger than those of modern apes.

It was not until 1953 that Piltdown man was proven beyond all doubt to be a hoax. Fluorine dating showed a wide discrepancy between the ages of the jaw and cranium. The perpetrator of the hoax has never been identified with certainty. Partly because of the Piltdown hoax, paleoanthropologists are very cautious about accepting dates of newly found fossils until they are well established by more than one method. It is unlikely that so many scientists could again be so badly deceived for so long a time.

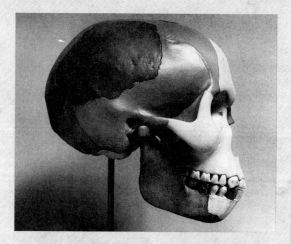

The Piltdown skull. The dark areas indicate the parts actually recovered at Piltdown—the cranium (that of a human) and the rear portion of the lower jaw (that of an orangutan). The orangutan's canine teeth had been removed and its molars filed down to simulate humanlike wear.

the study of how bones are deposited and come to be fossilized.

Pollen analysis, or **palynology**, is another useful tool for relative dating, provided a general picture of the evolution of vegetation in the area has been reconstructed. Tiny grains of pollen fall into the soil each year and can be recovered and identified many thousands of years later. While many plant species are typically represented in a given soil sample, the mix can vary considerably from time to time. Pollen samples firmly associated with a fossil skeleton can reveal, for example, whether the fossil was deposited during a rainy or relatively dry period, allowing the fossil to be associated with a particular time period.

Another relative dating technique is **fluorine dating**, which is based on the rate at which bone calcium bonds with fluorine in ground water. The rate of absorption may vary from site to site and over time, but two bone samples from the same site can usefully be compared to determine if they are the same age. This technique was crucial in determining that the Piltdown skull was a fraud (Box 6.1).

Amino acid racemization dating is based on the slow transformation of amino acid molecules from one form into another. These changes can be detected by passing polarized light through a solution containing the amino acid and determining the direction in which it is rotated. Living protein contains only left-handed molecules; after death, these molecules slowly change into right-handed molecules. The relative age of organic material can be estimated by the ratio of right-handed to left-handed amino acids in a sample. Because the rate of change rises with temperature, the technique is site-specific and cannot be used to determine absolute dates.

Absolute dating techniques may be based on the decay rates of radioactive isotopes, such as ^{14}**C** (radiocarbon), **K/Ar** (Potassium-Argon), and ^{238}**U** (radioactive uranium), or on other physical processes that occur at known rates or intervals. Each technique has specific limitations and yields estimates accurate within a given range (Figure 6.3). Ideally two or more techniques are used to estimate the dates of any particular object or stratigraphic layer. Some techniques are useful only when correlated with other dating techniques. Some techniques can be used directly on fossils or artifacts, while others can be used only on stone or soil samples found associated with such objects.

Radiocarbon dating is based on the fact that living organisms maintain a constant ratio of the unstable ^{14}C isotope to the stable ^{12}C isotope. After an organism dies, the ratio slowly changes as the unstable carbon decays through spontaneous fission into nitrogen. The half-life of ^{14}C is 5,730 ±40 years, so that in a given sample, about half of this isotope would have disappeared over this period. The radiocarbon technique can be used to date charcoal and other organic matter up to 70,000 years old (see Figure 6.3).

K/Ar dating is based on the decay of an isotope of potassium into a rare gas called argon. Radioactive

---

pronograde Parallel to the ground.

arboreal Adapted to living and moving around in the trees.

terrestrial Adapted to living and moving on the ground.

bipedal Habitually moving around on two feet, a characteristic of hominids.

quadrupedal Habitually moving around on four feet.

faunal analysis The archaeological analysis of animal remains.

taphonomy The study of how bones and other materials are deposited in the ground and of the processes they undergo after deposition.

palynology The study of pollen deposited in the ground in ancient times, useful in the relative dating of paleontological and archaeological sites.

fluorine dating A relative-dating technique based on the rate at which bone calcium bonds with fluorine in ground water.

amino acid racemization A dating technique based on the slow transformation of amino acid molecules from one form into another, a change that can be detected by passing polarized light through a solution containing the amino acid.

^{14}**C dating** An absolute dating technique based on the fact that living organisms maintain a constant ratio of the unstable carbon 14 isotope to the stable carbon 12 isotope.

K/Ar dating An absolute dating technique based on the regular rate of decay of an isotope of potassium into argon gas.

^{238}**U dating** An absolute dating technique based on the regular rate of decay of uranium into its daughter isotopes and elements.

Figure 6.3 *A comparison of the range limitations of six dating techniques.*

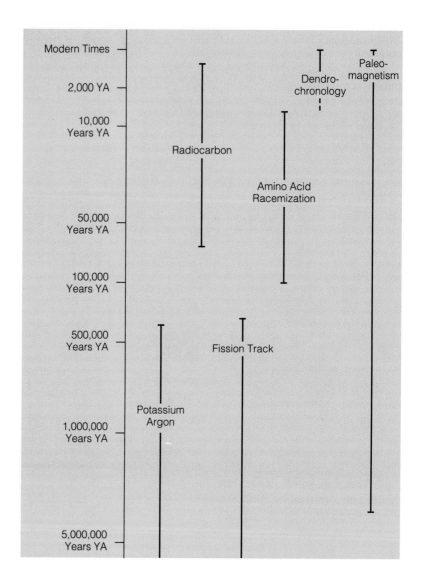

potassium (^{40}K) decays at a known rate; during 1.3 billion years half the ^{40}K trapped in rocks will turn into an isotope of argon. While porous bone releases argon into the environment, volcanic rock retains the gas as "frozen" crystals from the moment the **lava** spewed forth on the earth's surface and cooled into solid rock. The rocks can be heated to release the argon. The amount of argon given off by samples of volcanic rock and the ratio of ^{40}K to stable potassium isotopes can be measured to within a few parts per million by using a mass spectrometer. This dating

technique is indirect because it can only be done on adjacent rocks, not on the fossils themselves.

Paleomagnetism can be used when a sample of volcanic rock (lava) can be recovered in such a way that its spatial orientation at the site is known. The magnetic poles of the earth are known to have been reversed several times over geological time. The last such reversal is known to have occurred about 0.7 MYA. During more than 1.7 million years prior to that, there were several short reversals. The polarity prevailing at the time molten rock cooled or sediments were deposited can be observed through microscopic analysis of rock samples.

Fission track dating can be performed on naturally occurring glass, or obsidian. Tiny tracks left by spontaneously decaying ^{238}U are observable under the microscope. The more tracks visible in a sample of a given size, the longer the time period since the glass was last in a molten state (see Figure 6.3). Fission track dating can be used for samples up to 8 million years old.

Dendrochronology is a method of estimating the age of trees by analyzing the number of growth rings in a cross-section (or core sample) of a tree trunk. The range of accurate dendrochronology extends back only as far as trees or wood samples can be found, or about 7,500 years (see Figure 6.3).

During the Pleistocene, there was a sequence of glacial advances and retreats in certain regions of the world, especially Europe and North America. Geological evidence—such as the stratigraphic location of ancient beaches left behind by lakes and rising sea levels caused by melting glaciers—can be used to correlate these events with the deposition of fossils or artifacts. A sequence of alternating wet periods and dry periods in regions such as East Africa also provides investigators with useful information for dating sites and their contents.

Biochemical and Molecular Approaches. A variety of biochemical and molecular techniques can also provide information about evolutionary relationships. **Immunological** studies are the oldest kind of biochemical approach, having been used for about a century to determine whether it is safe for one person to donate blood to another. Certain blood types cannot be mixed with other blood types because the cells have an antibody that seems to recognize an alien protein and rejects it by causing the cells carrying it to clump. This immune reaction can be measured by observing the amount of solid that precipitates out when two samples of blood are mixed.

Measurements of the strength of antibody reactions show how closely two species are related. These blood serum chemicals are direct products of the genetic code. Such measurements are valuable in determining the sequence of evolution, based on the assumption that the stronger the immune reaction between blood samples from two species, the more distant the common ancestor.

During the past two decades it has become possible to estimate how closely related two or more living animal species are by comparing tissue samples. Now it is even possible to compare specific DNA sequences. Having two independent lines of evidence is invaluable for validating hypotheses. There is so much uncertainty in the identification, classification, and dating of fossils that the molecular evidence becomes a valuable independent data source and cross-check. Until now it has been impossible to obtain DNA from fossils, but very recent advances hold out the possibility that it may be possible to recover and test the DNA of ancient animal remains.

Understanding the structure of DNA molecules allows even more precise measurement of genetic distance between different species. In one method, known as **DNA hybridization**, single strands of DNA taken from the tissues of different species are mixed together and allowed to try to "match up" and form a double helix (see Chapter 5). Comparable genes find their match on the helix, while the remaining residue of genes can be washed out and measured by using a radioactive marking technique. The amount of residue is a measure of the genetic distance between the two species.

Now that specific genes can be isolated in the laboratory, it is possible actually to count the paired bases

---

lava Molten rock from volcanoes.

dendrochronology A dating technique for estimating the age of trees by analyzing the number of growth rings in a cross-section (or core sample) of a tree trunk.

immunological Pertaining to the immune system. Immunological studies measure the strength of antibody reaction to determine how closely different species are related.

DNA hybridization A technique used to measure genetic distance by taking strands of DNA from the tissues of different species, mixing them together, and then measuring the DNA that failed to bond with matching DNA from the other species.

one by one. This **gene sequencing** method compares actual **genomes** (the full complement of genes belonging to a given species) of tested species or of different populations of the same species to determine their genetic distance. Next, a computer program sorts through large amounts of this data to determine the most likely sequence of common ancestry linking the populations. In any given comparison the multiplicity of genes tested makes it possible to reconstruct various linkages through ancestors. In order to simplify the results the technique uses an assumption of **parsimony**, that is, it presumes the smallest possible number of linkages through time.

Most of the molecular studies show a very close relationship between modern *Homo sapiens* and chimpanzees (*Pan troglodytes*). It appears that *Homo* and *Pan* differ in only about 1 percent of the total number of genes. The relationship is so close, in fact, that one prominent biologist, Morris Goodman, has suggested that it is foolish to continue the separation of humans and apes into two separate families as is traditional in primate phylogeny (Lewin 1988).

The obvious limitation of these and other molecular techniques is that they are restricted to comparing living lineages. The same techniques cannot be used on most extinct populations because it is not possible to obtain live tissue samples. Thus molecular tests can tell us nothing directly about the relationships among extinct primates. For that we rely on inference and the concrete evidence of the fossil record. Furthermore, estimating dates of divergence between two or more groups of organisms from molecular evidence is not necessarily more accurate than using fossil evidence. The molecular techniques rest on assumptions that could invalidate conclusions based on them if they are incorrect. There are, in fact, serious discrepancies between the two lines of evidence. The fossil evidence suggests, for example, that monkeys and apes diverged more than 20 MYA. Some of the molecular evidence points to a split at about 10 MYA.

PRIMATE EVOLUTION

How did the human species evolve? To answer this question we must discard the notion that humans are unique in every respect or that they arose fully formed. Some characteristics of humans, such as their **prehensile** (grasping) hands, their ability to make tools, and even their reliance on learned behavior, are also found in other species. It is not necessary, therefore, to develop separate explanations for how these arose as purely human traits. They are ancestral traits,

Table 6.2 General Characteristics of Primates

Brains
1. Large relative to body size
2. Complex

Eyes
1. Overlapping fields of vision providing stereoscopic (3-D) sight
2. Color vision (except in many prosimians who, instead, have good night vision)
3. Eyes enclosed in a bony socket

Sense of smell
Relatively poor (more pronounced in nocturnal prosimians)

Face and jaws
1. Relatively flatter than most mammals
2. Smaller number of teeth than most mammals
3. Generalized dentition for a variety of foods

Locomotion, arms, and legs
1. Quadrupedal (most primates have some bipedal ability; humans are habitual bipeds)
2. Flexible limbs
3. Prehensile hands (and feet to some extent in many primates)
4. Opposable thumbs
5. Nails instead of claws (some prosimians retain claws on some digits)

Reproduction
1. One birth at a time (twins in a few prosimian species)
2. Long period of infant dependency
3. Long maturation period; relatively long life-span

Behavior Patterns
1. Emphasis on social relationships
2. Recognition of the individual and of differential status within the group
3. Relatively complex vocal and visual communication
4. Mutual grooming to help maintain group cohesion
5. Dependence on learned information
6. Flexible, highly adaptable behaviors

as defined earlier. See Table 6.2 for a summary of the traits common to both human and nonhuman primates.

Humans are members of the primate order, along with the prosimians, monkeys, and apes. Comparisons of information about contemporary primate species with paleontological evidence show that all primates descend from a common ancestral species. That is, primates make up a complex clade. (See the gallery of living primates in Figure 6.4.) Contemporary apes and monkeys are **lineages** related to humans as "cousins" at varying degrees of distance.

Modern humans are not descendants of modern apes. Rather we and other primates are codescendants of a common ancestor. If it were alive today, however, that common ancestor would probably be classified as an ape. Our task is to understand what environmental events and evolutionary processes could have selected for the upright posture, large brain, dependence on cultural behavior, and the other derived traits that distinguish human beings from other primates.

The Divergence of the Primates in the Paleocene

The class of animals known as mammals arose about 200 MYA during the Triassic period of the Mesozoic era (Table 6.3). At the end of the Mesozoic, mammals underwent an exuberant adaptive radiation. This corresponds to the period of maximum activity in **continental drift** as the separate continents began to split off from the once unitary land mass. With their relatively large brains, thermal regulation, extensive prenatal development, and live birth, mammals were probably more adaptively generalized than many other groups. The fossil evidence, though scanty, suggests that the first primates appeared during the **Paleocene** (65–53 MYA) geological epoch (see Table 6.3) in what is now North America. These tiny creatures resembled modern **insectivores** (insect eaters), another mammalian order that includes moles and shrews (Figure 6.5). The earliest primates may have taken advantage of niches made available by the rise of new plant species in the previous epoch and left open by the extinction of the dinosaurs that had filled many available ecological niches. During the Paleocene, humid tropical forests covered much of what are temperate zones today, including areas at the same latitude as modern Germany. Perhaps it was intense competition on the ground, as well as the extensive forest, that led some mammals to take to the trees.

Quite likely the first primates were **nocturnal** (active at night) and arboreal (tree living). It may be that early traits adapted for finding and catching insects were selected in this environment. Unlike other arboreal mammals, primates have flattened nails rather than claws. Thus while a squirrel can climb by sinking its claws into the bark of a tree, a primate must grasp the limbs of a tree. Grasping prehensile hands, feet, and sometimes tails (in the New World monkeys) are handy for jumping from branch to branch and holding on. Perhaps even more important, fingernails allow an animal to have sensitive fingertips that provide **tactile** feedback from the objects they touched

---

gene sequencing The comparison of genomes of tested species to determine their genetic distance.

genome The full complement of genes belonging to a given species.

parsimony The assumption that the simplest model of any phenomenon is preferred.

prehensile Grasping. Some New World monkeys have a prehensile tail for holding on to branches of trees while feeding.

lineage The direct descendants of a single ancestor.

continental drift Movement of the continents beginning in prehistory and continuing in the present.

Paleocene Geological epoch extending from 65 to 53 MYA, during which rodentlike primates began to evolve.

insectivore An animal that makes insects a large part of its diet.

nocturnal Pertaining to animals that are active at night and sleep during the day.

tactile Relating to the sense of touch.

Mindanao tarsier, native of the Philippines.
Bolivian red howler monkey.

Ring-tailed lemur, native of Madagascar.

Figure 6.4 *A gallery of living primates. The primate order is divided into two suborders, Prosimii and Anthropoidea. The former are small Old World animals and are considered the most primitive primates. The lemur belongs to this group, and the tarsier, a tiny, arboreal insect eater is normally included. The suborder Anthropoidea includes the Platyrrhinii (New World monkeys) and the Catarrhinii (Old World monkeys, apes and humans). New World monkeys, such as the howler monkey, are largely arboreal, and some have prehensile (grasping) tails for locomotion through the trees. Old World monkeys, such as the baboon, lack prehensile tails and may be partially terrestrial. Representative of the apes are the siamang, the orangutan, and the chimpanzee. Apes are tailless and may spend much of their time on the ground.*

Siamang, native of southeastern Asia.

Chimpanzees, found throughout Africa.

Mandrill baboon, from Africa.
Orangutan and baby, from Sumatra.

Table 6.3   Geological Eras

Era	Period	Epoch	Millions of Years Ago	Major Evolutionary Events
Azoic			4500–3500	The origin of life
Proterozoic			3500–570	Algae and early invertebrates
Paleozoic	Cambrian		570–500	"Explosion" of life; marine invertebrates
	Ordovician		500–430	Early vertebrates including jawless fishes; trilobites and many other invertebrates
	Silurian		430–395	First fish with jaws; land plants
	Devonian		395–345	Many fishes; first amphibians; first forests
	Carboniferous		345–280	Radiation of amphibians; first reptiles and insects
	Permian		280–230	Radiation of reptiles; mammal-like reptiles
Mesozoic	Triassic		230–180	First dinosaurs; egg-laying mammals
	Jurassic		180–135	Dinosaurs dominate; first birdlike reptiles
	Cretaceous		135–65	Extinction of dinosaurs; first birds and placental mammals
Cenozoic	Tertiary		65–1.8	
		Paleocene	65–53	First primates
		Eocene	53–37	Ancestral prosimians
		Oligocene	37–25	First proto-apes
		Miocene	25–5	First apes
		Pliocene	5–1.8	First hominids
	Quaternary		1.8–0	
		Pleistocene	1.8–0.01	Evolution of *Homo*
		Holocene	0.01–0	Neolithic revolution to contemporary times

Note: The Azoic and Proterozoic eras are often known collectively as the Precambrian.
Source: Relethford 1990, 268.

and handled. **Visual acuity,** an asset for an insectivore, would also be favored in the complex, multidimensional treetop niche. Eye sockets of primates rotated to the front of the skull, making true depth perception possible, and many primates developed color vision.

At the same time, the snout grew smaller, reflecting the reduced importance of smell, which is more useful for ground-dwellers than for arboreal animals. Movement through bushes and trees in pursuit of insects puts a selective premium on coordination of eyes, forelimbs, and hind limbs. Rapid, coordinated eye-hand movements of the sort needed for playing video games require an advanced neurological capacity to

Figure 6.5   *The skull of a* Plesiadapis *(top) reveals that this small primatelike mammal dating from some 60 MYA resembled a tree shrew (bottom), a modern insectivore.*

Figure 6.6   *A gibbon brachiating. The visual and manual dexterity required for brachiation may have been a step in the neural evolution of the apes and the ancestors of humans.*

rapidly analyze and respond to the information received through the eyes and to adopt appropriate action. This helps explain the selection among primates for an increase in relative brain size and brain complexity.

As primate groups diverged, a number of specialized adaptations arose. Some New World monkeys, for example, developed prehensile tails, enhancing their arborealism with a fifth grasping appendage. Gibbons and siamangs, the small apes of Southeast Asia, **brachiate**, swinging arm-over-arm through the trees like Tarzan (Figure 6.6). Other primates, like some African monkeys and the two African great apes (gorillas and chimpanzees), eventually adapted to a life spent largely on the ground.

During the Eocene (53–37 MYA), climates grew colder and the humid tropical forests that supported an abundance of primates receded, reducing the number of primate species. In the ensuing geological epoch, the Oligocene (37–25 MYA), however, a new adaptive radiation took place. As continents continued to drift and climates to change, new habitats and niches emerged. Primates disappeared from Europe and North America and proliferated in the southern landmasses, especially Africa. The Fayum region in Egypt yielded an array of Oligocene primates. These forms carry forward the trends of snout reduction, forward-facing eyes, and arborealism. One of the Fayum fossils, *Aegyptopithecus,* may be ancestral to all later Old World anthropoids.

---

visual acuity   Sharpness or precision of vision.

brachiation   Use of the arms and hands to swing through the trees.

The Miocene:
The Appearance of Hominoids

The **Miocene** epoch (25–5 MYA) was the dawn of the hominoid period, when the distinctive characteristics of modern apes began to emerge. One genus, **Proconsul,** from sites in Africa, was a generalized arboreal primate, not highly adapted to a narrow ecological niche. It had some traits in common with modern apes and others in common with modern monkeys. *Proconsul* is seen as a transitional form. Among Miocene hominoids were some that specialized in consuming high-bulk vegetable foods (primarily leaves), while others apparently fed on insects or high-quality vegetables (seeds and fruit). These differences are reflected in the teeth, jaws, and body structure of the fossil species. High-bulk vegetable foods require a longer, more elaborate digestive system than other foods. Similar variation occurs in the digestive systems of different modern primates. Most likely some Miocene primates began to exploit terrestrial as well

Figure 6.7   *Reconstruction of a skull of* Sivapithecus, *probably an ancestor of the modern orangutan.*

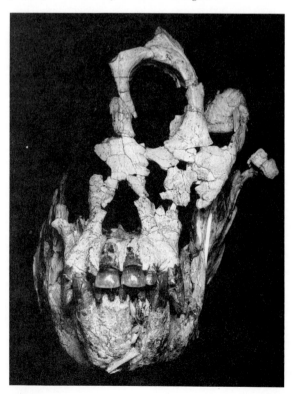

as arboreal resources, although they probably returned to the trees to seek safety and to sleep.

Two Forms of Miocene Apes.   Apes and monkeys were both present during the Miocene and gradually became more distinct from each other. The Miocene apes seem to come in two forms. One group of species is known as the **dryopithecines**. These are forest-dwelling animals, known mainly from teeth that suggest a diet of soft vegetable foods such as fruits, leaves, and shoots. The dryopithecines' range extended from Africa northward into Europe and eastward into Asia, as the specific climate permitted.

During the late Miocene, world climate changed so that the seasonal differences became greater (colder winters, hotter summers). Many areas once covered with continuous forest were broken up into forests interspersed with open woodland and **savanna**, grassland with widely scattered trees and shrubs. This change may well have brought about the extinction of many dryopithecine species. If the dryopithecines left any descendants, they are likely to be the African great apes, also largely humid tropical forest dwellers.

On the open savannas of Africa and Asia appeared the second new kind of ape, which was better adapted to the drier, more open environment. This form may well have branched off from some dryopithecine form. These apes lived in Africa and Asia from about 17 MYA to 8 MYA. Known as **sivapithecines** (or sometimes as **ramapithecines**), they appear to have adapted to a diet of harder, drier foods, judging from the thick enamel layer on their massive molar teeth and from their heavy-duty jaws (Figure 6.7). The tooth row of the sivapithecines, however, had a flaring shape instead of the parallel shape typical of modern apes (Figure 6.8). The sivapithecines lived on seeds, nuts, and roots they found on the savanna. In dry environments, these foods were typically covered with tough shells that evolved as protection against water loss and predation. For a time it appeared that some sivapithecine could have been *the* hominid ancestor, but later discoveries showed that its derived traits bear a remarkable resemblance to the modern orangutan. Additional discoveries suggest that the sivapithecines could not have been bipedal.

Divergence of Hominids.   The Miocene was a critical period in hominoid evolution. It was almost certainly

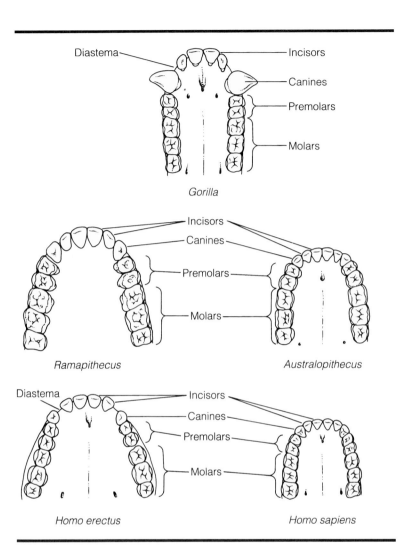

Figure 6.8 *Primate dental patterns. In modern apes (top) the tooth rows are parallel; in modern humans (bottom right) they are flared. The shape of the dental arcade is an important feature in determining the evolutionary status of fossil primates.*

during this period that the great apes and the hominids diverged. At some point during the African Miocene, selection favored a set of traits in at least one population of apes that characterize the hominids, —bipedal locomotion, greater manual dexterity, sharing of food and other resources, and, later, a larger brain. We don't know precisely which environmental features favored these modifications, but clearly certain key aspects of the environment did change, which led to more variegated vegetation and climatic zones.

Miocene   Geological epoch extending from 25 to 5 MYA.

Proconsul   An extinct genus of Miocene apes; ancestor and transitional form of both modern apes and monkeys; a generalized arboreal primate, found only in Africa.

dryopithecines   A group of forest-dwelling Miocene apes whose range included northern Africa, Europe, and Asia.

savanna   An environment that consists of grasslands with scattered trees and brush, usually in the tropics or subtropics.

sivapithecines   A group of Miocene apes that were more adapted to life in a drier, open savanna environment than previous apes and whose range included Africa and Asia.

ramapithecines   See sivapithecines.

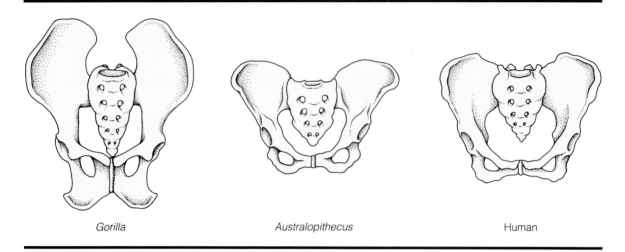

Gorilla   *Australopithecus*   Human

Figure 6.9   *The pelvic structure of a modern gorilla, an extinct australopithecine, and a modern human. Although it is different from that of the modern human, the australopithecine pelvis clearly belongs to a bipedal creature. The "blades" are flatter and more curved than those of the gorilla, forming a kind of basket to hold the viscera of an erect animal.*

These zones may have isolated some populations from each other. Evolutionary theory predicts that small isolated populations are more likely to diverge from each other through the process of genetic drift (see Chapter 5). A beneficial mutation has a better chance of becoming established in a small population that is reproductively isolated from other groups and subject to stringent selection. In other words, in a large population spread over a wide range, some individuals may escape strong negative selection whether because conditions are not equally harsh across the entire range or because the population includes some individuals whose genetic fitness is greater in the face of adverse conditions. A smaller population with a narrow geographical range is vulnerable to "all-or-nothing" conditions.

The identity of the earliest hominid remains a mystery. Unfortunately, there is a gap in the fossil record from about 12 MYA to 4 MYA, between the apes ancestral to hominids and the first hominids themselves. This is not the only "missing link" in paleoanthropology; however, it is a particularly intriguing one, because it covers the time when the transition to bipedalism occurred. Better knowledge of this period will provide evidence about the selective pressures that led to the development of the characteristic hominid traits.

The Evolution of Bipedalism

Many anthropologists believe that the earliest hominids evolved from a species that moved out of a forest habitat to a variegated woodland and savanna niche, occasionally coming out from under the cool forest cover into the blazing savanna sun. We might say that our ancestors "came down from the trees," since most of our primate ancestors were arboreal. However, we do not know whether the closest Miocene ancestor of the hominids was arboreal, terrestrial, or some combination. One possibility is that the early savanna-dwelling hominids were like modern baboons. They would spend most daylight hours on the ground and then seek the shelter of treetops for resting and sleeping.

The first trait that distinguishes the hominid line from the apes is not a large brain or the ability to make tools but specialized bipedalism. This adaptation required extensive modifications of the pelvis, legs, feet, and vertebral column (Figure 6.9). An ape has a hard time standing upright, partly because it is top-heavy. The design of the pelvis and spine pushes it forward onto all fours. Hominid pelvises, by comparison, are wider, providing a more stable base for erect posture (see Figure 6.9). The hominid vertebral column is unique among vertebrates. It forms an S curve, better distributing the weight of the torso and supporting

Figure 6.10 *The gorilla has difficulty walking upright because of the structure of its spine and pelvis. It has to use its arms and knuckles to support the weight of its upper body.*

the head. Consider the gorilla, a related primate that lacks the double-curved spine. For a gorilla, standing up requires constant strain to prevent the weight of its heavy torso, long arms, and head from pulling it over onto its face. The gorilla is not a good bipedal walker. Its normal gait is **knuckle walking**, with the forward weight carried by its curled-up fingers (Figure 6.10).

What selective pressures led to the development of bipedalism? Some anthropologists suggest that bipedalism adapted hominids to look over the tall savanna grass and scan the horizon for food and possible predators. Others have speculated that early bipedal hominids were more effective hunters because they could run down game, perhaps carrying weapons. Recent evidence suggests, however, that our earliest ancestors were not savanna hunters but scavengers, eating the remains of the prey of other predators or even animals that died naturally. Hunting was probably not part of their life-style and thus not a selective factor (Binford 1981, Walker 1981, Bunn and Kroll 1986, Box 6.2). If the forelimbs are not used for walking, they can be

turned to other useful purposes such as tool making and carrying food. But tool making and food carrying could not have been the original selective factors (see the discussion of teleology in Box 5.2), especially since we know that bipedalism occurred at least 1 million years before the earliest signs of tool use.

Other investigators disagree with the idea that bipedalism was adaptive to looking over high grass or running. Almost all primates can stand up at least to see over the grass, and many can climb trees for that purpose. Anthropologist Owen Lovejoy (1981) suggested that bipedalism need not give the hunter an advantage. The swiftest humans are far slower than many quadrupeds, including some monkeys. Lovejoy believes that bipedalism was selected because **birth spacing** (the interval between births) in the protohominids was shortened. This change could have been an adaptation to higher infant mortality caused by rapidly changing savanna environment and the harsher conditions. Living in the open without the protection of trees could have made infants more vul-

---

knuckle walking Semierect quadrupedalism, using the knuckles (instead of the palms) for support; an ape characteristic.

birth spacing The interval between births during the reproductive life of a female.

BOX 6.2

Man, the Hunter?

Perhaps the most enduring fallacy of human evolution is that humans are derived from carnivorous, bloodthirsty hunters. A number of additional ideas rest on this one. One popular notion is that human aggression derives from an inborn bloodthirstiness: Early humans were hunters and natural selection favored an aggressive, territorial nature that, in recent times, has turned inward against members of our own species (Robert Ardrey 1976). Closely related to these ideas is the theory that the fundamental instincts of women are different from those of men: Women tend to be passive and patient, tenders of fires and nurturers of babies, while men are the roving, aggressive seekers of game and defenders of the band.

Many of these ideas are based on inaccurate information about the actual behavior of hunting-gathering peoples. These are groups who subsist primarily by consuming wild animal and vegetable foods. They are known from a few contemporary examples and from archaeological remains. Only recently have detailed studies been made of the diets of these groups. The results have shown that, except for groups living near the polar zones, hunter-gatherer diets are based more on wild vegetable food than on meat. Second, in many hunter-gatherer groups, women are the primary providers of food, both in energy content and bulk. There are even some societies, such as the Agta hunters of the Philippines, where women do a significant amount of game hunting (Estioko-Griffin 1986). Third, many hunter-gatherer groups are not territorial, that is, they do not defend a defined area against outside intrusions. Often bands of hunter-gatherers cross over the customary ranges of other bands. Fourth, the composition of hunting bands tends to be unstable. People, usually family groups, move back and forth between bands as whim dictates or as food supplies fluctuate. Finally, contemporary hunter-gatherer males are not noticeably more aggressive or violent than the men of other societies.

Some viewpoints concerning early hominids were formed by comparing them to living groups of primates in environments thought to be similar to those of early hominids. During the 1960s, the predominant model was that of the group-living savanna baboon of East Africa. These baboons display a great degree of **sexual dimorphism**; the males are nearly twice the size of the females. Baboons are primarily **herbivores** (plant eaters), although they occasionally prey on small, defenseless animals. The large males, with their formidable canine teeth, play the role of defenders of the band. They face down and fight off, if necessary, leopards and other beasts as the band feeds on the open savannas. In some of the large bands, there is a well-developed hierarchy, with the males occupying all the top spots.

More recent research has tended to compare early humans to chimpanzees. Chimpanzees are apes more closely related than baboons to the hominids. They inhabit tropical forests in Africa, living in social groups. Sexual dimorphism is less pronounced: Females are nearly the same size as males, but selection for large males may be lower for the forest-dwelling chimps because nearby trees make it easier to escape from predators. Female chimps share food with their young and are highly protective of them. Like the baboons, chimps occasionally kill and eat other animals.

The evidence available so far suggests that early hominids were not sharply dimorphic. Some investigators (Tanner 1981, Zihlmann 1978) suggest that early hominid females were the first innovators of technology because of the heavy demands placed on them by subsistence pursuits, pregnancy, **lactation**, and child rearing. Nancy Tanner suggests that early stone tools were used not so much for cutting up game as for digging up, cutting up, and mashing plants. Bipedalism may have been particularly advantageous to females because it left the hands free for carrying children, food, and other materials from place to place. There is insufficient evidence to get much beyond these suggestions of female priority. Their utility lies primarily in forcing investigators to go beyond culture-bound gender stereotypes in thinking about human behavior.

nerable to predators and other hazards such as dehydration (even today, the major world cause of infant deaths). In this scenario, females would have spent more time caring for infants and would have been more dependent on mates for food during pregnancy and after childbirth. Bipedalism would have allowed females without infants and males to carry food to the less mobile females and offspring.

Sharing of food between a mated pair and between parent and offspring is common in wolves, several species of birds, and other species. Sharing allows for a "division of labor" in which one animal collects food while the other cares for the young. A major criticism of this hypothesis is its presumption of monogamous matings. Yet the basic scheme would work just as well if food were simply shared within a group consisting of various males, females, and juveniles.

Clifford Jolly (1970) offers a related hypothesis; he suggests that specialized seed gathering favored increased manual dexterity. This may have advanced selection for bipedalism, which frees the forelimbs for manual activities, and may have eventually led to tool use. These hypotheses are notable for the difficulty of testing them. Nonetheless, they may all have operated in the evolution of our basic hominid traits.

Whichever creature first ventured out of the forest onto the savanna came well equipped. It had good eyesight and good hand-eye coordination. It had a larger brain than most animals its size. It had hands and feet capable of grasping and manipulating objects and possibly even throwing things as some modern monkeys and apes do. Quite probably it was also a social animal, sharing food to some extent with members of its social group and depending on shared knowledge. On the other hand, its sense of smell was probably less acute than that of other terrestrial animals, because it had lost some of this ability during millions of years living in trees.

IDENTIFYING THE FIRST HOMINIDS

The first Plio-Pleistocene fossil identified as a hominid was the skull of a child about six years of age. It was found in 1924 at Taung, South Africa, and described by the late Raymond Dart, an anatomist by training. Since that time, thousands of fragments of these first hominids—named *Australopithecus,* or "Southern ape," by Dart—have been discovered in South Africa, Kenya, Tanzania, and Ethiopia (Figure 6.11). There are considerable differences among the fossils, and the total sample is still small. Only one nearly complete skeleton has ever been recovered—that of Lucy,

found in 1974 (see Chapter 1). The traits of these fossils, including bipedalism, fully erect posture, and relatively small teeth and jaws, are distinctive enough to separate them from other primate populations and to nominate certain of them as candidates for the ancestors of *Homo*.

By the late 1940s australopithecines had been found at five different sites in South Africa, with dates estimated at 3 to 1 MYA. The principal basis for dating has been the other fossils found nearby, but some of the hominid fossils still could not be dated firmly. The South African australopithecine remains were deposited not in neat sedimentary beds but in limestone caves formed by water and later filled in by dissolved minerals. The fossils had literally dropped in from above. One investigator speculated that these early hominids had been the meals of leopards who had dragged their prey up into trees and allowed the bones to fall off into the cave mouth.

The *Australopithecus* bones from South Africa belonged to creatures who had some apelike and some humanlike traits. Early australopithecines were chimp-sized animals who walked on two feet. Their heads, teeth, pelvises, arms, and legs all show important similarities to *Homo* and differences from other primates. But there are also many apelike features. The jaws jut forward, unlike the relatively flat faces of later hominids. The brain is about the size of a chimpanzee's (Box 6.3). A thick bone ridge appears over the eyes. The skulls of some of the larger australopithecines have a longitudinal ridge, or **sagittal crest**, that extended the area of attachment for massive jaw muscles (Figure 6.12).

The humanlike features include the pelvic bones (see Figure 6.9), which are wider and flatter than those of apes and serve as a "basket" to support a heavy load of internal organs within an upright torso. The bones of the legs and their attachment to the pelvis clearly belong to a habitual biped. Besides locomotion, perhaps the most human thing about the australopithecines were their teeth. Ape teeth are arranged in a U shape, with opposites sides roughly parallel. Hominid teeth form a parabola (see Figure 6.8). Aus-

---

sexual dimorphism   The occurrence of two distinct forms, based on gender, in the same species.

herbivore   A plant eater.

lactation   The production of milk from mammary glands.

sagittal crest   A ridge of bone that extends down the midline of the cranium and serves as a muscle attachment.

Figure 6.11   *The oldest known hominid fossils, the australopithecines, were all found in East and South Africa. There is little doubt that humans evolved in Africa, since no hominid fossils of this age have ever been found elsewhere.*

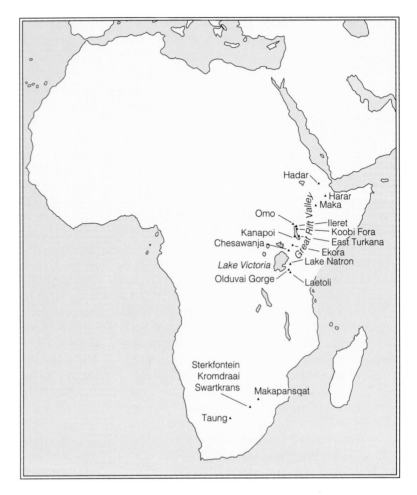

tralopithecine teeth are larger than those of modern humans, but the canines do not project beyond the level of the other teeth as they do in apes.

Gracile and Robust Australopithecines

As the fossil collections grew, it became evident that some South African australopithecines were larger and more ruggedly built than others (see Figure 6.12). When better dates became available, it appeared that the "robust" forms were later in time than the slighter "gracile" forms. The difference was large enough to lead anthropologists to divide the two forms into separate species, referred to as **Australopithecus africanus** for the gracile finds at Taung, Sterkfontein, and

Makapansgat and **Australopithecus robustus** for the larger forms found at Swartkrans and Kromdraai (see Figure 6.12).

The *A. africanus* fossils were generally smaller with lighter frames and more delicate bones and protruding jaws, while *A. robustus* had massive brow ridges, huge jawbones, and wider, flatter faces (see Figure 6.12). In the past anthropologists disagreed about the evolutionary relationship of these two forms. Recent dating, as well as the similarity of basic features such as brain size and their shared geographical location, suggest that the lighter (gracile) form is the ancestor of the heavier (robust) form. These australopithecines might be thought of as belonging to a single evolutionary line characterized by increasing robustness as an adaptation to an increasingly vegetarian diet as reflected in the large teeth and jaws of *A. robustus*.

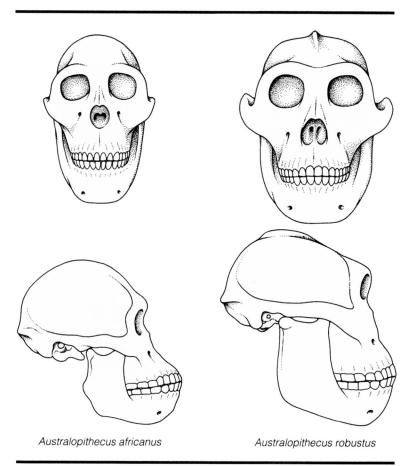

Figure 6.12 *The two major South African australopithecine fossils. On the left, A. africanus, the relatively light-boned, "gracile" form; on the right, A. robustus, the larger, heavier form. Note the wider face, massive jaws, and saggital crest of A. robustus, suggesting much heavier musculature. The robust forms had slightly larger brains than the gracile, but this may have been simply because of their larger overall size.*

Australopithecus africanus   *Australopithecus robustus*

The australopithecine question became even more complicated in 1959 when the famous Kenyan paleoanthropologists Louis and Mary Leakey found a robust australopithecine in the Olduvai Gorge, Tanzania. Olduvai is a deeply eroded canyon (Figure 6.13) with strata that are perfectly horizontal and provide what the South African sites could not: secure dates. Hominid finds were associated with fossils of established age. Moreover, because some of the layers were of volcanic origin, the potassium-argon dating technique could be employed. The robust form from Olduvai was dated 1.75 MYA, which was, at the time, the oldest verified date for a human ancestor.

The Leakeys named the fossil **Zinjanthropus boisei** ("Zinj" for short) to the dismay of other paleontologists, who thought it was too similar to the South African robust fossils to be considered a separate genus. Zinj was a very robust australopithecine, perhaps different enough to warrant a separate species name but not so different as to be placed in a separate genus. Eventually it was renamed *Australopithecus boisei.*

Australopithecus africanus Genus and species taxa for bipedal, gracile hominids that lived in southern Africa between 3 and 2.2 MYA.

Australopithecus robustus Genus and species taxa for bipedal, robust hominids that lived in southern Africa between 2.2 and 1.5 MYA.

Zinjanthropus boisei An extremely robust australopithecine that lived from 2 to 1 MYA; now called *Australopithecus boisei.*

BOX 6.3

What's in a Braincase?

Homo sapiens probably has the most complex brain of any organism. The evidence for this assertion comes primarily from a comparison of human abilities with those of other species. The human brain is capable of sophisticated symbolic communication, virtually unlimited information storage, and the complex thinking that underlies human social organization and developed technology. This comparative evidence is supported by careful examination of the thinking organ itself.

First of all, human brains are larger in proportion to body size than those of most other species. But human brains differ in more than just size. An ape brain does not look very different from a human brain: Both are "a pinkish-grey mass . . . perched like a flower on top of a slender stalk" (Campbell 1985, 48). Part of the difference lies in the **neocortex**, a thin gray layer that covers most of the surface of the brain. The neocortex plays a major role in problem solving, memory, abstract thought, the delicate movements of the hands that allow humans to make tools, and the vocal apparatus that allows them to communicate. This portion of the brain is much smaller in apes.

The neocortex constitutes 80 percent of the volume of the human brain. It is deeply folded, as if crushed to fit into the small space afforded by the skull. This is what gives the brain its convoluted appearance. So busy is the brain that its cells require 20 percent of the body's blood flow to supply the organ with energy and to carry off waste products.

Little is known about the functioning of the neocortex, but it is known to consist of billions of **neurons** (specialized nerve cells), joined by **synapses**, which allow very efficient, high-speed storage, retrieval, and processing of information. It is highly flexible in that it can be "reprogrammed" through experience to respond to new information flowing in from nerves elsewhere in the brain and throughout the body.

No computer ever built can come close to a single brain in storage and processing power. The way it processes data is unlike any computer ever built. Computer programmers have managed to design programs to make humanlike choices under restricted conditions, such as playing chess. But even the designers of artificial intelligence programs acknowledge that machines are far from achieving humanlike capabilities.

The human brain is the product of millions of years of evolution. Some information on its evolutionary development can be gleaned by comparing it with the brains of nonhuman primates and other species. But because it is a soft body part and consequently not preserved in fossils, there is little information about the specific path of development of the human brain to be found in the fossil record. The best information comes simply from the gross comparison of brain size measured by the interior volume of the brain case. The surface of the neocortex does, however, leave a faint imprint on the inside surface of the brain case. Studies of brain-damaged persons have enabled neurologists to identify two areas on the neocortex, **Broca's area** and

Australopithecus Afarensis

The picture was to become more complex following discoveries made by a joint French-American expedition exploring the Afar region of northern Ethiopia (see Figure 1.4). We have already heard part of that story in Chapter 1's section about Donald Johanson and Tom Gray's discovery of Lucy. Hadar, another desolate region of Ethiopia, yielded still more treasures: 200 hominid fragments representing at least 13 individuals, all with the same basic characteristics as Lucy. Johanson speculated that this may have been a family group that perished in a flash flood, hence the nickname "the first family." These remains were dated at 3.5 MYA, making them among the oldest hominid fossils known and nearly doubling the estimated age of the beginnings of bipedal walking. Their small brains and generally apelike features prompted Johanson to place them in a separate australopithecine species. Johanson called them *Australopithecus afarensis,* and he suggested that they represented the ancestors of all later australopithecines and *Homo.*

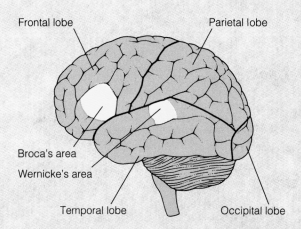

Frontal lobe   Parietal lobe

Broca's area
Wernicke's area

Temporal lobe   Occipital lobe

The development of the brain is probably the most important feature of human evolution. As the brain became more complex, humans were increasingly able to use their mental abilities to adapt to their environment. Among those abilities were language and speech, in which Broca's and Wernicke's areas of the brain play important roles.

Cranial Capacity of Representative Primates

Species	Cranial Capacity	
	Average (cc)	*Range (cc)*
Lemur	*	10–70
Chimpanzee	383	282–500
Gorilla	505	340–752
Australopithecus africanus	450	435–530
Australopithecus robustus	500	*
Homo habilis	680	*
Homo erectus	950	775–1225
Homo sapiens neandertalensis	1450	*
Homo sapiens sapiens	1330	1200–1800

*A missing value indicates that a representative population of this species has not been assembled and measured for the purpose of determining cranial capacity.

Wernicke's area, which are important in producing and comprehending speech, respectively. Some anthropologists now think they are able to identify these areas in the fossil **endocasts** of hominid brains (Hollo- way 1978). If these findings are verified, we might tentatively conclude that the neurological capacity for developed language occurred in *Homo* about 1 MYA, in the *Homo erectus* stage.

---

neocortex   The thin gray layer that covers most of the surface of the brain.

neurons   Specialized nerve cells.

synapse   The point at which nervous impulses pass from one neuron to the next. In humans synapses are structured to allow very efficient, high-speed storage, retrieval, and processing of information.

Broca's area   A portion of the neocortex, important in the production of speech.

Wernicke's area   A portion of the neocortex of the human brain, important in the understanding of speech.

endocast   A plaster cast of the inside of the brain case, used to determine the size and complexity of the brain.

Figure 6.13 *Olduvai Gorge in Tanzania, site of many important and well-dated hominid fossil finds, including "Zinjanthropus" and* Homo habilis.

In 1976 Mary Leakey discovered a remarkable set of footprints in ancient volcanic ash at the site of Laetoli, Tanzania. Examination of the prints showed that they were made by three bipedal hominids, two adults and a juvenile. The date of the ash indicated that these hominids left their prints 3.7 MYA (Figure 6.14). This was striking confirmation of Johanson's finding of bipedal hominids of great antiquity.

Homo Habilis

To complicate matters even further, another fossil hominid turned up at roughly the same stratigraphic level as *A. boisei* in the Leakeys' 1959 discovery at Olduvai. This discovery required a reinterpretation of an entire period of hominid evolution. The new fossil was similar to *Australopithecus* in several respects: It had large teeth, heavy ridges over the eyes, and a low cranial vault. But the pockets between the eyes (best seen from a top view of the cranium) were shallower, and the skull itself had thinner walls. This left room for a larger brain, 680 cc, versus an average of 450 cc for *Australopithecus*. Before the discovery of this fossil and others like it, paleoanthropologists had somewhat arbitrarily set a threshold brain size of 750 cc for membership in the genus *Homo*. But the **hablines**, as they were known, were distinct from the australopithecines in the respects mentioned above. They also had hands and feet that were similar to anatomically modern *Homo,* although the hands are unusually muscular. Although dating from 2.5 MYA, these fossils were just too much like humans to be seen as australopithecines.

Figure 6.14 *Hominid footprints at Laetoli, probably the most studied footprints in history. They were formed by hominids walking through freshly deposited volcanic ash. A light rain wet the ash and it set like cement. The footprints demonstrate that human ancestors living 3.7 MYA walked much as modern humans do today.*

Hablines have been unearthed in various East African sites, but there is still considerable controversy surrounding them. Louis Leakey's interpretation suggests that *Homo* and the australopithecines coexisted in Africa for as much as 1 million years, until finally the smaller-brained hominids became extinct and the larger-brained *H. habilis* continued to evolve, leading eventually to *H. erectus* and *H. sapiens*. If this is so, we may wonder how the two got along for all that time, especially if their niche requirements were similar.

Early Hominid Culture

The most remarkable thing about the Olduvai bed that yielded *Australopithecus boisei* and *Homo habilis* was the discovery of crude stone tools (Figure 6.15) with the same date as the fossils, 1.75 MYA. Unfortunately, neither genus was associated directly with the stone tools, so it cannot be determined who made them. Leakey concluded that it was *H. habilis,* which is why he dubbed the fossils *Homo habilis,* or "handy man." Many anthropologists agree, but there is no way currently of confirming this. After the Leakeys' discoveries at Olduvai, even older tools dating to 2.6 MYA were found in the Afar region of Ethiopia. Similar tools occur at Lake Turkana, Koobi Fora, and other Kenyan sites dating from 2.0 to 1.5 MYA. These **pebble tools** are generally called **Oldowan choppers.**

These earliest of all stone tools are known as **core tools.** They were made by striking a pebble core with another rock, a technique known as **percussion flaking.** If the blow was correctly aimed, it knocked chips

---

hablines Members of the species *Homo habilis,* dating from 2.5 to 1.5 million years ago; probably the first tool makers.

pebble tools See Oldowan choppers.

Oldowan choppers Relatively simple stone tools associated with *Homo habilis* at a site dated to 2 MYA, made by striking a few flakes off a stone core to make a sharp edge.

core tools Stone tools made from the core of a pebble by striking off flakes to create a sharp edge.

percussion flaking Production of stone tools by striking a hammerstone against a core.

of rock off the edge of the core, leaving it sharp and suitable for cutting or chopping (see Figure 6.15). The flakes struck off the core could also be used for such jobs as scraping animal skins and cutting soft material. Simple **hammerstones** (made with little or no flaking) were used to crush bone or seeds. The quality of workmanship suggests that these tools were made not by specialists but by the same individuals who used them, without great care.

Archaeologists have learned to produce close replicas of 2-million-year-old tools. These replicas are capable of cutting through the thick skin and sinews of large animals like giraffes and of crushing bones to expose the edible marrow (see Figure 10.7). Other tools made with the same technique can be used to scrape animal skins, crush nuts and seeds, punch holes in wood or hides, and perform other tasks. The sharpness of these tools depended partly on the type of stone used and partly on the skill of the maker. These tools were hand held rather than **hafted** (attached to handles or shafts). Although crude and of limited use, these **lithic assemblages** (collections of stone tools) are the earliest known examples of cultural artifacts, clues to the existence of a socially transmitted cultural tradition.

We don't know whether early hominids used fire. Anthropologists C. K. Brain and Andrew Sillen (1988) have described charred animal bones on the floor of a South African cave. These bones, deposited in little piles in different parts of the cave, were dated to 1.5 MYA. These are the earliest evidence yet of the deliberate use of fire by hominids, but there is considerable skepticism about whether these very ancient fires were actually set by hominids.

For many years, the weight of opinion was that early hominids subsisted primarily by hunting (see Box 6.2). This theory, known as **central place foraging** (CPF), is based on the idea that early hominids were bipedal, tool-using hunters who lived in central campsites, went out hunting, and brought back their kills to the camp to share with others. One of the most carefully studied sites to yield data on this topic was the Olduvai Gorge, which was meticulously excavated by Louis and Mary Leakey. In one location, called DK, Bed I showed a stone ring about 5 m (16 ft) in diameter. Inside and around the circle were found numerous bone fragments of extinct cattle and other animal species, along with various Oldowan tools such as choppers, scrapers, and hammerstones (see Figure

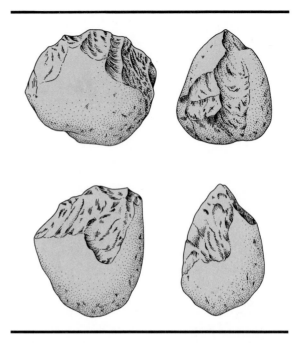

Figure 6.15   *Oldowan tools, dating from 2 to 1.5 MYA. These earliest stone tools were made by striking flakes off a rounded "core," usually of lava or quartz, to produce rough cutting edges. They could have been used for such tasks as cutting through bone and muscle, scraping meat from skin, and sharpening sticks. Making these tools required knowledge of appropriate materials, accuracy in striking the rock, and skill in exerting the right amount of force.*

6.15). The Leakeys and other investigators concluded that the site was a central campsite to which hunters dragged their prey and where they worked on tools, butchered the meat, and shared it with others. This practice, if confirmed, would represent a major step in social evolution.

Beginning in 1981 a number of investigators began a series of **taphonomic** studies to evaluate in detail the fashion in which the bones found at Olduvai and other sites happened to be deposited. Are there any other conditions, other than hunting and transport by hominid agents, that could account for the high density of animal bones mixed with tools? In a particularly searching reevaluation, archaeologist Lewis Binford (1981) compared the scatter of bones left by other contemporary hunting peoples and predatory animals. His conclusions were as follows:

> The only clear picture is that of a hominid scavenging the kills and death sites of other predator-scavengers for abandoned anatomical parts of low food utility, primarily for purposes of extracting bone marrow. . . . There is no evidence of "carrying food home." Transport of the scavenged parts away from the kill site to more protected locations in a manner identical to that of all other scavengers is all that one need imagine to account for the unambiguous facts preserved in Olduvai. [Binford 1981, 282]

Subsequent microscopic analyses of the bone fragments themselves showed that many of them had been chewed on by carnivores, although the question of whether the hominids or the hyenas got first crack at the bones is not easy to resolve. It now appears that early hominids were probably not hunters at all but scavengers, like hyenas or jackals, arriving after the kill to glean the scraps left behind by larger predators that were better equipped for hunting, killing, and ripping open the prey. "Anatomically, the early hominids were not well equipped for ripping apart and eating large pieces of raw meat. They may have used flakes of chipped stone to accomplish this, although this question is controversial" (Bunn and Kroll 1986).

On the other hand, there is little evidence that the early hominids were heavy consumers of plant seeds or grasses. Grinding down seeds or tough blades of grass would have caused considerable wear on their teeth. Microscopic analysis of australopithecine teeth does not reveal this kind of wear. If early hominids were neither game hunters nor intensive gatherers, what did they eat? It is possible that early hominids were omnivores like the chimpanzee, but dental evidence indicates that they relied primarily on tender morsels of meat, young shoots of plants, roots and tubers, and occasionally nuts and seeds.

The evidence concerning early hominid patterns of sharing and social interaction, habitation, and other behavior is even thinner. Binford asks, "Did early man sleep on the ground and consume food at a 'base,' or did he simply range, consuming food where it was found, sleeping in the trees as do most other primates?" (Binford 1983). We do not yet know.

Interpretation of the Early Hominids

What was the relationship of the various hominid species that lived in Africa during the Plio-Pleistocene period? As you recall, species are populations unable to interbreed with other populations and produce viable, fertile offspring. It is impossible to determine whether extinct organisms interbred or not, so the investigator is left to make educated guesses. A well-confirmed ecological generalization, the **law of competitive exclusion**, states that two organisms with identical niche requirements cannot coexist in the same habitat. To settle the matter once and for all about the early hominids requires more knowledge than we now have about their diets and other environmental requirements. But we are able to draw some tentative conclusions on the basis of their anatomy, their geographical locations, and the general features of their environments, though anthropologists are by no means in complete agreement.

Most anthropologists agree that *H. habilis* deserves a place as the ancestor to all later *Homo* species. They disagree, however, about the relationship between the hablines and the australopithecines. The late Louis Leakey and his supporters place *Homo* very early in hominid evolution, so that all varieties of *Australopithecus* come later and none is ancestral to *Homo sapiens* (Figure 6.16). If they are right, earlier *Homo* fossils should eventually be found.

---

hammerstone   A stone showing little or no modification by humans, used in percussion flaking and crushing seeds and bones.

hafted   Attached to a handle or shaft.

lithic assemblage   The array of stone tools found at an archaeological site.

central place foraging (CPF)   The theory that early humans were bipedal, tool-using hunters who made base camp-sites, went out hunting, and brought their kills back to share at their campsite.

taphonomic   Pertaining to the process of deposition of bones and other materials at an archaeological site.

law of competitive exclusion   An ecological generalization stating that two organisms with identical niche requirements cannot coexist in the same habitat.

Figure 6.16 *Alternative phylogenies proposed by Richard Leakey and Donald Johanson to explain Lucy's place in hominid evolution, as well as the timing of the split between the australopithecine and Homo line. The number of known fossil hominids is still so small that the data support a large number of alternative explanations. As new discoveries are made and better analysis is done, it gradually becomes possible to discard certain theories and refine others.*

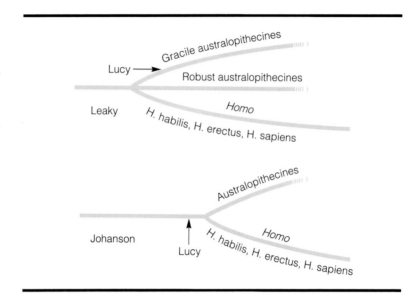

On the other hand, Johanson and a majority of paleoanthropologists place *A. afarensis* at the base of hominid evolution with *H. habilis* as a descendent and a bridge to modern *Homo*. *Australopithecus africanus* and *A. robustus,* as in Leakey's scheme, are also descendants from *A. afarensis* that became extinct. This picture seems to be the most widely accepted for now. Some investigators, however, still place *A. africanus* in the lineage leading to *H. sapiens* (Skelton, McHenry, and Drawhorn 1986). Some of them see *Homo habilis* simply as an advanced form of *Australopithecus africanus*.

The arguments proceed on different levels with appeals to many different sources of evidence and methods of interpretation. Some paleoanthropologists seem to have a vested interest in seeing fossils they discovered themselves viewed as directly ancestral to modern humans. What many people assume to be a dull, tedious occupation has attracted some of the most flamboyant personalities in modern science; these individuals defend their points of view passionately. The remarkable thing is that the entire debate on the australopithecines and early *Homo* is based on a small collection of fossils. Only a few dozen well-preserved early hominid skulls have been found. Hundreds of teeth exist, but very few long bones, ribs, or vertebrae have been collected.

As more hominid fossils are discovered, many of these issues may be resolved. Right now it is often hard to tell whether the differences among the fossils represent variation among species or within a species. All species vary, sometimes to a great extent. If we were to examine skeletal populations of modern people, from an area as large as South and East Africa, we would be impressed by the wide range of variation in such features as body height, size, and even cranial capacity. However, since we know the degree of variation within our species, no one would suggest that these people represent different species. How this applies to the hominids of 4–1 MYA remains to be shown conclusively.

The farther back in time the inquiry reaches, the smaller the number of primate fossils available for study. For this reason, whenever a new fossil hominid is found, the chances are great that it lies outside the known range of variation for fossils of comparable age. So for each discovery, researchers must reevaluate established evolutionary relationships, based on the assumption that the fossil represents a new group. If, however, the find is a deviant individual of an already established group, or even a fraud (see Box 6.1), the evaluation changes again. Paleoanthropology is a highly dynamic field, then, with dramatic shifts of opinion as new discoveries are made, analyzed, and reanalyzed.

SUMMARY

- The ancestors of humans can be set in a taxonomic context in different ways, depending on a choice of methodology.
- Humankind arose in Africa after a Miocene divergence between the ancestors of modern monkeys, apes, and hominids.
- There is a dearth of fossil evidence for the period 12 to 5 MYA, the very time when the hominids split off from the pongid line.
- The earliest bipedal primates are from East and South Africa from about 4 to 1 MYA. Collectively known as the australopithecines, these chimp-sized, small-brained, bipedal hominids lived on the open savannas, ate fruits and vegetables, and possibly scavenged for meat. Some interpretations attribute near-human qualities to them. Others see them as more like modern apes than humans.
- It is not certain how many australopithecine lineages there were, or which one was ancestral to *Homo*. The genus *Australopithecus* may include some species such as *afarensis* that were ancestral to *Homo*. But others, such as *A. robustus,* probably died out without leaving descendants.
- We are reasonably certain that *Homo habilis,* with its enlarged brain case and possible use of stone tools, was an ancestor of *Homo erectus.*

GET INVOLVED

1. Go to your local zoo. Make a survey of all the primates there (including *H. sapiens*) and photograph or videotape each one's mode of locomotion. Your images should include details of limbs, hands, feet, and eyes and any variation observed in the behavior of a given species (for example, gorillas sometimes walk on two legs). Consider how the zoo habitat may restrict the range of behavior you are able to observe.

2. Visit your local natural history museum and find out what paleontological collections are available. Pick one of the collections that is fairly extensive and try to get permission to examine it. (Research museums normally have collections much larger than are on display. A museum may not wish to grant access to a person without specific training, so you may need to approach a professional and volunteer your time to get such access.) Using a standard lab manual in paleontology as a guide, or with help from a professional paleontologist, try your hand at measuring some parameter that reflects evolutionary change over time. From the evidence you gather, try to determine what selective influences may have led to the evolutionary change you observed.

SUGGESTED READINGS

Blinderman, Charles. 1986. *The Piltdown inquest.* Buffalo, N.Y.: Prometheus.

Cartmill, Matt, David Pilbeam, and Glynn Isaac. 1986. One hundred years of paleoanthropology. *American Scientist* 74:410–420.

Ciochon, Russell L., and John Fleagle, eds. 1987. *Primate evolution and human origins.* New York: Aldine de Gruyter.

Fossey, Dian. 1983. *Gorillas in the mist.* Boston: Houghton Mifflin.

Goodall, Jane. 1971. *In the shadow of man.* Boston: Houghton Mifflin.

Lewin, Roger. 1987. *Bones of contention: Controversies in the search for human origins.* New York: Simon & Schuster.

Strum, Shirley. 1987. *Almost human: A journey into the world of baboons.* New York: Random House.

ANTHROPOLOGISTS AT WORK

The 2-Million-Year-Old Ancestor

Currently an assistant professor at Rutgers University, Robert J. Blumenschine spent 11 months in the Serengeti National Park and Ngorongoro Crater, Tanzania, studying modern scavenging behavior of African plains animals. On the basis of this data, he offers the following picture of the foraging behavior of early hominids.

Robert Blumenschine examining a carcass.

Imagine you are 4½ feet tall and weigh 100 pounds—one of the bigger members of your small group—and that you cannot speak about the past or future but can only convey anger, alarm, or pleasure about incidents and objects before you. Your thick body hair is your only protection against the night's cold, and your ability to climb trees is your only real safety from the predators that search for food below. True, you are skilled at producing knifelike slivers from rocks to butcher carcasses and jagged-edged blocks to shape sticks for digging out tubers, and you have pitcher Nolan Ryan's aim when throwing lime-sized cobbles at threats. You are also intimately familiar with your range, especially the locations of food and water sources, stone for tools, refuge trees, and predator hangouts. Sometimes you stare uncomprehendingly from your nighttime perch amid wispy acacia branches toward the setting sun; your gnawing stomach, domineering half-brother, itchy flea bites, or the saber-toothed menace below are less evident than the blaze of color you hope to see again in the morning.

Stripped of our clothes, half our neurons, and all but the most rudimentary elements of material culture, and placed in a remote wildlife area of the vast savanna woodlands of tropical Africa, we might begin to imagine what life was like for our ancestors 2 MYA. These earliest members of the genus *Homo*, found mainly in East Africa, are known from a small number of fossils and archaeological sites containing the earliest stone tools, often interspersed with the fragmented bones of animals such as fish, antelopes, pigs, and giraffe.

Attempts to reconstruct the extinct life-styles of early *Homo* are complicated by the extremely sparse and fragmentary nature of the fossil evidence. The hominid fossils indicate a generalized, omnivorous diet, a bipedal gait, a tree-climbing ability greater than ours, and manipulation and intellectual skills greater than those of any living ape. The archaeological sites bear witness to behaviors different in degree, and perhaps in kind, from those seen in our closest extant relatives, including production of flaked stone tools transported from remote locations to places where large animals were butchered and consumed. The sediments in which the hominid fossils and stone artifacts are found indicate that hominids were spending at least part of their time in lakeside or riverine settings. But there is no direct fossil evidence conveying information about life-style, such as whether meat was hunted or scavenged, how large social groups were, or what kind of relationships prevailed among individuals. The task of physical anthropologists and archaeologists trying to understand early hominid life is like trying to reconstruct a modern human's life experience from some tattered dental and medical records, an incomplete shopping list for the grocery or hardware store, written in a language that no one speaks, and some blurry and underexposed videos of the places the person lived and visited.

How can we go beyond the limited direct evidence for ancient life-styles? Much recent paleoanthropological research has focused on

Sunset in the Serengeti

deciphering the behavioral signals encoded in fossils and artifacts. To do this we must observe modern behaviors and other processes that produce or modify the kinds of traces we find in the fossil record.

My own work in the Serengeti National Park of Tanzania is designed to answer questions about how the animal bones found at archaeological sites can reveal whether early hominids acquired meat and marrow through hunting or through scavenging. Hunting has traditionally been assumed to be the method used by hominids, and as such has been heralded in the "man the hunter" model as the fundamental driving force behind the evolution of human tool use, intellect, and cooperative social organization. Scavenging, on the other hand has been assumed to be too risky, unprofitable, and irregular to account for the bones at the early sites and to have influenced the course of human evolution.

For almost a year I observed the location and condition of carcasses, from antelopes to elephants, to see if the amount of food left on them by lions, spotted hyenas, cheetah, vultures, and jackals would provide food for a scavenger that foraged during the day with stone tools.

I found that carcasses consumed by spotted hyenas only rarely provided a scavenging opportunity. Hyenas typically feed in large groups and are able to consume all edible parts, including marrow contained in the long bones and brains of even large animals, because of the prodigious bone-crushing ability of their robust teeth and powerful jaws. Animals killed in open plains habitats by lions and cheetah, which have weaker jaws and are therefore unable to access the marrow and brains of larger animals, still provide poor feeding opportunities, because hyenas are common on the plains and will quickly and completely scavenge any food that remains. During dry

periods, however, lions often ambush prey seeking water in the woodlands surrounding rivers and lakes. Because hyenas do not frequent such riparian woodland habitats, abandoned lion kills, which are defleshed but still contain high-calorie marrow and brain, persist as rich food resources for longer periods.

After my year in Africa, my student John Cavallo, another dirt-archaeologist lured to the Serengeti, documented how the leopard's habit of storing kills in trees and abandoning them for long periods during the day may have provided early hominids with an additional source of marrow and meat. Such a dual, arboreal-terrestrial scavenging strategy may have been sufficiently predictable, productive and safe to account for many of the animal bones at the early archaeological sites. Such a strategy could have selected for tool use, planning, and coordination among members of hominid groups usually attributed to a hunting way of life.

Relating the feeding habits of predators to the bones they leave behind allows us to predict the types and condition of bones that should occur at archaeological sites if hominids scavenged on a regular basis. The validity of our behavioral reconstructions must ultimately rest on tests against the fossil evidence and not upon analogy to the life-styles of modern animals like ourselves. But we can only hope to learn how to read the most cryptically encoded behavioral signals if we can conceive all aspects of prehistoric life-styles. I have often pondered some of these while relaxing on a hilltop overlooking a stream during a Serengeti sunset, when the predators emerge in force and the primates go to sleep.

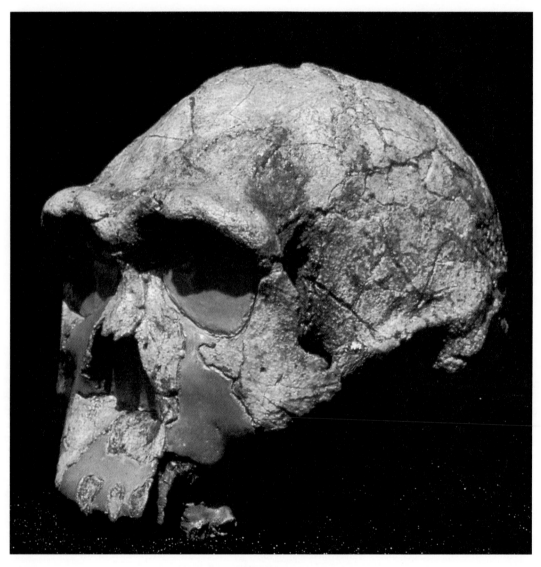

One of the oldest Homo erectus *skulls discovered to date, KNM-ER-3733, was found at Lake Turkana, Kenya, and dates to about 1.6 MYA.*

7

THE RISE OF THE GENUS *HOMO*

▲▲▲

ost of the animals we discussed in the last chapter were located along the evolutionary pathway that led to *Homo sapiens,* but they were not humans. If Lucy were to be found walking around downtown Toledo, she would probably be a disappointment to anyone who tried to interview her. In behavior, and possibly in ability to communicate, she might be more like modern apes than humans. Still, Lucy and her kind set the stage for future advances. From a quadrupedal, tree-dwelling creature emerged a bipedal, ground-dwelling, toolmaking, and possibly fire-using creature that may have had advanced social and communication skills. Its brain was only slightly larger than a chimpanzee's, but it may have had a greater capacity for socially learned (cultural) behavior than other apes. There is no evidence for such familiar artifacts of culture as shelter, clothing, language, art, or a complex division of labor, but some of these may have been present. We can be sure, however, that *Australopithecus* was a far cry from modern humans.

It may be helpful to elaborate on what we mean by *human,* before carrying the discussion further. We shall assume the principal characteristics of early hominids, just mentioned, and focus on the incremental traits that are distinctively human. Humans have a precision grip that gives them a broader range of abilities than other primates. This is related to their larger, more complex brains. Human babies come into the world largely undeveloped. They must undergo a long period of physical and social growth before they are able to fend for themselves. Thus, human social groups are highly organized and rely on a store of socially transmitted information and habits (that is, culture) that includes the manufacture of tools, devices built to solve certain problems. In brief, humans are bipedal, large-brained, toolmaking, tool-using, social primates with stereoscopic vision and prehensile, opposable thumbs, born undeveloped and requiring a long socialization period during which they acquire a large body of socially transmitted knowledge.

Taken together these traits describe humanity. The traits did not appear at the same time, nor are they exclusive to our species. Some of them, like stereoscopic vision, prehensile hands, and social cooperation, are characteristic of most primate species. Other traits, such as toolmaking, occur in only a few species.

Some people prefer the definition of *human* to refer to spiritual and intellectual qualities. Evidence of **spir**ituality—understood as a belief in the soul and in powers beyond the material forces of nature—can be seen in ritual burials made by Neandertals (early *Homo sapiens*) as far back as 50,000 years ago (Solecki 1971). It may be that humans are the most spiritual of all animals. They may also be the most *rational.* Spirituality and rationality are difficult to define precisely, however, and we cannot identify exactly when they arose in our evolution. We also cannot communicate well enough with other species to determine how rational or spiritual they may be. Because there is no scientific way of defining such traits, anthropologists do not generally include them in the definition. They rely instead on measurable traits, such as mode of locomotion and size of braincase.

Contemporary theorists interpret the major events in the origins of humans in terms of natural selection. That is, the environment shaped the species as it developed and made it what it is today. However, the evolution of humans was not inevitable; and given different conditions, it might not have occurred. Moreover, we should not suppose that *Homo sapiens* is the ultimate product of evolutionary change. Evolution is still going on in human populations, as shown in chapters 5 and 8. There is no scientific reason for believing that *H. sapiens* is the most perfect product of nature.

EVOLUTION AND EXPANSION: *HOMO ERECTUS*

Australopithecus either died out or evolved into another species. After about 1.5 MYA, all hominid fossils are clearly *Homo* with its large brain and lithic tool traditions. The best known early humans are called *Homo erectus* (upright man). It is clear, however, that in spite of the name, *H. erectus* was not the first hominid to stand up on two legs. When *H. erectus* appeared on the scene, hominids had been walking bipedally for over 2 million years. But however well the australopithecines walked, they apparently never walked out of Africa. The dispersion of *Homo* to the remainder of the Old World (Europe, Africa, and Asia) was left to *H. erectus.* While all early hominid sites discussed so far are in East and South Africa, *H. erectus* sites are also found in China, Java, North Africa, and Europe (Figure 7.1).

Compared to the complex situation of the earlier hominids, that of *H. erectus* is simple. Based on mor-

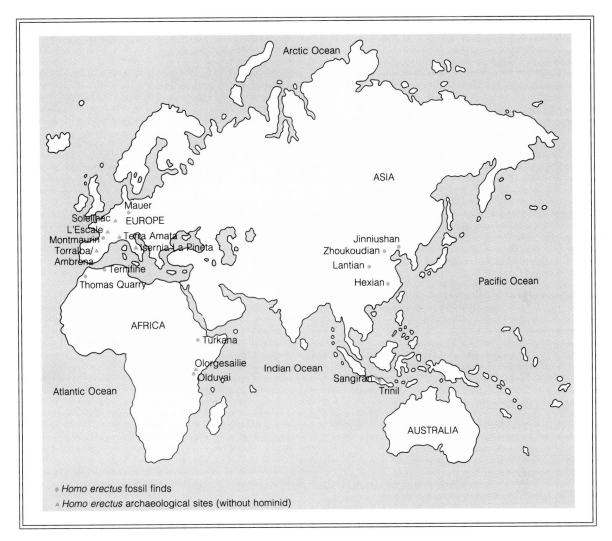

Figure 7.1   Homo erectus *sites have been identified in many areas of the Old World. No fossils of comparable age have ever been found in the Americas or Australia.*

phological characteristics, all forms designated *H. erectus* are clearly members of a single species that is either a lineal descendent or an offshoot of a lineage beginning with *Homo habilis*. The species originated in Africa at least 1.6 MYA, spread throughout the Old World, and lasted until 400,000 and perhaps as late as 250,000 years ago (YA). During that time, though some regional variation exists, *H. erectus* showed remarkably little change either across space or through time. It was a period of stability in human evolution.

The Pleistocene epoch, which lasted about 2 million years and ended only 10,000 YA, was a period of relatively rapid fluctuation in temperature, rainfall, and water levels. The best-known feature of the Pleistocene was the advance and retreat of massive glaciers from the polar regions, hence the name Ice Age. When they advanced, the glaciers covered much of the

spirituality   A belief in the soul and in powers beyond the material forces of nature.

higher latitudes with ice, gouging out lakes, flattening mountains, and transporting millions of tons of rock from place to place. Even in areas not directly touched by glaciers, there were major effects on climate, plants, and animals. During the interglacial periods, ice melted, sea level rose, and water covered many areas exposed to the air during the glacial highs. As a result, habitats were radically modified, leading to the extinction of certain species, such as many of the large Pleistocene mammals (or megafauna) of North America, after the last glacial retreat.

Fossil Finds

The first *Homo erectus* fossils to be found were identified in 1891 in Java, then a Dutch colony, by Dutch physician Eugene Dubois. Dubois drew inspiration from Darwin's suggestion that humans must have evolved in the tropics because their closest relatives, the great apes, all live in tropical zones. Africa, homeland of the chimpanzee and gorilla, was the logical choice to Darwin. But Dubois could only get work in Java (today part of Indonesia), so he looked there. Along the Solo River he found a skullcap and, nearby, a femur (thighbone). He called his find *Pithecanthropus erectus* (upright ape-man). After six years in Java, Dubois returned to Europe to announce his discoveries to the scientific world. Unfortunately the world was not ready to accept *Pithecanthropus*. Dubois was publicly ridiculed for claiming he had found human ancestors. He was told he had only found some old gibbon skulls. Dubois abandoned his work and died a bitter man in 1940.

After Dubois's initial find, many more examples of this stage of human evolution were unearthed, often associated with the tools they made. They have been dated to the middle Pleistocene, approximately 700,000 YA. These finds supported Dubois's contention that they represent a human ancestor included in our genus as *H. erectus*. *H. erectus* had a cranial capacity ranging from 800 to 1100 cc, considerably larger than any australopithecine, and larger even than *H. habilis* (see table in Box 6.3). The teeth resemble modern teeth and are smaller than those of *Australopithecus*. Curiously, a **diastema**, a gap between the canines and second incisors appears in some *H. erectus* fossils. This gap occurs in apes but is absent in all but the earliest australopithecines. The skulls have a heavy brow ridge with a shallow trough behind it followed by a sloping forehead. There is also a heavy ridge at the back of the skull, indicating heavy neck muscles (Figure 7.2). *H. erectus* was also larger than any earlier hominid, and the difference in size between males and females was less pronounced.

Perhaps the best known *H. erectus* fossils are those found near Beijing, China, beginning in 1927. First known as *Sinanthropus pekinensis* (Peking Man), the fossils were later included in *H. erectus*. By this time Dubois was so embittered that he refused to recognize the similarity of these fossils to the ones he had found in Java. The Beijing fossils disappeared in 1941, when Japanese troops invaded mainland China, and have never resurfaced (Shapiro 1974, Janus 1975). Fortunately, detailed casts, drawings, and descriptions of the originals were made and still exist.

The Chinese fossils are younger than those from Java, dating between about 460,000 and 250,000 YA. From the caves where the remains were found also came evidence of the use of fire and of the butchering of animals with stone tools. The treatment of some of the human skulls led some investigators to conclude that the Chinese *H. erectus* practiced cannibalism. The bases of some skulls appeared to have been broken open possibly to extract the brains. However, other investigators have reanalyzed some of the Beijing material and concluded that the treatment of the skulls was consistent with the actions of nonhuman scavengers (Binford and Ho 1985). More recently several other *H. erectus* fossils were found in China, dating to about 800,000 YA.

Louis Leakey made the first African *H. erectus* find, near the top of Bed II at Olduvai Gorge. Known as OH9 (Olduvai Hominid 9) and dating to 1.1 MYA, this *H. erectus* had a cranial capacity of about 1000 cc and in every other respect was like the Asian *H. erectus* fossils. Over the last 30 years or so, other *H. erectus* fossils have been found in Africa, perhaps the most important being the oldest. Discovered by Richard Leakey in 1984 at Lake Turkana in Kenya, these remains of a boy about 12 years old are nearly complete and dated at 1.6 MYA.

Stone Tool Technology and the Lower Paleolithic

Homo erectus fossils, or stone tools associated with the species, have also appeared in North Africa, Germany, Italy, France, and Spain. It may have been *H. erectus*

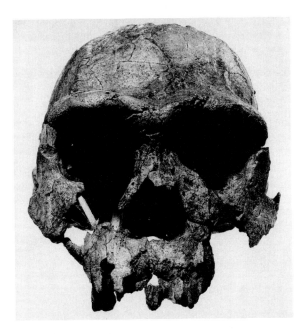
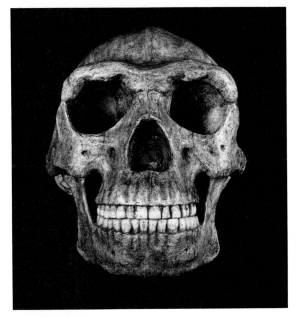
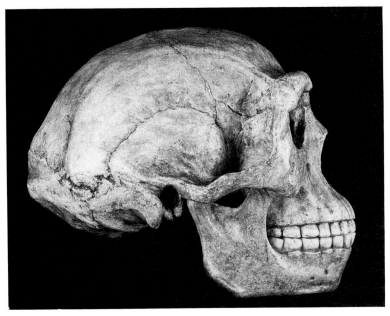

Figure 7.2 Homo erectus *skulls. At top left, a skull catalogued as KNM-ER 3733, from Lake Turkana, Kenya, dating to 1.6 MYA. At top right and bottom, front and side views of a skull from Zhoukoudian, China, familiarly known as Peking Man.* Homo erectus *had a much bigger braincase than* Australopithecus, *a face more like a human than an ape, and teeth roughly the size of modern human teeth.*

who began to have a noticeable impact on the environment, for there is some evidence that hunting may have begun to be a major part of subsistence. The nature of the stone tools and patterns of tooth wear suggest the *H. erectus* was a meat eater who did some bone crushing with its teeth. Louis Leakey showed

that a large biped in reasonably good condition can reliably hunt antelope and similar game species using only hand-held stone tools.

The **Paleolithic** (Old Stone Age) is the first culturally defined period in human history. It refers to the styles and traditions of stone tools made by hominids

---

diastema A gap between the canines and second incisors in the maxilla.

Paleolithic The Old Stone Age, an era that covers the earliest human cultural tradition, stretching from 3 MYA to 10,000 YA.

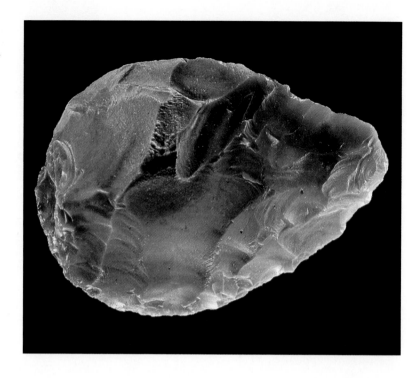

Figure 7.3 *Acheulean hand axe. Pieces were flaked off both faces of a pebble core to form a symmetrical tool, useful for cutting and chopping. The Acheulian tradition probably arose in Africa 1.5 MYA and spread throughout much of the rest of the Old World or was reinvented by Homo erectus or early Homo sapiens populations.*

and later humans from the earliest tools to about 10,000 YA. It is usually divided into lower, middle, and upper periods. The lower Paleolithic was the longest period, lasting well over 1 million years, and is associated mainly with early hominids and *H. erectus*. The middle Paleolithic is mainly identified with *H. erectus* and Neandertals. Associated with *H. erectus* is a toolmaking technique that became known as **Acheulean** after an early site found in St. Acheul, France. This type is known by its flaked stone hand-held axes chipped away by sharp blows, probably from other stones held in the hand (Figure 7.3). Acheulean tools occur throughout most of the Pleistocene extending from Africa into much of Europe and Asia, though not necessarily as a single unified tradition. In fact Acheulean tools may not represent a tradition at all; they may represent a technique for making stone tools invented again and again by different people at different times and places.

New Patterns of Subsistence: Hunting and Gathering

As we saw in the last chapter, many people assume the earliest hominids were game hunters, although little evidence supports this conclusion. The development of a more efficient technology and the abundance of game in some times and places gave an opportunity to an expanding population to rely more heavily on meat. To see what this new pattern of subsistence was like, let us consider two examples of hunting and gathering peoples from the archaeological record.

Ambrona and Torralba. The archaeological sites of Ambrona and Torralba in Central Spain have been known since 1888. They are located in a mountain pass between the winter and summer pastures of several species of large prehistoric animals. At these sites there are multiple layers of occupation dating back to the late Pleistocene (about 500,000 YA). These sites yielded thousands of stone tools and many thousands of crushed and split animal bones. The archaeologists found no hominid remains or shelters, but many anthropologists assume that the hunters at Torralba and Ambrona were *Homo erectus*. Most of the animals found are large species that were abundant in Spain during the Pleistocene, such as elephant, deer, wild horse, oxen, and rhinoceros. Very few small animal bones appeared except those of a migratory bird species found seasonally in the area.

The sites are large and may have been occupied by up to 100 people at a time. The animals whose bones occur at Torralba and Ambrona were apparently killed elsewhere, butchered, and then transported to these two sites for sharing and processing. The bones were crushed and split with stone tools to extract the edible marrow. Significantly, very few of the massive skulls of elephants were found. Presumably the hunters cracked them open at the **kill sites** to remove the edible brains.

Near Torralba and Ambrona archaeologists found kill sites where hunters had used fire to drive animals into traps, especially bogs where the beasts became mired in deep mud and could be killed easily. Outside the narrow mountain pass, on the mountain flanks and on the broad Castillian plain, other sites can be found. Some of them were quarries where stone was obtained for tools. Judging from the shallow depth of cultural material, others were temporary campsites that lasted a few days to a few weeks while their inhabitants foraged nearby for animals both large and small. Perhaps these hunters, like many modern hunters, preferred to go out at daybreak and return before dark with their kill, if any. When the game around a given campsite became scarce, they would break camp and move on to a new site.

Archaeologist Karl Butzer, who studied the Torralba site, concluded (1982) that Torralba and Ambrona were seasonal campsites occupied during the fall and spring migrations of big game. The outlying sites could be divided into kill sites, temporary campsites, and quarries. During the winter and summer hunting seasons, Butzer suggested, the hunters broke up into smaller groups wandering from place to place in search of game. Each year they returned to the mountains to prey on big game animals migrating through the narrow mountain pass. In the large campsites in the valley below, there may have been other activities, including finding mates and cooperative hunting expeditions. Some evidence at the site suggests that the hunters at Torralba used fire to drive game toward other hunters lying in wait. Butzer concluded that the Paleolithic residents of Spain varied their activities according to the season, moving where they could obtain the most game with the least effort,

a practice known as **scheduling**. They also cooperated in hunting, killing, transporting, and sharing the game.

It is impossible to verify Butzer's model down to the last detail. We know too little about the outlying kill sites and temporary campsites. Dating techniques are not precise enough to determine whether they were synchronized with the seasonal campsites. Archaeologists will continue to collect and analyze information on Torralba and Ambrona to determine if these sites fit Butzer's model. Another important way of testing such models is to observe the behavior of modern hunter-gatherers to discover whether their adaptive patterns are similar. Some ethnographic studies suggest a pattern of scheduling among such groups as the Inuit (Eskimo) of the Arctic circle, the !Kung San, and the indigenous peoples of Central Brazil, in which settlements are located near particular resources in season. Settlement size may have fluctuated seasonally as groups came together where resources were temporarily abundant and then split into smaller groups to exploit other areas where resources were scarce.

Terra Amata.   A well-known Acheulean site from a later period is found on the French Riviera at a site known as Terra Amata. More than 300,000 years before the area became a popular seaside resort, humans visited this spot annually to hunt land animals and collect seafood and land plants. France was colder in those days. Year after year the people of Terra Amata built (or rebuilt) dwellings. These were huts up to 15 meters (49 feet) long made of rows of slender tree trunks buried in the ground and bent together at the top to form a roof (Figure 7.4). The fact that these shelters were considerably larger than the 1.8 million-year-old shelter found at Olduvai suggests a larger camp size.

Shelter is an important means by which the hominids adapted to a wide variety of habitats and a broad range of temperatures and climates. Shelters provide protection from the heat of the sun, the cold of winter,

---

Acheulean   A toolmaking tradition of *H. erectus* (1.6 million to 250,000 YA) in Europe and Africa. It includes handaxes, cleavers, and flake tools made by percussion flaking.

kill sites   Archaeological sites where slaughter and butchering of animals occurred.

scheduling   A social group's practice of varying activities according to the seasons, optimizing access to resources.

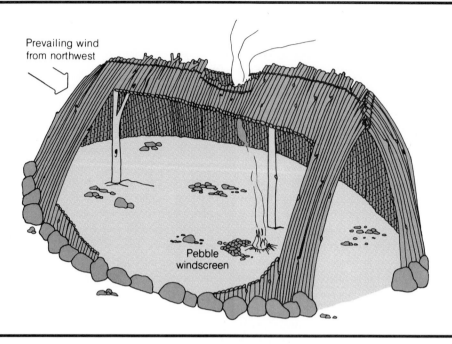

Prevailing wind
from northwest

Pebble
windscreen

Figure 7.4   *An artist's rendering of a shelter at Terra Amata on the French Riviera. The hut was built out of stakes bent inward to meet at the top and braced at the foot with large stones.*

wind, rain, and snow. They also serve as storage places for food, tools, and other goods and as protected environments for the young. Shelter is not unique to humans or even hominids: Such diverse species as bees, termites, birds, bears, and wolves erect structures or modify natural ones to provide protection from the elements.

People lived, worked, ate, and slept inside the huts at Terra Amata. Some people busied themselves manufacturing stone tools. At certain spots in the huts, French archaeologist Henry de Lumley found whole pebbles—apparently gathered on a nearby rocky beach—flakes, and discarded tools. In a few instances a core with a missing piece could be reunited with the flake which had been struck from it. One point was made from a type of volcanic rock found 30 miles or more from Terra Amata. In addition to stone tools, the archaeologists discovered an elephant leg bone hammered to a point and other pieces of bone resembling awls (for punching holes) and hardened by fire. The people who used this site (possibly *Homo erectus,* but no fossil humans have been recovered at this site) used tools for hacking animals apart, cutting up meat,

breaking open bones for their marrow, scraping animal skins, and possibly making other implements from wood, bone, and hide. A few of the stone tools may have been projectile points, such as arrowheads, showing that the people used the flakes of stone chipped from a core as well as the cores themselves.

Among other things, Terra Amata and other *H. erectus* sites represent a stage in the evolution of technology. Tools were made out of materials found locally or imported from other places. Toolmakers worked at home, and it is possible that some people were specialists in toolmaking. Tools came in a variety of shapes and sizes, probably reflecting the different uses to which they were put. Terra Amata and similar sites from the same period reflect the emergence of a technological society. Here, tool use and toolmaking became separate, specialized activities. These activities required developed skills, transportation of materials, and specialized sites for manufacture. Behavior became more complex, and people became dependent on each other for specific skills. Cultural repertoires— the sum total of knowledge and learned behavior available in a population—became increasingly im-

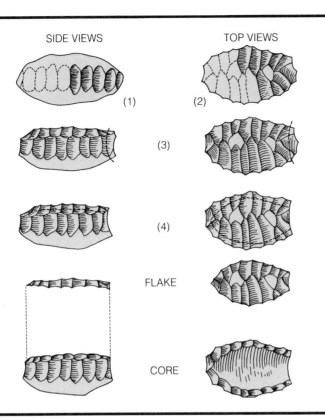

SIDE VIEWS   TOP VIEWS

(1)   (2)

(3)

(4)

FLAKE

CORE

Figure 7.5 *The Levallois tool technique. In this technique, the first step is the trimming of the sides of a stone pebble with direct blows (1). Next, the top is trimmed (2). Then a striking platform is prepared at one end (3). Finally, flakes of uniform size and shape are struck from the prepared core (4). The Levallois technique was more efficient and reliable than earlier techniques, but it also required more practice and skill.*

portant as a means of adaptation and the basis for organization. While *Australopithecus* and other early hominids were probably differentiated primarily on the basis of sex and age, individual skills and knowledge probably became more important in *H. erectus* populations with their dependence on tools, fire, cooking, and shelter.

ARCHAIC *HOMO SAPIENS*

The next stop in human evolution was *Homo sapiens.* From about 300,000 YA forward, fossils found in Europe, Africa, and Asia are enough like modern people to warrant classification in the same genus and species as modern *H. sapiens.* All the principal features of their form and structure are within the range of modern

skeletal populations. Of course, we still have no way of comparing the soft body parts or behavior, which may have been very different from modern *H. sapiens.* Compared to *Homo erectus,* archaic *H. sapiens* had a larger brain (averaging 1166 cc, about 10 percent larger that *H. erectus*) and a generally less robust skeleton.

Early archaic *H. sapiens* is generally found in association with an Acheulean toolkit, varying in composition from place to place but generally consisting of crudely worked stone and bone tools, including choppers, scrapers, and some tools made from animal bones. About 200,000 YA, however, a major advance occurred in stone toolmaking techniques. One technique was named **Levallois** for the suburb of Paris where some of the first finds were made. The technique involves a prepared core (Figure 7.5) with a

Levallois A toolmaking tradition, dating from about 150,000 YA, that involved striking uniform flakes from a stone core with a striking platform.

striking plate that will permit several flakes to be struck off the core much more predictably. Stone tools were produced by the steady application of pressure, allowing for more control than the Acheulean percussion flaking. The technique is more precise, efficient, and productive than earlier stoneworking techniques. It also produces tools better adapted to a particular task, such as skinning animals, filleting meat, and sharpening sticks. Out of this advance grew a family of related traditions known as the **Mousterian**, which reflect local traditions and perhaps the individuality of the artisans who produced the tools.

The Neandertals: Fossil Finds and Interpretations

Perhaps the best-known, and most widely debated, group of archaic *Homo sapiens* are the **Neandertals**. They lived during the late Pleistocene from about 130,000 to 35,000 YA. They are identified with the Mousterian toolmaking traditions and with some of the earliest known evidence for ritual behavior.

The Neandertals got their name from the earliest recognized find, made in 1856 in a limestone quarry in the Neander Valley near Düsseldorf, Germany. At the time of the find, no early hominid fossils were generally known, so the contrast with modern human skeletons appeared greater than it does today. The skeleton had thick, robust bones and skull, a protruding jaw, a slanted forehead, and heavy brow ridges. It was unmistakably human but unlike any human known at that time. Darwin's *Origin of Species* had not appeared yet, so the idea of any human evolution was controversial. Neither had any of the African hominid fossils yet been discovered. Scientists proposed all manner of explanations for the bones. An eminent anatomist from Bonn declared that the skeleton belonged to an early barbarian race that lived in Europe before the Celtic and Germanic tribes arrived. The bones were but a few thousand years old, he declared, and certainly were from a diseased individual.

In 1908 perhaps the best-known Neandertal discovery occurred at La Chapelle-aux-Saints in southern France. This hominid appears to have been deliberately buried in a flexed or fetal position. A bison leg was set on his chest, reminiscent of the burial customs of many contemporary peoples who provide food for the deceased to use on the journey to the afterlife.

Buried with the body were the bones of other extinct late Pleistocene animals and several stone tools of the Mousterian tradition. Marcellin Boule, a French anthropologist, described the skeleton in detail in 1913. In Boule's reconstruction the "old man" of La Chapelle walked in a shambling fashion, with legs bent, back curved, and head thrust forward (Figure 7.6).

Later investigations revealed that the skeleton was that of a 40-year-old male who evidently suffered from osteoarthritis, a degenerative bone disease. Boule either overemphasized the effects of the arthritis or, perhaps, simply wanted to show the Neandertals as primitive. His interpretation cast doubt on the possibility that modern humans could belong to the same lineage as the Neandertals. He helped create the image of Neandertals as apelike numbskulls. To this day, most people identify the word *Neandertal* with archaic attitudes, ignorance, and brutishness.

As other Neandertal fossils were unearthed, however, it became evident that these fossils, although powerfully built and with some primitive cranial features, were not brutes but people, with behavior much like modern *H. sapiens*. At La Ferassie, also in southern France, Neandertals were decently buried in what seemed to be a cemetery with several shallow, mounded graves. The skeleton of one male was buried with stone tools, the head and shoulders covered with a flat stone slab. A female was buried head-to-head with the male. Three children and an infant were buried nearby. All this took place about 60,000 YA. In other European Neandertal sites there are signs of special arrangements of cave bear skulls suggesting the existence of a ritual cult surrounding those animals. The evidence supporting such notions is rather thin, however; the accumulation of human and animal remains has also been interpreted as a natural accumulation.

In Shanidar Cave, Iraq, archaeologist Ralph Solecki found Neandertal remains buried with elaborate ceremonial preparations. The bodies had been colored with red dyes discoloring the bones, and the soil around the burials was full of flower pollen. Flowers do not grow in dark caves so they must have been placed there. Solecki concluded that the Shanidar Neandertals of 50,000 YA had buried their dead with flowers, similar to Western burials today (Solecki 1971). The Shanidar people lived in social groups, made and used tools, and cooperated and shared with each other (Trinkhaus 1983).

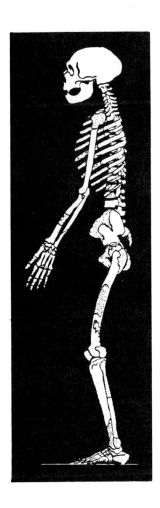 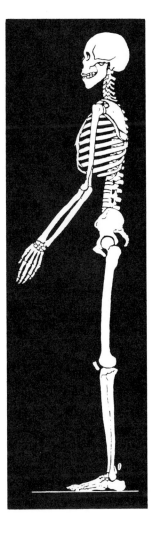

Figure 7.6   *Marcelin Boule's reconstruction of the Neandertal skeleton found at La Chapelle-aux-Saints (left) in comparison with the skeleton of a modern human (right). Boule overlooked the obvious signs of arthritis in the skeleton and depicted it with bowed legs and head thrust forward, creating the impression that these early humans were primitive and apelike.*

Some authorities suggest that Neandertals supported the sick and elderly long after they had ceased to be physically useful to the group. The implication was that there was respect for the aged and that they were recognized for the knowledge and wisdom they could provide. One Shanidar individual, who was missing an arm, lived several years after the amputation, although he could not have contributed much to subsistence. Recent evidence, however, indicates that most Neandertals died in their 30s, so, even if some members were cared for, such a practice was not widespread or always successful (Trinkhaus 1983). Furthermore, some critics suggest that the pollen around the Shanidar burials was blown into the cave on the wind, and they challenge the evidence for social cooperation (Gargett 1989). Nevertheless, the prevailing view today is that the Neandertals were fairly advanced *H. sapiens,* sharing many traits with modern humans.

This is not to say that there are not significant differences between Neandertals and modern *H. sapiens* in both physical appearance and life-style. Neandertal

---

Mousterian   A toolmaking tradition of the middle Paleolithic, associated with archaic *Homo sapiens* in Europe.

Neandertals   Archaic *H. sapiens* that lived during the late Pleistocene, from 130,000 to 35,000 YA.

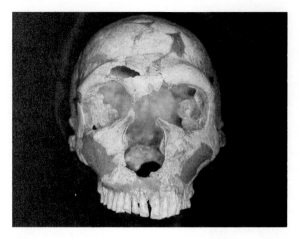 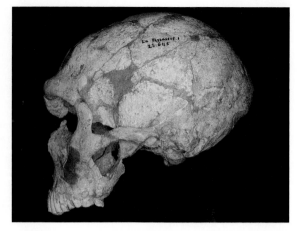

Figure 7.7 *Frontal and side view of a Neandertal skull from La Ferrassie in France. Note how large the teeth are compared to those of modern humans.*

teeth were large compared to those of modern *H. sapiens,* and the facial musculature was massive (Figure 7.7). Apparently the teeth were often used as a vice for holding objects to be cut or pulled apart. The teeth of many individuals are heavily worn down as if used for more than just chewing well-cooked food. Since the region had cold winters at the time, some investigators suggest that Neandertals used their teeth to soften animal skins for use as clothing in the manner of modern Eskimos. The Neandertal skeletons are exceptionally robust, suggesting that they relied heavily on physical force to accomplish many tasks. In general many Neandertal physical features fall outside the range of modern humans. Finally, the toolkits associated with the Neandertals are not as elaborate as those of non-Neandertal people living at the same time. Thus, while it is clear that Neandertals possessed a developed culture and social organization, the evidence suggests that they may not have developed the same dependence on tools and social cooperation as modern *H. sapiens.*

The Place of Neandertals in the Evolution of *Homo Sapiens*

Many questions about the status of Neandertals remain to be answered. While they are clearly not the brutes of popular myth, neither were they identical to modern humans. If they occurred in time between *Homo erectus* and modern *Homo sapiens,* gradually shading into each adjacent species at the extremes of their time period, they would fit neatly into a gradualist scenario. The problem with this scheme is that investigators have found anatomically modern *H. sapiens* of comparable age to Neandertals. How can a species be transitional unless it falls in the middle of a sequence from earlier to later forms?

If, on the other hand, Neandertals were a separate species, what accounts for their differences, and what happened to them? Some investigators suggested that the "classic" Neandertals of western Europe (those with an extreme expression of the typical Neandertal traits) were adapted to the intense cold of the Pleistocene glaciations. However, there is no reason why the unusually large, heavy skulls and torsos of these people were better adapted to cold than the smaller bodies of modern humans. The Neandertals could have developed their differences simply because they were reproductively isolated from other hominids through geographical or social separation. But there is no hard evidence that this isolation occurred. Some anthropologists point out that Neandertal-like features such as heavy brow ridges are still found in modern populations. They suggest that the Neandertals were merely a regional version of *H. sapiens* that was finally absorbed, through gene flow, into modern populations. The trend of thought today seems to focus on the differences between the Neandertals and modern humans and to consider the archaics as a subspecies of *H. sapiens* that became extinct.

A NEW VIEW OF HUMAN EVOLUTION: MOLECULES LEAD TO "EVE"

If it is the case that archaic *Homo sapiens* is a distinct lineage, where did "anatomically modern" *Homo sapiens* come from, and when? *Anatomically modern* refers to people whose skeletons fall within the normal range of variation found in the skeletons of people today. Until quite recently the fossil evidence led most investigators to accept the following sequence for the evolution of modern *H. sapiens*: About 1 MYA, *Homo erectus* migrated out of Africa into Asia and Europe. The evidence for this is strong. Different populations of *H. erectus* evolved in different directions due to isolation from each other, different environmental conditions, and genetic drift over hundreds of millennia. However, there was enough gene flow among populations to prevent speciation from occurring. Modern *H. sapiens* evolved out of this dispersed population, passing first through an archaic phase; in each region, *H. sapiens* reflected some of the traits of the ancestral population from which it descended.

Much variation exists among modern humans, including differences in stature, skin pigmentation (see Chapter 8), hair form, facial features, blood types, and other traits. These differences might suggest that distinct populations formed in widely separated regions around the globe. This idea provides a neat explanation for the emergence of what are commonly thought of as the races of humankind. A problem with the theory is that human populations did not develop into separate species as would normally occur after prolonged isolation. That this did not happen can be demonstrated by the fact that all known human groups are able to mate with each other and produce viable, fertile offspring.

Recent molecular studies have challenged some of these traditional assumptions. The basic idea that

modern humans are descended from *H. erectus* stands unchallenged. But molecular evidence and analysis suggest that *all* modern *H. sapiens* are recent descendants of African ancestors. If this is so, there had to have been two founding migrations out of Africa, the first involving early *H. erectus,* about 1 MYA, the second involving *H. sapiens,* perhaps as late as 200,000 YA. For this to have happened, the African *H. sapiens* would have had to replace all the hominid populations everywhere they found them.

This startling assertion was made in 1985 by a group of researchers at the University of California at Berkeley. They had done a study involving DNA sequencing on a sample of populations from Africa, Asia, Australia, New Guinea, and Europe. Rather than examining DNA from the cell's nucleus, they used **mitochondrial DNA** (mtDNA). The **mitochondria** are structures in the cell that provide energy for cell functions. They contain DNA molecules different from nuclear DNA. Nuclear DNA reflects the mating patterns of a population, because each individual inherits DNA from both parents. Mitochondrial DNA is inherited only in the female line because sperm do not pass on mtDNA. Thus mtDNA reflects only the maternal influence in a continuous line, changed only by random mutations, unbroken by genetic recombination, and not affected by selection acting on the whole organism.

The Berkeley team sequenced mtDNA from a sample of 147 women. They then attempted to construct the simplest possible model relationship among these people. The model they constructed assumed the least possible number of mutations to link all 147 together. The descent tree that resulted from this exercise led to some remarkable conclusions (Figure 7.8). First, it demonstrated the great degree of similarity among all the populations studied. The "races" are simply not genetically very different. Thus their divergence is probably quite recent. In addition, judging by the differences that showed up, the sample was divided into two groups: sub-Saharan Africans and everyone else.

Finally, there was greater genetic diversity *within* the African group than within any other geographical

---

mitochondrial DNA (mtDNA) Genetic material contained in the mitochondria of cells.

mitochondria Structures in the cell that provide energy for cell functions.

Figure 7.8   *Microbiologist Rebecca Cann (left) and her colleagues studied the pattern of mutations in the mitochondrial DNA of 147 women from around the world. The data they uncovered is presented in the simplified diagram below. Different symbols are used to show the continent of origin of each woman in the study, with lines of descent drawn from inside the horseshoe-shaped figure. The descent lines were provided by a computer that determined the closest match between each person tested and all the others. Africans appear to be the common ancestors of all the groups.*

group (Gould 1987). Geneticists have long assumed that a center of diffusion can be identified by the greatest within-group diversity.

Thus the interpretation presented by the Berkeley group strongly suggests an African origin for modern *H. sapiens.*

How recently were our ancestors united in Africa? The researchers assumed a constant rate of mutation for mtDNA. They calculated that a common ancestor for the entire sample population had lived between 140,000 and 285,000 YA. By the same technique they estimated the common ancestor of the non-African group at 90,000 to 180,000 YA. If this is correct, all the known diversity in living human populations arose from a single, relatively recent African origin that occurred about 200,000 YA. Modern *H. sapiens* populations first evolved in Africa and then migrated elsewhere (180,000–90,000 YA), replacing archaic *H. sapiens* wherever they went. The popular press picked up the idea and soon headlines screamed that research had found a single female from whom all humanity was descended. Someone called her a "mitochondrial Eve."

The paleontological and archaeological data on the rise and diffusion of modern *H. sapiens*—as opposed to the molecular data—are not quite so clear. However, there is some paleontological evidence that supports the notion of a recent African origin (Stringer and Andrews 1988). Some specialists disagree (Wolpoff et al. 1988), feeling that the single-origin model implies a kind of "Pleistocene holocaust" in which modern *H. sapiens* came out of Africa exterminating every other hominid in its path. The jury is still out on this issue.

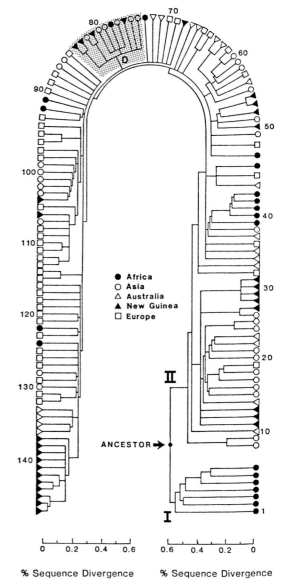

● Africa
○ Asia
△ Australia
▲ New Guinea
□ Europe

% Sequence Divergence   **% Sequence Divergence**

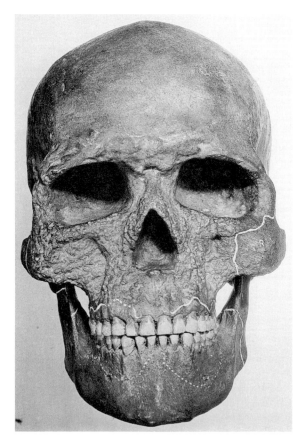 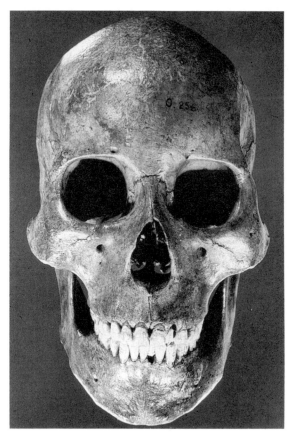

Figure 7.9   *A Cro-Magnon skull (left) and a modern* Homo sapiens *skull (right). The Cro-Magnons had skulls entirely within the range of contemporary humans.*

MODERN *HOMO SAPIENS:* FOSSILS BECOME PEOPLE

In 1868, workmen building a railway near the village of Cro-Magnon in the Dordogne region of France found a burial under an overhanging rock. In it lay the remains of five people together with stone tools dated to about 30,000 YA. This site is in the same region where the French Neandertals were found. **Cro-Magnon** was clearly different from Neandertal. The fossils had high foreheads suggesting expansion of the frontal lobes of the brain. The brow ridges were slight,

the faces short, and the cranial vault higher and rounded (Figure 7.9). Cro-Magnon became a "type fossil" used as shorthand for many other anatomically modern fossils of the same period. Similar fossils from the upper Paleolithic occur in other parts of Europe and in Africa, Asia, and Australia. Though sometimes conserving a few archaic traits, these remains would be hard to distinguish from the bones of modern *Homo sapiens.*

Anatomically modern *H. sapiens* was widely distributed throughout the Old World by at least 38,000 YA. These populations may have differed

---

Cro-Magnon   Fossil of anatomically modern humans found in Europe dated to 25,000 YA.

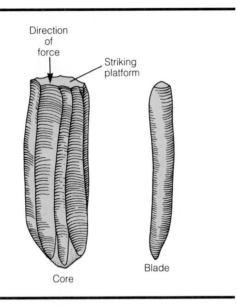

Figure 7.10 *The punch-blade technique—in which a stone is broken to create a striking platform and long vertical pieces are struck off its sides—enabled toolmakers to produce more sharp-edge flakes from a single stone core than was possible with earlier techniques.*

slightly from each other because of genetic drift or local adaptations. The groups were probably small and quite isolated, conditions that favor divergence and minimize gene flow. No one doubts, however, that all these groups were reproductively compatible. Given the wide dispersion of human populations and the extreme diversity of environments to which they adapted, why did they not evolve into several different, reproductively isolated populations, even separate species?

Gene flow, helped by migration and possibly trade, was one explanation for species unity. Another part of the explanation may be that adaptation occurred increasingly at the cultural level. Human populations became culturally specialized rather than diverging biologically into species. Natural selection at a biological level did not cease. But cultural adaptation became just as important as bioevolution in shaping the species.

Upper Paleolithic Culture and Tools

Associated with these modern humans, beginning about 40,000 years ago in Europe, North Africa, and Asia, was a new stone tool technology. Once again there was a leap forward in technique. The basic technique was similar to the Levallois technique except that the toolmaker selected relatively long, cylinder-shaped cores. Using a punch, the stoneworker directed a sharp blow to the end of the cylinder, striking off a long blade, hence the name **punch-blade** technique (Figure 7.10). A single core weighing 2 to 3 pounds could produce 75 feet of cutting edge, up to ten times more cutting edge than with the Levallois technique alone. Some of the blades were carefully sharpened on cutting edges. Upper Paleolithic tools were produced increasingly by the steady application of pressure rather than the less controlled banging

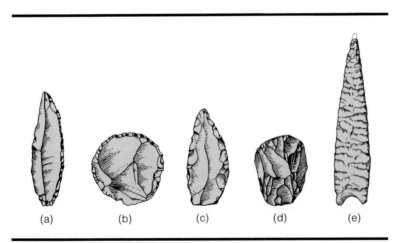

Figure 7.11 *Upper Paleolithic stone tools are more varied, sophisticated, and specialized than earlier tools. Shown here are a knife (a), a scraper (b), a point (c), a scraper (d), and a point (e).*

(a)   (b)   (c)   (d)   (e)

Figure 7.12 *An upper Paleolithic harpoon from the Magdalenian tradition shows that objects were being made with aesthetic considerations in mind. This period was characterized by the rise of artistic styles and traditions.*

together of rocks. Tool types differed from one place to the next and over time, reflecting different conceptions of how a tool should look. To some extent these changes were also the result of the changing environment. The Pleistocene was a period of alternation between relatively cool glacial periods and warmer, moister periods.

The upper Paleolithic toolkit also contained items made from antlers, wood, and bone. For example, the people of the French Perigord region developed a wooden spear-throwing device that greatly increased the range and accuracy of a spear. This made it possible to stalk animals from a greater distance. The earliest representations of the bow and arrow come from North Africa about 30,000 years ago. The bow was widely used in Europe in late Paleolithic times and has been used up to the present day in South America and southern Africa. The bow momentarily stores up energy from the archer's muscles in a springy piece of wood, releasing it with great accuracy in the flight of the arrow.

Upper Paleolithic tools were more specialized than earlier tools. The prevailing archaeological opinion is that these traditions represent increasing specialization by hunters and gatherers alike (Figure 7.11). As the Pleistocene epoch ended, hunters concentrated on specific game species, such as bison, reindeer, and mastodons, rather than the more generalized pursuits practiced by their forebears. Perigordians hunted reindeer almost exclusively; inhabitants of the Pyrenees Mountains during this period lived mainly on mammoths; and the Solutreans relied on wild horse meat. Magdalenians developed a heavy dependence on fishing, and their technology reflects this with a variety of harpoons, nets, and **weirs**, or fish traps (Figure 7.12). During each of these upper Paleolithic periods, new

punch-blade An upper Paleolithic (about 40,000 YA) technique for making stone tools by using a punch to apply intense pressure on a very small area of a core.

weirs Fish traps.

stoneworking techniques were added, until in the Magdalenian—the crowning period of the Paleolithic—we find exquisitely worked harpoons, knives, projectile points, punches, awls, and scrapers, whose many shapes follow not only the dictates of the use each tool served but also an artisan's conception of style, symmetry, and perhaps beauty. Many of the tools found in different sites resembled each other enough to suggest that the toolmakers followed a conventional or standard design.

The history of stone technology is best known in Europe and the Middle East, but there were similar developments in other parts of the world, including the Far East, India, Africa, and the New World. The pattern in each case was different, yet the basic sequence of events was roughly the same. A crude biface tradition came first, followed by a phase in which prepared cores were used and then a series of styles representing more specialized modes of toolmaking. The development of lithic technology came along with population growth and specialization in other areas as well. These traditions were not necessarily connected with each other and their timing was not synchronized. In Africa, for example, the period corresponding to the upper Paleolithic in Europe came later and did not last as long as it did in Europe.

Artistic developments were also striking during the middle and upper Paleolithic. As far back as 30,000 YA, artisans sculpted small portable statues and painted scenes on cave walls and cliffs. The artistic impulse in the Paleolithic was primarily expressed in the naturalistic representation of everyday objects, such as game animals, celestial bodies, and human figures, but there is also an element recognizable as symbolic of spiritual beliefs. The artists' intentions in creating these works are unknown; some experts suggest that the famous cave paintings of antelope and bison had a magical significance and were meant to attract game. Whatever the intent, these artifacts of the Paleolithic stand as monuments to human creativity and artistic representation that are today treasured as among the greatest legacies of humankind (see Chapter 23 for further discussion of this topic).

Population Patterns and Trends

The technological developments of the upper Paleolithic, or of any other period, were not simply a function of the inventiveness of a few individuals. Instead, technology is linked to broad social and ecological patterns. The environment influences the directions taken in technology, but technology can also play a role in shaping the environment. For example, the development of projectiles and devices to propel them gave weapons greater efficiency and probably contributed to the reduction or extinction of game populations in some areas. This could have led to enlarging the range of hunting groups that pursued the game over longer distances. The use of fire in hunting also had an important environmental effect, probably destroying mature forests and maintaining vegetation at an early stage of ecological succession.

Toward the end of the Pleistocene, the last severe glaciation lowered sea level so much that dry land may have been present where today there is open sea. The weather grew milder: drier in some places, moister in others. At the same time, humans were moving over much of the earth's surface. During the period of about 30,000 to 10,000 YA, the first human populations arrived in the Americas, Australia, and New Guinea, and populations grew significantly.

The Perigord region of Southwestern France, where the prehistoric chronology is well known, reveals an increase in the number of settlements throughout the upper Paleolithic. The earliest phase, known as the **Chatelperronian** (37,000–30,000 YA), saw no increase in the number of settlements over the previous 35,000 years. During the next period, the **Aurignacian** (30,000–17,000 YA), the number of known settlements in the same region more than tripled, and in the following phase, the **Magdalenian** (17,000–12,000 YA), that number doubled again. Not only the numbers of local populations but also their size increased during the upper Paleolithic, judging from the area covered by the sites. For every person alive in the Perigord 70,000 YA, there were ten people alive 12,000 YA.

Although there are clearly relationships between population growth and technological advancement, they are correlational and don't tell us which causes which. Many anthropologists argue that technological change drove population growth (Childe 1951). As new, more productive technologies became available, populations expanded to take advantage of them. This view suggests that technological advances led to increased food production and consequently to larger populations. Another, more recent view (Boserup

1965) holds that population growth created the conditions that led to technological change. In this view, excess population exerted pressure, which led to the development and diffusion of new technologies. This view is consistent with the adage that "necessity is the mother of invention." We shall meet the same question again in Chapter 12, when we consider the question of intensification in food production.

The Peopling of the New World

Humans probably did not enter the New World before 30,000 YA at the very earliest. This was when the last major advance of the glaciers created dry land out of much of the Bering Strait between Siberia and Alaska. Some early stone tools have been found, but the earliest confirmed human remains are fairly recent. Some examples are 11,000 YA for Tepexpan in Mexico and Marmes in Washington State, and 12,500 YA for two sites in southern California. There are many claims for earlier human remains in the Americas, such as tools dated at nearly 40,000 YA, but they are not widely accepted. The best evidence available for human presence in the Americas points to dates of less than 15,000 YA. All the human remains found in the New World are of anatomically modern *Homo sapiens*. Investigators believe that they migrated into the Americas following the vast herds of late Pleistocene game animals, some of which (the mastodon and giant sloth, for example) they may have later hunted to extinction.

Dental evidence suggests that there were at least three separate waves of migration into the New World, arriving at different times. The first may have arrived about 15,000 YA, founding the Eskimo-Aleut population. A second group may have come 3,000 years later, specializing in hunting large land animals such as mammoths and mastodons. The descendants of this group of migrants was responsible for peopling much of North and Central America and all of South America (Turner 1987). A third migration occurred

much later, giving rise to the native groups of the Alaskan interior and moving down the Pacific Coast to northern California and to the North American Southwest, where they are represented by the Navajo and Apache peoples from about A.D. 1500. This scheme, based on dental traits, is also supported by linguistic evidence.

The humans who peopled the Americas probably came as seminomadic hunter-gatherers. There is no evidence for complex social organization among the indigenous migrants to the new world. They settled into many different regions and developed specialized cultural adaptations to the new environments. As we will see in later chapters, these settlers eventually created elaborate social and cultural forms, including several developed civilizations.

The Growing Importance of Cultural Adaptation

The rate of cultural change among human groups accelerated during the late Pleistocene. The technologies of Plio-Pleistocene and mid-Pleistocene populations changed little for long periods, and they were fairly uniform over wide areas. They can be classified under a few broad categories such as Oldowan, Acheulean, Mousterian, and so on. Late Pleistocene stone technologies are much more diversified. Where there were two or three stoneworking traditions in the earlier periods, the later periods show a proliferation of traditions. The new techniques were also more effective. For example, in the manufacture of stone tools, upper Paleolithic technologies produce three times more sharp edges from a given quantity of flint than the Mousterian technology.

The increase in technological effectiveness and diversity provides evidence for the increasing importance of the cultural dimension of adaptation. Why should the *rate* of sociocultural change increase? Was it because brains became larger and with them the size of learned cultural repertoires? Or was it because the genetic potential for cultural behavior was aug-

---

Chatelperronian Earliest phase of the upper Paleolithic (37,000 to 30,000 YA).

Aurignacian Middle phase of the upper Paleolithic (30,000 to 17,000 YA).

Magdalenian The final phase of the upper Paleolithic (17,000 to 12,000 YA).

mented? These questions cannot be ignored, but the evidence suggests that the biological foundation for rapid cultural development was laid down *before* the rate of change accelerated. Paradoxically the accelerated rate of change was likely a direct result of culture itself. Cultural adaptation need not await the exceedingly slow process of genetic transmission and natural selection. It proceeds by the transmission of knowledge to people who are receptive and able to act on it. Each successive change called forth new changes, so that culture change became a major source of further culture change.

SUMMARY

- *Homo erectus* is generally considered a bona fide ancestor to modern humans, living from 1.6 MYA to at least 400,000 YA. It extended from Africa into East Asia and Europe.
- *Homo erectus* had a larger brain than the australopithecines. It is associated with different toolmaking traditions, hunting, and the use of fire.
- Archaic *Homo sapiens* appears in the fossil record about 400,000 YA.
- From 125,000 to 40,000 YA the Neandertals lived in Europe and the Middle East. This "archaic" form has the big brain of modern humans but differs significantly in features of the skull and in body build.
- The Neandertal was a robust hominid, depending heavily on physical strength for survival but also on relatively sophisticated stone tools.
- There is some evidence that the Neandertals developed a complex social life, shared food, and possibly held religious ideas.
- Molecular studies suggest that modern *H. sapiens* arose in Africa as late as 200,000 YA and spread rapidly throughout the world, displacing other hominids. If confirmed, this hypothesis would eliminate the contribution of all non-African *Homo* species to the modern human population.
- The general trends of human evolution have been the reduction in facial muscularity; decreased reliance on the teeth for holding, carrying, ripping,

and tearing; long periods of socialization of the young; and the development of complex social life based on shared repertoires of symbolic behavior.
- The history of technology through the Pleistocene reflects gradual increases in specialization both in terms of tool production and specialized tool types.
- Parallel sequences of cultural development, such as the development of lithic technology, have repeated themselves in various parts of the world.
- Increasing population density in some areas may have driven technological change, while technology itself may also have facilitated the expansion of population.
- There is no doubt that the first people to enter the New World were anatomically modern although culturally simple *H. sapiens.*
- *Homo* became progressively more dependent on culture as an adaptive mechanism. During the Pleistocene, culture became both cause and consequence of evolutionary change.

GET INVOLVED

1. Visit a museum or university archaeology department with an extensive stone tool collection. Make a set of drawings or photographs of the tools characteristic of a particular period and region. Go to the literature on stone tools and on the particular tools you examined and see what you can find out about how such tools were made and what the different tool types were used for.
2. Rent copies of three or four movies that depict early stages of human evolution, such as *Clan of the Cave Bear.* Enjoy the movies for their entertainment value, but while you watch them keep a running list of the unproven and downright false assumptions they make about early *Homo sapiens.* Write a review of these films from an anthropological perspective.
3. Read a book on discovery and interpretation of famous fossils, such as Johanson and Edey's *Lucy,* Harry Shapiro's *Peking Man,* Richard Leakey's *People of the Lake,* or Charles Blinderman's *The Piltdown Inquest.* Consider how the circumstances of the discoveries and the anthropologists' personalities affected the subsequent interpretations of the finds.

SUGGESTED READINGS

Johanson, Donald, and Maitland A. Edey. 1981. *Lucy: The beginnings of humankind.* New York: Simon & Schuster.*

Lewin, Roger. 1984. *Human evolution: An illustrated introduction.* San Francisco: W. H. Freeman.

Pilbeam, David. 1984. The descent of hominoids and hominids. *Scientific American* 250 (no. 3): 84–96.

Simons, Elwyn. 1989. Human origins. *Science* 245:1343–1350.

Tierney, John, Lynda Wright, and Karen Springen. 1988. The search for Adam and Eve. *Newsweek,* Jan. 11.*

* This selection is anthologized in *Applying Anthropology,* 2d ed., ed. A. Podolefsky and P. J. Brown (Mountain View, Calif.: Mayfield, 1992).

The What, Why, and How of Forensic Anthropology

Douglas Owsley is a curator at the National Museum of Natural History, Smithsonian Institution. His osteological research concerns demographic trends and disease patterns in prehistoric and historic populations of North America. As a forensic anthropologist, Owsley assists law enforcement with the identification of human remains.

The forensic scientist sometimes plays the liveliest role, sweeping in at the moment of greatest confusion to help solve the mystery . . . a sort of human catalyst who ties together the loose ends of an unraveled plot. [Joyce and Stover 1991, 42–43].

As curator in the Smithsonian's Department of Anthropology, I deal with bones, principally those of the human skeleton, although occasionally animal bones play a part in my investigations. My research covers a time span from some 10,000 years B.C. to the present, from studies of aboriginal inhabitants of the Americas to immediate problems of identification in cases of violent death or missing persons. This last is the domain of forensic anthropology, a specialized applied field of physical anthropology. Just as each individual is unique, so each forensic case represents a different set of circumstances and physical characteristics, offering new challenges to the physical anthropologist.

From examining a skeleton, the physical anthropologist can derive information on sex, race, age at death, time elapsed since death, stature, build, and handedness, as well as on pathology, such as infections of bone, fractures, amputations, dental anomalies, and, often, cause of death. Such data, together with those derived from clothes or other belongings found with the skeleton, are crucial in establishing positive identification in cases of disappearance,

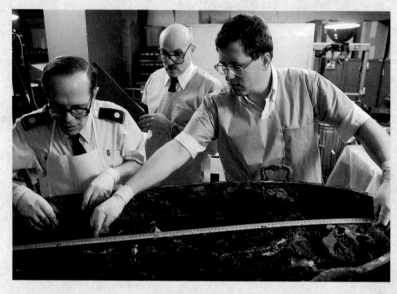

Douglas Owsley (right) and pathologists of the Armed Forces Institute of Pathology examine the skeleton of a 31-year-old Civil War veteran.

disfigurement, disguised identity, accidental death, and homicide. Comparison of premortem and postmortem X-rays, superimposition of photographs of premortem facial features and the skull, and computer analysis of points of correspondence or divergence supplement osteological examination.

But the physical anthropologist brings other types of expertise to forensic investigations. In field recovery of human remains, methodology makes all the difference in how much information is preserved. Locating a burial typically requires ground survey and probing for subsurface irregularities, often with special instruments such as a proton magnetometer and electrical resistivity techniques. Once located, the burial site is thoroughly searched for items dropped when the grave was dug, then photographed and mapped. Investigators carefully remove soil by trowel and brush, exca-

vating no bone until the entire grave is exposed and photographed. Data collected include dimensions of the grave, orientation of the body or bodies, presence of any fauna or vegetation, amount and type of clothing and other artifacts present, and condition and characteristics (such as presence of stain) of the bone. If the state of preservation is poor, investigators remove blocks of soil encasing parts of the skeleton to prevent fragmentation. They place the bones or soil blocks in labeled plastic sacks and transport them to a laboratory for cleaning and analysis.

Examples, rather than general description, can best convey the nature and diversity of forensic anthropology. In one case law enforcement authorities sought assistance from physical anthropologists when the body of a woman washed up on a river bank. Death had resulted from two shotgun blasts, one to the left side of the head, and the other to the

Owsley assists in excavating a 19th-century iron coffin from a family burial ground.

right side of the chest. The latter had fractured the upper right arm (humerus). Investigators found six minute fragments of bone in a truck belonging to the chief suspect. The suspect claimed that he used his truck on hunting trips and that the bone found in it was deer, not human. So small were the fragments that microscopic examination was necessary to identify those characteristics that distinguish human from animal bone. Results indicated that the bone was indeed human and from the humerus of the murdered woman.

In another case a murderer confessed his crime four years after he had committed it and offered to lead authorities to the burial site. As thick underbrush had grown over the area and the murderer's recollections were confused, physical anthropologists had to use a variety of techniques to locate the body. Once they located the site, they recorded data on the site and began excavation. As

they removed soil, items described by the murderer (e.g., plastic cover, blanket around the body) came to light. Following excavation, the skeleton was transferred to a laboratory. Information on sex, age, race, and other physical characteristics derived from skeletal analysis tallied with medical and other data on the alleged victim. In the upper left side of the skull (parietal) was a cluster of perforations that had been caused by projectiles moving from interior to exterior. The breakage pattern of the maxillae and mandible and the other cranial bones indicated that the gun blast that caused death was from a shotgun placed within the victim's mouth. This finding, together with cut marks on bones of the victim's arms and chest that were inflicted at the time of death, corroborated the murderer's story.

The third example deals mainly with the physical anthropologist's contribution to sociocultural and medical knowledge. When a small

19th-century family burial ground was threatened by surrounding development, the family obtained a court order to relocate the burials, with study of the osteological remains and associated artifacts specifically included as part of the complete relocation plan. The Smithsonian Institution, Armed Forces Institute of Pathology, University of Maryland, and Manassas (Virginia) Museum cooperated in the resulting study, which centered on one of the 24 excavated burials that contained an iron coffin. A marker identified the grave as that of Walter J. Weir, who died in 1870 at 31 years of age. Although the face plate had collapsed, admitting water to the coffin, the skeleton and clothing were in an excellent state of preservation. The skeleton was that of a white male, 5'7" in height, of medium build, and in his early 30s at the time of death. There was no evidence of arthritis or bone disease, trauma, or congenital or developmental abnormality. Dental analysis, however, showed that at the time of death Weir suffered from a severe abscess that had caused the loss of a molar shortly before death, and the infection had spread to an adjacent tooth. In that preantibiotic era, such an abscess could also have spread to the brain or into the neck and heart and could have caused the death of this healthy young man who had survived four years of active service in the Civil War unscathed. The clothing and cast-iron coffin itself provided information on the life-style of a mid-19th century, plantation-owning family, and biochemical analyses of bone samples yielded data on immunoglobulins (antibodies) and DNA that will contribute to a better understanding of the incidence and transmission of disease in the 19th century.

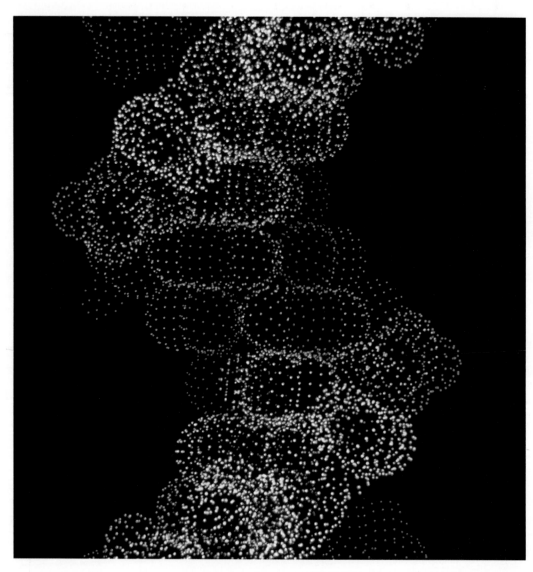

A computerized image of DNA, one of the major factors in human variation.

HUMAN VARIATION

▲▲▲

he last chapter brought us up to the present in the story of human evolution: *Homo sapiens* emerged about 200,000 YA and has been the sole human species for at least that long. Even though we are one species, however, anyone can see that there is tremendous variation among humans, both among individuals and among entire geographical populations. Humans come in a variety of shapes, sizes, and colors, with different eye and hair shape and color, facial characteristics, susceptibility to disease, and so on. This chapter examines how these differences came to be and their significance in terms of the past, present, and future evolution of the human species.

Looking at human variation and its role in evolution presents an interesting paradox: When we look at the past, the fossil record provides a long view of human biological history, reflecting major shifts but lacking the finer details. We are often missing precise information about the conditions that led to each major adaptive change, and we lack much information about the anatomy and physiology of organisms that we know only from their mineralized remains. On the other hand, when we look at contemporary human populations, we get a microscopic view of environmental conditions and genetic changes, but the time frame is too short to reveal long-term evolutionary trends. Evolutionary processes may unfold over many generations and many of the measurements we now make have only recently become possible. For example, physical anthropologists can use blood types to understand certain genetic processes because of their clear relationship with genotype. Blood types are generally traits whose expression is unaffected by environmental factors. Blood typing, necessary to compare donors to recipients of blood transfusions, has been possible only since 1900.

Nevertheless, the evidence is strong that human evolution driven by natural selection shaped our species in the past and continues to do so in the present. Evolution acts opportunistically on the variation that exists in a population. Environmental conditions exert pressure on the expression of particular genes, eventually affecting the frequency of those genes in a population. Variation in a population is thus both the raw material on which natural selection acts and the outcome of the ongoing natural selection process. The variation presently observable in human populations gives us insights into how human evolution took place in the past.

GENOTYPE AND PHENOTYPE: "HARD-WIRED" INFORMATION, "SOFTWARE," AND "DATA"

Before we examine the role of variation in the human species, let us review the ideas of genotype and phenotype. Inheritance determines the genotype of an organism and defines its genetic potential. Phenotypes, the observable expressions of genes, depend on the environment as well as the design contained in the gene. For example, an individual may carry a gene for a certain level of melanin in the skin. High melanin means dark skin color; low melanin means fair skin. The actual skin color of an individual, however, also depends on the amount of exposure to sunlight. Thus, not all phenotypic variation among individual humans can be understood in terms of genotypic variation.

One useful way of considering any change is to consider how permanent or reversible it is when it occurs. Some phenotypic features are firmly set at the moment of conception. Whether a person will be born with black or blond hair is determined irreversibly when sperm fertilizes egg. Other phenotypic features may be affected during the development of an individual from fetus to adult. For example, an individual's size can be influenced by **intrauterine factors** (the environment in the mother's womb). There is evidence that diet, smoking, alcohol, and other influences can affect the size, health, and behavior of the fetus and of the baby. Once an individual reaches 18 years of age, however, he or she normally has reached maximum height and will not grow any taller regardless of diet or other influences. Finally, there are traits that are changeable over time. Body weight, for example, can fluctuate during a person's lifetime.

Some biologists draw an analogy between biological traits and the ways in which information is encoded in a computer. Some information is built into the computer in the form of "read only memory" (ROM). Such "hard-wired" information cannot be changed without building a new computer. A "software program" contains information that can be changed, but not while the program is running. A third kind of information—usually called "data"—must be "fed in" to a computer. This information usually can be changed, copied, or erased easily. We can compare these three types of information to biological systems. Genotypes are the "hard wiring" of organisms, phenotypes are the "software programs," and short-term or cyclical changes in variables, such as

Figure 8.1 *An Inuit hunter and the seal he has shot are both protected from the Arctic cold by warm fur coats. The difference between their adaptations is that the seal's is biological and the human's is cultural.*

slow or rapid breathing, are the "data," the most easily changed characteristics.

Another way of looking at the question of adaptive variation is to consider the time required for changes to occur. Some adaptive changes require a genotypic change and therefore require the passage of many generations before they can become widespread in a population. Other changes can occur above the genetic level and therefore are faster. For example, people in Peru who move from sea level on the coast up into the highlands may develop greater lung capacity and other changes that help them adjust to the lower availability of oxygen at high altitudes (discussed in detail later in this chapter). These changes can take place within the lifetime of a single individual and thus are not direct expressions of genotype. However, the potential for these changes is genetically determined and is an inherited trait. Other changes, such as the shift to a more rapid breathing rate of someone who is exercising vigorously, can occur in a matter of seconds.

Earlier chapters stress the versatility of humans compared to other animals. This is largely because *Homo sapiens* relies, more than other species, on cultural adaptations—learned behavior and technology—to adjust to the environment. A simple example can be found in the adjustment of certain land mammals to the extreme cold of the arctic environment. The polar bear and the arctic fox have thick fur that helps insulate them from the cold. Humans have also developed an adaptation to the arctic habitat (Figure 8.1).

---

intrauterine factors Environmental factors influencing the development of the fetus within the mother's womb.

The Inuit (Eskimo) and other northern populations manufacture clothing, dwellings, and other devices to protect them from the bitter cold. Without these devices humans would die of exposure during the long arctic winter. Nowadays people from many other parts of the world travel to the polar regions. These visitors are not obliged to repeat the long period of trial and error that taught the Inuit to make suitable clothing; they can quickly adopt the dress style necessary for survival. A pattern of dress, since it is a learned cultural response, can change rapidly, independently of the genetic and physiological traits of those who use it. It can also diffuse rapidly to other people. This is not to say that cultural change is instantaneous. Indeed, some kinds of cultural change require generations to become widespread.

Humans are widely distributed over the earth. There is much evidence of movement and mating over long distances. For example, hundreds of thousands of people in the United States are descended from Chinese, Japanese, and Southeast Asians. Many of these people have mated with people of other ancestry. Genetic interchange has been going on for a long time, but gene flow on a large scale has only been a major factor during the past 500 years. This mixture of genes tends to reduce the average genetic "distance" between different populations. Still, there are strong, persistent heritable differences among populations in different parts of the globe. Let us look more closely now at the nature of these differences and their role in evolution.

IS THE HUMAN SPECIES DIVIDED INTO RACES?

To most people, human race is so obvious that it hardly needs definition or explanation. Yet to many anthropologists the idea of race is so problematic that they suggest it simply does not exist. Scientists are not ultimately concerned with whether something called *race* exists or not. They are concerned with finding and testing models to explain variations in human populations. However, *race,* unlike *genotype,* is a term used in popular discourse, in political and social debates, and in other contexts. It is frequently confused with *ethnic group* and other designations. Let us look closely at the term *race* and its scientific and social usages.

The Biology of Race

One common view is that the world contains a fixed number of human races, each one having a distinctive set of heritable characteristics. In the past this idea led to the attempt to describe and name major races of the world. One scheme that is still fairly popular in the West divides humanity into five major races: **Caucasoid,** (European), **Mongoloid** (Asian), **Negroid** (African), **Australoid** (Australian and Melanesian), and **Pygmoid** (usually referring to central African populations characterized by short stature). This classification, although first proposed by scientists, has no sound biological basis. So, how many races are there?

To answer the question, we have to look at how population biologists define human populations in genetic terms and what kinds of traits they use for their classifications. A biological race would be a relatively homogeneous breeding population that persists through time. The only way to characterize entire populations by heritable traits is to examine a group of people and count the frequency of specific genetic traits, such as **blood groups,** within populations. We may begin by noting that there are very few genetically homogeneous populations in the world. If there are any such populations, they should be small, isolated groups living away from the major pathways of population movement. Studies in small, relatively isolated tribal populations in South America show a degree of diversity comparable to large European and American cities. Nevertheless, statistically speaking, small populations are relatively homogeneous for some genes. For example, the indigenous people of South America nearly all have type O blood. The frequency of type A blood is high among the aboriginal (indigenous) people of Australia and the Lapps of Norway and Finland. These same populations are highly mixed for other genetic traits, however.

Maps showing the distribution of genetic traits may be misleading. They show sharp lines dividing populations with contrasting gene frequencies. In reality there are rarely any sharp lines. In humans, as in other widespread species, there usually are gradual changes in frequencies from one place to another. These gradations are known as **clines.** Figure 8.2 shows the clinal variation in type B blood in both Europe and central Asia. Not all clinal distributions are like this one, but this kind of information helps make two things clear.

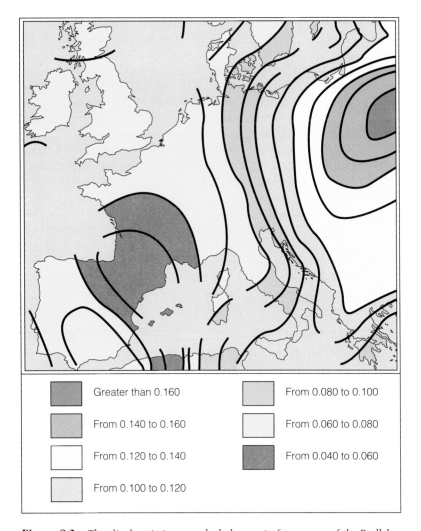

Figure 8.2   *The clinal variation—gradual changes in frequency—of the B allele of the ABO blood group system in Europe and central Asia. Type B blood is much more common in Asia, decreasing in frequency as the clines move westward into Europe.*

Caucasoid   A common category in racial typology for people of European ancestry.

Mongoloid   A common category in racial typology for people of Asian origin.

Negroid   A common category in racial typology for people of African descent.

Australoid   A common category in racial typology for people of Australian and Melanesian origins.

Pygmoid   In racial classification, an ideal type used to label people of short stature who live in the tropical areas of Africa (Pygmies), Southeast Asia, and the South Pacific (Negritos).

blood groups   A classification of blood types based on characteristics that are genetically inherited. Some types of blood are more common in certain racial groups than in others. The most commonly known is the ABO blood group, but there are many others, including Duffy, Rh, and Diego.

cline   A gradient or gradual change in gene frequency from one geographical location to another.

First, genetic traits may be continuously variable over space. We do not generally find sharp breaks in genetic traits between one place and another. This is partly the effect of mixing that occurs when people mate outside their own local groups, partly the result of migration, partly the result of new genes arising through mutation, and partly a reflection of the fact that selective forces may themselves be gradually distributed.

Second, accurate characterizations can be made in terms of frequencies of specific genes in particular populations, but such frequencies do not apply to individuals. For example, looking at the map in Figure 8.2, we see that between 6 and 8 percent of the people of the British Isles have type B blood. This information is useless for classifying individuals. An individual is either 100 percent type B or 100 percent some other blood type. All that it tells us is that if we pick an individual at random from the population of the United Kingdom, there is a chance of 6 to 8 in 100 that he or she will have type B blood.

These points apply to single traits. But most people think of races as clusters of different traits. One biologist, R. D. Lewontin (1984), tried to find out how homogeneous the commonly recognized racial groupings actually are. Rather than looking at a single trait at a time, he chose 17 different **polymorphic traits** (genes with more than one allele) for which he could find accurate data for a large sample of world populations.

Lewontin used seven conventional racial categories for his test: Caucasians, sub-Saharan Africans, Mongoloids, South Asian aborigines, American Indians, Oceanians, and Australian aborigines. He sorted the data with a computer and found that the major racial groupings helped him account for about 6 percent of

---

BOX 8.1

Social Race and the State

Race is a pervasive idea that shows up in nearly every aspect of life. In many societies there is much political manipulation of racial ideas. The Nazis pumped up German nationalism by declaring that the Aryan or Nordic race derived from the original Caucasian stock was a pure race with special characteristics that gave it the right to dominate other races. The myth of the Aryan "master race" provided the Nazis with their rationale for herding members of supposedly inferior races, including Jews and Gypsies, into concentration camps and murdering them as part of a eugenic program in Germany and occupied countries during World War II. Cultural Jews and non-Jews alleged to have Jewish ancestry were all caught up in the slaughter.

Social racial ideas are not always used to abuse other people. In the contemporary United States the government has established several programs designed to reduce the discrimination to which racial groups, particularly African Americans, have historically been subjected. In the name of affirmative action, for example, some cities and states have set up a double standard for admitting people to certain job categories. This can create some paradoxical situations. Consider the case of the Malone brothers, reported in *The New York Times*. These light-skinned, fair-haired twins of Irish-American descent were fire fighters in the city of Boston. In 1975 they took a civil service test to apply for promotion to captain, but their scores were not high enough to be accepted. The following year they reapplied, but this time they listed their race as Afro-American. In support of this claim they produced a sepia (brownish-tinted) photograph of their great-grandmother, who, according to their mother, was Afro-American. Although their scores again failed to meet the minimum requirements, they were eligible for appointment as minority applicants under an affirmative action program, and they were accepted. In 1988 they again applied for promotion, and their names appearing on a list of Afro-American fire fighters prompted questions about their race. At this point, they were fired for having lied on their applications. They sued for reinstatement, and the matter was taken up by the courts.

Regardless of the legal issues, the incident reveals the social and cultural component of racial classification in the United States. As one lawyer put it, "It's entirely possible to look white but be black." Whatever their motives and sincerity, the Malone Brothers were taking advantage of the cultural construction of race in the United States.

the variation in his sample. In other words, if Lewontin had tried to guess the 17 genetic traits of individuals based on their conventional racial grouping, he would be wrong 94 times out of 100. Even using a finer classification of "local races" (such as northwest European, East African, northern Chinese), he could have accounted for only 15 percent of the variation in his sample. This can be taken to mean that race, in a strict biological sense, does not exist. A more precise statement is that there is little biological basis for the conventional racial groupings recognized by most people, because they are not genetically homogeneous. This does not mean that there are no significant genetically based differences among human populations. Rather, it implies that these differences do not come "packaged" as the groups conventionally known as races.

Race as a Social Construct

Although race does not have a firm biological basis in our species, it does exist as a social construct. It is probably impossible to visit any major U.S. city without confronting the issue of **social race**. Americans conventionally classify each other as white, black, hispanic, Asian, American Indian, and so on. Entire neighborhoods, schools, and churches are characterized by race. These are social usages, found in informal speech, but such distinctions may also appear on official forms (Box 8.1). They designate categories that may determine eligibility for government programs, special consideration for employment, and so on. These labels also act to help or hinder people seeking employment, housing, educational opportunities, and other social goods.

Such groups are real and socially significant, but they cannot be defined in biological terms. For this reason, they are known by anthropologists as social races (Wagley 1968). Social races are identified in physical and cultural terms by such features as skin color, language, musical styles, food preferences, and clothing style. In Peru, for example, a person known as an *indio* (Indian) may have a full brother considered to be a **mestizo** ("mixed blood") because he speaks Spanish and wears non-Indian clothing.

People may believe that there is a heritable biological basis for certain differences and act accordingly, regardless of the scientific validity of their beliefs. When they use such beliefs to justify discrimination against another social group, they are practicing **racism**. We will discuss the meaning and significance of social race in Chapter 18. For the time being, we should simply take note of the fact that *race* has both a scientific and a social meaning and that it is important to separate the two.

NATURAL SELECTION AND HUMAN VARIATION

There is little doubt that human evolution is an ongoing process, and many of the polymorphic traits found among human groups can be explained by the principle of natural selection. One of the most striking differences observable among humans is in skin color (Figure 8.3). Skin color is frequently taken as a diagnostic racial trait, although we now know that the biological concept of race is quite different from the social conception. Let us consider skin color in terms of environmental adaptation and natural selection, *not* as a racial trait.

---

polymorphic traits Characteristics determined by genes that have more than one allele. For example, the ABO blood group is a polymorphic trait because there are three possible alleles.

social race A group of humans defined within a given social tradition as having common physical characteristics, such as skin color, language, musical styles, food preferences, and clothing style.

mestizo In Latin America, a person of mixed Hispanic and Indian racial descent. The term usually carries a negative connotation.

racism The practice of acting in a discriminatory manner against an entire social group based on its definition as a social race.

Figure 8.3   *Human phenotypes. Compared to many other species, human beings exhibit extraordinary phenotypic diversity. Some phenotypic variables apparent here are hair color, melanin content of skin, and nose, lip, and eye form (note the epicanthic eye fold in the woman at top center). There are many other visible phenotypic features, such as stature and shape of incisors.*

The Case of Skin Color

Unlike blood groups, pigmentation is polygenic, that is, under the control of several different genes. We also know that environment as well as genotype affects skin color. Greater exposure to the ultraviolet radiation in sunlight encourages greater **melanin** concentration in the skin (tanning). Ultraviolet radiation also stimulates the production of vitamin D, which is necessary for proper bone development. However,

excessive exposure to ultraviolet radiation can lead to serious damage from sunburn and eventually, in some cases, to skin cancer. High melanin content in the skin helps filter ultraviolet rays and prevents damage, although it also inhibits vitamin D production.

Let us consider a hypothesis about the worldwide distribution of skin pigmentation: *Natural selection favors dark skin (high melanin levels) closer to the equator where exposure to sunlight is greater.* There seems to be good evidence for the hypothesis: Africans from

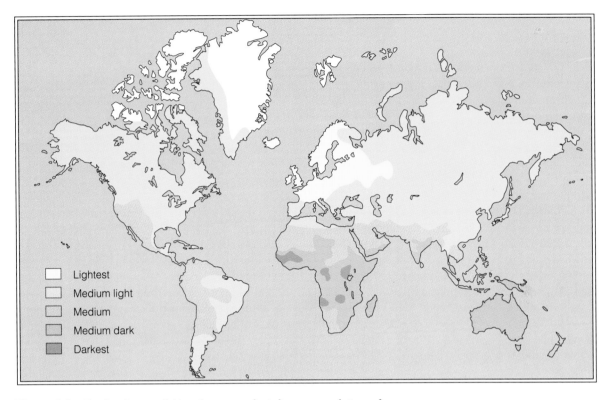

Figure 8.4   *The distribution of skin color among the indigenous populations of the world.* Indigenous *refers to the predominant population occupying an area at about* A.D. *1500. If the map reflected migration after that date, much of North America and Australia would be keyed the same as northern Europe.*

south of the Sahara, Melanesians, and others dwelling near the equator are generally dark in color. Northern Europeans (such as Scandinavians) and northern Asians (such as Siberians) are light skinned (Figure 8.4). Native North Americans appear to conform to the predicted correlation except for a skewing from northwest (where people are darker) to southeast (where people tend to be lighter).

South America reveals a more complicated pattern. There is a band of more highly pigmented people along the West Coast, compared with the Amazon basin to the east. The explanation for this may be that there is greater exposure to ultraviolet radiation at the high altitudes of the Andes than in the dense forests of the Amazon basin. Another exception is found in the Pacific, comparing Australian aborigines to the peoples of New Guinea just to the North. The theory predicts that the Australians, farther from the equator, will be less pigmented, but the reverse is true. Perhaps the fact that New Guinea has greater forest cover, while much of Australia is a treeless desert, is sufficient to explain this exception.

---

melanin   A pigment that darkens the skin and has protective effects for people exposed to ultraviolet radiation, as from bright sunlight.

In Africa the map is again more complicated. The !Kung San (see Figure 8.4), who inhabit a semidesert in southwest Africa, live outdoors under intense sunlight yet are fairly light skinned (although they have other skin characteristics that may provide greater protection from ultraviolet rays). They are surrounded by much darker people at the same latitude, altitude, and vegetation cover. Some of the darkest-skinned people of Africa live in thick tropical forests, where they are exposed to relatively little sunlight even though they live close to the equator. Some of the exceptions can be explained by migration. The heavily pigmented peoples of central African forests may have moved into these forested areas recently (within the last 2,000 years). Their pigmentation may therefore reflect an adaptation to open land where deep pigmentation would have been advantageous. The !Kung San may be a remnant population that once covered much of southern Africa at fairly high latitudes.

We have only limited success in explaining a particular phenotypic variation (skin pigmentation) in terms of natural selection. There are several reasons for this:

1. Skin pigmentation is not regulated by a single gene. The selective forces operating on each gene may be different.
2. The selective factors may have changed over time as people moved from one environment to another.
3. Through their culture, people have modified the environment to a great extent. In cold climates, people generally wear heavy, tight-fitting clothing that limits their exposure to sunlight. People who wear clothes and live in shelters in effect regulate their exposure to sunlight so that latitude would not be a good measure of the amount of exposure.
4. A particular phenotype may be adaptive to an environmental feature that is no longer present.

There may be a valid explanation for the distribution of skin pigmentation in terms of natural selection. But we should not expect it to be a simple one, given all the factors just considered. The same thing is true of such traits as a pronounced **epicanthic fold** (see Figure 8.3), blue eyes, peppercorn hair, a flat nose, or thin lips. Natural selection has influenced the development of people's physical features, but there is no simple relationship between these features and the environment.

Disease as a Selective Factor

Understanding the relationship among genotype, environment, and phenotype is much simpler when we examine cases where a single gene is involved and the interaction between phenotype and environment is known. In one instance, a disease, malaria, selects for a gene that carries both advantages and disadvantages. This is the allele for the gene that specifies the composition of hemoglobin.

Hemoglobin gives blood its red color and allows it to bind oxygen molecules for transport to other cells, an essential body process. A mutation at a single site on the chromosome can produce a variant allele, **hemoglobin S**, in an individual carrier. Hemoglobin S molecules crystallize when the oxygen level is low, and they twist and distort red blood cells into a sickle shape, which causes anemia (Figure 8.5). During anemia crises these crumpled blood cells accumulate at the joints, causing painful swelling or even death. Anomalies like hemoglobin S may arise repeatedly in human populations through mutations, but their carriers are less fit and generally produce fewer children. Thus there is a tendency in any population for hemoglobin S genes to be reduced through natural selection.

Malaria is a serious disease, widespread in tropical Africa, India, Asia, and, until recently, southern Europe. It is caused by a parasite (genus *Plasmodium*) transmitted to humans through mosquito bites. The parasite is capable of reproducing with terrific speed in the human bloodstream; in its active stage it causes high fever, chills, liver damage, even death. It is difficult to treat or prevent malaria infection, so prevention efforts have focused on the eradication of the mosquito **vector** (transmission agent). Over the past 20 years, however, heavy use of insecticides such as DDT has resulted in insecticide-resistant mosquito strains because of unintended natural selection in the mosquito population. During the 1970s malaria increased until it became a leading cause of death in many African and Asian countries.

During the 1950s human geneticists found that there was an excess of hemoglobin anomalies, including hemoglobin S, in certain human populations. These were located in western and central Africa, parts of the Arabian peninsula, and southern India. These are also areas of high endemic malaria. They found that the fragile blood cells of persons with sickle-cell anemia are inhospitable to the malaria parasite, often bursting before the parasites could mature. Of the different possible genotypes, those homozygous for the sickling trait (SS) are subject to negative selection because of severe anemia. Those homozygous for normal hemoglobin (AA) are vulnerable to malaria attacks. Heterozygotes (AS), however, are less susceptible both to severe anemia and to malaria attacks. With this combination of factors, there was positive selection for heterozygotes, in other words for both alleles (A and S) simultaneously. In this fashion, both genes were maintained in the population, wherever there was malaria, even though each one was deleterious. This is a balanced polymorphism, that is, one in which the selective forces are opposed and tend to cancel each other out.

Another important discovery is the role that human culture played in the spread of malaria and the balanced polymorphism. Malaria was probably not widespread in Africa until about 2,000 YA. Before then, most Africans lived in dry, open country and moved around frequently. When metal tools and root crops became available, people moved into the humid tropical forests of central and eastern Africa, cutting down trees and planting gardens for food. Their settlements became larger, more permanent, and more densely populated. The gardens, planted in the midst of steaming jungles, left standing puddles of water where mosquitoes could breed.

People modified their environment in a way that favored the occurrence of malaria, though not deliberately. Many people of African descent now live in North America (and elsewhere) where malaria has been all but eliminated. These people still have higher than average rates of hemoglobin S, although lower than in malaria-endemic areas of Africa. In North America sickling has only disadvantages, no advantages. One would expect, therefore, that carriers of the sickling trait are genetically less fit in nonmalarial areas and that this negative selection will eventually reduce the frequency of the gene in the population.

Human Activity as a Selective Factor

Hundreds of other changes brought about by human activity are contributing in unknown ways to human evolution. One that we have already mentioned is the introduction of thousands of new chemical substances to the environment, some of which probably have a selective effect analogous to that of malaria. One example is asbestos, a chemical once used in the manufacture of items such as roofing and fireproof insulation but now banned in the United States. In the past ten years, asbestos has been shown to be a cause of cancer, lung disease, and other maladies. No one knows for sure how exposure to asbestos affected each one of the thousands of workers who were once exposed to it. But the effect on many workers exposed in the past was severe; many became sick or died from their exposure.

The effect of asbestos is variable: Some exposed people live healthy, normal lives, while others are afflicted with the diseases that are connected with asbestos. Some differences may be accounted for by different degrees of exposure, but it seems increasingly likely that genetic differences underlie some of the variation in response. What is not known yet is the effect of asbestos on the ability to bear and raise children. If, for example, asbestos-related disease affects mainly people who have completed reproduction (are

---

epicanthic fold A protective fold of skin covering the inner border of the eye, characteristic of Asian peoples.

hemoglobin S One of the hemoglobin alleles, which originated from a mutation. A person who is homozygotic for hemoglobin S will have sickle-cell anemia. A person who is heterozygotic for hemoglobin S will have "sickle-cell trait." Heterozygotes are less susceptible to malaria and severe anemia.

vector An agent that carries and transmits a disease, such as the anopheles mosquito which transmits malaria.

Figure 8.5   *The distribution of the sickle cell allele in the Old World is shown at bottom left; compare the high-frequency areas of sickle cell with the regions where falciparum malaria is common (bottom right). Sickled red blood cells (top left) are less hospitable to the malaria parasite than normal red blood cells (top right). The sickle cell allele is a selectively advantageous trait in malarial areas.*

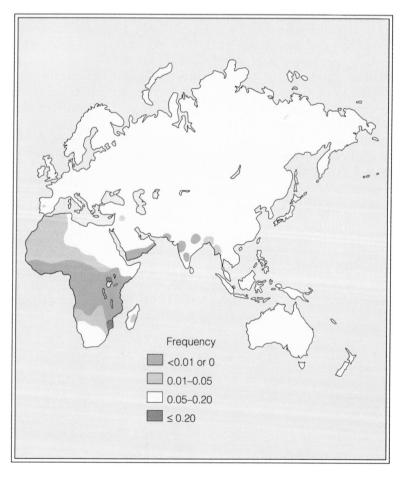

Frequency

- <0.01 or 0
- 0.01–0.05
- 0.05–0.20
- ≤ 0.20

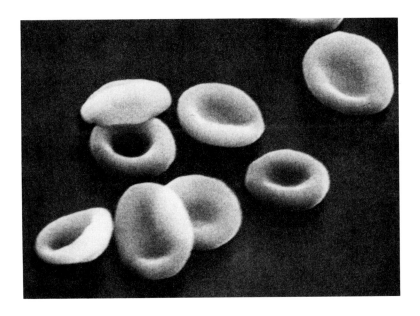

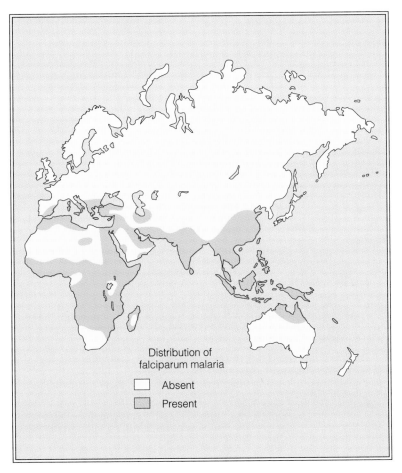

Distribution of
falciparum malaria

☐ Absent

▨ Present

beyond child bearing), it will have little effect on fitness. Asbestos will have an evolutionary impact only if it affects the reproductive potential of persons exposed to it. If it does not, asbestos would be considered a hazard but not a selective agent.

The environment to which humans adapt today is largely of their own making. Deficient diets, disease, crowding, pollution, stress, and other environmental features are the leading selective factors influencing the ongoing evolution of our species. On the other hand, some selective pressures have now been relaxed thanks to modern sanitation and medicine, food production and storage techniques, and machine technology.

Diet as a Selective Factor

Another important selective agent is diet. All mammals, including humans, are dependent on milk in the early stages of development. Milk contains **lactose**, a sugar that must be broken down in the body for it to contribute to nutrition and growth. Lactose cannot be absorbed by the body unless **lactase**, an enzyme secreted by the wall of the small intestine, is available. Most people have lactase during infancy but lose the ability to produce it at about four years of age. These people have **lactase deficiency.** Other people produce lactase throughout their adult lives. Lactase-deficient adults are unable to digest milk efficiently. When they drink milk, they suffer from gas pains and diarrhea.

Like hemoglobin S, lactase deficiency is not distributed evenly throughout the world. Between 2 and 20 percent of Europeans and their descendants in the Americas are lactase deficient. But more than 70 percent of African Americans and over 90 percent of the populations of Thailand, China, and Japan are lactase deficient. Studies show that lactase deficiency is especially high among people for whom milk was historically not an important source of nutrition after weaning.

Europeans, who are generally descended from **pastoral** (cattle-raising) people, show low levels of lactase deficiency. Many Asian and African people, and their descendants, have not depended on milk from domestic animals as a food. In a few cases there are people who are lactase deficient yet use milk products heavily in their diet. In most of these cases, however, people consume milk in the form of yogurt and cheese, products in which some of the lactose is absorbed by bacterial action, leaving other nutrients available for absorption.

Lactase deficiency is a recessive genetic trait. Populations with a history of cattle raising, using unfermented milk products as food, tend to have low levels of lactase deficiency. It appears that natural selection has favored people able to tolerate lactose in the diet whenever milk was readily available. Where it was not, there was less selective pressure and lactase deficiency remained a frequent pattern. In this case again, natural selection appears to have resulted in significant adaptive differences among populations. Here,

---

BOX 8.2

Genetics and Foreign Aid

There is a practical consideration connected with the story of lactase deficiency. Because milk is one of the most complete foods known—rich in protein, carbohydrates, fats, vitamins, and minerals—it is often included in diets prepared for people with nutritional deficiencies. The United States exports great quantities of surplus powdered milk to countries where there are nutritional problems. It also exports "know-how," including recommendations that people use more milk in their diets. It turns out that some of this generosity is misplaced, because lactase deficiency is high in many populations around the world. Billions of people are simply unable to take advantage of this rich source of food unless it is processed into cheese or yogurt, products much harder to store, ship, and distribute. Some "experts" suggested that the Chinese and other peoples were "irrational" because they were unwilling to expand milk production or to use low-priced powdered milk. These well-meaning people may not have understood that most of the world's human adults are unable to digest milk.

the selective agent was not disease, but cultural practices: keeping cattle and consuming milk products (Box 8.2).

THE ROLE OF NON-DARWINIAN FACTORS IN HUMAN EVOLUTION

Darwinian natural selection is not the only factor that explains genetic differences among human populations. Other processes can produce changes in human populations, both at the genetic level and at the physiological level. To the extent that so-called non-Darwinian factors are at work in human evolution, we need not expect to find that every single genotypic trait in *Homo sapiens* is the result of natural selection. As we will see, however, the conditions under which non-Darwinian factors act on the genome of populations are quite restricted. Thus, while we can acknowledge the existence of non-Darwinian factors, we should not expect to find them of great importance in determining the shape of our species.

Genetic Drift

Genetic drift may be responsible for changes in gene frequencies that are not caused by natural selection or gene flow (mixture). We have already discussed drift in Chapter 5. Drift may occur when a **breeding population** is reduced to a small size by epidemics, warfare, shipwreck, or other situations causing physical or social isolation. In some situations social factors lead to the reproductive isolation of a small segment of a larger population. One example is the practice of inbreeding among royal families who restrict marriage to other royalty. In small breeding populations, the

contribution of a single individual to the gene pool may be disproportionately large. After a few generations, that individual's genes may spread throughout much of a small population. This is the way hemophilia became common among European royalty. If a single male mates with a large number of women in a small population, in village societies practicing **polygyny** (see Chapter 14), for example, a similar effect can occur (Neel 1970).

According to some anthropologists, genetic drift is responsible for many of the major differences found among world populations today. This assumes that the major groupings had their origins as small, isolated populations and remained isolated long enough for drift to "take hold," leaving a distinctive genetic heritage. It is unlikely, however, that major human populations were ever completely isolated for more than a few generations. The fact that all human groups are able to interbreed suggests that there has been sufficient gene flow, even across the vast distances separating human groups during the Pleistocene, to maintain human groups as a single species. Recall, too, the molecular evidence (Chapter 6) indicating that modern *Homo sapiens* is only 200,000 years old. Thus any notion of a "pure race" will meet with the same difficulties as the notion of a "pure language." Neither one exists.

Nonrandom Mating

Another non-Darwinian factor in genetic change is **nonrandom mating**. Most population biology rests on the assumption of random mating. But mating, especially among humans, is seldom random. People may be quite "choosy" about who mates with whom. Economic, religious, ethnic, and other factors influence mate selection. In the United States, for example,

---

lactose A sugar contained in milk.

lactase Enzyme secreted in the small intestine that is required for the proper digestion of lactose, a sugar in milk and milk products.

lactase deficiency A recessive genetic trait reflected in the body's inability to produce the enzyme lactase, which is required by the body to digest milk or milk products.

pastoral Pertaining to a way of life based on the raising of herd animals such as cattle, sheep, or camels.

breeding population A group of individuals in a given species that occupy a local area and have the potential for interbreeding.

polygyny The marriage of one man to more than one woman.

nonrandom mating Mating that is influenced by nonrandom factors such as economic class, religion, or ethnicity.

Figure 8.6 *At an altitude of 12,000 feet in the Peruvian Andes, people are exposed to thinner air, extreme temperatures, and limited types of food. Individuals respond to these conditions through both physiological acclimatization and cultural adaptation.*

people are more likely to marry people of the same relative height. Such preferences tend to reduce the randomness in mating and to create relatively isolated effective breeding groups changing the frequency with which some alleles occur. As mentioned above, in some societies some men have access to more sexual partners than others. This is true in polygynous societies, but also in class-based societies (see Chapter 18) in which high-status men have sexual access to many women.

Acclimatization

Not all adaptation takes place by genetic modification. As we have seen, genetic changes take many generations to occur and they are not reversible unless the selective environment changes. The high rate of sickle-cell anemia among African Americans is an example of this. In other cases *Homo sapiens* has adapted in a fashion that does not involve changes in gene frequencies.

As an example of nongenetic adaptation, consider the response to stress caused by living at a high altitude. From the Himalayas of Asia to the Andes of South America, millions of people live at altitudes over 3,700 m (12,000 ft). At this altitude the density of the atmosphere is only two-thirds its density at sea level. The lungs must work harder to oxygenate the blood. People who move to high altitudes after a lifetime at low altitudes suffer from fatigue, dizziness, loss of appetite, and other symptoms.

At 5,500 m (18,000 ft) the ability to perform work falls to about 50 percent of that at sea level. This is probably the upper limit of human ability to adapt. Mountain climbers, such as the people who scaled Mt.

Everest (8,800 m or 29,000 ft) carry supplementary oxygen supplies. High altitudes also involve other stresses. Temperatures are generally lower at high altitudes: Even though the Andes are near the equator, temperatures during the day may hover close to freezing.

How do people adapt to such environments? There is evidence that people living at high altitudes for generations have **physiological adaptations** to high altitude stress. Individuals adapted to high altitudes have greater lung capacity, greater chest size ("barrel chests"), larger hearts, and higher blood pressure in the lungs. These adaptations allow people to take in a greater volume of air and get more oxygen from it than the average sea-level dweller. Other adaptive adjustments include a larger placenta, which is probably beneficial for supplying more oxygen to the developing fetus. High altitude dwellers also adapt through their behavior and other cultural aspects. In the Andes, Quechuas living at 4,000 m (Figure 8.6) specialize in animal products and crops adapted to high altitudes and trade with other people for goods more easily produced at lower altitudes. Since food energy is in short supply in their diet, they conserve energy. One way to conserve is to assign children—who are more energy efficient because of their small size—to herd cattle and other tasks that do not require adult size or strength (Thomas 1973).

How can we know whether these traits are genetic or acquired in each generation? Clearly the cultural traits are learned, and there is no reason to suggest that they are genetically encoded. The physiological traits, however, could be the result of natural selection. To find out, investigators did a series of studies in Peru comparing people who were born in the lowlands and then migrated to the highlands to people who were born in the highlands and then migrated to the lowlands. Lowlanders who moved to the highlands early in childhood showed most of the same adaptive adjustments as persons born in the highlands. Highlanders who moved to lower altitudes in early childhood did not develop the barrel chests and other features of highlanders raised in the highlands.

Those who moved in either direction later in life tended to retain the traits acquired in childhood.

The evidence supports the conclusion that adaptation to high-altitude stress can be better explained by physiological **plasticity** than by genetic change. In other words, the populations studied have the general capacity to adjust within their lifetimes to high altitude. This kind of adaptation is called developmental **acclimatization**. The earlier in life the individual moves to a given altitude, the more complete the adaptation. Those who move later in life do not acquire the full range of adjustment (Frisancho 1970).

It would be incorrect, however, to state that genetic factors are unimportant in adaptation to high altitude stress and other forms of acclimatization. Evidently the genotypes of Andean and other populations *allow* the degree of plasticity that they display. Phenotypic plasticity is "built in" to the genotype. There may be variation among populations in the degree of plasticity when faced with high altitude and other kinds of stress. Those with higher plasticity will be better able to adjust to sudden environmental changes.

Natural selection, mutation, genetic drift, migration, mixture (gene flow), and cultural influences probably all had an influence in shaping the current distribution of genes and phenotypes in the earth's human population. No single factor can account for all the diversity found in the world.

INHERITANCE AND INTELLIGENCE

The idea that some groups of people are inherently more intelligent than others is very old. Before the early 20th century, most scientists did not distinguish between race and culture, and they often used the term *race* to refer to any distinctive group of people, such as the "German race" or the "Jewish race." Although early writers on the subject had a scientific understanding of inheritance, they nevertheless suggested that many traits now thought of as cultural were inherited from parents. Almost invariably these

---

physiological adaptations Changes in the body resulting from adjustment to the physical environment.

plasticity The range of adaptability to varying conditions.

acclimatization Physiological adaptation that occurs within the lifetime of an individual.

traits were connected with the idea of superiority and inferiority. When Europeans referred to other human groups, they often called them "lower races." In similar fashion, Chinese scholars often referred to the non-Chinese as "barbarians."

Some writers offered evidence in favor of their beliefs. They argued (erroneously) that civilization never emerged among dark-skinned peoples; they suggested that certain human groups were more closely akin to apes than others because of differences in skin color, protrusion of the jaw, "height of the brow," and other features; and they suggested that writing systems, science, advanced technology, and great art never evolved outside of Europe. These beliefs were ethnocentric and self-serving in addition to being false. The attempt to present scientific evidence to support the inherent superiority of certain groups over others is **scientific racism**. Scientific racism rests on the **hereditarian** viewpoint, whose advocates tend to assume that all traits are hereditary, or genetically encoded.

Each generation has seen new proposals that purport to link the inheritance of social racial groups with some basic human ability, especially the ability to reason. In recent times, much of the debate centers around the question of "intelligence." Beginning in the last century, psychologists developed measures for evaluating human intellectual ability. This is known as intelligence testing or IQ (for **intelligence quotient**) testing. Before we examine the relationship between race and intelligence, it is helpful to consider how scientists use the word *intelligence* itself. *Intelligence* is one of many words used in social science that is also used in everyday speech. As with other terms, the scientific definition of *intelligence* is narrower than the conventional one.

The IQ Test

In their everyday lives, people evaluate intelligence in different ways. To a psychologist, intelligence refers to scores on standardized IQ tests. The Stanford-Binet tests (which most of the readers of this book have probably taken) consist of a set of tasks including word analogies, spatial perception, and problem solving. The score is based on how fast and accurately the test taker performs each task. IQ is computed by looking up an individual's score on a table giving the range of scores for a given age group. For example, two children may have identical test scores but the younger one will have a higher IQ score.

IQ tests are like other scientific instruments. They must be standardized and calibrated for **reliability**, the ability to yield similar results from similar measurements, again and again. Tests like the Stanford-Binet have been administered to millions of people and have been refined to a point where they are highly reliable instruments. When people are tested and then retested a short time later, the average difference in their IQ scores is small. Thus, when tests are properly administered and scored, IQ scores are reliable.

Another major concern is the **validity** of a measure. How do we know that a test is measuring what we think it is? In medicine, for example, a temperature higher than 37.5°C (98.6°F) usually indicates that the patient has an infection. But one can also run a fever without an infection. Temperature is not a perfectly valid measure of infection. One way of estimating validity is to cross-validate a measure with another one based on the same theoretical variable. In the medical example, a doctor might order a blood test for a patient running a fever to see if there is an elevated number of white blood cells, another indicator of infection.

IQ scores were originally designed to predict success in school, and they do generally correlate with academic success. In other words, people who succeed in school also tend to have high IQ scores. Some people believe that this correlation validates the IQ test, although it does not answer questions about how either IQ score or success in school is related to intelligence.

Why is there so much controversy over IQ testing? The reason is that reliability and correlation with success in school *do not* bear on the question of whether IQ is a measure of innate intelligence. High scores and academic success may both be more the result of culturally acquired abilities (Box 8.3). The question then becomes, are IQ test scores equally valid measures in all cultural contexts?

Is Intelligence Inherited?

If inherited at all, intelligence is certainly a polygenic trait. There is, however, evidence that whatever it is that IQ measures, it is at least partly heritable. In certain extreme cases, low intelligence can be explained by a genetic trait. Persons born with Down syndrome, an inherited disease, have below-normal intelligence and cannot perform normally in school. Down syndrome is caused by having three of the 21st chromosome, instead of having the normal pair. An extra chromosome, of course, involves hundreds of genes, so the phenotypic traits of a person with Down syndrome are highly polygenic.

In other extreme cases, however, it is difficult to show what portion of test-measured intelligence is genetically inherited. The reason is that the IQ test instrument depends on culturally encoded symbols and is usually given in a particular sociocultural setting. These factors interact with the background of each tested person. There are no words, symbols, or ideas that are completely culture free. Therefore, the IQ test is invariably mediated by social and cultural variables that can affect the outcome. In other words, it has a built-in cultural bias.

The issue of IQ heritability is best approached by comparing IQ scores of close relatives who have been subjected to different cultural environments during their formative years. Until recently the accepted evidence on this topic came from the work of Sir Cyril Burt, a British educational psychologist, who tracked down and tested **monozygotic** (identical) twins who had been reared apart. Monozygotic twins have the same genotypes, but in these cases they had been exposed to different formative influences. Thus, any difference between the two could be attributed entirely to environmental factors. If IQ is heritable, the difference in score between a pair of identical twins should be significantly smaller than, say, between fraternal twins, siblings, or unrelated persons.

Burt reported that the average IQ difference between the twins he studied was about 8 points, lower than the differences between **dizygotic** (fraternal) twins. Presumably this difference was entirely due to statistical random error and influences after conception. His results seemed to bear out the notion that IQ is heritable. Recently, however, it came to light that Burt had fraudulently modified his data to support his preconceived notions about the heritability of intelligence. The question is still unanswered, though most parties to the debate agree that what IQ tests measure is partly under genetic control and partly environmental. The question then becomes, how much of each?

With this in mind, the next point we need to consider is whether there are biologically based differences in intelligence as measured by IQ tests. The hereditarian position is that there is a significant genetic factor underlying the distribution of IQ scores in different social-racial groups and that the measuring instrument, the IQ test, is *not* biased. How well do these assumptions stand up against evidence?

Most of the discussion in the United States centers around the genetic potential of African Americans versus whites. There has also been discussion about the innate abilities of other minority groups. The greatest single application of intelligence testing of its time came in 1918 when the United States was involved in World War I. A Harvard professor of psychology, Robert M. Yerkes, designed a set of intelligence tests to be administered to all U.S. Army recruits. The tests were presumed to be useful in determining assignments for soldiers. Yerkes succeeded in having 1.75 million men tested at induction centers around the country.

The first analysis of this mountain of data seemed to provide statistical underpinning to many prejudices. Analysts compared the IQ scores of different nationalities. The average score for Russian immigrants was 11.34, Italians 11.01, and Poles 10.74. African Americans had the lowest average scores of all (10.41). Many scientists took these findings to mean that there are innate differences in intelligence among these various ethnicities.

Remarkably, Yerkes' principal report did not consider differences in the command of standard English, number of years in the United States, number of years

---

scientific racism The use of scientific evidence to support the notion that some social races are inherently superior or inferior to others.

hereditarian A viewpoint based on the assumption that all traits are genetically encoded.

intelligence quotient (IQ) A standardized measurement of human intellectual ability.

reliability The tendency of a measure consistently to give the same results under the same conditions.

validity The extent to which a measure captures what it purports to measure.

monozygotic Pertaining to identical twins, who originate from the same fertilized egg.

dizygotic Pertaining to fraternal twins, who originate from two different fertilized eggs.

BOX 8.3

Is the IQ Test Culturally Biased?

Many schools and other institutions use IQ and aptitude tests to determine the level at which a person can be expected to perform in certain settings such as school. People with low IQs are not expected to be as capable as others in certain tasks. Many other kinds of tests, such as the Scholastic Aptitude Test (SAT), are given in the United States. Like the IQ test, the SAT is designed to test not what students know but what they are capable of. Students with low IQ or SAT scores may be shunted off into less academic courses and placed on a track that does not lead to college. Teachers expect less of these students, who therefore do not try as hard. (Some studies show that students do better when teachers expect more of them.) In the United States these tests reflect the American preoccupation with individual achievement and competition.

The IQ test is a cultural product like a piece of music or a painting. The designers of the test draw the content of the questions or tasks on the examination from their own culture. Let us examine some of the tasks that examinees must perform on standard IQ tests given in the United States. There are many kinds of tasks required on an IQ test. Some of them involve looking at sketches and filling in missing parts (Figure). Others involve looking at various geometric shapes and determining which are similar and which are not. Others use numbers, as in the following example:

Look at the sequence of numbers given below. Then choose the letter that corresponds to the next number in the sequence.

　　　3, 6, 7, 14, 23, 46, 17 . . .

Answers:

　　A. 22 B. 29 C. 34 D. 23 E. 35

In this example, the sequence consists of pairs of numbers. The second number in each pair is twice the first, so the correct answer is C. This is a common type of question on an intelligence or aptitude test. It tests the examinee's ability to perceive a pattern, an ability that many people believe is important for clear thinking and understanding. But the item also depends on kinds of information that had to be learned for the examinee to see the pattern in the sequence. It depends on the ability to recognize numbers, the ability to make accurate computations (addition or multiplication would do the trick here), and possibly also familiarity with the ellipsis (. . .), a mark signifying that something is missing. Successfully performing this or any other task presumes certain acquired knowledge. The test cannot penetrate the thicket of cultural meanings that we use to communicate and tap directly into a person's innate intelligence.

In other test questions, the presumption of knowledge is more specific than in the example just given. In one IQ test second-grade children in a city school were given 30 illustrations to be matched with words. In one item, a picture of a log was followed by

A. goal B. log C. leg D. make.

Most of the children had never seen a log or a fireplace, so many of them saw the log as a rolled up carpet. Not finding *carpet* or *rug* among the answers, they got this item wrong (Fine 1975, 247).

Cultural bias can run both ways. James Loewen devised an intelligence test to show white Americans how it might be to take a test written from an African American perspective. One question reads as follows:

Saturday, Ajax got an LD. [This might be followed by . . .]
　　A. He had smoked too much grass.
　　B. He tripped out on drugs.
　　C. He brought her to his apartment.
　　D. He showed it off to his fox.
　　E. He became "wised up" (less dense).
　　[Quoted in Strenio 1981, 207]

If you don't know the definition of *LD* (Cadillac Eldorado) and *fox* (girlfriend), you probably could not answer the question. But these are terms that African Americans from urban areas recognize readily, while other terms used in actual IQ tests are not.

Another source of bias in standardized tests is the identity and behavior of the tester. Studies show that African American children get higher IQ test scores when they are tested by an African American examiner than when the examiner is white.

Tests that presume knowledge specific to a particular cultural tradition are **culture bound**. Tests may also be **class bound**, that is, they may relate to areas of experience that pertain to a particular socioeconomic group. One intelligence test used for 13- to 14-year-olds asks this question:

Sonata is a term used in:
A. drawing B. drama C. music D. poetry E. phonetics

The examinees were divided into high- and low-status groups based on their parents' income and profession. Of the high-status group, 74 percent knew the right answer, while in the low-status group only 29 percent knew the answer (Fine 1975, 49).

Other data show that there is a close correlation between IQ and economic rank. In 1974 the organization that administers the SAT presented data on the relationship between family income and SAT scores. A strong positive correlation was evident. What accounts for this correlation? One interpretation is that higher income gives an advantage on the SAT test. The advantage of wealth lies in better schools; better-educated parents; access to various cultural opportunities, such as books, music, art, and drama; and, perhaps most important, higher expectations. An opposite interpretation—also supported by the data—is that more intelligent people earn higher incomes. This explanation stretches credibility, for there are many intelligent and well-educated people who are not rich. Conversely there are plenty of rich people who inherited their wealth but not necessarily the intelligence that may have made their parents wealthy. Other interpretations are possible, but the environmental interpretation seems preferable to the hereditarian one.

In recent years many people have begun to object to the stress laid on intelligence and aptitude testing as a means for selecting candidates for advanced classes, colleges, and many professions. The premise behind the tests is apparently a very democratic one: Let an objective instrument determine who are the most qualified. The problem that has emerged is that the "objective" tests may be culture bound and therefore discriminate against certain minorities. Some critics argue that IQ and aptitude tests do not provide equal opportunity but enshrine the privileges of particular social and ethnic groups.

Part of the 1921 Beta test used by the U.S. Army for measuring innate intelligence among illiterate recruits. The examinee was asked to "fix" each drawing within three minutes by drawing in the missing parts. For example, the boy in item 1 needs a mouth, the woman in item 3 needs a nose, and so on. The amount of specific information needed to respond correctly varies from one picture to another. Someone from a warm climate might recognize a chimney (item 5) but might not notice that the chimney does not pass through the roof. Many will see that the cat in item 14 has no shadow. But would someone who has never played cards realize what is missing from the jack-of-diamonds in item 20?

culture bound   Characterized by the presumption of knowledge that is grounded in a specific cultural tradition.

class bound   Characterized by the presumption of knowledge that is grounded in the experience of a specific socioeconomic group.

of schooling, or other social and environmental factors. A series of later analyses of the same data, however, showed that environmental factors had an important influence on scores. For example, Yerkes found that the longer an immigrant had been in the United States, the higher his score. Another study showed that African Americans living in urbanized, industrial states had scores equal to whites living in rural, agrarian states. Literate New York African Americans, for instance, had about the same scores as literate Alabama whites.

In 1969 Arthur Jensen, an educational psychologist, wrote a long article claiming that even after discounting environmental influences there was an "irreducible" 15-point gap between the average IQ scores of African Americans and whites. He concluded that compensatory education aimed at enriching the cultural environment would never close the gap between these two groups. It is important to note that Jensen's presumption of the heritability of IQ was based on Cyril Burt's work, which has now been discredited.

Jensen also committed the fallacy of making inappropriate comparisons. To explain this fallacy, consider this example offered by S. J. Gould (1981). Suppose that we can establish that body height is highly heritable in a well-nourished North American population so that we can predict the height of a son from the height of his father with 95 percent accuracy. Could we then make similar predictions in another population, say one where there are nutritional deficiencies? The son of a tall man in this population might be stunted due to poor nutrition. We could not, therefore, safely predict the same relationship between genotype and phenotype in the second group. While it may be valid to compare IQ scores *within* groups, the nature of the test is such that the so-called gap between groups in different cultural settings cannot meaningfully be explained.

In order to sort out the effects of environment and genes on IQ, we would need to design another sort of experiment comparing identical twins, one of whom was raised as an African American and the other as a white. However, the likelihood of finding a significant number of twins raised with separate social (racial) identities is so small that the experiment will probably never be done.

Another difficulty is the lack of a sound biological basis for the comparisons Jensen and others make. Many of the studies (including Jensen's) that compare IQ scores of racial groups, searching for the extent of racial influences, use the social definition of race. This is because very few people are able to give a reliable report of their genotype. The best most people can do is tell you whether they *consider* themselves to be African American, white, Asian, or some other designation, since they are unaware of what specific genes they carry.

There is, furthermore, much gene flow between the socially defined races of the United States. Although there have been many African American–white matings, a cultural rule known as **hypodescent** assigns people of mixed ancestry to the black race (see Chapter 18). There is no way of knowing how much of this gene flow has taken place in the past 400 years of African-European contact in the United States. To treat the social racial classifications as if they were distinct breeding populations is biologically unsound. So not only are the measures of *intelligence* questionable, the definition and determination of *race* are also uncertain, and the controversy continues to obscure the issue of the heritability of intelligence.

Kinds of Intelligence

We should consider the idea that, as part of different cultural environments, different groups may recognize and favor different expressions of intellect. African Americans and whites in the United States generally belong to different subcultures; they speak distinctive dialects and have different dress styles, religious practices, and dietary preferences. There is some evidence that African Americans and whites also evaluate intelligence in different ways.

While both groups value verbal ability, African Americans put a special stress on verbal competition in a manner lacking in most white groups. In the urban United States, African American children and adults participate in a tradition known as "playing the dozens." The dozens consists of rhymed couplets made up on the spot to ridicule someone else, often by making disparaging references to that person's mother. A good dozens player can reply in short order to these playful insults with another even more scandalous response, maintaining the same meter (poetic rhythm) and rhyme. Two good dozens players will keep at it for several verses, possibly drawing a crowd of admirers around them on a street corner. Roger Abrahams, who studied the dozens, wrote that "ability with words is as highly valued as physical strength"

(1964, 62). Thomas Kochman (1970) writes about these verbal games in Chicago:

> Real proficiency in the game comes to only a small percentage of those who play it. . . . These players have the special skill in being able to turn what their opponents have said and attack them with it. . . . The "best talkers" from this group often become the successful . . . story tellers who deliver the long, rhymed witty narrative stories called 'toasts'. . . . [This tradition] has also produced entertainers such as Dick Gregory and Red Foxx, who are virtuosos at repartee, and preachers whose verbal power has traditionally been esteemed.

Americans can see this verbal power in the form of rap music and in public discourse in the speeches of Martin Luther King, Jr., and, more recently, Jesse Jackson, the preacher and civil rights leader who sought the Democratic presidential nomination in 1984 and 1988. Jackson's remarkable ability as a speaker is partly the product of a cultural background that values this ability highly.

While white poets and speakers certainly value the same verbal abilities, the African American cultural stress on verbal competition rich in metaphor and poetic devices clearly involves a unique expression of these abilities. Such an expression may not be tested on standard IQ examinations. Differences like this in cultural style could help explain some of the variation in average IQ.

An entire industry has grown up around testing people for intelligence. These tests are used as measures for people's basic abilities, especially in school settings. Some people feel these tests measure a real, tangible quality that is part of the individual and that will predict individual success in school and other situations. Others feel that disparities in test scores reflect differences in the environments of different social groups. Some investigators suggest there are different kinds of intelligence and that IQ tests measure only a narrow range of abilities that different groups value and cultivate. Some writers have suggested that there are many different forms of intelligence, including musical intelligence, logical intelligence, and spatial intelligence. Regardless of the source of IQ differences, we can see that social race is not a reliable method for distinguishing the abilities of individuals.

Eugenics: Can Breeding Improve the Human Species?

The debate over IQ and other phenotypic features has often arisen within the framework of eugenics. **Eugenics** is the study of improving the human species through breeding, eliminating less desirable traits from human populations and favoring more desirable traits. One assumption often made by eugenicists is that human social behavior is improvable through breeding. If only the world had more intelligent, reasonable people, their reasoning goes, the chances for wars, famine, and violence would be diminished.

History has shown, however, that eugenic theories can actually promote violence. The Nazis believed themselves to be part of a "master race" and sought to preserve it by wiping out "inferior races." Eugenic thought is also found in countries that prevent mentally retarded persons from breeding by forced sterilization, imprisonment, or other means. People may also seek to promote genetic improvement by positive rather than negative means. Recently the prime minister of Singapore announced a program to encourage college graduates to marry each other on the theory that this would promote intellectual excellence.

Eugenic theories rest on assumptions about the heritability of intelligence and other desirable traits. They also assume that by selecting for desirable traits, certain improvements will come about, but there is no evidence that intelligence has any relationship to how reasonable, greedy, or violent people are. Intelligent people will not necessarily make the world a better place. The idea that one can selectively breed for moral qualities, such as honesty, has no basis in biology. Finally we should recognize that many individuals do not realize their full potential, including the potential for creative solutions to problems. Before we embark on selective breeding of human beings, it might be well to determine whether we can make better use of the human potential we have at hand.

---

hypodescent   A cultural rule common in the United States that assigns children of African American and white matings to the black social race.

eugenics   The study of improving the human species through breeding, eliminating less desirable traits from human populations and favoring desirable traits.

SUMMARY

- In the course of human evolution there has been divergence due to many natural and cultural processes. Some of these processes fit the classical Darwinian model of natural selection. Melanin content in the skin appears to fit a natural selection model, although it involves several different genes and multiple environmental features.

- Human cultural behavior plays an important role in the process of human biological evolution. The development of agriculture in Africa was chiefly responsible for the spread of malaria in the tropical forest region, because it multiplied potential breeding spots for the malaria vector. Malaria, in turn, selected for the otherwise deleterious sickling trait. Raising dairy cattle appears to have selected for lactase production among pastoral peoples.

- Human evolution is also affected by non-Darwinian processes, including genetic drift, migration, and acclimatization.

- There is evidence that human evolution is an ongoing process, despite the fact that humans now control many of the selective influences of the environment.

- The relatively small, relatively isolated populations of the past are disappearing, swallowed up by population growth and the ease of migration. The kinds of variation arising from genetic drift will probably decline in importance.

- For hundreds of years, people have attempted to justify discrimination by suggesting that certain groups are naturally inferior.

- Scientific racist theories have been elaborated to explain differences in intelligence between populations.

- Because of the elusive nature of intelligence, it has been impossible to demonstrate a genetic basis for average differences based on standardized tests. There is evidence that there are environmental factors at work in the determination of the IQ. We cannot say for sure what these measures mean about basic human potential.

- The weight of scientific opinion is that racial groupings are not accurate predictors of innate ability or the social expression of intelligence.

GET INVOLVED

1. Make a collection of racial classifications used in your environment, such as those used on job applications, in university admissions, in popular speech, and in the mass media. Do these different usages correlate with each other? What is the biological and social basis for each classification?

2. Do a study of marriage patterns in a familiar community. If extramarital sexual relations leading to the birth of children are common, include them. Try to determine the extent to which there are nonrandom factors influencing the selection of mates, such as social and economic class, residence, religious and ethnic divisions, and college attended. On the basis of this try to determine how broad or restricted the mating pool is for the average individual in each group. Pay attention to intersecting variables such as social class and ethnic group.

3. Hold a discussion with a group of students in your community. How many times have they been tested for aptitude or intelligence? What are the testing instruments used? What has been their experience with such testing? Do they feel that the tests are fair or biased? Do they feel the tests are valid measures of what they are supposed to measure? If possible get copies of the testing instruments used and examine them for signs of cultural bias.

SUGGESTED READINGS

Frischano, A. R. 1979. *Human adaptation.* St. Louis, Mo.: Mosby.

Gould, Stephen J. 1981. *The mismeasure of man.* New York: Norton.

Molnar, Stephen. 1983. *Human variation: Races, types, and ethnic groups.* 2d ed. Englewood Cliffs, N.J.: Prentice-Hall.

Rensberger, Boyce. 1981. Racial odyssey. *Science Digest,* January/February.*

Thomas, R. Brooke. 1973. *Human adaptation to a high Andean energy flow system.* University Park: Pennsylvania State University.

Wagley, Charles. 1968. The concept of social race in the Americas. In *The Latin American Tradition,* ed. Charles Wagley. New York: Columbia University Press.

*This selection is anthologized in *Applying Anthropology,* 2d ed., ed. A. Podolefsky and P. J. Brown (Mountain View, Calif.: Mayfield, 1992).

An Evolutionary Perspective on Childbirth

Wenda Trevathan, a biological anthropologist, is an associate professor of anthropology at New Mexico State University. Her research interests focus on the evolution of human reproductive behavior with special emphasis on childbirth and sociosexual effects on ovarian functioning. She has received midwifery training and is the 1990 recipient of the Margaret Mead Award.

Wenda Trevathan.

In the 1970s and 1980s there was a great deal of concern about the way childbirth was experienced in the United States. There were complaints about the medicalization of childbirth and the impersonal way it was handled by obstetricians and other hospital personnel. In partial response to this concern, many women chose to give birth at home with midwives. One of the most important functions that midwives fulfill, which was missing in most hospital births, was the ability to provide emotional support throughout labor and delivery. The need for emotional support during childbirth is recognized in almost every culture in the world. In fact one of the few examples of the rare "cultural universal" is the practice of women assisting other women during childbirth.

Birth was probably a challenge for our ancestors even before we were hominids. Primates are characterized by large brains relative to body size. This means that birth is difficult for most monkeys who have large-brained infants. With the origin of the hominids, delivery of the already-close-fitting head became an even greater challenge because of the narrowing and reorientation of the pelvic canal associated with the evolution of bipedalism.

What are the major differences in births of monkey and human infants? The monkey infant enters and exits the birth canal facing toward the front of the mother's body. Once the head has emerged, she reaches down and pulls the infant toward her chest with the normal flexion of its body. The human bipedal pelvis, however, is oriented so that the infant must enter the birth canal facing to the side and then must rotate to emerge facing toward the mother's back. If she pulls the infant from the birth canal toward her chest, she risks damaging the nerves of the neck because she pulls it against the normal flexion of its body. Early hominid females who sought assistance at birth probably had fewer infants die than those who tried to deliver alone, as is the general primate pattern. Simply having another person present to help "catch" the baby once the head was born would have made the difference between life and death for many babies.

With the origin of the genus *Homo,* characterized by increasing brain size, childbirth became even more challenging. It is likely that the greater degree of infant helplessness in humans compared to monkeys originates in selection for larger brain size in the genus *Homo.* Because neonatal brain size was probably already at a maximum for safe birth, any increase in brain size had to occur after birth. This means that members of the genus *Homo* have typically given birth to infants with less-developed brains and a greater dependence on their mothers. Larger brains in adults probably also meant greater awareness of vulnerability at birth. Thus having someone provide emotional support for the mother during childbirth would likely be as important as having someone there to catch the baby. I believe that women have been seeking assistance from other women at birth for several million years.

For the past ten years, I have been talking with midwives, obstetricians, and others who work with pregnant women and newborn infants to explain why I think the desire for more humane birth practices is deeply rooted in our evolutionary past and is not simply a passing fad. My evolutionary perspective, which has arisen from my studies in physical anthropology, coupled with my training and experience as a midwife, have convinced many of these practitioners that my assessment may be right. It doesn't surprise me that women in the United States are asking to deliver in familiar surroundings with the support of their closest friends and relatives, including their husbands. The pattern has existed for millions of years and is in stark contrast to the recent pattern of giving birth in a strange place surrounded by unfamiliar people. Pregnant women in the United States today are simply wishing for the care that women have received for millions of years. The fact that they are getting it in many hospitals today shows that our efforts have been successful.

PART FOUR

SOCIETY & ADAPTATION

What are the means by which our ancestors managed to survive, both as individuals and as a species? Early humans avoided extinction thanks to a blend of physical traits and capabilities that allowed them to adapt creatively to their environment. One of their most effective adaptations was the development of an intense social life, a characteristic they share with other primates and with some other animals. Studies indicate that the elements of social life—living in groups, caring for the young, dividing labor, communicating, establishing social roles and hierarchies, defending the group from predators, regulating reproduction, and so on—are the products of evolution just as physical characteristics are. These various forms of social behavior proved to be successful adaptations for many species besides our own.

The earliest means by which humans satisfied their subsistence requirements—food, water, and the resources with which to make tools, shelter, and clothing—was foraging (also known as hunting and gathering), or the harvesting of wild foods. The behaviors and activities of early humans thus effectively balanced their social needs and their economic requirements, probably for millions of years. Then, as populations grew and people began to settle down in permanent locations, a new adaptation appeared—the domestication of wild plants and animals. With this development, human beings gained unprecedented control over the environment, including the ability to produce food and to regulate the reproduction of certain animal species.

Part Four addresses these basic human adaptations. Chapter 9 looks at the elements of social life, especially the social behaviors we see in the nonhuman primates that so resemble our own behaviors. Chapter 10 describes foraging as a way of life, showing how even today it can be a successful adaptation to certain environments. Chapter 11 explores a broader range of transactions between people and nature, including such methods of habitat management as slash-and-burn horticulture and pastoralism (herding). Chapter 12 describes the social and cultural factors surrounding the development of food production about 10,000 years ago, otherwise known as the agricultural revolution. Together, these chapters describe the basic adaptations by which human beings have secured their biological and social survival.

An Australian aborigine man with five of his eleven wives and their children pose after a successful hunt near Maipi.

THE ELEMENTS OF
SOCIAL LIFE

▲▲▲

The previous chapter considered the ongoing biological evolution of *Homo sapiens*. The human species presents an almost incredible variety of physical traits. Turning to human behavior, there is also a dazzling variety in language, social habits, **foodways**, settlement patterns, and ceremonial and religious life. This chapter focuses on the evolution of social behavior.

Unlike physical traits, **behavior** is something that happens, can be observed momentarily, and then is gone forever. Turning the page of this book is behavior. But it cannot be measured and recorded in the same way as more tangible physical properties like hemoglobin S. The most common means used by anthropologists to record behavior—note taking—is not always very precise, and of course it can't be used unless the observer is physically present when the behavior occurs. Researchers can partially preserve behavior for future study by using tape recorders, videotape, or film. They can also observe and record behavior by means of the physical traces it leaves behind. Cutting down trees, for example, leaves behind tree stumps and perhaps stacks of firewood or lumber. Some kinds of behavior, such as making stone tools or building cities, leave behind physical traces that can last for centuries and provide anthropologists with clues about the behavior that produced them. You will recall from Chapter 7, for example, that analysis of the Shanidar Neandertal skeletons suggested care of invalids, since some individuals seemed to have survived several years after crippling injuries. But such information is always just a partial record of the behavior that occurred at the time. In general, information about early language, belief systems, and social organization is sketchy and hard to obtain because there is little material evidence to go on (Box 9.1).

This chapter is concerned with **social behavior**, or any behavior involving interactions between two or more members of a species. There are many forms of social interaction. Usually people must be physically close to each other to interact, but they can also do so over long distances by sending gifts or communicating by mail, telephone, or computer. Social behavior creates social groups characterized by some degree of permanence in either membership or patterns of behavior. Social groups have a powerful influence on behavior. Individuals do many things in groups that they would never do alone. Thus, among humans, more than practically any other species, there is a social environment that influences nearly every other aspect of behavior and stamps it with unique qualities.

Studies of nonhuman primates and other animals show that social behavior is the product of evolution. Natural selection has favored intense social life among some species, and the primates seem particularly well suited to this adaptation. Many social patterns that have evolved must have been adaptive in specific environments. Looking at primate social behavior can help us better understand human social behavior and what purposes it might serve.

SOCIAL BEHAVIOR: LEARNING AND INSTINCT

All primates and many other mammals are **social** animals, acquiring and maintaining behaviors for **cooperation**, **division of labor**, and other kinds of social interaction. Primates are intensely social, living in small groups whose membership is relatively stable through time. Many insects, such as the honeybee, are also social. In the hive honeybees work at different tasks, such as guarding the door, cooling the hive with their wings, or gathering nectar from plants. But most scientists who study the subject believe that there is a wide gap between the sociality of insects and that of higher animals.

The most complex insect societies are heavily under genetic control. Different bees play specific **social roles**, behaviors patterned to fit into a network of differentiated activities. The specific roles of different bees in a hive are determined by the age of the bee and the amount of food it can get while an adult. As we saw in Chapter 4, bees communicate through dancing. But bee dancing is capable of little more than indicating the location of nectar sources surrounding the beehive. Insect societies are based on relatively narrow repertoires of social roles that do not vary from one family group of insects to another. Bees and other social insects seem to be born knowing what to do. "Decisions" seem to be based on exchange of chemical signals, the stage in life cycle, the availability of food, and standardized gestures. Insects acquire few additional capabilities during their lives.

BOX 9.1

The Evolution of Handedness

Artifacts can provide extraordinary amounts of information if we know how to look at them. Archaeologist Nicholas Toth studies the most ancient stone tools known, those found in East Africa dating to 2 MYA. To understand the ancient tools better, Toth taught himself how to make them. In the course of his experiments, Toth, who is right-handed, made an unexpected discovery. He found that slightly more of the stone flakes he struck off had a crescent of weathered rock on the right edge. A left-handed toolmaker would rotate the core from which chips are being struck in the opposite direction, producing slightly more left-side crescents. Out of 1,569 flakes Toth made himself, about 56 percent had a right-hand bias. When Toth examined a sample of stone tools from Lake Turkana, he found roughly the same skewing: 57 percent of the tools were right-hand biased. This indicates that like most people today, most of the hominids who made these tools were right-handed. This insight in itself is not highly important, but it indicates that one inherited trait has been part of the hominid genotype for at least 2 million years.

Prehistoric stone cores and flakes from left-handed toolmakers (left) and right-handed toolmakers (right).

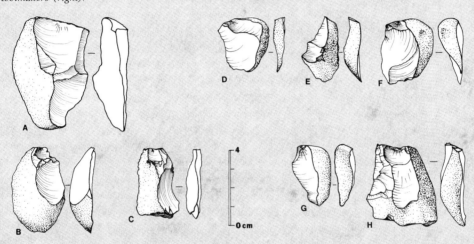

foodways   The habits and customs surrounding the production and consumption of food in a particular cultural tradition.

behavior   Any activity by any organism with an observable environmental effect.

social behavior   Behavior involving coordinated activities or communication among two or more members of a species population.

social   Living together and exhibiting behavior such as cooperation, division of labor, and other activities that require the interaction of two or more individuals from the same local group.

cooperation   Social behavior directed toward a goal, such as gathering food, hunting, or surveillance.

division of labor   Specialization of tasks within a social group, reflecting a degree of interdependency among the group's members.

social roles   Behaviors patterned to fit into the network of differentiated activities within a species.

Social life in higher animals is different. Mammals learn a great deal between birth and full maturity. Often this learning occurs under the supervision of parents or other older members of the society. It prepares the young for social roles and for a wide variety of situations that they may one day confront. While instincts are also important among wolves, baboons, and other social mammals, there is a much larger role for learned behavior among these species than among the social insects. Among mammals, selection favored a capacity for learned repertoires of social behavior, not specific behaviors. This capacity helps account for the ability of mammals to adapt to many different environments.

The Hereditarian View

During the 19th century, many scientists accepted the hereditarian theory, which suggested that specific human customs, such as religious practices, were part of a "racial" heritage. Early 20th-century anthropologists found it necessary to correct some positions taken by their predecessors. To set anthropology on a firm scientific footing, they asserted the independence of culture from biological inheritance. It seems obvious to us today, but it was not obvious to everyone in 1917 when anthropologist Alfred Kroeber wrote,

> In the last few years human beings . . . attained the power of [flight]. But the process by which this power was attained and its effects on the species are as different from those which characterized the acquisition of flight by the first birds as it is possible for them to be [Kroeber 1917, 24].

Only since the 1950s and 1960s have anthropologists and other behavioral scientists reopened the issue of the biological basis of human behavior, with studies emphasizing the biological and evolutionary significance of such human behaviors as those involved in courtship, sexuality, and reproduction.

Two Levels of Evolutionary Change

Behavioral evolution occurs on two levels that are easy to distinguish in theory but hard to tell apart in practice. Level 1 of behavioral evolution is **biogenetic evolution**, in which the process of natural selection favors certain types of behavior that became "hard-wired" into human chromosomes. Some examples of behavioral evolution are easy to classify: Upright walking behavior became possible only after level 1 modifications in the structure of the legs, pelvis, vertebral column, and skull had occurred. Until these physical changes happened, an early hominid would have had a tough time learning to walk even if there were benefits in doing so. Walking upright on two legs, then, is "hard-wired" into human genes and is an example of level 1 behavioral evolution.

Certain facial expressions may also be genetically based, along with the ability to acquire language and the hunger and sexual drives. Edward Wilson, a biologist specializing in the evolution of behavior, suggested that even responses like the fear of snakes may be inborn human tendencies (1984). Most of these behaviors are broadly defined and vary according to the setting. While there is a genetic basis for facial expressions, each social tradition seems to develop a set of expressions that can be interpreted only within that particular tradition (Figure 9.1) (Birdwhistle 1970).

Figure 9.1 *Some facial expressions can only be interpreted within a particular social tradition. This expression, used by a modern Maori warrior, is part of a ritual salute to a person of high rank.*

Level 2 of behavioral evolution is **cultural adaptation,** in which behavior is selected through a process of learning. This level includes all behavior selected and established through nongenetic processes. Some of this behavior pertains only to individuals, but most of it pertains to the social context in which two or more organisms interact. While the ability to communicate through speech is inherited, speaking French, Russian, or any other language is not inherited but learned. Social behavior may be acquired without any change in the genetic structure of the population. All a society's members need are the inborn abilities to interact in social groups and to learn from experience.

As an example of level 2 behavioral evolution, consider the belief in ancestor spirits found in many societies. There is no reason to think that belief in ancestor spirits was acquired at the genetic level. Nor is there a gene for monotheism (the belief in a single, all-powerful god) or matriliny (the tracing of descent through women). These traits occur in many separate societies around the world. Whatever influences selected for the occurrence of these traits did not operate at the level of genes.

On the other hand, there is a learned component in nearly all behavior. People are not born knowing how to walk or feed themselves; we speak of these capacities as "learned," even while we recognize that they have innate aspects. The simple motions involved in putting food into your mouth involve many learned aspects. They vary, depending on whether you are trained to eat with your fingers, with silverware, or with chopsticks. At level 2 there must be a set of inborn capacities in place before any animal is prepared to acquire learned behavior. As we saw in Chapter 4, some linguists believe that there is a gene for language. It is well known that a particular sector of the brain controls speech. There is a basic biological capacity underlying every learned capacity, from speaking French to playing guitar. Human biology provides

the foundations of behavior on which each society builds its traditions. The bottom line is that nearly all behavior has both a learned and a genetic component. It is not easy to separate the two.

FACTORS IN SOCIAL ORGANIZATION

Let us briefly consider some of the principal factors in social organization and look at how they may be adaptive for the species that practices them. **Social organization** consists of patterns of interaction between two or more animals in which each adjusts its behavior to the others. Social organization is adaptive when it contributes to the fitness or survival of the individual organisms. Some of the social patterns found among many species are parental care, dominance, division of labor, communication, altruism, pair bonding, and territoriality.

A word of warning: We sometimes describe animal behavior in everyday language, but when we do, the terms take on a special sense. It is important not to **anthropomorphize** animal behavior, that is, describe and analyze nonhuman animal behavior in human terms. You should be aware that use of a term like *dominance* in a scientific description of animal behavior does not carry all the connotations that the term may have in everyday speech. When it refers to behavior, a term may be borrowed from everyday usage, but in science the term acquires a narrower, more specific definition.

Adaptation in Social Behavior

Let us review some of the most common forms of social behavior found not only among humans but also among other animals. In each case, the behavior

---

biogenetic evolution   Level 1 evolutionary change, or adaptation, such as bipedalism in humans, which is part of the genome of a species.

cultural adaptation   Level 2 evolutionary change, or adaptation based on learning, not genetics.

social organization   Patterns of interaction between two or more animals, in which each individual adjusts its behavior to the other members of the social group.

anthropomorphize   To attribute human characteristics to an animal or other entity.

is adaptive in that it enhances the fitness of the animals that exhibit it.

Parental Care. One of the most common forms of social interaction is **parental care.** Parental care includes all kinds of behavior by adult animals that favors the well-being of their offspring. This includes nursing (suckling), bringing or sharing food, carrying, playing or supervising play, **grooming** (cleaning the fur of another animal), and defense. Many species seem to have a "maternal instinct," but males of many species also give parental care to infants and young animals. Males and females alike may give care to infants other than their own. It is possible that males in many species, such as baboons, do not recognize their own offspring, although they do participate in care by disciplining juveniles.

One problem with the term *maternal instinct* is the connotation that mothering is inborn rather than learned. There is evidence from primate studies, however, that maternal skills are partly acquired through practice, which includes "babysitting," or caring for infants by females that have not yet given birth. In one wild population of vervet monkeys, primatologist J. S. Gartlan found that females differed in their ability to care for the young. He observed some females carrying infants upside down or in other awkward positions (Gartlan 1968). On closer inspection he found that all these females were immature. Another primatologist, Harry Harlow (1959), raised baby rhesus monkeys in captivity without contact with a live mother to study the importance of the mother-infant relationship in the development of behavior. Instead of live mothers, Harlow provided cloth-covered mother dummies that baby monkeys could cling to and suckle, but which obviously gave no care to the infants. Female monkeys raised with dummy mothers rejected and mistreated their first offspring, but most gave adequate care to their second infants. Apparently there was some instinctual basis for caregiving; but to be effective mothers, monkeys had to learn either from their own mothers or from their mistakes.

Figure 9.2 *The same species may be organized in different fashions in different environments. On the Serengeti plain in Kenya, where food is relatively plentiful, predators abound, and trees are scarce, baboon troops tend to be large and elaborately organized (left). In the Ethiopian semidesert environment, where there is less food, less predator pressure, and more accessible refuge in trees, baboon troops tend to be small (right).*

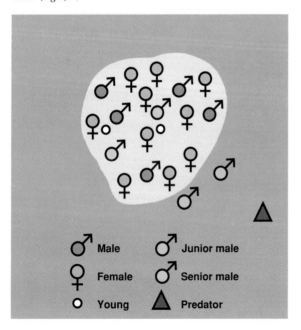

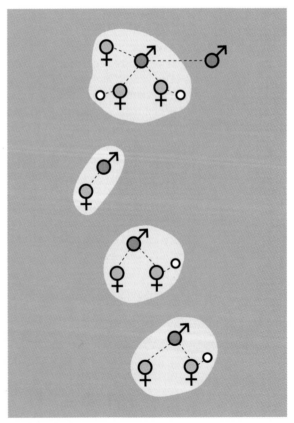

Social Groups. Many animals form social groups, coming together in herds, packs, swarms, or troops. Social groups may contribute to defense, group hunting, the regulation of reproduction, the socialization of the young, and possibly the sharing of information about the environment (as in bee dancing). There is great variety in the form and basis of groups in different species. Zebra herds consist of "harems" of females held together by individual males. The red deer of Europe live in herds led by an old female and consisting of a group of related families also led by females. Some species come together only periodically, such as birds that swarm at dusk or dawn or the giant herds of arctic caribou that form during the annual migration.

Sometimes large troops have an advantage over smaller groups because they can defend themselves better against predators. This may be so for the baboons of the Serengeti Reserve in Kenya, where lions and other predators will pounce on a lone baboon but hesitate to attack a troop of 40 or so animals. Other baboon groups in Africa, where predator pressure is lower, are much smaller and lack the elaborate hierarchy of the Serengeti baboon troops (Figure 9.2). In other words, baboons, like many other primates, display a high degree of variability in social organization.

Biologists and anthropologists often tend to assume that all social behavior is adaptive and to conclude that any social behavior must be advantageous. This is not necessarily true. If social behavior were always adaptive, every species would be social. But some animals live most of their lives alone, rarely interacting with others of their species. Social groups may have benefits; for example, a pack of African wild dogs can hunt more effectively than a single dog. Social groups also have costs: Forming and maintaining hierarchies, for example, requires time and energy that could be used in finding food, reproduction, and caring for the young.

For selection to favor social behavior, the benefits for fitness must outweigh the costs. This does not always happen. Some biologists suggest that social behavior among animals is not a normal but an exceptional state of affairs that occurs only under unusual conditions. Under most environmental conditions it may be preferable to the individual to refrain from social life because of its high costs.

Dominance and Animal Hierarchies. **Dominance** is the term used to describe patterns in which one animal forces others to submit. **Dominance hierarchies** can be seen in the "pecking order" among barnyard chickens, where the least dominant animal can be pecked by any of the other chickens and the most dominant can be pecked by none. Dominance can be expressed symbolically, for example in the "yawning" of the baboon (Figure 9.3). This gesture, in which the animal bares all its teeth, might be misinterpreted as boredom by humans. It usually occurs when one baboon comes too close to another or a male approaches a female in heat while a more dominant male is nearby. While yawning rarely ends in an actual fight between the animals, it is usually sufficient to communicate to the encroaching individual that it should stay clear.

There are also "surrender rituals." Male hamadryas baboons that live in East Africa and Arabia display dominance by lunging at one another. If one baboon turns his head exposing his neck in a gesture of submission, the aggressor halts immediately. Thus the reciprocal of dominance is submission, which is often symbolically expressed by **presenting** as if to receive a sexual advance (Figure 9.4). Dominance behavior may occasionally erupt into actual violence as animals compete for better positions in the hierarchy. Nevertheless, for a species in which dominance is important, the hierarchical order and discipline may be adaptive. They contribute to effective defense against attackers from the same or other species, and they may help limit aggression within the group. While these needs may be found to some extent in all

---

parental care The social behavior of adult animals that contributes to the well-being of a juvenile.

grooming Behavior in which one animal cleans the fur or skin of another.

dominance The ability of one animal to force others to submit.

dominance hierarchy A social pattern in which members of a social group are arranged in a continuum from most to least dominant.

presenting In dominance hierarchies, a social behavior that symbolizes submission. Among some primates, presenting involves symbolically assuming the posture of sexual receptivity to ward off a hostile attack.

Figure 9.3 *A symbolic expression of dominance. This "yawning" behavior is generally interpreted as an aggressive display and suffices to warn less dominant baboons to keep their distance. Rarely will this gesture result in an actual fight.*

Figure 9.4 *A symbolic expression of submission. When two baboons enter into conflict, the subordinate animal frequently turns around and "presents" its anal region as if to invite a sexual advance. The dominant baboon may "mount" the other briefly as a gesture of superiority.*

Behavior ("Roles")	Adult Males	Adult Females	Juvenile Males	Subadult Females	Infants
Territorial display	.66	0	.33	0	0
Vigilance, lookout behavior	.35	.38	.03	.12	.12
Receiving friendly approaches	.12	.46	.04	.27	.12
Friendly approaches to others	.03	.32	0	.47	.15
Chasing of territorial intruders	.66	0	.33	0	0
Punishing intragroup aggression	1.00	0	0	0	0
Leading in group movement	.32	.49	0	.16	0

Source: Gartlan 1968, 300.

Table 9.1 Social "Roles" among Vervet Monkeys, Shown as Frequencies of Behavior by Age-Sex Classes in Different Categories

groups, those in an environment with many predators would probably feel the strongest selective pressure for dominance.

Division of Labor.   Division of labor refers to an allocation of functions among individuals within a social group. The division of labor is determined to some extent by biological category. Female mammals are equipped by anatomy and physiology to give nourishment to infants. But care and protection of juveniles may be a male or female task. In many bird species males take a leading role in care and protection of the young. Male wolves provide for their young, swallowing food while on the hunt and then regurgitating it for their cubs back in the den.

Distinct activities can be analyzed independently of the particular animal doing them. Social roles are behaviors patterned to fit into a network of differentiated activities. Roles are usually discussed in terms of **functional categories,** that is, by the task they accomplish. Some examples of functional categories are infant care, defense of the group, and grooming. J. S.

Gartlan analyzed the behavior of vervet monkeys into the seven categories shown in Table 10.1. Some roles are played exclusively by adult males, such as punishing aggression within the group. Other roles are distributed across different age and sex groups, such as serving as "lookout." Juvenile males seem to avoid standing guard duty most of the time.

Communication.   **Communication** is a kind of social behavior that occurs in many species. Communication refers to behavior in which information flows through some medium to other animals. This can be done through gestures, as in the beaver's tail slapping the water; through **vocalization,** as in the howler monkey signalling danger (Figure 9.5); or visually, as in the male peacock's display of tail feathers before a female. As you will recall from Chapter 4, no other species on earth has a language or other communication system as elaborate as that of humans. Language, with its capacity to encapsulate and transmit experience from person to person, probably played a major selective role in human evolution.

---

functional categories The classification of roles or artifacts according to the tasks, goals, or uses they serve.

communication Behavior in which information flows through some medium to other animals.

vocalization Communication through the medium of the vocal apparatus.

◀ **Figure 9.5** *The howler monkey emits a low, pulsating sound that can carry for miles through the jungle. Heard most frequently at sunset and in the early evening, the vocalization may communicate the location of the troop to its scattered members or warn other animals of the howler's home range.*

Sexual Behavior

In most animal species, we can observe rules governing how and when animals form a sexual union. These rules of **courtship** may be adaptive if they regulate reproduction. Courtship behavior is exemplified in strutting, posing, display of plumage, mock aggression, or actual fighting. These behaviors are symbolic in that they do not contribute directly to a specific material outcome. They may, however, be indicators of the ability to breed successfully and to feed and defend the young. There must be a relationship between the symbolic aspects of courtship and fitness for courtship to have a selective advantage.

In some species successful courtship leads directly to copulation, after which the animals separate. In other species, such as cardinals, wolves, and humans, a mated pair may remain together for long periods after copulation. This phenomenon, known as **pair bonding**, is not the same as human marriage because it is a link that may be formed for a lifetime or only a few weeks and it does not have the symbolic trappings of marriage. But there is a similarity between the prolonged relationship maintained by pair-bonded animals and a similar relationship established between humans. Pair bonding is most adaptive when there is high **parental investment** in the young and a small number of offspring. Under these circumstances, it pays to leave one parent behind to "guard the nest"

while the other goes off to obtain and bring back food (Ember and Ember 1979).

Territoriality

One much-discussed aspect of social organization is **territoriality**. As it is used in biology, the term refers only to the active defense of boundaries, not to the customary use of a particular area. By this criterion, very few animals are territorial. Many animals do have **home ranges** or areas that they customarily and habitually use either as groups or as individuals. Other animals, such as colonies of honeybees, simply maintain a space between themselves and others. Having access to space may be important for getting resources, as well as for mating. The male red grouse of Scotland attempts to "stake out" and defend a small area of meadow. Those birds that do not establish territories are unable to mate and thus fail to reproduce.

THE SOCIAL LIFE OF PRIMATES

Ethology is the study of animal behavior in the natural habitat. Ethologists may be trained in anthropology, psychology, or zoology. Ethology often demands long hours of quiet observation and note taking. A primate ethologist may spend days sitting on the ground in a rain forest, straining his or her eyes for a glimpse of tiny monkeys in the canopy overhead. Some anthropologists believe that the behavior of free-ranging primates provides a model for the life of the ancestors of *Homo sapiens*. Others feel that ethological studies are valuable for understanding how selection acts on behavior but that this knowledge is not directly applicable to early hominid social life.

---

courtship Behavior that is aimed at attracting a member of the opposite sex for purposes of mating. It may include strutting, posing, displaying plumage, threatening rivals, or actual fighting.

pair bonding A reproductive behavior in which a pair of animals remains together for a time after copulation.

parental investment The effort that parents put toward the raising of offspring, including time and energy that cannot be applied to other pursuits.

territoriality The active defense of boundaries by a social group.

home range An area habitually used by an individual or a social group, which may or may not be defended.

ethology The study of animal behavior in its natural environment.

Figure 9.6 *Jane Goodall (left) and associate with chimpanzees in the Gombe Stream Reserve, Tanzania. Her close observation and long-term study of the wild chimpanzees was possible only after months of patiently waiting for them to grow accustomed to her presence. Goodall has been almost continuously observing the chimpanzee society here since 1960.*

Chimpanzee Society

Chimpanzees, the closest living relatives to humans, have been studied by many ethologists in the African rain forests where they live. Chimpanzees spend about half their time on the ground and half in the trees, where they make sleeping nests. Perhaps the best-known wild chimpanzees are those in the Gombe Stream Reserve of Tanzania, which were the subjects of a long-term study by Jane Goodall beginning in 1960. To observe the chimps Goodall decided to "introduce" herself to them and allow them to get used to her presence. Sometimes she fed them bananas to at-

tract them to convenient viewing areas and to see how they used the food. Gradually, the chimpanzees adjusted to Goodall, allowing her to sit close by and take notes for hours on end. She and her coworkers became familiar with individual chimpanzees and were able to follow them through several generations (Figure 9.6).

Goodall learned that chimpanzees have two major units of social organization. The **troop** is a loose combination of 30 to 80 animals occupying a home range over a period of years. The home range of one troop may overlap with that of another, although each troop may have a portion of the range that is exclusively its own. The other unit of chimpanzee organization is the **party** of animals that are together at one time. Troops are usually split up into several parties; the membership of parties is very fluid and may change from one day to the next. Parties of chimpanzees move through the home range searching for fruits, shoots, and other vegetable foods, insects, and occasionally small animals. Troops may encounter each other from time to time and such meetings are generally peaceful. Aside from the troop, the only enduring social tie among chimpanzees is that between mother and infant. This relationship may last well past weaning. Sometimes females move from one troop to another, but it seems that those with infants will generally move back to the troop they came from.

Chimpanzees communicate with each other through vocalizations (calls), gestures, drumming on trees and logs, embraces, and touching. Chimpanzee behavior includes patterns of dominance. If two chimpanzees approach a piece of food at the same time, the lower-ranking one will give way to the higher-ranking one. The lower-ranking or "subordinate" animal shows submission by reaching out with a hand to touch the lips, thighs, or genital area of the superior.

Female chimpanzees are **promiscuous**, meaning that while they are sexually receptive they will **copulate** with nearly any male, regardless of its rank. A female may copulate with several different males in succession. (This is very different from baboons, where a dominant male may have exclusive access to a female during estrus. If another male baboon approaches a female in estrus, he risks a violent attack from her **consort**.) After giving birth, however, a female chimpanzee is not sexually receptive again until her infant is weaned, a period of up to four years.

Unlike humans, animals do not have an **incest taboo**, a cultural rule forbidding sex between relatives. Some species seem to avoid sexual relations between parent and child and between siblings, although there is undoubtedly close interbreeding in many animal societies. In Chapter 13, we evaluate some of the theories about the incest taboo, including one suggesting that the taboo was biologically selected to prevent the deleterious effects of close inbreeding.

Grooming is common to all primate species. Grooming is the reciprocal of aggression; it might be called the tender side of primate life. Among animals like chimpanzees, grooming seems to be a means of providing reassurance. Chimps may groom a frightened or agitated chimp until it has calmed down. In baboons, grooming is a clear expression of dominance relations. Dominant baboon males are groomed more frequently than other males (Figure 9.7). While grooming to remove dirt and lice is beneficial to health, the behavior also has a symbolic value like the threat displays described above. Among chimpanzees grooming has a different value: Higher ranked chimpanzees are no more likely to be groomed than others.

Some aspects of social cooperation are particularly well developed among chimpanzees. Other species almost never share food, except between parent and infant. Chimpanzees, however, will sometimes offer bits of food to others while they eat, particularly if one chimp "begs" for it by staring and touching another's lips. Chimpanzees sometimes seem to coordinate their hunts by ganging up on small baboons and tearing them to bits. When they are stalking an animal, the usually noisy chimps do not make a sound. After killing game, dominant males will stand aside and allow others to partake of the kill. While this is a far cry from human sharing, it reflects a tendency to cooperate and share.

Chimps have the ability to make and use tools. While many animals use rocks or sticks, chimpanzees take this one step further, modifying their tools to suit their needs. Observers have seen chimps find little

---

troop One of two units of social organization among chimpanzees, the other being the party; a loose combination of 30 to 80 animals occupying a home range over a period of years.

party One of two units of social organization among chimpanzees; a momentary, fluid gathering of chimpanzees. A party is a subunit of a troop.

promiscuity Sexual behavior in which females may copulate with nearly any male during their period of sexual receptivity.

copulate To engage in sexual intercourse.

consort A sexual partner.

incest taboo A cultural rule that forbids sexual intercourse between certain categories of relatives, such as parents and children. Such rules are characteristic of humans only.

Figure 9.7   *Baboon grooming reflects the dominance hierarchy; dominant males are groomed by females. In a captive setting, however, the hierarchy may not be adhered to; a male at the San Diego Zoo (right) grooms a female. Among chimpanzees (left), dominant males are just as likely to groom as to be groomed.*

twigs, strip off their branches, moisten them with saliva, and use these slender devices to "fish" for termites in termite nests (see Figure 9.8). Of course, the ability to make rudimentary tools does not make chimps the intellectual equals of *Homo sapiens,* but it suggests a continuity across the two species.

Goodall found that different chimpanzees had distinct "personalities" (perhaps the word should be *chimpanzalities*). She observed that while one chimp was nearly always easygoing, another might be more fretful and aggressive. Some females seemed to be competent mothers, while others were inept, even abusive, to their offspring. Goodall once witnessed a mother kill her own infant for no obvious reason.

Primate Culture

Besides the differences in behavior among individuals, there are also differences among groups. Some primates may even have traditions. In one study a Japanese ethologist, Itani (1961), may have inadvertently stimulated a group of Japanese monkeys to adopt a tradition. In order to observe the animals more easily,

he lured them out of the forest onto a nearby beach by leaving sweet potatoes and wheat grains on the sand. One day a young female found that she could remove the gritty sand from the potatoes by washing them in a stream flowing through the beach. Other monkeys began to imitate her until the practice had spread through a large portion of the troop. Other animals began to float the wheat on the water with the same effect. This habit also spread throughout much of the troop. It passed from one animal to another over several years, finally reaching monkeys born after Itani had first observed potato washing. There is no evidence that Japanese monkeys ever washed food before. Thus Itani was able to observe the birth of a tradition through individual **innovation**. He followed the **diffusion** (transmission or spreading) of the new behavior throughout the group and generalization from one practice to another. This kind of traditional behavior occurs in a wide range of species, as well as primates. Domestic cats, for example, have learned to pass through special pet doors and have passed the custom to later generations.

Early ethological studies of primates created the impression that each species had an innate form of

Figure 9.8 *This chimpanzee is fishing for termites with a simple tool he made from a twig, stripped of its branches and moistened with saliva to trap the termites.*

social organization. As we saw in the discussion of baboons earlier in this chapter, primate behavior varies according to the setting. Now that primatologists have studied the same species in different settings, ethologists find that there may be considerable **plasticity** in social organization within a single species or between two closely related species.

Primate Language

A particularly intriguing aspect of social behavior in primates is the possibility that they are able to communicate via language. Most primates studied in the wild possess a repertoire of calls and gestures used to signal to other animals of the same species, sometimes over long distances. These signals may be used to mark territories, threaten, warn of danger, beg, show distress, invite another animal to play, initiate or reject sexual contact, and perhaps accomplish a variety of other purposes unknown. There is little evidence, however, that primates combine signals into longer utterances or that they have the property known as grammaticality (see Chapter 4). Many anthropologists have asked whether primates have the same abilities that humans have to learn and understand symbolic languages with complex grammars.

Since the 1960s several primate specialists have been doing experiments with captive primates to learn the linguistic ability of primates. Why does anyone want to teach apes or other primates to use language? The primary question is how different humans are from other primates. If humans are not unique in their ability to use language, a major link can be established between humans and their nearest living relatives. Other scientists hope that attempting to teach apes language will uncover the basic mental capacities that might underlie human linguistic ability. As we saw in Chapter 4, some linguists believe that there is a unique genetically encoded human ability for language, while others feel that language is wholly acquired after birth.

One of the earliest studies was reported in 1969 by R. A. and B. T. Gardner (1970), who raised a young

---

innovation The appearance of a new invention or an adaptation of an old one.

diffusion The spread of an item of culture within a social group or from one social group to another.

plasticity Ability to take on more than one form according to changes in environment.

female chimpanzee, Washoe, in a house trailer. The Gardners taught Washoe American Sign Language (Ameslan), a system widely used among those with hearing impairments in North America. Chimpanzees and other primates cannot produce humanlike speech because they lack the vocal apparatus to produce human speech sounds. After more than four years of training, Washoe learned 132 signs and was able to converse in Ameslan with her trainers. She learned to construct sentences, including sentences to which she had never before been exposed, an ability known as **productivity**. She also learned to generalize from what she knew to cover new items. For example, Washoe invented the term *water bird* to refer to a duck.

Other experimenters taught different animals language in other ways. David Premack devised a language by using colored pieces of plastic stuck magnetically to a board. The pieces had different meanings and included verbs, nouns, and prepositions. Premack and his associates taught a young chimpanzee, Sarah, to construct a wide variety of sentences by arranging the plastic pieces on the board (Premack 1971). Another group at the Yerkes Primate Research Center in Atlanta, Georgia, constructed a machine with colored buttons standing for words. They taught a female chimpanzee, Lana, to use the machine, which was linked to a computer. The scientists programmed

the computer to recognize correct sentences and reject grammatically incorrect ones in the made-up language that the team called Yerkish (Rumbaugh 1977). Other studies on language have been carried out with gorillas, orangutans, and pygmy chimpanzees. All of these studies seem to show that apes have the ability to learn and use language with a structure similar to human language, although they are limited to the level of very young humans. These findings seem to reduce the distance between humans and other animals. They also seem to weaken Noam Chomsky's claim (see Chapter 4) that language ability is uniquely human.

Skeptical of some of the claims of Chomsky and other proponents of transformational grammar, H. S. Terrace trained a chimpanzee he named Nim Chimpsky (Figure 9.9) to use Ameslan and then carefully recorded his behavior on videotapes (Terrace 1979). After close study of the tapes, Terrace's team found that most of Nim's utterances closely followed utterances by the trainer. Terrace also analyzed the grammar of Nim's utterances and found that many of them were ambiguously grammatical. Some could have been genuinely grammatical utterances, while many could have been conditioned by the training system.

Terrace and other critics suggested that language use among the apes is not true language but simply

Figure 9.9 *Nim Chimpsky uses American Sign Language to sign "open." In this study, experimenters concluded that the chimpanzee was mimicking the trainer and not truly using language. Other researchers suggest that apes can use grammar to construct sentences. Studies of language acquisition and ability in nonhuman primates continue to raise more questions than they answer.*

complex chains of behavior reinforced by the trainers through operant conditioning (the systematic use of rewards and punishments to favor certain kinds of behavior). In other words, the animals were simply mimicking the trainers to get food and other rewards. Their behavior was, in Terrace's view, not conclusive evidence for language ability among apes. While animals appear to be able to recombine a limited number of signs into new utterances, they seem unable to produce languagelike messages outside the context of the training session. The question of just how different apes are from humans in their ability to acquire and use language still fascinates anthropologists, psychologists, and linguists.

These studies of nonhuman primates have forced anthropologists to rethink their previous views of culture. *Homo sapiens* was once defined as the only cultural animal, that is, the only tool user and the only animal, capable of using a symbolic language. Primate ethologists have shown that there is not such a wide qualitative gap between humans and other species as once seemed clear. Their studies have also brought about a reevaluation of the biological significance of social behavior, how it evolves, and what it means.

THEORIES ABOUT THE EVOLUTION OF SOCIAL BEHAVIOR

As we observed earlier in this chapter, anthropological theory turned away from a biological explanation for social behavior early in this century and returned to it only in the 1950s. At first there was concern that anthropology might undergo a new attempt to explain *all* of human culture in biological terms. But such fears were unfounded. No reputable anthropologist has suggested that all or most cultural behavior has a specific genetic basis. Let us turn to a few theories that

have been proposed to explain the evolution of social behavior.

Reproductive Strategies and Parental Investment

Every species has a **reproductive strategy**. This is not necessarily a deliberate plan; it is a set of behaviors connected with reproduction, viewed as if they were aimed at certain goals. Darwinian theory suggests that reproductive strategies are selected for achieving the greatest reproductive fitness. That is, each organism seems to strive to reproduce as successfully as possible. Depending on the structure of the organism and the environment, that strategy can take different forms.

Consider the different reproductive strategies of rodents and primates. The rabbit, a typical rodent, seems to aim for quantitative success. A female rabbit can bear a litter every 60 days and up to 30 young in a single year. With so many young to tend to, she cannot spend much time nursing and caring for them. Rabbits are not able to defend the young against predators except by hiding the nest in thick brush. Under such circumstances, many baby rabbits are likely to end up in a predator's stomach, but there are so many babies that some will probably survive to reproductive age and carry on the genetic pattern inherited from their parents. This reproductive strategy is known as **R selection** (Figure 9.10). It is most adaptive in unstable environments in which the survival chances of any particular individual are low. Parental investment is correspondingly low.

In contrast, primates have relatively few offspring over their reproductive span, and parental investment is high. Biologists call this reproductive strategy **K selection**. Chimpanzee females have a gestation period of 11 months, and they nurse their young for up to

---

productivity In language, the ability to produce new, grammatical sentences that the speaker has never been exposed to before.

reproductive strategy A set of reproductive and parenting behaviors that determine the fitness of the individual within a given environment.

R selection A reproductive strategy involving the production of as many offspring as possible, relatively little parental investment, and a brief period of dependency for offspring.

K selection A reproductive strategy involving the production of a few offspring, great parental investment, and a lengthy period of dependency for offspring; characteristic of primates.

Figure 9.10   *These newborn rabbits will be nursed by their mother for a few weeks, after which they will be on their own. By contrast, baby primates like this chimpanzee will be nurtured by their mothers and other adults for several years until they reach maturity. These different reproductive strategies seem to ensure the greatest reproductive fitness of each species.*

four years, during which time they are unreceptive to sex. Thus in a typical life span of 25 years a single female can bear no more than about five young chimpanzees. On the other hand, chimpanzees do much more parenting than rabbits. A baby rabbit is out of the nest and on its own within weeks after birth. A baby chimp depends on its mother for milk, protection, and care for four years or more. During this period of dependency, the chimp learns a great deal that prepares it for adult life in a social group. Much of this learning is by imitation. Chimps are born mimics, one of the reasons they are so appealing as circus performers. Like other primates, young chimpanzees also play a lot. Much of the rough and tumble play of juvenile primates is a rehearsal for later roles without the consequences that mistakes can bring later in life.

Some biologists suggest that primates are divided by sex into those who practice R selection and those who practice K selection. Females invest more than males in any given infant because of the long periods of pregnancy and breast-feeding. To achieve maximum fitness, females need to choose their mates carefully; have few, well-spaced pregnancies; and invest maximum care and nurturance in a few offspring. Males, on the other hand, achieve greater fitness by mating with as many females as they can, producing as many offspring as possible. A simplified, but controversial, form of this statement is that female reproductive strategy aims at quality, while the male's aims at quantity. This dichotomy has interesting—and still highly controversial—implications for studies of human behavior.

Reproductive strategies may vary within a species. It is well known that in many disadvantaged human populations, women often bear many babies, even though the survival rate of children is low. In more affluent populations, on the other hand, the birthrate per female may be lower. As usual, the situation among humans is more complex than in other species. The reproductive behavior of humans is related to their tendency to share and exchange goods more than any other species. One theory holds that poor women have more children not to enhance their fitness but as a form of insurance in their old age. Having many children could increase the likelihood that some will survive and help care for their parents when they can no longer care for themselves.

It is impossible to say whether the slower pace of reproduction among primates is a cause or an effect of the long period of maturation and learning. It is probably more accurate to say that both are the joint results of selection in an environment where learned social behavior and increasingly complex symbolic repertoires of behavior were advantageous. The intense social lives of chimpanzees and other primates are compatible with learning complex social roles, cooperation, communication, and even toolmaking.

Altruism and Sociobiology

In the 1950s and 1960s, ethologists began to try to explain the significance of many forms of social behavior in biological terms. They sought to explain the adaptive significance of such behaviors as swarming and flocking. One approach that arose in the 1950s was known as **group selection.** This approach begins with the Malthusian observation that animal populations have the possibility of reproducing much faster than the food supply can expand. Yet most animal populations do not expand up to the limit of the food supply and other resources. The group selection theory suggests that social behavior that communicates information about the size and **density** (number of animals per square kilometer) of the local population to its members is favored by natural selection. When the population expands beyond tolerable limits, adjustments in **vital rates** (births and deaths) occur, bringing the population size back within those limits and thus preventing resource depletion. This theory was appealing to conservationists because it suggests a kind of balance in nature and the ability of animals to regulate themselves.

Self-regulation means adjusting **fertility** (number of fertilized eggs per 1,000 population) and **mortality** (number of deaths per 1,000 population) rates to keep population size and density within tolerable limits. One influential proponent of group selection, V. C. Wynne-Edwards, suggested that the massing of great swarms of birds every day at sundown yielded information for self-regulation by providing visible and audible cues indicating the size of the local population. By some unknown process, these cues could be interpreted by individuals, who would then act appropriately. Territorial behavior among birds like the grouse could have the similar effect of preventing mating by males who fail to secure territories. These kinds of behavior would be selected at the level of the group, not the individual, since the group would be the primary beneficiary. Group selection seemed to hold the key to many kinds of social behavior, such as group defense, suicidal attacks by bees, and others.

Group selection is particularly compelling in humans because of the vast repertoire of cultural behavior found in most human groups. While this knowledge is not necessarily shared equally among all individuals, neither is it necessarily linked to the fitness of an individual.

Sociobiology and Inclusive Fitness

After some time, other biologists raised a serious objection to group selection: It could not work within the framework of Darwinian theory. They pointed out that *populations* do not mate and reproduce, *individuals* do. Self-regulation of population at the group level implies that some animals sacrifice their individual fitness to improve the fitness of the group. This is known in biology as **altruism** (Figure 9.11). Critics of the group selection model pointed out that the model presents a paradox within the Darwinian framework.

---

group selection A theory suggesting that certain types of social behavior, such as swarming or flocking, can induce individual behavior that contributes to overall group fitness; according to the theory, these types of social behavior are favored by natural selection.

density Quantity per unit volume, such as number of animals per square kilometer.

vital rates The rates of births and deaths and other variables related to population growth and reproduction.

fertility The number of fertilized eggs per 1,000 population.

mortality The number of deaths per 1,000 population.

altruism In biology, the sacrifice of individual fitness to improve the fitness of the group.

Figure 9.11   *Are animals capable of true altruism? One explanation of mass whale strandings holds that the group protectively surrounds a sick member and stays with it even when it wanders into shallow water.*

An organism programmed by nature to sacrifice its own fitness would suffer negative selection, eventually eliminating any inborn tendency to altruism from the population. If natural selection worked as evolutionary theory suggests, altruistic behavior could not emerge. The scientists who raised these objections became known as **sociobiologists** and their ideas became known as the theory of the "selfish gene." This is because Darwinian theory stipulates that, in the struggle for survival, individuals with the highest reproductive success would pass their genes on to future generations. In this context the terms *altruism* and *selfish* should not be understood in their everyday sense.

The sociobiologists had to explain some apparent exceptions to their theory. Consider, for example, the honeybee worker, an animal that toils diligently for the common good, caring for future generations although its fitness is zero. In honeybee society only the queen bee can reproduce; the barren workers are pushed out of the hive to die when their usefulness is at an end. Consider also the baboon troop of the Serengeti plains in Kenya studied by Irven DeVore. When threatened by a predator such as a lion, the subordinate young males array themselves in front facing the threat. Behind them stand the females and juveniles and in the center of the group, farthest from danger, are the dominant males. How could such "unselfish" behavior have evolved if it exposed certain animals to a higher likelihood of injury and death?

The sociobiologist's answer to these apparent exceptions is that they are not true cases of altruism. The honeybee worker is a sibling or descendent of every other bee in the colony. The young baboon male is likely to be a close relative of the females and dominant males he is helping to defend. In other words, the animal helping to defend or care for others may be increasing its own fitness if the animals benefited by its sacrifice are closely related. Even though it may give its life for the good of the group, its genes will live on, transmitted by others. This notion is called **inclusive fitness.** It differs from group selection in that it preserves the Darwinian notion of the struggle for existence. Most sociobiologists admit that group selection may also operate among intensely social animals such as humans. Group selection could operate even in a strictly Darwinian system where there is a high dependency on learned behavior and a high **extinction rate** (high likelihood that certain genes might be eliminated from the genome of a population).

Recently, however, sociobiologists have been applying their theory of inclusive fitness to human behavior within a Darwinian framework. For example, Monique Borgerhoff-Mulder (1988) examined the practice of **bride price** among the Kipsigis of East Africa. Kipsigis men, as in other African peoples, must make a payment to their bride's family as compensation for permission to marry her. Borgerhoff-Mulder wanted to see whether the size of bride prices paid had any relation to the reproductive potential of the bride. She found that younger, plumper, healthy, never-married females fetched higher bride prices than older, thinner, formerly married females. These preferred women are likely to have higher reproductive potential than others. Since a man presumably seeks to achieve the greatest reproductive success through his wife, sociobiological theory correctly predicts that men are willing to make a higher payment for a woman who would help him achieve this. The Kipsigis may not see the matter in exactly these terms, but the study suggests that reproductive success is somehow encoded in social customs. This suggests not that the custom itself is genetically encoded, but that social evolution has favored customs that promote maximum fitness.

Criticisms of Sociobiology

Some anthropologists are opposed to sociobiological explanations of social life. They feel there is a danger of reducing social behavior to biological formulas as was done in the hereditarian anthropology of the past. More to the point, they wonder whether sociobiological explanations are necessary at all, since much of the behavior they seek to explain can be understood in terms of other models of social behavior, such as an ecological framework (see Chapter 11). Common sense and casual observation show that not all behavior is driven by a selfish biological imperative. People regularly contribute to the welfare of unrelated persons, even strangers thousands of miles away. In many societies, parents adopt unrelated children and invest heavily in their welfare. Inclusive fitness can explain adoption of close relatives but not unrelated persons. There may also be good explanations for customs like the Kipsigis bride price that do not invoke sociobiological principles. Therefore, it is necessary to find tests of sociobiological models that will discriminate between sociobiological and other explanations for behavior.

Another objection to sociobiological explanation is that it is not always clear whether the underlying biological factors in behavior are universal or restricted to specific populations. Generalizing from the Kipsigis example, we might expect to find that men everywhere evaluate potential mates similarly to Kipsigis males. In the United States, for example, do men prefer younger, plumper, healthy, never-married women? Or are there environmental differences that make these choices biologically less compelling?

While inclusive fitness may have some explanatory power in small, animal societies, in which most of the local group are related, it may be more problematic in others. Among primates, for example, a mother will usually recognize her offspring because they are attached to her from birth onward. A father cannot necessarily identify his own offspring, especially in a society where females are promiscuous. If it is difficult for the primates, consider how much harder it is for ethologists to determine which animals are related closely and which are not. This simple problem greatly complicates the matter of understanding behavior from a sociobiological perspective (see Anthropologists at Work: Kinship among Monkeys).

---

sociobiology   The study of behavior from the perspective of evolutionary biology, with emphasis on how social behavior affects Darwinian fitness.

inclusive fitness   The idea, current in sociobiological thought, that behavior that appears to be altruistic enhances the genetic fitness of the individual by contributing to the fitness of closely related individuals.

extinction rate   In population genetics, the rate at which certain genes are eliminated from the genome of a population.

bride price   A payment by the husband or his family to the bride's family in compensation for their losing her.

SUMMARY

- Studies of nonhuman primates and other animals show that social behavior is the product of evolution.
- Natural selection has favored intense social life among some species, and the primates seem particularly well suited to this adaptation. Primates may have elaborate patterns of parental care, dominance, cooperation, communication, and other social patterns that are adaptive in specific environments.
- Human females have cycles of ovulation regulating their fertility, but, unlike other primates, they are continuously sexually receptive. This acts as a powerful incentive to form long-lasting bonds with males, behavior that may be adaptive for the nurturance and socialization of children.
- Primate behavior is highly variable, showing plasticity within a single species. Evidence shows primates and other species have traditions and are able to use tools. There is a lively debate over whether primates are capable of using grammatical language.
- Better understanding of the biological significance of behavior has led biologists and anthropologists to reconsider the genetic basis for social behavior.
- Proponents of group selection suggested that populations are self-regulating through social behavior. Sociobiologists argue that this is unlikely. They suggest that true altruism would suffer negative selection and that most behavior can be explained by postulating the quest for inclusive fitness.
- Human behavior has many aspects that seem to reflect group selection, particularly in the area of information shared in communication.
- There are still many unanswered questions about the causes and significance of primate social behavior. The Darwinian model can no longer be ignored in considering human behavior, but neither should we expect it to become a dominant approach in explaining sociocultural behavior.

GET INVOLVED

1. Take some time to learn about social organization in some nonhuman social group. Ideally you will spend some time observing behavior firsthand, in a bee hive, an ant colony, or another group of social insects, for example. Other social animals you could observe include certain bird species, some deer species, and beavers. Alternatively, you could consult the literature on the species you select. Try to distinguish specific roles played within the group. Can you determine whether the same animals always play the same roles, or whether an animal can play more than one role? Focus on a particular age or sex category. Try to determine the extent of variation in performance of a social role. Can you detect any variation from one animal to another? If so, what is the significance of that difference?

2. There are endangered primates in many parts of the world, such as the gorilla in Africa and the orangutan in Borneo. The reasons they are endangered are complex, but the primary problem is habitat destruction by human activity. Find out what primates are currently endangered in Africa, Asia, and South America. The World Wildlife Fund, the World Wildlife Federation, and many other organizations and government agencies are trying to preserve primates. Get involved in one of these organizations and find out what you can do to help preserve the endangered species of primates.

SUGGESTED READINGS

Dawkins, Richard. 1976. *The selfish gene*. New York: Oxford University Press.

Konner, Melvin. 1982. *The tangled wing: Biological constraints on the human spirit*. New York: Harper.

McDermott, Jeanne. 1986. Face to face. It's the expression that bears the message. *Smithsonian* March 16.

Shepher, Joseph. 1983. *Incest: A biosocial view*. New York: Academic Press.

Smuts, Barbara. 1987. What are friends for? In *Applying Anthropology: An Introductory Reader*. A. Podolefsky and P. J. Brown, eds. Mountain View, CA: Mayfield Publishing.*

Wilson, Edward O. 1978. *On human nature*. Bantam: New York.

* This selection is anthologized in *Applying Anthropology*, 2d ed., ed. A. Podolefsky and P. J. Brown (Mountain View, Calif.: Mayfield, 1992).

Kinship among Monkeys

Carolyn Ehardt, Associate Professor of Anthropology at The University of Georgia and Affiliate Scientist with the Yerkes Regional Primate Center, has studied social organization in several nonhuman primates. These include the rhesus and Japanese macaques of Asia and the African mangabeys and vervets. Her major interests include the degree to which kinship structures social behavior in monkey groups and the interdependence of aggressive and affiliative behavior.

The fascinating social behavior of large, complex groups of various African and Asian monkeys has been my primary research area within biological anthropology. Because I work with both free-ranging and captive social groups, I am keenly aware of the need to relate captive studies to those done in more natural circumstances. Captive colonies, however, permit us to ask significant questions about social behavior that would be extremely difficult or impossible to ask in a field situation.

A common theme to my research with these monkeys has been the degree to which kinship structures social interaction among group members. Do close kin (for example, siblings) groom one another more or spend more time in close proximity than nonkin? When fights break out, are the antagonists' kin most likely to come to their aid? Inclusive fitness theory would suggest that the answer to such questions is "of course!" Many people, unaware of the pitfalls of anthropomorphizing, might also predict from personal experience that nonhuman primates would be kin-biased in their social behavior. But are they? Is preference for kin a primate universal?

The various monkeys I have studied live in complex social groups (both sexes, all ages), and mating is

Carolyn Ehardt studying a troop of Japanese macaques.

promiscuous. We therefore cannot easily determine who is the father of a particular individual, but knowing who an infant's mother is permits documentation of matrilineal kinship. For some groups these genealogies go back more than 20 years, documenting who all the offspring of particular adult females are; who their maternal siblings are; and who their maternal aunts, uncles, nieces, nephews, cousins, and grandmothers are. It is extremely rare to have this depth of kinship knowledge in wild groups; important questions about kinship are best answered with captive colonies.

For affiliative ("friendly") behavior, if we contrast interaction of all kin with one another and interaction with nonkin, behavior like grooming another monkey's fur is more frequent among kin in the groups I have studied. But is it just a monkey's *closest* kin that account for this higher level of association? When I looked more closely at the African mangabeys, for example, I found that removing from the data any cases of affiliation between mothers and their young (less than one year) offspring

nullified the kinship preference. More distantly related kin (such as adult female siblings), and even mothers and older offspring, did not affiliate more with each other than with nonkin group members.

What about aggression? Although you might predict that kin would fight less among themselves than nonkin, in rhesus monkeys kin actually show more aggression toward each other than toward nonkin group members. That seems odd, but it is a function of older kin, especially mothers, to use threats, slaps, or even bites to modify the socially unacceptable behavior of their offspring or young relatives.

In terms of aiding others, do kin defend one another in fights with nonkin? Rhesus monkeys do, especially mothers rushing to defend (at considerable risk) young offspring squabbling with other, perhaps older and more dominant monkeys. But do nonkin also aid one another? Absolutely, with an excellent example being a number of unrelated adult females joining in defense of another female threatened by a large, dominant adult male.

So kinship does structure the social interaction of these nonhuman primates, but not to the extent the sociobiologist might expect. Sociality is the ecological adaptation of primates, making other factors linking nonkin very important in their social organization. These factors go beyond inclusive fitness or other aspects of sociobiological theorizing. Much remains to be learned about primate sociality; the questions to be asked are numerous and exciting. Anthropology will play a large role in understanding the behavior of our distant primate relations and in helping to preserve them as part of the world's biodiversity.

*A Mekranoti family of Brazil harvest
sweet potatoes.*

THE FORAGING LIFE

Foraging, or hunting and gathering, is the oldest economic activity practiced by humans and their ancestors. It is a way of life based on the harvesting of wild food resources and consists of three different activities: hunting wild game, fishing, and gathering wild foods such as roots, fruits, or shellfish. Humans were dependent on foraging throughout all the geological epochs during which they lived. **Food production**—the use of domesticated plants and animals—did not begin until about 10,000 YA.

Even though foraging dates to prehistoric times, there are still some groups of pure foragers around the globe today as well as many groups who depend partly on foraging for food. Many groups plant crops as their primary source of food energy but rely on hunting and fishing for protein. Even technologically advanced food-producing societies rely partly on foraging for ocean fish.

It may be tempting to treat contemporary foragers (hunter-gatherers) as though they represented our distant ancestors, but such comparisons should be

---

BOX 10.1

Our "Living Ancestors"?

From time to time there is a story in the news that a group of people has been discovered in Australia, Brazil, or New Guinea who are described as "living fossils," or "Stone Age people." One such discovery were the Tasaday of the Philippines, a foraging people who lacked cultivated crops and even metal tools. According to first descriptions published in the 1970s, they lived exclusively on small animals, roots, fruits, and grubs and were a small remnant group that avoided contact with outsiders for many years.

In 1988 news stories broke stating that the Tasaday were a "fraud." They were not Stone Age people after all, but part of a larger linguistic and cultural group that practices agriculture, possibly even imposters set up as a publicity stunt. Some anthropologists agreed that information on the Tasaday had been highly filtered and that some of the claims made about them were not substantiated. Other anthropologists argued that the Tasaday were a distinctive cultural group speaking a unique dialect. An entire session was devoted to these arguments at the 1989 Annual Meeting of the American Anthropological Association.

The Tasaday were not the first group to be described as "living ancestors." For years, the !Kung San of Southern Africa were described as bearers of a Paleolithic culture 10,000 years old. The Kreen-Akrore of Brazil, first contacted in 1966, were also described as a "Stone Age" culture, partly because of a film about them that showed stone axes found in one of their abandoned camps.

In each of these cases evidence has come to light that the people in question were not so isolated as it first appeared. The !Kung San, for example, are the remnants of a people once spread over much of southern Africa. The Tasaday are closely related to agricultural peoples and have probably always traded with them. The Kreen Akrore had practiced food production since long before their discovery by outsiders. The idea of a **relict population** forgotten by time is certainly charming and exotic, but such a group is unlikely to exist in modern times. Foraging groups today share full humanity with ourselves.

Tasaday display food staples of tadpoles and crabs.

made with caution. Contemporary foragers are unlike our ancient Paleolithic ancestors in several ways (Box 10.1). We know this from various lines of evidence. First, the archaeological evidence for foraging does not match contemporary behavior perfectly. Groups with a life-style like that of the hunters of Torralba, Ambrona, or Terra Amata (see Chapter 7) have never been directly observed. The people themselves who used those sites were probably not *Homo sapiens*. All modern hunters are fully modern *H. sapiens* who happen to practice a foraging life-style.

Second, the environment has changed since the Pleistocene. The bogs where animals were trapped are now dry land, for example, and the valley below Torralba and Ambrona is colder than it was then. Third, the social environment of the Paleolithic foragers was a very different one. A wider set of habitats was open to them than is available today, with dense, highly concentrated resources. Hence forager communities could have been much larger and more highly organized than today. Modern foragers, in contrast, live in only a few remote areas that are inhospitable to agriculture or herding. Everywhere else there are cultivators. Thus the exact patterns of prehistoric hunter-gatherers could not exist today. But until 10,000 YA, the world belonged to them.

WHY STUDY FORAGERS?

Many anthropologists have studied modern foraging peoples, such as the Inuit of the Arctic Circle or the !Kung San of Botswana. Anthropologists are interested in modern foraging peoples for a variety of reasons. For one thing, their behavior provides clues about previous adaptations. Many adaptive strategies practiced by modern foragers serve as background to contemporary behavior, not only that of modern foragers

but also that of agriculturalists. For example, foragers **schedule** their activities throughout the year to minimize the costs and maximize the benefits of securing resources. There are, however, serious limitations to such studies. For one thing, most contemporary foragers survive only in areas that have no interest to agricultural peoples, such as the Kalahari desert or the Arctic Circle. For another, they often trade with other groups having different life-styles, obtaining tools, food, and other items that they cannot produce themselves.

Another reason anthropologists study foragers is to examine the relationship between adaptive strategies—strategies for surviving in a particular environment with a given technology—and social organization. Foraging by itself doesn't produce any particular social system. A group's social organization grows out of a set of interacting factors, including the environment, the nature and distribution of the resources, the technology and demographic makeup of the group, patterns of exchange with other groups, and the influence of neighboring peoples.

Some foraging societies, for example, organize themselves in small groups having few possessions and moving about often. They have little or no tendency to form social classes, although there are distinctions among people. There may be great differences in such personal attributes as prestige, influence, knowledge, or ability, but these differences do not translate into discrepancies in wealth or power. In these **unstratified** societies, there are no governments, no rulers, and no armies or police departments. Neither are there rich and poor. There are very few unstratified societies in the world today, although contemporary societies evolved from unstratified or less-stratified backgrounds. Learning about the organization of behavior in unstratified societies reveals a dimension that we could not observe if we restricted ourselves to stratified societies.

---

foraging The harvesting of wild food resources by hunting animals, fishing, and gathering plants and other nonfood items.

food production The use of domesticated plants and animals.

scheduling An adaptive strategy employed by foragers involving a patterned round of food-getting activities based on the availability of resources in different places in various seasons of the year.

unstratified Societies lacking social classes.

Are Foragers "Closer to Nature"?

Some anthropologists suggest that because of their dependence on wild foods and lack of power technology foragers are "closer to nature" than agriculturalists or those in industrial society. This is a fallacy. Foragers certainly must be closely attuned to certain aspects of nature to make a living. They learn the habits and behavior of animals, the signs they leave behind, and where to find them. They observe and classify plants, learning which ones are edible, when and where to find them, and how to harvest and prepare them. But cultivators also study nature carefully. They may, for example, need to learn the habits of insect crop pests to combat them effectively. Unlike foragers, they do have techniques for manipulating the reproductive rates of the animals and plants on which they depend, and their mode of adaptation involves forms of organization that are unlikely to occur among foragers. But even though they manipulate the habitat to a degree, they ultimately have no more control over the environment than foragers do. They cannot control rainfall, the appearance of crop diseases, insect pests, or any other natural factors that have an impact on their way of life.

Foragers also create a **cultural environment** populated with other groups, ideas and values, beliefs in the supernatural, and so on. While this cultural environment contains elements of the natural environment, such as animals and plants, the nature and arrangement of these elements are devised by human minds. For example, the curing spirits to which the !Kung San appeal when they are sick are not necessarily more "natural" than the idea of God speaking from a burning bush in the Old Testament or the rules of the New York Stock Exchange. In each of these cases, people have elaborated on natural themes, yielding cultural artifacts that are part of the **effective environment** to which they adapt. Close parallels can be drawn between foraging and industrial adaptations. Many people in New York City, for example, schedule their lives around the "alternate side" parking rules that require them to keep their cars off the street for specified periods each week. The search for a parking space during these periods is remarkably similar to a fisherman's quest for fish. Experts develop space-hunting skills, roaming the streets in systematic search patterns and paying close attention to minute details (a pedestrian reaching into his pocket for a car key) that may lead them to their elusive quarry.

Do Humans Have a Hunting Instinct?

The idea that hunting instincts are basic to human nature is widespread. The search for an instinctual basis for human behavior has led some writers to exaggerate the importance of hunting in early hominid adaptations. The ethologist Konrad Lorenz believed that early hominid hunting was a factor in the selection of aggressive behavior in humans. He saw reflections of a primordial "killer instinct" in much contemporary human behavior. Some writers have carried this idea to an extreme, even suggesting that the behavior of businessmen is predatory and aggressive because of a "hunter's blood instinct."

Anthropologists generally reject this view for three reasons. First, the hunter's instinct notion depends on the assumption that early hominids and Paleolithic humans were primarily hunters. But evidence from physical anthropology, archaeology, and ethnography has shown that gathering vegetable food, eggs, insects, and grubs, hunting small animals, and scavenging the kills of other predators were equally important activities.

Second, anthropologists are skeptical of accounts that attribute current behavior to primordial instincts from the distant past. Humans are so dependent on learning that it is difficult to sort out what is learned from what is innate, especially because behavior is so variable within and across societies. Aggression and cooperation among individuals are highly variable from one human group to the next. Whatever behavior may be drawn from our past is mixed with behavior adaptive to contemporary conditions. The idea that the competition among businessmen springs from the same instincts that led our ancestors to kill antelopes for food ignores the obvious differences. If humans had uncontrollable predatory instincts, they might kill each other's pets. If their aggressive instincts were not under strict cultural control, they might ambush and murder their business rivals and smash their tennis rackets over each other's heads.

Third, a look at the subsistence behavior of our closest primate relatives, the chimpanzees and gorillas, shows that they are not primarily hunters but gatherers of vegetable food. While chimpanzees occasionally hunt animals, hunting is rare and contributes very little to their total diet. Even the formidable male gorilla uses its large size and teeth primarily to threaten, not to attack other animals.

THE ECOLOGY OF FORAGING

Ecology is the study of the interrelationships between organisms and their physical environment. (Chapter 11 contains a more detailed discussion of ecology.) **Human ecology** focuses on the role of people in **ecosystems.** Every human population has a distinctive relationship to its environment. There are certain features distinctive to the human ecology of foraging. To begin with, let us briefly discuss the needs of all human groups.

Subsistence requirements are the basic needs that people have simply to sustain life.

- First and foremost, humans need food and water to stay alive. Their **nutritional requirements** include protein, carbohydrates, fats, vitamins, and minerals.
- In many environments people require protection from the elements. To build the simplest hut, people need building materials, such as stone, bone, or wood to support the structure and skins or thatch to cover it. They may fashion clothing from animal skins or natural fibers and burn fuel, such as wood, dung, or tallow, to keep warm and cook food.
- Many subsistence systems require a set of tools, or toolkit. To make tools, people need a source of stone, bone, wood, ore, fuel, and other resources, such as poisons for hunting arrows.

All these needs are satisfied through natural resources if people have the knowledge and technology to exploit them.

The behavior of foragers must be adjusted to the distribution of the resources they exploit. Resources may be distributed in different ways. They may be densely distributed, with many plants or animals packed into a given area, or they may be sparsely distributed like pearls in oysters. Another distinction can be drawn between uniform and patchy distribution. **Uniform distribution** occurs when resources are spread evenly over an area. **Patchy distribution** occurs when resources are unevenly bunched together in an area. Sometimes the resources themselves are mobile, such as herd animals that migrate seasonally. It is also important to consider the distribution of resources in time. Most environments have some seasonal fluctuation in the abundance of resources between winter and summer and rainy and dry seasons. A **pulsed environment** is one that undergoes regular or predictable fluctuations, such as the alternation of the seasons in temperate regions. An **unstable environment** is one in which fluctuations are unpredictable, such as the occurrence of hurricanes in the Caribbean.

Lacking control over resource distribution, a forager's job is to be at the right place at the right time to obtain resources. The primary means of adaptation for foragers are movement, scheduling, and storage. We saw some of these adaptations in the foraging patterns of the Paleolithic hunters at the archaeological sites of Ambrona and Torralba in Spain (Chapter 7). The objective in foraging is not to get rich or "corner the market" but to "stay in business." Foragers try to get the most desirable resources for the least possible effort, not because they are lazy but because energy and time are limited. If they cannot easily obtain the best meat or vegetable foods, they may settle for less tasty or nutritious foods that are easier to obtain. Every forager follows a strategy that makes the best of available resources under existing limitations. The optimal use of one resource may interfere with the optimal use of another. For example, a group that relies on a patchily distributed game species of low density may be unable to settle at a spot with a dense and stable supply of

---

cultural environment   The environment as it is shaped by the values and beliefs of a specific culture group. It may include natural objects, other people, and supernatural beings.

effective environment   That part of the environment that directly affects or sets limits on behavior.

ecology   The study of the interrelationships among organisms and between organisms and their physical environment.

human ecology   The study of how humans relate to their ecosystems.

ecosystem   A community of plants and animals in a shared physical environment.

subsistence requirements   The basic needs of people to sustain life.

nutritional requirements   The basic food categories needed to support life, including protein, carbohydrates, fats, vitamins, and minerals.

uniform distribution   A pattern in which items are spaced at regular intervals without bunching.

patchy distribution   An uneven pattern of items over a given area.

pulsed environment   An environment characterized by regular, predictable changes—four seasons in temperate climates.

unstable environment   An environment characterized by unpredictable changes like hurricanes, tornadoes, and droughts.

vegetable resources. Any subsistence strategy is a compromise among conflicting requirements.

Foragers have to balance not only physical and subsistence needs but also the activities required to maintain a suitable environment for biological and **social reproduction.** Social reproduction requires a source of marriage partners, defense against enemies, information about the environment and other people, and sources of goods that people cannot produce for themselves. A solution implies a particular deployment of labor, time, and energy. Even the simplest hunting group has a division of labor. Men and women and people of different ages invariably have different roles, but there is also a division in terms of different abilities and preferences. To satisfy all the needs of a foraging group, a balance must be struck among them.

Foraging in a Semidesert: The !Kung San of Botswana

Today foragers survive mainly in areas where resources are sparse and dispersed. Most live in small, nomadic groups that range widely over the habitat to obtain resources where they can be found in season. One well-known example of such a group is the !Kung San of Botswana in southern Africa (Figure 10.1). (The exclamation point signifies a glottal "click" at the beginning of the word, a sound that does not occur in English or any other European language.) The Kalahari Desert where they live is a region of scrub forests and open plains with a short, unpredictable rainy season. The !Kung adjust their movements to the seasons. During the rainy season water collects in shallow pans in many parts of the Kalahari. During

Figure 10.1 *The area in southern Africa inhabited by living groups of the !Kung San.*

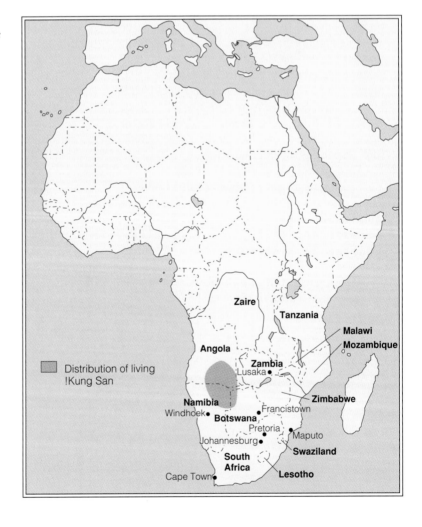

the dry season, surface water evaporates and the !Kung cluster around the few permanent water holes. From November to April, when most of the rain falls, many foods become available. From April to October the weather is very dry and the foliage withers. Both the people and the herds of grazing animals (antelope, buffalo, etc.) schedule their activities around the availability of water at certain locations. In historical times part of the region has also been occupied by herding peoples who trade with and sometimes employ the !Kung San.

!Kung San foragers live in small groups ranging in size from 10 to 30 people. Two or more camps may stay close together near a water hole for a time, but they are separate social units. Each camp is organized around a core of related older people, such as siblings or cousins. There is no formal leader of a camp, but there may be greater respect for the core group. These people are said to be the "owners" of the water hole near which they camp during part of the year. Most of the others in the camp are related to the owners, either by blood or by marriage. People visiting a water hole are supposed to ask the "owner" for permission to drink, but the owners never deny permission. While the core group of a camp is stable over time, the other camp members frequently move back and forth among camps.

The !Kung San hunt many game animals, including the warthog, porcupine, giraffe, hare, many varieties of antelope, and several kinds of birds and fowl. They also collect bird eggs, tortoises, snakes, insects, and caterpillars (Figure 10.2). Altogether, the !Kung eat about 80 different species of animals. But they do not eat everything. The !Kung do not eat some animals because they do not like their flesh. Others are too small to be worthwhile, because the return in meat is so low compared to the effort of capturing them. The !Kung usually do not hunt large carnivores such as lions, leopards, and cheetahs, and they don't hunt bats, elephants, rats, mice, hyenas, or wild dogs.

Even in years of low rainfall, game is abundant. Meat provides about 40 percent of the energy in the diet, although this amount fluctuates with the luck of the hunters. A single eland (a large antelope) can yield 227 kg (500 lb) of meat. When one is killed, everyone in the camp eats meat, as much as 2 kg (4.5 lb) per person per day for several days. On such occasions, several camps may join to consume the kill. They cannot keep meat very long after it is killed, and they move about frequently. Hoarding meat without sharing is unthinkable to them. When the hunters have no luck, many meals may go by without meat.

The Importance of Gathering

Although there is a great emphasis on hunting among the !Kung San, gathering by the women provides most of their food. The !Kung San collect about 30 species of wild fruits and berries, 18 species of edible tree gum, and more than 40 kinds of roots and bulbs. Women find and gather most of these important resources. They also carry them back to camp, prepare them, and serve them to their families.

The mongongo nut, the fruit of a large tree found in many parts of the Kalahari (Figure 10.3), is an important food resource for the !Kung. Mongongo trees are patchily distributed in groves. Their nuts are highly nutritious, but the thick outer shell makes it difficult to prepare them for eating. Women spend hours gathering nuts in the mongongo groves and carrying them back to camp in 20-kg (44-lb) bundles. There they prepare the nuts by roasting them over a small fire and then cracking them. To cut down on the work of carrying, the !Kung San may camp temporarily in the mongongo groves while they gather and process the nuts. The groves, however, may be located far from permanent water supplies. During the dry season, the stay in the mongongo groves is short, limited by the amount of water people can carry in ostrich egg canteens. During the rainy season, however, the !Kung San can camp near the groves for longer periods (Figure 10.4).

---

social reproduction   Activities that sustain a pattern of social life over time, including education, myth, technology, and so on.

Figure 10.2 *Some of the mammals commonly hunted and eaten by the !Kung San and the average weight of their edible parts: (top left) gemsbok, 108 kg; (top right) kudu, 108 kg; (center left) wildebeest, 114 kg; (center right) warthog, 39 kg; (bottom left) duiker, 10 kg; (bottom center) steenbok, 5.6 kg; and (bottom right) hare, 1.4 kg. The !Kung San also kill and eat several kinds of birds, tortoises, and insects. The bulk of their food, however, consists of the wild roots, fruits, nuts, and bird eggs gathered by the women.*

Figure 10.3 *The mongongo tree is a bountiful and reliable source of food for the !Kung San. A well-aimed stick (top left) is used to dislodge the nuts from the upper branches. Women spend hours gathering the nuts and then carry their 22-kg bundles back to camp for the preparation process (top right). The nuts are roasted first to soften the tough outer shell and then cracked open. A !Kung San woman must instruct her daughters in how to prepare the nuts for eating and cooking (bottom right).*

Figure 10.4 *During the dry season, a !Kung San campsite can be constructed among the mongongo trees by the women in under an hour. The simple huts are used as windscreens and storage for the few possessions of each family. Most waking hours are spent outside the huts—often around the cooking fire, preparing and eating food and engaging in endless conversations.*

Adaptive Strategies: Mobility and Sharing

The !Kung San also concern themselves with year-to-year fluctuations in rainfall and resources. The differences can be striking. In one year, five times more rain may fall than in the year just past. The fickle rains may fall in one place but not in another a day's walk away. The !Kung habitat has a lot of uncertainty built in, which elicits a cautious attitude among the !Kung San. Anthropologist Richard Lee (1979) comments that it makes no sense for a !Kung camp to claim permanent and exclusive rights to a specific piece of land. The land claimed might be precisely the area where no rain falls next year. It makes more sense to keep up ties with the neighbors so that they will be likely to help in an emergency. Thus the !Kung are not territorial; they do not defend their hunting and gathering grounds for their exclusive use. They are generous with their resources, and they expect others to be generous as well.

Frequent movement between camps is a form of sharing and an adaptation to fluctuations in the habitat. !Kung families frequently move from one camp to another, affiliating with another core group of owners. As long as they have some kinship tie or other close bond with one of the owners, outsiders are welcome. They can stay as long as it suits them. If food is scarce in the area, or if there is a dispute, a family can join another group. Later, when things get better, they can move back.

Another way in which people move around from camp to camp is embedded in !Kung marriage patterns. Camps tend to be **exogamic** (marrying outside the group), because in a small group it is difficult for a male or female of marriageable age to find a suitable mate. After marriage the !Kung expect the groom to provide meat for his in-laws' camp until the couple have two or three children. Only then is the couple free to return to the groom's camp, although they can also elect to stay. This custom is known as **bride service.**

Another feature that keeps the membership of camps unstable is the !Kung San way of settling disputes. People may argue over meat distribution, gift exchange, laziness, or stinginess. Serious physical fights may be provoked by accusations of adultery. There are also occasional cases of murder. The outcome of these incidents is, more often than not, that the camp will split up, each party going its own way.

The Hunting Role

Hunting is the main occupation of men. Looking for game in the Kalahari is a complex business requiring knowledge, strength, skill, sharp senses, and great patience (Figure 10.5). Before he can hunt effectively, a boy must learn a vast amount about animal habits, poison and its effects, weapons, stalking, and tracking. A hunter learns to notice tiny disturbances in the vegetation (a bit of trampled grass, a broken twig) to track animals. Hoof prints yield valuable information about the number of animals, how tired they are, which way they are travelling, and whether one is wounded.

Hunters carefully prepare their bows and arrows and the arrow poison that will bring down a large animal if the small arrow penetrates its skin. Hunters may spend days away from the home camp searching for game animals. Once they locate game, the hunters stalk their prey carefully, sometimes crouching for hours in tall grass to avoid being seen by sharp-eyed prey or carefully staying downwind of animals with a good sense of smell. Kudu, wildebeest, and other African antelope species are fast runners, so if a hunter gets close enough for a shot, he will not get a second chance. Even after a hunter shoots an animal, he may be obliged to follow it for hours or even days until the poison finally brings the animal down.

After he has killed both a male and a female kudu, a man goes through the first buck ceremony, in which superficial cuts are made on his chest, back, arms, and face. The !Kung believe this ritual ensures that the hunter will continue to be successful. A hunter who is down on his luck may also use magic to improve his chances.

While every man is expected to master basic hunting skills, there are differences in ability. Richard Lee surveyed 127 hunters and found that nearly a third of them had never killed a kudu (1979). About a third had killed ten or more. Because of differences in ability, hunters cooperate, forming small groups for hunting expeditions. Older, experienced hunters are useful for their knowledge of game habits. Another hunter may be an expert stalker or a swift runner, and still another may be a good marksman.

Game belongs not to the man who shoots it but to the owner of the arrow that killed it, and he has the privilege of distributing the meat. Every hunter carries arrows made by three or four different men. A good arrow maker may gain the right to shares of meat without even going on the hunt. Lee comments that this practice serves to "defuse bitterness over meat distribution." A hunter can be proud of his kill but often must hand it over to another for distribution. This practice also enforces sharing of meat.

The !Kung value hunting very highly. Good hunters enjoy prestige and their exploits are told and retold around the campfire. However, although the !Kung admire good hunters, they systematically belittle each other's achievements. Richard Lee found this out the hard way when he paid to have a fat ox butchered as a Christmas present to a !Kung San group. Instead of showing gratitude the !Kung told Lee that the ox was skinny and that they would still be hungry after eating it. Later the !Kung explained to Lee that they always did this to hunters to keep them from getting swelled heads. A hunter who gets too arrogant may forget that he is just as dependent on others as they are on him. A !Kung told Lee,

> . . . when a young man kills much meat he comes to think of himself as a chief or a big man and he thinks of the rest of us as his servants or inferiors. We can't accept this. We refuse one who boasts, for someday his pride will make him kill somebody. So we always speak of his meat as worthless. This way we cool his heart and make him gentle (Lee 1969).

---

exogamic   Pertaining to social groups that mate or marry outside their own group. *Group* may mean camp, caste, race, clan, religion, or class, depending on the society in question.

bride service   A social custom requiring a groom to provide services for his in-laws for a specified period of time as part of the marital contract.

◄ **Figure 10.5**   *An older man is not out of place on a !Kung San hunt. His knowledge and experience may be as valuable as the abilities of a younger, more athletic man, such as the one shown here, who can stalk and shoot the fleet-footed wildebeest.*

Table 10.1   Work Hours per Week per Person at Dobe Water Hole, July 1964

	Subsistence (Foraging)	Toolmaking and Fixing	House-work	Total
Men	21.6	7.5	15.4	44.5
Women	12.6	5.1	22.4	40.1
Average of both sexes	17.1	6.3	18.9	42.3

Source: Lee 1979, 278.

Work and Leisure

Modern technology is able to do so many tasks that we sometimes wonder how people got along without it. It might seem that primitive foragers, who lacked power technology, agriculture, and domesticated animals, must have worked harder than modern people just to eke out a living. In 1964 Richard Lee tested this notion by observing the daily activities of all the !Kung in the main camp at Dobe water hole. He recorded everyone's main activities for about a month. This was in an unusually dry year, which made life a bit harder than normal.

The data (Table 10.1) show that the !Kung work less than the average person in a developed society. The average !Kung adult spent 23.4 hours a week foraging and fixing and making tools. Adding housework (such as food preparation and collecting firewood) brings the total up to an average workweek of 42.3 hours per person. People did not work constantly. Half or more of the adults in the camp did not go out to forage on any given day. The !Kung spent many hours relaxing, playing with children, telling stories, and participating in ceremonial activities. Child care also took up a great deal of time not counted in these figures.

Figure 10.6   *This scene from* The Gods Must Be Crazy *points up the contrast in dress and material possession between the !Kung and the white inhabitants of southern Africa.*

Does this mean the !Kung are lazy? The !Kung San have no reason to work any harder. There is no wealth to accumulate and no way to work for some other valued thing. Are the !Kung San therefore poor? Not necessarily, because there are no rich !Kung. Compared to their neighbors, the Herero cattle herders, they are poor because they have no cattle. They are also poor in relation to the glittering society of white South Africa (Figure 10.6), a contrast emphasized in the film *The Gods Must Be Crazy*. But the evidence suggests that the !Kung San at Dobe in 1964 had an adequate diet and a relaxed life-style. The foraging life is not necessarily a constant struggle for food. Some foragers work so little that they may be the "original leisure society," in the words of Marshall Sahlins (1972).

Reproductive Strategies

The !Kung San's quality of life no doubt rests on the fact that there are sufficient resources in the Dobe area to support the population even in drought years. The abundance of resources is related to the size of the consumer population and the intensity with which they use them. In 1968 Richard Lee made a census of the Dobe area and found that about 730 !Kung make full- or part-time use of the Dobe area of about 9,000 km² (3,475 mi²). There were an additional 340 Herero cattle herders in the area. This works out to about 8.4 km² (3.2 mi²) of land per person, more if one leaves out the Herero. This is a low population density even compared to such lightly populated areas as Wyoming, where there is about 0.5 km² per person.

Nancy Howell, a **demographer**, studied the Dobe !Kung and determined that their fertility (number of pregnancy episodes per woman) is low for a population that does not use contraceptives. Figuring in the death rate, the Dobe !Kung population is growing at 0.5 percent per year (Howell 1979). At this rate the population would require 126 years to double in size. Some of the practices of the !Kung probably contribute to low fertility. For example, !Kung women voluntarily refrain from sexual intercourse for one year after giving birth. In addition, they may nurse their babies for more than two years, a practice that often causes **amenorrhea** (absence of menstrual periods), which makes them infertile. This custom tends to increase the space between pregnancies and lower the fertility rate. Having babies closer together could cause serious problems for a woman who must carry her infants over the long distances covered by the !Kung on their travels. Perhaps for this reason some !Kung women practice infanticide, allowing babies to die when they are born with birth defects or too soon after another.

The characteristic !Kung San way of life—foraging in an unstable environment with scattered, patchily distributed resources—is reflected in every aspect of their culture. **Social rank**, the relative amount of prestige, for men is connected with hunting skill, although they are careful not to allow any man to elevate himself over the others. Magic and ceremonials are also connected with hunting, as are the major stages in a man's life. Many customs require people to share and prevent anyone from becoming "bigger" than everyone else. A good hunter has a better chance of finding a wife, because women and potential in-laws find him more attractive. But even a poor hunter can share in game by making arrows or simply through family ties. Sharing and exchange are part of !Kung social structure. There are strong negative **sanctions** (social punishments) for people who do not share.

The !Kung San adapted to an environment with sparse and fluctuating resources by maintaining freedom of movement, allowing the group to fluctuate, and encouraging the frequent movement of people from one camp to another. Their environment and technology set certain limits on their activities. The !Kung San have no way of conserving or storing meat or carrying large quantities of it when they move from place to place. Consequently, whenever there is a large kill, everyone in the group shares in the meat. Their social system promotes exchange and sharing.

Wide spacing between births inhibits population growth. By maintaining a population size below the number the habitat can support, the !Kung San maintain an existence that, while not luxurious, is comfortable and secure. Let us look now at a foraging adaptation to a very different kind of environment.

FORAGING IN A HIGHLY PRODUCTIVE, PULSED ENVIRONMENT: THE KWAKIUTL

The peoples of the northwestern coast of North America (Figure 10.7) lived in an environment where at certain times of the year food was remarkably abundant. Thanks to the relative isolation of the area and the difficulty of growing crops, the area was left to Native American foragers until the early 20th century, when commercial fishing and timbering by white North American society became dominant. There were several different tribal groups living in the region, including the Kwakiutl, the Tsimshian, the Haida, and the Nootka. Those on the coast and major waterways lived in substantial wooden houses in settlements of up to several hundred inhabitants. Their subsistence was based primarily on fish, marine mammals, shellfish, fruits, and berries. In our discussion we focus mainly on the Kwakiutl society, which still exists, but we use the past tense in referring to them, because the social and subsistence system described here no longer exists.

Perhaps the most important aspect of the Pacific Northwest coastal environment is the Japan Current (see Figure 10.7), which brings warm water from the South Pacific northward to the southern coast of Alaska. There it turns southward down the West Coast. The current moderates the regional climate, which would otherwise be bitterly cold, and releases water vapor that falls on the slopes of the steep mountains of the region as heavy, year-round rainfall.

The Japan Current brings with it halibut, cod, herring, smelts, and five species of salmon. Every year the salmon migrate from the Pacific up the many rivers and streams of the Pacific Northwest to spawn (lay eggs). Until quite recently the salmon "runs" were so heavy that the streams seemed alive with fish struggling to get upstream. During these times, it was easy to spear, net, or trap salmon. In a few days of work, a person could obtain enough fish to last an entire year.

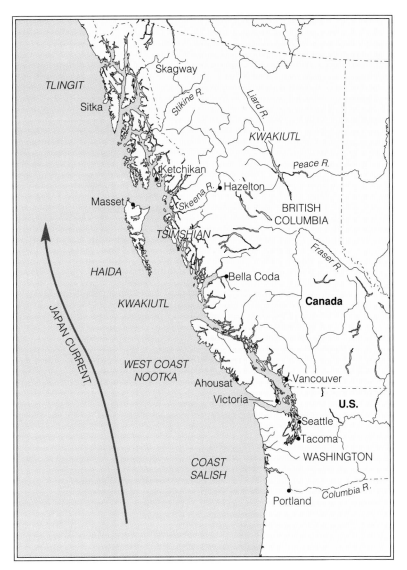

Figure 10.7 *The Pacific Northwest coast of North America. The rugged coastline offers a wide variety of ecological niches in which many different species of fish and shellfish abound. The salmon that run upstream each year to spawn were perhaps the most significant food source of many of the groups who once dominated the area, such as the Tlingit, Tsimshian, Kwakiutl, Haida, Nootka, and Salish.*

Nowadays, overfishing, dam construction, and pollution have contributed to great reductions in the fish runs.

Besides salmon and other fish species, the Pacific Northwest abounded in marine game, including the hair seal, sea lion, sea otter, porpoise, and whale. On shore, there were deer, elk, and mountain goats, as well as water fowl that passed through the region in great numbers on annual migration. The native peoples of the region could also gather shellfish in great

---

demography A branch of social science that studies population trends such as fertility, birth and death rates, and migration.

amenorrhea The absence of menstrual periods, which can accompany breast-feeding and produces temporary infertility.

social rank The relative amount of prestige accorded an individual.

sanctions Social rewards (positive sanctions) or punishments (negative sanctions) that show approval or disapproval of specific behavior.

Figure 10.8 *These remarkable watercraft, carrying a Kwakiutl wedding party, were made entirely with hand tools by traditional Kwakiutl craftsmen in the 19th century. A single craft could carry several dozen people or large cargoes of fish, blankets, or other goods.*

numbers. Finally, although vegetable foods were not abundant, many species of wild berries were available in season.

Not surprisingly, most of the native peoples of the region looked to the sea for subsistence and developed an elaborate technology to extract marine resources. They built several types of water craft, including canoes capable of carrying several dozen men (Figure 10.8). To capture fish the Kwakiutl made harpoons, fishing lines and hooks, nets and seines, and several different kinds of traps that could be set under water (Figure 10.9).

Much of the Kwakiutl technology made use of the abundant timber resources of the area. In addition to their canoes made from whole tree trunks, the Kwakiutl built houses from wide wooden planks and carved totem poles marking the rank and descent of

important chiefs. For land hunting they made wooden bows and arrows and spears, and they also fashioned buckets, vessels of all kinds, ladles, and other utensils out of wood.

Adaptive Strategies: Storage and Villages

Perhaps the most serious subsistence problem faced by the Kwakiutl was how to convert the seasonal abundance of fish and other resources into food for the entire year. They solved the problem with various storage techniques. For example, they dried fish near a fire, or smoked it, and stored it in baskets. They also boiled candle fish and seals, skimmed off the edible oil, and stored it in jars made from dried kelp.

Figure 10.9 *The Pacific Northwest coast peoples had an elaborate technology that heavily emphasized the capture of fish. In addition to weirs, they often used nets, as these Tlingit are doing here.*

Their elaborate equipment and need for storage space kept the Kwakiutl from moving about freely. Indeed, there was no advantage in doing so, since the major subsistence resource, fish, was highly localized and reliable. Individual groups claimed specific spots along streams that they defended against other groups. Although the Kwakiutl relied on wild animals and plants just as the !Kung San do, they were quite different from the !Kung San, because they used storage rather than movement as an adaptation to the seasonal unevenness of food supply and they defended specific **territories.**

Kwakiutl social organization was also markedly different from the !Kung San. Where the !Kung stress flexibility and mobility, Kwakiutl society assigned people to specific ranks based on both their ancestry and their deeds. Where !Kung San culture tends to reduce and blur individual differences, Kwakiutl customs reinforced them. Every person in a Kwakiutl village was ranked as either a chief, a noble, a commoner, or a slave. Slaves were mainly war captives; however, they could be obtained in trade for other goods. Slaves could be ransomed by their relatives, or they might be killed as a gesture of their owner's

territories Land whose borders are actively defended by a social group against outsiders.

Figure 10.10 *Scene from a Kwakiutl potlatch. The potlatch was a form of "fighting with property." The object was to give away more than one's adversary had and thereby to humiliate him. Some scholars think that the potlatch was an adaptive device that transferred resources from groups with more than enough to others that were in need.*

greatness. Otherwise they were expected to do menial labor.

Each of the other three groups had its own internal ranking system. **Ranking** refers to socially recognized differences in prestige among individuals. The boundaries between the ranks of commoner and noble and between noble and chief were not sharply marked. A local group was a kinship group in which everyone was said to be descended from a distant ancestor in either the mother's or the father's line. The theory of the system was that the closer your relationship to the ancestor, the higher your status.

Distributing Resources: The Potlatch

The chief, or head of the local group, was custodian of all that the group owned, including the fishing spots along the stream, the hunting grounds, the berry-picking grounds, and the stores of dried fish, oil, and blankets. He could use this wealth to help out needy members of the group or members of other groups he desired as allies. The more wealth accumulated by the chief, the greater his importance. Lower-ranking men contributed smoked fish, blankets, oil, and other wealth to the chief to help him aggrandize himself and share in his greatness. The chief, in turn, would take some of the goods entrusted to him and give them away at feasts known as **potlatches** (Figure 10.10).

Some writers (Piddocke 1965, Vayda 1961) suggest that the potlatch was a way of channeling resources from groups with excess resources to groups undergoing shortages. There is some evidence that the abundance of marine resources on the Pacific Northwest coast was not constant from year to year. According to their own legends, the Kwakiutl were no strangers to starvation. Fluctuations in the size of salmon runs could leave some groups with temporary food shortages for the rest of the year. The potlatch could have helped to redistribute resources from the wealthy to the needy. Later the wealthy group itself might fall on hard times and need help.

Another interpretation of the potlatch was that competitive giving away was a substitute for warfare and violence between groups. At these feasts the invited group felt shame and humiliation at the generosity of their hosts. In fact the hosts made a point of the shame they were inflicting on their "enemies" by giving them gifts. The only way the guests could retaliate was to give a bigger and better potlatch the following year and turn the tables on their hosts. Anthropologist Ruth Benedict quotes a Kwakiutl chief at a potlatch boasting (1934),

I am the great chief who makes people ashamed. I am the great chief who makes people ashamed. Our great chief brings shame to the faces. Our great chief brings jealousy to the faces. Our chief makes people cover their faces by what he is continually doing in this world. Giving again and again oil feasts to all of the tribes.

The shame felt by the losers and the prestige gained by the winners may have been incentives to produce more food than a group needed for its immediate needs. This motivated people to collect enough food to buffer other groups against shortages when they occurred.

During the late 19th century Kwakiutl potlatches became virtual orgies. Some chiefs did not simply give away goods but also destroyed great amounts of property in their quest to humiliate their adversaries. Some writers held up the potlatch as a textbook case of irrationality in a "primitive society." But anthropologist Marvin Harris (1974) stressed that the exaggerated and wasteful form of potlatch occurred only after the Kwakiutl and other related groups had suffered major population loss and were severely demoralized.

The Kwakiutl represent an extreme case among modern foragers; although they had no cultivated plants or domesticated animals, their subsistence system was productive and reliable enough to support an elaborate social system based on competitive exchange. This achievement was made possible by the bountiful environment of the Pacific Northwest coast and the Kwakiutl's ability to capture and store large quantities of food for long periods of time. Unlike the !Kung San and other foragers, the Kwakiutl did not have to travel long distances in search of food. Much of their food came to them in the form of annual fish migrations. While the Kwakiutl are unusual when compared to other contemporary foragers, they might well resemble Paleolithic foragers who lived before food production began. Living in the highly productive environments now occupied by food producers, Paleolithic foragers may have achieved even more complex levels of social organization.

SUMMARY

- It is tempting to treat contemporary hunter-gatherers as though they represented our distant ancestors, but such comparisons should be treated with caution. All of today's hunters-gatherers are fully modern *Homo sapiens* who happen to practice a foraging life style. They live in pockets neglected by food producers, but they cannot escape the influence of food producers and power technology in the vicinity.

- Although they rely on wild sources of food, foragers are no closer to nature or less civilized than anyone else.

- Even the simplest foraging camp has a social organization characterized by the sharing of food, resources, tools, and information.

- Foragers have no control over the reproduction of the plants and animals on which they depend. They must adapt to this reality by moving around to where resources are available, by scheduling their activities around the availability of resources, or by preserving and storing food.

- Hunter-gatherers must solve many other problems aside from the quest for food. They must camp near a good water source, and they require firewood, wood for bows and other tools, sinew and fiber for cords, and many other things. They must also maintain a suitable environment for social reproduction. The solution to the multiple problems faced by foragers is always a compromise among competing needs in the particular environment of the group. There is no universally applicable solution. It seems likely, however, that some solutions are more successful than others.

---

ranking   The hierarchical arrangement of individuals within a society according to their prestige.

potlatch   A form of competitive feasting among native peoples of the Pacific Northwest of North America that involved shaming one's guests by giving them extravagant quantities of food, blankets, and other goods.

- It is not foraging by itself that produces a social system. The structure grows out of a set of interacting factors, including environment, the nature of the resources, the technology and demography of the group, the influence of neighboring groups, and the possibility of storage resources.
- Foraging groups living in environments with sparse, widely distributed resources rely on mobility to make a secure living. They have little property; they live most of the year in small camps; and they show little tendency to form permanent social hierarchies. The !Kung San are one example of this kind of group.
- Foraging groups that rely on dense, patchily distributed resources that are available seasonally must store food to make a secure living. They live in permanent villages and have many forms of property, and their social organization may include hierarchical ranks. The Kwakiutl are an example of this kind of group.
- There are many other possible adaptations of foraging groups, depending on distribution of resources and relationship to other groups. Many of these possibilities appear in the ethnography of specific groups.

GET INVOLVED

1. Find out what is known about hunter-gatherers who lived in your general region (where you live or go to school). In North America there is a considerable amount of archaeological evidence about non-agricultural people. What evidence is available in your area? How did these people subsist? Learn as much as you can about subsistence, technology, shelter, settlements, health, religion, and the transition to agriculture.

2. Investigate the potlatch ceremony more carefully. Was it an example of cultural "pathology," as some people have suggested? Did it change over time? How did the potlatch vary from one Pacific Northwest society to another? Are there any examples of ceremonies practiced in our society that resemble the potlatch?

3. There are still several hunting-and-gathering societies around the world, struggling to survive in an increasingly hostile environment. Some examples are the Awá-Guajá of northeastern Brazil, the !Kung San of Botswana, and the Agta of the Philippines. Find out about organizations, such as Cultural Survival, that are working to help preserve these people and their way of life. What obstacles are there to the survival of these groups? What changes need to happen to guarantee their survival?

4. Indigenous peoples of the United States and Canada have acquired legal rights to fish and hunt in their traditional territories or areas designated by treaties. As a consequence these groups refuse to accept limits on hunting and fishing imposed by others. For example, the Chippewa of northern Wisconsin refuse to accept state catch and bag limits in areas where they are legally entitled to hunt under 19th-century treaty rights. Go to the law library nearest you and learn about the legal struggles between native peoples and the government in Michigan, Wisconsin, Ontario, and other areas. Are the legal rights of indigenous people compatible with the responsibility of the state to conserve fish and game populations and other natural resources?

SUGGESTED READINGS

Binford, Lewis. 1983. *In pursuit of the past.* New York: Thames and Hudson.

Dahlberg, F., ed. 1981. *Woman the gatherer.* New Haven: Yale University Press.

Friedl, Ernestine. 1978. Society and sex roles. In *Applying Anthropology,* ed. A. Podolefsky and P. J. Brown. Mountain View, Calif.: Mayfield.

Harris, Marvin. 1974. Potlatch. In *Cows, pigs, wars and witches.* New York: Random House.

Lee, Richard. 1969. Eating Christmas in the Kalahari. In the Dobe !Kung. New York: Holt, Rinehart and Winston.

* This selection is anthologized in *Applying Anthropology,* 2d ed., ed. A. Podolefsky and P. J. Brown (Mountain View, Calif.: Mayfield, 1992).

ANTHROPOLOGISTS AT WORK

Hunting with the Agta Women

Currently a historic preservation specialist working for the Department of Land and Natural Resources in the state offices in Hawaii, Agnes-Estioko Griffin spent two years living among the Agta of the Philippines. She recounts here her experience hunting with the Agta women.

Agnes Estioko-Griffin interviewing Agta women of the Philippines.

My husband and I, along with our 12-year-old son, lived among the Agta foragers in the northeastern Philippines for two years. We were there to investigate the nature of women's participation in hunting and other subsistence activities and their roles as mothers and wives.

The Agta are foragers who live in small groups of related families. Depending on the season, their camps may be located in the forest, along dry riverbeds, or near the mouths of the rivers along the beach. Both men and women are capable hunters, fishers, gatherers, gardeners, and traders. The women are not only active producers but also devoted and loving mothers and wives. They are the main caregivers to children. And, most importantly for me, they live and act as equals and partners with their men.

Simple daily successes and failures in forager food getting led me to value the Agta women's experiences. I recall hunger in our rainy season camp along the beach, when for days no luck in hunting meant no meat. The rivers were flooded and unfishable. The diet of sweet potatoes or cassava from the Agta gardens was, in a word, tedious. The men had been gone two nights, traveling deep into the mountains hoping to find wild pig, deer, or monkey. Women and children were left in the camp, along with the anthropologists. Teams of women and dogs made day-trips into the forest to track

game. On Christmas morning I accompanied Abey, a grandmother about 55 years old, her 12-year-old niece, and her three dogs to the edge of the forest. Abey carried her hunting knife, which she preferred to bow and arrows, and her **betel** pouch. Another team of two sisters, Littawan and Taytayan, and their five dogs chose to go upriver. The other women and children stayed in camp.

We spent six hours walking on slippery trails and chasing after the dogs through thickets of thorns and vines. This was interrupted by only a few minutes of rest to chew betel and catch our breath. Finally Abey decided that it was another unlucky day, and we returned to the camp. I was greatly disappointed at our lack of success because, like the Agta, I was looking forward to having meat for Christmas dinner. I apologized to Abey for joining them, thinking that my presence might have hampered her pursuit of the game. She insisted that it was not my fault and blamed her dogs for their inability to hold down the game until our arrival.

We arrived in the camp tired and hungry. The men, who had been away for two nights, also returned empty-handed. Later in the evening, however, Littawan and Taytayan

walked into the camp, each carrying a pack containing about 20 pounds of butchered wild pig. They appeared tired after having been gone for nearly ten hours. The meat was immediately divided among all the families in the camp, including us. Although it was evident that everybody was pleased with the sisters' success, no one immediately expressed praise for their accomplishment.

During our fieldwork it was typical for men, women, and children to gather in our house after dinner to record stories and chants. The highlight of the recording session that night was the story of the sisters' hunt. Everyone enthusiastically listened and asked questions. The men apparently felt no resentment of the women's hunting success.

This experience was not unusual during our stay with the Agta. It was repeated many more times when most of the food for the day was the product of the women's efforts. Women spend nearly as much time as men in subsistence activities. The Agta value hard work, and husbands and wives are equal partners in ensuring the survival of the family.

After the fieldwork, I returned to America with my husband and son. The equal treatment and respect between Agta women and men made me rethink my own ideas of gender relations. The Agta experience showed me that women can make an equal contribution to a society and gain respect without demanding it. The Agta men value the women's contributions, no matter how insignificant, and do not take them for granted. The Agta women have been an inspiration to me, a woman who grew up in a gender-stratified society of the Philippines and has for the past 15 years been living in the gender-stratified society of America.

*Coins—one medium of exchange—
were first issued about 2,700 YA in
Anatolia (the area corresponding to
Turkey today). Shown is a silver coin
from Phoenicia, a nation of extensive
sea-traders that flourished over 2,500
YA in southwestern Asia along the
eastern coast of the Mediterranean Sea.*

11

ECOLOGY AND EXCHANGE

▲ ▲ ▲

In human society there are two kinds of transactions: those between people and nature and those among people. Human beings are part of nature, and they interact with the environment in many of the same ways as other animal species. In some ways, however, the interactions are different. While animals rely heavily on biological adaptation to the environment, humans rely heavily on cultural adaptation, a capability that allows them to live almost anywhere on the globe.

Transactions among humans are also different from those that occur among other species. Every human society has an **economy**—a system of production, exchange, and consumption—that satisfies human needs and wants. Economies operate by means of exchanges among the members of the society. Human exchange systems are much more elaborate and extensive than the exchanges that occur among other species.

In the last chapter, we presented two extended examples illustrating how two foraging groups, the !Kung San and the Kwakiutl, adapted to different habitats. We saw that adaptation involved transactions both with nature—adjustments to the natural habitat—and with other people—sharing, cooperation, division of tasks, and so on. If you recall, a !Kung San hunter usually hunts with arrows made by another man. If he kills a large game animal, the hunter gives it to the arrow owner, who has the right to divide the meat. This custom assures a broad distribution of game within the social unit. This chapter provides a framework for understanding a wider variety of transactions with nature and among people. First we consider transactions between people and nature, looking at how environmental systems operate and how humans act on the environment. We then turn to the variety of systems of transactions that exist among people.

THE ECOSYSTEM

The interrelationships in nature can be better understood by thinking in terms of ecosystems. An **ecosystem** is an area of nature containing one or more communities, or assemblages of plants and animals occupying a particular habitat. Ecosystems are defined in terms of variables related in such a way that a change in one causes a change in the others. Ecosystems do not occur with neat borders around them,

although some, like islands and ponds, are more clearly bounded than others. Ecosystems are **open systems**, meaning that they exchange energy and materials with external systems (Figure 11.1). One way to describe an ecosystem is to view it as a set of energy and material flows.

Energy Flow

Energy is the ability to do work; it occurs in many forms, as radiant energy (e.g., light), kinetic energy (e.g., movement), and potential energy (e.g., fuel). The principal energy source of natural ecosystems is sunlight. Through **photosynthesis**, plants capture solar energy and transform it into the sugar **glucose.** Glucose is a stored form of energy that powers the growth, development, maintenance, and reproduction of plants. When a plant metabolizes glucose, it releases energy through a chemical process called respiration, which is analogous to the burning of fuel in an engine. All consumers, even the Inuit, who dine mainly on seals, fish, and whales, ultimately depend on **primary producers**, or plants, as an energy source.

Ecosystems obey the same **laws of thermodynamics** as physical systems. The first law of thermodynamics, known as the **conservation law**, states that energy may be transformed, but it is neither created nor destroyed. The second law of thermodynamics, the **entropy law**, states that in all transformations energy is degraded from a concentrated to a dispersed form. In ecosystems, energy enters through the medium of primary producers, or plants, which capture energy directly from the sun. This energy can be converted by **primary consumers**, or herbivores, into animal **biomass**, the weight of living tissue of a given class of living organisms. These animals may in turn be consumed by **secondary consumers**, or **carnivores**, that prey on herbivores. Each feeding level constitutes a **trophic level**, whose size is measured in biomass produced per unit area over time. In each transformation from one trophic level to the next, some energy is dissipated in respiration. The energy remaining after deducting for respiration may contribute to the biomass of the **consumers** (see Figure 11.1).

The biomass at one level is limited by the efficiency of exchanges between levels. No more than 10 percent of the energy available at one trophic level can be converted into biomass at the next level. No energy is actually lost in conversion, but so much is dissipated in respiration, decay, and transport that the higher levels on the food chain are considerably smaller than the levels on which they rest, hence the pyramid shape of the ecosystem (see Figure 11.1). All other things being equal, a particular habitat can support a larger human population on seeds, such as wheat, than on seed-eating animals.

The entropy law means that the environment sets limits on ecosystems. Energy flowing through the ecosystem along the food chain dissipates gradually until only a fraction remains. A tiny part of the solar energy falling on the earth's surface is captured by plants. Only a fraction of that can be captured by humans or other animals.

Materials Flow

The flow of **materials**, or nonenergetic substances, through ecosystems follows a different pattern. Rather than being degraded and lost to the system, materials such as water and nutrients can be recycled and used again and again. To grow and reproduce, plants and animals require many different elements and compounds, such as phosphorous, nitrogen, calcium, and iron. Some ecosystems recycle materials locally, while others rely on constant imports.

A mature **tropical forest**, like that of the Amazon basin in South America, is a complex ecosystem (Figure 11.2). In the tropical forest, many species of trees, shrubs, herbs, and other plants grow close together on a single patch of land. Tropical plants have elaborate but shallow root systems. When a plant part drops to the ground, decay begins quickly with the participation of bacteria, fungi, and insects. These "decomposer" species use some of the nutrients in the dead vegetation and deposit chemical compounds in the soil as waste. A dense web of roots, blanketing the ground just below the surface, quickly takes up these nutrients and uses them for growth and maintenance. Many animals, including birds and insects, live in the upper canopy of the forest, in the trunks of trees, on the ground, and in burrows under the ground. Many of these animals eat the shoots, leaves, and seeds of the plants. Their waste products and their decayed bodies when they die also replenish the nutrients in the soil.

In the tropical forest there are few nutrients in the soils but they are abundant in the lush vegetation. Nutrients cycle rapidly through the tropical forest because of the warm climate and high rainfall and humidity. In **temperate zones** (at higher latitudes),

---

economy Social activity that provisions society through production, exchange, and consumption.

ecosystem A community of plants and animals living in a shared physical environment.

open systems Systems that have relatively permeable boundaries with external systems.

energy The ability to work. Energy may take the form of light, motion, or fuel.

photosynthesis The capture and storage of solar energy by plants in the form of glucose.

glucose Sugar; stored energy.

primary producers Plants in an ecosystem.

laws of thermodynamics Physical laws pertaining to the behavior of energy.

conservation law The first law of thermodynamics, which states that energy may be transformed but neither created nor destroyed.

entropy law The second law of thermodynamics, which states that in all transformations energy is degraded from a concentrated to a dispersed form.

primary consumers Herbivores, or animals that eat only plants.

biomass The total weight of living tissue of a given class of living organisms.

secondary consumers Carnivores, or meat-eating animals.

carnivores Meat-eating animals.

trophic level A distinct feeding level, occupied by primary and secondary consumers. The size of a trophic level is measured in biomass produced per unit of area over time.

consumers Animals in their role as agents that capture energy by eating other organisms. The two types are primary consumers (herbivores) and secondary consumers (carnivores).

materials Nonenergetic substances, such as water and nutrients, that can be recycled.

tropical forest A complex ecosystem with a wide variety of plant, shrub, herb, and tree species growing closely together, characterized by warm climate, heavy rainfall, and humidity.

temperate zones Environments located in the higher latitudes where there are sharply differentiated seasons.

Portion of sunlight energy flows in the ecosystem

Production (Plants)

Decomposers ← Consumers

Respiration

Energy leaves the ecosystem (for example as low-grade heat)

◄ **Figure 11.1** *The flow of energy through a typical ecosystem. Energy enters the system when solar energy is captured by plants during photosynthesis. Energy then flows through the system by way of consumers and decomposers; in each transfer the available energy is degraded through such metabolic activities as respiration.*

environments may be pulsed, with sharply different seasons. Nutrients may remain in the soil for some time before being taken up by plants. The rhythms of life are keyed to fluctuations in the environment, and many organisms become dormant during prolonged cold or dry periods, when certain nutrients are scarce and life processes slow down.

Ecological Niches

Figure 11.2 *The tropical rain forest of Brazil is an example of a complex ecosystem in which nutrients and other materials are constantly and rapidly recycled by trees, shrubs, fungi, insects, birds, and other plants and animals.*

Every organism has a range of habitat conditions in which it can live and reproduce. For example, reptiles cannot internally regulate body temperature, so they

Figure 11.3 *Humans can meet their survival requirements in a wide range of ecological niches: A Netsilik man hunts by spearing salmon through a hole in river ice (top left); Chinese men plow their mountain-top fields with draft animals (top right); a Chiapas (Mayan) woman shepherds her flock up a rocky hillside (bottom left); and U.S. farmers use mechanized methods to harvest wheat on the broad American plains (bottom right).*

must seek out places where they can maintain temperature within tolerable limits. As explained in Chapter 5, an organism's requirements and its means for obtaining them are known as its ecological niche. Ecologists distinguish the term *niche* from the term *habitat,* which is the location or range inhabited by an organism. A metaphor for this is to say that the habitat is an organism's "address," while the niche is its "profession."

There is no single human ecological niche; humans have adapted to many different niches, from arctic hunting to farming in equatorial forests, from herding camels to digging irrigation canals (Figure 11.3). Humans everywhere have requirements for nutrients, shelter, and social contact, but there is a wide variety in how these requirements can be met. There is also some physiological and anatomical variation within *Homo sapiens* that allows populations to adjust to specific habitats. We have already discussed the role of skin pigmentation in adapting to varying levels of ultraviolet light (see Chapter 8). There may also be variations in the ability to metabolize certain foods, store nutrients, and resist certain diseases.

Cultural adaptation is the most important mechanism by which humans adjust to an ecological niche. There is a kind of "fit" between habitat and cultural pattern. For example, foragers who depend on sparse, scattered resources are apt to live in small nomadic groups linked by kinship and marriage. To suggest, however, that a cultural pattern arises just to fit a particular niche would be to fall into the fallacy of teleology (see Chapter 5). Cultural patterns are selected from a repertoire of cultural performances. Thus wheat farming in Kansas did not arise purely from the confrontation between a human population and the prairie; it emerged from a background that included an ancient European tradition of consuming bread; a preexisting agricultural technology; and the availability of transportation, distribution, marketing, and baking facilities. There is room in this scheme for human invention and creativity, but most cultural patterns arise from a rearrangement of cultural patterns within limits set down by the environment.

Competition and Cooperation

When two species have the same requirements, competition occurs and some adjustment takes place. If one species uses a given set of resources more efficiently than another, it frequently eliminates the other. As discussed in Chapter 6, this principle is known as the law of competitive exclusion which states that two species cannot coexist in the same habitat when their requirements are identical. This may have been an important factor in early hominid evolution, assuming that *Homo habilis* came into competition with *Australopithecus.* Another outcome is **niche compression,** which occurs when two species specialize to reduce the overlap in their niche requirements. Ecological studies show that the requirements and abilities of closely related species are always different in some respect.

In relatively stable environments, where habitat fluctuations are small and predictable, competition produces a greater diversity of species, sometimes with narrowly defined niches. In unpredictable or fluctuating habitats, niches are not so compressed. Where organisms are not in competition, they may be neutral, or there may be a **symbiosis** between them, as in the case of the bacteria that inhabit the human gut and aid in the digestion of food. Human populations may be symbiotic with others, as is the case with many herding peoples and cultivators who exchange animal products (meat, milk, butter, and skins) and grain.

Genuine cooperation, where organisms join forces for the benefit of others, seems to occur only within species populations. And although other species, such as ants, bees, beavers, wolves, and lions, may cooperate, humans far outdistance them in the complexity and variety of their cooperative systems, both in their

---

niche compression Specialization, reducing competition between species.

symbiosis A mutually advantageous relationship between two different life forms.

ability to store, transport, and exchange goods and in their ability to accumulate and share information.

Ecological Succession

Ecological succession is a sequence of growth in plant and animal communities after a mature community is disturbed. For example, if a patch of mature temperate forest is cleared, the first species to grow back are usually **pioneers**, hardy, fast-growing, leafy plants. They are followed by shrubs and other woody species, then fast-growing trees, which gradually give way to slower-growing trees until finally a stable community develops. Other organisms, including people, adapt to the particular stage of succession. Each stage of succession is associated with a different mix of animals. As the forest develops, the soil deepens and a greater number of species occurs with each stage. People manage different stages of succession for different purposes, such as cropland, pasture for animals, hunting grounds, places for gathering wild plants, or parks. **Fallowing** is the practice of leaving fields idle for a year or more, during which nutrients can be restored through the process of succession.

HABITAT MANAGEMENT

Every population must adapt to the energy and nutrient flows and successional cycles in its environment. As part of human adaptation, people use technology and information to modify the environment. This is called **habitat management**, and all human groups practice it to some extent. Chapter 10 explored the ways in which foragers use movement, scheduling, and storage to adjust to their environments. Foragers usually manage resources by adapting to the natural cycles of the species on which they depend. They behave like other predators, taking game and plants in quantities that do not deplete them.

Foraging, a Low-Intensity Adaptation

Many foragers appear to follow rules that protect the species on which they depend. The Tukano people of Colombia, for example, observe many rituals that they believe promote the replacement of each game animal they kill (Reichel-Dolmatoff 1971, 50). Their beliefs prevent them from killing more animals than they need. Hunters also modify their environments. Hunting an area intensively may affect the environment. For example, some hunters use fire to drive game. The native Americans of the Great Plains burned off large areas of prairie in hunting the bison (Figure 11.4). The fires destroyed some kinds of plants while promoting growth of the tender herbs that herbivorous animals prefer.

Food Production: Degrees of Management Intensity

Low-energy adaptations like foraging are known as **extensive management**; adaptations that involve greater environmental modification are known as **intensive management**. Food producing generally falls into the latter category. Wherever people plant seeds, they usually become involved in modifying different aspects of the ecosystem. Poking a seed into the ground is a small modification of the habitat, but it is the beginning of the elaborate system of modification that is agriculture. The term **horticulture** is used by anthropologists to refer narrowly to planting and harvesting of domestic crops, often combined with foraging. **Agriculture** is defined as farming with domestic plants and animals, specialized tools, and, usually, complex systems of exchange. In the most elaborate form, agriculturalists manage the habitat intensively through forest clearance, grading and terracing to change the contours of the land, mechanical preparation of the soil, application of chemical fertilizers to promote growth, application of other chemicals to control pests and kill weeds, mechanical tillage to loosen the soil and control weeds, irrigation to provide adequate water, and many other practices. Agriculture is discussed in greater detail in Chapter 12.

Slash-and-Burn Horticulture: A Form of Extensive Management. To see how people adapt to ecosystems and manage habitats, let us explore in greater depth a common form of horticulture practiced in many parts of the world. **Slash-and-burn** is currently practiced mainly in the tropics of Africa, Southeast Asia, and Central and South America. In Neolithic times, slash-and-burn was a common form of production in Europe. In slash-and-burn horticulture, the

Figure 11.4 *Native Americans often used fire to drive game. At this site in Montana, prehistoric hunters drove buffalo over the cliffs, a precipitous drop that killed many of the animals. The bison were butchered in the area below.*

fallow period is longer than the period of cultivation. The cycle begins when forest is cleared for planting and then burned over. The ashes from the fire fertilize the crops, reduce the soil acidity, and help remove additional undergrowth. A field may be cultivated for two or three years and then fallowed for a period ranging from a few years to a few hundred years. During this period, the soil develops and deepens, the forest regrows, and the number of different species increases. When the field is needed for planting again, the secondary growth is cut down, allowed to dry, and burned over, and the cycle begins again. Slash-and-burn horticulture is adapted to natural cycles in the ecosystem. The fertility of the soil is maintained by

long fallows, during which ecological succession slowly restores the nutrients. Slash-and-burn is particularly adaptive to humid tropical areas, where topsoils tend to be thin and acidic. In the tropics plots are typically invaded by weeds too thick to manage after two or three years of cultivation.

Slash-and-burn produces high yields for relatively low labor inputs. The number of worker hours or energy spent per acre for slash-and-burn is much lower than for more intensive forms of agriculture. While a North American farmer may spend 40 to 60 hours a week working in the fields, maintaining equipment, and so on, a Mekranoti native in Brazil spends an average of 8.5 hours a week working on a slash-and-

ecological succession The sequence of plant and animal communities after a mature community is disturbed.

pioneers In ecological succession, the first plants to grow back after the vegetative cover has been cleared.

fallowing The practice of leaving a field uncultivated for one or more growing seasons so that it can replenish its nutrients.

habitat management The use of technology and information by humans to modify their habitat.

extensive management A low energy ecological adaptation such as foraging, pastoralism, nomadism, and horticulture.

intensive management A high energy human ecological adaptation, such as agriculture, which involves substantial environmental modification.

horticulture The production of domestic crops using simple technology (e.g., a digging stick).

agriculture The production of domesticated crops and animals.

slash-and-burn A system of horticulture in which natural vegetation is cleared and burned over before cultivation.

Figure 11.5   *Slash-and-burn cultivation is commonly practiced among the Mekranoti of Central Brazil. This form of extensive management requires relatively little effort and is highly productive over the short run, but it can be used only in areas of low population density.*

burn plot to produce plenty of food for the household (Gross et al. 1979). The difference is even more dramatic when we compare the food energy yield to the calories of work energy expended. A slash-and-burn cultivator may reap from 15 to 50 calories in food energy for every calorie of energy spent gardening. A modern farmer produces less than one calorie in food energy for each calorie invested. While industrial high-tech agriculture gets high yields per acre, ancient forms of horticulture obtain higher yields per unit of effort. Slash-and-burn and other extensive forms of horticulture require larger amounts of land available to cultivators than are actively cultivated at any moment in time (Figure 11.5).

While slash-and-burn and other forms of extensive management are efficient uses of labor, they cannot

support dense populations. As the demand for food becomes more intense, the management regime is typically intensified, perhaps by shortening the fallow cycle. Because soil fertility is related to the length of the fallow cycle, shortening the fallow period lowers yields per acre. Today slash-and-burn is found mainly in areas of relatively low population density in the humid tropics. In most other places where it was once practiced, slash-and-burn horticulture has been replaced by more intensive forms of agriculture.

Other Forms of Extensive Management. Slash-and-burn is one of many forms of extensive management. Another is **pastoralism**, which involves herding animals like sheep, goats, cattle, and camels. Pastoral adaptations include **transhumance**, in which the

Figure 11.6 *The Kurds of Iraq, pictured here, practice transhumance, a form of pastoralism involving seasonal migrations between different pasture areas. Pastoralism is an adaptation in which people use animals as "converters" of energy in plants into foods humans can consume.*

herders follow a fixed cycle of migration, rotating among pastures through the various seasons. The Kurdish herders of Iraq and Iran graze their sheep and cattle in mountain valleys during the winter and then take their animals up the steep slopes of the surrounding mountains to take advantage of the pastures available in the summer months (Fig 11.6). True **nomadism** (wandering in a random pattern) is less common. The Karimojong camel, sheep, and cattle herders of East Africa, who do not follow a fixed pattern of movement among pastures, are a nomadic group.

Pastoral nomads and transhumants live on animal products, consuming the milk, blood, and flesh of their animals. They may also use animals to carry or pull loads. Although pastoralists are commonly viewed as highly independent and self-sufficient, this view is probably inaccurate (Lees and Bates 1974). Few, if any, pastoral groups are self-sufficient in food.

---

pastoralism The herding of animals, such as sheep, goats, camels, and cattle.

transhumance An environmental adaptation by pastoral people who follow a fixed migration pattern from one pasture to another according to the season.

nomadism Migration or wandering without a fixed pattern.

Figure 11.7 *Irrigated rice paddies in China. As a form of intensive management that increases the amount of food produced per unit of land, irrigation is associated with permanent settlements and a stable social system.*

Either they practice cultivation as well as pastoralism, or they exchange animal products (cheese, yogurt, and animal hides) for agricultural products such as grain. More intensive pastoral practices include selective breeding, preparing pastures, planting forage crops (such as hay or alfalfa), and storing foods for cattle to eat during the winter.

Intensive Management. More intensive forms of habitat management also take advantage of natural nutrient cycles, succession, and energy flow, but they involve greater modification of the environment. In intensive systems people expend greater amounts of energy per unit area. In both extensive and intensive management, activities are aimed at limiting the

growth of weeds and other undesirable species and promoting the growth of those that provide food, fiber, and other items people need. In many parts of the world today, farmers rotate crops to maintain soil fertility. **Crop rotation** means that a given plot is planted in different crops each year. In more extensive forms, a field may simply be allowed to lie fallow for a year or more. Planting a variety of crops together in the field (**simultaneous polyculture**) or successively over time may help restore soil nutrient balance. Leguminous crops such as beans or peas restore to the soil the nitrogen that other crops tend to remove. In a more intensive agricultural system, a fallow field may be temporarily converted to pasture to allow the manure of domestic animals to accumulate and enrich the soil.

Irrigation is a common form of agricultural intensification that has been used for thousands of years in the Nile Valley, China, Peru, and southwestern Asia (Figure 11.7). **Irrigation** is the practice of capturing water from streams, wells, or other sources and diverting it to cultivated fields. Irrigation brings nutrients and moisture to bathe the roots of growing plants. Extensive hydraulic works designed to provide adequate drainage for crops were also important in some situations, as in the area around present-day Mexico City. Even relatively simple irrigation or drainage systems require considerable investment in canals, reservoirs, pumps, and other technology. Therefore people who practice irrigation are likely to be settled permanently in a single place and to defend their investment against encroachers. Irrigation may also require a great deal of coordination among farmers to share the water equitably and maintain the system. (Canals often fill with silt and weeds and must be cleaned regularly.) Therefore irrigation presupposes not only a large investment but also a stable social system.

Some anthropologists maintain that irrigation underlies the development of all the early empires or **civilizations.** Irrigation was practiced in ancient times in Sumeria, Egypt, China, and Peru. Anthropologist Julian Steward (1955) argued that recruitment of great amounts of labor to construct and maintain reservoirs and canals led to the development of strong centralized states. Karl Wittfogel (1938) argued that irrigation underlies the development of a particularly rigid, despotic kind of state due to the great amount of regimentation involved. More recent studies indicate that in some places the great expansion of irrigation networks occurred only after expansion in the power of the state had occurred. There is no question, however,

that the managerial requirements for the construction and maintenance of dams, canals, and other engineering works reinforced the need for strong, centralized administrations (Adams 1966).

All forms of intensification involve increased energy expenditure per unit area. While intensification may increase agricultural yields, the increase may not be proportional to the increased energy and effort invested. Some studies (Pimentel et al. 1973) show that while maize yields have increased under modern techniques, the energy efficiency of agriculture has declined. In the most intensive modern agricultural systems, machines perform nearly every operation from plowing to harvest. Chemical fertilizers are used to supplement the nutrients in the soil, creating an environment hospitable to growing plants. Pesticides and herbicides are applied to eliminate pests and weeds. These processes and products require high energy expenditure to produce and use.

Are Human Societies Self-Regulating Systems?

We are familiar with self-regulating systems at the level of organisms. For example, most mammals are **homeothermic,** maintaining a constant body temperature. A **homeostat** is any mechanism that acts to maintain a system value within certain limits. A thermostat, for instance, regulates temperature in a room, switching the heater on when the temperature drops below a preset level and off again when it reaches that level. This is an example of **negative feedback**, a self-correcting mechanism. **Positive feedback** refers to changes that tend to move the value of some variable

---

crop rotation The successive planting of two or more different crops on the same piece of land.

simultaneous polyculture The practice of planting a variety of crops on the same patch of land at the same time.

irrigation The capture and diversion of water from a stream, well, or other source to a cultivated field.

civilizations Early empires, such as those in Egypt, Sumeria, and China. Some anthropologists have theorized that irrigation was the basis for the development of all early civilizations.

homeothermic Maintaining a constant body temperature regardless of environmental changes.

homeostat A mechanism (e.g., a thermostat) that operates to maintain a system value (e.g., temperature) at a constant level.

negative feedback A self-correcting mechanism that returns system variables to a determined range.

positive feedback A mechanism that drives a system value beyond a given range, causing instability and ultimately a changed system.

Figure 11.8   *A Maring pig festival in New Guinea, at which great quantities of meat and other goods are given to guests. This ceremony is held to propitiate the ancestors, but it also plays a role in redistributing resources and regulating the environment.*

beyond a given range, such as hyperventilation, which may cause you to faint, or a prolonged drought, which results in the replacement of one plant community with another.

Many social scientists believe that social systems may also be self-regulating. Some common theories of self-regulation involve a homeostat described as a "safety valve." Consider the average North American high school. In a large high school there is a great deal of tension caused by overcrowding, anxiety over grades, awakening sexuality, drugs, and worry about college acceptance. Some people believe that intramural sports and "school spirit" help to relieve that tension by acting as a safety valve. This approach is known as **functionalism,** the explanation of social institutions in terms of the functions they play.

A number of anthropologists have suggested that human populations are self-regulating in relation to the environment. We have already discussed Wynne-Edward's theories of social regulation among animals (Chapter 9). He argued that social mechanisms operate to keep animal populations in balance with resources. Anthropologist Roy Rappaport gave an example of self-regulation through negative feedback mechanisms in his study of a highland Papua New Guinea population (1968). The Maring are slash-and-burn cultivators living in high population densities along the steep slopes of a mountain valley. They also raise pigs, but slaughter them only on ritual occasions

(Figure 11.8) to propitiate the ancestors at times of sickness, death, or impending battle. Maring women feed their pigs substandard sweet potatoes from their gardens. If conditions are good, the population prospers, sickness is rare, there are few sacrifices, and the pig population can grow unchecked.

Negative feedback sets in when the pig population reaches high levels, the pressure on resources increases, and women begin to complain to their husbands about the heavy loads of sweet potatoes they must carry from the gardens to feed the pigs. The expanding pig population may begin to invade gardens, causing damage and further adding to the tension. At this moment, a ritual cycle may begin, which culminates in large-scale pig sacrifices and the beginning of warfare. Wars are fought to avenge killings that took place in previous wars. The celebration of this ritual is important both as a way of propitiating the ancestors of the local group and as a way of rewarding neighboring groups who may be allies in the war. The Maring will not go to battle until the necessary ritual preparations have been made.

Fighting takes place between neighboring groups, each of which mobilizes allies from among relatives in other groups. The allies are invited to pig festivals and are rewarded with gifts of pork, a rare delicacy in this area where meat is scarce and protein deficiencies are common. A war can end in a draw, but when there is a clear victor, one group drives another from its territory. When this happens, the victors may be able to take over the loser's land after a waiting period. Through this complex mechanism, the size of the pig population acts as a homeostat, regulating how often Maring groups go to war and how intensively the land is used.

The Maring themselves do not regard their use of pigs as connected with resources. They explain the pig sacrifices as a response to a demand by the ancestors. The ancestors demand to be fed, and they will accept only pig flesh. Even when people eat the pork, the Maring believe they are appeasing the ancestors. The Maring do not see their ritual system as a means of regulating their environment. For them it is a matter of fulfilling social and religious obligations.

EXCHANGE SYSTEMS

Now that we have considered exchanges between people and their habitats, let us look at the kinds of transactions that take place among people. The exchange of goods and services among people and groups of people takes many forms. Anthropologists have identified three major modes of exchange in social units: reciprocity, redistribution, and market exchange. These modes often coexist within the same society, although one of them generally dominates. We will examine each of these modes in turn. This description overlaps somewhat with formal economics, although most college courses in economics deal mainly with the theory of market exchange.

Reciprocal Exchange

Reciprocal exchange can take place between individuals, households, or other social units. In reciprocity any individual is as likely to give as to receive. For example, greeting cards are exchanged reciprocally among North American families at Christmas time. Reciprocity may be immediate, as when a Yanomamo native gives a hunting dog to a friend and receives a hammock in return. More often reciprocity is delayed; a gift is not returned immediately. Birthday gifts between spouses or siblings are examples of delayed reciprocity. Reciprocity is balanced when, over a period of time, the value of items given is equal to the value of items received. Friends who exchange Christmas gifts are often careful to match the gifts they give with the value of the gifts they receive from a given exchange partner. Although accounts are usually not kept, exchange partners may be embarrassed when they feel they have given a gift of lesser value than they received. The important thing about reciprocal exchange is that it is not centrally administered or regulated. Reciprocal exchange often supports other aspects of social relationships. For example, if you ask people why they exchange Christmas gifts, they may respond that the gifts in themselves are not important but are tokens of the love, friendship, or esteem that people have for each other.

Generalized reciprocal exchange occurs when the cycle of gifts and countergifts is open ended. Ethnologist Allen Johnson studied reciprocal exchanges among worker households on an agricultural estate in northeastern Brazil (1971, 105–107). He found a system of delayed, generalized reciprocity in effect:

> We are dealing here with exchanges between . . . persons of roughly equal status. . . . Small exchanges . . . occurred constantly. Women came to visit and spun cotton for their hostess as they gossiped. Liters of beans, folk remedies, pieces of pork fat, cigarettes, squashes, the loan of a milk goat for an infant, piglets, and a host of other items appeared endlessly as "gifts." It is clear that a great many goods and services were being exchanged.

Johnson distinguished three categories of exchange goods: The first were relatively expensive items such as bicycles, radios, watches, and sewing machines. These goods were never exchanged as gifts. Whenever they changed hands, they were bought or sold for a

---

functionalism Theoretical perspective that considers social phenomena in terms of their contribution to social stability.

reciprocal exchange A system of trading gifts, in which any individual is as likely to give as to receive; also known as reciprocity.

generalized reciprocal exchange An open-ended cycle of gifts and countergifts.

price, even among friends. The second and most common category of exchange goods was necessities, such as basic foodstuffs and labor assistance. The third category consisted of small luxuries such as meat, tapioca, fruits, and vegetables; these were the closest thing to "pure gifts."

Workers frequently exchanged labor, usually to accomplish a major task in a short time, such as clearing a new garden quickly before the rains began. A worker in that situation might invite several others to assist him in the task. He then had the obligation of helping the others in some way some day in the future. Johnson stresses that "labor exchanges usually occur between persons who have established a relationship by other means (e.g., gifts of meat)" (1971, 107).

Figure 11.9 *An example of reciprocal meat exchange on a Brazilian plantation. Kinship and proximity seem to be the main factors determining which households will exchange meat with each other. Note the partially closed "network" of exchange among households 3, 4, 9, 5, 6, and 17.*

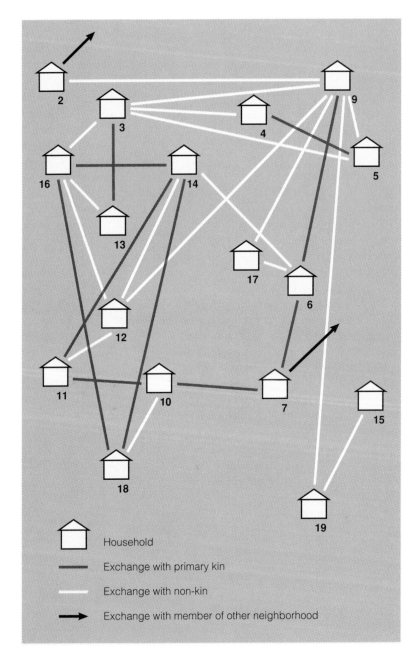

Johnson was unable to keep track of exchanges of basic foodstuffs, such as beans and rice, because they were so frequent. Meat exchange was easier to trace because meat is a scarce and highly valued food and it stands out in people's minds:

> The usual chain of events begins when a household slaughters a pig or goat. That same day, it sends gifts of meat to several other households. There is no immediate gift return or attempt at repayment with some other commodity. Eventually, a household that received meat will repay the gift with a roughly equivalent gift, but the delay may be several months. [Johnson 1971, 107]

Johnson kept track of meat exchanges among households for a year and found that certain households formed more or less closed exchange networks (Figure 11.9). The community formed by this **generalized reciprocal exchange network** was not based on any formal organization or central leadership. It was a loose collection of **dyadic** (one-to-one) relationships between households. This kind of generalized exchange provides a powerful form of "cement" that binds communities together. While it is economic in nature, exchange is frequently embedded in the social structure of a community and is inseparable from it.

Redistributive Exchange

A second major mode of exchange, **redistribution,** occurs when goods are collected by a central agency and then doled out to recipients, sometimes the same people who contributed them. In Chapter 10 we examined one case of redistribution, the Kwakiutl potlatch. In the potlatch people contribute fish, fish oil, blankets, and other goods to a local chief, who may use them to throw a competitive feast for another group or within the group or simply distribute them to needy people within the group. Each contributor to

a potlatch will very likely be a recipient of such goods as well, and the exchange may balance out over time. Redistribution differs from reciprocal exchange in that the goods are controlled by a central agent, such as a chief (Figure 11.10).

Redistribution is found in some form in most societies. In the United States, the Social Security Administration is a redistributor, collecting payroll taxes in a central fund and paying out benefits to retirees, disabled workers, and survivors. Most socialist societies are based primarily on a redistributive model, with the state playing the role of redistributor. Redistribution also occurs in families where a household head collects the income (cash, crops, or other items) in a single pool and then uses it to feed, clothe, and house the family.

In most cases of redistribution the redistributor is not the owner of the goods and may not distribute them as he or she pleases. A redistributor is usually a leader bound by a legal or moral code to conserve the collected wealth for some socially approved purpose. Redistributors may use their control over goods to aggrandize themselves, even to humiliate their enemies, as in the Kwakiutl potlatch, but they cannot expend them for their own benefit. Like reciprocity, redistribution is embedded in the social life of a community or society, expressing common values and goals.

Market Exchange

A third form of exchange is **market** exchange. In this system goods have values that fluctuate according to supply and demand. In the United States, for example, fruit prices are generally low when the fruit is in season and high when it is out of season and must be imported from distant places. In nearly every society things have an **exchange value**—what something is worth in units of some other thing—that is distin-

---

generalized reciprocal exchange network The web of dyadic social relations involved in generalized reciprocity, not based on any formal organization or centralized leadership but promoting social cohesion.

dyad A pair.

redistribution A mode of economic exchange based on the collection of goods by a central agency, or actor, that in turn distributes them to recipients (e.g., the Kwakiutl potlatch).

market A social institution in which goods are exchanged at prices that fluctuate according to supply and demand.

exchange value The worth of a good stated in units of some other good.

Figure 11.10 *Redistribution of goods in China. Bullock meat is being divided into 72 equal portions for the members of the group.*

guishable from their **use value**—the intrinsic benefit derived from using or possessing a thing. This distinction is illustrated by the Yir Yoront aborigines of Australia (Sharp 1952). This group relied on implements handmade from stone and other locally available materials until the 1930s, when the steel axe was introduced. Since stone for axes was not found in Yir Yoront territory it had to be imported from another area. The ethnographer Lauriston Sharp describes the trade network as follows (1952, 19):

The stone they used came from quarries 400 miles to the south, reaching the Yir Yoront through long lines

of male trading patterns. . . . Almost every adult man had one or more regular trading partners. He provided his partners in the south with surplus spears, particularly fighting spears tipped with the barbed spines of stingray that snap into vicious fragments when they penetrate human flesh. For a dozen such spears . . . he would receive one stone axe head. Studies have shown that the stingray barb spears increased in value as they moved south and farther from the sea. One hundred and fifty miles south of the Yir Yoront one such spear may be exchanged for one stone axe head. . . . Farther south, nearer the quarries, one stingray barb spear would bring several stone axe heads. Apparently people who acted as links in the middle of the chain and who made neither spears nor axe heads would receive a certain number of each as a middleman's profit.

The use value of stone axes and stingray spears is probably the same across the entire area, but the exchange value changes. Even though stingray barbs are no more useful in the interior than on the seacoast, they "cost" more for the simple reason that they are scarcer.

What Sharp described is a simple form of what economists call a market. A market is a social institution in which goods are exchanged at rates that vary according to supply and demand. Markets need not be localized in a single spot, and money is not a feature of every market, as is illustrated by the Yir Yoront case. The key aspect of a market is that it sets **prices** (exchange rates) for goods. The "perfect market" that economists sometimes idealize is one in which buyers and sellers have complete knowledge of the products, their quality, the demand for them, their availability, the cost of producing them, and so on (Figure 11.11). Markets therefore act as sources of information for decision making. Perfect markets do not exist, but the model is powerful enough to explain many aspects of behavior, including behavior that is not, strictly speaking, "economic." (Some economists have begun to use economic models to explain marriage behavior, the allocation of time, and many other features of life where cash markets are not directly involved.)

The minimum conditions for a market are met when the interaction between buyers and sellers affects the exchange rates for goods. In this sense market economies are found nearly everywhere. Many anthropologists prefer to restrict the term to situations where the market mode of exchange is dominant. In capitalist economies nearly everything may become a commodity on the marketplace, including food, land, labor, and ideas. There are, however, levels of market penetration, ranging from very little among groups like the Yir Yoront to the all-encompassing market society found in contemporary North America.

Developed capitalist economies have some distinctive features. Perhaps the main feature is the tendency for capital and monetary exchange to enter every nook and cranny of the society. Consider, for example, the kinds of goods and services available for sale in the United States: kennels for boarding pets, computer dating services, stock brokers, hot tubs, caviar, pinball machines, paging services, drive-in movies, dune buggies, prefaded jeans, passion fruit juice, swimming pool service, resumé writing services, psychotherapists, premium unleaded gasoline, tomato pickers, baby-sitters, photocopiers, and so on. Consider what the use and exchange value of any of these products is. Almost any good can be converted into a cash equivalent, such as so many dollars for a suntan. In such a society people often convert their hopes and plans into monetary equivalents. They consider their happiness as closely tied to their credit balance. In this context money takes on a life of its own (Taussig 1977 and 1980). Banks advertise, "Let your money work for you." Stock prices may "soar," "move sideways," or "dive." Wealthy people seek out "tax shelters." We even say that "money talks."

Some anthropologists consider this state of affairs to be alienated. They feel that people in a capitalist society forget the use value of things and focus purely on exchange value. They object to the use of terms like *profit* and *loss, price* and *cost,* in descriptions of nonmarket economies, declaring that such terms impose the standards of the capitalist world on societies that are noncapitalist. Other anthropologists feel it is reasonable to conduct economic analysis of societies that lack formal market economies. The reason is that all people must economize.

Economizing is part of capitalism, but it is also part of everyday life in noncapitalist societies. When a worker saves money by taking the bus to work instead of driving, she is economizing. When a factory owner tries to cut costs he is economizing. But economizing is much more than saving money. Consider the situation of a !Kung San woman who goes out with her baby strapped to her back to dig up edible roots. She is limited by how far she can walk with her baby and a load of roots. Therefore she looks for roots as close to the camp as possible. As the supply of roots nearby becomes depleted, she is obliged to travel farther from

---

use value The worth of an object in terms of the benefit derived from its use or possession.

price An exchange rate, which is established only in market economies.

economizing Lowering costs, maximizing return on effort.

Figure 11.11 *An open-air market in Huehuetenango, Guatemala. Sellers of similar goods are grouped together in one place, making it possible for buyers to compare as they shop. This is the "information" function of markets.*

the camp each day unless the campsite is moved. Searching for resources nearby and moving a campsite when are depleted are both forms of economizing.

These behaviors can also be seen as **maximization**, getting the highest possible return for a given unit of effort. What is maximized is the return on effort. It is not the same as maximization of profits because a !Kung San woman stops working as soon as her needs are satisfied, while a capitalist is generally never completely satisfied with the level of profits. Nevertheless, in these and many other activities people make decisions to get maximum return on their effort. Maximization is not necessarily motivated by either greed or need. It could be considered a part of nature, decreed by the struggle for existence discussed in Chapter 5.

As Karl Marx admiringly observed, capitalist exchange is one of the most powerful forces in the modern world. It is the system that spawned the first great world empires and the first industrial systems. It unleashed forces that have transformed the face of the earth. The relentless search for profits created by modern capitalism has also created many problems. Maximization of profits has led to severe exploitation of workers in some instances and to the despoiling of the environment. A great deal of controversy currently surrounds the expansion of capitalism into the developing world. Some view it as a blessing; others regard it as an evil. Anthropologists have led the way in describing the effects of capitalist expansion in the developing world (see the Anthropologists at Work sections "Fishing in Panama," at the end of this chapter, and "Studying Tubuai Agriculture," in Chapter 12).

SUMMARY

- Like all other animals, people live in ecosystems. An ecosystem is an area of nature that can be described in terms of flows.
- Energy and materials behave differently in ecosystems. Energy flows in one direction and is degraded in each transformation, while material flows are cyclical.
- Ecosystems change in regular sequences over time.
- Like other animals, people must adapt to energy and material flows in the ecosystems. They adjust their behavior, growth rates, food requirements, and reproductive strategies to the opportunities presented by the particular habitat in which they live. They must also adjust to other species present in the habitat.
- Organisms adapt to competition within species by competitive exclusion or niche compression. Different species are sometimes mutually beneficial.
- Ecosystems obey the same laws of thermodynamics

as other physical systems. Energy is conserved as entropy (energy dispersion) increases.
- Human groups enter the food chain at different trophic levels. Some humans are primary consumers. Those who depend on animal converters for a large part of their diet are limited by the low efficiency of trophic conversion of energy.
- Human groups rely on technology and information to adapt to the habitat. All adaptations make use of natural cycles and energy flows.
- Adaptations that involve greater environmental modification are referred to as intensively managed, while low-energy adaptations such as foraging and slash-and-burn are referred to as extensively managed. Neither adaptation is superior to the other. Intensive management uses up resources, especially energy, at a higher rate and permits higher population densities. Extensive management involves lower rates of resource use and lower densities.
- All forms of management involve environmental modification. When the environment is modified, people must adapt to the changes.
- Some changes in the environment lead inevitably to further changes (positive feedback). Other perturbations may set self-correcting mechanisms into motion, restoring a previous state of affairs (negative feedback). Some studies suggest that self-regulation takes place at the population level.
- People differ from animals in the complex ways they exchange goods and services.
- Reciprocal exchange, redistribution, and market exchange are the three major modes of exchange; they can coexist in a single society, but one mode tends to dominate.
- Simple societies like the !Kung San rely heavily on reciprocal exchange.
- More complex societies like the Kwakiutl may have redistributive economies.
- Market exchange predominates when goods are valued by their relative supply and demand.
- All exchange systems are embedded in the social behavior and values of a society.

maximization Behavior directed toward producing as much as possible of a given good.

GET INVOLVED

1. Do an investigation of one ecosystem in your area. What are the primary producers, primary consumers, and higher trophic levels? What are the primary constraints on production? Is energy limiting? What nutrient cycles are present? What part do humans play in this ecosystem? What changes have people made over time in the ecosystem you are analyzing? What adaptive changes have occurred in the human populations dependent on this environment? In the long run, are the primary human activities in the area sustainable? If not, what changes are likely to take place?

2. In recent years, there has been movement—organic farming, alternative agriculture—toward reduced energy use in general and reduced use of chemical fertilizers, pesticides, and herbicides in agriculture. What are the reasons for this movement? What are the chances that these tendencies will become more general? What economic factors influence these choices?

3. Make a survey of all the forms of nonmarket exchange that occur in your community. Include both monetary and nonmonetary forms of exchange, such as helping with homework, exchanging Christmas presents, and the college health service. What are the rules underlying gift giving? Are all gifts truly "free"? Briefly analyze each of these systems to see how they function. Are they based on reciprocity, redistribution, or something else?

SUGGESTED READINGS

Diamond, Jared. 1987. The worst mistake in the human race. *Discover Publications* (May):64–66.*

Goodman, Alan H., and George J. Armelagos. 1985. Death and disease at Dr. Dickson's mounds. *Natural History* (American Museum of Natural History) 94, no. 9.*

Harris, Marvin. 1974. Pig lovers and pig haters. In *Cows, pigs, wars and witches*. New York: Random House.

Monaghan, John. 1990. Reciprocity, redistribution, and the transaction of value in the Mesoamerican fiesta. *American Ethnologist* 17:758–774.

Sharp, Lauriston. 1952. Steel axes for Stone-Age Australians. *Human Organization* 2:17–22.

*This selection is anthologized in *Applying Anthropology*, 2d ed, ed. A. Podolefsky and P. J. Brown (Mountain View, Calif.: Mayfield, 1992).

ANTHROPOLOGISTS AT WORK

Fishing in Panama

John R. Bort is an associate professor of anthropology at East Carolina University. He works in Central America with traditional rural populations involved in small-scale fisheries, aquaculture, and agriculture.

I am interested in how contemporary small-scale fishermen gain their livelihoods and what factors promote change in the way they exploit their environment. The rapid development and continual increase in the importance of international seafood marketing in Panama have influenced rural coastal populations. Developing an understanding of the ways in which traditional populations cope with rapid change and the new forces influencing their lives is crucial to anticipating and avoiding serious environmental and economic problems in the future.

Humans have lived along the coast of Panama's Azuero Peninsula for over 1,000 years. Archaeological evidence indicates that marine resources have always been important in the area. Today they remain important, but the patterns of resource exploitation have changed rapidly in recent years.

In the past fishermen sold most of their catch fresh in the local area. They preserved some fish by salting and sun drying and sold them to buyers who eventually resold the dried fish in areas farther from the coast. The overall market for fish was small and did not extend beyond the central region of Panama. Historical records indicate that this pattern persisted and remained stable from the colonial era until the middle of this century. The abundant shrimp stocks, which are by far the most important resource today, were not exploited historically because no market existed. Local people preferred fish to shrimp.

Bort (right) and a local Panamanian examine a cayuco, a dug-out canoe made from a single log and used for small-scale fishing, as they discuss local fishing activities.

In the late 1950s the pattern of resource exploitation began to change very rapidly. Panama began developing a thriving shrimp industry oriented toward international markets. (Typically about 90 percent of the commercial shrimp catch is exported to the United States.) Shrimping continued to expand rapidly during the 1960s and 1970s. The combination of good prices and abundant untapped wild shrimp stocks resulted in a rapid shift in emphasis among established fishermen away from the traditional fish species to shrimp. It also attracted very large numbers of new fishermen. For example, the number of fishermen in one community grew from a modest 20 to 25 individuals to over 400 in a period of 15 years. Pressure on the environment has become very heavy in recent years, and, as a result, the catches of indi-

vidual fishermen have declined. More and more fishermen have had to divide up the limited stocks of wild shrimp.

Still another important change is taking place today. Fishermen are now beginning to combine aquaculture with fishing, raising shrimp in artificial impoundments. Market demand for shrimp remains high, and aquaculture provides a means of producing more shrimp than by fishing alone. Aquaculture promises to be increasingly important in the future, but it raises many difficult questions. The potential for environmental damage as fragile mangrove areas are exploited is not clearly understood, but there may be serious long-term consequences if the use of these areas is not properly controlled. In addition the people are becoming economically dependent on a single product. Thus fluctuating international shrimp prices and events far removed from the Azuero Peninsula have a very direct impact on them.

My work with the fishermen of the Azuero Peninsula spans ten years. This long-term research has yielded insights into the ways in which the local population adapts to unpredictable economic and environmental fluctuations. Their highly successful adaptive strategies are based on the diversification of productive pursuits; an extensive, kinship-based system of mutual assistance; and the flexibility to alter activity patterns rapidly to exploit unexpected opportunities and cope with often precipitous setbacks. The traditional resilience of the local population will remain very important in the future as these small coastal communities develop more links to often volatile international seafood markets.

Rice is the leading staple of the Philippines, and the Ifugao people of northern Luzon, Philippines, used a sophisticated technology to develop irrigated rice terraces in their mountainous environment.

12

INTENSIFICATION AND TECHNOLOGY

▲▲▲

or the past half million years, the world has been filling up with people. The population of the world today is fast approaching 5 billion. Overall world population density is about 32 people per square kilometer. Until the end of the Pleistocene (10,000 YA), the number of hominids alive at one time probably never exceeded 200,000, even after *Homo* had migrated throughout Africa, Asia, and Europe. A half million years ago, hominids were scattered throughout the **Old World** (Europe, Africa, and Asia) at a low density, probably less than one person per 100 square kilometers. The density was higher where abundant, stable resources were available, but there were large uninhabited spaces between such places. A Paleolithic male who survived early childhood had a life expectancy of around 30 years; a female's was lower. How did hominids expand so much that today they are the most numerous large animal species on the globe?

POPULATION GROWTH

Human populations did not increase smoothly; they grew in jumps (Figure 12.1). We can identify three great moments of change. The first was the **agricultural revolution** that occurred around 10,000 YA. The second was the **demographic transition** when the mortality dropped sharply and the birth rate leveled off. This transition began in the 18th century at the time of the expansion of sanitation services in urban areas and the beginning of industrial production and dynamic world trade. A third major population event is the explosive increase, occurring now, of populations in the developing world as a result of their having undergone a partial demographic transition.

To explain the fluctuations and trends in human population, demographers concern themselves with vital rates. The **birthrate** is the number of babies born alive per 1,000 people per year. The mortality (or death rate) is the number of people who die per 1,000 people per year. The **growth rate** of a population equals the birthrate minus the mortality, not counting migration in and out of the population. It can be positive or negative in a given year. For example, a population that has a birthrate of 40 and a mortality of 30

will grow at the rate of 10 per thousand, a 1 percent growth rate. For the larger view of any particular population, we must also consider the effect of migration in and out.

Fertility refers to the rate at which females bear young. Theoretically a woman could have a child as often as once a year, starting at age 15 and ending at about 44. However, no known population has ever reproduced at this theoretical high limit of fertility. If it did, the average woman would have about 20 pregnancies during her reproductive span. Nearly two centuries ago, Thomas Malthus noted that populations are capable of expanding much faster than the food supply. Malthus was correct in saying that ultimately a population is limited by the amount of food available, but human populations do not often bump up against this limit. Something prevents people from attaining the theoretical maximum of fertility and growth. To understand how these processes work and to examine the steady growth of human populations, let us begin with the Paleolithic period, when *Homo* was a forager.

Figure 12.1 *The growth of human populations from the lower Paleolithic to the beginning of the modern period. The smoothness of the curve is deceptive.*

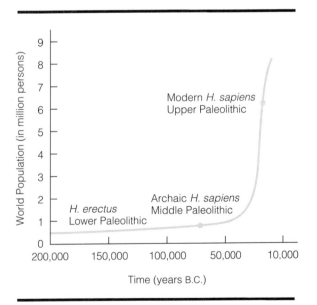

Table 12.1 Doubling Time of Populations at Different Growth Rates

Growth Rate (percent)	Doubling Time (years)
0.001	70,000
0.01	7,000
0.05	1,400
0.1	700
0.3	240
0.7	100
1.0	70
2.0	35
3.0	24
5.0	14

have been very high, as is common among other animal species. There was likely a good deal of fluctuation in the composition of local groups. A small foraging camp group with 15 to 20 members would be particularly vulnerable to random events and accidents. Events such as the injury of a good hunter, the death of a woman in childbirth, or the loss of several children to disease could have a devastating effect on the life of the group. Without a parent to care for them, small children might starve; without enough hunters, a group could suffer a shortage of meat. A small group could compensate to some extent for such disasters by seeking help from another group, perhaps merging with it temporarily. But in many cases, especially when there were problems across an entire region, such as droughts, random events could cause populations to collapse.

Population during the Paleolithic

From the appearance of the first australopithecines, hominid populations grew slowly. Let us suppose that 3.5 MYA the ancestral population of australopithecines consisted of 100 individuals. Three million years later, at 500,000 YA, the total hominid population stood at 200,000. This increase could have occurred in a population that grew at a rate of .002 percent per year, doubling in size every 35,000 years. A look at Table 12.1 shows that this is an extremely low rate of growth. By comparison, Mexico's population is now growing at the rate of 2.9 percent, doubling every 25 years.

Low fertility alone would not account for the slow rate of growth during the Plio-Pleistocene. There must also have been a high mortality rate. With births and deaths in close balance, it is probable that the population fluctuated with some setbacks and some leaps forward. At times of recovery, the growth rate may

Factors Affecting Fertility

While the !Kung San are not representative of Paleolithic foraging populations in many ways, some aspects of their reproductive behavior may illustrate early human reproductive behavior. As in all human groups, fertility and mortality are regulated by a combination of social and biological factors. These are in turn tied to the environment of the group. Populations that depend on movement as an adaptive strategy may have spaced births widely primarily because of the difficulty of transporting small children. Richard Lee estimates that !Kung San women walk about 2,400 km (1,500 mi) per year in their foraging activities. When the camp moves, they must carry all their worldly belongings as well as their babies. It is small wonder that the !Kung San women do not conceive while they are still carrying babies on their backs.

In most human populations, females have the responsibility not only of carrying and caring for babies

---

Old World Africa, Asia, and Europe.

agricultural revolution The invention of agriculture and its effects, which first occurred in the Fertile Crescent about 10,000 YA, at the end of the Pleistocene.

demographic transition The dramatic decline in mortality and stabilizing of the birth rate, which first occurred during the 18th century.

birthrate The number of babies born alive per 1,000 people in a year.

growth rate The percentage of change in a population, calculated as the birthrate plus (or minus) the death rate, excluding migration in and out of the population.

Figure 12.2 *A Hausa woman of Nigeria and her daughter. Strong taboos on post-partum sex are part of Hausa folklore, but they also have a solid basis in biology.*

but also of feeding them. The basis for this lies primarily in the fact that mother's milk is the only available baby food. No soft, nutritious foods were available during the Paleolithic, and many modern societies also lack them. For this reason women in many places breast-feed children for up to three years before they wean them completely to solid foods. Among the !Kung San, for example, children with a full set of teeth, who can walk and digest solid food, often continue suckling at their mother's breast.

The relatively low birthrate of the !Kung San can be explained by several factors. In addition to the postpartum amenorrhea that most females undergo after childbirth and while they are suckling a baby, the !Kung San, like many other societies, have rules forbidding sexual intercourse for a year or more after childbirth. Such **postpartum sex taboos** are common in a wide range of societies today, including the Hausa of West Africa. Consider the following remarks by a Hausa woman (Figure 12.2):

A mother should not go to her husband while she has a child she is suckling. If she does, the child gets thin, he dries up, he won't be strong, he won't be healthy. If she goes after two years, it is nothing, he is already strong before that, it does not matter if she conceives again after two years. If she only sleeps with her husband and does not become pregnant, it will not hurt the child, it will not spoil her milk. But if another child enters in, her milk will make the first one ill [Smith 1954, 148].

Although this informant didn't know the Western biomedical explanation, she recognized that pregnancy causes problems for a nursing baby. The reason is that as pregnancy progresses and the mother's hormonal balance changes, the production of milk is inhibited and eventually ceases. People in many parts of the world explain their postpartum sex taboos in similar ways. They are "folk beliefs" that have a sound basis in nutrition.

Some anthropologists believe that infanticide plays a role in regulating population. If a !Kung San child is born too soon after a sibling, a mother may take the baby out into the bush and kill it. As we saw in Chapter 2, the Tapirapé of Brazil may kill a child born with a physical deformity. In some cases infanticide takes the form of neglecting rather than actually killing the infant.

There is evidence that some societies kill (or simply allow to die) more girl babies than boys (DiVale and Harris 1976, Miller 1981). Such practices are difficult to detect, partly because people do not readily admit to them. In some cases they may even be unaware of the practice. However, the higher female mortality may be reflected in statistics, such as hospital admissions. Barbara Miller (1981) showed that more than twice as many boys as girls are admitted to hospitals in northern India. This means either that boys get sick much more than girls or that parents are less likely to take sick girls for treatment. Reducing the number of females in a population could lower the birthrate, although the effect would be felt only over the long run. Some investigators, such as Richard Lee, who studied the !Kung San, believe that natural child mortality and such practices as birth spacing were sufficient to control the population of hunter-gatherers.

Factors Affecting Mortality

Mortality in foraging societies is also affected by both cultural and biological factors. Most experts agree that infectious disease was not a major factor in mortality as long as people lived in small, relatively isolated groups that kept moving. There were, no doubt, infectious diseases during the Paleolithic, but the isolation of populations from each other prevented the spread of epidemics over large portions of humankind. Death from starvation was probably also relatively rare. The principal causes of death for adult male *Homo erectus,* archaic *H. sapiens,* and early modern *H. sapiens* may have been injuries sustained in hunting animals and

fighting with one's own kind; the principal causes for females were the hazards of childbirth. Some prehistoric skeletal populations show high levels of traumatic injury, lending support to this hypothesis.

Many cultural factors affect mortality. In some Inuit (Eskimo) groups, for example, old people who were unable to accompany the group on the spring migration asked to be left alone. An old person alone in the Arctic had little chance of survival.

In many societies, violent conflicts where people attack, injure, and kill each other may be major contributors to mortality. Among the Yanomamo of Venezuela and Brazil, for example, one study showed that 30 percent of adult male deaths were due to warfare (Chagnon 1974). On the other hand, like all social behavior, warfare is bounded by rules. The Dani people of Papua New Guinea engage in battles in which each side shoots arrows at each other. At the first sight of blood, however, the combatants leave the field and the war is over for a time. As warfare has evolved and weapons have become more effective throughout much of the world, the magnitude of killing has increased until a single weapon can take hundreds of thousands of lives at once.

The treatment of disease is another cultural factor influencing mortality. Some indigenous therapies help save lives and reduce mortality. Surgery is performed in many technologically simple groups, such as the Inuit and the Chippewa in arctic sections of North America, who amputate frozen fingers, and the Masai of East Africa, who are able to suture wounds and blood vessels and even perform abdominal surgery. Modern medicine with its arsenal of antibiotics and other drugs can save many lives that otherwise would have been lost.

Some therapies, however, may *raise* mortality. In many societies, for example, mothers withhold water from children suffering diarrhea, thinking that they must have too much fluid in their bodies. These children often die of dehydration, the leading cause of death among children in many countries. Another example is bleeding, an accepted therapeutic practice

---

postpartum sex taboos Negative sanctions, which forbid sexual intercourse for a given interval after the birth of a child. These rules may reduce the birth rate in some societies, such as the !Kung San.

in Europe and North America until the 19th century. George Washington is said to have died from loss of blood caused by therapeutic bleeding. Of course, not all traditional therapies are dangerous.

Sedentization and Population Growth

Most investigators agree that sedentization (settling down) was the single most important influence on population growth before the development of agriculture. On the one hand, sedentization probably led to an increase in mortality due to disease. As long as people lived in small groups and moved around frequently, they would leave before the accumulated waste in their settlements became a health problem. As they began to settle down, people began more and more to live in close proximity with their own refuse. This refuse, consisting of human excrement, food wastes, and possibly shelters covered with skins or thatch, exposed people to disease vectors and higher risk of death.

On the other hand, sedentization also led to higher fertility. There is evidence that birth spacing is lowered when populations become sedentary. Richard Lee compared !Kung San women who were highly nomadic to others who were more settled. The more nomadic women gave birth at average intervals of 44 months, while the more settled women gave birth at average intervals of 36 months (Lee 1979). All other things being equal, this would increase the birth rate.

Because of these two processes (the higher incidence of disease and the narrowing of birth spacing), sedentary societies lacking modern public sanitation (clean drinking water, closed sewers, and pest control) typically have both high fertility and high mortality. The growth of such populations is kept in check by mortality. While many children are born, many die in the first few years of life. Infant mortality has a particularly important effect on future births because the children who die do not live to reproduce. In societies with good sanitation and health care, mortality occurs mainly in the older age groups, among people who have already been able to reproduce. This can be represented graphically by using pyramids (Figure 12.3). For many years, archaeologists believed that fully sedentary life occurred only after the development of horticulture. Evidence from both the Old

Figure 12.3 *Age-sex pyramids for three populations—the !Kung San, Brazil, and the United States—showing the percentage of the population in each age cohort.*

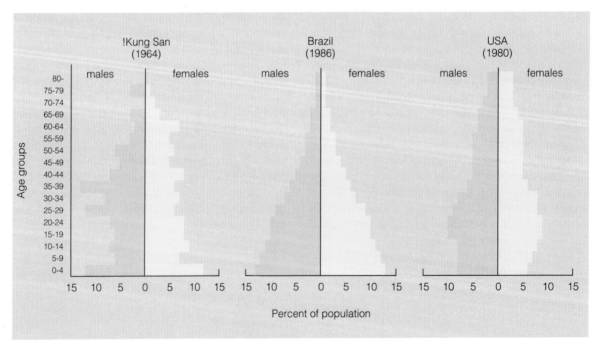

World and the New World now shows that substantial settlements whose populations did not move around with the seasons were already in place before plants and animals were domesticated.

The development of **technology**—the use of tools to solve problems—also had an impact on population trends. Many anthropologists have suggested that technological change drove population growth. According to this view, as new, more productive technologies became available, populations expanded to take advantage of them. Another view (Boserup 1965) holds that population growth is a cause not a consequence of technological change. This view fits the adage that "necessity is the mother of invention." (The relationship between population growth and technological development is discussed in detail later in this chapter in the section "The Consequences of Food Production").

Figure 12.4 *A rice farmer in South Korea uses modern equipment to harvest his crop. Through the use of mechanical devices, chemicals, and scientific information, industrial agriculture has raised per acre productivity to levels unimaginable a century ago.*

INTENSIFICATION

If a population is running short of food or other resources, it can increase production by two different means. The first is to exploit a wider area of land with the same techniques already in use. This is an extensive form of habitat management (see Chapter 11); it involves extending the range of exploitation without changing the means of exploitation. Among foragers and slash-and-burn horticulturalists, this may mean that, as the local population grows, communities undergo **fission**: New groups "bud off" and move to a new location. This extensive approach reduces the pressure on resources at a particular location, but it requires additional land.

The second alternative is to intensify, raising production *without* increasing the area of land in use. As we saw in Chapter 11, intensification involves spending more energy per unit area of land. Intensification may take place in any subsistence system. A foraging population may intensify production by searching more systematically for food within a given area,

working harder to capture food, or expanding **diet breadth** (the number of types of food it typically searches for and eats). The most potent weapon that humans bring to intensification is their use of technology. Technology extends and augments human capacities for manipulating nature. Agriculturalists can intensify by plowing, by careful weeding, or by using fertilizer. Often intensification depends on technological innovation, such as the use of the plow, irrigation, agricultural terraces, or hybrid seeds (Figure 12.4).

Different habitats respond differently to intensification. Some habitats reward extra effort with higher production. The Great Plains of North America, for example, have yielded more and more grain per acre with the development of better and better agricultural techniques. Other habitats, particularly fragile ones, quickly reach a point of diminishing returns, where additional efforts are not rewarded with increments in production. Where resources are scarce and slow to be replenished, greater effort may simply drive the resource to extinction. This is particularly true of slow-breeding wild animals.

---

technology The use of tools to solve problems.

fission The splitting off of a small social group from a larger one. It may occur as the result of overpopulation and declining material resources.

diet breadth The diversity of food items commonly consumed within a year by a given population.

Figure 12.5 *Many sites in and around the Fertile Crescent have yielded important information about the rise of domestication.*

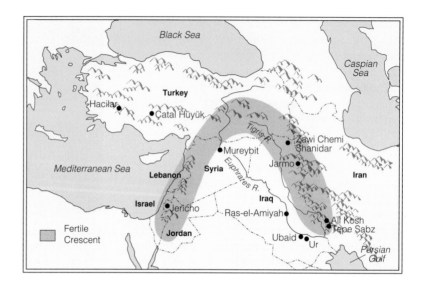

The Broad Spectrum Revolution

One of the richest laboratories for the study of intensification is southwestern Asia (modern Iraq, Iran, Syria, and Jordan). The **Fertile Crescent** is an arc of mountains and lowlands with rich, arable land beginning in Jordan and extending northward through Syria into Turkey and then west and south into Iraq and part of Iran (Figure 12.5). At the end of the Pleistocene, there were herds of wild gazelle, sheep, goats, cattle, and pigs living here. Wild wheat, barley, and other grains grew in natural meadows. At lower elevations, fish, waterfowl, and other useful food species were available to hunters. On the flanks of the mountain ranges were areas of rich soil. This region was the setting for the first known transition to food production in the world.

Thousands of upper Paleolithic archaeological sites in southwestern Asia show a fairly consistent picture: Small, temporary camps dated to this period, inhabited by 15 to 20 people, are littered with pieces of stone tools, the bones of large animals such as gazelles and wild cows, and the ashes from cook fires. After about 18,000 YA the remains found in these camps changed in subtle but important ways. Certain species that occurred rarely in earlier sites began to appear frequently, especially smaller animals such as birds, mollusks, and snails and a variety of plants. Small

sickles made with **microliths** (tiny stone blades) set in stone or bone were used to harvest wild grasses, including the ancestors of modern wheat. Grinding stones were used to break open the tough outer shell of the grass seeds (Figure 12.6).

Archaeologists refer to this increase in food varieties as the **broad spectrum revolution**. It appears that competition among different groups for wild game and other resources forced people to exploit foods they had overlooked before. The broad spectrum revolution could have been a consequence of increased population density, the overhunting of large game species, or climate change. There is some evidence for all of these. This period corresponds to the end of the Pleistocene, which in southwestern Asia was characterized by a drying trend and the local extinction of many species of animals.

Many of the ecological niches available to stone tool users were filled. Movement among resource zones may have become more difficult, especially since there were more people and greater demands for resources. Groups that had once moved about seasonally began to settle down permanently, often building more elaborate shelters. Several groups underwent niche compression, exploiting a narrower range of resources more intensively than before. In short, many people may have found it necessary to make better use of available resources than they had in the past.

Figure 12.6 *Tools of broad spectrum revolution: A Neolithic sickle (left), in which tiny stone blades would have been set, used for cutting grasses, and a Neolithic basalt plate and grinding stone (right), used for crushing seeds. Such tools of intensification enabled people to increase their land's productivity.*

Domestication

Domestication is the process of breeding wild species to control their rates of reproduction. In ecological terms domestication is a symbiotic relationship between people and biological species in which people modify the environment to favor the growth of the species they use. This involves the **selection** of naturally occurring varieties that have desired characteristics for human use.

Paradoxically, human selection left plant and animal species less fit biologically than before domestication. The seeds of wild grasses, such as wild wheat and barley, are attached to a segment of the stalk called the **rachis.** Under natural circumstances, this segment becomes brittle as the seed ripens, and eventually it can be dislodged by a passing animal or strong breeze. This is what allows the seeds to be detached and the plant to reseed itself. A brittle rachis

makes it difficult, however, for people to harvest the ripe grain because the plant tends to dump its load of seed on the ground at the first touch of the sickle.

When people began to domesticate wheat, barley, and other grasses, they selected the occasional plant with a flexible rachis that did not release its seeds easily. These plants would have failed to disperse their seeds under natural conditions and so would suffer negative selection. In other words, plant and animal domesticators bred out some of the very characteristics that allowed species to survive and reproduce successfully under natural conditions.

From the ecologist's perspective, most domestication involves "simplifying" the natural environment by reducing diversity. To do so requires the constant application of energy to keep the local ecosystem in an early successional stage. Human history since 10,000 YA has been a succession of technologies designed to accomplish this control.

Fertile Crescent A fertile region of the Middle East that spreads through modern Jordan, Turkey, Syria, Iran, and Iraq; archaeologists have found the earliest evidence of sedentization and agricultural origins here.

microliths Tiny, sharp stone blades, embedded in wood or bone handles and used for harvesting wild grasses.

broad spectrum revolution The increase in the number of different food resources that were exploited by humans toward the end of the Pleistocene.

domestication The breeding of wild plants and animals to control their rates of reproduction and other traits.

selection The choice of certain plants or animals by humans for domestication based on some trait such as hardiness or productivity.

rachis The segment of the stem to which the seeds are attached in wild grasses such as wheat or barley.

Figure 12.7 *The site of a Natufian house, dating to about 10,000 YA (right). The round shallow pits in the floor may have been storage pits, and smaller structures at these sites may have been storehouses for wild grains. Compare the settlements of the Malinke of Sierra Leone (below), in which the ruins of ancient buildings stand adjacent to modern dwellings (flat-topped) and granaries (with thatched roofs).*

Natufian Culture

At about 10,000 YA the first sedentary communities appear in the archaeological record even though there still were no domesticated plants or animals. In other words, intensive food gathering in the Fertile Crescent was sufficiently productive to allow small permanent settlements to form. A well-known tradition of this period is the **Natufian culture**, represented by many sites in the western end of the Fertile Crescent (Figure 12.7). Natufian sites had as many as 50 circular houses, ranging from 2.5 m (8 ft) to 9 m (29 ft) in diameter. The living floors of these houses were partly sunken below ground level, and the lower walls were lined with rocks around the outer perimeter. Some of these huts were probably used for storage, indicating that the Natufians did not immediately consume everything they harvested. These settlements are similar to those of a modern African people, the Malinke of Sierra Leone, although the latter are agricultural (see Figure 12.7).

Settling down and building substantial houses brought other changes. In addition to many hand tools, the Natufians made carved stone vessels, decorative objects, figurines depicting women and animals, and other objects suggesting specialized craft production. There is evidence that Natufians traded shell, **obsidian** glass, and other commodities. They may also have exchanged perishable items like salt, skins, and food with communities where these items were more abundant. The Natufians buried their dead under the house floors in a manner suggesting a concern with the afterlife.

The Natufians brought the Fertile Crescent to the threshold of plant domestication, and perhaps they stepped across. Mureybet, a village of the Natufian phase on the upper Euphrates River in northern Syria, was first occupied 8,600 YA. The refuse deposits of this village include grains of wild wheat and barley.

The nearest place where wild wheat and barley could have been found was 160 km (100 mi) north of Mureybet in the high slopes of the Taurus Mountains of Turkey (see Figure 12.5). It is possible that these grains were transported to Mureybet from where they were harvested. But it is more likely that the people of Mureybet had begun to plant the grain nearby. Later sites provide even more convincing evidence that people had begun to plant grains far from the place where they grew wild.

Early theories of how agriculture developed suggested that people began to plant when they became so familiar with the environment and its species around their villages that they began to attempt to control these familiar processes. More recent thinking, influenced by such evidence as that from Mureybet, holds that plant domestication became a reality when people moved a relatively unfamiliar but desired species to a new habitat. In a new habitat a species is subject to new selective pressures and undergoes adaptive changes. In other words, people accelerated the selection process by transferring plants to new habitats.

THE DEVELOPMENT OF FOOD PRODUCTION IN THE NEOLITHIC

The **Neolithic**, or "New Stone Age," is the period when humans began to depend more heavily on food production than on food gathering. The Neolithic revolution took place in more than one place. Similar events occurred in southwestern Asia (modern Iran, Iraq, and Syria), the Indus Valley in India, Central Mexico, the Andean region of South America, and Southeast Asia. The transition to food production was not identical everywhere it occurred, although there are some remarkable parallels.

Natufian culture A cultural tradition in the western end of the Fertile Crescent, dating to about 10,000 YA, and one of the earliest permanent human settlements reflecting sedentization based on intensive food gathering without agriculture.

obsidian A naturally occurring volcanic glass used in prehistoric times to manufacture very sharp tools.

Neolithic The "New Stone Age," or the period when humans began depending more on production of domesticated food resources (agriculture and animal husbandry) than on gathering wild food resources. This period started about 10,000 YA.

No one knows when people first thrust seed into the ground in the expectation that plants would sprout. Many lay people think that the discovery that seeds grow into plants was the major achievement of the Neolithic. Few archaeologists share this idea. Throughout the Paleolithic and Mesolithic (10,000–8,000 YA), people gathered and ate seeds. During the upper Paleolithic in southwestern Asia (18,000–10,000 YA), seed gathering became a highly specialized activity. It is likely that these people were aware of the fact that seeds grew into plants long before they began to cultivate them.

It may be impossible to determine with certainty what the "trigger" variable was in the Neolithic: It may have been population growth and pressure on resources; climatic change; or technological change. Or it could have been a combination of factors. What is clear, however, is that, as groups became more sedentary and more dependent on domesticated plants and animals, and as populations grew, the entire system of human life underwent dramatic changes.

These changes made it impossible for most people to revert to an earlier life-style. The habitat was modified too drastically for hunting and gathering to be viable in most places. There were now too many people. The Neolithic changed more than people's habits. It changed their minds as well. Once people became accustomed to the sedentary life-style, it would have been difficult for them to adjust to the life-style of foragers again. Just as we have come to value our own hearths and homes and to depend on such comforts as our own beds and all of our familiar belongings, it is easy to imagine the same thing happening in the Neolithic.

The southwest Asian Neolithic was not a unique moment in history or the result of a single inspired discovery. It was a process that grew out of a tendency, perhaps a need, to intensify production. In this period people began to modify their habitat more drastically and, in turn, to adjust to the resulting changes in the environment. In Chapter 11, we discussed processes of negative feedback, in which cultural behavior keeps a set of environmental variables within tolerable limits. The Neolithic was a period of positive feedback, where a change in one variable in a system causes changes in all the others and thus transforms the entire system. Once the process began, there was no turning back.

A Southwest Asian Neolithic Site: Ali Kosh

Ali Kosh is located in the Deh Luran Plain in Iran (see Chapter 1). This arid, windswept location was greener when it was first occupied by people about 9,900 YA. A marshy area near the village was always moist, replenished by winter rains. In its earliest occupation Ali Kosh occupied about 1 acre of small rectangular houses built of unfired clay bricks with roofs made from woven mats. During this period, the inhabitants collected wild plant foods. They also hunted gazelles, wild oxen, wild asses, wild pigs, and water fowl in season. Fish was available in the swamp pools. Clearly food gathering was still quite important in early Ali Kosh.

The people of Ali Kosh were also food producers. In the damp soils adjacent to the marsh, the inhabitants of Ali Kosh planted wheat and barley varieties not native to the area. Excavations have also turned up large quantities of goat bones. These bones were identical to those of the wild goats that inhabit the region, but the archaeologists noted that most of the goats were killed fairly young. Only a third of the flock lived as long as three years and most of the longer-lived individuals were females. This distribution of sex and age is interpreted as evidence for an early stage of animal domestication. Wild goats were probably captured and kept in corrals or pens for slaughter. Certain female goats were kept alive longer for breeding purposes but most of the males were slaughtered as soon as they reached full size. The investigators found no seeds or animal remains from species that would have been present during the summer. This could mean that the villagers took their goat herds and migrated to summer pastures elsewhere in the region.

In later phases at the Ali Kosh site, the proportion of cultivated to wild grains increased. The consumption of goats increased, and their bones show increasing differences from wild species, which suggests that selective breeding led to a distinctive domestic breed of goat. The people of Ali Kosh bred goats with smaller horns, probably to reduce the danger of injuries among the penned animals. In the wild, male goats with large horns probably had higher reproductive success since they used them to fight other males to establish mating rights with females. Frank Hole and his associates charted the size and shape of goat horns over nearly 4,000 years of human settlement on the Deh Luran Plain (Hole and Flannery 1969). Over time male horns became smaller and female horns disappeared almost entirely.

Even as their dependence on domesticated plants and animals increased, the people of the Deh Luran Plain continued to hunt and gather, as shown by plant and animal remains among the refuse. As grazing land increased to accommodate more domesticated animals, natural vegetation was cleared for pasture. Farmers also had to weed their crops more carefully to maintain yields. In other words, intensification caused habitat change which, in turn, provoked more changes, an example of positive feedback. By 7,500 YA Ali Kosh had expanded to cover nearly 3 acres with a population of perhaps 170 people. There may have been two or three similar settlements nearby. There is evidence for long-distance trade, possibly during the summer migrations, in the form of stone tools from 500 miles away and cowrie shell beads from 200 miles away.

Beginning around 7,500 YA the villagers of the Deh Luran Plain launched a new phase of intensification. They moved their villages from the edges of swamps to places near streams flowing out of the mountains. The water from these streams could be diverted through ditches into fields in a simple irrigation scheme. This put agriculture on a more secure basis, since it did not depend on the rainfall to moisten the soil. Villages grew as large as 1,500 people. Extension of cultivation led to more land clearance, reducing the natural pasture available to the gazelle and other wild species, which began to decline in number.

Although carved stone figurines are known from upper Paleolithic sites dating from nearly 30,000 YA (see Chapter 23), **fired** clay vessels appeared for the first time about 7,500 YA. By its fine quality, it appears that it was manufactured by full-time craft specialists. Large, sedentary villages with rudimentary **craft specialization** must have presented a challenge to the informal organization of smaller groups. Could a single leader coordinate the activities among so many people, settle disputes, and manage relations with other groups?

The Neolithic in the New World

The transition to food production occurred in the Americas independently of, and later than, similar developments in the Old World. The pathways to domestication and intensification differed in important ways. First, sedentary communities in the Fertile Crescent developed before agriculture. In Mexico, however, **maize** (corn) was cultivated as early as 7,000 YA, yet the first sedentary settlements appear only 5,000 YA. There is little doubt that New World domestication is independent of Old World origins. The plant and animal species were different, and the knowledge required to domesticate them was different as well. Another significant difference is that the Old World Neolithic was based on domestication of many animal species and a relatively few plants, while in the New World there were relatively few animals domesticated but many different plants (Figure 12.8 and Table 12.2).

Some of the similarities between Mesoamerica (Mexico and Central America) and southwestern Asia can be explained by the operation of similar principles. Population growth seems to have played an important role in the development of domesticated plants and animals in southwestern Asia. In Mesoamerica the evidence for population growth is not adequate to support this theory, although it is possible. Much less is known about conditions in Mesoamerica than is known about the Fertile Crescent.

One of the few areas of Mesoamerica whose prehistory is well known is the Tehuacán Valley, a semidesert in the Central Highlands of Mexico. A North American archaeologist, Richard MacNeish, excavated a number of sites in Tehuacán over many years. Tehuacán was a cultural backwater compared to the elaborate empires of the Olmecs, the Mixtecs, and the Aztecs (all native cultures that arose in Mexico),

---

fired   Tempered by intense heat, fired pottery appeared for the first time about 7,500 YA.

craft specialization   The manufacture of specific crafts by full-time specialists.

maize   Corn; maize was one of the first grasses domesticated in the New World, beginning about 9,000 YA.

Figure 12.8   *Worldwide distribution of centers at which plant and animal domestication appear to have originated.*

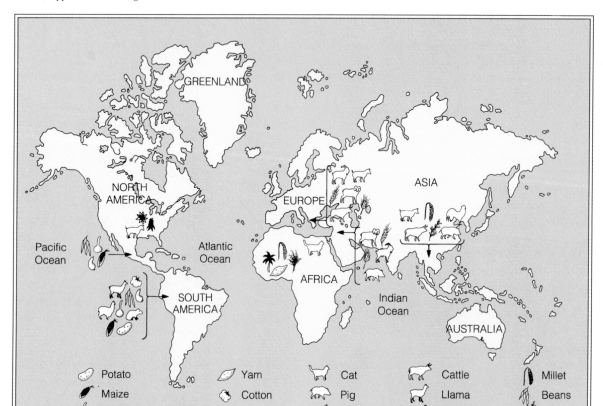

but it was not the small temple mounds or ceremonial burials that sparked MacNeish's interest. Tehuacán seems to have been close to the site where maize was first domesticated. MacNeish found 28 separate cultural layers preserved in the dry, sandy valley. The patient work of MacNeish and coworkers from various disciplines uncovered a clear sequence leading from small foraging groups to settled agriculturalists over a period of more than 8,000 years (Figure 12.9).

The earliest phase of Tehuacán dates to 12,000 YA and reveals a simple, nomadic hunting society living in small bands, camping in caves, and eating rabbits, gophers, turtles, rats, and occasionally deer. The entire population of the Tehuacán Valley probably did

not exceed 24 people. The next phase (9,200–7,200 YA) reveals a shift toward specialized gathering of plant foods, with the appearance of grinding and milling stones used in processing plants and their seeds such as wild squash, chiles, and avocados.

By 7,000 YA the people of the Tehuacán valley were planting small amounts of maize, chiles, avocados, gourds, beans, and other plants in little canyons on the edge of the valley. They must have sowed the seeds and then gone off to hunt and gather, leaving the plants to grow on their own. Some of the crops must have been lost to pests each year. This phase was distinguished by the larger seasonal camps containing as many as 100 people. Groups this size could not

Table 12.2 A Chronology of Domestication

Years Ago	Mesoamerica	Southwest Asia	East Asia	Southern Europe	South America	North America	Africa
1,000–							
2,000–					White potato		
3,000–						Sunflower, marsh elder, amaranth	Cat (Egypt)
4,000–			Chicken (south-central Asia)				Yam, oil palm
5,000–		Camel		Horse (Eurasia)	Llama, alpaca maize, cotton (white potato?)		Millet, sorghum
6,000–			Cow, pig millet				
7,000–	Maize, beans, peppers, gourds				Gourds, squash, lima beans, common beans, guinea pig		Sheep, goat
8,000–			Rice	Wheat, barley, lentils, sheep, goat, dog			
9,000–	Squash	Wheat, barley Goat, dog, cow	Dog	Cow Dog			
10,000–							
		Sheep					
11,000–		Dog				Dog	

Figure 12.9 *The evolutionary nature of the adoption of agriculture in the Tehuacán Valley can be seen in this graph. The slowly growing percentages of domesticated food contributions to the diet demonstrate the long process of agricultural development.*

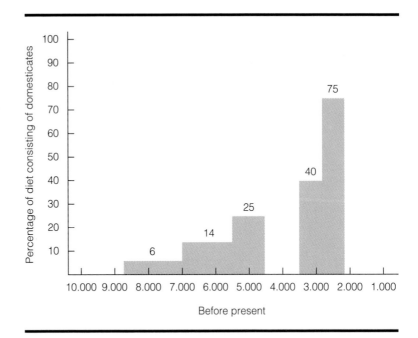

BOX 12.1

The Annual Meeting: A Phase in Human Social Evolution

The early foragers of the Tehuacán valley spent most of the year wandering from camp to camp in groups of a dozen or so people. Once a year, however, several small groups came together in a single place where resources were temporarily plentiful. This may have been a time to hold ceremonies, arrange marriages, and transact important business. To come out of the arid countryside into a camp of 100 or more people must have been equivalent to the thrill of a small-town American seeing New York City for the first time.

One can imagine the excitement of these annual gatherings when food was abundant. One could see old friends, catch up on the news, and share important information about where resources could be found. We have ethnographic reports from contemporary societies with a similar life-style. Many of the native peoples of the Great Plains of North America hunted in small, mobile units for most of the year. But during the time of the great bison migrations, they formed camps of up to 1,000 to hunt the vast herds of bison. Some aborigines living in the central desert of Australia also gathered for an annual festival known to some as a coroboree. In central Brazil many of the native societies spent much of the year on "trek," gathering in large central villages at harvest time.

In all these examples, the period during which dispersed groups gathered together was a time of feasting and relative plenty. Important ceremonials, such as initiations, took place at this time. In these societies, children initiated together formed a lasting bond, which often endured throughout their lives. These **age classes**, as well as other social groupings based on shared names or other commonalities, created the basis for social cooperation because they cut across family and camp lines. There was no strong or permanent leadership in such groups; coordination was achieved primarily through regimentation for ceremonial purposes through the cross-cutting organizations.

We cannot know how the temporary village aggregations in the Tehuacan Valley were organized. But it is possible that they too had cross-cutting groups and ceremonialism allowing for cooperation among the component groups. This type of organization may represent a transitional phase between the dispersed, family-based foraging group and settled villages. These meetings occurred where resources and technology available could support larger aggregations of people for short periods. For the rest of the year, it was much easier for people to split into smaller groups that made extensive use of resources.

have supported themselves by foraging, because resources were too scarce most of the year. MacNeish decided that these must have been temporary groupings of people who came together to socialize and exploit seasonally available resources (Box 12.1). The greatest part of the diet, however, was still from wild plants through this and the succeeding phase, which lasted from 5,400 to 4,300 YA.

MacNeish believes that sedentary village life began about 5,400 to 4,300 YA. Some of the earliest pottery found in Mesoamerica dates to 4,300 to 3,500 YA, but it is not known for sure if fully sedentary villages were making and using the pottery. (The earliest pottery in the New World comes from the Pacific Coast of South America.) New varieties of maize appear in this period, which MacNeish describes as one of an accelerating pace of cultural development. After 3,500 YA, settled village life is clearly present, pottery techniques are improved, and small figurines (Figure 12.10) are found in the sites, perhaps representing some form of worship or ancestor cult.

Just as in late Ali Kosh, the people of Tehuacán began to irrigate their cornfields by diverting streams starting about 2,850 YA. Population density rose sharply and there are many signs that Tehuacán people were trading extensively with people outside the valley. There are clear signs of influence from the Olmec people of the Gulf Coast. From this point on, it appears that the Tehuacán Valley was incorporated into one of the several empires that ruled southern Mexico until the time of the Spanish conquest in A.D. 1532.

Of all the plants used in Tehuacan, maize was surely the most important (Box 12.2). Maize was first domesticated in the New World, but since the late 16th century A.D. it has diffused around the world (Crosby 1972). Today, maize is the world's third most important food crop (after rice and wheat), and it is a mainstay in the diet of millions of people in the Americas, Africa, Asia, and Oceania. Maize contains many important nutrients, including starch, oil, vitamins, and protein. It does not contain an ideal balance of proteins, however, because it contains relatively little of the **essential amino acids** lysine and tryptophan.

Figure 12.10 *A ceramic figurine from the Ajalpan phase of development at Tehuacán, Mexico, dating to about 3,500 YA. By this time, people were living in stable settlements and some forms of agriculture were established.*

---

age class People who were initiated into adulthood as a group, such as a school graduating class.

essential amino acids Amino acids such as lysine and tryptophan that are necessary in the human diet.

BOX 12.2

The Origins of Maize

There is no doubt that maize (scientific name *Zea mays*) is a New World plant. In 1953 drillers using special bits drew cores of rock from the lake bed surrounding Mexico City. Microscopic analysis of these sediments revealed pollen very similar to that of maize. The layer in which the pollen grains were found was 80,000 years old. Pursuing another line of research, Dr. Paul Mangelsdorf, a geneticist, suggested that maize descended from an ancient form that grew in loose pods, which could be self-seeding. But, unlike the wild strains of wheat and barley found in contemporary southwestern Asia, the ancestral forms of maize have never been found. Mangelsdorf explained this by suggesting that the ancestral species had been "swamped" by natural hybridization with domestic maize over thousands of years, and had ceased to exist as a separate variety. Mangelsdorf "reconstructed" ancestral maize by "back-crossing" modern varieties until he came up with a primitive plant looking much like some of the tiny ears of corn excavated by Richard MacNeish at Tehuacán and dated to 7,000 YA.

In 1972 another geneticist, George Beadle, suggested that there never had been a wild maize and that a well-known species of grass, teosinte, was the true ancestor of corn. Teosinte (*Zea mexicana*) is a wild grass growing in disturbed upland areas of Mexico. Frequently found near peasant maize fields, it is able to cross-breed with domestic maize. The new theory was accepted by some botanists who never felt comfortable with the disappearing ancestor proposed by

The evolution of maize at Tehuacán. The cobs are dated, from left to right, at about 7,000 YA, 6,000 YA, 5,000 YA, 3,000 YA, and 2,000 YA. The cob at the far right is identical to a modern variety.

Mangelsdorf and who felt that Mangelsdorf's reconstructed ancestor was unlikely to have survived as a wild plant. Beadle's supporters suggest the 80,000-year-old pollen from the basin of Mexico could just as well be teosinte as maize. The argument between Mangelsdorf and Beadle has continued for nearly two decades; neither side appears likely to concede the point.

Source: R. S. Peabody Foundation for Archaeology.

When eaten with beans and chiles, however, maize provides balanced protein nutrition. It is noteworthy that these three native American crops are frequently found together both in archaeological sites and in contemporary societies throughout Mesoamerica.

Biological anthropologist Solomon Katz found that preparing maize with lime (calcium carbonate) improves the utilization of its proteins. Katz (1974) further found that lime tends to be used in maize processing wherever there was no other major source of protein available in the diet. The mixing of maize, beans, and chiles and the distribution of lime processing of maize suggest that people may be able to recognize and adopt practices that are beneficial to nutri-

tion, even though they may not be aware of the properties of foods from a modern nutritional point of view. It is possible that early Mesoamericans accurately observed the effects of different diets and were attracted to the diet that was most beneficial.

The Consequences of Food Production

Tehuacán was probably not the area where maize and other crops were first domesticated in the New World. Neither was it the earliest area of settled village life, craft specialization, ceremonialism, or social stratification. However, Tehuacán provides a window into these linked processes, and the bits of seed, bone, and human artifacts excavated in the caves and open air sites of that high, dusty valley allow the reconstruction of eight millennia of cultural evolution in Mesoamerica. The parallels with Old World domestication are remarkable. Let us review some of them.

- Specialization in gathering activities, especially seed gathering, precedes domestication.
- Domesticated plants and animals are usually familiar species moved into new habitats, where they are subject to new selective pressures, including selection by humans.
- Domestication eventually leads to an increase in population density.
- Settled village life combined with domestication leads to rapid increases in population, craft specialization, ceremonial activity, and hierarchical social organization (stratification).
- As settlements increase in size and population density rises, new forms of intensification occur, such as irrigation and terracing.

There is little doubt that **states**—complex societies characterized by a division of labor, social and economic classes, urbanism, trade, literacy, and other features—would not exist without food production. While foraging can be intensified to some extent, the size and density of population that are necessary conditions of complex societies can be achieved only with food production. Agriculture can be intensified to support growing populations. The use of animals to pull plows, draw wagons, turn mills, and so on increased the productivity of farmers. When power technology (such as tractors, combines, and pumps) began to be used in agriculture, there were further gains in productivity.

In societies where agriculture is technologically simple, one cultivator feeds four or five people. In the most advanced agricultural societies like the United States and Canada, one farmer feeds 50 or more people (Figure 12.11). However, in developed countries each farmer is supported by a great number of services in research, manufacturing, finance, transport, food processing, marketing, and food preparation, which employ many people. Thus the ratio of food producers to food consumers in advanced countries is not as high as it might seem. Still, the inescapable conclusion is that highly intensive agriculture frees people for other activities such as manufacturing.

Stability and Reliability

Many writers suggest that food production led to a more stable, reliable food supply. This seems reasonable considering that food gatherers rely on what they can find, while food producers have some control over how much they produce. For a number of reasons, however, the relationship between food production and stability is not so simple. Food producers are at least as vulnerable as food gatherers to weather, pests, water availability, and other factors beyond their control. Most food producers experience crop failures, invasions by crop pests, animal diseases, and other hazards to production. In addition, food gatherers and other extensive producers often maintain an **undegraded** environment. By keeping population growth in check and by using resources extensively they can avoid depleting the habitat. In contrast, food producers tend to increase more rapidly and to extend their production system to the limits of the habitat. To keep up with population growth, food producers tend to intensify their production constantly, placing higher and higher demands on resources. Furthermore, food gatherers are generally self-sufficient, feeding themselves with what they produce and depending little on others. On the other hand, as production expands, food producers tend to become specialized in certain products, obtaining other needed goods through exchange. As they become involved with external markets, their production goals are linked less to their own needs and more to market demand and exchange rates. For all these reasons, food production is apt to be less reliable and more unstable than food

---

state A complex society characterized by division of labor, social and economic classes, urbanism, trade, political organization, and other features, usually occupying a definite territory.

undegraded An environment where rates of resource use are sustainable over long periods without major changes in ecosystem structure or function.

Figure 12.11 *Agricultural workers as a percentage of all workers in selected countries (1982 data).*

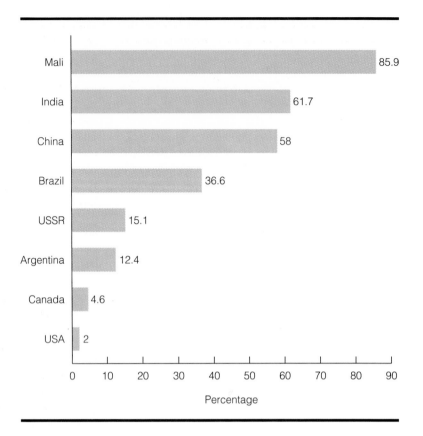

Figure 12.12 *Fluctuations in food production per capita in selected countries between 1979 and 1984. Food production actually tends to be less reliable than food gathering.*

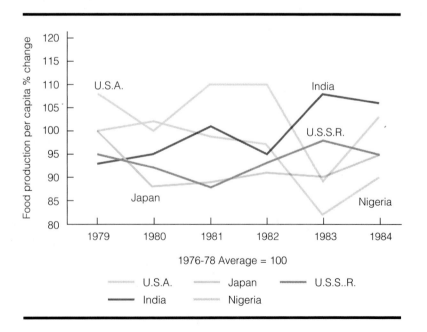

Table 12.3 Types of Technology

Mechanical / body-extending	Physical / chemical energy-capturing	Information / mind-extending
Bow and arrow	Fire	Abacus
Steel plow	Smelting iron	Calendar
Sailing ship	Cooking food	Printing press
Spiral screw	Fertilizer	Radio
Auto transmission	Gasoline	Computer

gathering. Figure 12.12 shows the fluctuations in food production over the same period in different countries to illustrate this point.

TECHNOLOGICAL DEVELOPMENT

Tools extend human capabilities and make it possible for people to do more work with the same or less effort. Many tasks become possible only with technological devices. For instance, the bumper jack makes it possible for an ordinary person to lift a car weighing more than a ton. The abacus allows people to do more complex computations than they could do in their heads. Other devices make use of power outside the human mind and body. The harness and plow allow the use of **draft animals** such as horses to turn over soil for planting, which is far more effective than a person with a hoe. A sailboat captures power from the wind to move through the water. There is an endless list of technological devices for solving problems. Most technological devices can be classified as one of three types: (1) mechanical/body-extending, (2) physical/chemical energy-capturing, or (3) information/mind-extending (Table 12.3). All these technologies may be used to transform nature in ways that suit us (Figure 12.13). Agricultural technologies include ex-

amples of all these technology types, such as the plow, chemical fertilizers, and techniques for land surveying. Industrial technology similarly includes such devices as mechanical drills, refineries, calculators, and computers, which use each of these three types of technology.

Lithic technology is discussed at some length in Chapters 6 and 7. Here we focus on two of the most important technological developments leading to the rise of industrialism: **metallurgy**, the refining of metals to fashion them into tools and other useful goods, and successive revolutions in energy technology.

Metallurgy

Humans were probably familiar with naturally occurring minerals long before they began to experiment with the smelting of metals. **Smelting** is a process in which heat is used to separate metals from **ores**. Until people began to experiment with metals, they made most of their tools with their own muscle power, striking, shaving, carving, and grinding with their hands. When they began to smelt metals, they harnessed the power of fire to purify and transform metal ores. The earliest known metal objects are simple, hammered copper pieces dating from about 9,000 YA in southern Turkey. By about 6,000 YA copper was widespread in the Middle East, primarily in the form of pins and bracelets.

Metallurgy arose independently in several different parts of the world. In the northern Balkans (Albania, Greece, Yugoslavia, Romania) people began to hammer out artifacts from naturally occurring copper found in the area around 5,000 YA. Copper is too soft to make many useful tools, so the items were limited to decorative amulets and a few tools such as fishhooks, daggers, and awls. A thousand years later, heaps of **slag** (waste products of the smelting process) around archaeological sites demonstrate that people

---

draft animals Animals such as cattle and horses that can be used to pull a plow or haul loads.

lithic technology Systematic knowledge about making tools from stone.

metallurgy The process of refining metals and fashioning them into tools and other useful goods.

smelting The process of separating metals from ore by using heat.

ore A raw material from which a metal can be extracted.

slag The impurities that are left after smelting.

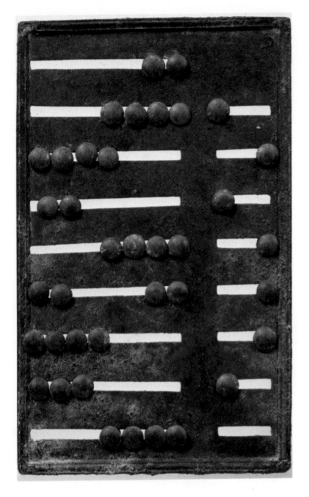

Figure 12.13 *Technological devices designed to manipulate information and extend the capacity of the human mind. On the left, an abacus, possibly of Babylonian origin, used for computing and keeping records; the abacus is still used today in some parts of the world. On the right, a quipu, knotted strings used by the Inca of Peru to keep quantitative records.*

in the area had learned to smelt metal. They also dug shafts up to 80 feet deep in search of silver, gold, lead, and antimony ores. Still later, similar industries can be found around the Aegean Sea and in Italy and Spain. By 4,500 YA, the metalsmiths of Europe were adding tin to copper ore to produce bronze, an **alloy** that is much harder than copper.

Copper and bronze ages occurred in several different places at different times. When the Spanish arrived in South America in 1532, they found people using objects made of bits of unsmelted copper hammered into ornaments and a few tools. They also found that Andean peoples were smelting gold. Andean silver and gold became the greatest single incentive for the Spanish to invade and dominate South America. They devised ways to force the native peoples of the Andes to work in the mines.

Iron smelting derives from the knowledge gained from working with copper and bronze. Iron smelting did appear in some places where there had been no copper or bronze smelted, but in these cases, the know-how came from elsewhere. Although iron is more easily corroded than copper and bronze, it is a harder, more durable metal that is suitable for making cutting and chopping tools. Iron ore is also 500 times more plentiful in the earth's crust than copper. The earliest evidence for iron smelting is from 4,500 YA in the Near East, but iron did not come into its own until about 3,200 YA. In most places, the earliest known metal objects were used for decorations or ritual purposes (Figure 12.14). In the early European iron age, armaments consumed most of the metal; only later did it begin to be used extensively for agricultural tools such as axes, picks, and hoes.

In Africa iron was associated primarily with agriculture rather than with militarism. The iron age reached Africa about 2,500 YA as many new food crops diffused into the areas south of the Sahara desert. Iron tools were employed in clearing forests for planting millet and sorghum (crops originating in North Africa) and bananas, yams, and taro (crops entering from Southeast Asia). Again, technology not only helped the population adjust to a new environment but also transformed the environment. Moreover, the ways in which the new material was incorporated into a society depended on the social and political context. Technology shapes society but it is also shaped by it.

While the development of metal owes something to its superiority to stone, it also bears witness to important social changes. Stone can be worked by people who go out in search of the raw material and transform it into tools single-handedly. Metallurgy demands more organization. To mine ore, transport it, build smelters, produce fuel (charcoal), smelt metal, produce alloys, and work the metal into finished products requires specialization and coordination beyond the abilities of a small group. Thus the copper and bronze ages of Egypt, Europe, the Mediterranean, and China were as much social and political events as technological breakthroughs. They were based in societies in which some people were able to accumulate the knowledge necessary to produce metals, probably on a full-time basis. There is also evidence of long-distance trade in ores, metal **ingots** (molded bars of smelted metals), and finished products between widely separated points, such as Ireland and the southern Aegean. Trade in ores and unfinished metal products meant that some people specialized in shipping and that ocean craft capable of carrying heavy ingots were available. These points underscore the interrelatedness of technology and social organization. In some cases a technological breakthrough had to await the development of organizational means for exploiting it. In others the developing technology may have provided the momentum to develop ways of using it.

The Energy Crisis

Perhaps the greatest technological revolution in modern times was the rise of fossil fuel power in the 18th century. Until then **power technology** depended on **renewable energy sources**, principally wind, water, and wood fuel. These sources harnessed available energy allowing far-reaching changes in transportation and manufacturing. Nevertheless, most forms of renewable energy depended on proper location; a water wheel, for example, must be near a river. Truly dynamic changes awaited development of **nonrenewable energy sources**, especially **fossil fuels** (coal, natural gas, petroleum, and their fuel derivatives). These energy sources revolutionized metallurgy, transportation, and every other industry. They could be transported to the site where they were needed and applied to a specific need, such as an iron smelter or a railroad engine.

The use of fossil fuels gave power technology a greater influence over the environment than ever before. Forests that once yielded gradually to the woodsman's axe could be decimated at a much higher rate with chain saws and powerful tractors. The horse-drawn plow was superseded by mechanized plowing in many places, modifying landscapes thousands of acres at a time. Fossil fuels also brought undesirable side effects. Burning them gives off sulphur dioxide,

---

alloy A substance made by mixing two or more metals, usually to give some desirable characteristic, such as the combination of tin and copper to make the stronger alloy bronze.

ingot A molded bar of smelted metal.

power technology The harnessing of nonhuman energy for human goals.

renewable energy sources Energy sources that can be replenished, such as wind, water, and wood.

nonrenewable energy sources Energy sources that cannot be replenished, such as fossil fuels.

fossil fuels Energy sources—primarily coal, natural gas, and petroleum and its derivatives—that result from ancient depositions of organic materials in the earth's crust.

◄ **Figure 12.14** *With the development of metallurgy, people begin to use copper, bronze, and iron to make tools, jewelry, weapons, and decorative and religious objects. This archaic bronze axe head from China dates from about 3,000 YA.*

carbon monoxide, carbon dioxide, dirty particles, and other pollutants. Long before the pollution problems that we are familiar with, such as acid rain, burning fossil fuels caused catastrophic conditions in cities where coal was burned extensively as a heating fuel. In 1909, for example, a cloud consisting of natural fog and gases and particles descended on Glasgow and Edinburgh and killed more than 1,000 people with respiratory afflictions. Eventually London and other cities passed laws to control coal burning and the air

quality improved. As power technologies diffuse rapidly to less developed parts of the world, the danger of environmental catastrophes increases (Figure 12.15), because these countries have less time to adjust to the danger of power technology by passing appropriate legislation and educating their citizens to the danger.

Because fossil fuels are nonrenewable, for each unit of energy extracted, the remaining fossil fuels became more expensive to find and extract. Nuclear power seemed to offer a cheap, clean, unlimited source of energy as an alternative to fossil fuels, but in recent years, critics have raised many questions about nuclear safety. Of course all forms of energy conversion present danger; coal mining and burning cause more deaths each year than nuclear accidents. But the accidents at Three Mile Island in 1979 and Chernobyl in

Figure 12.15 *A chemical leak at the Union Carbide plant in Bhopal, India, in 1984 caused thousands of deaths and injuries, including blindness. Environmental catastrophes tend to be more devastating in the less developed countries than in the developed countries, partly because modernization and development have outpaced controls.*

1986 made it chillingly clear that a serious nuclear accident has a more lethal potential than accidents in conventional fossil-fueled power plants.

Worries about nuclear power are tied up with the **energy crisis**. For some time, technologically advanced regions of the world have been using up world supplies of energy faster than they can be renewed. The energy that drives the transportation system, runs the factories, and heats, cools, and illuminates homes and offices in the industrialized countries comes primarily from fossil fuels. Modern agriculture is also highly dependent on fossil fuels. These fuels derive from decaying plants and animals locked into geological formations for thousands of years. Once plentiful and relatively easy to find, they are becoming more difficult to find and extract. Some experts predict that fossil fuels will be exhausted within the foreseeable future.

The vulnerability of societies dependent on fossil fuel came into sharp focus during the "oil shocks" of 1973 and 1979. In the first oil crisis, a cartel of oil producers called the Organization of Petroleum Exporting Countries (OPEC) temporarily stopped shipping oil to many consumers to protest Israel's role in the Middle East. Shortly afterward the price of crude oil more than doubled. In 1979 the same cartel decided to quadruple the price of oil. While supplies were not actually cut off, the attempts of countries and companies to reallocate the flow of oil created temporary scarcities in the availability of petroleum products, especially gasoline and heating oil. Prices shot up suddenly. In the United States, gasoline prices went from around 40¢ per gallon to over $1.30. There was a similar abrupt price increase early in 1991 during the Persian Gulf crisis. This time, however, prices fell back when it became evident that there was no oil shortage.

These changes had far-reaching effects on lifestyles, especially in the oil-dependent developed countries. The private automobile, long a symbol of affluence and comfortable life-style in many countries, became a luxury. Large gas-guzzling cars gave way to smaller, more efficient cars. People accustomed to cruising the countryside in their automobiles for fun began to stay at home more. A night out at the movies gave way to a night at home around the television set. In the United States smaller, more efficient, Japanese-built cars displaced the larger, American-built models, precipitating a crisis in the U.S. automobile industry.

The gradual shift to smaller cars meant lower demand for steel, and many steel mills closed. Many of the large urban centers of the eastern United States that depended on steel and other "smokestack" industries went into decline, and many workers became unemployed. High energy prices were a major factor in accelerating inflation even as the economy of the country slowed down. The resulting "stagflation" created a political and economic malaise that contributed to social tensions.

In many U.S. homes people saw their heating and cooling bills climb to nearly the same level as their rent or house payments because of the higher price of electricity and heating fuel. People living in older, uninsulated homes found they could not afford to heat them in the winter. Some people were forced to move. Many bought wood stoves and spent the winter hauling wood just as their grandparents once had. Other people set back their thermostats and closed off entire rooms to save on heat. In poor areas of large cities, landlords reduced the amount of heat and hot water and sometimes cut it off entirely. Tenants resorted to the dangerous practice of turning on ovens continuously to heat their apartments.

Many features of life that people in the United States had taken for granted—large, comfortable houses, leisure use of large cars, year-round temperature control for maximum comfort, highly paid industrial jobs in the steel and automobile industries, opportunities for minorities and migrants—became prohibitively expensive as a result of the energy crisis. There are signs that some of the more wrenching adjustments to the energy crisis are nearly over, but the underlying problem—dependence on a dwindling, nonrenewable energy source—remains. It will continue to be an issue in the 21st century.

Developing countries have also had to make painful adjustments. Higher energy costs have pushed up prices of imported goods needed to increase production. Recessions caused by oil price shocks in 1973 and 1979 reduced the markets for many commodities produced by the developing countries. While the wealthier countries could adjust by giving up some leisure comforts, the poorer nations suffered severe deprivation of basic goods, especially food. The energy-intensive system of agricultural production practiced in North America cannot diffuse to the rest of the world without severely depleting the remaining reserves of petroleum.

Figure 12.16   *Natural environments transformed by human technology. On the left, hills terraced and irrigated for rice cultivation by the Ifugao of the Philippines. On the right, giant green circles created by central pivot irrigation in Texas, U.S.A. Sometimes technology produces far-reaching environmental changes, which themselves become the stimulus for further adaptive changes.*

Because technology has the power to transform the environment, human activity has become a factor in evolution (Figure 12.16). Environmental change caused by the application of technology may become a selective factor. There are major debates the world over about the role of technology in society. Is technology like the "sorcerer's apprentice," a magical helper that, when switched on, runs out of control and creates a disaster? Or is technology a servant to humankind? Does technology arise because someone perceives that we can do something better than we used to? Or is technology developed in response to social and biological requirements over which we have little or no control?

energy crisis   A situation created by the rapid depletion of fossil fuel and other energy sources and concerns about the safety of energy generated by nuclear fission.

SUMMARY

- Thomas Malthus raised the possibility that the human population might outrun its food supply.
- The hominid population of earth has been growing steadily for 3 million years. For most of that period, however, it did not grow quickly.
- There were many checks on population growth including high mortality and low fertility. Some of the checks were biological, such as infectious disease and postpartum amenorrhea. Others may have been cultural, such as taboos on sexual intercourse or rules about maximum family size. We can see some of these factors at work among some modern populations, like the !Kung San who depend on foraging for a living. The necessity for frequent movement may lead foraging populations to space births widely because women cannot carry more than one infant on long treks.
- When people sedentized, new factors became important in population regulation. On the one hand, permanent settlement brought increased risk of exposure to disease because people began to live in close proximity to their own waste. On the other hand, sedentary peoples had no need to space births widely.
- Generally speaking, sedentary populations grew faster than foraging ones.
- In some places, the increased pressure on resources brought by larger populations may have accelerated the process of incorporating new resources and domesticating plant and animal species. In other words, a process of positive feedback was set in motion, leading to further, irreversible change. This seems definitely to be the case in southwestern Asia, the site of the earliest known domestication.
- Humans are distinctive for their heavy dependence on technology, which extends and augments human capacities for solving problems and manipulating the environment.
- There is little doubt that population growth is related to technological development, but the precise relationship is much debated.
- The Neolithic was not a single moment in history but a process that occurred again and again. It is part of a broader process of intensification in which

people began to depend on a broader spectrum of natural resources and to develop new technologies for exploiting them.
- In southwestern Asia there is good evidence that population pressure led to niche compression and eventually to domestication, but this is not so clear in other areas.
- Domestication everywhere involved modifying a species or several species by applying new selective pressures to it, usually by moving it to a new habitat. The result was a species that yielded greater harvests than its wild ancestor.
- Food producers can invest more time and energy in production and reap larger harvests. But the process also has limits, because it can exhaust soils, water, and other natural resources.
- Fixed settlements evolved in some places without domestication, but populations began to grow rapidly only when sedentized communities began to practice agriculture. This set into motion a number of processes that are still working themselves out.
- Settlements grew in size until cities formed. Social institutions appeared in order to provide coordination and control of new, more densely packed populations.
- Some people began to specialize in crafts such as stonework, ceramics, and house building and in artistic, healing, and ritual roles.
- As full-time specialists arose in nonagricultural roles, there was more pressure on cultivators to produce enough food for those who did not cultivate. Gradually the ratio of cultivators to noncultivators declined until, in modern industrial societies, noncultivators outnumber cultivators.
- Like many other technological innovations, metallurgy arose independently in several parts of the world.
- Metallurgy illustrates the relationship between technology and social organization. Certain forms of metallurgy became possible only after societies had achieved a degree of centralized control over labor.
- Energy capture has evolved through various forms over the last 10,000 years, beginning with the use of firewood for cooking and other purposes and continuing to the present, when firewood and fossil fuels are still dominant. Nuclear and renewable energy sources are also available but involve exposure to new risks.

- To understand technology, we must understand the social setting in which it is used.

GET INVOLVED

1. What has been the effect of medical technology on population? How have individuals and governments used technology to affect the reproductive process? Some examples you might examine are the use of abortion to end unwanted pregnancies in the United States and China and the use of prenatal diagnosis—through amniocentesis—to select the sex of the unborn child in India.

2. Keep a record of your own food intake for a week. Analyze it in terms of protein, carbohydrates, fats, and total energy (calories). How does your diet compare to that of known hunting and gathering peoples in terms of these nutrients?

3. Select a particular technology that has appeared relatively recently, such as robots in the assembly line, word processing, satellite communications, fax machines, or genetic engineering. What social preconditions had to be fulfilled before this technology could emerge and be applied? What have been the social and economic consequences of this technology? Has the technology given rise to cultural change, such as a modification in world view? (For example, in recent years, the proliferation of mass-produced goods, such as toys, clothing, and processed food, has led to increased interest in homemade and handmade products.)

SUGGESTED READINGS

Bartlett, Peggy F., and Peter J. Brown. 1985. Agricultural development and the quality of life. *Agriculture and Human Values.**

Binford, Lewis. 1983. *In pursuit of the past.* New York: Thames and Hudson.

Boserup, Esther. 1965. *The conditions of agricultural growth: The economics of agrarian change under population pressure.* Chicago: Aldine de Gruyter.

Cohen, Mark N. 1977. *The food crisis in prehistory: Overpopulation and the origins of agriculture.* New Haven: Yale University Press.

Miller, Barbara. 1981. *The endangered sex: Neglect of female children in rural northern India.* Ithaca, N.Y.: Cornell University Press.

* This selection is anthologized in *Applying Anthropology*, 2d ed., ed. A. Podolefsky and P. J. Brown (Mountain View, Calif.: Mayfield, 1992).

Studying Tubuai Agriculture

Victoria Lockwood is an assistant professor of anthropology at Southern Methodist University. She conducted fieldwork on Tubuai in 1980–1981, 1985, 1987, and 1991. Her research has focused on the social impact of rapid agricultural development on a traditional Polynesian society.

Tubuai is a rapidly modernizing, rural Tahitian island located about 700 kilometers due south of Tahiti. When I first went to study the island's agricultural development, I knew that Tubuai islanders were hard-working taro farmers and fishermen who had recently begun cultivating cash crops. Although some islanders held jobs with local government service agencies, agriculture was the mainstay of the island economy and the major activity of Tubuai families. I was surprised that when I told Tubuaians I wanted to study their agricultural system, they quickly responded that it was not very interesting and such a study would be a waste of time. They went on to say that the "interesting" agriculture was to be found on the main island of Tahiti, where farmers plant European crops using all of the latest Western methods and techniques.

The islanders' point was that Tubuai farming was certainly not "state of the art" in agriculture, at least not in how they had come to understand modern agriculture from agricultural extension agents. Although they are now learning to use fertilizers, insecticides, and tractors, they also spend much of their time applying the "primitive" techniques passed down to them by earlier generations of Tahitian farmers. These techniques include planting and harvesting by the phases of the moon and relying on traditional technology, including the digging stick, in indigenous subsistence gardens. As a result, agricultural officials tend to accuse Tubuaians of backwardness, and islanders are embarrassed to describe their own agricultural practices to outsiders.

I gave up trying to convince islanders that their agricultural system was worthy of study and simply went about trying to learn about its novel form and effectiveness. After spending a great deal of time talking to farmers, mapping their household gardens and fields, and actually working in the fields myself, I concluded that island farmers were not being overly conservative in their adherence to "tradition," although it probably looked like that to agricultural officials. Instead, Tubuaians have effectively created a *new* agricultural system that integrates the wisdom of their own agricultural system, particularly its sensitivity to nature, with the innovations of Western agriculture. The Tubuai system merges what islanders consider to be the best elements of both, and it works equally well for indigenous crops like taro (planted in swamplands) and for European vegetables and potatoes (planted in Western-style fields).

The system of cultivating European potatoes, the island's most recently introduced cash crop, illustrates the nature of the islanders' farming system. The farmers clear and prepare their fields and obtain seed potatoes from the local agricultural service. Following ancient prescriptions they plant the potatoes (and other root crops) on the day of the new moon (or three days before or after). According to Tahitian cosmology, this timing will cause the potatoes to be large and long. The farmers systematically apply insecticides and fertilizers according to detailed directions supplied by the agricultural service. According to principles followed for centuries, women who are menstruating do not enter the field for fear the plants will die from the powerful natural force embodied in menstrual blood, a force related to reproduction, birth, and death. At other times, both women and men work in the fields weeding, mounding potatoes, and fertilizing. When the potatoes are mature, island families harvest the crop only when the moon is auspicious for that purpose.

When Tubuaians plant swamp taro, the indigenous staple food, they also follow the prescriptions of the moon and the prohibitions on women. But no islander considers applying fertilizer or insecticide to taro because this crop is so well adapted to the island's natural environment (the product of centuries of cultivation) that it flourishes on its own; islanders say that even if one used these products they would have no impact. For Tubuaians, taro's natural productivity demonstrates that nature has the power to provide abundant crops without outside help and that in some cases Western technology may be both superfluous and impotent. The Tubuai taro farmers pass up the Western shovel and spade to cultivate their patches with the Tahitian wooden digging stick. This tool has been used for centuries, and islanders assert that it is much more effective in a swampy taro patch than Western tools.

After spending many months on Tubuai, I learned that the islanders have concluded that Western technology alone is insufficient to ensure successful cultivation, because it

Victoria Lockwood measuring a taro garden in Tubuai in 1991.

does not embody a concern with the powerful and unpredictable forces of nature (including the Christian God). In the islanders' view, it is these forces, not chemical fertilizers and insecticides, that ultimately control the productivity of crops, and these forces are in tune with the moon and cosmos. It is nature, for example, that controls the heavy rains that strike unexpectedly, swamp potato fields, and destroy the crop, and it is nature that controls the apparently random infestations of insect pests against which Western insecticides may or may not prove effective. The forces of nature can

also cause the potato harvest to be small even though the farmers have applied fertilizers as directed. When islanders perform ancient Tahitian agricultural practices, they are striving to fill the gap that they perceive between nature and Western technology.

The last decade of agricultural development on Tubuai has shown that Tubuai agriculture is indeed successful. Using their own brand of farming, the approximately 180 Tubuai families who cultivate potatoes are now exporting over 130 tons of potatoes to Papeete markets every year, a feat at which agricultural offi-

cials marvel. And, at the same time, farmers are able to feed their families with relatively little effort from their household taro gardens and tree crop plantations (coconuts, bananas, papayas).

It is unfortunate that agricultural officials do not appreciate Tahitian perspectives on the world and agriculture, and that islanders have learned to be embarrassed by them. Indeed, Tubuaians have found that there is wisdom in being both sensitive to the natural world and skeptical about the omnipotence of Western technology.

BASIC SOCIAL & CULTURAL PATTERNS

Every society establishes rules and customs for handling the problems inherent in the human way of life. People living together in groups, for example, have to establish ways of regulating relationships, getting tasks done, settling disputes, making decisions, and so on. Although many of these problems are universal, the solutions devised by human groups are almost endlessly varied, related as they are to environmental, economic, social, and other factors.

In Part Four we looked at the behaviors, traits, and capabilities that enabled human beings to adapt successfully to their environment. In Part Five we consider how humans have elaborated those adaptations into patterns of behavior and forms of social organization that further enhance their ability to survive. Noting both the tremendous variation and the common threads running beneath the differences, we look at basic social and cultural patterns in three areas: gender and sexuality; marriage, family, and kinship; and leadership.

Chapter 13 looks at how different societies handle such sex- and gender-related questions as, Who is allowed to have sexual relations with whom? How exclusive is sexual access? What personality and behavioral traits are (or should be) associated with men versus women? Do men and women have different roles and tasks in society, and if so, on what are the differences based? Chapter 14 looks at social issues related to marriage, family, and domestic arrangements: Who is allowed to marry whom? Who chooses a person's marriage partner? Where do married couples live and who lives with them? How do they pass on property to their children? How do they trace their ancestry and reckon their relationships with other members of the group? And Chapter 15 takes up questions of order, cooperation, and leadership, the rudiments of political behavior: How are decisions made? How are tensions diffused and disputes settled? What qualities are desired in a leader? Are women as likely to be leaders as men, and if not, why not? Our examination of issues in these three areas once again underscores the great diversity of solutions to human problems.

Cultures, like individuals, have different ideas about what makes a person attractive to a member of the opposite sex. This New Guinea woman incorporates both Western and non-Western articles in her dress.

13

SEX, GENDER, AND SEXUALITY

▲▲▲

As we have seen in previous chapters, humans are social animals. They possess **social structures**, or networks of interconnected social roles. Human groups have specialized roles for individuals of different ages and for males and females. Perhaps the most explosive and complex issues in anthropology today involve the differences between men and women, the different roles they take, and whether these differences are hereditary and instinctive or learned and cultural. This chapter addresses some of these issues and then goes on to examine sexuality in general and sexual access in particular, setting the scene for discussions of kinship and domestic arrangements in the next chapter.

SEX AND GENDER ROLES

In every social tradition there are differences between male and female roles, that is, typical and expected behavior for boys and men versus girls and women. A common belief is that the role differences between males and females derive from sexually specific physical traits. This view emphasizes the fact that humans are sexually **dimorphic**; that is, males and females differ in anatomy and physiology. Females are generally smaller than males. The bodies of males and females have different levels of **estrogen** and **testosterone**, hormones that are responsible for contrasting **secondary sexual characteristics**, that is, the distribution of hair, fatty tissue, and musculature in the body. The reproductive organs of males and females are distinctive, as are their corresponding roles in biological reproduction.

These sexually specific physical traits are seen as determining the kinds of tasks that males and females will perform and the rights and responsibilities accorded to them in society. However, evidence is accumulating that the *social* roles of males and females do not always follow the lines set down by biology. These roles are built up of elements that have little to do with the biological difference between the sexes. For this reason, when referring to differences between males and females in society, anthropologists now prefer the term *gender* to *sex*. **Gender** refers to the aspects of male and female roles that bear no necessary relationship to biologically based differences. Every society socializes children to be either boys or girls, but the social meanings and behavior attached to these roles are not the same in every society.

Some evolutionists have interpreted human sexual dimorphism as being a result rather than a cause of the different roles played by males and females over the course of human evolution. According to this theory, males had to be larger to hunt effectively and defend females and juveniles from attack. Female anatomy was based on the female's primary function in life, to bear and raise children, and to gather and prepare food. This viewpoint is flawed by the confusion of sex with gender role assignments. There is no denying that women are fitted by nature to bear children and to feed babies at the breast, but there is nothing about preparing meals or gathering food that would select for female anatomical characteristics. What then is the relationship between dimorphic traits and gender roles in human societies? To approach this question, let us first consider sex roles in our closest biological relatives, the nonhuman primates.

Primate Sex Roles

The view that sex roles are determined by anatomy might find support among the savannah-dwelling baboons of Kenya (see Figure 9.7). Baboons are highly dimorphic: Male baboons are nearly twice as large as females. While walking in open savannah, the dominant senior males take a position between a possible source of danger and the juveniles and females. The dominant males of a troop maintain their dominance by aggressively threatening any other animal that appears to usurp their role. During **estrus**, dominant males have exclusive access to sexually receptive females.

Recent studies among forest-dwelling baboons, however, give a different picture. Forest baboons lack the dominance hierarchy of the savannah baboons. Older females appear to lead the troop as it wanders; males do not form the core of the troop but frequently drop out of one group to join another. While in the forest larger males do not play the role of defender; in fact when danger threatens, they are frequently the first ones to leap into the trees, because they are quicker than females encumbered with infants (Rowell 1972). Thus baboon sex roles vary according to the habitat.

Species (Location)	Sexual Dimorphism	Dominance Behavior	Sexual Life	Aggression
Gibbon (S.E. Asia)	None	None	Infrequent copulation, pair-bonding	Frequent in defense of territory
Gorilla (Africa)	High	Slight male dominance	Rare events of copulation	Mainly symbolic
Chimpanzee (Africa)	Moderate	Weakly present	Frequent, non-exclusive	Moderate
Orangutan (S.E. Asia)	High	Male dominance	Highly aggressive males	Not territorial
Homo sapiens	Moderate	Variable	Variable	Variable

Table 13.1 Sexual Dimorphism and Sex (Gender) Roles in Five Anthropoid Species.

Highly dimorphic species like the orangutan show a tendency toward male dominance over females, while the equally dimorphic gorilla does not.

Turning to the anthropoid apes, we find no correlation between physical dimorphism and distinct sex roles (Table 13.1). Male and female gibbons, for example, grow to approximately the same size (6–7 kg) with no secondary sexual characteristics. Gibbons live in mated pairs that exploit a fixed range of forest. Gibbons copulate only when the female is neither pregnant nor nursing; otherwise males make no attempt at sex, and females are not receptive. A gibbon male defends his territory against intruders by actual aggression on occasion (Figure 13.1).

Orangutans, which also inhabit tropical forests, are much larger than gibbons, and they are highly dimorphic. Male orangs weigh an average of 70 kg (160 lb); females weigh only half as much. Orang females occupy stable ranges of forest, but males range much more widely. Males are not attached to a particular female, and in spite of their great size and formidable canine teeth, males are not protective of females or their young. On occasion, male orangs have been observed to copulate with unreceptive females, an event comparable to rape among humans.

Gorillas are the largest apes, with males weighing up to 270 kg (600 lb) and females up to 180 kg (400 lb). Senior males—sometimes known as **silverback males**—exercise leadership over a group of females and young males. Some younger males wander off alone, but females never do. Gorillas seem indifferent to sex, copulating only rarely. Individual groups are not territorial, and there appears to be little competition for food, territory, or access to females.

In chimpanzees the difference in size between males (averaging 70 kg, or 150 lb) and females (averaging 60 kg, or 130 lb) is less than that between male and female gorillas. Male chimpanzees are more interested in copulation than male gorillas, but they do not

---

social structures Networks of interconnected social roles.

dimorphic Having two different shapes or forms. Humans are sexually dimorphic in that males are generally larger than females.

estrogen A female sex hormone, responsible for triggering female secondary sexual characteristics, among other effects.

testosterone A male sex hormone, responsible for triggering male secondary sexual characteristics, among other effects.

secondary sexual characteristics Contrasting patterns for distribution of hair, fatty tissue, and musculature in men and women, caused by the sex hormones.

gender Classification as male or female on the basis of social roles rather than biological characteristics.

estrus The period of female sexual receptivity.

silverback males Dominant males in the gorilla social hierarchy; they exercise leadership over females and young males.

Figure 13.1 *Gibbons are not dimorphic, but males are slightly more aggressive than females and defend their territory against intruders. Orangutans are highly dimorphic, with females about half the size of males, but the male orangutan does not defend a territory.*

attempt to prevent others from copulating with the same female.

In the four living species most closely related to *Homo sapiens,* then, sex roles are not clearly correlated with physical dimorphism. There are relatively few ape populations in the world, and their behavior has not been studied under a wide variety of circumstances. Baboon studies, however, suggest that there is wide variation within a single species, which may represent social adaptation to different habitats. In other words, a species may be capable of a number of different kinds of social behavior, an adaptability known as plasticity. This plasticity of sex roles does not mean that sex roles have no basis in genetics, only that other factors must also be taken into account. This appears to be the case with humans as well.

Human Gender Roles

Like their primate relatives, humans exhibit a great deal of plasticity in male and female behavior differences. The assumption that men throughout prehistory were the primary subsistence providers has been challenged on many grounds. First, most foraging groups rely more heavily on gathering than on hunting for food, and gathering is more often a female activity. Although women are commonly held to be

less rugged than men, sometimes they occupy the more strenuous physical roles in a society. For example, among the Yahgan of Tierra del Fuego in South America, women were responsible for collecting the dietary staple, shellfish. This meant long periods of exposure to the frigid waters of the Antarctic sea. Yahgan women also steered and paddled canoes and had to swim back from deep water moorings because Yahgan men generally could not swim. There are also examples of women who are land hunters. (See "Anthropologists at Work" in Chapter 10.) One study shows that

> among various groups of Agta foragers of northeastern Luzon, the Philippines, many women . . . actively hunt game animals, traversing difficult terrain, often with considerable exertion, duration, and distance. These same women are successful mothers and engage in a full range of maintenance and other subsistence activities. They are not identical to men in their tasks, nor are men as active in housekeeping as some women are in hunting. [Estioko-Griffin 1986]

Many anthropologists have focused on gender roles in different societies. The best-known study to date is Margaret Mead's study in New Guinea. Mead worked in highland New Guinea among three culturally distinct but neighboring groups, the Tchambuli, the Arapesh, and the Mundugamor. Her study focused on the roles assumed by males and females in each of the three groups, with special emphasis on the psychological attributes of gender. Mead's descriptions were based primarily on what informants said was socially approved. This is referred to as the normative approach to behavior.

Among the Tchambuli, Mead reports, "we found a genuine reversal of the sex attitudes of our own culture, with the woman the dominant, impersonal, managing partner, the man the less responsible and the emotionally dependent person" (1935, 259). Mead states that Tchambuli men were primarily artists, obsessed with beauty and with decorating their elaborate ceremonial houses. Men also spent considerable time working on their ceremonial outfits, practicing the flute, dancing, and pursuing other artistic and ceremonial activities. Tchambuli women, by contrast, were the steady economic providers of their society; they did most of the subsistence labor. Women were socially more at ease than men, who were likely to be uneasy when outside their usual surroundings. There was a tradition of headhunting, and until shortly before Mead's visit, every boy was expected to prove himself by killing an enemy. Boys did so reluctantly, however, and only at the urging of their fathers. Women manufactured woven bags for trade, but men did the actual trading. A man might take two days before closing a deal on the sale of the bag; apparently the negotiation was part of the fun. Mead wrote, "The women's attitude toward the men is one of kindly tolerance and appreciation. They enjoy the games that men play . . . particularly the theatricals. . . ." Unlike the men, the women rarely quarreled. They shaved their heads and had little concern for their own physical appearance. They were at the center of things in the household; men lived in a men's house away from their mothers, wives, and children.

The second group studied by Mead, the Arapesh, subsisted by slash-and-burn horticulture, cultivating sago palms and raising pigs. Mead describes them as a "cooperative society" where violence was rare and greed and jealousy were suppressed. The Arapesh were trained from childhood to be sensitive and responsive to the needs of others, and men and women were similar in this regard. Mead states that men accepted leadership roles and even affected arrogance during their early years, but they were only too happy to give up these pretenses as soon as their eldest child reached puberty. Men and women shared the tasks of child rearing, including such tasks as feeding babies and cleaning up a child's feces. While Arapesh boys and girls were subjected to different experiences and had different responsibilities as adults, their training led them to behave in much the same manner. They suppressed and condemned aggression and did not admire people who took revenge. Thus, while gender differences existed, the ideal temperament for both men and women was the same. In Western terms, both Arapesh men and women could be described as "maternal, womanly, unmasculine" (Mead 1935, 162).

Mead's third research group, the Mundugamor, subsisted by fishing, gardening, and cultivating coconut and sago palms. According to Mead, the Mundugamor had "standardized the behavior of both men and women as actively masculine, virile, and without any of the softening and mellowing characteristics [that Westerners think of as] womanly" (Mead 1935, 162). The words *hostility* and *distrust* are found on practically every page of Mead's description of the Mundugamor. Brothers could scarcely live near each other, so great was their mutual hostility. Men of influence in Mundugamor communities acquired large families by marrying many wives—a practice known as polygyny—thereby depriving other men of women. They humiliated their enemies in the manner of the Kwakiutl by giving large feasts that the enemies could not reciprocate. Communities tended to be unstable, and Mead notes that practically the only thing that united them were the periodic headhunting raids culminating in cannibalistic feasts (although Mead never observed such a feast).

Among the Mundugamor, hostility was even a component of love making. Before marriage it was common for young boys and girls to have brief affairs. The sexual foreplay that began these events consisted of the lovers scratching and biting each other, breaking each other's ornaments, tearing their clothes, and smashing their weapons. The young people were expected to keep such affairs a secret, however, because girls were supposed to be virgins when they married. As with the Arapesh, boys and girls grew up with different experiences and had different economic roles. Like the Tchambuli, the Mundugamor had separate men's clubhouses. But the Mundugamor socialized both males and females to treat others with distrust and hostility, even brothers and lovers, as we have seen. Women were not tender even to their small children. Men were indifferent to children.

These three sharply contrasting gender patterns occurred in societies with much in common who lived within a radius of 160 km (100 mi). Assuming that Mead's observations were valid, she was justified in her conclusion:

> If these temperamental attitudes which we [in the United States] have traditionally regarded as feminine—such as passivity, responsiveness, and a willingness to cherish children—can so easily be set up as the masculine pattern in one tribe and in another be outlawed for the majority of women as well as for the majority of men, we no longer have any basis for regarding such aspects of behavior as sex linked. [Mead 1935, 259]

Mead's work has recently been criticized as relying heavily on subjective judgments. Nowadays most ethnographers would try to operationalize terms like *hostility* or *tenderness* and to measure these variables with much greater precision. Anthropologist Debra Gewertz, who restudied the Tchambuli in 1974–1975, pointed out that Mead characterized her subjects by using Western models of gender roles that do not correspond to how these people see themselves. Gewertz also points out that the "aggressive" behavior of Tchambuli women may have been influenced by the absence of more than half of the adult males, who were away working on plantations. Mead herself pointed out that there were many deviations from the cultural ideals she described. However, her conclusion, that cultural norms outweigh biological factors in determining gender roles, is still widely accepted.

Male-Female Differences

Many explanations of the sexual division of labor refer to the indispensable role of females in bearing, nursing, and otherwise caring for children. Although the reproductive function of females is essential in every society, it is often not prestigious or influential work. In a study of the Mekranoti people of central Brazil, Dennis Werner (1984) showed that women's influence decreases as they spend more time caring for children. However, this lack of influence may be tied more to the social role of mother than to physiological factors. Women can share child care, including nurturing infants, with other women, with children, and with men. Middle-class women in Western countries

have found that they can combine demanding professional careers with motherhood, although it is often stressful. Menstrual pain, considered by some to be an obstacle to participation in certain activities by women, is controllable. Agta women in the Philippines, for example, engage in strenuous hunting activities during their menstrual periods. In the face of growing evidence that extreme separation between male and female roles and abilities has more to do with socialization than biology, the argument for a "natural" sexual division of labor based on anatomy and reproductive function is less and less convincing.

However, it would be a mistake to conclude, as some now do, that there are no major differences between males and females aside from their separate reproductive functions. While the evidence for cultural patterning of gender roles may be overwhelming, there still may be innate differences between males and females. There are studies that suggest the existence of inborn differences in the average ability of males and females to orient themselves in space, for example. Physical anthropologist Stephen Gaulin (1986) suggests that this difference is related to the fact that during most of human history males typically wandered farther away from home than females. This explanation may have validity, but it is not directly testable. Gaulin presented some experimental evidence comparing nonhuman animal species that wander far and wide to others that do not. Since humans are so learning dependent, and since learning begins so early, it is difficult to test any theory about innate behavior or its causes. This kind of debate is likely to continue for some years.

Another trait that may be innately different in males and females is aggressiveness, which some scientists believe is related to the male hormone testosterone. Greater aggressiveness may in turn be related to political power. Men hold positions of greater public power in every society on earth about which we have reliable information. Is this the result of innate biological characteristics, such as a higher level of testosterone? If so, how can we account for variation in gender-specific political equality among different populations? There is no evidence for culture-specific differences in testosterone levels. Several studies point out that in many different cultures boys are socialized to compete with other boys, while girls tend to be socialized to conform to social norms. So it is more likely that learned behaviors underlie the different arrangements of political power between men and women.

There is an active debate among anthropologists about why women are more influential in some societies and less in others. A great deal of the debate centers on the role of women in production outside the domestic sphere. The more important women's subsistence roles are, the argument goes, and the greater control women have over what is produced, the more influential they will be in matters of public interest. This topic is discussed in greater detail in Chapter 18.

Finally there is no scientific basis for arguing that biology dictates how gender roles *ought* to be structured. If there is a biological basis for certain male-female differences, these are *average* differences and there may be considerable overlap across genders in a given population. Some men, for example, are smaller, weaker, or less aggressive than most women, and some women are larger, stronger, or more aggressive than most men. Also, the plasticity of human learning ability means that an individual can often compensate for and even offset any built-in limitations. Men, socialized to be aggressive and unforgiving, may not have the ideal traits for raising children. However, there are certainly instances in which men have learned to be nurturing and have successfully raised children, even without a woman to help, and there are many women in positions of power in business, government, and the professions who compete successfully with men.

SEXUALITY AND SEXUAL EXPRESSION

It is difficult to imagine a topic that excites people more than sex. It is the stuff of many dreams; it is often the cause of deep despair. In the United States and other Western countries, sex is a powerful persuader. People can be induced to desire products because advertisements hint that they will make the buyer more sexually attractive. People may risk their lives, spend fortunes, even betray their countries, in return for sexual favors. Sex is a pervasive theme in

Figure 13.2 *The male bowerbird of Australia builds an elaborate chamber, or bower (shown here), arched over with grasses and twigs and decorated with bright objects—all to attract a female.*

the lives of people outside the West as well. We will limit ourselves here to the question of the sex drive and **sexual access** viewed in a biocultural context.

Among mammals, the male and female must copulate (the act of mating) for a sperm to fertilize an egg. Biologists treat the sex drive as a universal among sexually reproducing animals. The sex drive in mammals is regulated in part by **androgens**—hormones that motivate animals to mate. There are other motivations for mating that have probably been derived by natural selection. The intense pleasure that people find in sex almost certainly has a biological basis, although varying psychological and cultural factors have created a wide range of sexual pleasures.

In theory, natural selection is based on random mating among members of a population. But truly random mating rarely occurs. Darwin discovered in many species a nonrandom process he called sexual selection. Sexual selection has two aspects: (1) competition among males for mates—among the savannah baboons of Kenya, for example—and (2) the element of choice by members of one sex in selecting a mate. In many bird species, for example, the males develop behaviors or physical traits, such as brilliant plumage, that have no other function than to attract females, who then choose among potential mates (Figure 13.2).

---

sexual access Availability for sexual intercourse.

androgens Hormones that motivate animals to mate.

Figure 13.3 *Pop star Madonna uses provocative sexual symbolism to attract attention and sell her image to her fans. Many products are promoted through the use of sexual images, as in the men's underwear advertisement (above). Different groups vary in the degree to which they use and respond to sexual imagery. In some, nearly every human act contains a symbolic reference to sex; in others, sex is a topic that is almost never raised.*

Sexual selection occurs in *Homo sapiens* as well, although we do not know its biological effects. In no other species has the sex drive been elaborated into so many different symbolic themes and channeled in so many directions (Figure 13.3). Psychoanalyst Sigmund Freud referred to humans as "polymorphous perverse," meaning that humans are able to find sexual satisfaction in a variety of ways, including heterosexual sex, homosexual sex, and masturbation.

There are many complex psychological overlays associated with sex. In every society sex is more than simple reproduction. In some societies, such as the Dani of New Guinea, sex is not highly sought after. In other societies, such as the Mehinaku of central Brazil, sex is a form of recreation. Elsewhere, such as traditional rural Ireland, sex is repressed almost as if it were a crime. In a few instances, sex is suppressed altogether. The Shaker religion, which flourished in the United States during the 19th century, did not permit sexual intercourse, a fact that probably con-

tributed to the disappearance of the Shakers. Some societies, such as the Trobriand Islanders of Melanesia in the Pacific, do not recognize a connection between intercourse and pregnancy. In some societies homosexual sex is permitted or even promoted for certain people. Anthropologist Gilbert Herdt (1981) reported that boys of the Sambia (a pseudonym) of New Guinea are secretly initiated into homosexual activities from the age of seven or eight, progressing later to heterosexual intercourse.

Sexual Access: The Incest Taboo

Every society regulates sexual access in some way. Written or unwritten codes regulate who may have sex with whom and under what conditions. While societies vary greatly in the amount of freedom they allow in sexual matters, males nearly always have more sexual latitude than females. Perhaps this is re-

Figure 13.4 *This Mehinaku woman belongs to a cultural group in which attitudes toward sex are open and accepting. Nevertheless, the incest taboo is strongly in force among the Mehinaku.*

lated to the fact that intercourse can have a more serious outcome for females, namely, pregnancy. When societies regulate sex, they also regulate fertility.

The most widely recognized code regulating sexual access is the incest taboo, the societal prohibition on sex with close relatives. People everywhere have a horror of incest and condemn it, although they define it differently. For example, the tragedy in the play *Oedipus Rex* by the ancient Greek dramatist Sophocles is that King Oedipus unknowingly married his own mother. So great was his shame that Oedipus blinded himself. The Mehinaku of central Brazil have no written laws and are fairly relaxed about sex. They have frequent extramarital affairs, and the fact that a man or woman has taken many lovers is an open secret in their village. Nevertheless the Mehinaku feel that close relatives should not have sex (Figure 13.4). In one Mehinaku myth a boy, Araukuni, has intercourse with his sister, who becomes pregnant. The myth teller describes the reaction:

Oh, the mother was angry. She struck Araukuni and beat him with a club. She cut down his hammock and burned it. She burned his bow, his arm bands and his belt. All of these she burned. She would not make bread for him. She would not give him manioc porridge or fish stew. All she would do was beat him, beat him, beat him. All the time she beat him . . . Araukuni grew sad. Araukuni went off into the forest. In his village, Araukuni's family and friends said it was so much better that he had gone. "Good riddance," said the father. "He had sex with his sister." [Gregor 1985, 180]

People who commit incest, especially within the nuclear family, may be executed, as is true among the Ashanti and Ganda peoples of Africa, or they may be banished, as was the case in 19th-century Japan. In the United States most states have laws prohibiting incest. A person convicted of an incest charge could draw a prison term, but in most cases judges refer the responsible individual for psychiatric treatment.

All known societies prohibit sexual intercourse between parents and children and between brother and sister. This is known as **nuclear incest**. The condemnation of incest is universally more stringent in relation to nuclear family members and less stringent in regard to other kinfolk. The taboo is universally extended to other kin but not always to the same kinfolk. For example, the Mehinaku prohibit sexual relations between the children of two brothers or two sisters (**parallel cousins**), but a man's children are expected to marry his sister's children (**cross-cousins**). In other societies the taboo may be extended to all cousins. In spite of the taboo, incest does occur in all societies.

Explanations of the Incest Taboo

How can we explain the taboo on incest? Because some kind of incest taboo is universal, some anthropologists suspect that it is genetically encoded or innate. But the taboo is also culturally encoded, and the extension of the taboo to different kinfolk varies with the cultural context. The taboo therefore presents a challenge to anthropological explanation. The first difficulty that arises is due precisely to the fact that the nuclear incest taboo is universal. It would be helpful to use an experimental model comparing cases where the incest taboo is present to others where it is absent. But since it is universally present, this is impossible.

There is another difficulty in explaining the incest taboo. It is important to distinguish between explanations for the genesis (or beginning) of a custom and explanations for whatever maintains the custom in society. In Chapter 3 we traced the beginnings of the U.S. Halloween tradition to a Celtic custom in which evil spirits were driven out with bonfires. Belief in evil spirits is not prevalent in today's United States, yet the holiday observance persists. Similarly, with the incest taboo, the explanation of the genesis of the taboo is not necessarily the same as for its persistence in modern society.

Let us examine the leading explanations of the incest taboo. The issue is still being debated. The experts have not yet agreed on how the taboo originated, or why it persists. There are many theories about the incest taboo, most of which can be summarized under four headings: (1) inbreeding, (2) family integration, (3) aversion, and (4) cooperation.

Inbreeding Theory. In Chapter 5 we saw that deleterious genes may be maintained in populations in recessive form. A recessive gene is expressed only when an individual is homozygous for that allele. Homozygosity is more likely if the parents are **consanguines** (blood relatives). The chance that full siblings have identical copies of a given gene at a particular locus on the chromosome is high. If siblings mate, there is a 25 percent chance that their offspring will be homozygous for a given gene. If the gene is deleterious, the offspring will suffer the consequences. If first cousins mate, the risk of a child born with identical genes from both parents drops to $\frac{1}{16}$th. Note that **inbreeding** itself is not harmful and is not the cause of disease; it is dangerous only if the parents carry deleterious genes.

The rate of inbreeding depends on the size of the breeding population and how isolated it is. A population may be isolated geographically, such as one living on a remote island. A group may also be technologically isolated. Until the invention of the bicycle, most Englishmen living in the countryside probably found their spouses within a radius of about 5 miles from their homes, the distance a man could walk to court a woman and return home the same day. When the bicycle was introduced, in the 19th century, the "courting radius" was expanded to 25 miles, and the size of the breeding population grew accordingly. Societies can be socially isolated as well. The Old Order Amish, who are settled mainly in Pennsylvania, Ohio, and Indiana, are a highly inbred religious isolate because their religion calls for **endogamous marriage**, or marrying within the group (Figure 13.5). Studies show that the Amish suffer from a relatively high frequency of genetic disorders, including dwarfism, albinism, and muscular dystrophy.

Inbreeding theory suggests that the incest taboo reduces the amount of consanguineous mating in human populations. Throughout most of prehistory people lived in small, relatively isolated communities and probably found spouses close to home. The incest taboo would have prevented the most dangerous kind of inbreeding, mating with close consanguines. In a cross-cultural survey of contemporary societies, anthropologist Melvin Ember (1975) showed that people permit marriage with consanguines when the selection of mates is small; otherwise they are likely to condemn it. The data are consistent with the theory that the taboo reduces inbreeding, but they do not

Figure 13.5 *Genetic disorders are relatively common among the Amish of the American Midwest because of their practice of endogamous marriage. Inbreeding theory suggests that the incest taboo exists to reduce the occurrence of such genetic problems.*

explain how the taboo could have been adopted, unless people could recognize how the taboo benefited them. Ember believes recognition is possible. He points out myths in several societies in which the offspring of incestuous unions are born as monsters or with other defects.

However, inbreeding theory does not help us understand why many societies distinguish between cross- and parallel cousins. In many societies sex and marriage are permitted between cross-cousins but defined as incestuous between parallel cousins, even though the probability of homozygous offspring is the same for both. Another difficulty with inbreeding theory is that it suggests that people recognize the health benefits of the taboo. Mortality has been high throughout much of human history, and it would have been difficult for people to distinguish between individuals dying from genetic disorders and those afflicted with infections or other diseases.

Family Integration Theory.   The family integration theory suggests that incestuous relations would disrupt the unity of the nuclear family. The human nuclear family probably evolved during the Paleolithic. It arose as a response to the long maturation period among humans, the increasing specialization of subsistence activities, and the heightened importance of sharing. The role relationships within the nuclear family provided for teaching and learning, the care and socialization of the young, the sharing of food and other goods, and the satisfaction of sexual needs. In short, survival depended on the coordinated efforts of family members.

Ethnologist Bronislaw Malinowski suggested (1927) that if parents were allowed to have sex with their own children, and sisters with brothers, the role relationships within the nuclear family would be disrupted. What authority would a father have over his daughter if they were also lovers? This theory is based

---

nuclear incest   Sexual intercourse between parents and children or brothers and sisters.

parallel cousins   The children of same-sex siblings, such as children of two sisters.

cross-cousins   The children of cross-sex siblings, that is, a brother and a sister.

consanguines   Blood-related kin.

inbreeding   Sexual reproduction among closely related consanguines.

endogamous marriage   Marriage to a person from the same group, such as a clan, caste, class, or religion.

on the assumption that relationships between sex partners are so powerful that they will overwhelm and distort other relationships.

Sigmund Freud, the founder of **psychoanalysis,** proposed a theory of the origin of the incest taboo related to his theory of the mental personality. Freud suggested that people are born with strong **drives** for food, sex, and affection. He argued that growing up involved repressing these elemental drives. **Repression** was necessary for people to get along and assume their respective roles as members of society. Young boys grow up near their mothers, from whom they receive most of their food, affection, and nurturance. As a result, according to Freud, the first object of a boy's sexual desire is his mother. In his fantasy life, a boy dreams of eliminating his father and possessing his mother, a set of ideas and impulses Freud called the Oedipus complex. This fantasy fills the boy with guilt and fear. A boy achieves manhood when he represses his fantasies and turns to a woman other than his mother as a sex partner. His guilt over his fantasies never wholly leaves him, however, and this forms the core of the horror of incest. A similar fantasy about her father presumably underlies the development of a girl's rejection of incest; Freud called this the Electra complex.

Malinowski's and Freud's theories are both plausible, yet they leave many questions unanswered. Human role relationships are flexible, and people can assume many different roles in life. Many husbands and wives and parents and children work together in a professional context and seem to have little difficulty in adjusting their behavior to the context. A woman who serves as her husband's attorney, for example, would not address him in court the same way she does at home at the breakfast table. Why could people not regulate sexual relationships in similar fashion? Theoretically mothers could have sex with their sons on weekends and with their husbands on weekdays. The strains of such **role conflict** could be eliminated by strict enforcement of rules. The fact that this idea is patently absurd demonstrates that a strong taboo exists, but it does not actually make it intelligible. Neither Freud's nor Malinowski's theory helps us understand the taboo on brother-sister incest. Finally, these theories may not be testable because there is no evidence that would falsify them.

Aversion Theory.   Nearly 100 years ago, anthropologist Edward Westermarck suggested that children who are raised together have no attraction for each other when they become sexually mature. Something about contact in early childhood seems to reduce sexual interest. The idea was repeated by a few later anthropologists, but it did not attract many adherents because it related only to the taboo on brother-sister incest, not to parent-child or other forms. Unlike other incest theories, Westermarck's did not assume that people naturally desire to have sex with consanguines. But why is it necessary to prohibit something that no one wants to do anyway?

Ethnologist Arthur Wolf noted that in China people sometimes marry someone with whom they were raised. These "minor marriages" occur when a family wishes to avoid the trouble and expense of an elaborate wedding for their son. A young girl, herself often from a family too poor to support their daughter, is adopted by the boy's family, usually before she is three years old. The boy and girl are raised like brother and sister, but upon reaching the appropriate age, they are married. Wolf (1966) collected data on large numbers of marriages in Taiwan. He found that couples in minor marriages had, on average, fewer children and higher rates of adultery and divorce than married partners raised separately. Wolf concluded that lower fertility and marital problems were consequences of an aversion people feel when raised together in the same household from an early age.

Anthropologist Melford Spiro (1958) studied Israeli collectives (**kibbutzim**) where children were raised cooperatively rather than in a family setting (Figure 13.6). He found that the boys and girls raised together had little sexual interest in each other and were unlikely to marry. Another anthropologist, Yonina Talmon, also studied marriage patterns among the second generation on established kibbutzim. She confirmed Spiro's conclusion, stating "we did not come across even one love affair or one instance of publicly known sexual relations between members of the same peer group who were co-socialized from birth through most of their own childhood" (Talmon 1964, 493).

Aversion relates the incest taboo to a basic biological process. **Imprinting** is an inborn learning process in which a particular stimulus, experienced early in life, establishes a behavior pattern relative to that stimulus. For example, there is some experimental evidence from rats that sexual arousal is greater between rats that have been raised apart than between rats raised together. Still, the Chinese and Israeli data

Figure 13.6 *Israeli kibbutzim children are raised together almost like sisters and brothers. Aversion theory suggests that they, like biological siblings, will be uninterested in each other sexually.*

are subject to other interpretations. The lower fertility and marital problems associated with minor marriages, for example, may be related to the lower prestige of that form of marriage.

People feel repelled by the mere thought of incest, but that feeling may be the result of socialization rather than instinct. For aversion theory to yield a comprehensive explanation of incest, it would have to provide more and better evidence that aversive imprinting occurs in various contexts and to suggest a mechanism by which it occurs. It might be helpful to examine the instances in which brother-sister incest does occur. We would want to know whether the same process operates between parents and children. It would also be useful to learn what factors could have selected for such an instinct.

Cooperation Theory. The cooperation theory is widely accepted by anthropologists, even though

there is little evidence for it beyond its intrinsic plausibility. Basically the idea is that the incest taboo reinforces a rule of **exogamous marriage** (marrying outside one's group), thereby obliging a group to become dependent on others. The classic statement of this position was made in 1889 by E. B. Tylor, one of the founders of anthropology: "Again and again in the world's history, savage tribes must have had plainly before their minds the simple practical alternative between marrying out and being killed out" (Tylor 1889, 267). Tylor meant that local groups of people would have had little basis for cooperation and alliance if they had not married outside the local group. Tylor's idea was particularly attractive to mid-20th-century anthropologists on both sides of the Atlantic who wanted to make a case for the primacy of social over psychological and biological causes in human affairs. Leslie White, an influential figure in American anthropology, suggested that the incest taboo was the foun-

---

psychoanalysis A method developed by Sigmund Freud and others for the treatment of psychological disorders based on the belief that innate drives of the personality are denied by the conscious mind but become part of the unconscious mind through repression.

drives Basic needs pressing for satisfaction, such as hunger, thirst, and sexual desire.

repression The denial of some psychological drives, which is required for people to assume roles in society but also responsible for some disorders.

role conflict Conflict that arises as a result of a person's assuming more than one social role.

kibbutz (plural kibbutzim) An Israeli collective community in which production, consumption, and sometimes child rearing are communally organized.

imprinting An inborn learning process through which a behavior pattern becomes established due to an early stimulus.

exogamous marriage Marriage outside a defined group, such as a clan, caste, class, or religion.

dation of social evolution because it furthered exchange between otherwise splintered groups. We have seen how the !Kung San camp group benefits from multiple ties to other groups (Chapter 10). If the water hole that one group depends on dries up, its members can seek another one where relatives live. If a group finds that it has more girl babies than boys, it can find husbands in another group.

For ethnologist Claude Lévi-Strauss the rule of exogamy bolstered by the incest taboo lays the foundation for what he calls the most "elementary form of kinship": the exchange relationship between brothers-in-law. Lévi-Strauss suggested that the most precious gift a man could make to another was a sister or daughter. The recipient, or his family, would be obligated to reciprocate with a payment or perhaps with another woman for a man of the other group. The two men would become bound into a relationship of mutual support and respect. Lévi-Strauss argued that the entire structure of kinship was built up on the relationships between brothers-in-law, as shown in Figure 13.7. We will discuss this model further in Chapter 14.

A central problem with this approach to incest is that it confuses the incest taboo (a sexual prohibition) with exogamy (a marriage rule). Incest prohibitions refer to persons with whom one may not have sexual relations. Exogamic rules refer to persons one may not marry. There is often considerable overlap, although incest cannot have a broader scope than exogamic restrictions—no society permits marriage between partners who are prohibited from having sex by the incest taboo.

Some anthropologists have recently suggested that rules of exogamy may come first and incest rules later. They suggest that the value of exogamic marriage was so great that it was adopted as an explicit rule by some societies. If this were true, however, we should not expect the incest taboo to be universal, and the exogamic rule should be more widespread. It is theoretically possible, however, that incest prohibitions and exogamic rules could be separate. People could obtain sexual satisfaction within the family and still marry outside it. Another difficulty with cooperation theory is that cooperation among families is not an equal necessity in all types of societies. In modern industrial societies, for example, it is possible for families to isolate themselves from others, giving and asking little. Finally it is important to remember that no empirical test of cooperation theory has been made.

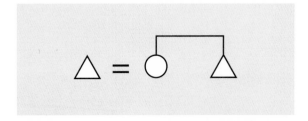

Figure 13.7 *The "elementary structure of kinship," according to French ethnologist Claude Lévi-Strauss: exchange between brothers-in-law.*

Incest Behavior

There are several explanations of the incest taboo supported by good, logical arguments. Possibly no single theory will account for the origin, persistence, and extension of the incest taboo. The theories we have considered do not exclude each other; if one is true the others are not necessarily false. Thus the incest taboo may be one of those phenomenon that is **overdetermined**, the joint consequence of a number of different causes or conditions. Another possibility to be considered is that the incest taboo is not one but a collection of human institutions that should be examined separately. The parent-child taboo may be governed by different principles than the brother-sister taboo. Finally we must recognize that in every society incest does occur, in spite of the taboo.

Recognition that incest does occur has led to increased awareness of incest as a social problem. As social service agencies have become more concerned in the United States, and as better data become available, estimates of the frequency of incest have risen. At the turn of the century, the rate of incest was estimated at 1.2 to 1.9 cases of incest per million inhabitants in the United States. This would work out to no more than 450 per year based on today's population. More recent estimates place the incidence of incest in the United States at 25,000 to 45,000 cases per year (Phelan 1983), or more than 100 cases per million population. Still, because of the deep shame people feel concerning incest, many cases are never brought to light. Current estimates of the occurrence of incest in the United States may still be too low.

A number of researchers have addressed the determinants of incest in U.S. households, but the results so far are not revealing. Incest is no longer thought to be the result of poverty and deprivation; it is known to occur in all social classes. Many case studies of incest have linked its occurrence with certain psychosexual disorders or with family pathology of various sorts. For example, a dominating but insecure father and an unassertive mother are frequently present in a family where incest occurs. However, when incest cases are compared to control groups, drawn at random from similar populations, it is not possible to predict the psychological or family conditions that will lead to incest. Perhaps the most striking finding in incest studies in the United States is that the incidence of father-daughter incest outweighs all other types combined. Often the father is a stepfather or a father who has been absent from the household. One recent finding is that the incestuous father is often one who has had little close contact (such as holding, feeding, diapering) with his daughter while she was growing up (Parker and Parker 1986). This finding might be interpreted as supporting aversion theory.

At the current state of knowledge, there is little in the data about incest behavior that unravels the question we are considering: the origin and persistence of the taboo. The simple fact that incestuous behavior is prevalent—possibly more than current statistics show—suggests that incest may not be such an unspeakable crime in everyone's mind. Most of our thinking about incest has been based on the assumption that the taboo is universal and that behavior followed suit. The possibility that the horror of incest may be a variable and not a constant may require rethinking of the incest question.

SUMMARY

- This chapter forms a bridge to the consideration of social organization in contemporary society. However, we find ourselves once again raising questions about the biological nature of human sexual differences and the possible biological meaning of the incest taboo.

- Human sex roles may be related to the reproductive differences between males and females, but they are elaborated in a cultural context.

- Human sexual dimorphism is not a simple key to understanding behavioral and psychological differences between male and female humans. Our closest relatives, the apes, show no clear correlation between sexual and behavioral dimorphism.

- Men and women show great plasticity in the varied economic, social, and political roles they play in different societies. Stereotypical views of women and men are not defensible against the evidence of the variety of behaviors found across world cultures.

- Sexual behavior among humans is much more than reproductive behavior. It is overlaid with symbolic and psychological meanings and has an effect on all other aspects of culture.

- All societies have codes governing sexual access. Some societies are relatively relaxed about sex, while others impose extremely rigid restrictions.

- The incest taboo is a universal code of access that forbids sex between nuclear family members (except husband and wife) and between other relatives as well.

- Inbreeding theory explains the incest taboo as a means of preventing consanguineous matings. Integration theory explains incest avoidance as a way of protecting the structure and function of the nuclear family. Aversion theory approaches incest as an instinctual aversion between persons raised together, regardless of consanguinity. Cooperation theory suggests that incest restrictions evolved to oblige groups to become interdependent.

- Some of these theories explain the persistence but not the origin of the incest taboo. Others fail to explain all aspects of the taboo, such as brother-sister versus parent-child taboos. Some theories cannot be tested empirically, so we cannot evaluate their validity. Perhaps incest is so overdetermined that we cannot isolate a single explanation but must accept several of them.

- Incest violations do occur, but their occurrence is poorly understood and does not shed light on the taboo itself.

---

overdetermined   A phenomenon with more than one cause or condition.

GET INVOLVED

1. The women's movement has focused sharply on gender equality over the past 20 years. Get involved in an organization taking a position on a major issue of special concern to women, such as affirmative action, equal pay, child care for single parents, maternity and paternity leave, date rape, pornography, abortion. What is the social and moral basis for the position taken? What steps is the organization taking to get its point of view across? What has been accomplished and what remains to be accomplished? What are the obstacles to achieving its goals?

2. Increasing attention is being focused on incest as a form of child abuse in the United States and other countries. Because it is tabooed, incest tends to be hidden from view and is almost certainly underreported. What are social agencies doing to deal with this problem? How are the children who are victims of incest treated? What about the parents who commit incest?

3. What has been the influence of AIDS on sexual behavior? Which groups and populations (at home and in foreign countries) have altered their habits and which have not? Can you design a public information campaign that will help bring the message to those who do not yet understand the disease?

SUGGESTED READINGS

Margolis, Maxine L. 1984. *Mothers and such: Views of American women and why they changed so much.* Berkeley: University of California Press.

Martin, Joann. 1990. Motherhood and power: The production of a women's culture of politics in a Mexican community. *American Ethnologist* 17:470–490.

Mead, Margaret. 1928. *Coming of age in Samoa.* New York: William Morrow.

———. 1935. *Sex and temperament in three primitive societies.* New York: Dell Publishing.

Murphy, Yolanda, and Robert Murphy. 1985. *Women of the forest.* 2d ed. New York: Columbia University.

Spiro, Melford E. 1958. *Children of the kibbutz.* Cambridge: Harvard University Press.

Sex, Gender, and the Mehinaku Division of Labor

Thomas Gregor is a professor of anthropology at Vanderbilt University. He has conducted research among the Mehinaku of Brazil's Xingu National Park over a cumulative period of two years. His research has focused on gender relationships and the peaceful intertribal system that unites the native Xingu societies.

Thomas Gregor receiving a ceremonial name from the Mehinaku.

My work as an anthropologist has been among the Mehinaku, a tropical forest people living in Brazil. I first visited the Mehinaku in 1967 as a graduate student working on a doctorate in anthropology. Compared to many tribal peoples, the Mehinaku were easy to reach. I took a Brazilian air force plane to the Xingu National Park, where I was put up at the Indian Post. There I met some of the Mehinaku. They agreed to take me to their village, which took only three hours by canoe and an hour's walk along a forest trail.

The Mehinaku loaded my 200 pounds of equipment, gifts, and food into a large dugout canoe, and we set off for their port. As we paddled, I wondered how we were going to transport my luggage to the village. To my surprise, the Mehinaku women cheerfully hoisted my duffel bags and trunks onto their heads for the hike. The village chief walked alongside me carrying only my rifle, which was an item of great prestige.

When we arrived in the village, the chief distributed dress material and other gifts I had purchased for the villagers. Several hours later I found the men sewing the cloth into dresses for their wives. For me this experience was a lesson in gender relationships that I have not forgotten. In our culture men usually carry heavy objects and women sew. If biology strictly determines gender, the Mehinaku read the facts of life very differently than we do.

My discovery about the arbitrariness of the division of labor is typical of many societies: Men's work in one culture may be women's work in another. Moreover, most cultures allot tasks to either men or women, but not indifferently to both. Very few jobs in the average society (only 7 to 12 percent of tasks in one broad, cross-cultural study) are assigned without respect to sex. Work is gender coded, and men who do women's work, or women who do men's, may find themselves ridiculed. A Mehinaku man who must fetch water (a woman's job) may do so after nightfall so he will not be seen.

What explains the arbitrariness of the division of labor? Why not allow everyone to do what he or she does best, whether it is "gender appropriate" or not? Émile Durkheim first proposed an answer in his sociological and anthropological classic, *The Division of Labor in Society*. To grasp Durkheim's solution, consider the case of Yuma, a Mehinaku man.

I recall that Yuma was the saddest of villagers. I came to know him quite well because he was always around at mealtime, trying to beg some of my food. I noticed that he seemed to be poorly nourished. His hammock (the Mehinaku do not have beds) was in tatters, and he never wore the arm bands and belts that were essential to proper dress. To the Mehinaku he was socially marginal, an object of pity and contempt. What was wrong? The villagers explained that he was a bachelor. Lacking a wife or other close female kin, he had few of the things that women produced, such as hammocks, cotton, and manioc flour.

Yuma's plight was evidence in favor of Durkheim's solution to the puzzle of the arbitrariness of the division of labor. Durkheim maintained that the assignment of different tasks to men and women is socially adaptive. In small tribal societies gender roles provide a material incentive for bringing men and women together in enduring relationships. The division of labor among the Mehinaku and in other simple societies may therefore not be as arbitrary as it seems. Establishing *une différence* between men and women makes them dependent on one another. Neither is socially complete without the other. The division of labor thereby supports marriage and family as basic human institutions.

Parents the world over have devised means of carrying their infants, like this Guatemalan baby in a rebozo on its mother's back, so they can go about their daily routines.

14

MARRIAGE, FAMILY, AND KINSHIP

▲▲▲

Scientists search for fundamental units in nature. Physicists use the molecule to understand matter and energy. Biologists treat the cell and the gene as basic units. Social scientists have tried to find an appropriate basic unit for social analysis. One such unit is the family. Is the family or any other unit the "molecule" of human society? This chapter addresses several topics related to the family: marriage, household, postmarital residence, social rules for organizing kinship groups, and the representation of kinship in language.

MARRIAGE

Most North Americans think of marriage as what happens when a man and a woman meet, fall in love, formalize their bond, live together, and raise a family. This voluntary form of **monogamous** marriage is common in contemporary Western societies, but it is relatively rare around the world. Marriage patterns vary so widely that anthropologists sometimes wonder whether there is a single institution that can be called by that name. The definition of **marriage** that fits most societies is a "contract (written or unwritten) that establishes the social identity and legal status of any children." The contract may also grant rights of sexual access and regulate how property will be shared. These contracts involve more than a couple; in most societies third parties play an important role in marriage decisions.

There are also variations in the form of the marriage union. Many societies permit polygamous marriages, most often polygyny, in which a man may take more than one wife. Marriage is not always even contracted between a man and a woman. In some societies, a woman can marry another woman.

Consider the Igbo people, a major ethnic group of southeastern Nigeria. While most Igbo marriages are between a man and a woman, an Igbo woman may take another woman as a wife if she can live up to the same financial obligations as any prospective bridegroom. This may happen if a woman is childless or if she acquires wealth on her own. The wife of a female husband may bear a child (by a man of course), but the female husband or her own male husband has paternity rights over the children. Thus an Igbo child may have a female father (Uchendu 1965). Man-man

marriages also occur, such as when homosexual couples wish to have the same legal relationship as heterosexual married couples (Figure 14.1). Men may marry very young girls in many societies; in some societies, such as the Yanomamo, a girl may be promised to a man even before she is born.

Attitudes on the topic of sexual exclusivity vary widely. They range from the severe disapproval of adultery among the Xavante of central Brazil or punishment among the Puritans of 18th-century New England to the acceptance of adultery by the Mehinaku of central Brazil (see Chapter 13). Although marriage contracts usually bind the partners to sexual exclusivity, people in many societies carry on sexual affairs with different people before and after marriage. Among the Nayar warrior caste of India, for example, a woman may have sex and bear children only after she is formally married (Gough 1959). Once married, however, she is free to take as many lovers as she

Figure 14.1 *A wedding ceremony between two gay men in the United States. Such formalized unions are legal for gay and lesbian couples in some states. What couples seek is legitimacy for their children and social recognition of their relationship. Same-sex marriage occurs in other societies as well and is just one of many forms the marriage contract can take.*

Figure 14.2   *In some societies a bride brings a dowry to her marriage, representing her share of the family inheritance. Here, married women carry a bride's possessions to her new home in a traditional wedding in Czechoslovakia. In other societies wealth passes from the groom's family to the bride's in the form of a bride price.*

pleases, including her husband. If she bears children without marrying, the Nayar consider the children illegitimate.

Marriage practices also vary within societies. In some societies there are several different forms of marriage. In Brazil the highest-status marriage is a combination religious and civil wedding; the lowest-status marriage is a "consensual union," with no formal ceremony. Children of consensual unions may encounter legal problems in receiving an inheritance, but they are socially recognized as belonging to their parents.

Economic and Social Aspects of Marriage

Marriage generally involves the transfer of valued items such as money, material goods, labor power, rights in children, and membership in social groups. A bride price paid by the groom's family to the bride's is common in some societies, such as the Igbo or Dinka of Africa. Bride prices compensate the bride's family for the loss of her labor and her reproductive power. In some societies, such as the Nuer of the

---

marriage   A contract (written or unwritten) between two or more people that establishes the social identity and legal status of any children, governs property rights, and sets out rules and obligations between the parties.

monogamous   Pertaining to a marital union involving only two partners.

Sudan, the husband of a woman who does not have babies may return his wife to her family and demand a refund of the bride price. In many societies, women find they are not well accepted by their in-laws until after they have borne children.

In other societies the bride's family must provide a **dowry** (Figure 14.2). Without it, she cannot marry well. Dowries are wealth transfers from the bride's family to the groom or his family. They are most common in situations where women's potential contribution to the husband's household is not highly valued. In India, families of young women who can afford it pay dowries to make them more marriageable. A woman may marry into a higher status if her father can offer a substantial dowry. The custom was declared illegal in 1961, but it continues nevertheless. As grooms' families demanded higher and higher dowries, the families of young women went into debt to make dowry payments. When they could not meet the payments, the families of some husbands murdered the bride, usually by dousing her with kerosene and setting her afire. In 1977 the New Delhi police received 311 complaints of women burned under suspicious circumstances; in 1983 the number of "wife burnings" had risen to 690 (*Washington Post* 1984, A10).

Sometimes the exchange of valued goods is reciprocal. In **bilateral cross-cousin marriage** (see "Types of Kinship Terminologies" later in this chapter), two kinship groups exchange women with each other. One man may offer his daughter in marriage to another lineage. In return his son may be betrothed to a girl from that lineage.

With so much exchange going on, many people have a stake in marriage arrangements. Marriage contracts almost universally concern the partners' immediate families, but they are of concern also to wider kin groups such as clans and lineages, local communities, and the state. In complex societies the state usually regulates marriage. In the United States, for example, most states require a marriage license and set requirements concerning the age, physical condition, and relatedness of the couple. The marriage ceremony is usually a public event in the United States. The ceremony is conducted by someone empowered by the state to perform weddings. In this ceremony the couple declare their desire to be married and their acceptance of the terms of the contract, emphasizing the voluntary nature of marriage.

The Diversity of Marriage Patterns

A few examples from different parts of the world will illustrate the social ramifications of marriage. Thomas Fraser, Jr., studied Malay fishermen in South Thailand. He wrote (1966, 29):

> Marriage arrangements are *always* made by the parents of the prospective couple. . . . During the time that a boy is approaching marriageable age, his father remains alert to potential mates. . . . The main criteria for choosing a daughter-in-law are beauty, family background, wealth and religious training. . . . Fathers seeking daughters-in-law . . . must balance objectively the assets of their sons against the assets they are seeking in his mate. When the field has been narrowed to one or a few suitable girls, the boy's father seeks the assistance of an intermediary, a man who is known to both families. It is this man who either arranges for a surreptitious viewing of the girl by the boy and his father, or enters directly into negotiations with her family. When the negotiations have been completed, the girl is informed by her parents of her impending marriage.

Anthropologist Francis Madang Deng described marriage customs among his own people, the Dinka of Sudan (1972, 94):

> The first step is "seeing" the girl. Usually this means that after a period of friendship with a girl, a man decides to marry her and consults his relatives. This is often the subject matter of cathartic songs in which young men request their elders to authorize them to look for brides or to consent to proposed marriages. While some fathers urge their sons to marry, many . . . may delay their sons' marriages until they reach an age when marriage can no longer be postponed. The usual reason given is insufficiency of cattle and the need to accumulate more wealth.

Norma Diamond, an ethnographer who worked in a village in Taiwan, described the traditional marriage pattern (1969, 51):

> Ideally, marriages are arranged by families, not by individuals. When parents feel it is time for their son to marry, they call in a traditional matchmaker. . . . Theoretically, the young couple play no part in these arrangements and are rarely consulted. As filial children, they rely on their parents to make the correct

decision and they do not expect to see their prospective spouse until the day of the wedding. . . . The suitability of the match is decided . . . by consulting a specialist in the city or by presenting the horoscopes at the village temple and soliciting an opinion from the village gods. . . . The money sent to the bride's family at the time of the formal engagement is used to purchase dowry items. Thus, it is not really a bride price because the young couple receive it back again in the form of household goods and clothing that maintain them for the first few years of their marriage.

Another study examined Chinese marriage in a nontraditional context. Anthropologist Lydia Kung reported data from a survey of factory girls in Taiwan living in dormitories away from parental authority. None of the girls surveyed expected to decide independently whom they would marry, and nearly 20 percent expected their parents would decide for them. The remaining 80 percent thought they might choose themselves and then request their parents' permission (Kung 1983).

With so much emphasis on contracts, transfers of wealth, and legal rights, our discussion of marriage may seem to have ignored what most North Americans feel is the essence of marriage: love and commitment between two people. In fact, North American marriage patterns *are* different from those in most of the world. In the West people feel marriage rests on love, and many people feel that the love and support they enjoy in marriage is the foundation of their entire lives. In other societies, however, women often feel that love may develop in marriage but is not a requirement before marriage; this is the case in traditional China.

Even in North America, where romantic love is heavily stressed, love is only one element of marriage. Marriage is a legal contract that must be recognized by the state. While financial exchanges are not normally part of marriages, middle- and upper-class Americans, especially the parents of the bride, often expend large sums on wedding festivities. Weddings support a large industry composed of caterers, photographers, musicians, dressmakers, and other specialists. While Americans often state that they "married for love," most Americans marry within their own social, religious, and ethnic groups. They choose partners acceptable to their families and give consideration to the prestige and earning potential of their future spouses.

While the institutions surrounding marriage are highly diverse, nearly all societies regulate marriage as an exchange of valuable goods, of labor power, and of reproductive services. In many societies, children born to unmarried women suffer serious consequences. They may, for example, be ostracized by others or be ineligible to inherit property from their fathers. The broadest definition of marriage, then, is one that recognizes its social, contractual, and economic nature.

FAMILY AND HOUSEHOLD

The **family** is a useful unit for comparing societies. It can be defined as the smallest kinship unit in a society. A kinship group is a social unit based on a metaphor of biological relatedness. The metaphor of relatedness is not equivalent to biological relatedness for two reasons. The first is that people can belong to families without any biological tie. A common example is an adopted child or anyone who marries into a family. The second is that societies have different ideas about relatedness. The Mehinaku of Brazil, for example, believe that a child is descended from all the men who had intercourse with the mother but not from the mother herself (Gregor 1985, 88). Families, then, are part of a class of kinship groups that are based on the idea of biological relatedness. They are not necessarily biological units; rather, they are social units based on cultural rules.

---

dowry   Compensation from the family of the bride to the family of the groom, or to the groom himself, for taking on the responsibility for the bride's welfare.

bilateral cross-cousin marriage   The exchange of spouses in marriage between two descent groups in which one ideally marries a cross-cousin.

family   A social unit based on a metaphor of consanguinity (blood relations) and affinity (marriage relations).

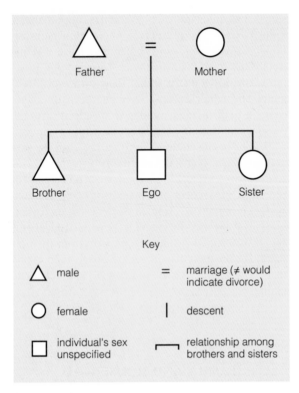

Figure 14.3 *Kinship diagram of a nuclear family. Although the nuclear family is a common form, many other family forms and arrangements exist.*

The most common form of the family is the **nuclear family**. This is a unit consisting of one or two parents and their dependent children (Figure 14.3). The nuclear family is universal, but only in the sense that everyone needs two parents to be born. From the perspective of social structure, the nuclear family is not universally found. In each society the basic family unit includes some relatives and excludes others. For example, the typical nuclear family of white Americans excludes grandparents. In many other societies a person's family includes grandparents. In many societies individual nuclear families are part of an **extended family**.

Not every society recognizes the nuclear family. The Mehinaku, according to their ethnographer, Thomas Gregor (1985), have no word for *family*. Nevertheless, nuclear family groups hang their hammocks near each other in the communal dwellings, and each one has a separate fireplace where they cook their food. By contrast, consider the case of the people of Ulithi, a group of small islands in the western Pacific Ocean, as described by their ethnographer, William Lessa (1966, 21):

> The nuclear family is strongly dependent in character, for it must compete with three other kin groups—the extended family, the commensal group, and the lineage. These other groups assume some of the roles of the nuclear family, which . . . often is scattered among other units for purposes of eating and sleeping. Adding to these impinging influences are the extremely common practices of adoption and remarriage. These practices cause shifting about of the personnel of the family with the result that biological members are often replaced by purely sociological ones. The result of all this is that the feeding, sheltering, training, and other services which the family provides the individual are so dissipated that his nuclear family loses much of its importance in his life. [Nuclear family] members do not always eat together even when [they live] under one roof . . . an individual may eat in a group in which there are no individuals whatsoever with whom he lives.

On the Israeli kibbutz, a collective residential and economic unit, the nuclear family is recognized, but it is primarily a group that provides identity and some companionship to offspring. On many kibbutzim, children eat, sleep, play, and learn apart from their parents from early infancy.

As a final example, let us return to the polygynous Igbo. The ideal Igbo family is a "big compound," a walled-off area with several dwellings in it. The "family" in a big compound consists of a man, his wife or wives, his unmarried daughters, his sons, and their wives and children (Figure 14.4). In big compounds, a child grows up with full siblings in the same house and half siblings next door.

Family membership, because of the biological metaphor, is an example of **ascribed status**. *Status* refers not only to differences in prestige but also to the normal behavior expected of a position in society. An ascribed status is one that could have been predicted from birth, such as being Japanese, being born deaf, or being born to a royal family. The family and other kinship ties bestow a social identity on an individual. These are characteristics recognized by others that include obligations and expectations. People may strive to acquire a certain social identity, such as cheerleader, college graduate, or merit scholar, because of the prestige it brings. People may also seek to shed a certain social identity, such as ex-convict, when it brings shame or discrimination. The social position of the family often shapes people's attitudes and interactions with each other. Americans identify important aspects of a person simply from his or her family name. The names Vanderbilt, Kennedy, and Barrymore, for example, connote wealth, political influence, and theatrical glamour, respectively.

In other societies kinship connections may determine whether a person is destined to a life of privilege and luxury or one of struggle and poverty. Even where there are no royal lineages or formal elites, kinship ties are crucial in determining the opportunities an individual will have. Some sociologists have suggested that societies that stress ascribed status based on kinship are less able to cope with change than those that are based on **achieved status,** which grows out of an individual's experiences through life.

Functions of the Family

An early theory, now discarded, held that the nuclear family had certain universal functions: legitimation and socialization of the young, provision of basic needs such as food and shelter, economic cooperation, and procreation. Anthropological research has shown that these functions can be assumed by other social units. Children can be socialized outside the family, as in some Israeli kibbutz where children are raised, fed, and housed communally. Few anthropologists today focus on discovering universal functional roles for the nuclear family. More often they are concerned with analyzing how the form of the family changes in relation to its environment.

Family ties—kinship in general—establish other aspects of social role. One important way in which

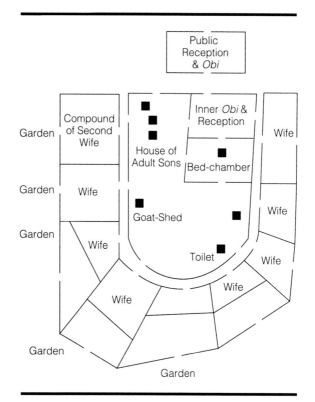

Figure 14.4 *A "big compound" of the Igbo people, housing a man, his wife or wives, his unmarried daughters, and his sons and their wives and children. Each wife has a separate hut; husbands rotate among their wives' huts. For most purposes, an individual considers the family to be all the people who live within the walls of the compound.*

this occurs is **inheritance.** Nearly every society has rules of inheritance. These rules determine how property, such as cattle, cash, houses, land, stocks and bonds, and many other valuable goods, passes down from person to person or from group to group. Not only property but also titles, membership in groups, political leadership, and specialized roles, such as healer, can be transmitted through inheritance.

---

nuclear family A type of family consisting of one or both parents and their coresident offspring.

extended family A family unit consisting of segments larger than a single nuclear family.

ascribed status A position in a social structure that can be predicted from birth, such as nobility.

achieved status A position in a social structure that is determined by life experiences.

inheritance Rules that determine how property, titles, leadership positions, and so on are to be handed down from one individual to another or from group to group.

Figure 14.5 *A family shrine in China. The eldest son in a traditional Chinese family is responsible for maintaining the ancestral hall dedicated to the memory of his ancestors in the male line. The family that worships in this hall forms a corporation that jointly owns the hall and possibly other assets such as land. The eldest son is the manager and chief custodian of the hall and its assets.*

Family and kinship rules also prescribe obligations for the individual. For example, some Igbo are born to be "slaves" while others are "freeborn." Today, there is no actual slavery among the Igbo, but the slaves can marry only within the slave group. Other kinship obligations involve ritual observances, such as maintaining an ancestral shrine, which is the responsibility of the eldest son in a Chinese family (Figure 14.5).

Anthropologists do not think of families as social units recognized by every society in which status is defined by metaphors of biological relatedness. Families establish and maintain role relationships that allow them to fulfill many essential functions. Families are basic units of adaptation in many societies, so they change in form and function as conditions around them change.

The Household

The **household** is a social unit defined by the activities of its members. Like the family, its composition and functions vary from one society to another. The particular activities vary in different societies, but they commonly include food preparation and consumption, construction and maintenance of shelter, nurturance and socialization of children, sleeping, and leisure activities. Households may be units of production when members work together to make a living. Often they are units of consumption when they live under a common roof and eat from a common pot. Note that *household* is an etic, or observer-oriented, term; it is defined in terms of activities. The definition we give to it may not be the same as a native informant would give.

Households usually consist of family groups, and the household typically occupies a single dwelling unit, but there are exceptions. Adult men of the Mundurucu society of central Brazil, for example, do not take meals, sleep, or spend most of their time in the houses where their wives and children live. They live in a central facility that functions as a men's clubhouse.

The **developmental cycle** of a household is the pattern of changes through which households move as their members pass through life stages and different roles connected with those stages. The developmental cycle of a typical middle-class family in the United

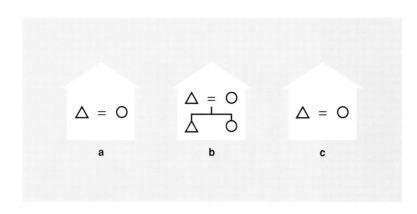

Figure 14.6 *The developmental cycle of a typical American middle-class family. In the first stage, a couple marries and establishes a separate dwelling (a). Next, the couple has children (here, a son, △, and a daughter, ○) who live with them for 18 to 22 years (b). When the children leave home, the couple is once again alone in the household (c). In recent years there has been an increase in the number of single-parent households with children and in nonfamily households in the United States, partly as a result of high divorce rates.*

States is shown in Figure 14.6. In a stable society, these cycles are repetitive, and at any moment in time different households in the same society are at different stages in the cycle. Households are woven into the fabric of society as threads in a larger whole. They are sensitive indicators of social change. Changes in social roles within households or changes in the developmental cycle itself may reflect long-term changes in the society at large.

Anthropologist Thomas Arcury (1984) studied the changing composition of households in Ridge County, Kentucky (a pseudonym), using census data from 1900 to 1980. Arcury wanted to test the hypothesis that industrialization and urbanization lead to simpler households. Arcury could not identify specific households across the 80-year gap, but he could examine aggregate changes in kinds of households at the two dates.

In 1900 most of the population of Ridge County was involved in growing food for home consumption, **barter**, and sale. Gradually the economy of the county was linked to the growing regional and national economies by improved communication and the rising importance of commercial exchange. By 1960 most of the workers were still farming, but farm output was

oriented more toward sale than home consumption. In the mid-1960s the first factories were built in Ridge County, and the welfare of people was linked to government income maintenance programs such as Social Security. In 1980 farming was a primary occupation of only 25 percent of the work force, while employment in commerce, manufacturing, and service industries had grown to over 60 percent. In other words, Ridge County had become more tightly tied to the national economic system, and its economy had become more complex.

Arcury's data indicates that industrialization and integration into the national economy led to shrinkage in household size and complexity. Arcury suggested that differences between 1900 and 1980 reflect changes in the developmental cycle of the household. Arcury used age of the household head as an indicator of stage in developmental cycle (Figure 14.7). In 1900 the proportion of complex family households increased with the age of the household head. Arcury suggests that in 1900 young families tended to start out on their own as nuclear families. As they developed, grew older, and acquired wealth, many developed into complex families with more than one married couple under one roof. In the 45–54 age bracket,

household A social unit defined by a variable combination of common activities, including coresidence, economic production, food preparation and consumption, construction and maintenance of shelter, and nurturance and socialization of children.

developmental cycle A pattern of changes that a household experiences as its members go through life stages and changes in social roles.

barter The exchange of goods or services without the use of money.

Figure 14.7 *Changes in the developmental cycle of households in Ridge County, Kentucky, between 1900 and 1980. Broad social and economic changes occurring in the region were reflected in changes in the size and complexity of individual households. Complex households were much less common in 1980 than in 1900.*

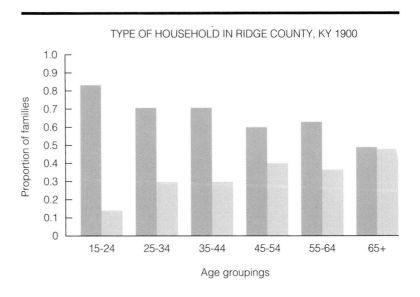

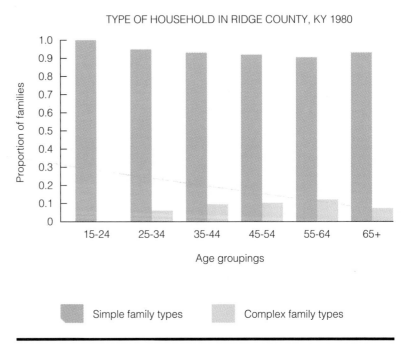

about 40 percent of the households are complex. In the next age bracket, 55–64, the number declines, probably as a result of married children moving out of their parents' homes. In the highest age bracket the proportion of complex families increases again, perhaps as older people move in with their children in their retirement years. In 1980 the tendency to form complex households is much lower; the developmental cycle has been simplified, reflecting the greater autonomy of nuclear family households in a service industry–oriented economy, as opposed to a rural agricultural economy.

The example illustrates how households respond to social and economic changes in the greater society. Viewing social change from the perspective of the household allows us to see how economic and political change influences the lives of ordinary people. Like cells in a living organism, households are a basic unit, or building block, of society. They are often structured by the emic rules of kinship. Households are also linked to other units and social groups and to political and economic currents, adapting to changes in the larger society.

Postmarital Residence Patterns

The prohibition of incest and rules of exogamy lead people to look outside the family for mates. This encourages the formation of new households. As children grow older, find mates, and begin families of their own, they form new households or add to existing ones. Every society has rules or preferences about how households are to be set up. These are **postmarital residence rules** that express a preference or requirement for where marriage partners will reside after marriage. Actual **residence patterns** depend on the availability of housing and other factors and may deviate from the prevailing residence rules. In many societies, people recognize a residence rule specifying where a couple ought to live after marriage. A residence pattern, on the other hand is the observed distribution of marriage partners. Some residence patterns are fixed for life, while others change as the marriage partners mature and have children.

Patrilocal residence is a pattern in which the couple lives with or near the husband's family. This is the preferred rule in traditional Chinese society. When a woman marries, she typically resides with her husband's family. Together with her husband and other in-laws of her husband's generation, she falls under the authority of her father-in-law (Figure 14.8).

Households organized around blood relatives of two or more generations are **stem families**. When the male head of household dies, his surviving sons may elect to go on living as a **joint patrilocal extended family**. More often they will decide to split up the household, with each brother going off with his wife, unmarried daughters, sons, and daughters-in-law. The patrilocal household reproduces itself in this way. Ethnologist George P. Murdock compiled a list of 858 societies around the world that have been ethnographically described (Table 14.1). Of that list, more than two-thirds are patrilocal.

Matrilocal residence occurs when the couple lives with or near the wife's family (see Figure 14.8). The western Apache, who live on a reservation in Arizona, are matrilocal. A single nuclear family household lives in a spot known by the Apache as a *gowa*. What distinguishes the Apache pattern as matrilocal is that the gowa are clustered into groups of related women known as *gota*. J. B., an Apache, described his family history to anthropologist Keith Basso (1986):

> When I got married, I moved to where my wife was living with her parents. We stayed there for about one year but it was too crowded. Then my wife's mother said we should live where my wife's sister used to live [a gowa about 75 yards away]. After we came to this place, I used to get homesick for where my own people lived down the creek. I used to go down there a lot. . . . Now I am used to living up here. It's a pretty good place and my children like it. Now I am like one of these people around here and I only go back when someone dies or they sing for someone who is sick.

Although the matrilocal rule appears to be a simple opposite of the patrilocal rule, there is an important social difference. In patrilocal households women marry in from outside, and the male household head exercises authority through his sons and grandsons. In matrilocal households men marry in from the outside, and the core of the household is a group of re-

---

postmarital residence rules An ideal pattern governing where marriage partners will live after marriage.

residence patterns The actual patterns of postmarital residence, which may be different from a society's postmarital residence rules.

patrilocal residence A social pattern in which marriage partners live with or near the family of the groom.

stem families Households organized around two or more generations of consanguines (blood relatives).

joint patrilocal extended family A pattern in which brothers, their wives, and their children live together as a household.

matrilocal residence A social pattern in which marriage partners live with or near the family of the bride.

362

Figure 14.8 *Postmarital residence patterns vary from one society to another. In the patrilocal extended family pattern, typical of Chinese families, a new couple lives with the husband's family. In the symbolic representation of this pattern, the family consists of a husband and wife, their unmarried daughters, their sons, and their sons' wives and children. In the matrilocal extended family pattern, typical of Navaho families, a new couple lives with the wife's family. In the symbolic representation of this pattern, the family consists of a husband and wife, their unmarried sons, their daughters, and their daughters' husbands and children.*

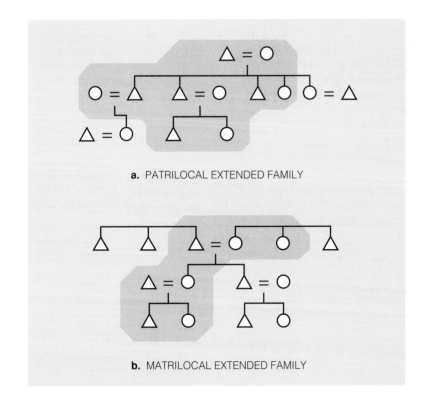

a. PATRILOCAL EXTENDED FAMILY

b. MATRILOCAL EXTENDED FAMILY

Table 14.1 Prevailing Rules of Residence in a Worldwide Sample

Rule	Number	Percentage
Patrilocality	588	68.5
Matrilocality	112	13.0
Neolocality	40	4.7
Other	118	13.8
Total	858	100.0

Source: Murdock 1967.

lated women. Women in matrilocal systems may be influential, but in most cases it is still a male—usually the husband of the senior female—who has the most authority.

The prevalent residence rule in North America and Europe is **neolocal residence**; that is, a couple establishes a residence independent of both bride's and groom's families. While neolocal residence is the preferred pattern in the United States, there is a minor tendency for couples who cannot afford the ideal of a home of their own to live with or near the bride's family. This is an example of a contradiction between the prevailing rule of residence and the actual pattern.

Why do some societies favor one form of residence over another? The most popular explanation is that residence follows gender lines in the division of labor. If men are the primary contributors to subsistence, residence is patrilocal; if women are primary, residence is matrilocal. The underlying model is social cooperation. If women are the primary contributors to subsistence, it will be helpful to have a group of cooperating women stay in the same household (or nearby). The same should be true for men.

Carol and Melvin Ember made a cross-cultural test of this hypothesis with a worldwide sample of societies. They developed a measure to determine which gender contributes the most to subsistence, and they coded a large number of societies on this variable and on postmarital residence rules. The results failed to confirm the hypothesis. Men were the main subsistence producers in patrilocal societies less often than they would have been by chance, and the same was true of women in matrilocal societies.

In spite of this failure, the Embers still felt that the division of labor by sex had some effect on residence rules. But they wondered if the effect was obscured by some other factor. They decided to examine the effect of warfare on residence. The explanatory model they developed can be summarized as follows: Unless something else interferes, men will do more subsistence labor than women. If a community is constantly at war, sometimes with close neighbors, each community will try to keep its men close by to defend it. Therefore patrilocal residence will predominate. If, however, warfare is sporadic, and the group fights only with distant enemies, men will be away from their own communities for longer periods, leaving the women behind to do subsistence work. Under these conditions the sexual division of labor will determine the residence rule.

To test the model, the Embers distinguished between societies who fight against neighbors and societies who fight exclusively with distant outsiders. Their model predicted that neighborhood fighters would be patrilocal. Residence among outside fighters would depend on who contributed more to subsistence, the original failed hypothesis. Table 14.2 shows that the cross-cultural data in their sample support their model.

In nearly every known society men are the main fighters, or soldiers. If we assume that men prefer to fight alongside close male relatives, matrilocality poses a problem because it tends to draw men away from their relatives into their wives' families. On the other hand, if related men are scattered among different households or communities, it could be easier to mobilize different households and communities against a common external enemy.

neolocal residence A social pattern in which marriage partners select their residence independently of the partners' family location.

Table 14.2   Type of Warfare and Residence Patterns*

| | Residence Pattern | |
Type of Warfare	Matrilocal	Patrilocal
Purely external	5	3
Internal	1	24

*A cross-cultural test of the relationship between warfare and residence. The numbers are societies coded as either matrilocal or patrilocal and on two patterns of warfare. The distribution of cases is highly unlikely to be due to chance and lies in the predicted direction. The data tend to support Ember and Ember's hypothesis.

Source: Ember and Ember 1971.

DESCENT RULES AND DESCENT GROUPS

A **descent rule** is a belief about how people are related and how different kinds of relatives are classified. **Unilineal descent** rules mark off connections between people related only through males or only through females. Some societies have nonunilineal, or **cognatic**, descent rules. A common form of cognatic descent is **bilateral descent**. Familiar to Europeans and Americans, this form is one in which a person traces descent equally through both the male and female line.

Of the two unilineal forms, the **patrilineal descent** rule states that people are related to each other through males. **Matrilineal descent** occurs where people trace descent through females. Women are part of patrilineages but they are not considered in tracing kinship links. The same is true of men in matrilineages. Two women can be patrilineal relatives, if for example, they are daughters of brothers. Their children are not patrilineally related. See Figure 14.9 for a comparison of the two descent forms.

Descent rules define how a society transmits property, status, personal names, social obligations, and other things from one generation to another. In the Trobriand Islands, for example, a boy inherits goods from his mother's brother, who, in their matrilineal system, is closer to the boy than his own father. The rules are not always consistent. In the United States,

surnames are usually transmitted patrilineally, while property is transmitted bilaterally. This means that most Americans inherit their father's surname, but they inherit property from both father and mother.

Descent Ideologies and Residence Rules

Unilineal descent **ideologies** probably have a basis in residence rules. A matrilocal descent pattern brings people related to each other through women together in the same place (see Figure 14.8). Households consist of related females, their husbands, and other unmarried males (brothers and sons). This means that the core of the household or local group is formed only by female consanguines. Patrilocal residence has a similar effect, except that it groups males together. The overwhelming majority of patrilineal societies have patrilocal residence, and most of the matrilocal societies have matrilineal descent.

Some additional factor is probably responsible for the formation of unilineal descent groups. There is some evidence that unilineal descent arose in situations characterized by unilocal residence and competition for resources. Unilineal descent is one convenient way of determining who may or may not have rights to some important resource, such as land, water, or cattle. Unilocal groups may arise where fighting is prevalent among different communities; according to a study by Ember, Ember, and Pasternak (1974), groups in this situation are more likely to have unilineal descent rules.

Descent Groups: Lineages, Clans, and Kindreds

Anthropologists usually classify descent groups according to the way an individual traces his or her kinship to others. This individual is referred to as "ego" and represents a typical individual in the society. Lineages are descent groups whose members can trace a relationship to common ancestors according to a specific descent rule. **Clans** are descent groups whose members claim descent from a common ancestor but are unable to trace the linkage. Lineages and clans are sociocentric because they can be recognized as distinct social groups. A descent group that owns or controls property is a **corporate descent group**.

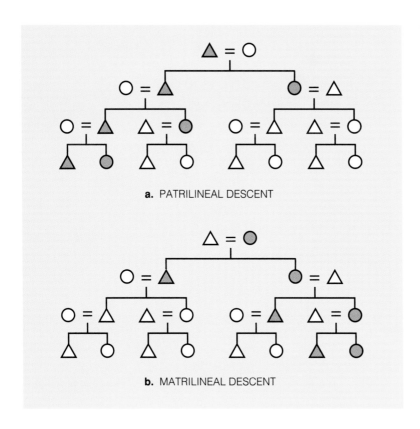

a. PATRILINEAL DESCENT

b. MATRILINEAL DESCENT

Figure 14.9 *Symbolic representations of two descent forms. In matrilineal descent, people are related through the female line to a common ancestor; only those who are in this line of descent are considered to belong to the same kin group. The same rule applies in patrilineal descent, except that people are related through the male line.*

Even when people trace kinship links, there is almost always some judicious pruning of the family tree. A genealogy collected from an informant will conveniently leave out individuals—criminals and idiots, for example—whom the informant prefers to forget. Ethnographer Napoleon Chagnon has described how his Yanomamo informants sometimes disguise or omit certain features of their genealogies. Sometimes this is to avoid leaving the appearance that someone is in an incestuous relationship. Since the Yanomamo intermarry a great deal, there are different ways a person can trace a relationship to another person.

Segmentary societies are large populations in which all the descent groups are linked by descent. These are societies in which the lowest level descent groups can all trace their relationship to each other by going back through enough ascending links. For ex-

---

descent rule A belief about how people are related and how different kinds of relatives are classified.

unilineal descent A descent ideology that traces relations through either male or female ancestors.

cognatic descent Nonunilineal descent.

bilateral descent A form of cognatic descent in which kinship may be reckoned equally through male and female ancestors.

patrilineal descent A form of unilineal descent in which kinship is reckoned through males and children belong to the kin group of their fathers.

matrilineal descent A form of unilineal descent in which kinship is reckoned through females and children belong to the kin group of their mothers.

ideology A set of beliefs that express the goals and standards of a society or social class.

clans Descent groups whose members claim descent from a common ancestor, although they may be unable to trace the specific linkages.

corporate descent group A descent group that owns or controls property.

segmentary societies Populations in which all the groups are linked by descent principles.

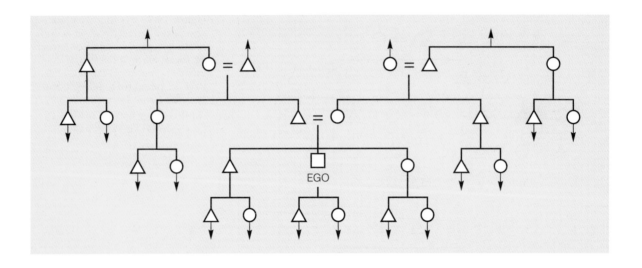

◄ **Figure 14.10** *A kindred is an ego-centered group whose membership changes as an individual proceeds through the life span, gaining and losing relatives through birth, death, and marriage. The large family reunion is an example of a bilateral kindred group in which people trace descent through both parents.*

ample, in a segmentary society there might be four clans: Turtle, Eagle, Wolf, and Bear. The Turtles and Eagles both claim descent from a distant ancestor, Thunder, while Wolf and Bear claim Black Rock as their ancestor. Thunder and Black Rock, according to legend, were brothers. By reaching back far enough in time, it is possible to mobilize large segments of a society to confront a common enemy. Thus, in a dispute between a Turtle and an Eagle, two clans are pitted against each other, while in a dispute between an Eagle and a Wolf, two pairs of clans might become parties to the dispute. In a dispute between a Wolf and someone from another tribal group, all the clans would unite against the common enemy. Anthropologist Marshall Sahlins (1961) suggested that segmentary societies are more successful in warfare against other groups because of this ability.

Other kinship groups are **egocentric** because they define themselves in relation to a specific individual. Whenever people trace descent bilaterally, each individual possesses a unique **kindred.** Kindreds cannot be organized by unilineal descent. Kindreds are ego-oriented rather than ancestor-oriented. My kindred consists of my parents, aunts, uncles, cousins, children, and grandchildren, and perhaps other relatives. No one else (except my brothers and sisters) has the same kindred as I.

Kindreds may appear to be similar to sociocentric kinship groups. Kindreds like the "Kennedy clan" are not true clans in the anthropological sense but rather bilateral kinship groups centered around the late President John F. Kennedy and his siblings (Figure 14.10). Because he and his siblings were so prominent in American life, they have a unique social identity as a family. If you are a North American, you can imagine

how a kindred is defined if you consider how difficult it is to decide whom to invite to a family reunion. There are no rules telling you to invite your mother's or your father's relatives. Your choice would probably depend on your personal preferences, where you live, whom you see frequently, and so on.

Where there are unilineal descent groups, the situation is quite different. In the late 19th century, the western Apache consisted of five subtribal groups each within territorial boundaries. Within each subtribe there were two to four bands (or camp groups) encompassing 50 to 750 members with rights to farmland and hunting territory. The band was also a political unit under the leadership of a chief who led it in raiding, food-gathering expeditions, and farming. Bands contained local groups composed of several *gota,* a large matrilocal extended family. The gota consisted of up to a dozen nuclear families, each of which included a woman related as a daughter or sister of an older woman in the group. These women constituted a matrilineage, the core of the family cluster. Husbands of these women married in from other groups.

Even though membership in the Apache lineage was reckoned in the female line, leadership was always in male hands. Each gota had its headman, usually an outsider who had married in. Western Apache lineages were linked together into clans. Clan members believed they shared common (female) ancestors, but they could not actually trace the relationship. The 62 western Apache clans had no territorial base; each was scattered across the Apache country. The Apache required all marriages to be outside the clan. Beyond marriage regulation, clans functioned primarily in large-scale ceremonial contexts such as burials.

An Apache informant born in the 1850s gave a vivid impression of how the system worked. His words were taken down by anthropologist Greenville Goodwin in the 1930s (quoted in Basso 1986, 11).

Over at Ash Flat where I was born, I used to live. This was before the White soldiers came. . . . When I was growing up, my mother told me I had many relatives from all over this country, but I guess I didn't think

---

egocentric Pertaining to a kinship group that defines itself in relation to a specific individual (ego) rather than an ancestor.

kindred A kinship group that is unique to each individual and her or his siblings.

about it. Then when I was six years old, my mother's brother, a chief, got sick and died. It was winter when he died, but right away everyone from around the camp where we lived came to the place. [Some people said], "It is not right to bury that man now. Right now, in places far from here, his relatives are getting ready to come here. We should wait to bury him so his relatives can see him."

In the morning some *iya'aiye* [a clan name] came in. These people were of my uncle's clan, my clan. First there were some men on horses and, after that, women. They were walking and carrying baskets with food. . . . On the same day, many people came from the north. Some of these were *iya'aiye,* but mostly they were *kiya'an* and *tu'agaidn* [clans in the same collection of related clans as *iya'aiye*].

Pretty soon there were lots of people there. Many I had never seen and some of the men looked mean and made me afraid. I told my mother, but she said: "No, don't be scared. These people are your relatives and that is why they have come here. Even though they are not living with us, they have come to help us out."

The next day some other people came—maybe 100 of them. There were *iya'aiye* with them but most of them, I think were *dzctadn* and *tlukadgaidn* [clans related to ego's]. Three of those women began to cry and yell. "Our brother is dead, has gone away." After my uncle was buried, all those people stayed at Ash Flat for two days. They helped make food for our people who lived there. Then they went back to their own camps. Some had a long way to go. After that, I knew I had relatives from all over this country. I saw many of them after I grew up. It was that way. If someone was in trouble or needed help his relatives would come a long way to help them out. And he would try to do that for them.

This story makes it clear that the Apache felt that the chief ought to be buried by his matrilineal kin. The informant did not know the extent of his clan and related clans until after his uncle, the chief and part of his matrilineage, had died. He also learned about the obligations that clan members had to each other. The Cibecue Apache are still matrilocal, and nonlocalized matrilineal clans and the gota are still significant social units among the Cibecue Apache as described by Keith Basso in the 1970s. What has changed are the bands with their distinct territories.

We can best understand descent as a set of beliefs (an ideology) based on a biological metaphor of kinship. It is a major aspect of the organization of society, especially in societies with unilineal descent groups. Until recently many anthropologists taught that simple societies were structured primarily by kinship and that kinship was not a major feature in the organization of complex societies. This generalization is no longer readily accepted. There are many small-scale societies that possess important non-kin-based institutions such as age grades, ceremonial societies, and warrior societies, which we explore in Chapter 15. There are also complex civilizations, such as China, where kinship is an important determinant of status and role. Descent groups may be egalitarian without major divisions in wealth and prestige. However, in other cases—again, China is a good example—there may be major differences in wealth and prestige within a descent group. These matters are discussed further in Chapter 18.

KINSHIP TERMINOLOGY

Kinship terminologies are a kind of egocentric status terminology used to refer to relatives in a kinship system. **Kin terms** are terms used in actual speech by people referring to relatives. A kin term may refer to a specific relative, as in the English term *mother*. Most kin terms refer to more than one relative. The English term *uncle* can refer to a consanguine (such as father's brother) or to an **affine** (someone related by marriage). Anthropologists use a standard "grid" of **kin types** (a relative standing in a particular relation to ego, such as "mother's sister") to describe the range of relatives to which a given term applies. This grid is largely independent of the specific cultural context. We will use the abbreviated notation presented in Box 14.1 to refer to kin types. The English kin term *uncle* refers to the following kin types: MB, FB, MZH, FZH. In English all these relatives are "equated" or subsumed under a single kin term. **Terms of reference** are those used by ego when referring to relatives in the third person. Examples are "mother, father, grandmother." **Terms of address** are those used to speak directly to the relative. Examples are "Mom, Dad, Grandma."

To collect kinship terminologies, ethnographers use the genealogical method. First the interviewer asks an informant to list as many relatives as possible. The ethnographer records all the names and the relationship to ego, then asks what kin term the inform-

---

BOX 14.1

Kin Types and Kin Terms

Rather than ordinary English terms such as *sister* or *husband,* anthropologists use the following set of abbreviations to designate the relationships known as kin types.

These terms allow for greater descriptive precision; they can also be combined to refer to other relatives. Father's sister, for example, is abbreviated as FZ. The corresponding English kin term is *aunt.* Keep in mind, however, that these abbreviations are used to specify a genealogical relationship to ego; they do not refer to terms as they are used in everyday speech.

M = mother

F = father

S = son

D = daughter

B = brother (ego's MS and/or FS)

Z = sister (ego's MD and/or FD)

O = older than ego

Y = younger than ego

H = husband

W = wife

---

ant uses for each of them. Suppose ego calls his MZD "Jessica" and refers to her as his "cousin." The procedure must be repeated with several informants, because a single family rarely possesses all possible kintypes. Informants sometimes disagree with each other, particularly about remote kintypes. Americans, for example, may disagree about what to call an FBSS. Some will say, "second cousin." Others will say, "first cousin, once removed."

Meaning of Kinship Terms

Anthropologists have been studying kinship terms for over 100 years, since Lewis Henry Morgan, a lawyer turned anthropologist, collected kinship terms from societies across the world. Morgan thought that kinship terms reflected different forms of marriage that represented stages in the evolution of society. Although he was mistaken in many details, his work still inspires important research today.

Morgan's fundamental discovery was that kinship terms form coherent systems with an underlying logic. He focused particularly on **terminological equations** (different kin types grouped under the same term, such as FZD and MBD, which are both *cousins* in English). We analyze these systems in terms of models that help us understand the properties of the system. Models need to be compared to actual behavior to determine whether they are helpful in understanding how people think and behave with their relatives.

---

kinship terminologies Egocentric status terminologies used to refer to relatives in a kinship system.

kin terms Labels used by people of a particular society in actual speech to refer to or to address their relatives, such as "Mother," "Dad," "Uncle."

affine A person who is related by marriage.

kin type An etic label used by anthropologists to describe a specific relative in relation to ego; for example, "mother's brother."

terms of reference Kin terms used by ego to refer to relatives in the third person.

terms of address Kin terms used by ego when speaking directly to relatives.

terminological equations Different kintypes subsumed under the same kin term. For example, Yankee terminology equates MB, FB, MZH, and FZH by referring to them as *uncle.*

Figure 14.11   *The Chinese-American detective Charlie Chan, a popular movie character in the 1930s, was often assisted in solving crimes by his "number one son." The term is actually a rough translation of the Mandarin Chinese kinship term* da er zhi, *referring to the firstborn male child.*

Some anthropologists believe that kinship terminologies are clues to attitudes and behavior. Others think that kin terms hold the clue to the rights and obligations a person holds in society. A third group of anthropologists think that kinship terminologies reflect little more than the human tendency to lump some things together and split others apart, in short, the urge to classify things. This last point of view is represented by ethnologist Alfred Kroeber, who discovered a series of eight **binary** distinctions that could be used to describe virtually all known kinship terminologies. Each terminological system falls on one side

or another of a two-sided distinction. The distinctions are (1) generation (same as ego or other), (2) lineal versus collateral, (3) difference of age (older or younger than ego), (4) sex of relative, (5) sex of ego, (6) sex of linking relative, (7) consanguineal versus affinal, (8) condition of life (living or dead). Every known kinship terminology can be analyzed and classified according to its position on each of these distinctions.

Let us illustrate with an example from Chinese kinship terminology, which observes the relative age of a kin compared to ego. Mandarin Chinese, for example,

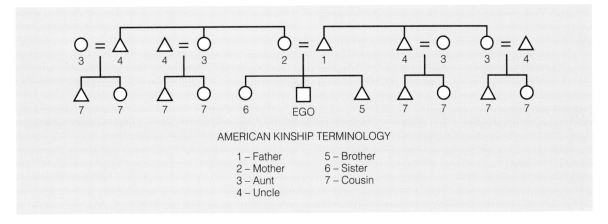

Figure 14.12 *Lumping and splitting in American kinship terminology. Some kin types have a unique kin term, such as father (indicated by 1 in this diagram) or sister (indicated by 6). Others are lumped together under a classifying term, such as aunt (3) or cousin (7).*

distinguishes between a firstborn son ("Da Er Zhi") and a second-born son ("Er Er Zhi") (Figure 14.11). These differences are important in Chinese families, because older sons traditionally have considerable authority over their younger brothers. Most European terminologies, including English, do not observe this distinction.

Another binary pair is the difference between **lineal** and **collateral** relatives. Lineal relatives are those in ego's direct line of descent, that is grandparents, parents, children, and grandchildren. Collaterals are blood relatives who are not in ego's direct line, such as uncles, aunts, cousins, nieces, and nephews. Some terminologies, such as the Yanomamo's, override the lineal-collateral distinction by referring to some lineal kin types by the same terms as collaterals. The Yanomamo use the same term for father and father's

brother, for example. Other terminologies, such as English, distinguish between lineal and collateral relatives.

Types of Kinship Terminologies

Let us look briefly at some of the principal features of some of the major types of kinship terminologies. American English kinship terminology is known as **Yankee** or **Eskimo** because its pattern is the same as the Inuit terminology. Like all kinship terminologies, Yankee lumps some kin types and splits others. For example, the Yankee term *cousin* lumps together FBD, FBS, FZD, FZS, MBD, MBS, MZD, MZS (Figure 14.12). On the other hand, some terms refer to a single individual, such as *father, mother, wife, husband,*

---

binary Based on sets of twos.

lineal Related to ego through a direct line of descent or ascent, as grandparents, parents, children, and grandchildren.

collateral Related to ego but not through a direct line of descent or ascent, as uncles, aunts, cousins, nieces, and nephews.

Yankee terminology A pattern of kinship terminology used by North American English speakers, Eskimos and many Europeans—that distinguishes lineal and collateral relatives and equates collaterals on the mother's and father's sides.

Eskimo terminology Kinship system similar to Yankee terminology.

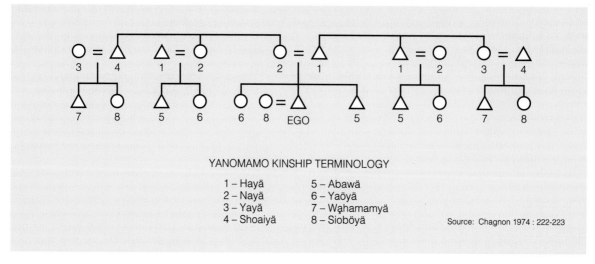

YANOMAMO KINSHIP TERMINOLOGY

1 – Hayä	5 – Abawä
2 – Nayä	6 – Yaöyä
3 – Yayä	7 – Wạhamamyä
4 – Shoaiyä	8 – Sioböyä

Source: Chagnon 1974 : 222-223

Figure 14.13 *Yanomamo kinship terminology. Lumping and splitting in this system follows the pattern known as Iroquois. Lineal and collateral kin, such as father and father's brother, are classified together and identified by the same kin term. Similarly, siblings and parallel cousins are lumped together and referred to by the same term.*

mother-in-law, and *father-in-law.* The pattern of lumping and splitting provides a kind of map of how people divide up genealogical space. In Yankee terminology, lineal and collateral relatives are always distinguished. Collaterals on ego's mother's side are lumped with those on father's side. These features are consistent with a society with bilateral kinship in which the nuclear family is set apart from other kin. Yankee kinship treats kin on mother's and father's sides as equals. Nuclear families are the predominant household form, and family-managed resources are relatively uncommon. The isolation of the nuclear family and lineals in general is mirrored by the terminology. Collaterals are highly aggregated on both mother's and father's sides, reflecting the relative unimportance of the extended family in North American society. Yankee terminology also occurs among speakers of French, German, and Spanish, although there are some differences.

For a contrast, let us examine the kinship terminology of the Yanomamo of Venezuela and Brazil. Yanomamo live in villages of up to 250 people, usually dominated by two exogamous patrilineages that intermarry. The Yanomamo practice **preferential cross-cousin marriage.** This means a Yanomamo man considers his FZD or his MBD to be a potential wife. Indeed, a man calls these kin types by the same term used for *wife* (*sîböyä*). Likewise a Yanomamo woman refers to her FZS or MBS by the term *husband* (Figure 14.13). The Yanomamo kinship terminology follows a pattern of lumping and splitting known as **Iroquois** and found in dozens of different societies.

Yanomamo terminology also overrides the lineal-collateral distinction. F, FB, and MZH are all called by the same term, and M, MZ, and FBW are, too. The ethnographer Napoleon Chagnon explains this as follows (1977, 88):

> [P]eople can stand in a child relationship to a number of individuals; that is, it is possible to have multiple "mothers" and "fathers" in Yanomamo society. The term for mother and father conveys as much of a social as a biological relationship between individuals and in the daily activities of the Yanomamo it is the social implications of the kinship roles that are most important.

When we look at ego's own generation, we see that there are basically two sets of terms. One set, *Abawä* and *Yaöyä,* refers to ego's own sister and brother and

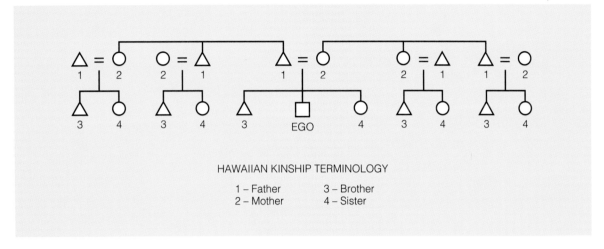

Figure 14.14 *The Hawaiian kinship system. Kin types are distinguished mainly by generation.*

to ego's parallel cousins (FBS, FBD, MZS, MZD). One way of interpreting this is by the logic of the system itself. Since ego calls MZ and FB by the same terms as M and F, it follows that ego calls their children by same terms as B and Z.

Another way of understanding this equation is to consider the descent and marriage system in which exogamous patrilineages (or matrilineages) regularly exchange spouses with each other (bilateral cross-cousin marriage). For convenience, let us label the lineages "Mason" and "Dixon." Every Mason will have a Mason father and a Dixon mother. A Mason woman will marry a Dixon man and their children will be Dixons. From the point of view of any individual, the world is divided into us and them, Mason and Dixon. Thinking of the system in these terms helps us understand the articulation of the kinship terminology, de-

scent groups, and marriage preferences. Ego calls FBS "brother" and FBD "sister," because they belong to the same patrilineage as ego. MZS and MZD are also called "brother" and "sister," because their father is likely to be from the same lineage as ego's. Carried out for several generations, this system will produce balanced exchange between two lineages.

There are several other major types of kinship terminologies that lump and split kin types in different ways. They are named for one of the societies in which the particular system prevailed. The **Hawaiian** pattern (Figure 14.14) lumps virtually all of ego's blood relatives, distinguishing only by generation. At another extreme, **Sudanese** (Figure 14.15) distinguishes between nearly every possible kin type. Mandarin Chinese belongs to the Sudanese type. **Crow** (Figure 14.16) and **Omaha** (Figure 14.17) systems are com-

---

preferential cross-cousin marriage A kinship ideology in which the marriage of a man to his FZD or his MBD (or a woman to her MBS or FZS) is the preferred pattern.

Iroquois terminology A pattern of kinship terminology that equates certain lineal and collateral relatives, such as F = FB, M = MZ, and FBD = MZD.

Hawaiian terminology A pattern of kinship terminology that distinguishes kin types mainly by generation.

Sudanese terminology A pattern of kinship terminology that distinguishes many possible kin types without blurring lineals with collaterals.

Crow terminology A pattern of kinship terminology, similar to Iroquois, in which matrilineal relatives are more differentiated than patrilineal.

Omaha terminology A pattern of kinship terminology, similar to Iroquois, in which patrilineal relatives are more differentiated than matrilineal.

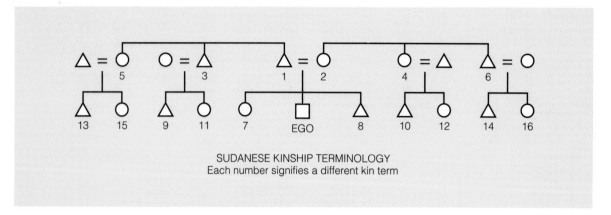

Figure 14.15   *The Sudanese kinship system. Nearly every kin type is distin-guished by a separate kin term, indicated here by different numbers.*

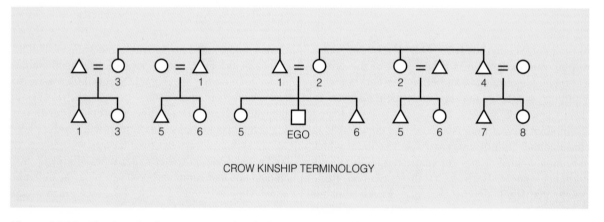

Figure 14.16   *The Crow kinship system. Matrilineal relatives are more differen-tiated than patrilineal ones.*

Figure 14.17   *The Omaha kinship system. Patrilineal relatives are more differen-tiated than matrilineal ones.*

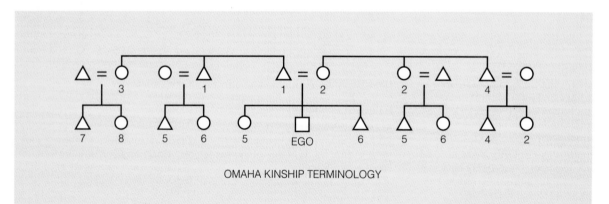

plex forms similar to Iroquois kinship that seem to occur when matrilineal or patrilineal kinship, respectively, is well developed.

The real world is not nearly as perfect as the kinship diagrams. Women do not always have a perfectly matched number of boys and girls. The underlying organization of groups may change while the kin terminological system lags behind. Many other things can upset the ideal functioning of these kinship systems. No one has ever observed a kinship system in a real village that functioned exactly like the model on the pages of a textbook.

FICTIVE KINSHIP

We have seen that kinship in human society is not a simple matter of biological relatedness. Beginning with a biological metaphor, people elaborate kinship into symbolic systems that find expression in social organization and systems of thought. **Fictive kinship**, or "ritual kinship," goes beyond the biological metaphor as a basic principle. Fictive kinship may be based on a metaphor of brotherhood, parenthood, or other kin ties. It may be established by ceremonial means or because of some connection between people, such as sharing the same name. A common form of fictive kinship found in nearly all Roman Catholic communities is **godparenthood**, known as *compadrazgo* in Spanish.

In Catholic countries, *compadrazgo* ties are formed in connection with rituals of consecration, such as baptism, confirmation, and marriage. All over southern Europe and Latin America, parents are expected to baptize their children in the church. The parents select a godfather (in Spanish, *padrino*) and a godmother (*madrina*). The godparents often provide the baptismal clothes for the child and hold it during the baptismal ceremony. Godparents are responsible for the

child's spiritual welfare and, if anything happens to the parents, they agree to adopt and care for the child. An important bond is also formed between parents and godparents. They become "coparents." In Spanish, they address each other as *compadre* or *comadre* and treat each other with special reserve and respect. The incest taboo is extended to *compadres*.

Frequently the godparents are socially or economically better off than the parents, and are chosen with that in mind. They are expected to provide support and help to the child and its parents. A godparent may help pay for the education of his or her godchild. The godparents may also benefit from the loyalty and assistance of their less fortunate *compadres*. For example, employers who become *compadres* to their workers can expect greater loyalty and hard work from them. Ritual kinship in Latin America creates special obligations among people with important social and economic dimensions. The obligations provide for an exchange of goods and services between persons who are socially and economically unequal. Thus ritual kinship in Latin America plays valuable functions supplementary to kinship.

SUMMARY

- Marriage contracts that regulate sexual access and what happens to children are practically universal, but that is about the only valid generalization about marriage.
- Anthropologically, marriage is best understood as a contract between two or more parties that regulates sex and reproduction. Only rarely is the contract made between two individuals. More often the

fictive kinship   Ritual kinship, such as godparenthood in Latin societies.

godparenthood   Known as *compadrazgo* in Spanish, a form of fictive kinship in which a person agrees to act as a coparent for a child; this status implies certain rights and obligations on the part of the child and the godparent.

contract is between families or lineages; frequently it involves religious authorities and the state. In most of the societies of the world, marriages are arranged by parents or others.

- The family is a class of social units that are conceived of as based on biological reproduction.
- There are no universal functions and there is no universal form of the family.
- Households are units defined by observers in terms of activities such as coresidence or food sharing.
- Households have developmental cycles that repeat themselves over generations.
- Households are units of adaptation, changing their form, size, and function to accommodate social and economic change.
- When residential households are formed, they tend to group certain kinds of kinfolk. There is some evidence that the basic rule of postmarital residence is determined by the pattern of warfare in a society interacting with the gender division of labor.
- The residential groupings formed by residence rules provide the basis for the development of ideologies of kinship. There is some indirect evidence that competition for resources is the additional factor responsible for the emergence of kinship ideologies.
- Kinship ideologies are beliefs and organizing principles about how people are related to each other.
- Patrilineal ideologies stress the links between males, matrilineal between females.
- Lineages, clans, and other descent groups may own property, regulate marriage, and provide reciprocal services to each other.
- Kindreds are ego-centered kinship groups in which kinship is traced bilaterally; they are rarely corporate.
- Kinship terminologies may provide clues to the functioning of kinship systems. Kinship is one of the best studied domains of culture. The study of kinship provides a unique opportunity to study social behavior in its adaptive context, as a basis for the formation of groups, as an ideology of relatedness, and as it is represented in language.

GET INVOLVED

1. Collect the kinship terminology used by persons in your environment having different native languages. Use the genealogical method, identifying by name each of the relatives known to your informant and then asking what term they use to refer to and to address that relative. See if you can analyze each of these systems in terms of one of the main terminological types presented in this chapter. What social groupings or other behavior does each terminology appear to reflect?
2. Make a genealogy of your own family, or that of a friend, going back as many generations as you can. Observe where the gaps are and attempt to explain the reasons for those gaps.
3. Make a survey of all the families currently (or recently) appearing on network television shows, such as the Huxtables ("The Cosby Show"); the Svornaks, Nylands, and Devoreaux ("Golden Girls"); the Bunkers ("All in the Family"); the Conners ("Roseanne"); and the Keatons ("Family Ties"). Make a kinship chart for each family. What trends in modern North American life are reflected in the structure of each family?

SUGGESTED READINGS

Beattie, John. 1960. *Bunyoro: An African kingdom*. New York: Holt, Rinehart and Winston.

Fox, Robin. 1983. *Kinship and marriage: An anthropological perspective*. Cambridge: Cambridge University Press.

Fraser, Thomas M. 1966. *Fishermen of South Thailand*. New York: Holt, Rinehart and Winston.

Goldstein, Melvyn C. 1987. When brothers share a wife. *Natural History* 96(3).*

Radcliffe-Brown, A. R. [1924] 1965. The mother's brother in South Africa. In *Structure and function in primitive society*. New York: Free Press.

Schneider, David. 1968. *American kinship*. Chicago: University of Chicago Press.

* This selection is anthologized in *Applying Anthropology*, 2d ed., ed. A. Podolefsky and P. J. Brown (Mountain View, Calif.: Mayfield, 1992).

ANTHROPOLOGISTS AT WORK

Family Life in Bengali Culture

Lauren Anita Corwin is an Associate Professor of Anthropology and Asian Studies at Cleveland State University. She has done research in Mahishadal and Calcutta, India, and has published many articles on Bengali life. Corwin recently adopted a Bengali child.

Lauren Corwin with her Indian "aunt."

When I was a graduate student preparing to do fieldwork in India, I associated mainly with other students of Bengali, studying the Bengali language and trying to experience as much Bengali culture as possible. We went to Bengali films and festivals together and carried out Bengali religious rituals. Our first such ritual was *rakshi bandhan,* or the brother-sister ceremony. A sister ties a shiny paper charm on her brother's wrist and he presents her with a gift. The ritual symbolizes the strength of the brother-sister bond. I tied my charm around the wrist of a Bengali graduate student, Tarasish. After that, he addressed me as "sister" and I addressed him as "elder brother."

A year later I was in Calcutta trying to set up a research project. I was having difficulties, so when I received a telegram from my advisor reading "Go to your father's house," I set out for my "elder brother's" father's house. A trip by train, bus, and cycle rickshaw brought me to a large brick house where an elderly man waited on the veranda. He greeted me, saying "Oh, daughter, you have come at last. Your mother and brothers are waiting for you." He escorted me upstairs, where I met my family.

To my surprise my "father" had already taken charge of my research. "No daughter of mine can live in a village. It is not suitable," he said. "You will study a town. I have chosen three you can choose from. We will start looking tomorrow." I opened my mouth to object, then shut it again. An unmarried Bengali female

is under the control of her father. I decided to go with the Bengali system, as it seemed unwise to go against it.

I chose the town of Mahishadal as a research site, and my father was pleased with my choice. He informed me that he had already made arrangements for me to live with a well-known town family of high status. He had also chosen a research assistant for me. And so I began to live with the Chatterji family.

Bengali kinship is patrilineally oriented, although in practice it is almost bilateral. The Chatterji household consisted of a patrilocal extended family. The head of the family was recently deceased, and since his elderly widow was still alive, I received my mail care of the late Mr. Chatterji. His son, in his 50s, was not yet head of the household. His wife and five children lived in the household. Two sisters were visiting home on a long-term basis, and a nephew also lived there. The family was a close one and they spent many hours a day together. Whenever I was not outside gathering data, I spent my time with the family.

The day began with tea at 5:00 A.M. and ended after dinner at 10:30 P.M. The household seemed to run smoothly. Children went to

school and did their homework. The grandmother read religious stories as we sat around a kerosene lantern in the evening. I was adopted into the family kinship terminology system.

Life in this joint family seemed serene. I never heard an argument or saw a child cry. But gradually I became aware that the relationship between the widow and the daughter-in-law was strained. Unkind remarks flew back and forth. Six months into my study a child was slapped for whimpering and admonished, "Careful, she will put it in her book." At that time I realized that everyone had been on special behavior because I was living there. But they could no longer suppress the tensions created by the strains of daily family life.

Now the stress broke through to the surface. The children quarreled. The widow and daughter-in-law shouted at each other, and the visiting sisters joined in. One day the daughter-in-law moved out of the house, taking the baby to a collapsed mud structure behind the house. She shouted that she preferred to live with the large python there than with her mother-in-law. After day-long negotiations, she finally came back home.

On a later occasion I saw the two brothers of another joint family in a fist fight in front of their house. I asked the Chatterji family what they thought of such behavior. They were dismayed that the fighting had taken place in public, but they acknowledged that fighting did happen. They agreed that if brothers fight, it should be inside the house, so that outsiders can't see it. That way the proper image of the family is maintained. As in my case, they were expressing the belief that the real dynamics of family life should not be allowed to tarnish the public image of the family.

Symbols of leadership come in many forms, including the red feather that Chief Fon of Cameroon in central Africa affixes to the cap of this new nobleman.

15

FOLLOWING THE LEADER

▲▲▲

In many western movies there is a scene in which an old chief addresses his people. Arms folded, staring straight ahead, the chief solemnly gives commands. The young warriors obey him unquestioningly, perhaps going into battle against incredible odds to fight soldiers or settlers. Most people who see these movies find them quite believable. They know that the characters are being portrayed by Hollywood actors, but they do not question the image of the authoritarian chief, able to command hundreds of followers. The stereotype of unquestioned authority is probably inaccurate in most cases. Father John Cooper, an ethnologist in South America, wrote, "the chief has but to give a command, and everybody does as he pleases." In *Dances with Wolves,* a popular film that aimed at authenticity and a respectful view of a tribal people of North America, the Sioux chief was shown not so much as an absolute monarch as a first among equals.

Why does it seem natural that native Americans had powerful leaders and loyal followers? Perhaps the idea arises from the biased view that tribal peoples are driven by irrational superstition and blind respect for authority. The knowledge we have of tribal societies does not support this view. Leadership, authority, and political power are relatively undeveloped in such societies. Many tribal peoples have no strong chiefs, no absolute rulers. They may have leaders but usually no supreme leader. Formal leadership may be temporary, activated only during times of war or major ceremonials. Leaders may be born to their roles, or they may acquire them through knowledge, political ability, or force. As societies become larger and more complex, political leadership takes on a different character.

Leadership may be defined as the ability a person has to influence the behavior of others, especially in matters of public concern. **Authority** is the recognition by others of a leader's right or obligation to influence them. **Power** is the ability to force others to behave in certain ways. Authority and power are variables in leadership. Not all leaders have authority, and those with authority may have little or no power. This chapter examines the different types of leadership that develop in different social and political contexts; it also looks at how leaders arise and how they lead.

EGALITARIAN LEADERSHIP

Egalitarian societies, those in which everyone has roughly equal access to power and resources, tend to have leaders with little power. They may not even recognize authority in a formal sense. This form of leadership tends to be characteristic of groups that are not settled in one place, do not defend fixed property, and have fluctuating membership. It is typical of such nomadic and foraging groups as the !Kung San and the Inuit of Canada and Alaska. In some hunting groups, there are simply no leaders.

Richard Lee wrote of the !Kung San (1979):

> I made enquiries in the Dobe area in 1964 to find out who was the headman or chief at each waterhole. The answers the people gave were almost entirely negative. The younger people didn't know who, if anyone, was the headman, and the older people were obviously puzzled by the question. . . . Finally I discussed the question with K"au, a senior /Xai/xai man. . . . "Before the Tswanas [a cattle herding people] came here," I asked, "did the San have chiefs?" "No," he replied. "We had no one we set apart like a chief; we all lived on the land." "What about /Gaun!a? Was he a chief of /Xai/xai?" I asked, citing the name of a man whom the Hereros [another cattle-raising people] had mentioned as a former San headman. "That is not true," K"au responded. "They are mistaken. Because among the Bantu the chief's village is fixed; you come to him, speak and go away. . . . But with us San, we are here today, tomorrow over there, and the next day still elsewhere. How can we have a chief leading a life like that?" . . . Years later I was speaking with /Twi!gum, one of the owners of !Kangwa [waterhole], and I casually asked him whether the !Kung have headmen. "Of course we have headmen!" he replied, to my surprise. "In fact we are all headmen," he continued slyly, "each one of us is headman over himself!" [pp. 346–348]

The !Kung San have hereditary figures who are the nominal owners of waterholes, but they have no more authority than any other family head. In fact the !Kung San, like many other egalitarian peoples, take pains not to assert themselves too strongly in public, to avoid stirring up displeasure among their comrades. You may recall from Chapter 10 how the !Kung San put down hunters who show the slightest sign of pride or arrogance.

Under such circumstances, how can the !Kung San make decisions? Every society, no matter how small and nomadic, occasionally must make some decisions. Should the local group move to a new waterhole or stay put? Should a ceremony be held? Should the group tolerate someone's antisocial behavior? Should someone try to break up a fight? How are such decisions made?

One outcome frequently observed in egalitarian groups like the !Kung San is the avoidance of decision making. The people are reticent about being assertive, and there are so few mechanisms for forcing people to do what they do not wish to do that people simply "vote with their feet," moving away to a new location and leaving the disagreement behind them.

George Silberbauer studied a group of nomadic foragers known as the G/wi who also live in the Kalahari desert of Botswana, and this is what he observed of their decision-making process (1981):

> The band is reluctant to come to a decision under the sway of strong feelings: If discussion becomes too angry or excited, debate is temporarily adjourned by the withdrawal of the attention of the calmer participants until things calm down. Withdrawal is not usually physical—to get up and move away is . . . a gesture of rejection. . . . Members signal their lack of sympathy with the heated mood by . . . [pretending to tend a] cooking fire [or pretending to extract] an invisible thorn from the sole of [the] foot. . . .
>
> Band decisions are arrived at by consensus. . . . Consensus is not unanimity of opinion or decision. [Neither is it] a synonym of democracy. . . . Consensus is arrived at after a series of judgments made by people who all have access to a common pool of information. [pp. 29–31]

The G/wi reach consensus largely because of their shared outlook on life. No chasms of belief separate them as in stratified or ethnically diverse societies. Coercion and threats have no place because people

can simply take their families, pick up their belongings, and move away at any time. In short, people do largely as they please.

People in such societies are elaborately respectful of each other and carefully observe rules of common courtesy known to everyone. Sharing is a powerful norm and envy is avoided and suppressed. When all of these mechanisms break down, the most frequent outcome is separation; people with different opinions "agree to disagree" and move off to live elsewhere with other people.

Some of the confusion about native tribal peoples arises from the imposition of leadership roles on otherwise leaderless peoples by colonial conquerors. Anthropologist Mary Shepardson used early visitors' accounts and other sources to reconstruct the traditional authority system of the Navajos of the southwestern United States. She wrote (1963):

> The traditional authority system of the Navajos before the conquest differed in important respects from the authority system that was established on the reservation. In the first place, the Conquest eliminated an important group, the raiding party with its power role of "war chief." Second, before the Conquest, members of the tribe acknowledged no external superordinate authority; afterward they were forced to. The United States Government conferred authority on headmen or chiefs who were appointed . . . to serve as contact officials with members of the tribe. [pp. 118–145]

The Big Man

In egalitarian societies where there is more differentiation, particularly where there is more property and greater competition for resources, leadership may take other forms. Ethnologist Marshall Sahlins described a kind of leader known as the **big man**, common in Melanesia and the South Pacific. The big man (Figure

---

leadership   The ability a person has to influence the behavior of others.

authority   The recognition of a leader's right or obligation to have influence on others.

power   The ability to force others to behave in certain ways.

egalitarian societies   Societies in which everyone has roughly equal access to power and resources.

big man   A form of leadership common in tribal societies in Melanesia and elsewhere. The big man is able to mobilize people for social and political ends, but his status must be validated constantly through generosity and the exercise of leadership.

Figure 15.1 *A Melanesian big man. Generosity, eloquence, and wealth are among the qualities required for leadership in this type of egalitarian society. Big men do not inherit their status and may be obliged to validate their position on a daily basis.*

mind. Philip Newman studied the Gururumba people of highland New Guinea. He wrote (1965):

> "Big men" are men of prestige and renown; men whose "names are known," as the Gururumba put it. The characteristics essential to becoming a prestigeful person include physical strength, demonstrated ability as a warrior, heading a lineage, oratorical skill, success in manipulating a rather complex system of economic exchange, an ability to determine and express group consensus, and a forcefulness or assertiveness of character exceeding that of most men. [p. 44]
>
> In the course of daily affairs, big men are not particularly noticeable. . . . Their dress is not distinctive except on ceremonial occasions when they appear in *less* resplendent costumes than other men. They wear no badge of office, do not carry any symbol of authority, nor is their place of residence distinctive. [T]hey become noticeable [in] the settlement of disputes, food exchanges, certain kinds of ritual, and discussions concerning matters affecting the group as a whole. If disputes [involve] lineages, villages, sibs, or phratries [related clans], the "big men" . . . will attempt to arrange a meeting. . . . [T]hey tend to stay in the background while the disputants in the case speak. . . . If the issue seems to be reaching an impasse, they frequently resort to long, rambling speeches full of historical illusions, generalities about their own or their group's past achievements, and references to the strength of the group. [p. 43]

Leaders in egalitarian societies like the Gururumba have no more wealth at their disposal than other people. On the contrary, they tend to live modestly and to be generous with what they have. Leopold Pospisil, who studied the Kapauku of Irian Jaya (Indonesian New Guinea), learned of a case in which a wealthy man who failed to be generous was assassinated for his selfishness (1963, 49). The Kapauku big man lends out cowrie shell money, and his debtors become part of his support group. Kapauku men use money to buy food, animals, land, and tools and to pay for ceremonials and services such as healing.

Karl Heider, writing about his study of the Grand Valley Dani of Irian Jaya, made the following observations (1979):

> What seems to characterize the important men more than anything else is their skill in manipulating the exchange system . . . the degree to which they have

15.1) tends to be a man with a large extended family or clan. Where there is polygyny, the big man is one with many wives. The primary role of a big man is to mobilize the labor and support of other people to achieve public goals, such as by sponsoring important ceremonies, organizing labor parties to fence a garden, or mobilizing fighters for battles with an enemy. The big man does not have a better standard of living than anyone else; he may acquire a great deal of wealth, but he must spend it to maintain his position. His rank is not permanent. He may lose it suddenly if he fails to maintain the loyalty of his followers or if he is successfully challenged by another big man. Big man status is not inherited, although a big man's son may learn his father's skill.

Let us look at some cases of the sort Sahlins had in

Figure 15.2 *A !Kung San band at a camp in the mongongo nut groves. An egalitarian society, the !Kung San live in small groups where leadership is quite informal. Leaders have little power to coerce others. Anyone with a grievance that cannot be easily settled may simply pick up and move to another location, joining another band.*

established ties with many others through the exchanges. . . . For example . . . Egali . . . was very much of a loner and not nearly as important as Um'ue. He had more pigs in his sty than did Um'ue but they were always the same pigs. While Um'ue was continually giving and receiving pigs and shell goods at funerals, Egali held on to his. So although Egali at any one moment had more pigs on hand, Um'ue was worth more in a social/economic sense. [p. 70]

With so few privileges and so much responsibility, one is led to wonder why anyone would accept a leadership role in an egalitarian society. French ethnologist Claude Lévi-Strauss asked this question in regard to the Nambikwara, a central Brazilian people he studied. Nambikwara leaders accept many risks in return for a single privilege: the right to have plural wives. He concluded that the sexual gratification and prestige afforded by many wives did not offset the problems of a leader. Why then do men agree to lead? Leadership, Lévi-Strauss suggested, has its own rewards, but only a few men are fit to accept it. Perhaps

there is an analogy in modern society to political leaders. The salaries for many of the highest governmental offices in modern nations are far below those paid to nongovernment corporate executives and top professionals.

Special Purpose Leadership

As we have seen, the amount of power and authority a leader has seems to be a function of the size and permanence of the local group. Smaller groups, such as those found among the !Kung San and the Inuit, tend to have informal leaders with little power, as do groups who move around a great deal (Figure 15.2). When decisions are required, they act by consensus. Such leaders as do exist function through personal influence in face-to-face situations on a daily basis.

Larger groups, on the other hand, tend to have leaders with more power and authority. One reason for this is that they have greater potential for conflict than smaller groups. Consider a small hunting camp with 20 people in it, 6 of whom are adult males. In most tribal societies, the greatest potential for violence is among adult males. Among the 6 males in our hypothetical group, there are 15 potential **conflict pairs**, or pairs of men who might enter into one-on-one conflict. In a group about four times larger (25 adult males) there are *20 times* more conflict pairs. Perhaps the most frequent cause of conflict in societies like the !Kung San or the Yanomamo is fights between men over women. In a larger group, there is much greater potential for such conflict because the number of pairs, hence possibilities for adulterous affairs, is so much greater. The need for strong leadership or for some other mechanism to maintain cooperation and control is therefore greater in a large group than in a small group.

Although small groups and large groups have different leadership requirements, some societies have both large and small groups and two corresponding patterns of leadership. This is the case in societies with a pattern of seasonal aggregation and dispersal, that is, populations that disperse into small groups during part of the year and aggregate into large groups during other parts of the year (see Box 12.1). In these groups a single informal leader can scarcely hold sway over the entire group because they may be too numerous for him to know and understand. The participants in large temporary gatherings are too independent to be subordinated to a central authority. The possibility of an individual altercation escalating into violence is great. How is this situation handled in societies with such a seasonal pattern?

Warrior Societies: The Cheyenne.   The Cheyenne of the Great Plains of North America were a seasonal patterned group. For many months of every year the tribe broke into groups of bilateral kindreds who coordinated activities and roamed the territory in search of game and pasture for the horses. But they had not always been nomadic hunters and gathers. In the 18th and early 19th centuries, the Cheyenne were sedentary agriculturalists who lived in earth lodge villages and grew corn, beans, and squash near the present border of Minnesota and the Dakotas. The introduction of the horse around 1760 was a major turning point for the Cheyenne. Horses, which had been brought to the Americas by Europeans, gave them greater mobility and speed than they had ever known. They began to specialize in bison hunting. Bison (often called buffalo) roamed the plains in vast herds

of tens of thousands of animals. A few bison kills could yield enough meat for a family to live through the winter, as well as hides for clothing and the conical tents known as *tepees*. By 1830 the Cheyenne had abandoned farming and become completely nomadic.

From late spring until the fall of every year, the Cheyenne came together to form a great communal village. Ethnologist E. Adamson Hoebel carefully reconstructed 19th-century Cheyenne life and wrote this beautiful description (1960, 6): .

> On a broad flat, near a good stream of water, where there is plenty of forage for the horse herds, the entire Cheyenne tribe gathers to renew its vitality. [It is late spring.] Eight hundred to a thousand tepees are raised in a great open circle, in the form of the new moon. They form a broad crescent with the gap between the horns facing the northeast, the point of the rising sun. The entrance of each family tepee also faces east, so that the sun's first rays will shine into the lodge. In the clear, open space of the great camp circle stand three isolated tepees. In the center is a huge, conical skin lodge, the Sacred Arrow Lodge. Off to the right is the lodge of the Sacred Arrow Keeper. At the edge of the open space . . . is the Offering Lodge which is the tepee of the pledger of the ceremony.
>
> In the great circle of family tepees, the lodges are grouped by bands. Each of the ten bands of the Cheyennes' camps together as a unit within the whole. Throughout the long winter, the bands, and even the family groups within the bands, have been scattered in smaller camps hidden in cottonwood groves along the watercourses, many miles apart. When spring was once more upon the land, an enterprising Cheyenne had made the rounds of all the camps. Sometime during the previous year, he had assumed the responsibility of organizing the Medicine Arrow Renewal Rite. He had made a pledge or vow to the supernatural forces to do this thing. His kinsman had helped him to accumulate the necessary food and gifts.

At the end of four continuous days of ritual observances, which renewed and purified life, the entire village went on a great communal bison hunt. The summer season with the whole tribe gathered would also be the occasion for a raid against another tribe or against the whites. By October the great village had broken up into the bands and smaller groups that would roam the territory throughout the winter months. In all their activities, Hoebel stresses, the Cheyenne attached great importance to tribal unity,

Figure 15.3 *The Cheyenne Council of Forty-Four (top), the major decision-making body of the tribe. The council was charged with keeping peace among the many internal rival groups, particularly during the summer when the whole tribe came together to form a "great village" (bottom).*

personal self-control, and nonviolence. Perhaps the greatest crime known to the warlike Cheyenne was the taking of another Cheyenne life. Still, such murders did occur, indicating that tensions and rivalries were common.

Cutting across the kindreds and bands were seven warrior societies. Cheyenne boys chose which society they wished to join, and most men remained members of the same society for life. The warrior societies played important roles in warfare and ritual but also served as a police force during the great tribal ceremonies and on the communal hunts. Each society had its own officers, plus distinctive dress, dances, and songs performed at ritual gatherings. The officers included two ritual leaders and two brave warriors who served as representatives to the Council of Forty-four, the supreme authority in tribal matters (Figure 15.3). This council consisted of "peace chiefs" who were generally

conflict pairs The number of pairs of men who might enter into one-on-one conflict.

proven fighters, but they had to resign from any other post in a warrior society to serve on the council, a term of ten years. While bravery in battle was the principle criterion for leadership in the warrior societies, a peace chief had to be known for being good-tempered, wise, kind, considerate, generous, and altruistic. A peace chief was expected to tolerate all events with equanimity.

Thus the Cheyenne had a system of checks and balances built into their tribal structure. Households were the main economic units, and bands were territorial and economic units; cross-cutting them were the warrior societies. A single band might have men from all seven societies. Thus a man's loyalties might be divided between his neighbors and relatives on the one hand and his comrades-in-arms on the other. The

warrior societies were important units in ritual and military life, yet the highest decision-making body of the tribe was the council, which had separate functions and was oriented toward peace and conciliation rather than military matters. Hoebel states, "The greatest of Cheyenne governmental and legal achievements has been the absolute and total elimination of feud" (1960, 50). In other words, the Cheyenne created a governmental structure designed to prevent the outbreak of segmentary rivalry with its destructive effects.

For a few decades the Cheyenne were supremely effective, maintaining their tribal unity, establishing lasting peace treaties with other tribes, and holding off encroaching whites. They participated with the Sioux in the annihilation of General Custer's troops at Little Big Horn in 1876. Subsequently they were rounded

Figure 15.4 *Young Xavante men in the first of six age-grades (age 7-12) undergo a ritual ordeal to become warriors through intimidation by the older men. Age-grades cut across kinship and local groups, undermining rivalries and discouraging violence in societies without hierarchical power structures.*

up and shipped off to a reservation in Oklahoma. Even then a group led by Little Wolf set off on a long march back to their homeland. A group of 300 Cheyenne kept 13,000 federal troops tied down until they were decimated on January 9, 1879. The remaining Cheyenne were assigned to reservations in Oklahoma and Montana.

Age Grades.   Other societies with patterns of seasonal aggregation and dispersal also possess organizations cutting across local groups organized by kinship. Such groups commonly possess **age grades**, groups of people, usually men, who are united by passing through a common ritual together. Often this is an initiation. The Xavante of central Brazil, who practiced a seasonal pattern of aggregation and dispersal until quite recently, have six age grades. The first, boys between the ages of 7 and 12, is a bachelor's group that lives apart from the boys' families in a separate hut. They receive instruction for five years, until they are ready to undergo a ritual ordeal that involves intimidation by the older men (Figure 15.4) and standing in a cold stream all night. After they are initiated, the young men become warriors.

Age grades, which are common in Africa, South America, and the Great Plains of North America, usually cross-cut kinship and local groups, uniting men of a given age cohort into an organization capable of united action. In addition to military duties, such groups have important ceremonial functions, helping maintain unity in a variety of settings. In other societies other organizations play similar functions. Some examples include ceremonial societies, feasting societies, ritual performers such as clowns or "mummers," groups of people who share the same names, and women's societies. In many cases multiple organizations cross-cut tribal segments in a variety of ways. Such groups set up cross-cutting loyalties that prevent segmentary rivalries and violence without a centralized hierarchy of political power.

These examples illustrate how societies can achieve unity, coordinate activities such as warfare, and prevent segmentary rivalry without a pyramidal leadership structure. Leaders may hold power in certain

situations but not in others, depending on which particular social unit is activated. The form and style of leadership varies from one unit to another, depending on the requirements of the situation.

LEADERSHIP IN RANKED SOCIETIES

Once people settle down and the local population grows beyond a certain size, new patterns of organization and leadership emerge. Such societies are **ranked**, meaning that people are placed along a scale of prestige and power. **Hierarchy**, lacking in egalitarian tribal societies, appears in the leadership patterns, so that individual leaders are not independent but are subordinated to more powerful leaders above them. Authority is not based on personal exploits or qualities so much as on the office itself. The individual who holds the office draws some of his or her authority and power from the office itself. The office may be surrounded with symbolic paraphernalia designed to distinguish its holder, including thrones, insignia, special residences, titles, deferential behavior such as bowing and forms of address, musical anthems, special vehicles (chariots, carriages, automobiles, ships, yachts, airplanes, etc.), and contingents of guards and retainers. If the office is hereditary, leaders are born to their status. Let us consider two examples of this kind of leadership in ranked societies.

Hereditary Chiefdoms in Polynesia

Besides the big man, ethnologist Marshall Sahlins distinguished a second type of leadership in Polynesia, hereditary chieftanship. His focus was on the South Pacific, but such leadership appears in many places and is similar in form to the royal lineages of Europe, India, and China. Sahlins points out that Polynesia, where hereditary chiefs once prevailed, had much larger political units than the villages and hamlets of Melanesia, with their big men. While big men might extend their influence over several hundred people at most, the politically organized groups of Tonga or

---

age grade   A group of people of about the same age united by passing through a common ritual together.

ranked   Pertaining to a society that places people in a hierarchy based on a scale of prestige and power.

hierarchy   An ordering in society such that individuals can be ranked higher or lower with regard to power or prestige.

Hawaii numbered in the thousands. This difference corresponds to a striking difference in the "geometry" of power.

> The . . . Melanesian "tribe" . . . consists of many autonomous kinship-residential groups . . . each of these tends to be economically self-governing. The tribal plan [found in Melanesia] is one of politically unintegrated segments—segmental. But the political geometry in Polynesia is pyramidal. Local groups of the order of self-governing Melanesian communities appear in Polynesia as subdivisions of a more inclusive political body. [Sahlins 1963, 286]

Hierarchy appeared in the leadership patterns in traditional Polynesia before European contact and early in the colonial period. In precolonial Polynesia, individual leaders were subordinated to other leaders on the basis of relative rank. These chiefs did not acquire their authority or status; they inherited leadership from their fathers or mothers. And they did not have to validate their leadership by lending money, doing favors, or demonstrating their superiority like the Melanesian big man. Their superiority was part of their birthright.

Polynesian chiefs maintained their power by redistribution of **tribute** collected from their subjects. The chiefs collected and stored goods, especially food, in a conspicuous place as a symbol of their affluence. This food could then be used to sponsor public ceremonies, to feed the needy, and to entertain royal guests. Polynesian chiefs also subsidized craft production so that artisans could devote full time to their work (Figure 15.5). Chiefs could also mobilize enough talent and labor to construct major engineering works such as irrigation systems or military fortifications. Many resources in the larger chiefdoms went to support a **priesthood** and religious structures. The tribute paid to Polynesian chiefs did not depend on the chief's prestige or ability to motivate people. It was paid because it was owed. Unlike the big men, Polynesian chiefs might live in grand style, with large houses, many retainers, and lavish finery to wear (Figure 15.6).

In many Polynesian societies, people believed that leaders possessed *mana*, a divine ability to lead and control things. Hawaiian chiefs were paid what one writer called "incredible respect." No commoner could touch an object belonging to a chief. All commoners were obliged to prostrate themselves on the ground before a chief. Chiefs also had the ability to prevent others from gaining access to resources they wished to control. For example, a chief could place a **tabu** (a Polynesian word) on a certain crop so that only he could use the harvest. Sahlins notes that the

Figure 15.5 *Fine Polynesian crafts, such as this Maori canoe prow dating from approximately 1840, provide evidence of political leadership and craft specialization in the hereditary chiefdoms of the South Pacific in precolonial times.*

Figure 15.6 *Queen Liliuokalani of Hawaii (1891–1893), the last of the Hawaiian monarchs. Polynesian rulers enjoyed a lavish lifestyle and controlled many symbols of power.*

ability to appropriate land and labor carried in it the seeds of discontent. If chiefs demanded too much, they stimulated rebellion against authority, and such rebellions were apparently common in Tahiti and Hawaii.

African Chiefdoms: The Nyoro

Chiefdoms are also common in Africa, although nowadays they tend to have less autonomy due to the influence of the central state imposed first by European colonizers and then by independent African governments. One well-known African chiefdom is the Nyoro people of western Uganda. There were well over 100,000 Nyoro when they were studied during the 1950s by the British ethnographer John Beattie (1960). The Nyoro were organized into nonlocalized patrilineal clans. Once primarily cattle herders, they are now mainly cultivators because their cattle were wiped out by warfare and disease. The highest leader of the Nyoro was the *Mukama,* or king. Below the Mukama was a graded series of chiefs: four district chiefs, subcounty chiefs in each district, local chiefs, and village headmen. Although it was modified by colonialism, the basic structure of the Nyoro state remained essentially unchanged from precolonial times.

---

tribute Payments exacted by a dominant society from a subordinate one or by a ruler from subjects.

priesthood Full-time religious specialists.

tabu A sacred prohibition that prevents others from touching or using certain people, objects, or places.

Beattie compares the Nyoro kingdom to a feudal state of medieval Europe in the sense that each member of the government was a **vassal** (a subject or servant) of someone at the next higher level. In return for the right to rule, each chief owed homage and services to his superior. The idea of ruling was an aspect of all social relations. Nyoro kings were not thought of as sharing kinship with their own people. The king had to be protected from certain dangers that emanated from the illness of others, as well as from low-status foods such as sweet potatoes and cassava (manioc). A cook could not have sexual intercourse before preparing a royal meal or else the food would be contaminated. The king was addressed with special language, and he had **regalia**, consisting of ancient crowns, drums, and spears, that symbolized his power. Many rituals signifying the purity, power, and uniqueness of the king had to be celebrated upon his accession to the throne and during his reign.

In the traditional Nyoro system, territorial chiefs held rights in land and power only at the pleasure of the king. The king could remove a chief at any time, although usually the office passed to the incumbent's son. A chief was obliged to maintain a residence near the king's palace, which was a way for the king to keep the chiefs under his thumb. Chiefs were generally selected from patrilineal groups that had given some special service to the king, but they might also be selected from the chief's maternal kin or even his affines (inlaws). Reforms introduced by the British administration, however, had led to increased private ownership of land, removing land from royal control. Chiefs were becoming less like vassals to the king than like local magistrates responsible for implementing central governmental policies. The king still had influence over the selection of chiefs, however, and most of the chiefs were in fact former appointees of the king or their lineal descendants.

While Beattie was in Bunyoro (as the kingdom is known), the system was in transition. Upper-level chiefs nowadays must be literate; they spend a great deal of their time doing paperwork, tending to permits, collecting taxes, serving as magistrates in civil and criminal cases, maintaining official correspondence, and other duties. Local chiefs and village headmen have less paperwork and more direct contact with their people and the daily activities of life. They give technical assistance to farmers, and serve court summonses.

One of the earliest insights of European political philosophy is that all government to some extent requires the "consent of the governed." Even despotic monarchies and dictatorships in which the general public has no representation at all must have at least passive acceptance for their authority. Even after the Nyoro King had lost much of his power, members of the royal clan, the Bito, were accustomed to receiving extra respect and deference from the common Nyoro people. The voluntary recognition and acceptance of a leader's authority is known as **legitimacy**. Functionalist theory in anthropology holds that political legitimacy is a function of wide acceptance of a common core of ideas. These ideas may be embodied in a charter, which is a formal document, an oral myth, or a ritual enactment. A good example of a charter is the Nyoro myth of how the king received his power (Box 15.1).

LEADERSHIP IN STRATIFIED SOCIETIES

The study of leadership in complex, stratified societies could occupy another entire chapter. As stated earlier, leadership roles become more formalized as societies become more complex. Often the exact rights and obligations of a leader are spelled out in a charter. For example, Article II, Section 2 of the U.S. Constitution makes the president of the United States commander-in-chief of the armed forces. With formalization comes greater precision in the specification of duties, although there is always room for maneuver in the most detailed regulations. For example, during the late 1980s Soviet president Gorbachev exploited his popularity and the widespread dissatisfaction with conditions in his country to make far-reaching changes in the formal and cultural structures of government. His job was made particularly difficult by the conflict between his country's charter and his goal. The Soviet Union is founded on the writings of Marx and Lenin, and until 1991 its strongest formal institution was the Communist party, while Gorbachev's goal was to steer the Soviet Union toward a market economy.

Charters set limits, which are subject to interpretation by leaders and by other specialists such as legislators and jurists. The outcome of a given situation depends on several factors, including the leader's true power, the acceptance of decisions by public groups, and the interpretation given to formal law. Many aspects of leadership in complex societies are the same as in simpler societies. Perhaps the greatest difference is that modern leadership depends heavily on delegation of authority and on a pyramidal chain of command. This sets up a field within which a great deal of political maneuvering can take place. For example, a leader can sometimes avoid being held accountable for actions by subordinates. Clever leaders try to take credit for successes and allow subordinates to take the blame for failures.

Anthropologist J. McIver Weatherford made an intriguing analysis of the United States Senate from an anthropological perspective. In *Tribes on the Hill* (1981) Weatherford describes a hierarchy of power in the Senate based on seniority. This principle, which is often important in simpler societies, operates to deprive junior senators of committee chairmanships, exposure in the media, and other kinds of power. Thus, while all senators are formally equal in power, the seniority system grants more power to second- and third-term senators. Weatherford compares the status rivalries, factions, initiation rites, and rituals in tribal societies to those found in the U.S. Senate. Like a Melanesian big man, only a senior senator will be found giving a major speech during a full session of the Senate. Junior senators will more likely speak to an empty chamber or simply request that written remarks be inserted into the record (Figure 15.7).

Weatherford classifies senators into three categories: shamans, warlords, and godfathers. Shamans are legislators who seek high visibility by making frequent pronouncements on matters of public concern, such as communism, big business, pollution, and crime. According to Weatherford, shamans rarely get important bills passed, but play a primarily "spiritual" role of exorcising demons and reducing anxiety. Warlords are senators who specialize in a particular area of government, such as health, science, or defense. Warlords try to build their influence by holding hearings and sponsoring legislation, primarily in their specialty area. Godfathers are senators who exercise consider-

Figure 15.7 *President Bush addressing the U.S Congress. Anthropological analysis suggests that an elaborate hierarchical power structure exists within this body of supposed equals.*

able power from behind the scenes by doing favors and collecting debts from other senators.

Weatherford's final judgment is harsh. He believes that U.S. senators are so deeply involved in ritual performances, the drive for publicity, and, above all, the quest for reelection that they neglect the work of making good laws for the country. As in tribal communities, the Senate is a small face-to-face community, and as Weatherford's analysis shows, there is a differentiation of roles within it. The analogy to tribal society should not be pushed too far, however, because the Senate differs from a tribal village in important respects. The extent and variety of the various local, ideological, corporate, and political interest groups that exert pressure on U.S. senators go far beyond anything known in tribal society.

Leadership in stratified societies has many facets. In neighborhoods, informal groups, and other face-to-

---

vassal In feudal states, a person or society that is subject or servant to a higher authority.

regalia Emblems or symbols of royalty or high leadership status.

legitimacy A quality of political leadership based on the voluntary recognition and acceptance of authority.

BOX 15.1
Political Origin Myths

The Nyoro people have an origin myth that explains for them the origin of humanity and of Nyoro social and political structure.

The first family was headed by Kintu who had three sons. Kintu wished to name his boys, so at the suggestion of God, he devised a test for them. Kintu told his sons to sit on the ground with their legs stretched out, each holding a full pot of milk in his lap. Kintu commanded them to sit in this position through the night without spilling a drop. Late at night, the youngest boy began to doze and spilled some of his milk. He begged his brothers to give him some of theirs. They agreed and each one poured a little of his milk into their brother's pot filling it up to the brim again. Toward dawn, the eldest brother fell asleep, spilling all his milk. He asked the help of his brothers, but they refused. In the morning, Kintu found the youngest boy's pot full, the second son's nearly full and eldest boy's empty. Kintu used this outcome to assign roles to his sons. He made his eldest son and all his descendents servants and cultivators. The second son who husbanded most of his milk and helped his younger brother was given the respected position of cattleman together with his descendents. Kintu made the youngest son "Kakama" or little ruler. His descendents became the kings of Bunyoro. Kintu ordered his elder sons to remain by their younger brother's side and serve him. [Beattie 1960, 11–12]

Myths contain clues concerning the ideal or proper behavior expected of persons occupying certain roles. In the Nyoro myth it is clear that boys are expected to help their brothers and, by extension, members of their patrilineal group. Nevertheless, a person is not expected to give away what he has to his own detriment. The youngest son's refusal to help his eldest brother is not condemned but actually rewarded. The eldest, who might have been expected to be the most responsible, was granted the lowest status, perhaps as a punishment. From this myth one could extract the following information about Nyoro values:

a. Brothers should help each other.

b. One need not help another to one's own detriment.

c. Older brothers bear heavier responsibility.

d. Leaders can be expected to manipulate others.

e. Cleverness is valued.

f. People are born to be unequal.

These ideas should be treated as provisional suggestions, not as certain truths. They can be tested against other information we have about the Nyoro and against Nyoro behavior in actual situations. If they do test out, we have gathered valuable information about Nyoro values from their myths.

Political origin myths may exist in any society. Some of the most cherished myths in the United States revolve around the character and abilities of its early leaders. For example, George Washington, commander of the Revolutionary Army and first president, is the subject of several myths.

---

face situations, it may resemble the egalitarian pattern, while in other contexts such as big cities and labor unions, leadership may share features with the big man pattern. In many countries leaders still have many characteristics of those in ranked chiefdoms. They surround themselves with the trappings of wealth and power and do their best to avoid formal constraints on their power. In stable nation states, the leaders of government and other large institutions are highly constrained by formal charters and rules. In many cases, however, leaders spend much of their time attempting to escape from the constraints imposed by constitutions and legislation. They may appeal on a personal level to their followers or voters, distributing favors to enhance their power. Or they may strengthen the institutions, such as the army and financial institutions, that can exercise control over people.

WHO WILL LEAD?

Leadership in practically all societies is partly achieved and partly ascribed. In some societies ascribed traits such as descent from a royal lineage are important; in others achieved traits are the most im-

American political mythology attributes unusual straight-forwardness and honesty to the first U.S. president, George Washington.

1. When George Washington was a small boy, he was given a new hatchet. Anxious to try it out, he cut down an ornamental cherry tree on his father's plantation. When asked about the tree, little George said, "Father, I cannot tell a lie. I cut down the cherry tree with my little hatchet."

2. Before he became president, Washington had a guest to dinner at his plantation. The guest was an uneducated backwoodsman and did not know how to behave at a planter's dinner table. The guest accidentally spilled his soup on the fine linen tablecloth. The children at the table giggled, turning embarrassment into humiliation. George Washington promptly spilled his own soup.

3. When George Washington was a boy, he had an amazingly strong arm. Once he threw a silver dollar across the Potomac.

Probably none of these events actually took place, but many Americans feel the literal truth of these stories is not important. One can draw several conclusions about American ideals of leadership from these myths.

a. Leaders should be honest even when it may invite punishment and disgrace.

b. Leaders must be humble. They may be better than ordinary people, but they should never act as though they think so.

c. Leaders are strong. They can do things ordinary people cannot.

It is interesting to compare the myths about George Washington and the Nyoro origin myth. While one myth legitimizes superiority, cleverness, and the privileges of the nobility, the other legitimizes equality and honesty. The myths do not necessarily reflect how leaders will actually behave in either society, or how people will judge them. Still, they may be accurate reflections of underlying values and ideals.

portant. Leadership in egalitarian societies seems to be informal and based on the personal qualities of leaders. In more complex societies leadership is based on fixed statuses; in sociological terms leadership is **institutionalized.**

Many studies show that as conditions change, different qualities are emphasized for the ideal leader. Leaders may be deposed when people perceive that they are no longer equal to their tasks or simply when an effective rival comes along. Styles of leadership also

institutionalized role   A pattern of behavior, common in more complex societies, that is based on fixed statuses within a formal structure, such as a royal court, a corporation, or a government.

change; sometimes leaders are aggressive and demanding and at other times they are conciliatory and compromising. Changes in the style of leadership can be observed clearly in the recent history of the American presidency. Franklin Roosevelt, who took power during the Great Depression, was a vigorous and innovative president who resorted to many unusual tactics to bring about major reforms. His successor, Harry S Truman, was flamboyant but stressed responsibility and authority. Dwight Eisenhower was an avuncular figure who led the country through quiet persuasion and delegation of power. John F. Kennedy was again a dynamic leader who urged people to accomplish more and to put their country before themselves.

Other criteria may affect the selection of leaders. In some societies leaders are invariably fairly advanced in age, while in others leaders may be young. Wherever leadership depends on physical strength and agility, leaders tend to be young or middle-aged. Where experience is important, leaders tend to be older. In some cases leadership is reserved for people who have a real or mythical relationship to the foundation of the society or the state. For example, virtually all the major leaders in the People's Republic of China took part in the Long March of Mao Tse-tung in 1949, when the Chinese communist revolution took place.

Rising to the Top in an Egalitarian Society

In most societies there are formal or informal criteria for assuming leadership roles, but there are exceptions to those rules. We have already mentioned some of the qualities that lead to recognition as a big man in New Guinea. Richard Lee refers to "paths" to leadership among the !Kung San, mentioning four attributes that are important: (1) seniority in a large family, (2) n!ore (water hole and surrounding territory) ownership, (3) marriage to a n!ore owner, and (4) personal qualities. It is clear that these are not rigidly applied. Three of the leaders of the /Xai/xai water hole group are a woman called Sa//gain!a, who is descended from several generations of water hole owners, her husband, and her niece Baun!a. These individuals achieved leadership status through ownership, descent, and marriage, but in each case there were personal qualities involved as well. A !Kung San who is

boastful, arrogant, selfish, or acquisitive is disqualified from leadership. People with these traits cannot command respect from the !Kung San. In many cases, persons who are quite senior and closely related by blood or marriage to n!ore owners are not themselves leaders, either because they do not have the appropriate personality or because they have moved away from the water hole where their ties are strong.

Anthropologist Dennis W. Werner used more exact measures of the criteria that account for inheritance of leadership among the Mekranoti-Kayapó of central Brazil. The Mekranoti live in a village of about 285 people on the upper Iriri River. They are generally egalitarian with no major differences in wealth, influence, or control over resources. The political life of the village revolves around two men's societies, which have civic, ceremonial, and recreational functions. Each society has a headman, one of whom is also the leader or chief of the entire village (Figure 15.8). Unlike leadership in most egalitarian villages, leadership in the Mekranoti village tends to pass from father to son. This may be a recent innovation. Werner believes that the idea of leadership inheritance may actually have been reinforced by outsiders.

The Mekranoti have been in contact with Brazilian society since 1958. To this day, however, very few of them speak Portuguese, and they have little contact with outsiders. Village leaders tend to be the primary go-betweens between the villagers and the officials of the government agency FUNAI, which has considerable influence over tribal villages and the services they receive. Because leaders have close and frequent contact with outsiders, their children are also more likely to have close contact with outsiders and to be more conversant with their behavior, language, and culture. Werner tells the story of a government official who worked closely with the village leader. One day the agent put his arm around the leader's son and said, "Oh, you'll be the next chief." Werner suggested that it was not just being a chief's son that made it likely a man would become chief, but his close contact with outsiders as a consequence of being the chief's son. Werner constructed a statistical test of his hypothesis. He tested the correlation among three variables: (1) closeness of descent from a chief, (2) knowledge of Brazilians and their customs, and (3) the strength of a man's reputation for influence (i.e., leadership). He found that knowledge of outsiders has a larger independent effect on influence than simple descent from

Figure 15.8 *A chief of the Mekranoti of Brazil. A chief's son may inherit his position, but there is little power or wealth to accompany it in this relatively egalitarian society.*

a chief. It appears that the tendency toward hereditary leaders was increased by contact with Brazilian society (Werner 1982).

Chiefly Succession

Leadership in chiefdoms is more developed than in egalitarian societies, and the criteria for assuming leadership are more clearly delineated. Among the Mende of Sierra Leone (West Africa), chiefs are selected by a council of noblemen from the senior males most closely related to the royal lineage. This seems like a cut-and-dried decision, but there are other factors as well. Ethnologist Arthur Murphy studied the Mende council debates to learn what features the Mende consider relevant. One factor concerns the candidates' claims of relationship to the royal lineage.

We have observed that genealogies are subject to different interpretations, especially when two or more people attempt to trace their ancestry back to a distant ancestor. Other factors the Mende discuss concern the candidates' fitness to rule the tribe. These matters are not usually discussed openly but in the form of a code that transforms the issue of competence into one of legitimacy.

In other cases of chiefly succession there might be a struggle for power among different contenders and their followers. For example, before the first contact (1778) with the English explorer James Cook, there were four separate kingdoms in Hawaii, each ruled by a leading chief and several subchiefs. In about 1780 the king of Maui, Kalaniopuu, handed the throne over to his son Kiwalao. He turned the guardianship of the important war god over to his nephew, Kamehameha. Kamehameha defied tradition and the new king by performing the sacrifice of a war prisoner himself instead of leaving it to the king. Kamehameha found it best to retire from his post, but soon five subchiefs encouraged him to lead a rebellion, which resulted in the death of King Kiwalao. After nearly 30 years of struggle, during which he vanquished his rivals one by one, Kamehameha succeeded in uniting all the Hawaiian islands under his rule for the first time in history. It is possible that firearms obtained from American visitors were decisive in Kamehameha's victories.

Succession in Stratified Societies

Social conditions in complex societies affect the criteria by which leaders are chosen, just as they do in simpler societies. Sometimes it appears that the criteria are quite rigid, yet they can change rapidly. Until the 1970s, for example, most observers believed it was impossible for a divorced man to be elected president of the United States. American values required that the president be a stable family man. Some pundits suggested that the late Nelson Rockefeller, who was divorced, could not be elected. In 1980, however, Ronald Reagan, divorced and remarried, was elected president in a landslide victory. This may reflect the fact that more and more Americans have experienced divorce in their own lives.

A second example of abrupt change in leadership criteria is the election of Pope John Paul II by the college of cardinals in 1978. Virtually all of the popes selected in recent years were of Italian origin. Suddenly, and against the expectation of the "experts," the cardinals selected a Polish pope. Many reasons can be given for this choice. Possibly the cardinals felt it was "time for a change"; possibly John Paul was a kind of compromise. On the one hand, his long-standing opposition to the Communist government of Poland made his selection a kind of political statement. On the other hand, John Paul is rather conservative in theological matters, which satisfied the conservative members of the church.

Powerful outsiders can also change the rules of the game, introducing new criteria for accession to leadership and altering the structure of power. Paradoxically, contact with a powerful outside society may increase the authority of leaders in egalitarian societies, while in ranked societies such contact may reduce the power of traditional leadership statuses. While women are sometimes leaders, there is no society where women are consistently chosen as leaders. We look at this question next.

Women in Power: Questions and Theories

When the anthropologists of the 19th century became aware of matrilineal descent, they assumed that it was a **survival** (a cultural vestige) from a time when women were dominant in society. This is technically known as **matriarchy.** We now know that there is no necessary relationship between matriliny and matriarchy. There is no evidence that women once possessed greater power than men in societies with matrilineal descent rules. Furthermore, no case of matriarchy has ever been confirmed: There are no known societies where women regularly occupied major positions of political power.

This is not to say that women are never powerful leaders. In the second half of the 20th century, there has been a handful of women heads of state, such as former prime minister Margaret Thatcher of England; the late Indira Gandhi of India; Sirimavo Bandaranaike, former prime minister of Sri Lanka; the late Golda Meir, prime minister of Israel from 1969 to 1974; Benazir Bhutto, former prime minister of Pakistan; Corazon Aquino, president of the Philippines; and Violeta Chamorro, president of Nicaragua (Figure 15.9). None of these societies has matriarchal tendencies, and these women are exceptions in the history of their countries. In the United States women have been virtually excluded from powerful leadership positions. Until Ella Grasso was elected governor of Connecticut in 1974, there had never been a woman governor except for a few elected as successors to their husbands. In 200 years, there have been only a few women in the U.S. Senate, one woman on the Supreme Court, and no women presidents or vice-presidents.

Women do hold formal and informal positions of power in many societies, but they are never the equal of men, either in terms of the number of positions they hold or the power they wield. What accounts for this difference? A number of theories have been proposed to explain it, although none is truly satisfactory.

Figure 15.9   *Violeta Chamorro at her inauguration as president of Nicaragua. Women in less developed countries sometimes have been able to attain positions of considerable power, possibly because they are less constrained by child-rearing duties than women in developed countries. However, such positions are generally restricted to the elite.*

A Biological Approach.   Some theorists have suggested that women are biologically less fit for leadership roles. Sociologist Steven Goldberg published a book in 1973 called *The Inevitability of Patriarchy.* In it he argued (1) that men's logical abilities are superior to women's and (2) that men are innately more aggressive than women; therefore, he said, patriarchy is inevitable.

In support of Goldberg's first contention, it can be said that men score higher than women on mathematics and spatial ability tests. But these differences do not translate into superior logical abilities or leadership qualities. Women generally score higher than men on verbal ability tests, a trait that is probably as important as logical ability in leadership. Leadership, however, is not a simple function of logical, spatial, or verbal ability, so that differences between the sexes in these areas cannot explain differences in leadership potential.

There is some evidence to support Goldberg's contention that males are innately more aggressive than females. Goldberg denies that differences in aggressiveness in males and females are the result of socialization; he argues that socialization for sex roles is simply a way of helping the individual adjust to the role that biology has prepared for him or her. A critic, psychologist Eleanor Maccoby (1973), pointed out that as humans mature and as society becomes more complex, the occasions in which pure aggression is used become rarer and other interpersonal qualities

---

survival   In culture, any behavior, belief, or object that is a vestige of a past stage of history.

matriarchy   A social order in which women dominate politically.

become valuable in achieving individual goals. These qualities include conciliation, compromise, persuasion, sharing, and cooperation. Adults in the modern world who lack these abilities are generally not successful. Goldberg's approach suggests that aggressiveness is the only necessary quality for leadership, but even our brief survey has shown that this is not the case. Different situations call for different styles and qualities of leadership. The ethnographic record suggests that no single quality is the universal prerequisite for leadership.

A Historical Approach.   Some anthropologists suggest that women once played major leadership roles in simple, non-Western societies. They cite evidence from such groups as the !Kung San showing the relative equality of men and women as leaders. They argue that women leaders disappeared soon after these small societies made contact with more powerful state-organized societies. According to this theory, the representatives of complex societies were so unused to dealing with women in leadership positions that they refused to deal with them. The relatively powerless tribal groups acquiesced by switching to exclusively male leaders. While this hypothesis is appealing, it is nearly impossible to test because the evidence for it, by the very terms of the argument, has disappeared.

The terms of this argument can also be reversed. As societies became more complex and stratified, more opportunities arose for women to move into leadership and other roles normally monopolized by men. At a theoretical level, it can be argued, complex societies create elaborate social statuses, something like job descriptions in bureaucracies, that are entirely independent of the individual that may fill the position. The very abstractness of the status definition, the argument goes, is what makes it possible for a woman or other nontraditional occupant to fill the role. In recent years, since the advent of **feminism**, some societies have legislated the equality of access by women to the scarce and valued positions of society. Of course for every case where this has happened, there are societies, such as Saudi Arabia, where women are legally prevented from occupying the same statuses as men.

A Symbolic Interpretation.   Sherry Ortner, a symbolic anthropologist, offered another explanation for the absence of women in leadership statuses (Ortner and Whitehead 1981). She rejects biological explanations but wonders why women are almost universally denied access to leadership positions. Her explanation rests on the symbolic value of women's reproductive roles. Women carry babies with them for nine months until they are born. Since the father's link to the baby is through a woman, and since women nurture babies at their breasts, Ortner believes that the women are almost always considered to be closer to nature than men. This closeness to nature becomes an obstacle to achieving a higher status in society, which, it can be argued, is a cultural construct. Being closer to nature puts women in an inferior position, and therefore they are considered unfit for leadership. This is an interesting argument and much anecdotal evidence can be found conforming to it. It is difficult to falsify, however, leaving it more in the realm of interesting speculation than testable hypothesis.

Reproductive Roles, Child Care, and Available Time. Another explanation for women's absence in leadership roles also relates to their reproductive roles. If we assume that leadership requires a great deal of interaction between actual or potential leaders and the people they would lead, leaders should have more time than others at their disposal for such interaction. Professional women in modern complex societies are disadvantaged if they interrupt their careers to bear and raise children. The same may be true more broadly of leadership in society. Since bearing and raising children frequently removes women from important arenas of social interaction and absorbs their time and attention, women may be less able to take on leadership roles.

Among the !Kung San, women do 90 percent of the work of child rearing and contribute more than twice as much as men to the food supply. They are sought after in marriage and men perform bride service in order to obtain a wife. As a result, wrote Richard Lee (1979),

> !Kung women's participation in . . . decision making is probably greater than that of women in most tribal, peasant, and industrial societies. But the level of their participation is not equal to that of men. The latter appear to do about two-thirds of the talking in discussions involving both sexes, and men act as group spokespersons far more frequently than do women. [p. 453]

Lee's overall impression was that while the status of !Kung San women is relatively high, in public matters the opinions and decisions of men carried more weight. Lee did not suggest a cause-effect relationship between child care and leadership, however.

Dennis Werner made a study of the relationship between child care and women's influence in the Mekranoti village (1982). Werner tested the hypothesis that women have lower influence because they must spend more time than men on child care in the private sphere and have less time available to build influence in the public domain. Werner observed that men generally had more political clout than women. Once while the village was out on an extended hunting trip, the women had a dispute with the men over whether to return to the village (the women's preference) or to go on hunting. The men prevailed and the hunt lasted several more weeks. It was difficult to test Werner's hypothesis. Werner could not make direct comparisons of women's influence to men's, because Mekranoti informants simply refused to compare them. When Werner asked informants to name people with influence, they gave only men's names.

Mekranoti men and women spend a lot of time in separate spheres. Men spent a great deal of time in the men's house at the center of the village, while women spent more time in residential houses arranged in a circle around the men's house (Figure 15.10). Men spent practically no time at all in child care and, of course, did not bear or suckle babies. Since cross-sex comparisons were not feasible, Werner decided to correlate variation in women's influence with time spent in child care. For his comparisons, Werner was able to make use of detailed spot-check data on how people use time (see Chapter 1). Werner hypothesized that women who spent relatively little time at child rearing would have greater influence. The data are consistent with Werner's hypothesis. However, some qualifications should be introduced. First, older women have more influence than younger ones, and younger women are more likely to have young children who demand their time. Thus the correlation between child care and influence may be a function of age. Second, because Werner could not compare women's influence directly to men's, his study may not have relevance for influence in the society at large. It is still possible that women's influence has nothing to do with child care.

The deceptively simple question of why men usually rule in society is still not resolved. It arises again and again in political and scientific discussions and involves questions of historical and evolutionary sequences, reproductive roles, and the symbolic status of women. Of all the varied hypotheses, those relating to the relationship between power and reproductive roles seem to be the most promising answers at the moment.

SUMMARY

- Leadership involves the acquisition and use of authority and power. Leaders are able to influence the actions of others in matters of public concern.
- In egalitarian societies leadership tends to be an achieved status. Small-scale egalitarian societies may not have formalized leadership statuses; leaders must earn the respect of others by acts of bravery, oratory, generosity, or other personal traits. Egalitarian leaders must constantly reaffirm their status through generosity and bravery.
- Some societies have "big men," who occupy leadership roles by building a loyal following, stimulating production, or leading successful raids on an enemy.
- In societies with a pattern of aggregation and dispersal, leadership may be diffused into different roles, setting up a system of checks and balances. Ceremonial elaboration results in cross-cutting loyalties and allows even large social entities to be self-governing.
- In complex societies, leadership roles become increasingly formalized. As leadership is institution-

---

feminism   The advocacy of equal rights and social status for women.

Figure 15.10 *A Kayapó village, with the men's house at the center of the circle and residential houses around the periphery. The men's house is an exclusive clubhouse, for men only, where many important political decisions are made. Women tend to dominate the residential sphere in this matrilocal society.*

alized in ranked and stratified societies, people respond less to the personal qualities of leaders and more to the authority of the status (or office) the leader occupies. Still, leaders must satisfy certain criteria in order to serve, and these criteria change over time in accordance with the values and needs of the society.

• Matriarchies are not known to exist, though there are individual cases of women assuming important leadership roles in some societies. In general, however, women are not prominent in leadership in simple or complex societies. There may be some relationship between women's reproductive and domestic roles and their relative lack of political power.

GET INVOLVED

1. Survey all the organizations and groups (formal or informal) of which you are a part. Who are the leaders? How are they selected? What are the formal and informal rules governing the selection of these leaders and their tenure in their role? Can you detect patterns of leadership characteristic of egalitarian, ranked, and complex societies?
2. Nearly all leadership is chartered in some way. That is, people have stories or explanations that justify the amount of power and authority a leader holds. Make a collection of constitutions, bylaws, myths, or legends that justify the power or authority of a leader.
3. Make a survey of the women who currently hold or have recently held leadership roles predominantly held by men, such as company or university president, federal or local legislator, military officer, or judge. What changes, if any, have occurred in the definition and recruitment to these statuses? What adjustments have the women who hold these statuses made to fit into what formerly was defined as a male role, including changes in dress, behavior, and management style?

SUGGESTED READINGS

Hoebel, E. Adamson. 1960. *The Cheyennes: Indians of the Great Plains.* New York: Holt, Rinehart and Winston.

Lee, Richard. 1984. *The Dobe !Kung.* New York: Holt, Rinehart and Winston.

Newman, Phillip L. 1965. *Knowing the Gururumba.* New York: Holt, Rinehart and Winston.

Sahlins, Marshall. 1963. Poor man, rich man, big man, chief: Political types in Melanesia. *Studies in Society and History* 5:285–303.

Weatherford, Jack McIver. 1981. *Tribes on the hill.* New York: Rawson Wade.

ANTHROPOLOGISTS AT WORK

Problem Solving and Collaboration: A Model for Applied Anthropology from the Field

Carlos G. Vélez-Ibañez is a professor of anthropology and director of the Bureau of Applied Research in Anthropology at the University of Arizona. He has conducted fieldwork in Mexico, India, and the southwestern United States. His research has focused on household formation, the impact of technological change, and regional development.

My studies in low-income Mexican households in Mexico and the United States have helped me understand the relationship between culture and citizenship and have provided my colleagues and me with insights useful in addressing problems of low achievement by Mexican American school children. My first challenge was to understand how in the most dire circumstances human beings survive in relatively good order. I first began to define the question (but not the way to resolve it) while I worked in a city called Ciudad Netzahualcoyotl Izcalli, some 17 km southeast of Mexico City. Ciudad Netzahualcoyotl was an ecological disaster; set on a former lake bed, by 1990 it comprised a 62-km² area of sandy soil heavily populated by 3.2 million people, mostly poor urban dwellers. The population suffered terribly: In the summer months strong winds blew dust and dried fecal matter from untreated sewage, and in the winter months heavy rain turned the area back into the lake it once was. Water sources became contaminated by improperly laid sewage lines so that human waste mixed with drinking water; in one neighborhood 75 percent of the deaths among children up to the age of four were due to dysentery and

Carlos Velez-Ibanez (seated) with graduate research associates
Anna O'Leary and Gerardo Bernarche at the Bureau of Applied
Research in Anthropology.

other water-borne diseases. Political violence was endemic, street gangs numbered in the hundreds in some areas, rates of unemployment and underemployment were about 50 percent, and land developers and realtors sold the same lots up to 16 times to different buyers.

Yet, for the most part, the inhabitants of Netzahualcoyotl expressed social and cultural values little different from those of other populations. In fact most households placed high values on traditional ritual marriage, extended family relations, and home ownership (77 percent owned their own homes). Literacy characteristics were above the national norm, a

large number of children attended school, and cooperation was the dominant social value within neighborhoods and families. Neighborhoods were also well organized as political interest groups.

As I was to find out during three years of fieldwork, the key to this social and cultural stability was the fact that people were "nested" within large household clusters of dense familial relations. This made possible small informal business enterprises, the frequent exchange of assistance and labor, and the reliance of one household on another for survival. These clusters rotated and exchanged labor, skills, and child care so that cooperation partially offset the effects of great scarcity and need.

Beginning in 1984, my colleague James B. Greenberg and I began to try to understand Mexican households in the southwestern United States. We had assumed that even though these households were "American," they would in fact appear not too different from those in cities like Netzahualcoyotl in central urban Mexico. Part of what we were interested in was the way added variables of discrimination and ethnocentrism would influence household formation.

We found that household formation was not greatly different from what we had previously studied in urban Mexico. We also developed an understanding of the manner in which knowledge was exchanged in household clusters. I called this *funds of knowledge* in reference to the strategic reservoirs of information and learning accumulated from the many experiences the Mexican population had had in the borderlands region of northwestern Mexico and the southwestern United States. These funds of knowledge included information about construction, mining, gardening, farming, ranching, medicine and healing, cooking, hunting, and the various abstract fields relating to them, such as basic chemistry, mathematics, geography, hydraulics, dynamics, mechanics, planning and design, and architecture. Strategic information about immigration laws and their various changes, legal regulations, city codes, finance rules, and hundreds of other institutional bits of information were also well represented in the households we analyzed.

We found that these funds of knowledge crisscross the actual border and are transmitted by cross-border household clusters. Mexicans on both sides of the border share a basic continuity of culture; where individuals are born does not make much difference in the sharing of a regional culture. This brought us to understand that the legal border separating the United States and Mexico is less significant than we had imagined. In other words, the differences in "ethnicity" between Mexicans south and north of the border are largely the creations of citizenship requirements, not cultural ones. Even Mexicans in the American Southwest who are monolingual English speakers (only 14 percent of the total, even though 76 percent of the population is U.S.-born) are socially and culturally Mexican, since they still operate in "clustered" households, have kin relations in Mexico, and share the strategic funds of knowledge specific to the borderlands.

It is the manner in which Mexican children are raised that is most telling in deciphering Mexican regional culture, and it speaks against equating citizenship and culture. We found that unlike Anglo-American children, Mexican children were never raised by the nuclear family alone. Infants, for example, were constantly picked up and handled by a variety of persons within the household clusters.[1] Mexican children had a variety of sources for access to funds of knowledge with aunts and uncles and significant others; both relationally and substantively, Mexican children regionally have "denser" social relations and "thick" volumes of information compared to Anglo-American children in the same region.

This brought us to a realization that there is a lack of recognition in the public school systems of the wealth of information that Mexican children in the United States carry to the classroom. This becomes crucial in seeking appropriate educational strategies for Mexican American children, who today suffer from very high dropout rates in elementary and secondary schools and who consistently are grade levels behind in achievement. We began to think that such knowledge could potentially enhance instruction.

Together with two other colleagues, we devised an intensive training program by which we taught teachers to become household ethnographers who could tap into the funds of knowledge of their students. So far this experiment has been a success, and teachers, parents, and students seem to have created a new respectful relationship between them in which *confianza* has been established, an appreciation of the children's knowledge gained, and "dense" and "thick" relationships established between them. For the long run, we are convinced that further development of this approach will improve the performance of Mexican American children in U.S. public schools.

---

1. Actual fieldwork on child rearing was carried out by Maria T. Vélez and appears in her Ph.D. dissertation, "The Social Context of Mothering: A Comparison of Mexican American and Anglo Mother-Infant Interaction Patterns" (Wright Institute of Psychology, 1983).

PART SIX

CONFLICT & FORMAL INSTITUTIONS

As human societies grow and change, basic social and cultural patterns often develop into social institutions—firmly established practices, relationships, and organizations—of increasing complexity. In a few instances in the past, for example, some patterns and combinations of conditions, including high population density, large sedentary settlements, intensive agriculture, occupational specialization, and developed leadership with political power, led to the development of the state, a form of political organization that today is the most comprehensive and influential social institution in the world. Similarly, as societies became more complex, disputes between individuals came to be a concern of society at large. To control conflict, societies established such formal institutions as law codes, courts, police forces, penal systems, and military organizations.

Part Six looks at the development of formal institutions in three areas: violence, warfare, and law; political organization; and social inequality. Chapter 16 explores some of the ways aggression and violence are controlled and regulated in different societies, showing how a society's legal codes and processes, its concepts of crime and punishment, and its approach to organized violence—war—are related to its size and complexity and embedded in its social system. The chapter also considers the evidence for and against several theories of warfare. Chapter 17 describes the development and characteristics of state-organized societies and considers several theories that attempt to explain the rise of the state. Chapter 18 looks at social inequality and how it becomes structured and institutionalized in different societies. It considers how social stratification, whether by class, ethnic group, gender, or some other factor, divides people along lines that have consequences for health, access to resources and power, personal freedom, and opportunities for self-fulfillment. The chapters in Part Six thus provide a look at some of the institutions and organizations that have evolved in human societies over the centuries as a function of growing social complexity.

This black basalt stone is engraved with the code of Hammurabi (depicted standing), a Babylonian king of the 18th century B.C. Found by archaeologists at Susa, Iran, in 1902, the code contains 282 laws whose basic principle is one familiarly attributed to Moses: "an eye for an eye, a tooth for a tooth."

16

WARFARE, VIOLENCE, AND LAW

▲▲▲

iolence and warfare are constantly before us in the daily newspapers, on television screens, and in everyday conversations. During the 20th century, hardly a year has gone by without major incidents of mass violence or warfare somewhere in the world. During the 1980s and 1990s, there have been major conflicts in El Salvador, Nicaragua, Colombia, Lebanon, Angola, Mozambique, Sri Lanka, Iran, Iraq, Kuwait, Afghanistan, and Northern Ireland. These conflicts have taken thousands of lives and have forced millions of people from their homes into refugee camps.

In this chapter we look at different forms of violence and warfare in human society. The scope and scale of organized violence vary from one society to the next. Although we often think of it as exceptional, even pathological, warfare is a regular part of the lives of many people around the world.

We also look at the many ways that societies control and regulate violence. Legal systems in tribal and egalitarian societies tend to be based on "private law." Violence and injuries are compensated by retribution by the victim or the victim's family. As societies become more complex, legal systems become more universalistic and concerned with public law. Crime and punishment nevertheless are subject to many cultural influences and reflect a society's standards.

VIOLENCE AND AGGRESSION

Some people think that warfare, violence, and aggression are simply gradations of the same thing. It is important to distinguish them from each other. **Aggression** refers to attacking behavior that is harmful or potentially harmful. **Violence** refers to behavior that physically harms or destroys people or things. Not all aggression causes violence; some aggression is purely verbal, as in a "battle of words." **Warfare** is socially organized violence aimed at political or public goals. However irrational and impulsive warfare may be, it is a social phenomenon organized around social norms and attitudes. In some societies many aspects of social organization revolve around warfare as an institution.

We keep these ideas separate to avoid falling into a familiar error. Many writers have tried to explain warfare in terms of basic instincts. Konrad Lorenz, a zoologist and a founder of modern ethology, wrote a book called *On Aggression* (1966), in which he suggested that warfare is an expression of innate aggressive tendencies present in all people. Lorenz, who spent a lifetime studying animal behavior, did not distinguish between simple aggression and warfare. He may have underestimated the extent to which social and cultural factors control natural tendencies, aggressive or otherwise. There are many situations in which people might give vent to aggressive tendencies. In American

Figure 16.1 *Super Bowl XIX. Is the aggression exhibited in a football game attributable to instinct or to culture?*

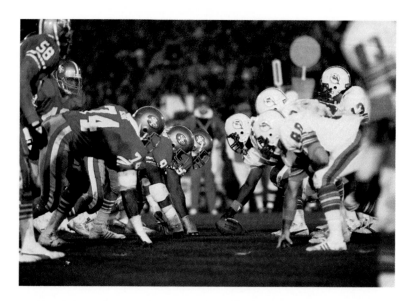

Figure 16.2 *"Locking horns" has become a figure of speech for hostile interaction. When these bighorn rams literally lock horns, their fight for dominance is at least partly controlled by instinct.*

football (Figure 16.1) a lineman is expected to be very aggressive toward his opposite on the other team during the plays. He should block, sock, elbow, and otherwise mistreat his adversary as much as possible before the whistle blows to end a play, but between plays and after the game, he must "turn off" his aggression, shake hands with his adversary, possibly even engage in friendly conversation. Aggression, the instinctively based attacking behavior, must be brought under tight control.

In thinking of aggression Lorenz may have had in mind the sort of physical encounters that animals have. When two mountain sheep lock horns (Figure 16.2), they are at least partly controlled by instincts. But human wars are not just outbreaks of aggression like fights in bars. In warfare the actual fighters usually have little to do with the decision to fight. The encounters often do not even involve physical contact between the combatants. Soldiers may sit in bunkers firing weapons at unseen enemies. More to

---

aggression Attacking behavior that is harmful or potentially harmful.

violence Behavior that physically harms or destroys people or things.

warfare Socially organized violence aimed at political or public goals.

the point, the people who send the troops into battle are rarely combatants. As the generals sit in secure offices far from the scene of fighting, sign orders, and talk to colleagues, are they responding to the same instincts as two men facing each other with swords? The activities of warfare, especially modern warfare, are highly compartmentalized and depersonalized. While inborn tendencies are in play, the social and cultural aspects are far more important. It seems more useful to deal with warfare and violence as aspects of social and political life, since instinct—although it is involved—is buried deep beneath many layers of social practice.

SMALL-SCALE VIOLENCE

According to the 17th-century political philosopher Thomas Hobbes, life in the "state of nature" is "solitary, poor, nasty, brutish, and short." For centuries this statement was accepted as a true description of life in tribal societies. In the 19th century another idea that gained currency was that "to a primitive, life is cheap." According to this view, human life is not sacred to the uncivilized. Such people are willing to sacrifice others in the pursuit of their own selfish aims. These ideas are typical products of ethnocentrism. They attribute qualities to other people that we deplore in ourselves. These stereotypes are not supported by evidence from non-Western tribal societies. There are, to be sure, some societies where killing is a normal part of life, but there are others where killing is unthinkable and warfare, as we define it, is not practiced.

Consider the Semai, an inland group living in the tropical forest of the Malay peninsula and subsisting on slash-and-burn horticulture and hunting. The Semai idealize nonviolence in social relations. They do not condemn anger; they deny it. Ethnographer Robert Dentan observes that the Semai appear carefree and timid to outsiders, although, like people everywhere, they do sometimes become angry. When Semai become involved in a dispute, the disputants seek out a mediator to help set things right. Until a dispute is resolved to everyone's satisfaction, the disputants avoid each other and resort only to nasty rumors about each other. Even mild forms of aggression, such as name-calling or threatening gestures, are avoided.

With so much repression and denial, one imagines the Semai would be seething with hostility. However, Dentan reports that even when drunk, the Semai refrain from hostility. Until 1950, when Malaya experienced a communist uprising, the Semai fled from every violent encounter. There were no raids and no warfare. When they were recruited into the militia by the British colonial authorities, Semai recruits seemed unaware that soldiers were meant to kill people (Dentan 1968). They were reluctant fighters and inefficient killers (Robarchek and Dentan 1987). They became disoriented at the sight of blood. After they returned to their own society the norms of nonviolence were restored and former soldiers became gentle and fearful of violence.

The fact that the Semai soldiers joined in the killing convinced some anthropologists that murderous instincts lurk just below the surface; they concluded that aggression and violence are human universals. Two leading Semai ethnographers published an article specifically to deny that the Semai data provide support for the universality of aggression (Robarchek and Dentan 1987). Dentan notes that official records show only a single case of homicide among the more than 12,000 Semai from 1963 to 1976. This works out to less than one homicide per 100,000 people per year, a remarkably low rate. The Semai may be exceptional in the degree to which they avoid violence. The !Kung San also avoid violence, but based on oral accounts of fights and homicides over a 50-year period, the San homicide rate works out to 29.3 per 100,000 population (Lee 1979).

Feud

Small-scale societies living in dispersed settlements like the !Kung or the Semai do not generally engage in warfare or organized violence. In some of these societies, however, a form of violence known as **feud** is fairly common. In a feud between two factions or two villages, each side attempts to attack and kill members of the other. The pretext for an attack is usually revenge for the death of a murdered relative. In other words, one killing leads to another in an endless chain. These raids and counterraids are known as **blood feuds.** They are dangerous in tribal societies because there is no centralized authority to restrain the conflict.

BOX 16.1

The Eskimo Song Duel

The Inuit or Eskimo people of Alaska and Canada generally shun aggression and socialize their children to repress their aggressive feelings, no matter how strong. To show anger is a great shame among the Inuit; if a person does display anger, he or she is likely to be ostracized, at least temporarily. In the early 1950s E. A. Hoebel studied the Inuit and observed that hostilities did erupt among them, particularly rivalries over women. Sometimes hostilities led to violence, homicide being the most serious outcome. To provide a means for releasing some pent-up anger and deciding the winner in a dispute, many Eskimo groups practiced competitive singing or "song duels" between the aggrieved parties. In one exchange of songs, a man was accused of taking another man's wife. He responded (Hoebel 1954):

Hi! You sing about my woman who was your
  wench.
You weren't so loving then—she was much alone.
You forgot to prize her in song, in stout, contest
  songs.

Now she is mine.
And never shall she visit singing, false lovers
Betrayer of women in strange households.

The objective of the songs was to ridicule and humiliate the opponent. According to Hoebel the duel displaced the anger and frustration of the contestants into a medium that could do little harm and would not lead to an escalation of violence. The outcome depended not on who had the better argument but on who sang the cleverest, most original songs. The winner gained prestige and the loser lost face, but no blood was spilled. In some Eskimo communities, song duels were accompanied by boxing matches or head buffeting.

Homicide was perhaps the only reason for going beyond the usual sanctions of humiliation or ostracism. The family of a murdered person might try to take revenge on the murderer or his family. If the murderer came from a different settlement, one settlement might raid the other. Only rarely did the Alaskan Eskimo go on raids for reasons other than blood revenge.

Blood feuds and raiding are often associated with factionalism. **Factions** are groups of a larger organized entity (village, party, school) who unite under a common leader to pursue common goals. Unlike political parties or religious groups, factions are not necessarily united by common beliefs or values. More often they come together to oppose another faction under another leader. The context is usually one in which there is competition for some resource or simply competition for dominance in the political arena.

In the absence of a recognized centralized authority the parties to a blood feud may go on trading attacks for a long time. Each new attack is justified as a retaliation for the last one. The logic of feuding is often **deterrence**: If an attacked group does not take revenge, the previous attacker may feel free to attack again. Revenge, however, turns the attacker into a victim who then feels obliged to retaliate. In some cases, the violence may be escalated as each side attempts to mobilize more and more people to attack the enemy.

In other cases, however, there may be a way to prevent the escalation or continuation of violence. The Eskimo Song Duel (Box 16.1) is a means of dis-

---

feud   A common form of violence involving attacks and counterattacks between factions, clans, villages, or other groups.

blood feud   A feud with the purpose of avenging the death of a murdered relative or group member.

factions   Groups within a larger organized entity (village, party, school) that unite under a common leader to pursue common goals.

deterrence   Prevention of action by one's enemies, usually by taking some action that keeps them from feeling they can attack with impunity.

Figure 16.3 *Yanomamö parade in body paint and adornment at a feast. Feasts can be the sites of both alliances and ambushes; a village with a particularly fierce feud with another may enlist the aid of a third village to host a feast, where the unwitting guests are attacked.*

placing potential violence. Another means is used by the Kapauku of New Guinea, among others: A battle may go on until one side has clearly won or until there is an equal number of deaths on each side. If there is any discrepancy, the side that lost more lives can press a claim on the other side. Before peace returns, the side that has lost fewer men must make a payment (in cowrie shells and pigs), known as **bloodwealth,** to the father and brother of any warrior on the other side whose death has not been avenged (Pospisil 1963, 61). Acceptance of the payment makes revenge unnecessary.

Feuds exist in many kinds of societies. Shakespeare's *Romeo and Juliet* describes a feud between two powerful families in Renaissance Italy. In modern times, we have heard many stories about feuds between the so-called "crime families." Feuds persist between such groups because they do not recognize any superior authority such as the state.

Tribal Warfare: The Yanomamö

Settled societies with larger local populations have different patterns of violence. The sporadic and limited feuds between households or factions give way to organized warfare under stronger leadership. In some tribal societies, warfare is a major focus of social life, and the socialization of boys is mainly devoted to developing future fighters. One such group is the Yanomamö of Brazil and Venezuela, whom we have met in several other contexts. The Yanomamö spend great amounts of time and energy preparing for war (Figure 16.3). They fight to punish other groups for attacks, to capture women, or to defend other groups against attack. Fighting takes a heavy toll. In one group, ethnographer Napoleon Chagnon found that warfare was the largest single cause of death among men, accounting for over 40 percent of male mortality (Chagnon 1966, 160).

The Yanomamö live in villages ranging from 25 to 250 people, typically all under a single roof built in a doughnut shape around a central plaza. They are slash-and-burn horticulturalists who have been expanding at the expense of other tribes for the past century. Each village is an autonomous unit led by a headman who is a senior male of the most powerful faction. There is constant tension between the Yanomamö's quest for security and stability, on the one hand, and meeting the need for garden land and marriageable women on the other. Yanomamö villages consist of two or three major exogamic patrilineal groups that intermarry with each other. Thus there is usually an exchange relationship between the two major lineages, following the pattern of **balanced reciprocity** (see Chapters 14 and 15). Men can promise their daughters and younger sisters to men in the opposite lineage.

The Yanomamö are "male chauvinists." They strongly prefer male children to female because of their emphasis on military defense. There is some evidence that Yanomamö women kill some girl babies, a practice known as **female infanticide.** This may lead to imbalanced **sex ratios.** In one group the ratio of female to male children under ten years old was about 64 females to every 100 males (Chagnon 1974, 159). The imbalance is even greater because high-ranking men among the Yanomamö may have several wives, while others have none. In the village of Mishimishimabowei-teri, there were three men who had six wives each, two who had four each, seven who had three each, and eight who had two wives each. There were not enough women to go around among all the men.

The constant threat of attack leads Yanomamö villages to maintain a strong defense. The best defense is a large village with plenty of warriors. However, large villages are unstable because there are frequent internal fights. Most of the disputes are over women and involve accusations of infidelity, wife beating, and jealous rivalry. Because of exogamy, men from the same lineage are in competition with each other for the same women. Men also fight over the theft of food or accusations of witchcraft. Once a fight begins it can escalate. A man may challenge his rival to a side-slapping duel (Figure 16.4); other men may join in, leading to a club or arrow fight. Deaths and injuries often result from these conflicts. Many Yanomamö men shave their heads to display scars from such battles. (See "Anthropologists at Work" at the end of this chapter.)

Like many tribal peoples, the Yanomamö do not have a strong political organization. The headman has little coercive power and leads mainly by example. In the documentary film *The Feast* (Chagnon and Ashe 1971), we see the headman trying to get his fellow villagers to clean up the plaza for a visiting village that will arrive later that day. He does not give orders but instead squats down to scrape away weeds with his machete, inviting others to join him.

In a large village with many possibilities for disputes, the tension sometimes becomes intolerable and the danger of violence too great. At such points a small, weak faction may decide it is wiser to leave the village. This is known as fission. The first to move are those in greatest danger. A man who has killed or wounded an adversary may gather his brothers and close supporters and move away with their families before the victim's family can take revenge. There are few mechanisms to heal rifts in the village once they have occurred. The headman himself may be deeply involved in one of the factions. No one can truly stand above these disputes.

Life among the Yanomamö seems to fulfill Hobbes's "nasty and brutish" stereotype. While many people regard all warfare as pathological and abnormal, the Yanomamö case gives us pause. Warfare is an integral part of their existence. Much of their social, political, and economic life seems to revolve around it. It is also self-perpetuating. Each of the features connected with warfare, such as the female infanticide or the intravillage side-slapping duels, can be seen as causally re-

---

bloodwealth Payments made by (or demanded from) a killer, or the killer's group, to compensate a victim's family.

balanced reciprocity A form of economic exchange that involves giving with the expectation of a return gift in the immediate or near future.

female infanticide The killing of female babies, common in societies where males are more highly valued than females.

sex ratio The ratio of males to females in a society.

Figure 16.4 *Fighting among the Yanomamö often escalates from chest-pounding and side-slapping to club fights, which, though subject to rules and regulations, are very violent and may result in serious injuries. Duels and warfare are an integral part of Yanomamö life.*

lated to all of the others, eventually leading back to the beginning. However, the interconnectedness of Yanomamö society does not lead us toward a scientific understanding of their warfare pattern, because it does not explain the conditions under which the pattern arose or the conditions that maintain it. Because of the high mortality from warfare, it seems maladaptive. What could account for the persistence of a social behavior so costly in terms of energy and human life?

Chagnon believes that Yanomamö warfare derives from the fundamental need of a Yanomamö village to maintain its autonomy. Other anthropologists suggest that Yanomamö warfare is related to the scarcity of resources in the tropical forests of Amazonia. Animal protein in particular appears to be in short supply. The main Yanomamö crops are low in protein, and there are no domestic animals for meat or milk. The lush tropical forest does not support abundant game

(Gross 1975). Large populations, or populations that remain sedentary for more than a few years, tend to "hunt out" their neighborhood, making it necessary for them to travel further and work harder to get an adequate protein supply. Good garden land and other resources may also be scarce, since Amazonian soils are thin and easily exhausted.

Under these circumstances, it is advantageous for groups to maintain small villages, shift their location frequently, and leave some forest areas fallow (no hunting, no gardening) for long periods. Warfare and the associated "male supremacist complex" (Harris 1984) may help maintain this state of affairs. As we saw, large Yanomamö villages are unstable and are likely to break up into smaller groups. Warfare may also lead to "no man's lands," unpopulated buffer zones between warring villages where game and garden land can regenerate through ecological succession. Finally, raids and counterraids force some groups to move their villages to escape danger (Gross 1975).

This model has not been confirmed, because it is nearly impossible to set up an experiment comparing Yanomamö conditions to a control. The proposed links between the system's parts are complex. Evidence to support the model will come not only from the Yanomamö but also from other South American groups. Many of these studies reveal traces of a former warfare pattern similar to that still practiced by the Yanomamö. They also show that long-term use of territory, even by small populations, reduces fish and game populations and garden fertility. Hopefully new ways of testing this model will be found.

While the model is not confirmed, it is useful to consider certain aspects of the "protein model." The model proposed is not necessarily similar to the model by which the Yanomamö understand their own behavior. The Yanomamö are not "fighting over protein." Their own reasons for fighting are probably what Chagnon asserts, to maintain their "sovereignty," to take revenge for past killings, and to capture women. It is possible, however, that these goals are tokens in a game that the Yanomamö are not aware of but must play to survive. The Yanomamö are an expanding population in a restricted environment. The fact that the Yanomamö and other relatively **unacculturated** (having assimilated relatively little of the culture of surrounding societies) tribal peoples of Amazonia are not now subject to protein deficiencies is evidence that the high cost of warfare is compensated for by successful adaptation to the environment.

Mediators and Segmentary Systems

Yanomamö warfare may be an extreme form because there are so many factors that encourage it and so few mechanisms to control it. In Africa there are a number of societies that have mechanisms for controlling the

extent of warfare. One such group are the Nuer people of the Sudan. According to their ethnographer, E. E. Evans-Pritchard, the Nuer are very fond of their cattle, talking and boasting about them almost constantly. Evans-Pritchard described the Nuer as an egalitarian society with no tradition of authoritarian leadership (1940, 181):

> The ordered anarchy in which they live accords well with their character, for it is impossible to live among the Nuer and conceive of rulers ruling over them. [The Nuer's] turbulent spirit finds any restraint irksome and no man recognizes a superior. Wealth makes no difference. A man with many cattle is envied but not treated differently from a man with few cattle. Birth makes no difference.

Like the Yanomamö and the Kapauku, the Nuer take matters into their own hands when a life is taken. Blood revenge must be taken whenever a relative is killed. Sometimes, the victim's family is satisfied with a payment in cattle for their loss. When a murderer fears for his life, he sometimes takes refuge in the home of a leopard-skin chief. Leopard-skin chiefs (Figure 16.5) are men held in high esteem; as long as the culprit is in the home of such a chief, no one will attack him. The leopard-skin chief can intervene in such matters and determine what compensation must be paid.

Furthermore, the Nuer are a segmentary society, that is, their kinship system divides them into lineages and clans balanced against each other but able to join together against a more distantly related or unrelated adversary. By memorizing lengthy genealogies, the Nuer can trace relationships through many generations and even between distantly related persons. In a sense, all of the several hundred thousand Nuer are related. In a conflict each side mobilizes its more closely related kin. As a conflict gathers force, each side recruits progressively wider circles of kinship until the ring that includes both parties to the conflict is reached. Only then can family authority be brought to bear, that is, when someone related to both of the

---

unacculturated Pertaining to traditional societies that have not been integrated into the dominant culture or that have not adopted Western cultural values and behaviors.

Figure 16.5 *Although the Nuer leopard-skin chief wears a distinctive symbol of his office, he wields little political power. His role is to mediate disputes, thereby averting serious outbreaks of hostility within the Nuer community.*

adversaries can enter the scene to mediate or decide between the opposing sides. The special role of the leopard-skin chief may have arisen because of the danger of a general conflagration between closely related segments, those who live in the same village and depend heavily on each other. Thus the Nuer have a mechanism for damping the most destructive kind of conflict. The ability of the Nuer and similar segmentary societies to mobilize a large number of segments also helps to explain their conquest of territory occupied by other tribes (Sahlins 1961).

WARFARE AND THE STATE

Tribal societies have relatively few means for controlling violence. More complex societies have more elaborate means for regulating violence. Chiefdoms and

monarchies can appoint magistrates or judges with police power to impose settlements and punish wrongdoers. States are societies with a complex division of labor, **social stratification** (that is, socioeconomic classes), and an organized government that claims a monopoly over the use of force (states are discussed in detail in Chapter 17). States typically attempt to regulate violence at every level: between individuals, between groups, and between states. Despite regulation, however, violent acts such as murder, assault, and revenge do occur in state societies. Classical political theorists like Hobbes and Jean-Jacques Rousseau held that the state emerged because life without the state is so insecure. According to these theories, the state's legitimacy is tied to its ability to protect its citizens from violence.

The control exercised by states takes many institutional forms. Police forces maintain internal order, deter lawbreakers, and apprehend criminals. Courts and the judiciary determine the innocence or guilt of persons accused of crimes and decide disputes between citizens. Legislatures make the laws, which are enforced by the police and the courts. Penal systems carry out the sentences imposed by the courts, such as imprisonment, fines, and corporal punishment. States raise armies of full-time soldiers to fight wars. In modern states these functions relating to order and social control are separate from each other, while in tribal and **intermediate societies** (societies organized as chiefdoms or monarchies with constituted authorities but without all the features of states), many of these functions may be combined in a single institution.

The military function is well developed in many states. In such states military roles are hierarchical. At the top, generals or war leaders recruit armies, plan strategy, and coordinate policy with civilian leaders. Below them are officers who are responsible for training soldiers, commanding men in battle, and seeing to it that they are fed and housed. Common soldiers occupy the lowest ranks. They do most of the physical work and run the highest risk of death or injury in battle. Highly militaristic societies have full-time professional armies and generals who also fill roles of political leadership. In some societies, the highest ranks are reserved for those who have distinguished themselves in battle. In such societies men of low social rank can rise through bravery or brilliance in battle.

Women are rarely soldiers. In some societies, however, women serve in the armed forces and have been

Figure 16.6   *Rarely do societies grant the role of warrior to women, although some do permit women to participate in warfare to a limited degree. Kapauku women of New Guinea (left) join the men on the battlefield and collect arrows for reuse. During the war in the Persian Gulf, women flew combat missions; a Kuwaiti woman in Kuwait (right) greets a member of the U.S. liberation forces.*

given some limited combat roles. For example, in 1991 women were authorized to fly combat aircraft in the U.S. military, but they are still not permitted to participate directly in land combat (Figure 16.6). Kapauku women accompany their men to the battlefield and help by gathering up arrows for reuse. The Kapauku have a code of warfare that prohibits men from shooting arrows at enemy women (Pospisil 1963).

The Aztecs

One complex society known for its warfare was the Aztecs of Mexico. The Aztecs arrived in the central valley of Mexico in the late 12th century and quickly adapted to the regional system, which was dominated by warring city states. States did not attempt to destroy each other, but victors obliged the losers to pay tribute in foodstuffs and other goods. If a conquering state itself were conquered, part of the tribute it collected would be owed to the new conquerors. As we saw in Chapter 2, Aztec religion required periodic blood sacrifice to satisfy the high god. Some sacrifices came from within the society itself, but most sacrifices were captives taken in battle. Sometimes noble members of the conquered group were invited to watch as hundreds of their own people were sacrificed on the altar.

The Aztecs established a permanent city, Tenochtitlán, where modern Mexico City stands, in about A.D.

---

social stratification   A hierarchical arrangement of a society into classes of people that have more or less wealth, prestige, and power; a characteristic of state political organization.

intermediate societies   Societies organized as chiefdoms or monarchies with constituted authorities but lacking many features of state societies, such as social classes.

1325. From then on their influence rose until, on the eve of the Spanish conquest in 1520, they dominated a vast area of central Mexico. The Aztecs had a hereditary noble class that reserved many privileges for itself. Only the nobility could own land privately. The only other routes to wealth and prestige were through the priesthood or success in warfare. Warriors who captured four captives alive acquired the title of *tequiua* and privileges on a par with nobility. The *tequiua* formed a council that advised the ruler in matters of war. While the Aztecs did not have a **standing army**, certain echelons of the army were on a state payroll.

As with the Yanomamö, the various parts of Aztec society, including warfare, reinforced each other. Aztec society was not self-sustaining economically. Tribute income was essential to the maintenance of the social structure, especially the opulent lives of its upper classes. The flow of tribute was maintained and augmented by continuous conquest. Aztec commoners led hard lives and had little chance of rising in wealth and prestige. The bloody ceremonials at which the gods were honored with human sacrifice and warriors were rewarded with prestige and honors were a way of consecrating the people to its warlike ideals. So important was warfare in creating a constant flow of tribute and captives that the Aztecs created pretexts—so-called flowery wars—for fighting even when conquests or greater tribute payments could not be expected. Soldiers were motivated to fight by promises of fame and glory. But they were also motivated by a desire not to end up as sacrificial victims themselves.

Modern Warfare

Nowadays there is a growing tradition that condemns all violence and seeks to dedicate humankind to peace. "Ain't going to study war no more," says an American folk song. Some people believe that social evolution will lead inexorably away from reliance on violence and toward peaceful resolution of disputes. In fact many people implicitly equate the term *civilized* with the term *nonviolent*. There is not much evidence for this belief, however. Most of humankind lives in states where war preparations are constant and special honor is reserved for citizens who serve their nation as soldiers. Warfare, arming and preparing for battle, and the spoils of warfare are integral parts of the struc-

ture of many modern societies. Warfare drives the development of technology, as in the case of nuclear power, radar, jet propulsion, laser guidance, satellite monitoring, and other innovations.

Evidence from tribal groups like the Yanomamö and complex societies like the ancient Aztec and Roman states shows that modern states are not unique in their preoccupation with warfare. Some anthropological theories suggest that warfare is adaptive. A society that is in constant readiness for warfare and motivates its citizens to embrace the military life will be better able to defend itself if attacked. If it goes to war, it may gain more territory or have access to more resources.

Other popular theories suggest that warfare is simply a consequence of human nature and that people have inborn violent tendencies. While aggression may be under partial genetic control, however, we have already seen that warfare is a social process that is triggered by political and economic events having little to do with instincts.

Another theory suggests that all warfare is a struggle for material resources. The recent war in the Persian Gulf might lend credence to such a theory. The president of Iraq, deprived of Soviet protection, apparently made a fatal miscalculation that the United States and its allies would not act against his invasion of oil-rich Kuwait. Cross-cultural studies now under way (Ember and Ember in press) suggest that scarcity of resources, as evidenced by famines and shortages, lies behind many warlike situations. The issue is complicated in the context of the modern environment, because the world struggle involves the search not only for raw materials like petroleum but also for markets and secure places to invest.

Finally, it is important to recognize the cultural component of modern national and international conflict. Recent years have seen a resurgence of conflict and persecution with an ethnic basis (Figure 16.7). There are conflicts between French- and English-speaking Canadians, Latinos and Anglos in the United States, Zulus and other ethnic groups in South Africa, Protestants and Catholics in Northern Ireland, Kurds and Iraqis in Iraq, Azerbaijanis and Armenians in the Soviet Union, Serbs and Croats in Yugoslavia, Christians and Muslims in Lebanon, Lithuanians and Russians in Lithuania, North Africans and French in France, Basques and Spaniards in Spain, Tamils and Sinhalese in Sri Lanka, Sikhs and Hindus in India,

Figure 16.7 *In recent years, ethnic conflicts have been erupting throughout the world with increasing regularity. Here, a Soviet paratrooper guards the television tower in Vilnius, Lithuania, after Soviet troops stormed it in January 1991, firing on the peaceful Lithuanian demonstrators.*

Jews and Palestinians in Israel, and indigenous and nonindigenous peoples in many Central and South American countries. The issues are numerous, including police brutality; oppression of minorities by elites in power; cultural autonomy, including language and customs; and economic issues.

It is a truism to say that people may fight when they do not share customs, language, and understandings, but in many cases the differences between the competing groups seem small or imperceptible to outsiders. It is clear that people do not fight simply because they are different. Ethnic conflict may be encouraged by the state because it serves the interests of leaders who want to divide their opposition, but this explanation applies only to a small number of cases. Perhaps the greatest challenge to social science in general, and anthropology in particular, is the understanding of culture-based conflict. We are only at the threshold of understanding what fuels these conflicts.

LAW

Every society has **laws** and **legal codes.** These are norms of behavior and prescriptions about how to settle problems that arise in the normal course of social life. They include rules to be followed, procedures for determining guilt or innocence, and sanctions to deal with people who violate the rules. A society's body of law may be an informal, shared set of views about acceptable behavior, or it may be a formal set of rules and procedures. Small-scale societies may function very well with an informal body of law. As societies grow larger and more complex, or as they come into contact with complex societies, laws and legal procedures tend to be formalized. Specialized lawmakers, mediators, judges, and councils arise to settle disputes, determine guilt or innocence, and mete out punishment. Matters that are settled privately in simpler societies become matters of public concern.

---

standing army A full-time, professional military organization paid by the state.

law A body of norms and commandments to which, by custom or imposition, people normally adhere, along with the customary or codified sanctions imposed for nonadherence.

legal code The formal body of law belonging to a given society; the standard of reference used by authorities to judge behavior.

Anthropologists have spent a good deal of time among nonliterate peoples trying to understand their legal codes and procedures from statements people make and from how they treat specific cases. This approach to law has a serious drawback, however, as anthropologist Robert Redfield has stated: "If we take [the case-study approach] we find ourselves concerned with all the complicated and varying considerations of personal motivation and social advantage or disadvantage which are involved in deciding to do or not to do what people expect of us. Following . . . this road, one has not too little to talk about but far too much" (Redfield 1964).

Redfield and other anthropologists adopted a "formal" approach to law that concentrated attention on those societies that possess a formal body of law, whether written down or not. Redfield defines law as "the systematic and formal application of force by the state in support of explicit rules of conduct" (1964, 4–5). By this definition, law in simple societies exists only in "incipient" and "rudimentary" form. In other words, Redfield believes that law exists only in the presence of a legal authority with the power to enforce its decisions.

This definition of *law,* while making it easier to identify the object, may be too restrictive. There are many examples of legal codes and legal procedures in simple societies, even though there may be no formal code, no police, and no code enforcement. We have seen a few cases where blood feuds can be settled by compensation paid by the killer's family to the victim's. Among both the Nuer and the Kapauku payments are set by convention, although the actual payment may be negotiated. There is, however, no superior authority to which an injured party can appeal if the payment is not made. In effect, the final resort in such societies is the injured party's ability to enforce a judgment. Redfield points out that the existence of a "code of indemnity" specifying payments to be made to compensate for deaths is "likely to occur in societies where forms of wealth are recognized and much status attached to its possession. There is something that may be given up, that people hate to give up, and that may be offered as equivalent to vengeance" (1964, 13).

Redfield wanted to distinguish the law from other aspects of social life concerned with good behavior, morality, and personal strategies. In doing so he may have overemphasized the significance of formal legal institutions and ignored the existence of informal legal institutions among simple tribal societies. But his stress on the connection between societal complexity and legal complexity seems correct. In societies with larger social units and greater possibilities for conflict and feud, formal legal codes are more salient.

Private Law and Public Law

As societies grew more complex, not only legal *codes* (sets of rules) but also legal *processes* become formalized. More complex legal systems provide for some impartial judgment to be made by persons who have no personal interest in the dispute at hand. This is an important development in social evolution, because it implies recognition that society at large has interests above and beyond the concerns of the parties to a dispute.

E. Adamson Hoebel, the ethnographer of the Cheyenne, distinguished between **public law**—legal rules considered of interest to the entire society and administered by public officials—and **private law**—rules dealing with conduct of concern to the injured party and only indirectly the concern of government. The evolution of legal systems could be viewed as the transformation of private law into public law. In tribal societies, for example, murder is generally a matter of private law. The main deterrent is the possibility that the victim's family will avenge his or her death. In many cases, victims are people who do not have large families or other support groups.

A social institution that creates an alternative to vengeance is a step toward public law. One such institution is found where the disputants allow a disinterested third party to mediate between them. The leopard-skin chief among the Nuer is an example of such a mediator. Mediators are also found among the Ifugao of the Philippines, whose elaborate legal code was described in 1919 by R. F. Barton, a missionary, in a book called *Ifugao Law.* The Ifugao are a tribal people but one with high population density based on intensive rice cultivation. Disputes are frequent and potentially violent. The first step in an Ifugao legal dispute is for the plaintiff or the accused to seek out a *monkalun.* The *monkalun* is a recognized legal specialist who acts as judge, prosecutor, defense attorney, and court recorder. He should not be closely related to either party to the dispute. He is entitled to a fee for his services; the fee is larger if a peaceful settlement is reached. The *monkalun* takes testimony separately from the parties to the dispute and their kinfolk. After he renders his judgment, he may use flattery, pleading, scolding, or other means to persuade the parties to accept it. He has no power to impose his judgment, however, and if the disputants refuse to accept it, they may resort to violence.

Another recognized procedure for settling disputes among the Ifugao is the **ordeal.** If a man is accused of a crime but refuses to admit it, his accuser may challenge him to an ordeal. In one version the accused is required to pluck a pebble out of a pot of boiling water and then put it back. He must do it slowly; undue haste is seen as a confession of guilt. In another version, the *monkalun* touches a hot knife to the hands of both parties. The Ifugao believe that the gods of war and justice will cause the knife to burn the hand of the guilty party more seriously than the hand of the innocent. This is apparently a way of translating a human judgment (made by the *monkalun*) into a supernatural one (Barton 1919).

A further step toward public law occurs when a serious offense like murder becomes a crime not just against a victim and his or her family but against society itself. In Chapter 15 we saw the role of the tribal council at the annual gathering of the Cheyenne. Hoebel claims that the Cheyenne completely eliminated feuds. Hoebel wrote, "The bulk of Cheyenne law is public law" (1960, 49). If a murder occurred, the Cheyenne took swift public action against the criminal. He was seen as "polluted" and thought of as having a putrid smell, offensive to people and to the bison. For the good of the tribe, the murderer was banished from the tribe. Hoebel shows that councils not only decided particular cases but also used the occasion of such decisions to lay down general rules for future behavior. Unlike the !Kung San, the Yanomamö, and the Ifugao, the Cheyenne had the organizational means to enforce decisions. They therefore represent a further development in the evolution of law: the capacity to enforce legal decisions.

The League of the Iroquois provides an example of "international law" in a tribal context. The Iroquois were a group of horticultural, village-based societies who, when the first Europeans arrived, were invading what is now New York State and displacing many Algonquian groups. The league is said by the Iroquois to have been founded by a prophet named Daganawidah who arrived on the scene about 1570. At that time the Iroquoian groups were frequently at war with each other. Daganawidah convinced the Iroquois to stop fighting among themselves and to live in peace and righteousness. It is possible that the formation of the league was also stimulated by the arrival of the French in the Gulf of St. Lawrence early in the 16th century.

The league was a confederacy that regulated contact among the five tribal groups that composed it. It was governed by a council representing the Onondaga, Cayuga, Mohawk, Oneida, and Seneca. These "peace chiefs" were men chosen by senior women from certain matrilineages in each tribe (Figure 16.8). The council had no jurisdiction within the tribes, but its ability to enforce peace and coordinate external warfare made the Iroquois a highly successful military force. From fortified villages in New York State they ventured against neighboring tribes, including the Huron and the Algonquians and their French allies in what is now Canada. Gradually the Iroquois were drawn into an alliance with the British in Albany, New York, on whom they depended for trade goods. They played an important role in controlling the hotly contested Great Lakes fur trade. Throughout the 17th century, the Iroquois successfully resisted the French, repulsing two major attacks in 1687 and 1689. The league was finally broken up in 1787.

Tribal societies like the Cayuga and Oneida are not as clearly defined as modern nation states. They often have no territorial boundaries, and they may speak a number of different languages. The League of the Iroquois is a somewhat unusual example of tribal peoples uniting for political ends. The fact that the league dealt only with military matters may be a key to its weakness and ultimate dissolution. If the tribal mem-

---

public law   Legal rules dealing with behavior of interest to the government and administered by public officials.

private law   Legal rules dealing with behaviors of interest primarily to an injured party and only secondarily to the state.

ordeal   A test of physical or mental endurance, used to initiate an individual in a rite of passage or to determine guilt or innocence in a trial.

Figure 16.8 *Cornplanter, a Seneca peace chief, represented one of the five tribal groups in the League of the Iroquois, a confederacy that flourished from the 16th to the 18th centuries in what is now New York State.*

bers of the league had developed other forms of cooperation, especially in production and trade, they might not have been divided so easily when the American Revolution came.

In modern times the state has become concerned with an increasing number of acts. Modern states make laws about every aspect of life, including food, sex, work, transportation, the use or exchange of every kind of commodity and service, and religious practices. Even as state interference increases, the distinction between public and private law continues to be relevant. For example, recently there has been controversy about whether the U.S. government should require the use of automobile safety belts. One side to the debate argues that if individuals wish to risk their own lives without harm to others, they should have that right. The other side argues that reducing fatali-

ties from traffic accidents is everyone's concern and that there is no inherent right to risk one's life.

Crime and Punishment and the Social Context of Justice

How different societies define and treat crime—**legal culture**—is one of the clearest indicators of cultural differences. We have examined the difference between public law and private law in tribal societies. Complex societies also present contrasts in how crimes are perceived and punished. Even the most explicit legal codes may not include the social background of law. Learning how to live in any society includes understanding the legal sensibilities and procedures in effect.

Legal systems reflect the social world that surrounds them. In 1976 a Brazilian "playboy socialite" known as Doca Street was accused of killing his mistress, a well-known actress. At his trial Street admitted shooting the actress but pleaded innocent on the ground of "defense of honor" because he had discovered that his mistress had been having a love affair with another woman. Street's defense was successful, even though there was nothing in the legal code that provided for such a defense, and he was acquitted of the murder charge. Later, however, the public outcry against the verdict was so great that he was arrested, retried, and sentenced to a jail term. Doca Street's acquittal and subsequent conviction testify to changing social and legal conditions in Brazil.

Legal Culture in the United States.   Americans are socialized to the law in many ways. Popular television programs and newspaper accounts provide detailed accounts of legal proceedings (Figure 16.9). Courtroom dramas are a popular genre for film and the theater. Many Americans serve on juries, act as witnesses in criminal proceedings, or bring suit in civil court. Some segments of the population acquire a very different outlook on the police and the court system because of their socializing experiences. African American youths in large cities, for example, have a much greater chance of being arrested than white youths of the same age.

A segment of the population that is particularly subject to arrest is the group of people who live on "skid row" and are commonly known as "bums," "der-

Figure 16.9 *Jimmy Smits portrayed trial lawyer Victor Sifuentes in the popular TV show "L.A. Law," which has familiarized millions of viewers with courtroom procedures and a host of legal issues.*

elicts," or "drunks." The men themselves often refer to themselves as "tramps." Often these people are arrested on charges of public drunkenness. Anthropologist James Spradley studied homeless men in Seattle, Washington. Examining court records for the year 1967, Spradley found that nearly 12,000 men were charged with public drunkenness, more than half the total arrests in Seattle that year. Spradley pointed out that although the men were usually charged with public drunkenness, the actual cause of arrest was urinating, sleeping, or drinking in a public place, behavior associated with the men's homeless situation and highly offensive to the general public.

Tramps have life-styles that ignore basic American values. They may go for days without bathing or shaving; they eat, sleep, and eliminate in public places; they do not have steady jobs or fixed addresses and do not strive to maintain a good reputation. Clever tramps learn to manipulate these values to avoid being locked up. Spradley recounted one case as follows (1971, 366):

> [One] inmate, when released from jail, went personally to the judge and pretended to be a contractor; he

told him that a man who had worked for him was in jail and he would employ him if he were released. The judge complied with the request, and the two tramps left town together—proud of their achievement, surer than ever that one of the best ways to beat a drunk charge was to understand the value of work in American culture.

Spradley found that, contrary to popular opinion, tramps hate confinement and feel that they are arrested to provide cheap labor. As prison "trusties," they work as cooks, janitors, and maintenance workers for the police department. After "doing time" once or twice in the company of other tramps, they learn the best ways of "beating the drunk charge." They lay careful plans to allow them to continue their life-style without being arrested or sentenced on drunk charges. From the perspective of the judges, these men are simply "con artists," but for the men themselves, winning freedom against the system is a skill, patiently learned from experience and fellow inmates.

From extensive interviews with tramps, Spradley compiled a list of the most common strategies used by men arrested on drunk charges (Table 16.1). Spradley did not suggest that it is bad to have a job, only that the conditions that influence the treatment of tramps are closely tied to widely held American values. Although the legal system has a formal logic of equality, fairness, and blindness to "extraneous" factors, the sight of a man urinating in an alleyway, sleeping on a park bench, or wearing torn and dirty clothing is disturbing enough to American values to prompt the authorities to arrest and imprison him. Thus it appears that the treatment these people receive is related more to American norms and values than to the formal legal system.

Legal Culture in the Soviet Union.   A view of a different legal culture comes from observer George Feifer, who spent ten days sitting in a People's Court in Moscow. Even if defendants were not sitting in the prisoner's dock, they could be identified by the fact that their heads were shaved, as required by Russian prisons. The language used in Russian courts was

legal culture   The sociocultural context in which crime, the legal process, and justice itself are embedded.

TABLE 16.1   Strategies for Beating a Drunk Charge in Court

1. Bail out (posting bail; usually $20, nearly always forfeited).
2. Bond out (posting an appearance bond).
3. Request a continuance.
4. Have a good record (conventionally six months or more without a conviction).
5. Use an alias (fake name).
6. Plead guilty (and ask for leniency).
7. Hire a defense attorney.
8. Plead not guilty (requiring a costly trial).
9. Submit a writ of habeas corpus.
10. Make a statement.
    a. Talk of family ties.
    b. Talk of present job.
    c. Talk of intent to work.
    d. Tell of extenuating circumstances.
    e. Offer to leave town.
11. Request the alcohol treatment center.

Source: Spradley 1971.

plain, everyday language without the "legalese" often heard in courts in other countries. But perhaps the most distinctive aspect of the people's court was the stress laid on Soviet doctrine by the magistrates. In one case a young man admitted stealing a hat from another passenger on the subway. The court learned he had quit his job and drifted about, drinking excessively. The judge berated the defendant saying, "How could you permit yourself to go for weeks without work? Where is your honor as a Soviet citizen?" Taking into account the defendant's disregard for his obligations as a citizen, the judge sentenced him to a year in a labor colony.

In another case a young man had been living in Moscow for nearly two years without a *propiska*, the permit required to live in a major city. He was arrested for swindling. He admitted guilt and was lectured by the judge before being sentenced (Feifer 1964):

> Young man, you have got to get a job, you have got to find yourself an honest place in our socialist society. And you cannot do it in Moscow. Do you understand you are living at the expense of society? Young man, you are a piece of fungus. You have done nothing with your life but practice the bourgeois creed of getting something for nothing.

With that the judge sentenced the man to four years in a labor colony. Feifer commented that the sentences were particularly harsh for poor, working class, and minority defendants, a somewhat unexpected outcome in a state created to uplift the working class. The Soviet example shows how a legal system reflects a set of "official values" promoted by the state and the myth on which it is founded, that is, that each citizen should contribute to society according to his ability and receive benefits according to his need.

A century ago, the German sociologist Max Weber distinguished between universalistic and particularizing tendencies in society. In tribal and intermediate societies, social norms are highly particularizing. As societies become more complex and based on abstract principles of administration, rules become more general and administration more impartial. An individual is not treated as an individual but as a member of a category. This dichotomy appears to be appropriate for many cases. The legal system in most developed countries is oriented toward public law; laws are written universalistically, applying to all citizens regardless of rank or status.

However, the briefest survey of modern societies like the United States and the Soviet Union shows that the ideal of equal treatment for all citizens is more of an ideal than a reality. Citizens with dark skin color, minority ethnic origin, or lower educational level or income generally do not receive equal treatment in legal proceedings. Some major strides have been made in the United States, such as requirements that defendants who cannot afford legal defense are entitled to a court-appointed defender. Most authorities agree, however, that the legal process is still deeply embedded in the social system as a whole.

SUMMARY

- Life in some tribal societies is dangerous and filled with violence. Elsewhere tribal life is peaceful and virtually devoid of violence.

- In societies with small, shifting local populations, such violence as does occur is restricted to individual fights, sometimes elevated to the level of family feuds. Societies with larger, more sedentary populations seem prone to a more organized form of violence, such as the blood feud.
- In some societies, it may be possible to stop a feud by making a payment (bloodwealth) to the victim's family. Other societies have mechanisms, such as mediators, for preventing violence from escalating.
- In segmentary societies opposing segments can be mobilized through the clan system, reaching a point where large portions of the population are arrayed against each other. Such societies can also unite their segments against an outside opponent.
- Organized campaigns of violence for political ends are known as warfare.
- Warfare is not the simple outgrowth of human aggressive tendencies because it is highly variable and dependent on cultural norms.
- In some societies, such as the Aztecs, warfare is an integral part of the social system, tied to rank and prestige, distribution of goods and services, and access to resources.
- All societies have codes of conduct and means for settling disputes. Some are more formalized than others.
- Private law consists of codes for the resolution of disputes by the disputants themselves.
- Private law becomes public law when an institution arises that involves nondisputants in the resolution of disputes. Under public law, leaders or the government become involved in determining guilt or innocence and meting out punishment.
- The ways in which different societies define crime and determine punishments are good indicators of the importance of social and cultural context in understanding the law.
- People everywhere are socialized into a legal tradition. This tradition, in turn, must be understood in a cultural context.

GET INVOLVED

1. Feuds are the predominant form of organized warfare in simple (egalitarian) societies. They are also present, however, in complex societies, especially in situations where the state will not or cannot intervene. Using the news media, direct interviews, and any other source of information, learn about some feud that has been going on for some time in your environment. What was the original cause? What events have prolonged the feud? What, if anything, limits the acts of the disputants? Remember that people feel very strongly about feuds, especially if they are still active. You should therefore exercise great discretion in your inquiries.

2. There are many cases in which the state's formal legal system comes into contact with informal legal codes. Some examples are colonial administrators with responsibility for indigenous or other traditional people, urban administrators or law-enforcement officers in contact with ethnic groups or organizations with their own internal organizational principles, even high school teachers in contact with students. Examine one of these cases as thoroughly as you can to learn what differences and conflicts exist between the formal legal system and the informal codes. How do people who accept the informal codes deal with the formal legal system? How do those responsible for enforcement of the formal code adjust to the informal code?

3. Much has been written about conflict and war and their causes, but little has been written about peace. See if you can identify any society or group that has been at peace for at least 50 years. Make a study of this society to determine how and why it has been able to keep peace.

SUGGESTED READINGS

Chagnon, Napoleon. 1983. *Yanomamö: The Fierce People.* New York: Holt, Rinehart and Winston.

Gibbs, James L. 1963. The Kpelle Moot. *Africa* 33 (1).*

Kertzer, David L. 1988. Flaming crosses and body snatchers. In *Ritual, politics and power.* New Haven, Conn.: Yale University Press.*

Podolefsky, Aaron. 1984. Contemporary warfare in the New Guinea highlands. *Ethnology.*

Robarchek, C. A., and R. K. Dentan. 1987. Blood, drunkenness and the bloodthirsty Semai. *American Anthropologist* 89:356–365.

* This selection is anthologized in *Applying Anthropology,* 2d ed., ed. A. Podolefsky and P. J. Brown (Mountain View, Calif.: Mayfield, 1992).

Fieldwork among the Yanomamö

Raymond Hames is an associate professor and chair of the Department of Anthropology at the University of Nebraska-Lincoln. He conducted fieldwork among the Yanomamö and Ye'kwana of Amazonas, Venezuela, in 1975–1976 and among the Yanomamö in 1985–1987. His research emphasizes behavioral ecology with a special focus on time allocation.

Before beginning fieldwork with the Yanomamö I was well advised through my readings and discussions with Napoleon Chagnon (an ethnographer with extensive experience among them) that the Yanomamö had a reputation for aggression ranging from verbal intimidation, through chest-pounding and club duels, to murderous intervillage raiding. I was also advised about their propensity to lie, especially to achieve a political goal or to put off an especially nosy ethnographer.

As I began to get to know the Yanomamö at my research site of Toropo-teri and other villages in the Padamo River basin, I was struck by the apparent lack of overt political hostility among these villages. One of the goals of the project of which I was part was to collect systematic information on settlement pattern history, demography, and genealogies in my area. This sort of information is key to understanding Yanomamö political dynamics, and it was beginning to show that there had been virtually no raiding or lethal dueling for more than 20 years. Nevertheless it quickly became clear that there were deep-seated animosities between the three villages (the Kowaci-teri cluster) in the middle of the basin and the two villages (the Shawarawa-teri cluster) that occupied the headwaters of the basin.

Raymond Hames uses a battery-powered computer and printer in the field to collect information from Yanamamö informants on settlement pattern history, including where they lived, how big the village was, and why they moved.

In the late 1940s the ancestors of these five villages had lived in a single village called Kowaci-teri. Oikomo, a prominent ancestor of many of those who now lived in the Shawarawa-teri villages, had killed Kumauwä, the headman of Kowaci-teri, who was ancestor to many of those who now lived in the Kowaci-teri villages. This precipitated an immediate village split, as the kin of Oikomo fled to the present locations of the Shawarawa-teri villages. Intensive raiding occurred between the groups for several years, ceasing only in the mid-1950s.

In August of 1975, just as I was beginning to piece together the major outline of political relations in the basin, all the men of Toropo-teri suddenly left for the village of Namaho-teri, the northernmost village of the Kowaci-teri cluster, to trade and to participate in a feast (*reahu*). It struck me as odd that none of the women went: The villages were at peace, and many of the women had close relatives in Namaho-teri. I was also disappointed that I had not been invited to accompany the men because I had visited with them before, and they knew of my interest in studying Namaho-teri. About one week later the Toropo-teri returned, and it became clear why I had not been invited and why their women had remained at home: Five men had been killed in a fight.

The real purpose of the visit was to engage in a series of club duels to settle a dispute. My Kowaci-teri informants claimed that several women from their villages who had married Shawarawa-teri men were severely abused and that one had been murdered by her husband, the brother of the powerful headman Naköshema. Accounts of exactly what occurred during the fight differed, predictably, along political lines. Kowaci-teri informants claimed that Naköshema, the leading headman of the Shawarawa-teri villages, entered Namaho at the head of his group and quickly shot and killed two allies (kinsmen visiting from a village outside of the river basin) of Kowaci-teri with his bow and arrow.

He was killed with a shotgun blast by the headman of my village, Baadawai. Two more Shawarawa-teri men were killed as they retreated.

Shawarawa-teri informants gave an account that blamed the Kowaci-teri. Naköshema indeed entered the village first at the head of his people, they said, but as he was strutting toward the center of the village plaza, Baadawai mortally wounded him with a shotgun blast. As he was dying, he managed to get off two shots, killing the Kowaci-teri allies, and two more Shawarawa-teri men were killed as they retreated back to their village. The only points of agreement between the two versions of what happened were who had died and who did the killing.

Claims have been made that Yanomamö warfare is designed to enhance protein consumption, but I believe that these sorts of killings cast considerable doubt on such ideas. The initial cause of the killings was a dispute between two political leaders that led to one killing the other more than 20 years ago. Although tense but peaceful relations developed between the descendants of the two headmen, none of the Kowaci-teri had forgotten who killed their kinsman. Then the despicable treatment of their female kin forced the Kowaci-teri to make a momentous decision: endure past and present outrages and expect more or seek immediate vengeance to deter further depredations.

The killings at Namaho-teri were immediately followed by a large raid that pitted the three Kowaci-teri villages and two allied villages outside the river basin against the village of Naköshema. Even though there were no further killings, Naköshema's people were forced to take refuge in a distant allied village. Some anthro-

pologists would argue that this is a clear demonstration of the adaptive value of Yanomamö warfare: It leads to displacement of the vanquished with the victors gaining access to vacated hunting areas.

There are at least three factors that cast doubt on an ecological interpretation of Yanomamö warfare. First, regardless of the cause of the conflict, in the face of overwhelming military superiority a weaker village has little choice but to retreat to make enemy raiding more difficult. Second, if hunting efficiency is the ultimate cause of warfare, why would the Yanomamö go through the charade of seeking vengeance for the murder of beloved kin as the motivation to fight? The Yanomamö have a long history of raiding for the canoes and steel goods belonging to neighboring tribal groups such as the Ye'kwana. The Yanomamö make demands, the Ye'kwana refuse them, and the Yanomamö resort to force without rationalizing it in terms of vengeance. Finally, there are vast and rich hunting areas open to the Kowaci-teri groups to the east and west of their villages. If chronic game shortages were severe adaptive constraints, relocation without the onerous burden of warfare would be a less costly and therefore more adaptive solution to the problem.

This is not to assert that gaining an adequate protein diet at a reasonable cost is not an adaptive constraint on the Yanomamö and other Amazonian groups. But there are cheaper and more effective alternatives to warfare. I believe the causes of Yanomamö warfare may be more productively pursued by examining the intense competition among males for wives and the nature of a political system that is poorly designed to break the cycle of revenge.

The city of Ur in southern Mesopotamia (now Iraq) was founded in the 4th
millennium B.C., and this ziggurat of
Ur dates to the 22nd century B.C. Not
a single straight line was used in its
construction; the builders employed
many subtle refinements, such as the
slightest of convex curves, to give the
illusion of strength.

17

THE RISE OF THE STATE

▲ ▲ ▲

T he rise of the state was perhaps the single most important event in human social evolution. There were no states 10,000 years ago; today nearly all of the 5 billion people on earth live in state-organized societies, making the state the preeminent social institution of modern times. Because states are so common, it is difficult to realize the degree to which they have transformed human life. In this chapter we ask what the state is and how it arose. Are there many different conditions that gave rise to the state, or was there a single cause? What are some of the ways in which states influence the lives and behavior of people living in or near them?

As mentioned in Chapter 16, the state is a form of political organization occurring in complex societies, encompassing many settlements or communities under a multilevel system of authority within a particular area. All states have governments, but the government is not the same thing as the state. The state is a total institution that includes citizens, a charter, laws, regional structures, communities, statuses, and roles. The **government** consists of the particular institutional arrangements for the exercise of power by the state. Governments come and go, but the state remains. For example, Iran recently was transformed from a monarchy to an Islamic Republic; the form of government changed, and so did the rulers. Of course, states may also disappear when they are destroyed by other states, as when the Aztec state was destroyed by the conquistadors of Spain.

THE POWERS OF THE STATE

States claim a monopoly on the use of force, both externally and internally. They use force to defend the borders of their territories—the fixed areas they control—and they may also extend control beyond their borders, as when imperial states use weapons and military force to impose their will. Internally states set up codes of conduct for their citizens, which they enforce through a police force and a judiciary. Much of the state's power is not overtly forcible, however; states can operate in subtle, even invisible ways.

Classifying People and Controlling Their Lives

States classify people in different ways, granting rights and imposing obligations. Sex and age are generally important dimensions of state classification, just as they are in simpler societies. In the United States the state sets age limits for voting, buying and consuming alcoholic beverages, driving a vehicle, attending school, purchasing firearms, retiring from work, holding political office, and other activities. For example, males between the ages of 18 and 25 are required to register for military service. The state may recognize differences in social rank, as in countries that distinguish between the nobility and commoners. Racial or ethnic factors may also be taken into consideration. For example, up until the 1960s some places in the United States had laws providing separate public facil-

Figure 17.1 *Until recently, black South Africans were not considered citizens in the land where they were born; these residents of a township near Johannesburg show the pass books they were required to carry.*

ities, such as schools and public restrooms, for African Americans and whites. Some modern states, like Israel and Lebanon, distinguish people according to religious background.

Like many ancient states, all modern states have a category of **citizen**, a legal classification that grants certain rights denied to noncitizens and imposes certain obligations. In the United States citizenship is primarily a matter of one's birthplace and the citizenship of one's parents. Citizenship rights may be differentiated. For example, until recently in South Africa the **apartheid** system granted citizenship only to people of European, Asian, or mixed descent. Black Africans were defined as citizens of native "homelands," even if they were born in South Africa to South African parents. They had to carry passports while on South African territory just like other foreigners (Figure 17.1).

While states differ from each other, there is virtually no area of life that states have not attempted to control at some time, including birth, death, health, nutrition, sex, reproduction, family life, production, finance, trade, religion, and ideology. For example, states intervene in family life by granting marriage licenses, recognizing the legitimacy of children, and limiting the number of spouses a person can have. States can have considerable control over social advancement by providing or withholding education or information.

States also define property and how it can be transferred. In the Aztec state, for example, only the nobility could own land. Commoners worked land owned by the state. In the United States, property can include "intellectual property," such as a computer program, a short story, or a patent. States encourage investment in some kinds of production and discourage investment in others. States control trade through regulations, taxation, and the construction of infrastructure (roads, harbors, airports, and so on) and socialize the young by operating schools. States create a standard of value and a medium of exchange of coining money and regulating its circulation.

Manipulating Information

All societies depend on information, but in complex societies information relates directly to power. Successful manipulation of information is a key to control. States define roles in terms of the information to which a person has access. Some information is available only to judges, generals, or people with a security clearance. States often practice **censorship**, restricting access to information. This is because a government's legitimacy—the acceptance of its authority by the people—is directly related to how people perceive it, which in turn is related to what people know about it and its leaders. All states control access to radio and television broadcasting, for example. States generate a great deal of information, such as censuses and economic data, that is important for political and economic control. States may also produce **propaganda** designed to convince people that the state is acting in their best interests.

The Power to Tax

States use the power of **taxation** to appropriate wealth to finance their activities, as well as to influence social and economic activities. There are many different forms of taxes. **Head taxes** are payable per individual or head of household. They have been used by colonial governments, like the British in Uganda, as a means of forcing people into the labor market who might otherwise work only for their own consumption. **Circulation taxes** are imposed on commodities

---

government The institutions that formally constitute the authority of the state.

citizen An individual having legal rights defined through birth, residence, or membership in a particular state.

apartheid The policy of racial segregation practiced in South Africa.

censorship Restriction of access to information, usually by the state.

propaganda The manipulation of information by states or parties to gain support for particular policies and activities.

taxation The imposition of assessments on wealth by the state to finance its activities.

head tax A tax that requires every individual or household head to pay a fixed amount (also called a poll tax).

circulation tax A tax imposed on transactions involving merchandise or services, sometimes for the purpose of controlling their production or consumption.

or merchandise; they provide a means of regulating the production or consumption of certain goods. For example, the cigarette and alcohol taxes in the United States limit the use of these products by making them more expensive to the consumer. **Labor taxes** are paid in services. The Inca government in Peru, for example, required every person to spend a certain number of days working on state plantations, maintaining irrigation canals, or doing other work.

Income taxes are collected on people's earnings. A **progressive income tax** can partially offset wealth differences by setting higher rates for people with higher incomes. **Estate taxes** on inheritances of land, houses, bank accounts, and other property can also be instruments for redistributing wealth. Some states, like Canada, have **pronatalist** taxation, reducing taxes on large families as a way of encouraging people to have more children. The People's Republic of China, on the other hand, has an **antinatalist** policy, adding to the tax burden of families with more than a prescribed number of children.

Distributing Power and Privilege

In all state-organized societies, political power is unevenly distributed. Typically there are also major differences in wealth, luxury, and access to resources. In other words, all state societies are stratified. (Social stratification is discussed in detail in Chapter 18). Some anthropologists define the state as a means of supporting the prevailing system of socioeconomic stratification. Examining the ways states use power to define categories of citizenship, to uphold property rights, to make and enforce laws, and to control information, we find that they nearly always act to maintain the prevailing system of stratification.

Karl Marx, the 19th-century political philosopher and revolutionary theorist, wrote that modern nations were simply **bourgeois states**, that is, states organized to protect the interests of the **capitalist class** (the owners of the investment capital, factories, land, and other means of production). Marx predicted that bourgeois states would be overthrown by the workers and eventually the state itself would "wither away." In the 20th century, several states based on Marxist principles established **command economies** in which all major production and distribution decisions were to be made by central planners, presumably to benefit the greatest number of people. These states have typi-

cally presented themselves as "classless." However, it appears that the state in these countries did not "wither away" as Marx predicted. They also have clear ruling classes. Modern socialist states seem to protect property and privilege as much as others, in spite of their ideological principles. During the late 1980s, many Marxist states in Eastern Europe, Latin America, and Africa underwent dramatic collapse, primarily due to the inability of the Soviet Union—the most powerful Marxist state at the time—to continue sustaining them. Most of these states (and many in the Soviet Union) are undergoing transitions to market economies. The role of the state as a redistributor is much smaller in market economies than in Marxist states.

A key variable among states is how power and privilege are allocated. The formal allocation of power provided for in a constitution is not necessarily the same as the actual allocation of power. For example, many states hold regular elections, but the leaders are still not accountable to the people. In every state there is an informal structure behind the formal structure. To understand how a state actually functions, we must understand both the formal and informal structures. For example, the formal structure of the United States Congress gives each representative a single vote. In fact, however, certain legislators have greater influence than others, stemming from favors they have done for other legislators.

Differences among States

Forms of government vary widely. Some states, such as Brunei and Saudi Arabia (Figure 17.2), are governed by monarchs. Others, like England, have a monarch as "head of state" but an elected prime minister as head of the government. Democracy is not a single type of government; there are many variations in the form of representation and the process of selection of leaders. Some states are **secular**, with separation between religion and state; others have a religious orientation. England, the Islamic Republic of Iran, and Israel have official state religions, although they may allow other forms of worship as well.

States differ in the extent to which they interfere in the lives of their citizens. Some states are **totalitarian**, using their power to control and sometimes to abuse their citizens. Throughout this century, social critics have raised concerns that the state may attempt to

Figure 17.2   *The Sultan of Brunei, Muda Hassanal Bolkiah, rules a small state on the island of Borneo. Brunei is a constitutional monarchy rich in oil and natural gas.*

fere in many aspects of life. Some states also have strong, centralized governments exercising tight control over outlying regions or areas. Other states allow some regional self-determination.

Nearly all modern states claim to defend freedom, but the idea of freedom varies from one place to another. In some countries freedom is defined in terms of individual rights, while in others freedom is defined in terms of the entire society. Marxist societies place a high value on freedom from want but place sharp limits on individual property rights and political rights. Similarly, almost every modern government claims to act on behalf of its people, but this claim can be justified in many different ways. Some governments claim legitimacy by holding popular elections for their leaders. Others derive legitimacy by adhering to a particular economic system or religious ideology that, the leaders assert, is in the best interests of the people. Most states are divided by economic, religious, regional, and ethnic cleavages so there is no uniform "popular will."

Resisting the State

control even the private, intimate thoughts of its citizens. Such questions arise in books like George Orwell's *1984,* Aldous Huxley's *Brave New World,* and Alexandr Solzhenitzyn's *Gulag Archipelago.* Other states have a "lighter touch" and do not actively inter-

Often people at one of the levels of organization in a state, whether a local community, a religious organization, or an ethnic group, find ways to resist the power and intrusions of the central state. They may do so by resisting taxation, keeping alive a minority language or cultural tradition, disobeying laws, or actively rebelling. In many modern states, there are organized regional or ethnic groups arrayed against each other and attempting to manipulate the power of the state in their own interest.

---

labor tax   A tax paid in the form of service to the state.

income tax   A tax based on the amount of income an individual or business earns over a given period of time.

progressive income tax   A form of income taxation in which rates are set higher for higher levels of wealth or income.

estate tax   A tax on inherited land, houses, bank accounts, and other property.

pronatalist   Policies that tend to encourage people to reproduce.

antinatalist   Policies that tend to discourage people from reproducing.

bourgeois state   A state based on the economic principles of capitalism.

capitalist class   The owners of the means of production or wealth-producing resources, such as property, land, factories, and businesses.

command economy   An economic system in which production and distribution decisions are made centrally.

secular   Nonreligious.

totalitarian   Pertaining to state institutions that exercise powerful central controls, in which the rights and opinions of citizens count for little.

In modern Lebanon, for example, Maronite Christians, Shiite Muslims, Sunni Muslims, Druse, and other ethnic groups compete for power and influence in the state. This is the result of the unraveling of a set of tacit agreements that had lasted for decades, granting the greatest amount of power to the Maronites with the participation of the Sunnis and Druse and the exclusion of the Shiites. Aggravated by the interference of Israel, Syria, and other nations, the fragile accommodation shattered, and open warfare broke out on the streets of once-peaceful Beirut. Some observers believe certain factions encouraged the ethnic rivalries as a way of maintaining their grip on power. As a result, the society has been ripped apart.

THE RISE OF THE STATE

In considering questions about the rise of the state, some anthropologists use the term *civilization* instead of *state*. The idea of a civilization refers to a broader set of features than those associated with state organiza-

tion. In common usage a civilization is a complex society embodying the state and a set of distinctive cultural traditions comprising technology, science, art, architecture, law, morals, literature, religion, and other features. Often the term *civilized* is used to make an invidious comparison to another, simpler group. The term *uncivilized* connotes a people who are crude and violent, lacking great artistic and intellectual traditions and true moral and legal codes. It is easy to see how this idea lends itself to ethnocentric bias.

Attempts to define civilization more rigorously often require arbitrary cultural judgments. For example, *civilization* is sometimes defined as a society possessing a system of writing. According to this rule, ancient Rome would be regarded as a civilization, while ancient Peru, which lacked a writing system, would not. The term *civilization* is avoided in this book because it is imprecise and carries these connotations of superiority.

Most of the ancient states we read about in history books were not the earliest states in their respective regions. The Incas, the Aztecs, the Han Chinese, the

Figure 17.3   *World map showing the location of ancient primary states.*

1. MesoAmerica
2. South American
3. Subsaharan Africa
4. North Africa
5. Southwest Asia
6. India
7. China

Greek and Roman states, and the states of Europe all arose under the influence of earlier states. They are **secondary states** because they borrowed state institutions from other states or had them imposed on them by outsiders. Most contemporary states are secondary states. A **primary state**, on the other hand, is one arising spontaneously from less highly organized origins. Primary states arose independently of each other in different parts of the world: southwestern Asia (including Mesopotamia), China, India, South America, Mesoamerica, North Africa, and sub-Saharan Africa (Figure 17.3).

Beginning in the 16th century A.D., Europe's influence was felt over most of the world, creating an illusion that Europe was the fountainhead of "advanced civilization." However, the states of Europe were all secondary in origin; in fact, until the 15th century, the states of North Africa, Asia, and the New World were technologically more advanced than those of Europe. There have been persistent attempts to demonstrate an Old World origin for the pre-Columbian New World states, and some writers have even suggested an extraterrestrial origin for the advanced features of New World societies (von Däniken 1969). It is as if some people cannot accept that the native peoples of South America and Mesoamerica were capable of developing complex state institutions, science, technology, monumental architecture, and writing on their own.

Secondary states do not arise simply because of contact with state-organized societies. There are tribal peoples and chiefdoms in many parts of the world, including Oceania, South America, and Asia, who live in contact with state-organized societies without adopting state organization. Often such peoples are overwhelmed and absorbed into state-organized societies. In such cases tribal organization is subordinated to state controls, as on U.S. tribal reservations. The conditions that lead secondary states to become independent states are similar to those that underlie the development of primary states. Among these conditions are productive and reliable agriculture, relatively high population density, at least some large settlements, and the development of specialized economic and political roles. Borrowing (diffusion) of institutions, then, is not a sufficient condition for state formation.

THEORIES OF STATE FORMATION

Most studies of state formation focus on primary states. Primary state formation was a relatively rare event; it may have occurred as few as six times. However rare they were, these events are important because they set a pattern for social evolutionary changes that were to encompass nearly the entire world. Before examining the leading theories of the origin of the state, let us survey some areas of widespread agreement. We can lay out a set of *necessary* conditions for the rise of the state on which most scholars agree. The disagreements arise when we attempt to specify necessary and *sufficient* conditions for the rise of the state.

Among the necessary conditions we can specify are the following:

- Intensive agriculture
- The ability to produce and store more food than immediately required for consumption
- High population density
- Some large sedentary settlements
- Some form of extralocal trade or exchange
- Occupational specialization
- Social stratification
- Developed leadership with political power

In surveying primary states we find that subsistence intensification generally preceded state formation (see Chapter 12). In southwest Asia, settled villages appear before the full development of agriculture. Within a few thousand years, the first evidence of state organization can be found. In Mesoamerica, maize was first

---

secondary state   A state whose origins are influenced by other states, such as through borrowing or imposition of their institutions.

primary state   A state that arose spontaneously and independently without influence from other states.

domesticated about 7,000 YA, but settled villages do not appear until after 4,000 YA and indications of state organization appear about 3,000 YA. The first settled villages in Peru appeared on the coast before domesticated plants were available.

Settled villages and agriculture interacted to promote **social complexity**. A simple model of state for-mation posits that settled villages or agriculture pro-moted population growth, because of either a reduction in birth spacing or a more abundant food supply (see Chapter 12). Population growth had a positive feedback effect (discussed in Chapter 11) of encouraging intensification in subsistence efforts. New settlements filled the space available wherever

Figure 17.4 *A model of the causes and effects of state formation as proposed by three theorists.*

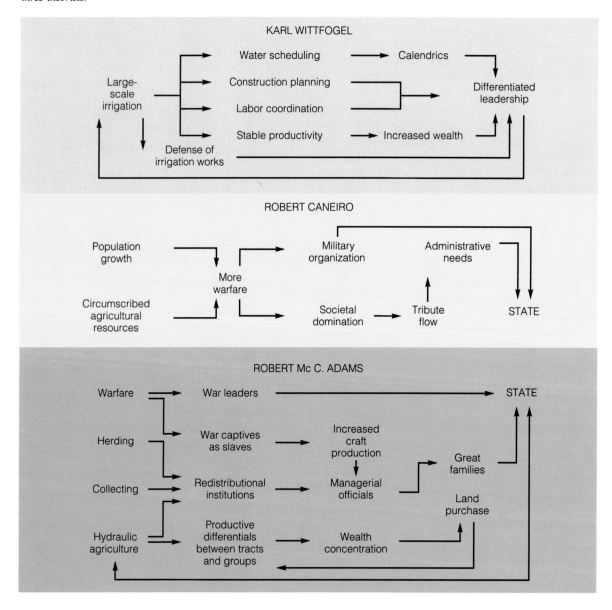

they were ecologically viable. Trade developed between settlements that had access to different resources. Sedentism and large populations also made it possible for some people to devote themselves full-time to craft production. Trade provided an outlet for their products. Of course someone had to feed these artisans, so farmers increased their output.

As population densities rose and populations found themselves "hemmed in" by natural barriers or hostile peoples on their borders, new ways had to be found to support rising populations. In several cases irrigation systems increased productivity and removed the barrier to population increase. Stronger political leadership arose in response to the need to mobilize large amounts of labor to construct and maintain canals and other infrastructure. This was another positive feedback effect.

Little of this model is controversial, although different theorists give different weight to different factors (Figure 17.4). But this model does not show *why* a society would become more complex. It only sets out conditions that logically would favor it. Most of these conditions can be found archaeologically in the development of the major primary states. But not every settled agricultural village is a step on the path to state formation. Many such village societies described in the ethnographic and archaeological record remained stable for long periods of time. Some additional feature or features gave society that extra "kick," leading to social complexity and state formation.

Hydraulic Theories

One of the earliest and most durable theories of social complexity suggests that the first states emerged from the need to control water (thus the descriptive term **hydraulic**). In the 1930s, Julian H. Steward, archaeologist and ethnologist, noted that several of the "cradles of early civilizations" were in arid or semiarid regions (southwestern Asia, Egypt, northern China,

northern Peru, and Mesoamerica). Comparing the archaeology of these areas, he found that there were comparable stages in each one (Steward 1949). Steward proposed a model with the following stages:

1. Rainfall agriculture reached the limits of productivity.
2. Irrigation was introduced, but the system of dikes, dams, and canals required a managerial class. Societies turned naturally to religious specialists, who already occupied positions of prestige and influence. Thus the early states were "theocratic" with heavy religious influence. Religious authority was combined with civil authority. These early states generally extended over a limited region.
3. As irrigated agriculture reached its limits, regional states began competing with each other for resources.
4. An age of conquest followed. The conquerors established empires and demanded tribute from the vanquished.
5. The demands on food producers in conquered areas were so heavy that eventually there were rebellions, plunging these empires into a "dark age."
6. The technology and social organization of highly productive irrigation agriculture was restored when outsiders, perhaps predatory nomads, invaded and reestablished the empires.

There is a remarkable similarity among Steward's five cases, once the superficial differences are swept aside. For example, Steward compared the Early Intermediate period in Peru to the Old Kingdom period in Egypt (Box 17.1). In each case, small, regional states were incorporated into a larger empire as a result of conquest. The capital of each empire could mobilize and feed large numbers of non–food producers: artisans, priests, soldiers, and courtesans. They were also able to mobilize thousands of workers to build enormous monuments in honor of the gods. These laborers were probably not full-time construc-

---

social complexity A measure of social development framed in terms of division of labor, patterns of economic production and exchange, political organization, legal system, social classes, and so on.

hydraulic theories Theories suggesting that the need to control water resources for irrigation or drainage led to the origin of the state.

BOX 17.1

Early Empires in Peru and Egypt

The Peruvian Early Intermediate period, beginning about 2,200 YA, saw the first truly large cities, with populations possibly as large as 100,000. Some were capitals of large regional states, and a few became the centers of empires. There are many archaeological indicators of intensive warfare from this period, including fortified towns and cities, weapons found in the excavations, the morbid representation of trophy heads, artistic renderings of soldiers and battles in tapestries and painted ceramics, and numerous headless bodies found in cemeteries. This was plainly not a period of small-scale feuding. Population had been expanding steadily for centuries and reached a high point at this period. Irrigation systems in several coastal valleys were extensive.

The Tiahuanaco empire developed late in the Early Intermediate period, beginning sometime around the time of Christ. Throughout the Early Intermediate, Tiahuanaco's influence grew until, by 1400 YA, it had extended its empire over what is now western Bolivia, southern Peru, and northern Chile, an area about the size of France. Tiahuanaco was not the only empire of that period; the Huari empire occupied much of the central and northern Andes. Neither empire lasted more than a few centuries, but both left an imprint on the areas they conquered. Tiahuanaco pottery and emblems representing Tiahuanaco gods are found on pottery and textiles throughout the region. Unlike later conquerors, Tiahuanaco allowed regional art styles to flourish alongside their own.

The seat of the empire was in the Andes at an altitude of 3,900 m (12,750 ft) near Lake Titicaca (in present-day Bolivia). By about 1300 YA, the city of Tiahuanaco had a population possibly as large as 100,000. The center of Tiahuanaco had great religious monuments and was dominated by a pyramid whose base is 210 m² (690 ft²). There are massive walls and sculpted monoliths made from red sandstone taken from a quarry 10 km away. One piece of sandstone used in the construction weighs 131 metric tons. A Bolivian archaeologist has estimated that 2,620 people would have been needed to drag a stone this large (one

of many at the site) from the quarry to Tiahuanaco. Visitors to Tiahuanaco have wondered how such an elaborate city, which obviously required thousands of workers and many years to complete, could have been supported in the cold, bleak *altiplano*. The answer may lie in an area of 8,000 hectares (20,000 acres) of irrigated farmland near Lake Titicaca, which probably furnished Tiahuanaco with food. We lack any written record about the form of government in Tiahuanaco or the religion that apparently inspired the giant stone monoliths.

The comparable period in Egyptian development is known as the Old Kingdom. The main geographical feature of Egypt is the Nile River, which flows through the arid North African desert. Crops can be grown on the banks of the river itself, or along the narrow flood plain with the help of irrigation. About 5,100 YA the Nile Valley was dotted with small regional states called *nomes*. These were united first into two separate kingdoms known as Upper and Lower Egypt and then, by 4,850 YA, into a single nation under King Menes who ruled from Memphis. Egyptian hieroglyphic writing (a local invention) records the earliest dynasties of rulers from this period. Many of the remarkable artistic creations for which ancient Egypt is so famous were produced in this period by specialists for the enjoyment of noble people and the adornment of their tombs.

Unlike Tiahuanaco, the Old Kingdom does not seem to have been an age of militarism, at least not in its early stages. Neither was there significant urban development. Irrigation agriculture provided the basis for reliable food production, and rulers undertook to store surplus grain for distribution to soldiers and to armies of workers. Evidence for this can be found in the construction of the Great Pyramid at Giza, which was built as a tomb for the ruler King Khufu. This construction is estimated to have required a labor force equal to 84,000 people working 80 days a year for 20 years. It was built from 2.3 million stone blocks weighing an average of 2.5 tons.

Both Tiahuanaco and the Old Kingdom collapsed rather suddenly. In Peru the population abandoned all

---

tion workers but rather peasants drafted to work during periods of low agricultural labor demand. They too had to be fed. In each empire intensive irrigation agriculture was part of the productive system.

These similarities led Steward to conclude that there were parallel processes at work in which like causes led to like effects. Box 17.1 presents relevant information about two of these cases. Steward sug-

The Gateway of the Sun at Tiahuanaco is adorned with the sculpture of a god thought to be the creator deity, Viracocha. Nearby are huge freestanding sculptures and massive walls with sculpted figures. The number of icons here suggests that Tiahuanaco was not only an important economic center but an important ceremonial center as well.

Over 80 pyramids still exist in Egypt, and these in Giza are the largest monuments in the world. As was true at Tiahuanaco, the labor force needed to move the stones into place was massive; a large population and elaborate bureaucracies to coordinate the building process would have been imperative at both sites.

the cities of the southern highlands and dispersed into the countryside. Although cities and regional empires arose elsewhere, southern Peru underwent a period of nearly 700 years without substantial urban development. There was a significant amount of trade during this period as well as feuding between small regional states. During the 14th century (600 YA) a small regional state in the Apurimac basin in Peru began a series of conquests of its neighbors. In 1428, the ruler Pachacuti defeated the neighboring Chancas and rebuilt Cuzco the fallen capital of Tawantinsuyu. In less than a century, these people, led by a royal lineage known to us as the Incas, succeeded in conquering most of western South America from present-day Colombia to northern Argentina, the largest empire known in pre-Columbian times in the New World.

In Egypt the Old Kingdom was gradually weakened by the increasing power of provincial leaders and the nobility, who busied themselves with wars against nomadic groups outside the Nile Valley. Beginning

about 4,160 YA there were great political and religious upheavals lasting more than a century. The old state religion of Re, the sun god, was eroded by the prominence of the cult of Osiris, and the political power of the central state was eclipsed by provincial warlords and rebellions. The power of the central state was restored and augmented with the establishment of the Middle Kingdom about 4,040 YA under Mentuhotep II. His successors restored the capital at Memphis and reduced the power of the nobles.

Some of these similarities may seem coincidental, but the parallels in development are so extensive as to make us wonder whether some specific factor was not responsible. We can rule out contact between the two centers with virtual certainty. They arose in different periods separated by nearly 5,000 years, and there was no linkage between them. Much work is still needed before we can determine just why these striking parallels exist.

gested that the primary factor that induced state formation was irrigation to improve agricultural production. Once a society embarked on this course, it required elaborate bureaucratic controls to recruit,

feed, and coordinate workers on large-scale construction projects. Irrigation requires dams to trap water, reservoirs to store it, and canals and ditches to deliver it to the crops. Irrigation systems also tend to spring leaks and clog with silt, so they require constant main-tenance, generally by hand labor.

Many writers observe that irrigation systems re-quire careful coordination and skillful government to ensure that every farmer whose land is hooked in to the system gets the right amount of water at the right time. Political theorist Karl Wittfogel developed a the-ory similar to Steward's (Wittfogel 1957) in which he suggested that irrigation created the need not only to mobilize large amounts of labor but also to manage information about water allocation, production statis-tics, storage records, labor demand, annual cycles of flooding and drought, and so on. The fascination that ancient complex societies had with **calendrics** and astronomy may be related to the necessity for timing complex agricultural and engineering operations (Fig-

ure 17.5). In early states some priests specialized in making astronomical observations. They determined when major phases in the agricultural calendar should begin. On a more ideological level, the idea of con-necting worldly events to the behavior of celestial bodies may have been an effective way of keeping a potentially unruly population under control.

Over the years since Steward put forth his model of hydraulic civilizations, the theory has drawn both support and serious criticism. Mayan society, an elab-orate state of southern Mesoamerica, seemed to be an exception to Steward's theory, because it was located in a region of abundant rainfall and irrigation was nei-ther necessary nor practiced. But recent discoveries showed that the Maya built vast areas of ridged fields, an elaborate system to promote drainage and water

Figure 17.5 *An Aztec calendar stone found in the sacred precinct of Tenochti-tlan, the capital city of the Aztec and now Mexico City. Dating to about 600 YA, the stone helped the Aztecs keep track of important cyclical events in both astro-nomical and agricultural spheres.*

flow (see Figure 2.1). In the broader sense of hydraulic development, then, the Maya case fits Steward's theory.

On the other hand, some evidence fails to show that the state developed *because* irrigation was adopted. Archaeologist Robert McC. Adams wrote a book comparing Mesoamerica and southwestern Asia. He asks, "Were [ancient irrigation systems] sufficiently large in scale or complex in managerial requirements . . . to have served as a stimulus to the growth of specialized political bureaucratic elites?" (1966, 67). His answer for both regions is no. In southwestern Asia, Adams wrote, irrigation was conducted on a "small-scale basis," and he concluded, "there is nothing to suggest that the rise of dynastic authority in southern Mesopotamia was linked to the administrative requirements of a major canal system" (1966, 68). Adams draws a similar conclusion for Mexico.

Another perspective on the problem is offered by ethnographer J. Stephen Lansing who studied "water temples" in Bali, an ancient kingdom that is now part of Indonesia. Lansing (1987) shows that while the Balinese state was very unstable over time, the water temples, which ritually regulate the flow of water through irrigated rice paddies, provide an element of stability. The temples form a network managed by priests who use a complex yet flexible calendrical system to regulate the flow of water through a vast network of interconnected canals and fields. All the farmers whose fields are within a certain network must meet periodically to decide when water will be admitted to the system. This is accomplished without any interference from the state. The decisions are coordinated by a hierarchical network of temples supported by the farmers themselves (Lansing 1987).

Steward's hydraulic hypothesis does not fare well under scrutiny. The parallels are there, but the details do not always point in the direction Steward suggested. Stratification and centralized political authority are not present in every case of elaborate irrigation

networks. In recent years researchers have learned more about small- and medium-scale irrigation systems built and maintained virtually without state involvement. However, early states did manipulate the productive system to produce food above the needs of the food producers themselves; to do so they had to convince the food producers to work harder. They used their organizational power to build or expand irrigation networks, increasing the amount of arable land and raising productivity. While irrigation or hydraulic development may not have been the sole cause of state formation, it is certainly closely tied up with its rise in several cases.

Demographic Theories

A major factor in the rise of the state was the increase in population density that accompanied its origin in every instance. Can rising population density itself cause development of new social and political forms? There are at least three different pathways by which higher population density could have influenced state formation. First, as we have seen, larger populations create more opportunities for conflict within and between groups. This requires creative solutions that may change the structure of the society. Second, larger populations create management problems that may require new forms of leadership and control. Third, denser populations put more pressure on resources and favor technological innovation, which in turn encourages further population growth. It is hard to find anything logically wrong with these three arguments, and separate archaeological tests of them have yielded positive results. Let us briefly examine each of these propositions.

Social Complexity and Warfare. Ethnologist Robert Carneiro is the best-known proponent of the idea that warfare is the prime mover in the origin of the state. While Carneiro does not believe that all warfare leads

---

calendrics A system of measuring time and seasons of the year, generally based on astronomical observations, that became especially important after the development of agriculture and the rise of the state.

to increased social complexity, he thinks that, together with other conditions, it was a significant factor in the rise of all the ancient primary states. Carneiro (1970a) suggested that a society undergoing population growth would normally expand through fission, increasing the number of settlements and keeping settlement size stable. In some areas circumscribed by high mountains, bodies of water, deserts, or other groups, fission was impossible. The next step would be agricultural intensification, which could take place until no further gains in productivity were possible. Within such circumscribed areas, competition would arise, eventually leading to warfare aimed at the conquest of territory. The vanquished would have nowhere to go so they would remain on their land, but as subjects of the conquerors, paying tribute in the form of agricultural produce. The defeated people become an inferior social class within an empire. To the victors go not only the spoils of war but also the need for administrators, a police force, and a standing army.

The principal inspiration for Carneiro's model lay in the regional states that developed in narrow river valleys of the western slope of the Andes in South America (see Figure 17.3). The rivers that flow into the Pacific cross a desert. Cultivation is possible only along narrow strips of land near the edges of rivers, and it is expandable only by irrigation. There is archaeological evidence in many of these valleys that as agriculture became more intensive, warfare increased, culminating in the domination of the entire valley by a single state. In other valleys, however, chronic warfare and conquest may have followed, not preceded, the development of complex society.

Perhaps the most important assumption in Carneiro's argument is that of continuous population growth. Not all societies grow continuously, and there is some evidence that many societies undergo long periods of relative stability during which population either does not grow or declines (Cowgill 1975a and b). We have seen evidence of practices that discourage population growth, such as long postpartum sex taboos, late weaning, long birth spacing, and infanticide. Prehistoric populations, even those in circumscribed areas, could have adapted by reducing their rates of population growth. The alternative—violent warfare and the threat of defeat and subjugation—must not have been very attractive. Why did people choose it? It may have seemed more desirable than

adopting any practices to limit populations, or perhaps people optimistically believed they would win wars, not lose them. Of course, we have no way of knowing that these alternatives appeared to people as choices.

Social Complexity and Information Management.

A second hypothesis suggests that new social and political forms arise as a result of the adjustments required by an increase in the volume of information that leaders have to manage. One of the clearest expressions of this idea came in 1955 when ethnologist Kalervo Oberg approached the problem of increasing complexity in South American tribal societies. Oberg accepted the importance both of growth in food production and of warfare on social structure, but he focused especially on information management.

Oberg suggested that when conditions require the coordination of the activities of large social groups, the whole is broken down into manageable parts, each identified by a name and, if necessary, directed by a leader. Each leader is subordinate to a higher leader who, in turn, may be the subordinate of a higher leader. These principles of organization are found in nearly all complex organizations, which are broken down into divisions, sections, departments, and so on. They derive from the need for coordination and control and our limited capacity to direct or even recall every member or segment of a large group of individuals.

These ideas have been given a different twist by archaeologist Gregory Johnson. Johnson's comparative research indicates that when local groups grow larger than a certain fixed size, they tend to be segmented into smaller subunits (1978). Johnson found fixed ratios between local group size and the number of subunits. Johnson explains this phenomenon in terms of modern **information theory**, an approach to modeling the flow and use of information in social systems. As organizations grow in size and complexity, the number of different sources of information also grows. Consider the situation of a chief in a growing ranked society. He receives information about craft production, local factions, fighting, trade, farming, animal production, and other activities from different specialists in all the local units (villages, lineages, clans) under his authority. At a certain point there is too much information of different kinds for an individual to absorb and act on.

This bottleneck has different possible outcomes. The local unit could split, greatly reducing the information load for any individual leader. Or the average size of units might increase through consolidation, reducing the number of units and thereby the number of information sources. A third possibility is **hierarchic elaboration** in which new levels of management appear, intermediate between the highest level of control (the chief or ruler) and the lowest (craft production units, warriors, households, and so on). The largest number of disparate units that can be coordinated by a single manager tends to be about six. Information coming from more than six dissimilar sources may create **scalar stress**—problems arising from the complexity of an array of information sources—and the breakdown of control. Another archaeologist, William Rathje, suggests that the complexity of a community increases at a higher rate than its size. A village of 100 people can be administered by a single leader. Ten villages of 100 people each, joined into a larger system, require more than ten managers.

These notions go beyond the multiplication of numbers of people and their effect on the environment. They deal with the mental and social requirements of managing information and people. They do not address the causal factors of population growth, warfare, occupational specialization, or the mutual relationship of population and habitat. The limits and potentials of human organization, however, are just as significant as the physical and biological limits on production and exchange.

Social Complexity and Population Pressure. Few theories have produced as much controversy as those that suggest population pressure on resources as the driving force of many of the key transformations in human history. Until the 1960s most anthropologists and economic historians accepted the Malthusian theory that populations are ultimately limited by the food supply (see Chapter 5). By this logic it was convenient to think that technological changes, such as the invention of the plow, the introduction of new crops, and irrigation, were the causes of population growth. The introduction of the South American potato to Ireland in the 18th century, for example, is regarded by some as the cause of rapid population growth there. The Irish potato blight—a plant disease that nearly wiped out the potato crop—and the subsequent famine and massive emigration are also viewed as the tragic results of technologically driven population growth.

In 1965 the Danish economist Ester Boserup suggested that technological change in agriculture was a *consequence,* not a *cause,* of population pressure on resources. Boserup's approach attracted many adherents who proposed new explanations for the rise of agriculture and the beginnings of complex societies. Boserup herself did not propose mechanisms by which population pressure would cause technological innovation. Nor did she suggest how complex organizations might emerge from population pressure. Anthropologists were quick to suggest social mechanisms to fill this gap in Boserup's work. Robert Carneiro, for example, suggested warfare as an intervening variable between population pressure and social complexity.

Another approach was suggested by archaeologist Ezra Zubrow, who constructed a mathematical model for prehistoric carrying capacity in a mountain valley in Navajo-Apache country in Arizona. By **carrying capacity** Zubrow meant the maximum population size that can be maintained indefinitely in a certain area (1975, 15). Zubrow's model attached special importance to increasing population density. As populations rise in areas where it is easy to make a living, they move off to more marginal parts of the habitat where they have to work harder but there is less competition. This situation leads to greater emphasis on trade to offset local shortages, specialization by entire villages in specific resource procurement, and greater cooperation in economic activities. These general fea-

---

information theory A systematic approach to the flow and use of information in social systems and institutions.

hierarchic elaboration In information theory, one of the possible resolutions to the problem of information overload, in which intermediate levels of information management are developed between the highest and lowest levels of control.

scalar stress Management problems associated with the growth in quantity and diversity of information sources.

carrying capacity The maximum population size that can be maintained indefinitely in a certain area.

tures lead to spatial aggregation of settlements and the tendency for settlements to become ranked according to their size, their location in a trade network, and the importance of the resources they control. In other words, Zubrow outlined a pathway toward social complexity. One interesting aspect of Zubrow's model is that he formalized it enough to allow him to simulate it on a computer. The computer model behaved in a way consistent with the archaeological data collected in Arizona.

It is important to keep the idea of population *growth* separate from that of population *pressure*. Populations may grow numerically and expand territorially without necessarily putting pressure on resources. There are many different ways of measuring these different factors. It is possible to measure the size of con-

temporary populations and collect data on fertility, mortality, and other vital rates through health, household, and census records. However, there are few records on such matters going back more than a few generations, so it is difficult to examine broad general trends using contemporary data.

To take a longer view, archaeologists must rely on data that have more time depth than recent censuses or household registers. Most such data come from prehistoric populations. Some archaeologists have become experts in examining human remains to determine sex, age at death, cause of death, nutritional status, and even disease history. New techniques of bone chemistry allow them to determine the principal components of the diet of prehistoric populations. Paleopathologists have developed techniques that

Table 17.1 Some Estimates of Population Growth During the Neolithic and in Contemporary National Societies.

Population	Growth Rate (%/Year)	Doubling Time (Years)
Prehistoric Cases		
Neolithic (various areas)	0.10	694
Diyala (Neolithic Iraq)	0.07	991
Egypt (5,000–2,150 YA)	0.05	1387
Aegean Region (Neolithic and Early Bronze Age)	0.04–0.16	1734–434
Ixtapalapa, Mexico (3,200 YA–500 YA)	0.13	534
Middle Eastern Neolithic	0.08–0.13	867–534
Contemporary Cases		
France	0.3	232
India	2.0	36
Jamaica	2.2	32
Japan	0.5	139
Nigeria	2.9	25
Switzerland	0.2	347
United Kingdom	0.2	347
United States	0.6	116

Sources: Hassan 1981, 221, 234. Modern values (1989) from Mark S. Hoffman, ed., (New York: Pharos Books, 1991).

allow them to detect certain kinds of nutritional deficiency disease in skeletal populations. Together with estimates of prehistoric population sizes and prehistoric environments, these data allow anthropologists to form a long-range view of the interaction of population and resources.

In recent years there has been a reaction against the population pressure theory of social complexity. Critics feel that proponents accepted the idea of constant population growth uncritically. Archaeologist George Cowgill, for example, compiled evidence (1975a and b) suggesting that ancient populations underwent periods of slow growth, no growth, and high growth. Archaeologist Fekri Hassan quotes various authors showing relatively low rates of population growth, even in the Neolithic (Table 17.1). If the estimates of population growth for the Neolithic are accurate, they indicate that population was rising gradually, leaving time for adjustments to be made in subsistence and living patterns. Rates of population growth in some modern countries are much higher (see Table 17.1). Another criticism reminds us that populations are not homogeneous. Even though a given population may have a relatively slow overall growth rate, there may be segments of that population that are growing quite rapidly, offset by other segments that are not growing at all.

The data on population pressure in ancient times do not point clearly in one direction. Did ancient populations outrun their resources, and if so, how was this stress translated into complexity? There will continue to be debate and research on the topic. Population increase almost certainly had some effect on the rise of social complexity and the state, but it is still impossible to say whether its influence was felt through warfare, scalar stress, pressure on resources, or some other factor.

Trade and Exchange Theories

Exchange had an important role in the evolution of social complexity. Reciprocal exchange, which is found in every society, does not favor complexity. But redistributive exchange does, because it enhances the status of the redistributor. Agricultural societies—especially grain producers—can accumulate and store a substantial amount of food in one place. Stored food can be used to gain prestige, to attract people to ceremonies, or to pay for public works (roads or canals) and monumental construction (tombs and temples).

Redistributive economies are limited in their potential, since typically only a few kinds of goods are exchanged and the flow pattern is simple. State-run exchange, like that of the ancient Peruvian Inca and modern socialist societies, creates the possibility for significant inequalities between people because those with control over resources such as food have so much power. Market exchange, particularly capitalism, allows great disparities in wealth because wealthy people and corporations can invest wealth to acquire even more wealth. These disparities in the modern world add up to great power in the hands of business, often rivaling the power of states.

Trade in Early States. Trade and social complexity go together. What role did trade play in the rise of the state? This question can be addressed through archaeological research because many of the items that circulated in ancient exchange systems can be recovered in archaeological sites. One of the earliest items widely traded in southwestern Asia during the Mesolithic and Neolithic was natural asphalt, **bitumen,** which bubbles up to the surface of the earth in a few spots. For millennia bitumen was used to fasten stone blades to wooden handles, to waterproof baskets, and to seal the bottoms of boats. Archaeologist Henry Wright sifted out the bitumen from dirt removed from different levels in the Farukhabad mound in Iran. In the deposits laid down in the 100 years from 5,150 YA to 5,050 YA, the amount of bitumen per ton of earth went from 1 pound to 8, indicating a rapid increase in its importance as a commodity and specialization in bitumen export at that site.

Another widely traded item was obsidian (Figure 17.6), a naturally occurring glass used to make sharp knives and other items. Different sources of obsidian can be distinguished through spectrographic analysis

---

bitumen Naturally occurring tar used in some ancient societies as a sealant and an adhesive.

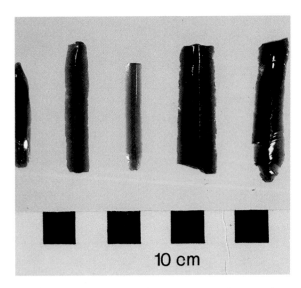

Figure 17.6 *Obsidian was an important trade commodity in early states. The volcanic glass was often used in cutting tools; the edge of an obsidian blade is more than 200 times sharper than a modern surgical steel scalpel.*

of its zirconium and barium content. Through this technique, obsidian found at the Ali Kosh site in Iran (see Figure 12.5) was identified as an import from the Lake Van area, 970 km (600 mi) away in eastern Turkey. The obsidian was probably brought on boats down the Tigris River, which rises near Lake Van and flows to within 65 km (40 mi) of Ali Kosh.

Trading Strategies.   The evidence for trade in these items raises two important issues. The first is the fact that exchange implies **demand**. There were people living in southwestern Asia who had no direct access to these materials but strongly preferred them to local substitutes. They were willing and able to produce something to exchange for them. The second issue concerns **production**. What could the buyers of rare or hard-to-get goods exchange for them? There were several possible strategies: (a) exchange some other rare goods obtained locally; (b) exchange rare goods obtained elsewhere; (c) exchange common goods such as animals, food grains, or pottery in quantities that would make it worthwhile for producers of demanded goods to part with them; or (d) exchange goods made precious by fine craftsmanship.

Probably all of these exchange mechanisms were found in southwestern Asia during the period of early state formation. If people in a community with access to obsidian desired bitumen, they could exchange obsidian directly for bitumen, which we shall call strategy (a). Since only a few places had access to rare goods, strategy (b) meant obtaining them elsewhere in trade. For example, an obsidian miner who had no direct contact with a supplier of bitumen might seek out a trader to serve as intermediary between the suppliers. There might be several such go-betweens. Such a **trading specialist** would need to get *more* bitumen for the obsidian (or vice versa) in order to cover the costs of locating supplies, transporting goods, and finding a buyer. Under strategy (c), the producer needed to find a way of producing more goods than were needed for local consumption to have enough left over to trade on the seller's side. In some cases, the amount of food or other goods offered for obsidian or bitumen might be sufficient to lead a food producer to give up farming and concentrate on producing **trade goods**. Strategy (d) required periods of apprenticeship and sufficient time for artisans to build the skills necessary to manufacture fine pottery, jewelry, or similar items.

Effects of Increased Trade.   All the trading strategies followed common lines. They all led to specialization, and they all provided an incentive for keeping costs down, raising productivity, and improving quality. Does this mean that early traders were all capitalists? In a limited sense, yes, because traders and producers had to invest their limited time and other resources in such a way as to earn profits to achieve their desired goals. On the other hand, it is unlikely that full-scale **capitalism** (a system in which land, labor, and capital all become commodities negotiable on the market with prices fixed by supply and demand) was part of the ancient world anywhere. In any case the demand for imported goods provides incentives to reorganize production in order to have something to exchange. Individual entrepreneurs may have played this role, but it seems plausible that civil leaders also took the initiative by recommending specialization, standardization, and increased productivity.

Specialization meant the development of centers of production where skilled craftsmen turned out products in a standardized form. **Standardization** had two advantages: (1) Production became repetitive and

Figure 17.7 *Yahya bowls from a site in western Iran. This popular, standardized trade item of 5,000 YA has been found within a 1,500-mile radius of its origin, often in temples and in graves of high-status individuals. In spite of their standardized form, the bowls may have been status symbols.*

specialize in carved stone objects, perhaps stimulated by an outside trading specialist. Skilled artisans began to turn out bowls of greenish chlorite (Figure 17.7). The bowls came in different sizes, but designs carved on them were highly standardized and repetitive. Apprentices may have roughed out the outline of the bowl, leaving the delicate carving to master artisans.

Archaeologist Philip Kohl made a special study of Yahya bowls (1974). They are found as far west as Syria and as far east as the Indus Valley, a total range of 2400 km (1500 mi). The bowls are found in temples and palaces and in the graves of high-status individuals. Science writer John Pfeiffer, compares them to the standardized emblems used by today's international elites, such as the Mercedes-Benz star on the hood of a luxury car or "designer" labels on clothing (1977). Curiously, there is no "upper-class" section of Yahya, which suggests that the local artisans were not getting rich from making them. Perhaps the people who traded them were. Also there is no indication of any luxury goods that might have been received in exchange for Yahya bowls; it seems that the artisans were paid in perishable goods like food.

Logic and the data agree that there was a close tie between the development of trade and the rise of complex societies and the state. However, the close interrelationship between the variables still does not establish a causal relationship between one and the other. Archaeologists Henry Wright and Gregory Johnson examined that question in a study of state formation in southwestern Asia. They examined a number of sites where there was evidence for long-distance trade in goods such as bitumen, obsidian, copper, and alabaster. Their data show that the volume of trade actually declined before the establishment of powerful states and was relatively limited for some years afterward (Wright and Johnson 1975, 277–279).

therefore more efficient, and (2) the exchange value ("price") of standardized goods was easier to set and agree on. Archaeologist Carl Lamberg-Karlovsky excavated a Neolithic site in western Iran that illustrates many of these points (1970). Yahya is a large mound first settled as a farming village about 6,500 YA. The farmers made some sculptures from a local stone called chlorite. About 5,000 YA, the village began to

---

demand   The desire and ability to purchase a commodity, or the quantity of a commodity that can be exchanged at a given value.

production   The creation of value by producing commodities.

trading specialist   A person who is a full-time trader or go-between.

trade goods   Commodities produced for the purpose of trade rather than individual or family consumption.

capitalism   An economic system in which land, labor, and capital all become commodities negotiable on the market, with prices fixed by supply and demand.

standardization   The production of goods to uniform measurements of quantity and quality, which greatly facilitates marketing and exchange.

Figure 17.8   *These bevel-rimmed bowls (right) found in a ceremonial site of southwestern Asia may have been used to issue rations to the workers who were drafted to construct the massive buildings of the Uruk period, such as the great ziggurat at Ur (below). The bowls may have been "mass produced" as a means of meeting the needs of the increasingly complex and populous state.*

On a local level, however, there is evidence that centralized production and distribution of certain crafts accompanied the extension of administrative control in the Early Uruk Period (about 6,000 YA). Wright and Johnson (1975) suggest that the centralized production facilities may have come into existence to meet fluctuating demands of nomads or others who came shopping at unpredictable intervals. One common kind of bowl that was "mass produced" and shipped out to smaller centers has been interpreted as a "ration bowl" by Hans Nissen (1970), a German scholar (Figure 17.8). Wright and Johnson (1975) suggest that the bowls were used to issue rations to labor **conscripts** drafted to work on ceremonial and administrative buildings. The most common bowl size holds enough grain to make the amount of bread eaten daily by a typical modern villager.

Again, there is no way to interpret trade in this context as the cause of social complexity. Trade does arise *with* social complexity, at least on a regional level. As with irrigation, there are probably feedbacks from trade to complexity with causal arrows running in both directions.

Other Factors Associated with Complex Societies

Certain other features have been associated with early states, including the development of writing and official religions. Although they are not suggested as causal factors in the rise of the state, they are clearly associated with growing societies.

Writing and Records. Trade helped stimulate the development of two activities often identified with complex societies: writing and record keeping. As trade grew more complex, involving a division of labor among producers, transporters, middlemen, and consumers and goods graded by prestige, utility, and quality, the need for record keeping became apparent. Some of the earliest recorded messages in southwestern Asia were impressions in soft clay made by tiny

Figure 17.9   Cuneiform *comes from the Latin word* cuneus, *meaning "wedge," which describes the characteristic impression of the symbols. This cuneiform script in clay records the sale of a slave in Mesopotamia about 5,000 YA.*

seals carved from stones. They seem to have served as "bills of lading" to help keep shippers honest. Without such a clay seal, the consignee of a boatload of grain might not know whether the grain received was the same amount shipped. These seals were followed by "cylinder seals," which made an impression with a repeating pattern when rolled over soft clay. It was only a short step from using clay seals to more complex symbols incised on soft clay. These symbols are known as **cuneiform** (Figure 17.9) and are perhaps

---

conscripts   Persons drafted into the service of the state, such as for military service or labor on roads or other state projects.

cuneiform   Wedge-shaped writing used in ancient Mesopotamia.

Figure 17.10 *The ground plan of the "Great Death Pit" at Ur. Made at the time of the excavation, the plan records the positions and relationships of the bodies and objects as they were found. The burials date to about 4,500 YA. Many precious objects were found among the bodies, including this "Ram in the Thicket" (below). The wood figure was covered with gold and silver leaf, shells, and lapis lazuli.*

the earliest form of writing. Around 5,500 YA in Uruk, an early state, there were about 2,000 different signs, but with a great deal of duplication and many different representations of the same thing. Within four centuries, the system had been standardized and the number of signs had been reduced to 400.

Writing systems evolved to serve different purposes in different places. In some parts of southwestern Asia, they were used to maintain genealogical records, presumably to keep people's rights and obligations straight. Early Egyptian writing, known as **hieroglyphics** seems to concern myth and religious affairs; early Chinese texts were concerned with **divination**, that is, supernatural ways of foretelling the future. Early Mayan writing dealt largely with the conquests of great leaders and deeds of war (Marcus 1976).

Religion and the State.   In every early state for which there is reliable data, there is evidence of an official **state religion.** In other words, there were beliefs in supernatural beings and worship practices that were officially mandated or required by the state. Characteristically the ruler was regarded as a descendant of the gods. Both the ancient Peruvians and the ancient Egyptians worshiped a sun god and believed their rulers were descendants of that god. The leaders had powers ordinary people did not have, and they had to be treated with special deference and respect. State religions arose along with professional religious practitioners, or priests. These were invariably handpicked men or women given special training in religious lore, calendrics, and other forms of knowledge.

We have already noted the relationship between calendrics and the priesthood. Religious specialists also held other kinds of specialized knowledge that gave them great influence. For example, at Anyang, the last capital of the first known dynasty in ancient China, the Shang excavations produced 30,000 inscribed "oracle bones," shoulder blades of oxen and tortoise shells. Scratched into them are characters recognizable as precursors of modern Chinese graphemes. These texts appear to represent communications with people who had died. They were the result

of a form of divination in which a religious specialist acted as an intermediary between a living person and a dead ancestor. The ancestors were consulted for predictions of the future and advice about pending decisions. Similar practices survive to this day in modern Taiwan and the People's Republic of China.

Many of the early complex societies developed beliefs in an afterlife in which the dead lived on in another realm. Burials provide evidence of these beliefs, for the dead were provided with many kinds of objects to accompany them to the other world. In southwestern Asia during late Uruk times, for example, rulers were buried with extraordinary wealth and pomp. Not only objects but also the servants of a dead monarch were sacrificed and placed in the tomb to continue their usefulness in the next world. In 1927 Sir Leonard Woolley excavated a tomb at Ur that became known as the "death pit." Woolley first came upon five bodies lying in a row, each equipped with a copper dagger, as if they were guards. Beneath them he found the bodies of ten women with ornaments of gold, lapis lazuli, and other precious jewels. Nearby were a bejeweled harp and the remains of the harpist, who wore a golden crown. Continuing down, Woolley's excavators found a chariot decorated with jewels, complete with donkeys and grooms. Other "guards," wheeled vehicles, and many heavily ornamented objects such as a model boat were found, until finally, at the bottom of the tomb, they came upon the body of the queen of Ur almost hidden by beads of gold, lapis, silver, agate, and other stones. This was but one of 16 royal burials found at Ur (Figure 17.10).

Similarly lavish burials have been found in both Egypt and China associated with ancient dynasties. Above these burials were massive buildings, tombs topped by temples that required many years and thousands of people to build. Are these elaborate burials evidence for a kind of spirituality among ancient peoples different from that found today? In some respects, these burials are consistent with modern practices and beliefs. Important leaders are buried with great pomp even today, although precious objects are rarely included in the burials. Many modern religions

---

hieroglyphics A system of graphemes used in writing in ancient Egypt.

divination Communicating with the spirit world to gain information for a living person.

state religion A religion sanctioned or supported by the state.

accept the idea of an afterlife. Ancient states seem to have involved the living in the death of monarchs to a great extent by building enormous tombs in anticipation of the ruler's death and manufacturing elaborate grave goods.

There are many theories about these practices. One suggests that tomb building was a way of keeping people busy and preventing them from engaging in other activities such as revolutions. Another suggests that the lavish grave goods removed valuable items from circulation and maintained the value of precious metals, gemstones, and so on. Like many functionalist theories in social science, these ideas are hard to refute but also hard to confirm. Another theory suggests that the tombs and the public plazas on which they were built were deliberately designed to impress the common people, particularly those from the countryside. It is plausible to imagine that rural folk who spent most of their days toiling on farms would have been awed and fearful in the presence of monuments that dwarfed them and finery beyond their wildest imagination. Religion, architecture, beliefs in the afterlife, and burial practices all conspired, according to this view, to make people docile by impressing them with the immense power of the state and its rulers and with the futility of resistance. These ideas are plausible, but it is difficult to devise a test of them. We will return to the theme of religion and the state in Chapter 22.

Nomads and the State.   Although we know little about them, it seems that specialized pastoral nomads played important roles in the development of the state in southwestern Asia. Pastoral nomads are people who keep animals, such as sheep, cattle, or goats, and migrate (usually in a regular seasonal pattern) from pasture to pasture. Some historians and archaeologists have suggested that states arose from the need of sedentary farmers to organize a defense against marauding nomads. Most specialists now agree that independent nomadism was not common in southwestern Asia until after the rise of complex societies and the state (Lees and Bates 1974). Nomads took advantage of ecological niches left unused by settled agriculturalists that furnished them with wool, hides, milk products, and meat. Nomads are never self-sufficient, however. They depend on farmers for grain, cloth, manufactured items, and, sometimes, protection.

Nevertheless, nomads played an important role in the development of the state because they raised the animals that provided services for traders, especially transportation of bulky goods like grain. After the introduction of the plow (about 5,000 YA) and wheeled vehicles (about 5,500 YA) in southwestern Asia, the role of nomads as suppliers of animals to farmers may have been even greater. Their animals also provided protein in the form of meat and milk, important elements in the diet of densely settled, urbanized people who had hunted out the wild game resources of their region. These services were probably crucial to the continued development of the state.

Nomads probably also caused trouble for settled peoples and state authorities. Since they were so mobile, they probably felt less loyalty to any particular territorial ruler, and they may have switched their allegiance from one state to another as it suited their needs. Nomads are famous throughout history as raiders and marauders, and there is some basis for this in the history of southwestern Asia. It is possible that some nomadic groups served as mercenary soldiers for warring states and that they attacked and plundered traders and cities.

Multicausal Theories

In recent years a number of researchers have decided that no single factor accounts for all cases of primary state formation. An adequate theory must be a multicausal one. This seems to be a practical solution: Social complexity does not have a single cause but a combination of causes that work together in different ways. Such statements are disarmingly seductive, but after we have agreed to them, what do we know that we didn't know before? In some cases they are simply admissions of ignorance. There is no avoiding the simple facts of state formation: Primary states arose in several different places, isolated from each other, within a relatively short time span, under similar circumstances (aridity, population growth, warfare, and trade). It seems unlikely that these were coincidences. If multicausal explanations have any value, they must still propose general principles of state formation that account for the variety of conditions under which states arose and that can be tested against data.

Archaeologist Kent Flannery examined the problems of state formation in the light of **general systems theory**, a body of ideas concerning how systems function. He proposed several ideas that may lead to a general theory of state formation. One such principle is that of centralization. Like Johnson's scalar stress, **centralization** refers to the increased demand placed on leaders in a community where there were numerous different spheres (**subsystems**) of activity, such as hunting, gathering, planting, herding, trading, and religion. In small-scale societies, a few part-time leaders could make decisions about how much effort should be allocated to each activity. In situations with more highly segregated activities, decisions also had to be made about the allocation of time and resources. As activities became more complex, leadership (that is, decision making) required leaders to spend more time acquiring information. A herder could not make good decisions about how much land cultivators should prepare for the spring planting. The point of Flannery's argument is that communities would need to support leaders who spent all their time on leadership activities.

According to Flannery, centralization and segregation take place through promotion and linearization. **Promotion** occurs when a control function, such as coordinating the use of land, is raised to a higher level. If a part-time leader becomes a full-time headman, promotion has occurred. **Linearization** refers to the process by which control over local decisions is passed up the line to successively higher levels of decision making. Decisions once made at a local level become higher-level decisions. For example, if a county school superintendent begins to make decisions formerly made by school principals, linearization has occurred. Delineating these processes makes it possible to generalize processes without referring to the specifics of trade, irrigation, or warfare.

Critics have suggested that systems theory does not really *explain* the processes of state formation but merely *labels* them in a convenient way. The problem seems to lie in the looseness of the ideas used. It is easy to attribute linearization or centralization to a social process; it is difficult to determine that it is present in a specific case, especially when the process cannot be observed first hand. Does systems theory lay out the necessary and sufficient conditions of the rise of the state? Or does it merely provide a series of plausible statements that flow largely from the very definition of the state? While systems theory does not appear to explain state formation, it helps set a standard of evidence for other hypotheses by reminding us of the interrelatedness of social, economic, political, and religious phenomena.

SUMMARY

- In its various forms, the state concentrates the power of human social organization in a way no other form can.
- States can assume great power over their citizens, people in other lands, the environment in general. They wield this power by defining categories of citizenship, writing and enforcing laws, collecting and allocating taxes, regulating the flow of information, and manipulating religious and political ideas.
- Most states are secondary in that they arise through contact with an already existing state. There may be as few as six primary states.
- There are many theories of primary state formation that emphasize different aspects of a fairly wide-

---

general systems theory   A theoretical approach that assumes the interrelatedness of the parts of a larger whole and attempts to describe that interrelatedness.

centralization   The increased demand placed on leaders in a community where there are numerous different spheres of activity.

subsystems   Relatively independent spheres of activity within a larger system.

promotion   In systems theory, the raising of a control function (for example, a leader) to a higher level (such as from part-time to full-time).

linearization   The process by which control over local decisions is passed up the line to successively higher levels of decision making; for example, from head of household to village headman to clan leader to chief.

spread process. The principal aspects of the process include the use of irrigation in agriculture, the influence of warfare, the influence of size and complexity, the influence of population pressure on resources, and the influence of trade on society. No single theory explains all instances of the rise of the state. Some writers have suggested multicausality, but this approach is so general that it does not satisfy the curiosity many people have about what factors were responsible for the rise of the state.

GET INVOLVED

1. Organize a debate on your campus about the relationship between religion and the state. Some topics that might be discussed are the rise of evangelical religion and the political involvement of evangelicals as compared to other religions; the abortion issue; and the creation of religious states in the Middle East. Be sure to get people with a wide diversity of viewpoints to participate.

2. What are the implicit social policies behind taxation in your country and others? For example, what is the purpose of providing exemptions for children to payers of U.S. income tax? What are the goals of the state with regard to family organization?

SUGGESTED READINGS

Adams, Robert McC. 1966. *The evolution of urban society: Early Mesopotamia and prehispanic Mexico: A comparative study of the great transformations.* Chicago: Aldine de Gruyter.

Carneiro, Robert. 1987. Cross-currents in the theory of state formation. *American Ethnologist* 14:756–770.

Johnson, G. A. 1978. Information sources and the development of decision-making organizations. In *Anthropology as a social science,* ed. C. L. Redman. New York: Academic Press.

Service, Elman. 1975. *Origins of the state and civilization.* New York: Norton.

Sampling the Uruk Past

Gregory A. Johnson is a professor of anthropology at Hunter College of The City University of New York. Since the early 1970s he has worked in various areas of the Middle East, concentrating on the development and organization of early states. His comments reflect problems archaeologists face in investigating large-scale political processes.

As sunset approaches, the Jazireh desert of northern Syria turns a rich gold against the deepening blue of the sky. Bedouin women in layered, brightly colored clothing light cook fires near their distinctive black goat-hair tents. Men and older children approach the camp with flocks of fat-tailed sheep and ever-hungry goats. A young boy enjoying an evening horseback ride leaves a lingering trail of dust across the middle distance.

I am sitting atop Chagar Bazar, a mound containing the remains of thousands of years of human settlement, where Max Mallowan and Agatha Christie once directed archaeological excavations. Looking around the horizon, I count some 40 other ancient sites dotting the landscape. This is a land of many people, a vast land, and an old land. These aspects of scale pose special challenges to the study of the past.

My research area is the fourth millennium B.C., when the state first appeared in and around Mesopotamia. Elites and commoners, priests and worshipers, bureaucrats, artisans, and laborers of all kinds initiated a political dynamic here that continues today. We call this culture the Uruk after one of the many major centers of this ancient people. That site, now called Warka, is in southern Iraq. It covers some 5 km², with deposits up to 40 m deep, so this single location contains many millions of cubic meters (m³) of archaeologi-

Gregory Johnson in the field at a site in southern Iraq.

cal remains. German teams have been working here, with interruptions for wars, for nearly 100 years. They have just gotten started.

Imagine what it would be like to do this work. A typical project might excavate 150 to 500 m³ in an intensive two-month season. If you moved quickly indeed, you could get out 1 million m³ in only 2,000 years. Of course you would not want to concentrate all your resources at a single location; instead you would disperse your efforts over sites of different kinds in different regions. You might rely on the classic strategy of picking the largest site in the neighborhood, climbing to its summit, and starting to dig. This strategy is productive, but it has resulted in our knowing much more about the architecture of a few Uruk public buildings than we do about such seemingly simple, yet essential, matters as what 99 percent of the population had for lunch.

Warka itself is only one of many hundreds of known sites containing the remains of Uruk occupation. By the late fourth millennium, about 5200 YA, Uruk settlements extended from the high valleys of the Zagros Mountains in Iran, through the rich alluvial plains of Khuzistan, across Iraq, and up the Tigris and Euphrates rivers through Syria to portions of southern Turkey—an area of about 500,000 km². We can never hope to study more than a small proportion of the evidence.

Uruk also had long-distance trade relations, and you would want to extend your investigations to the sources of lapis lazuli in Afghanistan, of carnelian and shell on the shores of the Persian Gulf, and of other commodities on the Nile Delta. You might also want to identify the sources, still unknown, of gold, silver, copper, and other valuable items, which certainly came from well beyond the Mesopotamian heartland, where raw materials were strictly limited. Your investigations would be further complicated by the interethnic and international conflicts that afflict the region today.

A final problem is time itself. Developments in Uruk culture spanned a period of nearly 1,000 years. Chronological refinement in excavation data is quite advanced, but many dates can be fixed only to within 200–300 years. Archaeologists also do not know what the relationship is between the data we have and the data still uncollected, so we can never have a statistically reliable sample of the Uruk past. This means that what we say about it is necessarily subject to continuing revision. Unlike the laws of Hammurabi, archaeological interpretations, especially those of events dating to 5000 YA, are not carved in stone.

North American powwows, such as this one in Calgary, Alberta, are celebrations that reflect tribal traditions and help reinforce the participants' ethnicity.

18

SOCIAL INEQUALITY

▲▲▲

Many think that inequality is part of human nature. Some people have more and some have less as a function of differences in ability, skills, interest, and luck. However, this view does not explain why societies differ in the degree of inequality they recognize. Some societies emphasize sharp differences in prestige, power, and control over resources. Other societies minimize such differences. Between egalitarian societies like the !Kung San and highly stratified societies like the United States there are many gradations.

A stratified society is one whose structure includes graded levels distinguished by access to goods and power. Ranked societies are also hierarchical, with sharp differences of prestige and power, but they lack **social strata**, or classes, based on access to resources. Egalitarian societies have a *relative* lack of hierarchy, and differences among people are not part of the structure of society. In an egalitarian society, prestige depends more on the quality of the individual than on the group or family to which he or she belongs.

To see how social stratification affects individuals and the social roles they play, consider the differences between the !Kung San **shaman** and the American medical doctor, both of whom serve as healers or curers in their respective societies. Medical doctors in the United States undergo a long period of training, after which they become associated with a special set of symbols, including special clothing and equipment and a particular life-style. In the United States, a person who becomes a doctor can expect to earn a high income, drive an expensive car, live in a big house, and enjoy power and prestige. People are careful to address medical doctors as "Doctor." Doctors can get special license tags for their cars and are permitted to violate certain parking rules. The high income and **social status** of the medical doctor in the United States is a source of motivation for admission to medical schools, and young doctors are willing to undergo many years of training and preparation to gain the privileges of a doctor (Figure 18.1).

Compare this to the social status of the !Kung San shaman. To become shamans, individuals must undergo a long and painful apprenticeship, during which they acquire the physical and psychological self-control to enter trance, heal the sick, ward off spirits, and train new healers. They also learn a body of dietary knowledge aimed at preventing illness (Lee 1984, 103–112). Although their knowledge can bring power and prestige, healers do not occupy a higher stratum in !Kung society. Male healers are more likely than the average man to have more than one wife, a sign of high status in !Kung society, but polygyny is not an exclusive right of healers. In most respects, healers engage in the same activities as other !Kung San, such as hunting, gathering, making weapons, and food preparation. They receive no payment for healing services, and they perform curing only occasionally. !Kung shamans are valued for their ability, but their role is not linked with power, wealth, or special privileges.

How does social inequality arise? The wide variety of social customs surrounding inequality makes it seem likely that it is not simply a response to instincts or universal tendencies. Structured social inequality tends to arise under certain historical conditions. Generally speaking, dense populations with a high degree of occupational specialization favor stratification. Some experts suggest that the ability to produce an excess of goods over the immediate needs of the producers—sometimes called a **surplus**—is what gives rise to an upper class. But others think it is precisely the concentration of power in a small group that motivates producers to produce more than they need for themselves. Since surplus production, increased population density, occupational specialization, and social stratification generally occur together, it is not easy to sort out what is cause and what is effect.

Does structured inequality have any function in society, or is it simply the strong taking advantage of the weak? Stratified societies vary in degree of internal harmony, but they are generally stronger than unstratified societies. In conflicts between stratified and unstratified societies, the stratified ones have emerged victorious. This may be because a class-organized society is better able than an egalitarian society to mobilize labor, soldiers, capital, and other resources.

SOCIAL CLASS: THEORIES AND APPROACHES

Most social scientists define a **social class** as a group of people who share similar life chances. More formally, social classes are groupings of people differentiated from each other by property, power, prestige, world view, and other features. There are different

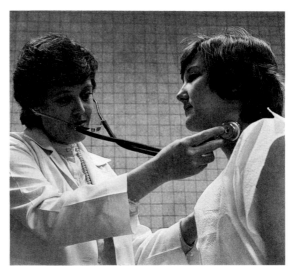

Figure 18.1 *The role of healer in an egalitarian and a stratified society. The !Kung San healer (shown here in a trance state, bending over his patient) has no more wealth or special privileges than any other member of !Kung society. By contrast, this in-house doctor for a U.S. pharmaceutical company enjoys a higher social status and income than many of the company's employees.*

ways of thinking about social class. Here we consider two of the most far-reaching and influential approaches.

Marx's Theory of Class

Karl Marx stated that class is based on ownership of the means of production. According to him, social classes form around economic interests. In each historical epoch the owners of the means of production (land, machinery, raw materials, and so on) formed the dominant class, while the peasants or workers formed the subordinate class. The principal cause of change is class conflict, which arises from a group's realization that it is being exploited and that the work it does benefits others more than themselves. Marx called this **class consciousness.**

In Marx's scheme, as consciousness rises, conflict increases until the entire structure of society is overthrown. For Marx a class is defined by a relationship to the "means of production," that is, property. Thus

---

social stratum (pl., strata) A homogeneous level of wealth and prestige within a complex society.

shaman A religious or ritual specialist, such as a healer, who fulfills the role of mediating supernatural forces.

social status The position of an individual in the social structure and its associated behavior and level of prestige.

surplus Production exceeding the immediate needs of producers; the tradable portion of any product.

social class A group of people who share similar life chances, differentiated from other groups by ownership of property, power, prestige, world view, and so on.

class consciousness In Marxist analysis, the understanding by a social class of its interests and the ability to act in behalf of those interests.

in feudal society there was a landlord class, a peasant class, and an artisan class. In later industrial societies, there tend to be three classes: the bourgeoisie (the capitalists), the proletariat (industrial workers), and the landowners. Just as the bourgeoisie replaced the feudal lords, Marx believed the proletariat would one day replace the bourgeoisie.

Marx's ideas were based largely on his analysis of the transition in Europe between feudalism and capitalism. In his day industrial organization was still fairly simple. Workers and owners were clearly distinguished. In today's industrial societies, more people belong to intermediate categories between labor and capital. Accountants, attorneys, engineers, teachers, computer programmers, civil servants, and many other specialists in information are not workers in the traditional sense and do not share a point of view with

workers on a factory assembly line. Nevertheless they are workers who do not own the means of production.

Marx believed that industrial class structure was inherently unstable, because the logic of capitalism led to increased exploitation of workers and eventually to revolution (Figure 18.2). The proletarian revolution that Marx predicted has not occurred, however. Workers in the advanced industrial countries are generally not revolutionary. Credit buying, employee benefits, public services, and union representation have made workers' lives far more comfortable and stable than they were in the early years of industrialism about which Marx wrote.

Marx also believed that rural producers were fundamentally conservative and unlikely to rebel. Yet the major revolutions of the 20th century occurred in

Figure 18.2 *Marx's concept of the proletariat is depicted by these workers at a shoe factory in Anshan, China. Marx had envisioned a proletarian revolution of angry, unsatisfied industrial workers wresting power from the bourgeoisie; in the 20th century, however, most major revolutions occurred in farming societies with significant peasant populations.*

agrarian societies—Mexico, Russia, China, Vietnam, Cuba, Algeria—with heavy peasant support. Some writers argue that Marxist class concepts apply not to specific countries but to the "international division of labor" that prevails today. According to this interpretation, capitalists in developed countries exploit workers abroad through a pattern of **dependent development**. This is a system by which the wealthy countries allow only part of a developed technology to take root in a developing country, thereby depriving it of the benefits of broadly based, balanced development.

Marx's scheme also has trouble accounting for societies like the !Kung San or the Yanomamo, where virtually everyone has control over the means of production. Marx left behind a few fragmentary writings on tribal and intermediate societies, but he apparently had virtually no concrete information about them, so he confined himself mainly to speculation about "primitive communism" and "precapitalist modes of production."

Figure 18.3 *In Weber's model, status and class don't necessarily go hand in hand. Someone with significant wealth and the trappings of a high class, such as a gangster like Al Capone, may have a low status in society if its members perceive the riches as disreputably gained.*

Weber's Theory of Class

Another approach to class came from Max Weber, a founder of modern social science, who distinguished class from status. Like Marx, Weber thought of class as an economic level or stratum. On the other hand, Weber said, status differences are those that depend on people's evaluation of others' prestige, or "social honor." Weber found it necessary to separate class from status to understand the position and behavior of particular groups. For example, when feudalism declined in Europe, people at first refused to consider merchants and other capitalists as equals of the landed aristocracy. While their economic position was higher than that of the nobility, their status was, at least temporarily, lower. Similarly, in the United States there are people who are quite rich but whose status is low because they made their money in a disreputable way, such as by drug dealing. Status may be defined in terms of different dimensions, which vary according to the values—basic orientations about what is good and bad—of a society. Class and status, as Weber defined them, are not the same, but they are linked (Figure 18.3).

There is no necessary contradiction between these different uses of the term *class*. Weber's emphasis was on social processes and the relationship between individuals and class, while Marx was more concerned with broad historical movements. Marxist definitions of *class* focus mainly on the organization of production in society and how different groups form around ownership of the means of production. For Marx class was primarily a matter of the economic position of a group in society. Classes changed the structure of society through struggle. Weberian definitions of class focus on the way in which people perceive status differences and how they act them out.

Marx's and Weber's approaches have led to different ways of studying social class. In the United States

---

dependent development In the developing world, increased economic production that depends on capital and technology from the developed countries.

sociologists focus primarily on **status groups** and on how people themselves think about status differences. Status has several dimensions in the United States, including wealth, occupation, ancestry, and educational level. Sociologists use income levels and consumption as measures of status because they are easily quantified and because Americans consider them in judging each other. In the Marxian sense, however, income is not a necessary indicator of class position. The income of different kinds of workers may vary, but, from the Marxian point of view, all workers belong to the same class.

Perceptions of Inequality and Markers of Class

Now that we have looked at how social theorists think about class, let us consider the topic in some specific societies. How do people perceive and understand differences in rank and power? The question of social inequality is loaded with strong feelings. In some societies differences in rank are very obvious. Consider the landowner class in the Andean region of Ecuador. The landowner class owns most of the productive land and a disproportionate share of farm animals, vehicles, and other productive goods. They hire peasants as laborers to grow crops and tend herds. They themselves do little manual labor. The landowners have enough income to eat well, live in comfortable houses, own cars, wear good clothing, and enjoy many luxuries. They are able to travel and to send their children to school. Peasants, who own little or no land, lack most of these advantages and have little hope of giving them to their children. In any dispute with a lower-status person, the landowner is likely to win.

Another society in which rank differences are stressed is Ponape, an island society in Micronesia. Before colonization, matrilineages headed by chiefs controlled the most important resource, land. Around the turn of the century, German colonizers took away the chiefs' control over land, drastically reducing their power. Ponapean chiefs retained their power to bestow honorific titles on loyal clan members. Chiefs can give titles as rewards for loyalty even though the titles no longer carry any special power or privileges. Ethnographer Glenn Petersen has noted that differences in wealth and power are relatively small, yet the Ponapeans attach great importance to titles (1982).

Ponapean titles are ranked on a scale of importance, and men can accumulate several titles. Title holders, like the lords and peers of Great Britain, still enjoy prestige. Some highly ranked titles include *Nahnipei* (Lord of the Altar), *Nahlik Lapalap* (Great Lord of the Exterior), *Oundolen Ririn* (Watchman of the Mountain of the Ladder), and *Nahnsou Sed* (Lord of the Masters of the Sea) (Riesenberg 1968). The highest chief of Ponape holds the title of *Nahnmwarki* (Lord of Controlling Titles). Petersen, who studied Ponape in the 1970s, found that even after lineage chiefs lost control over land, they remained strong and the matrilineages continued. The chiefs remained important leaders, and the competition for titles became even more intense (Figure 18.4). "Judicious use of this control is recognized by the Ponapeans themselves as the root of chiefly power and, again, it is titles, not property, that have the greatest impact on political activities today" (Petersen 1982, 23). More commonly, however, high status corresponds to control over resources, as in Ecuador.

In other societies, class differences exist but are masked by an ideology of equality. In the United States, for example, there are significant differences in power and wealth yet relatively few public markers of social rank. People may even deny they exist. In other words, the perception of equality and reality are two different things. Foreigners who visit the United States often comment that it is difficult to determine what stratum Americans belong to. In some countries dress styles and quality of clothing are clear markers of status. But nowadays, many Americans can afford to dress in a style that blurs class distinction, although mink coats and snakeskin boots are still distinctive. For a premium, any American can wear "designer" clothing, a privilege once reserved for the rich. Even low-ranked people of modest means can participate in some of the most extravagant rituals of privilege, if only temporarily. A high-school teacher can dine in an expensive restaurant next to a millionaire, and a bricklayer can rent a Cadillac limousine for his daughter's wedding.

Americans tend to minimize the class differences among themselves because of their ideology of equality. Differences in wealth and power are presumably based on what people achieve for themselves (Box 18.1). Americans do not condemn people who "earn" their power and privileges, but they tend to resent people who flaunt them openly. The idea of a lower class is so offensive to Americans that they have in-

Figure 18.4   *Among the Ponapeans of Micronesia, titles are more important than property holdings in establishing leadership and prestige. The chief (left) is distinguished from a commoner mainly by his titles.*

vented a set of euphemisms, such as *working class* or *underprivileged,* to identify people occupying the lower rungs of American society.

SOCIAL MOBILITY: OPEN AND CLOSED SOCIETIES

In every society life chances are determined by a combination of ascribed and achieved factors (see Chapter 14). Class societies vary in the degree to which status may be achieved. Some class societies, often referred to as "closed," are extremely rigid, with little opportunity for movement from one class to another. Other societies are more "open," allowing movement between classes. **Social mobility** refers to the possibility of movement upward or downward from one stratum to another based on achievement. Societies differ in how much mobility there is. In India, for example, it

is difficult and rare for a person to rise out of poverty and get an education and a good job as, say, an engineer or lawyer. In countries like Sweden, on the other hand, while there are still obstacles, social mobility is more likely. While mobility is difficult to measure directly, we can examine the social institutions that people use to achieve mobility.

Open Societies

In premodern Europe there was little social mobility. A person born a peasant was likely to remain a peasant for life. Some people achieved upward mobility by securing favors from a lord or monarch. In 16th-century Spain, for example, there were some nobles who held titles but no property. Some of these *hidalgos* sought to move upward by getting royal permission to go to the New World to search for gold. In open societies the ingredients of high status are typically varied and sometimes ambiguous. In many cases strategies for upward mobility depend on creating the *appearance* of high status. Trying to "move up" by attaching oneself to influential people has always been a common tactic. One strategy common in the United States is to move to an area with the "right kind of people." In universities faculty try to ingratiate themselves with the dean. In societies where warfare is important, social advancement may depend on one's ability as a fighter. In Chapter 16 we saw that practically the only avenue of mobility for Aztec commoners was to be a successful warrior.

Moving Up (or Down) through Marriage.   Kinship is often involved in social mobility. Perhaps the most common means of changing status is through marriage. As we saw in Chapter 14, in many societies people give careful consideration to the family of a potential spouse before agreeing to a marriage. The Betsileo of the Malagasy Republic (Madagascar) have ranked descent groups classified as "nobility," "commoners," and "slaves," although actual slavery does not currently exist. The Betsileo have strong feelings

---

status groups   Groups defined by social variables such as wealth, occupation, religion, consumption habits, ancestry, or education level.

social mobility   Movement upward or downward between social strata.

BOX 18.1

Money and Prestige

In societies with capitalist economies, wealth is a powerful means of achieving high status, whether by possession, consumption, or both. A classic example in the United States is John D. Rockefeller. Born in 1839, Rockefeller was a small businessman in Ohio who got into refining shortly after the first oil wells were drilled in Pennsylvania. He built his first oil refinery in 1863 and quickly moved to buy out his competitors, forming the first modern "trust." His company, Standard Oil, monopolized the oil industry until 1911 when the U.S. Supreme Court broke it up into several smaller companies.

Although he was not a popular figure, Rockefeller had immense wealth, which gave him the social power to influence events on a grand scale. With his money he influenced American finance, law, politics, education, art, and philanthropy for years to come. In 1891 he founded the University of Chicago. Together with his son and namesake, he also founded the Rockefeller Institute (now Rockefeller University) in New York City, the Rockefeller Foundation, and many other philanthropic, scientific, educational, and cultural institutions. He donated more than $3 billion to institutions he judged important.

Rockefeller's influence and wealth passed to his heirs, three of whom became state governors— Winthrop (Arkansas), Jay (West Virginia), and Nelson (New York). Nelson Rockefeller also served as vice-president of the United States. In every community in

John D. Rockefeller embodies what many consider to be "the American dream." His immense wealth gave him not only material possessions but power and prestige as well.

the United States there are people whose wealth has brought them prestige and social power, although few on the scale of a Rockefeller.

---

about people who marry out of their social rank. Ethnographer Conrad Kottak, who studied the Betsileo in the late 1960s, reports the case of a commoner, Felix, from Ivato, who married a woman without consulting his relatives (1980, 205):

> Felix contracted what more senior Ivatans regarded as a scandalous marriage. Betsileo custom required that at least his father and uncle travel to her village to ascertain her descent group affiliation and to scrutinize her ancestry for imperfections. In addition to slave descent, certain descent groups carry curses, and Betsileo believe that others carry hereditary maladies.

Felix clearly experienced downward mobility as the result of his marriage. His wife, on the other hand, moved up.

Marriage is an avenue to social mobility in the contemporary United States where people claim to be unconcerned with such issues. Americans are nevertheless familiar with such sentiments as "he married well—her father is a real estate developer," or, on the downside, "she married beneath herself." Marriages outside of a particular neighborhood or racial or ethnic group are often viewed as raising or lowering the status of the individuals concerned. Concern with the social status of a potential spouse begins in adolescence. Teenagers check each other over for signs of athletic, social, intellectual, and financial ability. They carefully examine each other's clothing and possessions for clues to social orientation.

Moving Up the Career Ladder.   In some social contexts, there is a prescribed route for social mobility. The military has specific "career ladders," which allow individuals to move up through the ranks through a combination of training and service. Each step up involves a new combination of benefits and badges, including housing, uniforms, insignia, and the use of a title, such as Sergeant or Lieutenant. Career paths are prescribed in nonmilitary contexts as well. University teachers move through the ranks from instructor to assistant professor, associate professor, and finally full professor.

In highland villages in Central and South America, there is an elaborate ranking system with a partially described career path. Successful peasant farmers are asked to become officials for the annual **fiesta** in honor of the local patron saint. Young men enter the system near the bottom, accepting a minor **cargo** ("burden") such as bell ringer. If a man prospers and keeps the esteem of other villagers, he may be given more important and prestigious burdens. The **mayordomo**, the highest cargo, must rent a house in town, buy gold coins or other finery to decorate the saint's image, hire a marching band, and buy liquor, food, and fireworks for the saint's day (Figure 18.5).

To fulfill this office, a mayordomo may spend as much as a year's income, so that it is not surprising that some men resist this "honor" (Harris 1964). Some anthropologists suggest that the fiesta is a way of maintaining solidarity within the community by keeping everyone poor and united. On the other hand, Frank Cancian, an anthropologist who studied the fiesta in Chiapas, Mexico, suggested that the Maya fiestas there do not erase inequality; rather, they are a social means of expressing it (1965).

Figure 18.5 *In the town of Yoshimel in Chiapas, Mexico, the Mayan mayordomo and his wife served the local saint for a year. They made biweekly offerings of flowers and incense and saw to the preparations of candles, food, and drink for the culmination of their office—the festival of the saint's day.*

Achieving Status through Wealth, Property, and Consumption.   In many societies one avenue to high status is to build up wealth and property. Of course to do so presupposes that there is some kind of wealth and property to accumulate. Not all societies have such items. The !Kung San, the Yanomamo, and the

---

fiesta In Central and South America, religious rituals that are centered around the veneration of a Catholic saint but that may also have functions in civil administration, dispute settlement, and so on.

cargo In the context of the fiesta, a rotating position or "burden" in the civil-religious hierarchy of a village. The holder of a cargo accepts a financial burden in return for prestige.

mayordomo The highest cargo in the civil-religious hierarchy of a fiesta system. The mayordomo bears the greatest burden at the time of the fiesta and gains the greatest prestige.

Semai are societies in which there is little personal property; hence one cannot gain prestige by acquiring property.

There are many strategies for using wealth to acquire high status. In ranked societies there is no class structure, but as we saw in Chapter 15, big men are obliged to accumulate great stores of goods in order to be generous. In the Trobriand Islands, village chiefs accumulate quantities of yams contributed by the villagers. The yams are kept in storehouses in the center of the village and symbolize the status and prestige of the chief (Figure 18.6). This wealth does not benefit the chief, who cannot exchange it for other goods. He must keep the yams on hand to assist the needy and to use for special occasions such as ceremonials, visits from other villages, and funerals. He validates his status by generosity. He is not so much the owner as the *custodian* of the yams (Malinowski 1922).

Wealth may also bring prestige through consumption. Economist Thorstein Veblen observed in his 1899 book *Theory of the Leisure Class* that people are willing to pay more for goods of inferior quality if owning them brings prestige. Tribal members in Brazil sometimes purchase and wear wristwatches, even though they are unable to tell time. Americans follow consumer strategies in which prestige is a very important ingredient. They purchase food, clothing, cars, and housing with great concern for what the product says about the buyer. They carefully examine other people's consumption habits to determine what social level they are striving to achieve (Box 18.2).

Product advertising reveals a great deal about class aspirations. Much advertising is designed to create associations between products and certain life-styles. Ads may attempt to link products with an upper-class life-style, which presumes a good income, a comfortable house, one or two cars, and leisure time for tennis, skiing, or sailing. The unspoken message is that the purchaser of these products will move to a higher status. People do not necessarily achieve mobility through consumption. Instead, consumption patterns are indicators of the consumer's goals. In a country like the United States, where consumption is carefully scrutinized, people will determine whether a person

Figure 18.6 *This storehouse of yams in the Trobriand Islands represents the wealth of the village chief, but it is used to achieve status rather than to exchange for personal property.*

BOX 18.2

What Does Your Car Say about You?

North Americans care a lot about their cars, and a great deal of car advertising plays on this concern. The ads try to tell you what kind of person owns each make or model. In general, the more money one has, the better (more expensive) the car she or he drives. However, there may be a point where this relationship becomes inverted. In a satirical book about class in America, Paul Fussell writes about automobiles as a mechanism for "outdoor class display."

> [I]f your money . . . allows you to buy any kind of car, you provide yourself with the meanest and most common [car] to indicate that you're not taking seriously so easily purchasable and thus vulgar a class totem. You have a Chevy, Ford, Plymouth, or Dodge, and in the least interesting style and color. It may be clean, although slightly dirty is best. But it should be boring. The next best thing is to have a "good" car, like a Jaguar or BMW, but to be sure it's old and beat-up. You may not have a Rolls, a Cadillac, or a Mercedes. Especially a Mercedes. . . . The worst kind of upper-middle-class types own Mercedes, just as the best own elderly Oldsmobiles, Buicks, and Chryslers, and perhaps Jeeps and Land Rovers, the latter conveying the Preppie suggestion that one of your residences is in a place so unpublic that the roads to it are not even paved.

Fortunately for the U.S. automobile industry, most Americans do not take Fussell's advice. They purchase between 5 million and 8 million cars each year, responding to such challenges as "Get behind the wheel!" "See the USA!" or "Move up to Buick." Nowhere are the aspirations of the buying public so clearly manipulated as in the images surrounding the purchase and ownership of automobiles. Americans are entreated to share in the power and cunning of a Cougar, the speed of a Mustang, the perfection of a Topaz, the grace of an Impala, the joy of a Sky Lark, or the majesty of a Regal. Japanese and Korean manufacturers are getting in on the act with models bearing Italian-sounding names like Diamante, Sonata, or Infiniti, which, to American ears, sound classier than Mitsubishi, Hyundai, or Toyota.

Most Americans are aware that the major manufacturers repackage the same cars over and over under different labels with superficial differences in trim and equipment. This allows consumers to cherish the illusion that they own a "personalized" machine, made to suit their own specific interests and personality. The annual rotation of models further stimulates demand by making previous models appear out of date. The anthropological interpretation is that auto manufacturers capitalize on Americans' concern with status as a way of inducing them to purchase more and more cars.

---

deserves the status associated with his or her consumption patterns. In some cases the strategy fails and a person is judged pretentious, a striver living beyond his or her means. For others the strategy is successful; the consumer achieves prestige, even adulation, for being "in style" and having "good taste."

Closed Societies: Caste

Caste is a form of social stratification in which class membership is ascribed from birth and is associated with a particular station in life. Castes are typically endogamous, meaning that people are expected to marry within the same caste. Castes are part of a hierarchical system in which higher castes are dominant over lower ones. Perhaps the most common castes are slave castes, groups obliged to perform slave labor for other groups. For example, the ancient Israelites were slaves in Egypt at the time of Moses. Slaves are often war captives or people sold into slavery by others who have power over them. Often the stigma of slavery lives on long after involuntary servitude has been abolished.

---

caste An ascriptive form of social stratification based on endogamous social classes.

Figure 18.7 *A woman of the "untouchable" caste sweeps the street in New Del-hia, India; a member of the Vaishnava Brahman caste sits in a temple corridor and studies palm leaf manuscripts. The caste system in India, according to Brahman thought, ideally provides for the care of the low-caste people by those in higher castes. Similar patron-client relationships occur in many societies throughout the world.*

India is well known for its caste system. Indian caste has a religious justification. Each caste is spoken of as an occupational group, such as priest, land-owner, farmer, clothes washer, woodcutter, and so on, although not all members of a group do the work associated with it. One caste is considered "untouchable" by members of all other castes. One approach (an emic approach) views Indian castes as a system of ideas, stressing the ways in which people justify the inequalities of the caste system. Another (etic) approach focuses on how wealth, privileges, and activities vary with caste membership.

An Emic Approach to Caste.   Hinduism divides society into ranked **varnas**. At the top are **Brahmans** or priests, followed by warriors, merchants, and servants. Untouchables fall outside the varnas altogether. Each caste is divided into local **jatis**, or subcastes. Jatis are ranked according to the foods they eat. The highest ranks belong to vegetarians, because they live according to the highest principles of Hinduism, without taking life. Members of one jati can eat food pre-

pared by a person from the same or higher-ranking jati but not that prepared by lower-ranking persons. Untouchables are so polluting that a Brahman will not eat food on which an untouchable's shadow has fallen.

Ideally, upper and lower caste relations would be governed by the **jajmani system**, in which lower-caste individuals attach themselves to high-caste persons and serve them faithfully as cultivators, shepherds, water haulers, woodcutters, or waste collectors (Figure 18.7). According to the ideal, upper castes care for the needs of dependent low-caste people when times are hard. This type of **dependency relationship**, often referred to as **patron-clientage**, occurs in many societies around the world. According to Brahman thought, the system is harmonious and provides for everyone's needs. The differences among people were created by God and are permanent and everlasting. There is therefore no reason to want to change them, especially since the lower castes will find relief from their hard lives in the afterlife. The justification of a system of stratification in religious terms is not unique to the Indian caste system.

An Etic Approach to Caste.   The etic view of Indian caste focuses on the actual practices involved in daily life in Indian villages. Researchers taking a regional view have observed that there is a great deal of variation in the activities and status of jatis from one region to another. Not all members of a given jati practice the profession identified with it. For example, members of a shepherd caste who have no animals may raise crops for a living on someone else's land. The goatherds of one region may occupy a low status, while in a neighboring region they will be higher on the scale. The flexibility of what seem to be rigid rules is apparent in the following passage from a study by ethnographer McKim Marriott (1968, 145):

> Sweepers and leather workers, for reasons of "pollution," should avoid casual trespass upon even the exterior platform of a house belonging to a person of high caste, yet they may enter the same house and have a purifying rather than a polluting effect on it, provided that they come on the owner's command to do their respective jobs of cleaning and repairing. Obviously the maintenance of rank, not pollution by proximity, is the issue on which action turns in such instances. A Brahman may walk into a leather worker's house to call him for work without incurring any pollution dangerous to the standing of the Brahman caste, but a leather worker may not enter a Brahman's house to call on him without exciting anger and possibly suffering a beating.

The position of a jati in the ritual hierarchy of a particular village can change through political and economic pressure brought to bear on priests (Marriott 1968). While Hinduism teaches acceptance of status, some untouchables are aware of the injustice of their situation. This may be phrased in the logic of the system itself, as in the case of the untouchable who told the ethnographer Gerald Berreman, "Englishmen and Muslims are untouchables because they have an alien religion and they eat beef. This is as it should be. We are Hindus and we do not eat beef, yet we, too are treated as untouchables. This is not proper. We should be accorded higher status" (1960).

Class Ascription by Social Race.   There are other social formations that resemble Indian castes but differ in key respects. Some writers have compared Indian caste to race relations in the United States (e.g., Dollard 1937). In both situations class membership is ascribed and there is preferential endogamy. The characteristics of dominance and subordination typical of Indian castes were found in relations between whites and African Americans in the southern United States from abolition to about 1960. As in India, the subordinate group was thought, at least by the upper class, to have a particular place in society from which it should not stray.

This idea was particularly clear in the sexual domain. In the southern states white men could have sexual relations with African American women without fear of punishment, but African American men having sexual relations with white women were subject to violent retribution if the relationship was discovered; consequences ranged from vigilante action (lynching) to legal execution. Under the latter category 405 men were legally executed for rape in the United States between 1930 and 1979; of these, 360 (89 percent) were African American, a disproportion that goes well beyond any difference in the actual rate of criminal involvement (Gordon 1984, 141). In India the same rules apply: Upper-caste men are free to have sexual relations with lower-caste women, but upper-caste women are carefully guarded from sexual contact with lower-caste men.

There are important contrasts between the Indian and American situations, however. The ideology that

---

varna   The four social strata idealized in Indian Hindu society: Brahman (priest); Kshatriya (warrior); Vaishas (merchant); and Shudra (servant).

Brahman   The highest of the Hindu varnas; people in this strata represent the priestly or holiest level.

jati   In India, a subcaste or village representative of a caste; jatis tend to be endogamous.

jajmani system   The system of dependency relations in Indian Hindu society, in which members of each caste are subservient to members of a higher caste, receiving favors and protection in return.

dependency relationship (or patron-clientage)   A social and economic relationship in which a high-status individual provides assistance to clients in exchange for services or political support.

supports racial discrimination in the United States is not as elaborate as the religious justification for Indian caste. The African American minority in the United States has developed a class structure parallel to the white class system with separation in terms of income, residence, education, political orientation, dress styles, and so on. The castes in India have no such internal stratification. Caste endogamy and pollution taboos tend to reduce mobility and possibly make the formation of class consciousness more difficult (Mencher 1980). Still the caste system of India is not merely a system of ideas; it delineates social groups that behave in distinctive ways and provide a basis for continuity in Indian society.

ETHNICITY

There are many other systems of belief that stratify societies. One of them is **ethnicity. Ethnic groups** are found in most complex societies. They are generally defined in terms of distinctive cultural identities or national origin. Ethnicity is an ascribed social status that depends on how individuals themselves and how others identify them. Each ethnic group has a distinctive inventory of diet, dress styles, language, religious beliefs, ceremonial practices, and other customs that set it apart from other groups. Ethnic groups are sometimes called minorities or nationalities. In the broadest sense, religious, racial, and national minorities are all ethnic groups to the extent that membership in them is ascribed.

Ethnicity is often a disguise for class stratification. While ethnic groups may present themselves in a context of equality, they usually occupy a place in a hierarchical structure of ethnic groups and relate to each other in different ways. In other words, they tend to be politically or economically superior or subordinate to other groups.

The Essentialist Approach to Ethnicity

There are two ways to understand ethnicity, the **essentialist approach** and the **boundary approach,** each of which reveals important aspects of the phenomenon. The essentialist approach defines ethnic groups in terms of *cultural content:* ideas, attitudes, and traditions that people carry around in their heads.

The essentialist view corresponds to the way most people think about cultural diversity. It sees people as having personal identities that are tied up with their ethnic identity. In the United States ethnicity is an important feature of social identity. If one American asks another, "What are you?" she or he will often respond using an ethnic label, such as Italian American, Scotch-Irish, Korean, or WASP (a colloquial abbreviation for White, Anglo-Saxon Protestant). In the Province of Quebec in Canada people are quick to signal whether they are Anglos or French-speaking Quebecois.

In Lebanon ethnic identity may be a matter of life and death. As we saw in Chapter 17, Lebanon is deeply divided into Maronite Christian, Shiite Muslim, Sunni Muslim, Druse, and Palestinian factions. All these groups speak a common language (Arabic) and have lived in close proximity for generations. The government issues identity cards listing the ethnic identity of the bearer, an indication of how seriously the Lebanese take ethnic group affiliation.

Essentialism views the persistence of ethnic groups as "nonassimilation" or "incomplete acculturation." An ethnic group may originate when a group is incorporated into another population as a result of migration or conquest. Ethnic groups usually assimilate some features of the dominant population, but they preserve distinctive traits from their native culture. The essentialist view presumes that cultural traditions are inherently conservative and that people cling to their life-styles as a means of preserving their social identity.

When a group begins to assimilate or merge with another group, essentialists assume that its identity has been weakened or that its traditions have lost their influence. Assimilation may occur when a group's ethnic heritage is "compatible" with that of the other group. When two groups maintain separateness, the essentialist approach explains the divergence in terms of the different content of each group's culture.

There are many other "badges" of ethnic identity that mark off boundaries between ethnic groups. Some of these badges are visible, like the hats, beards, and long black coats worn by Hasidic Jews and the turbans worn by Sikh men. Food preferences are also important ethnic markers. Religious Muslims refuse to eat pork, and many Hindus are vegetarians. These customs are generally justified or explained in various ways, aside from their function in marking off group identity. Orthodox Jews, for example, refrain from eating pork and shellfish or mixing meat and milk dishes because of prescriptions in their sacred writings. Some rabbis explain the dietary laws as a means of maintaining Jewish identity. But most customs that create boundaries between ethnic groups are also justified in other ways. There are many other explanations of food taboos (Douglas 1966, Harris 1985). Language is another common marker of ethnic affiliation: Accents and dialects distinguish speakers from others (see Chapter 4).

Ethnic Identity in the Essentialist View. Problems appear in the essentialist view when we compare how people view their own ethnic heritage with how outsiders view it. In the United States more than 15 million people are classified as Hispanic according to the Census Bureau. This category includes Mexican-Americans ("Chicanos"), Puerto Ricans, and other Spanish-speaking people from a variety of backgrounds, including Cuba, Colombia, the Dominican Republic, and Ecuador. Sometimes all these nationalities are grouped together by Anglo-Americans under the term, *Spanish* or *latino.* For members of these groups, however, these are not one group, but many. Cubans consider themselves quite distinct from Dominicans. Mexican Americans feel they are different from Mexican migrants. Some Puerto Ricans distinguish between "New Yoricans" (people of Puerto Rican descent born in New York City) and those born on the island of Puerto Rico. Not only do ethnic groups distinguish themselves from others, but they may also disagree on fundamental issues. If ethnicity is based on a sense of common identity, how can we say that it exists when there is no such identity?

Other problems in the essentialist view emerge when we consider **multiple identities**. Essentialism views ethnic identity as something attached to the individual and carried around like baggage throughout life. Some ethnic badges, such as a beard or permanent scars on the body, are difficult to remove. Others can be removed but may be worn constantly, such as a yarmulke or a Sikh's turban. But some signs can be used selectively, and in many situations an individual can choose to play or not to play the role associated with his or her ethnic identity.

In a multiethnic society people often manipulate their ethnic identity to achieve personal and social goals. For example, a fair-skinned, blue-eyed young women in Texas attends college on an American Indian scholarship although she has never before identified herself as an Indian or lived on an Indian reservation. She qualified because she has a Cherokee great-grandmother. In fact the 1990 census showed a large increase in the number of people who checked "Native American" under the race category. Another example is the case of a Peruvian man who speaks Quechua in his small village where only Indians live. When he goes to market in a nearby town, he wears his Indian cap but speaks Spanish. When he travels to more distant places, he wears a western-style hat and "passes" as a mestizo (a person of mixed Indian and Spanish ancestry).

The Origin and Persistence of Ethnicity in the Essentialist View. Another problem in the essentialist viewpoint is that its emphasis on the fixed inventory of cultural content leads it to ignore the degree to which ethnic identities are constantly being created and modified. The essentialist viewpoint tends to locate the origin of ethnic groups in places where groups with different geographical origins come together through migration or conquest. According to this view, the native American ethnic group originated when Europeans and others colonized the Americas. But ethnic groups also arise by other means.

---

ethnicity Social identity based on such factors as a common homeland, language, ancestry, religion, or racial characteristics.

ethnic group A group that shares an ascribed social identity based on such variables as homeland, language, ancestry, religion, or racial characteristics.

essentialist approach An approach to the study of ethnicity that defines ethnic groups in terms of their cultural content: ideas, attitudes, and traditions that people carry around in their heads.

boundary approach An understanding of ethnicity that focuses on the boundaries and relationships between ethnic groups rather than on the internal content of ethnic identity.

multiple identities The manipulation of ethnic identity by an individual adopting more than one social identity as the social context changes.

In differentiation, or **ethnogenesis**, a group detaches itself from another and assumes a separate ethnic identity. This has occurred recently in the United States as Brazilian immigrants have focused on their separate language and national background as a point of difference between themselves and other emigrants from Latin America, forging a distinctive ethnic identity against a background that tended to treat them as Hispanics. Differentiation can also occur through religious conversion or through rediscovery of separate "roots." In recent years many Americans have rediscovered their "roots" in a quest for personal identity, as in the case of the writer Alex Haley (1976) who traced his ancestry to an ethnic group in The Gambia, Africa.

Ethnic persistence presents a final problem for the essentialist viewpoint. If ethnic differences grew out of simple cultural differences, one would expect that over time adjacent groups would come to resemble each other more and more until they disappeared as separate entities. A simplistic view of the persistence of separate ethnic groups is that each group is isolated from the others and therefore ignorant of their ways. This view is hard to defend: There is scarcely any social group in the world that is truly isolated from others. Even relatively isolated groups like the Yanomamo and the !Kung San are well aware of the existence of other groups with different languages and customs, and there is considerable mingling with those groups, including intermarriage.

Bilingualism and multilingualism are very common, even in small-scale societies. The native peoples of the northwest Amazon Basin, for example, usually speak four or five different languages (Sorensen 1971). Many ethnic groups have remained separate for centuries, even while integrated into a greater society with a common language and a single government. In Spain, the Basques and Catalonians have maintained separate languages and separate identities for generations even though they are integrated into the modern Spanish state. Jews have maintained a separate identity, often in the midst of other cultural groups, over thousands of years. On the other hand, an ethnic group can gradually assimilate until it is indistinguishable from the majority population. This is true of many descendants of European emigrants to America. Isolation alone cannot explain ethnic persistence.

The Boundary Approach to Ethnicity

The boundary approach to ethnicity focuses not on how people think and behave within each ethnic group but on the kinds of relationships that are set up between ethnic groups. Anthropologist Fredrik Barth tried to approach the question of ethnicity in terms of what leads people to stress differences between themselves and others: "The critical focus from this point of view becomes the ethnic boundary that defines the group, not the cultural stuff that it encloses. The boundaries to which we must give our attention are . . . social boundaries although they may have territorial counterparts" (Barth 1969, 15).

According to Barth, if a person considers another person a fellow member of an ethnic group, each will presume that the other shares a series of ideas and goals, no matter how different they may actually be. On the other hand, if people perceive that they are members of different ethnic groups, they will apply different standards of judgment to each other and not assume common interests, even if they exist.

Ethnic Competition and Discrimination.   In nearly every complex society there is competition for resources. This competition may be among local groups or regions or among people of different backgrounds, languages, or religious groups. The resources competed for may be controlled by the state, such as public jobs, or by private groups, such as investors. While ethnicity may not be a factor in a given competition, it may become one as the competition heats up or as conditions change. In general, ethnic conflict seems to increase as resources become scarcer or one group perceives that another group has increased its share of resources at the expense of others. **Discrimination** is a social institution that operates on the individual level but may be supported by communities or the state. Discrimination consists of applying separate standards to people on a basis of social race, class, religion, gender, or ethnicity.

Consider the case of Ireland, a British colony until 1922, when the Irish Republic was proclaimed. The "Five Counties" of Northern Ireland (Ulster), however, remained under British rule, partly because its predominantly Protestant population would have become a minority in the predominantly Catholic Irish Republic. Catholics became a minority in Ulster, and their access to power, jobs, and other goods was severely limited. They also suffered discrimination at the hands of the law. The British support of Protestants created deep resentment among Catholics in Ulster, and since 1968 the two factions have been locked in a violent dispute.

Canada has had considerable strife over a linguistic minority. French speakers have long felt that they suffered discrimination for not using English. While official discrimination is illegal in Canada, there is still considerable informal discrimination against **franco-phones**. This has led them to seriously propose the secession of the Province of Quebec from Canada. The government has taken several measures to improve the situation, such as requiring the use of French alongside English in many contexts.

In the United States ethnic conflict has taken many forms. Perhaps the most virulent ethnic conflict in the United States is that between African Americans and whites in the prolonged aftermath to slavery. After a long period of officially sanctioned discrimination favoring whites over African Americans, the U.S. government, through legislation and the courts, outlawed discrimination in schools, public transportation, housing, voting, public accommodations (hotels and restaurants), and employment. In spite of these changes, discrimination continues at many levels. The life chances of African Americans in the United States continue to be significantly lower than those of whites, as measured by education, income, infant mortality, and life expectancy.

Governments can promote or condone ethnic conflict, and they can also suppress it. Overt ethnic conflict was thoroughly suppressed in the rigid regimes of the Soviet Union and other Eastern European countries. Bulgaria, for example, demanded that its citizens of Turkish descent adopt Bulgarian surnames and use the Bulgarian language. In the Soviet Union, the Russian language and cultural traditions officially replaced those of Georgians, Byelorussians, Azer-

beijanis, Armenians, Lithuanians, Estonians, Ukrainians, and other ethnicities, even though together these "minorities" outnumbered the Russian "majority." All religions were suppressed. In recent years, with **perestroika,** the central state relaxed its hold on the ethnic minorities (Figure 18.8), and now it has virtually collapsed in the face of the demand for independence by ethnically distinct republics. Conflicts that were submerged for generations have reemerged with startling violence. Ethnic Hungarians living in Romania, for example, feel seriously threatened under the Romanian regime installed in 1989. The Soviet government has felt obliged to intervene militarily between Armenians and Azerbeijanis to prevent a bloodbath.

Can Cross-Cultural Understanding Reduce Ethnic Conflict?

The essentialist approach, with its emphasis on cultural content, sometimes overlooks the political and economic factors in ethnic strife. In Northern Ireland and Lebanon, people point to the different religious systems of the parties in conflict. In Nigeria and other African countries, ethnic differences are described as "tribal conflicts." In many of these situations, concerned people attribute the conflict to a lack of understanding. They suggest that the parties to the conflict need to understand each other's cultural values better and to build sensitivity to cultural styles, such as patterns of speech, "body language," and taste in clothing and music. Canada, for example, has attempted to include French and English in school curriculums all over the country. The underlying assumption of these attempts is that discrimination and ethnic strife are the result of differences in cultural content. They assume that discrimination has its roots in ignorance and misunderstanding.

While building understanding across ethnic boundaries may be a desirable goal, it is not a solution in most cases of ethnic conflict. Reducing ethnic prej-

---

ethnogenesis The formation of a new ethnic group.

discrimination The application of separate (usually negative) economic, social, and political standards to individuals based on their social race, class, religion, gender, or ethnicity.

francophones French-speaking people.

perestroika Russian, "restructuring." A new policy that aims to restructure the economy of the Soviet Union toward the adoption of a market economy.

Figure 18.8 *Under the strict regimes of the Soviet Union, all religions were suppressed; with the advent of* perestroika, *these Muslims in Uzbekistan can worship openly for the first time in many years. Coming into the open along with religious sentiments, however, are long-suppressed ethnic conflicts.*

udice could possibly reduce the day-to-day friction between members of different ethnic groups. However, if the underlying causes of ethnic differences are economic and political boundaries set up by competing groups, reducing prejudice will have little effect on ethnic conflict. This has become evident in the United States.

For generations, Americans believed that prejudice could be overcome by building cross-cultural sensitivity. The primary tool for this purpose has been integration of schools and other public facilities. The general public has been sensitized to prejudice, and openly discriminatory attitudes are not generally acceptable in public. But ethnic conflict has not diminished. In recent years ethnic violence has erupted in most U.S. population centers. In spite of laws, policies, and affirmative action, there is still considerable discrimination against African Americans, Hispanics, and other ethnic groups in education, employment, and housing. Even though the public has become far

more sensitive to prejudice and there has been widespread exposure of African American and other ethnic cultural patterns to the majority public, discrimination is a continuing factor in American life.

The essentialist view has difficulty explaining how and why ethnic groups arise and persist. The view of ethnicity in terms of cultural content has to be balanced with attention to political and economic dimensions of ethnicity and the fundamental inequality it implies. Clearly the boundaries between groups are not purely a product of the differences in cultural content, although these differences help maintain the boundaries.

GENDER STRATIFICATION

In Chapter 13 we examined differences between men and women in different social contexts and found that there was some plasticity in how people are socialized to gender roles. Yet there are some systematic differences in male and female roles, one of which is the nearly universal tendency for men to be politically dominant over women. Does this amount to a form of stratification?

If we view social classes as groups sharing a common relationship to the means of production, it makes little sense to consider men and women as separate classes. In most societies women share the hardships and benefits of the class status of their fathers and husbands. Nevertheless, in most societies women's roles are different from men's, and in many cases men and women are divided along lines that have consequences for health, access to resources and power, personal freedom, and opportunities for self-fulfillment. Out of their separate experiences women may create a gender consciousness similar to class consciousness. The roles assumed by women in class societies may intersect with class-based roles in interesting ways.

The Role of Women in Egalitarian Societies

Let us first examine gender stratification in egalitarian societies. Among the Chimbu of Highland Papua New Guinea, men and women live separately. A hamlet consists of a large men's house where youths and married men gather and sleep. Women and children live in small, separate houses clustered near the men's house. In everyday life women work independently of men, even though they have husbands and families. Men prepare and fence gardens and then hand them over to their wives, who do most of the planting, weeding, harvesting, and food preparation. Women are also responsible for feeding and caring for domestic pigs.

Big men (see Chapter 15) often have several wives, whose garden work provides extra food for feasts and giveaways. Men meet daily in the men's house to discuss the affairs of the day and settle political issues that require group decisions. They make decisions about garden and house locations, cooperative projects, ceremony scheduling, and the beginning and ending of hostilities. Women have little part in these deliberations except as they can influence their husbands. There are major differences, then, in the activities, rights, and obligations of men and women. Al-

though they contribute heavily to subsistence, women have less influence than men over decisions affecting the entire group (Brown 1978, 133–137).

Distinctive economic roles are also characteristic of men and women in the native societies of central Brazil. Like the Chimbu, Mundurucu men, live in a central men's house in the village, where they participate in many secret rituals at which sacred flutes are played and from which women are excluded. Women who glimpse the sacred flutes stored in the men's house may be gang raped. In some central Brazilian ceremonies, women take over male roles and act out ritualized aggression toward men, a kind of gender class warfare. This "warfare" has a purely symbolic function, however. Men are not deposed from their positions of political power (Murphy 1959).

While men everywhere have more political power (control over public matters) than women, there is considerable variation in the degree of equality between the sexes. There are many other aspects to gender equality besides political power. For example, there is control over the domestic food supply. Like Chimbu women, Mundurucu women have control over this realm of life. Mundurucu women live in matrilocal extended families surrounded by close female relatives on whom they can rely for help with children and other housework. Murphy and Murphy, who studied the Mundurucu in 1951, argue that women are more secure and less reliant on symbolic expressions of their power like the sacred flutes (Murphy and Murphy 1985). Their study challenges the notion that gender inequality can be understood purely in terms of male symbols of power.

Social Complexity and Female Subordination

There are many studies on the degree of inequality between the sexes. Generally there is greater gender equality in egalitarian societies without market exchange. According to the prevailing theory, as societies develop market economies and the division of labor is geared to production for sale, men become increasingly dominant over women. Why should this be?

The sociologist Martin King White (1978) conducted perhaps the broadest study to date on the status of women in preindustrial societies. Using a cross-cultural sample of 93 societies, White concluded that there is no single variable that describes the status of women. He showed that they rarely have political leadership roles equal to men's, but in many cases they have rights equal to or superior to men's in property inheritance and in access to specialized roles such as that of shaman; they also usually have final authority in matters concerning young children.

White isolated a series of indicators of the status of women, such as contribution to subsistence, descent and residence rules, the presence of private property, and the presence of exclusive male groups, such as the Chimbu and Mundurucu men's societies. White showed that the various indicators did not come together in neat bundles. It has long been believed that the greater women's contribution to subsistence was, the higher their overall status would be. This conclusion is not supported by White's comparative data. Another indicator, the presence of exclusive male groups, is also not connected with lower status for women. Women seem to enjoy moderately higher status in matrilineal and matrilocal societies and generally lower status wherever significant amounts of private property exist. The strongest result in White's study was a positive correlation between societal complexity and low status for women. Women in complex societies tend to have less authority in the household, more unequal sexual restrictions, and fewer property rights than in simpler societies (White 1978, 172).

White believes that these features are connected in complex preindustrial societies with intensive agricultural systems. It is fairly well established that women's influence declines with the adoption of intensive agriculture. There are several possible reasons for this. In a cross-cultural study, ethnologist Carol Ember (1983) showed that when a society practices intensive agriculture, men do most of the agricultural labor. This may be because intensive agriculture involves the use of the plow and draft animals, which are almost universally handled by men. But Ember believes that the main reason is that women are "pulled away" from agriculture to do more work inside the household. Women's work involves food processing and child care. This may be a result of the fact that intensive agriculturalists have higher fertility and hence women have more child care responsibilities. Also, the cereal grains (rice, corn, millet, wheat, barley) commonly used by intensive agriculturalists require more processing; hence women spend more time grinding or pounding grain. Ember suggests that women who are tied down with child care and food processing are not able to link up with power and information networks that would allow them to gain broader influence in society.

The Role of Women in Industrial Societies

If intensive agriculture keeps women subordinate in complex preindustrial societies, what accounts for their subordination in industrial societies, where only a fraction of the population is involved in agriculture? Most evidence suggests that the status of women is higher in industrial societies than in complex agrarian societies, perhaps because technology frees women from repetitive, isolated labor, such as collecting firewood, hauling water, food processing, and so on. The situation is different in developing countries undergoing rapid urbanization and industrialization. In countries like Brazil and India, many middle- and upper-class women receive professional training and enter professions such as law, medicine, teaching, and science in spite of traditional attitudes relegating women to second-class status (Figure 18.9). It is actually easier for these women to manage careers and families than it is in developed countries, because inexpensive domestic help is available. The intersection of gender and class creates a situation where wealthier women may be more "liberated" than their counterparts in industrial economies.

Here again, however, there are no neat bundles of status. While women are well represented in the work force in the United States, they are underrepresented in many specific areas, such as law, engineering, medicine, and top management. In 1984 a woman (Geraldine Ferraro) was a candidate for vice-president of the United States for the first time in history. But in 1991 there were still only two women among the 100 members of the Senate, one female justice on the Supreme Court, a single woman state governor, no women cabinet officers, and only a handful of congresswomen and women mayors.

In other respects women are still subordinated. Women who work find themselves placed in roles that reflect traditional attitudes about women. Women's pay in the United States averages only 58 percent of men's pay. Men often expect women to play the same

Figure 18.9 *At the University of Cairo, these Islamic women receive what is still reserved only for men in many countries—professional training in science. Their traditional dress, however, indicates that long-standing attitudes about the status of women relative to men still prevail.*

roles they play in the household as wives and mothers at the same time that they are efficient workers outside the home. Women are expected to be compliant, cheerful, and willing to serve the coffee. This role conflict places women in a "double bind." If a woman is aggressive and ambitious, she is criticized for being "unladylike"; if she accepts a subordinate role, she is faulted for lack of ambition. And although more women work full-time, time allocation studies in the United States, Norway, and other developed countries show that working women still bear the brunt of housework and child care.

American women may have "turned the corner," moving toward a more equal place in society, although with many setbacks and obstacles. Anthropologist Marvin Harris (1981) believes that the feminist movement of the 1970s and 1980s is a product of the post–World War II industrial boom in the United States, when a number of factors converged to draw women into the work force. Urbanization reduced the incentive for people to have many children, since a large family was a liability in the city. American industry was geared to produce many consumer products once regarded as luxuries but now seen as "necessities." For example, American families began to desire comfortable suburban homes, air conditioning, cars, boats, telephones, televisions, stereos, dishwashers, and clothes washers and dryers. Recently the demand has expanded to include vacation homes, pools, recreational vehicles, videocassette recorders, and micro-wave ovens. Installment credit made it relatively easy to acquire these goods. Harris pointed out that the demand for goods was sustained in part by their shoddy quality so that, by the time a car or appliance was paid for, it was probably broken and in need of replacement.

The demand for some items, such as a second car, more clothing, and labor-saving household appliances, was stimulated by the rise of the two-earner household. Some women who took jobs to have "extra income," found that with rising inflation and rising expectations, they could not afford to stay at home any more. Harris interprets the women's liberation movement as the outcome of the realization that women were getting the short end of the economic expansion. They were being asked to retain their roles as mothers and homemakers and also to join the work force and accept poorly paid, dead-end jobs, while remaining docile and subservient to men.

THE STRUGGLE FOR EQUALITY

Since the beginnings of complex society, people have struggled against inequality and questioned its inevitability. The struggle has taken many forms. Many people have tried to suggest that inequality is part of the order of nature and that some people are destined by nature or misfortune to live in misery and want while others enjoy plenty. As industrialism became dominant in the West, however, the belief arose that industrial production would eventually provide a good living for everyone. Most of the debate has centered around inequalities in material wealth. However, inequality also involves access to power, education and other fulfilling experiences, and even to spirituality.

During the 20th century there have been two fundamentally different approaches in the West to the question of inequality. The **liberal approach** accepts the idea that complex societies are inevitably inequitable, because organized production requires different levels of reward depending on the degree of training, skill, and responsibility held by the individual. Liberals tend to be reformers, trying to make things more equitable and to allow everyone to compete with an equal chance of success. Liberals do not seek to overthrow the system itself. The radical or **utopian approach** suggests that inequality is an inevitable phase in human social evolution but that in a subsequent phase it will disappear. Utopians tend to be revolutionaries who believe they can play a role in bringing about the next major historical phase. They seek to replace the current system with a more egalitarian one.

Millenarian Movements for Equality

There are many forms of utopian struggle against inequality. Some of them are effective in modifying the system, while others have little effect. "Primitive rebel-

Figure 18.10   *These men marching with painted wooden rifles are members of a cargo cult on Tanna Island in the South Pacific. They reverently mimic the actions of the troops they saw during World War II in hopes that planes and troops will return and bring them great wealth.*

lions" against inequality sometimes take the form of **millenarian movements**, which may poignantly express the longings of a group but do little to achieve them. The name comes from movements formed several times in the history of Christianity by believers who thought the second coming of Christ was close at hand. In anthropological usage, the term also refers to non-Christian movements that focus on a great transformation that will reverse the relations between the oppressed and the oppressors.

Millenarian movements have appeared on every continent and although unconnected with each other, they take a similar form. Most millenarian movements arise within a suppressed minority group within complex or expanding state organizations. Many times these have been tribal societies that have recently been incorporated into states and have become demoralized and disoriented, unable to cope with changed conditions.

In Papua New Guinea and other parts of Melanesia a number of **cargo cults** were formed during and after World War II. Cargo cults formed around the belief that a mysterious ship or plane would arrive one day bringing fabulous wealth and other social transformations. The tribal groups who formed these cults lived in isolated areas with only rudimentary knowledge of U.S. and Japanese society and the conflict in which they were engaged. Much of their knowledge related to goods carried by Japanese or U.S. ships and planes, which sometimes crashed in the mountains or on the seacoast. Sometimes the tribal groups had direct contact with troops, who seemed to possess fabulous wealth as well as great destructive power. All of the energy of the cargo cult was devoted to bringing the day when the cargo would arrive, the people would become rich, and work would no longer be necessary (Figure 18.10).

A remarkable parallel occurred among the Kanela of northern Brazil. During the late 1950s, after a period of great conflict between the Kanela and Brazilian settlers, a leader emerged among the Kanela. She predicted that soon the Kanela would no longer have to work for the Brazilians; their food would be provided by Brazilians who would work for them. The Kanela would become white; they would become policemen and bus drivers and occupy other important positions in Brazilian cities. At the direction of their leader, they sang and danced and tried to hasten the day of the great transformation. No transformation occurred. Instead a Brazilian vigilante group raided the village and killed several of the Kanela (Crocker 1967).

Millenarian movements arise at moments of stress, after change has seriously eroded the quality of life of the inhabitants, who perceive a great difference in their own life-style and that of other groups in the same environment. Because millenarian movements are based on magical beliefs and are regarded as dangerous by those in power, they are doomed to failure. They express the longing and frustration of a group without advancing it toward the goal of sharing in the benefits of a more powerful society.

Liberal Movements for Equality

An example of a liberal quest for equality is the African American civil rights movement in the United States. African American self-help groups such as the National Association for the Advancement of Colored People (NAACP) had existed for decades, but by the

---

liberal approach An approach that accepts inequality in complex society as a normal state of affairs, though one that can be improved through reform.

utopian approach An approach that does not accept social inequality as a normal state of affairs in a complex society; instead of reform, utopians advocate radical change.

millenarian movements Religious or political movements that believe that a social transformation involving a reversal of unjust social relations will occur in the near future.

cargo cults Millenarian movements occurring among tribal peoples, especially in Melanesia during and after World War II, based on the belief that ships would arrive laden with cargo for the natives.

Figure 18.11 *Martin Luther King, Jr., accompanied by his wife Coretta Scott King, heads the 1965 Selma march, a nonviolent demonstration for civil rights.*

end of the 1950s little progress had been made in removing legal and traditional barriers to African American participation in education, employment, and housing. The official response to protests against discriminatory **Jim Crow** laws was that African Americans could be excluded if the facilities provided them were equal to those available for whites.

In 1954 the U.S. Supreme Court determined that racially segregated education was inherently unequal and ordered public schools to integrate. In the early 1960s, however, little progress had been made on school desegregation, and Jim Crow laws were still in effect in many other areas, such as public transportation, hotels and restaurants, public rest rooms, and drinking fountains. Manipulation of voting laws and gerrymandering (tinkering with the boundaries of election districts) made it difficult for African Americans to be represented in law-making bodies. Many jobs were unavailable to African Americans and other minorities because of discrimination by labor unions and employers. Regardless of income, African Americans could not rent or buy housing outside of segregated areas.

Against this backdrop, a new African American movement emerged in the 1960s based mainly on religious leadership, long the backbone of African American communities. Although whites sometimes joined in "sit-ins" and other protests, the major gains were won by African Americans themselves. One common tactic was for protesters to peacefully occupy an area, such as a segregated lunch counter for whites, challenging the police to arrest them.

Perhaps the most powerful leader of his generation, the Reverend Martin Luther King, Jr., was the major spokesperson for African Americans until he was assassinated in 1968 (Figure 18.11). King and his colleagues successfully used the tactic of nonviolence. Nonviolence proved to be a successful formula for achieving change in the mid-century United States, just as it had been in Mohandas Gandhi's successful liberation movement in India. The civil rights leadership perceived that if they used violence they would lose their national support and reinforce negative African American stereotypes. Nonviolence succeeded in the United States because national leaders were not willing to use violence against a largely defenseless minority. Local and regional leaders, who may have felt they had more to lose, did use violence against the protesters, but this only brought more sympathy for the African American cause and confirmed the effectiveness of nonviolent tactics.

A number of important reforms were gradually adopted, including voting rights acts, formation of a federal civil rights commission, and prohibition of discrimination in public accommodations. "Affirmative action" in hiring was implemented to redress the imbalance in minority hiring and later in women's employment. Nevertheless, the long-range goal of full equality is far from secure. In many areas of employment, African Americans and other minorities are still not represented in proportion to their numbers in the population at large. African American income is much lower than white income, and the gap between the two has increased.

It may be too soon to gauge the full effects of racial desegregation and affirmative action in the United States. Greater equality may come in a future generation. But there is evidence that racial attitudes that support discrimination have not changed in many places. New forms of discrimination have emerged to replace the legal forms that have been struck down. Some social scientists believe that the basis for racial discrimination is embedded in American society and that legal reforms alone are unlikely to make a difference.

SUMMARY

- Inequality exists in every society, but some societies permit much more institutionalized inequality than others.
- Social class can be defined narrowly as an economic stratum. More often it is defined multidimensionally in terms of economic position, prestige ranking, occupation, and so on.
- Some societies are deeply divided by class divisions yet tend to understate their existence. Others make more of social class even when the differences are relatively small.
- In open societies, individuals have greater social mobility, while in closed societies, most aspects of class are ascribed from birth.
- Castes are endogamous social classes defined by ascription, often with specialized economic roles. While Indian caste is based on an ancient religious

Jim Crow laws Discriminatory laws, once common in the United States, that sanctioned unequal access to public facilities, housing, and other goods and services for African Americans.

model of a harmonious society with interdependent parts, it functions as an elaborate justification for inequality and restricted mobility.

- Ethnicity is another face of social complexity and must be understood in the political context in which it arises.
- Ethnic groups are ascriptive statuses defined by actors in terms of cultural content and by observers in terms of a process of boundary formation between groups. They arise mainly in complex states and they may interact symbiotically or competitively, but only rarely do two ethnic groups interact as equals.
- Gender stratification occurs in many societies. While women are generally politically subordinate to men, there are other aspects of the relative status of women and men that vary from one society to another.
- Women generally have lower overall status in complex societies than in simpler societies.
- Industrial societies use ever greater amounts of female labor outside the domestic setting, and women in the West may be starting to organize to achieve greater independence and equal treatment.
- Industrial societies use ever greater amounts of female labor outside the domestic setting, and women in the West may be starting to organize to achieve greater independence and equal treatment.
- Reform movements created by liberal thinkers seek to achieve greater equality by allowing everyone to compete with an equal chance for success.
- Radical or utopian movements seek to overthrow the current system and replace it with a more egalitarian one.
- No movement, whether radical or reformist has ever succeeded in overthrowing stratification altogether. At most the movements have changed the degree of mobility in a society.

GET INVOLVED

1. Make a diagram of the system of social stratification in your community. Identify the class membership of all groups as clearly as possible. Remember that stratification is not simply a matter of prestige or wealth, but the sum total of life chances for individuals in a particular stratum. What role, if any, do ethnic or racial groupings play? Is the system you describe relatively "open," allowing mobility across class lines, or relatively "closed"?

2. Select a series of books or films that depict social life in a particular country or region over time. You may use fiction or history or mix the two. Use these documents as a mirror of the social system prevailing at each time. With the data you have available, try to trace the causes of social change and particularly changes in the system of inequality over time. You may wish to focus on a specific aspect, such as gender discrimination or social race. Try to distinguish the *causes* of change from the *mechanisms* of change.

3. Join and participate in a movement for social change in your community. Examples are community groups promoting the rights of minorities, women, gays and lesbians, or the homeless. As you participate, try to learn what the particular views of the group are concerning the prevailing social system and what supports it. How does the group propose to change conditions? Is its program consistent with the way it conceptualizes social conditions, and is its program realistic in the light of its views?

SUGGESTED READINGS

Eckert, Penelope. 1989. *Jocks and burnouts: Social categories and identities in the high school.* New York: Teacher's College Press.

Fernea, Elizabeth W., and Robert A. Fernea. 1979. A look behind the veil. *Human Nature,* January.

Freeman, James M. 1979. *Untouchable: An Indian life history.* Stanford, Calif.: Stanford University Press.

Harris, Marvin. 1964. *Patterns of race in the Americas.* New York: Walker.

———. 1981. *America now: The anthropology of a changing culture.* New York: Simon & Schuster.

Worsley, Peter M. 1959. Cargo cults. In *Magic, witchcraft and religion,* ed. A. C. Lehmann and J. E. Myers. Mountain View, Calif.: Mayfield.

Inequality and Exploitation in the Peruvian Amazon

A Professor at Washington State University, John Bodley is passionately concerned about the plight of indigenous peoples. He has written on the subject in Victims of Progress, *and he explains here how his interest began.*

In 1964, before I completed my undergraduate major in anthropology, I spent a summer as a free-lance collector of zoological specimens in the central Peruvian Amazon, the traditional homeland of the Ashaninka (Campa) Indians. By chance I met Alfredo Vela, an experienced local settler and skilled outdoorsman. I accepted his invitation to use his farmstead in the upper Pichis valley as my field camp for a month, and as it turned out, this event shaped my future anthropological career. I had only the faintest knowledge of rain forest Indians and no understanding of the political and economic inequalities that confront indigenous peoples in many parts of the world.

Alfredo was the last non-native settler on the upper Pichis river; his house marked the frontier between the national society and the vast and rugged Ashaninka homeland. Many scattered Ashaninka groups lived in the surrounding forested hills where they cleared small gardens and hunted with bow and arrow.

Alfredo proved to be an enterprising man, with visions of eventually turning his small clearing into a cattle ranch. He talked bitterly about how unreliable the Ashaninka were as laborers, complaining that they would work a few days and then simply disappear. On our excursions into the forests, we visited several isolated Ashaninka settlements. The Ashaninka, who wore red face paint and long, hand-spun cotton robes, regarded us suspiciously and remained haughty and aloof. One man drew his bow at me and then re-

John Bodley and three Campa Indians, a group recruited to work for a patron.

leased the string without engaging the arrow. When Alfredo began pointing out numerous Ashaninka who he claimed were "in debt" to him, it became clear why we were being treated as unwelcome outsiders. He had earlier advanced cheap merchandise such as cloth and cooking pots and then expected the Ashaninka to clear the forest, saw lumber, and tap wild rubber at his bidding. He viewed these people as his "peones" and was visiting to remind them of their obligations. However, these Ashaninka were still autonomous enough that they had little use for money or patrons.

I found it remarkable that Alfredo's subsistence life style differed little from that of the Ashaninka, yet he obviously considered them to be his social inferiors. During my visit, we lived entirely from hunting and fishing and garden produce. We travelled by foot and dugout canoe. The most valuable manufactured item Alfredo owned was a dilapidated shotgun. By national standards, Alfredo was a very poor man; yet relative to the Ashaninka, he saw himself as a powerful patron who was on his way up. In fact, the Ashaninka were far more self-sufficient. They could do quite well without him, but he was

virtually helpless without their labor, and yet he was an intruder on their home ground. My sympathies were drawn to the Ashaninka, and I decided to learn their side of the story.

Two years later, I returned to Peru as a graduate student to carry out fieldwork for my M.A. thesis. This time I conducted extensive interviews with many Ashaninka, collecting genealogies and life histories. When people realized that I was not a patron and that I was genuinely interested in what they could tell me, I was treated most kindly. What I discovered was a shocking history of abuse and exploitation. Many Ashaninka told of losing family members in attacks by slave raiders and of being forced into virtual servitude. One man told of working as a logger for two years to pay for a $25 shotgun given to him by a patron. The most critical problem was that settlers were steadily pushing the Ashaninka from their lands, while the government offered them no support and encouraged their exploiters.

After completing my thesis, I returned again for more extensive Ph.D. research, and in 1972 I published a carefully documented account of my findings, including a policy recommendation that the Peruvian government recognize Ashaninka land rights and guarantee their cultural autonomy. I argued that independent Ashaninka enjoyed a highly egalitarian existence as long as they remained in control of their territory, but they were rapidly impoverished when forced to compete from the bottom of a highly competitive and stratified national society. In the 1980s the Pichis valley became part of an internationally financed development project that further marginalized the Ashaninka, but they have formed political organizations to defend their interests.

PART SEVEN

CONTEMPORARY CULTURAL PATTERNS

When we look at the world today from an anthropological point of view, we see many contrasts, contradictions, and paradoxes. In some parts of the world, notably North America, Western Europe, and the Far East, we see unprecedented wealth, power, and privilege. But elsewhere we see millions of people living in poverty and deprivation, victims of disease, malnutrition, exploitation, and neglect. We see poor countries welcoming foreign development projects in hopes of catching up with the West, only to find that the projects have disrupted life in unforeseen ways and left people more impoverished than before. We note that much of the world's wealth is the result of the highly efficient mode of production known as industrialism, but we also know that industrialism restricts personal freedom, increases poverty, and threatens to destroy the natural environment with its waste products. Many anthropologists today are studying problems and patterns of contemporary life such as these. They hope to understand and perhaps help resolve some of the pressing issues that challenge our species—indeed, all of life on earth—as we stand at the brink of the 21st century.

Part Seven addresses some of these current concerns. Chapter 19 looks at issues of development and underdevelopment in the so-called Third World, focusing on the roles of colonialism and neocolonialism in creating and maintaining poverty, inequality, and deprivation. The chapter also considers the qualities of successful development projects and explores three theories of underdevelopment. Chapter 20 addresses urbanism, the predominant settlement pattern in many countries of the world today, and examines the adaptations people make to urban culture. The chapter also explores industrialism and its effects on people and nature as well as the role of the environmentalist movement in society. Chapter 21 looks at medical anthropology, one of the fast-growing areas of anthropological study today. It investigates the cultural components of health and disease, bringing into focus once again the complex interplay of biology and culture in human society. Together, the chapters in Part Seven offer a glimpse of some of the most dynamic areas in anthropology today. They also show how anthropological knowledge can be used to change current conditions and to predict the impact of change on society and its members.

In many tropical countries, economic
growth has taken place at the expense
of the environment and cultural values.
Whereas slash-and-burn agriculture
does not degrade the environment,
large-scale cattle ranching can devas-
tate entire forests.

19

DEVELOPMENT AND UNDERDEVELOPMENT

▲▲▲

conomic development is one of the central issues of our time. The modern world is divided, broadly speaking, into two halves: developed and underdeveloped. This split is sometimes described as "rich versus poor," "industrialized versus nonindustri-alized," "North versus South," or First World (developed market economies), Second World (socialist), and **Third World** (underdeveloped). There are various opinions regarding the causes of these differences, but there is no ignoring the gulf between the world's poor and those who are reasonably well fed, live in

Table 19.1 The World's 25 Richest Countries: Vital Statistics, 1988

	GNP per Capita, U.S. $	Life Expectancy*	Infant Mortality†
Switzerland	27,500	77	7
Japan	21,020	78	5
Norway	19,990	77	8
United States	19,840	76	10
Sweden	19,300	77	6
Finland	18,590	75	6
Germany, Fed. Rep. of	18,480	75	8
Denmark	18,450	75	8
Canada	16,960	77	7
France	16,090	76	8
United Arab Emirates	15,770	71	25
Austria	15,470	75	8
Netherlands	14,520	77	8
Belgium	14,490	75	9
Kuwait	13,400	73	15
Italy	13,330	77	10
United Kingdom	12,810	75	9
Australia	12,340	76	9
New Zealand	10,000	75	11
Hong Kong	9,220	77	7
Singapore	9,070	74	7
Israel	8,650	76	11
Ireland	7,750	74	7
Spain	7,740	77	9
Saudia Arabia	6,200	64	69

*Average age of death.
†Number of deaths between birth and one year of age, per 1,000 live births.
Source: World Bank 1990

Table 19.2 The World's 25 Poorest Countries: Vital Statistics, 1988

	GNP per Capita, U.S. $	Life Expectancy*	Infant Mortality†
Mozambique	100	48	139
Ethiopia	120	47	135
Chad	160	46	130
Tanzania	160	53	104
Bangladesh	170	51	118
Malawi	170	47	149
Somalia	170	47	130
Zaire	170	52	96
Bhutan	180	48	127
Laos	180	49	108
Nepal	180	51	126
Madagascar	190	50	119
Burkina Faso	210	47	137
Mali	230	47	168
Burundi	240	49	73
Uganda	280	48	101
Nigeria	290	51	103
Zambia	290	53	78
Niger	300	45	133
Rwanda	320	49	120
China	330	70	31
India	340	58	97
Pakistan	350	55	107
Kenya	370	59	70
Togo	370	53	92

*Average age of death.
†Number of deaths between birth and one year of age, per 1,000 live births.
Source: World Bank 1990

relative comfort, have access to education and health care, and are shielded, to some extent, from the worst effects of periodic economic downturns. The division exists not simply between the rich and poor nations but also within the populations of modern countries.

To grasp the magnitude of the difference, let us look at some statistical information collected by the World Bank on the wealth and poverty of different nations. Table 19.1 shows the 25 richest countries in the world as measured by **gross national product** (GNP)—the value of all goods and services produced in a country for a given year—per capita for 1988. The average GNP per capita for these 25 countries was $14,680. Table 19.2 shows the 25 poorest countries; among these countries, the average GNP per capita was $235. Another measure of well-being is **life expectancy** (the average age of death for a population), also shown in Tables 19.1 and 19.2. It can be seen that the average Japanese, for example, has a life expectancy of 78; the average person from Niger (West Africa) lives to only 45. Infant mortality is another sensitive measure of well-being (see Tables 19.1 and 19.2). In Mali (West Africa), for example, 168 of every 1,000 infants born alive in 1988 died before reaching the age of one year. In Sweden only 6 out of every 1,000 infants died in the same year. Infant mortality is negatively correlated with GNP.

Anthropologists are concerned with issues of wealth and poverty partly because many of them work among poor populations. They see poverty as participant observers and identify with its victims. Many anthropologists have made poverty itself a focus of study. They try to discover the causes of deprivation in particular settings and investigate how people adapt to scarcity and the lack of resources. Not every population that lacks modern technology is poor or underdeveloped. A population in which there are no great differences in wealth or life chances may be perceived as "poor" by outsiders, but this category may

be meaningless within it. Other populations *are* poor in that they are the subordinate part of stratified societies and deprived of equal life chances because of their status. Among such populations are many of the world's **peasants**, who, as the rural-dwelling, food-producing part of states, are frequently disadvantaged.

In this chapter we begin by looking at colonial domination and how it created a structure in which wealth was diverted from one region to another through the exertion of political and economic power. We then examine some of the leading theories of underdevelopment, distinguishing between growth and development and between underdeveloped and undeveloped areas. Finally we consider the role of anthropologists in planning, evaluating, and guiding the process of development to maximize its benefits and minimize its costs for the people involved.

COLONIALISM

Colonialism refers to the domination of one people by another through conquest, tribute, alliance, or dependency. This definition is broad and includes diverse relationships. Colonialism should be distinguished from **imperialism**, which refers more narrowly to political domination, generally by conquest. Both colonialism and imperialism are ancient phenomena in human affairs. In Chapter 17, we saw that imperial conquest is a constant theme in history. It has taken many forms, ranging from the relatively loose system of the Aztecs, which was aimed primarily at collecting tribute, to the imposition of elaborate bureaucratic controls, language, and an economic system, as in the Inca, Han, and Ottoman empires.

The Portuguese Empire, which began to be established in the 14th century with unprecedented feats of maritime navigation, stretched around the world from Africa to India and across the Pacific and lasted until

---

Third World Regions or countries characterized by a low standard of living, an extreme gap between rich and poor, a high rate of population growth, low per capita income, and general dependency on the First World (North America, Western Europe, and Japan).

gross national product (GNP) The annual value of the total output of goods and services of a country.

life expectancy At birth, the number of years an individual is likely to live.

peasants Rural dwellers who produce crops and livestock both for subsistence and for outside markets.

colonialism The economic and political domination of one people by another through conquest, tribute, alliance, or dependency.

imperialism Political domination of one nation by another, usually as a result of conquest.

Figure 19.1 *This 16th-century engraving of Columbus's landing at Hispaniola marks the beginning of European colonization efforts of the New World. Note how the Belgian engraver depicted the New World natives as European-looking and bearing gifts of European origin instead of the parrots and cotton they did offer.*

the 20th century. It did not, however, extend direct political controls over large areas. Like the Italian traders before them, the Portuguese were primarily interested in setting up **ports of trade** to tap indigenous systems of production of textiles and other luxury goods for sale in Europe. The extraction of natural resources such as **dyewoods** and precious gems and metals became a virtual obsession of the Spanish Empire, which overlapped Portuguese expansion from the 16th through the 18th centuries (Figure 19.1). The development of plantations and mines, beginning in the 16th century, required that colonizers establish greater controls over conquered areas, because it was necessary to marshall a substantial labor force, build a labor-intensive productive enterprise, and provide it with food and other necessities.

The British Empire

The British Empire was the last of the great world empires to impose direct rule on its colonies. Its activities included mining, agriculture, trade, and construction of railroads and other public infrastructure. More than any other European colonial system, the British Empire concerned itself with the expansion of the market for British goods, particularly in the 19th century, when industrial production in England expanded well beyond the ability of local markets to consume its products.

To achieve their goals, the British promoted a free trade system and banned the slave trade. These measures helped open up new areas for commercial expansion and expand the buying power of workers in the colonies. By banning slavery the British also reduced the possibility that other countries would soon compete with it in industrial production by using cheap slave labor. In some cases the British suppressed native industries to stimulate their own. In the late 18th century, for example, the British prohibited the **looming** of cloth in India, which until that time had a larger textile industry than England. This context adds meaning to Gandhi's suggestion in 1929 that Indians take up looming their own cloth.

The British also began to apply scientific knowledge to the development of empire. The Royal Botanical Gardens, known as Kew Gardens, became a major research and development center for perfecting the technology of plant transfers from one region to another (Brockway 1979). Cinchona, the tree whose bark yields **quinine**, was smuggled out of Bolivia and shipped to Kew Gardens, where researchers worked out how to cultivate it in India. Quinine was of critical importance in the conquest of Africa, greatly reducing malaria deaths among British troops. Englishmen also smuggled native rubber plants out of Brazil to Kew Gardens and later transferred them to Malaya (now Malaysia). Rubber became a plantation crop in Malaya and decimated the South American rubber industry in 1909 (Brockway 1979). The British put colonialism on a scientific basis and used anthropological knowledge to design suitable forms of administration in indigenous areas of Africa and Asia.

The Impact of Colonialism

It is difficult to exaggerate the impact of colonialism on the modern world. No people on the globe were untouched by its influence. By extending markets to distant places; transferring technology; introducing new crops and diseases (Crosby 1972); promoting massive migrations through land grants, slavery, and indentured servitude; and imposing new forms of social organization, colonialism affected every society on every continent. Colonialism also had an influence on the colonizers. We have already mentioned the impact of scientific research on colonial expansion. Many discoveries made in the colonial context had important influences on scientific progress in the mother country. For example, Charles Darwin's theory of evolution was a result of his two-year voyage of discovery aboard the HMS *Beagle,* which called at ports throughout the British Empire, as well as other places.

Anthropology itself can be said to be the offspring of colonialism. Explorers and missionaries who visited remote parts of the world from the 13th to the 19th centuries left a literature that was the precursor to modern ethnography. These descriptions of foreign peoples in physical, linguistic, and cultural terms, although often crudely biased and ethnocentric in viewpoint, gave Westerners a view of worlds beyond their own. Traveler and missionary accounts formed the basis for the first systematic comparative research in anthropology done by E. B. Tylor, the English scientist who, as we saw in Chapter 3, proposed the first anthropological definition of culture.

The British, and later other colonial powers, used anthropological knowledge to develop administrative and legal procedures in their colonies. British law did not cover such matters as polygyny, bridewealth, and blood feuds, so they commissioned studies designed to harmonize such practices with the British legal system. Several eminent British social anthropologists came from the ranks of the British foreign service. More recently the U.S. Peace Corps, founded in 1960, provided many Americans with their first exposure to foreign societies. Many former Peace Corps volunteers became professional anthropologists.

The primary impact of colonialism on the colonizers, however, was a dramatic increase in their wealth. Colonial exchange is, almost by definition, unequal exchange. The colonial power has the ability to extract more value from its colony than it returns to it. Colonial enterprises used the labor and resources of colonies and transferred the wealth to the mother country. The wealthy classes in the colonial countries used these resources to raise their standard of living, acquire new luxuries, reinvest in expanded colonial activities, and finance new economic activities at home. The industrialization of Europe and North America in the 18th, 19th, and 20th centuries was financed in large measure by the profits from colonial enterprises.

Neocolonialism

Today there are relatively few colonies under direct political control. Most of Latin America won political independence from Spain and Portugal in the 19th century. The 20th century has seen the decolonization of former British, French, Italian, Dutch, Portuguese, German, and Belgian territories in Africa and Asia. However, the removal of direct political controls does not necessarily create total autonomy, as can be seen in countries like Zaire (formerly the Belgian Congo) or Algeria (a former French colony). There is a wide variety of economic, financial, political, and military means by which the dominant powers maintain control over people, resources, and decisions. The label given to such indirect forms of colonial domination is **neocolonialism.**

What historical forces have led to this transformation? Following the cataclysmic events of the first half of the 20th century—two global wars and one prolonged worldwide economic depression—a new world order emerged. In the political realm, the post–World War II order was characterized by competition between two superpowers, the United States, with its capitalist economy, and the Soviet Union, with its socialist system. The spread of socialism to the entire world was an objective of the Marxist program and was enacted over most of Eastern Europe and parts of Southeast Asia, Africa, and the Caribbean (Cuba). The United States used its political and military power to

---

ports of trade Centers (usually seaports) established in undeveloped regions under the control of colonial powers for the collection and export of goods to the mother country.

dyewoods Tropical wood species that produce dyes for coloring cloth.

looming The weaving of cloth on a loom.

quinine A medicine made from the bark of the cinchona tree that plays a role in suppressing malaria.

neocolonialism The indirect domination of one group by another through economic, financial, political, or military means.

defend market economies in most of the Americas, Western Europe, and parts of Asia and Africa.

Parallel to this competition, there arose a set of opposed ideologies of development. Although phrased in the form of competing ideologies, many people see this competition simply as a form of neocolonialism. A rough balance between the two sides prevailed for most of the second half of the 20th century, until, in a dramatic turn of events, the worldwide influence of the Soviet Union collapsed, and with it the ideology it represented.

In the economic realm, the post–World War II world order was characterized by an array of technology, resources, and industrial and financial organizations that unleashed unprecedented growth and expansion, particularly in the West. Previously, Western capitalism had been primarily concerned with importing raw materials and exporting industrial products. Now the stage was set for a new kind of export: **capital exports** in the form of technology, industrial processes and equipment, and money. Many countries that had formerly imported motor vehicles from the United States and Europe, for example, now began to produce their own cars, generally through subsidiaries of Western companies.

One of the most powerful institutions of our time is the **multinational corporation (MNC)**. These giant firms (Figure 19.2) have acquired assets and power far greater than that of most of the less-developed countries (LDCs). For example, the total sales of the Exxon Corporation in 1983 were more than $88 billion, an amount greater than the GNPs of Indonesia and 105 other countries. Even after subtracting expenses, Exxon was left with a net income of nearly $5 billion, greater than the 1983 GNPs of Tanzania and 58 other countries.

MNCs are involved in manufacturing, mining, agriculture, commerce, and services. MNCs frequently take advantage of lower labor costs in LDCs. Their global reach allows them to transfer resources, capital, and know-how from place to place to achieve their aims. MNCs can shift assets and transfer profits from one country to another to get better tax treatment. The sheer size and extent of their operations make MNCs difficult to control, even by the powerful nations. In some cases MNCs have interfered directly in government activities in the countries in which they have interests. Executives in office towers sometimes wield more power than the most powerful generals of invading armies.

Figure 19.2 *Coca-Cola is a multinational corporation whose global reach extends to more than 170 countries. In 1990, the net income of the corporation exceeded $10 billion.*

Some LDCs have undergone significant growth spurts in the postwar period. South Korea, Brazil, Taiwan, Singapore, and Malaysia are examples of these "advanced developing countries." Growth in these countries did not follow the same pattern as in the countries that industrialized earlier. Workers' wages tend to be very low and income highly maldistributed in most of the advanced developing countries. Some have accumulated staggering foreign and internal debt as a consequence of ambitious development programs. For some this debt has become a major national issue as the people perceive that before they can emerge from poverty, they may have to work even harder to pay off their debts to banks from wealthier countries.

Even where developing countries are nominal democracies with elections and regular rotation of governments, they often are dominated by corrupt elites who become skilled at using public resources and public power for their own benefit. Developing countries are frequently governed by populist leaders who use public funds and public works to distribute jobs and largesse as widely as possible to maintain power. Such leadership patterns are often associated with unsustainable patterns of public expenditures; bloated, do-nothing bureaucracies; and gargantuan public works that soak up much of the wealth of poor societies. There has been a great deal of debate in anthropological and related literature about whether the social systems of developing countries are remnants of a feudalistic past or simply the products of partially modernized societies.

Financial institutions also exercise a great deal of power in LDCs. Since the 1950s major U.S., European, and Japanese banks have loaned billions of dollars to LDCs. When the world economy turned sour, many of these countries came close to defaulting on their loans. The International Monetary Fund (IMF), an international financial institution controlled by the wealthier countries, is able to assist these countries with further credit. But the IMF imposes strict rules on countries it assists and requires them to curtail public welfare, government subsidies, and other social programs in order to control inflation and balance their budgets. These requirements are not the same as direct political control, but they have much the same effect. They have had major impacts on LDCs like Jamaica, where food and fuel prices skyrocketed once government subsidies were removed. In 1982 Brazil adopted an economic austerity program recommended by the IMF. In the resulting recession, infant mortality rates rose sharply after having declined steadily for nearly ten years. Thus the effect of postcolonial institutions, though indirect, can be as powerful as more obvious actions.

GROWTH AND DEVELOPMENT

The contemporary debate concerning growth and development revolves around the recognition that rising levels of income and production are not always beneficial for all concerned. At one time economic growth—expansion in the per capita production of goods and services—was automatically defined as good. This was because a higher GNP means more wages, more money in circulation, more market transactions, and more products. But by the 1960s a number of studies showed that not all growth brought about improvement in the well-being of people. It also became clear that not all investments in LDCs resulted in growth. Today many experts distinguish between growth and **development.** They consider that development occurs when people can share more equally in the wealth a society produces. Many eyes are now focused on the overall consequences of investment and growth to determine who are benefited by these processes and who are not.

Growth without Development

During the 1960s and 1970s many anthropologists went to LDCs to study the effects of investment and economic growth on the lives of people living in villages and towns in the developing world. In many cases they concluded that, while economic expansion had taken place, very few people benefited from it. Some people became richer, but others remained poor or sank lower into poverty. This was often the case where peasants were induced to begin growing new crops for sale to take advantage of new markets.

The author investigated one case of crop introduction and **commercialization** in the arid interior of northeastern Brazil. Before 1950 cattle products were the main exports from this region, which is famous for the catastrophic droughts that come in cycles of about seven years and the consequent mass exodus of people to the coast. Beginning about 1951 state agencies in the northeast began to encourage farmers to grow sisal as a cash crop. **Sisal** is a thorny, drought-resistant plant, first used in the area as a hedgerow to keep

---

capital exports Financial and industrial resources exported by capitalist countries to be used in economic production.

multinational corporation (MNC) A private company with branches in more than one country.

growth In economics, increased production of goods and services and a consequent rise in income over time.

development In economics, an improvement in the quality of life for people. Viewed holistically, development can have several aspects, such as increases in production, income, or economic choices.

commercialization The production of goods and services for sale rather than local consumption; the increased use of money in trade.

sisal A plant native to Mexico whose leaves yield fibers used in the manufacture of rope and twine.

Figure 19.3 *Brazilian men use portable machines to strip away the fleshy cortex of the sisal plant and extract the fiber within. The introduction of this cash crop ultimately benefited only a small number of people in the region.*

livestock out of neighboring fields. The long leaves of the sisal plant contain a fiber used for twines on automatic hay-baling machines on farms in North America and Europe. The process of stripping away the fleshy part of the leaf to extract the fiber is called **decortication**. In Brazil decortication is low-paying, dangerous, demanding work, done with labor-intensive, portable machines (Figure 19.3).

Many small farmers whose crops of maize, beans, and manioc periodically failed saw a chance to escape the uncertainty of the drought cycle and earn profits by planting much of their land in sisal. After planting, however, they had to wait four years for the first harvest. During the wait they generally worked for wages as crews on decorticating machines. In this way, sisal created its own labor force.

When the plants matured, many farmers found that the price paid for sisal fiber had fallen too low to make it worth harvesting their fields. They were left with fields choked with sisal plants, which are difficult to uproot, and with no food crops to sustain their families. In 1968 nutritionist Barbara Underwood and the author collected food and cash budgets of sisal worker households (Gross and Underwood 1971). They found that even though many households spent most of their money on food, they did not earn enough to provide an adequate diet for their families.

Dependent children, too young to work themselves, were particularly affected. The study showed that children of sisal workers were more seriously malnourished than the children of other workers. The sisal workers did not deliberately deprive their children; they were trapped by the necessity of providing adequate calories for themselves to keep up their strenuous activity on the decorticating crews.

Sisal brought benefits for some people in the region, especially through increased commercial activity. People who once grew their own food now needed to purchase food, and sisal required machinery and fuel. A town middle class arose, occupied with the purchase and processing of sisal fiber, the operation and service of vehicles and agricultural machinery, and the marketing of food. The life chances of this group improved dramatically, and many of them were able to purchase cars, have apartments in the state capital, and send their children to college—things unheard of in past years. However, a majority of the population experienced a drop in their level of living. Peasants who stopped producing subsistence crops and planted sisal found that they had been transformed from small crop producers into wage laborers. They also found that they had traded the uncertainty of the weather for the uncertainty of the world market for agricultural fibers.

Figure 19.4 *The Kofyar people of Nigeria hold cooperative labor parties to help in the weeding and harvesting of the yams they'll later sell at market. Their commercial venture proved successful in part because the Kofyar devised a strategy for cultivation and marketing on their own terms, not as a result of government intervention.*

Grass Roots Development: A Success Story

A recent long-term study of the Kofyar people of north-central Nigeria (Netting, Stone, and Stone 1985) showed that commercialization and technological change do not always have negative results for peasant farmers. Robert Netting first studied the Kofyar in the early 1960s. The Kofyar had a population density as high as 200 people per km², and they were approaching the limits of the habitat's ability to support them, even though they used relatively intensive cultivation techniques. During the 1960s a significant number of Kofyar began to move out of their communities at the foot of a plateau into the forested plains, where they began to cultivate more extensively. They also began to grow yams for sale. Netting and two graduate students returned to the Kofyar in 1984. They found that the Kofyar had improved their level of living with no one becoming worse off as a result of their entrance into the market system.

One of the changes brought by the new settlement pattern and by yam cultivation was that a high **peak labor demand** had been created for weeding and harvesting. Kofyar migrants to the plains met the demand primarily through **cooperative labor parties**, informal groups of relatives and neighbors who meet to perform a specific urgent task in the agricultural cycle (Figure 19.4). The cooperative labor party is similar to the barn raising on the North American frontier. After

---

decortication The process of removing the cortex of plant leaves from usable fibers at their core.

peak labor demand A temporary period during which there is a high demand for workers, often the harvest period in agriculture.

cooperative labor parties Groups formed temporarily, usually without pay, to perform a specific task, such as plowing or barn raising, for a friend or neighbor on a reciprocal basis.

the task is completed, the beneficiary gives food and drink to the participants and accepts the obligation to help them in future labor parties. In other case studies the commercialization of peasant agriculture and uneven labor demand have led to increasing inequalities among farmers: Some come to rely on wage labor while others increase their holdings. Studies elsewhere point to the decline in cooperative labor as agriculture becomes commercialized and inequality grows. In the Kofyar case significant inequalities did not arise and the tradition of free mutual assistance continued (Netting, Stone, and Stone 1985).

Why was the Kofyar experience so positive when so many other peasants have suffered negative consequences from commercialization? Netting, Stone, and Stone offer the following reasons:

1. The Kofyar entered the market voluntarily and on their own terms, not as a result of government intervention.
2. The primary commodity the Kofyar produce is a food crop that they can sell, hold for future sale, or consume themselves. Prices are not regulated by the government.
3. The market for Kofyar yams is internal, and the demand is high due to food shortages in Nigeria.
4. Nigeria is a petroleum producer, so transport costs are relatively low.
5. The Kofyar have not gone into debt to acquire new technology. Whatever new technology they need, such as tractors, has been acquired at a gradual rate and at their own pace.

The researchers concluded, "One of the keys to Kofyar success was that they had never been subjected to the efforts of outsiders to improve their agriculture" (Netting, Stone, and Stone 1985).

The "Green Revolution": Lessons of Development Schemes

One of the most promising events in recent years was the application of modern plant-breeding technology to Third World agriculture in what became known as the **green revolution.** The green revolution grew out of the development of hybrid varieties of major staple crops, such as wheat and rice, at research centers sponsored by U.S. foundations. The new varieties gave significantly higher yields than traditional varieties; they were introduced to farmers in many countries, some with chronic food deficits, such as India, Indonesia, Morocco, the Philippines, and Mexico. The new plant varieties were not simply packets of seeds handed out to farmers. In traditional farming systems farmers do not use purchased **agricultural inputs;** they simply select some of the best seed from last year's crop and save it to plant the following year. Using the green revolution varieties meant adopting a total "package" that included seeds, fertilizers, water control, pest control, and special cultivation techniques.

The green revolution produced mixed results. Many farmers in the Philippines could not afford the new inputs. Those who could afford them produced good harvests; often they used the profits to buy out poorer neighbors who could not afford the total package. In other cases mice and other pests driven from fields treated with pesticides moved to untreated fields and devoured the neighbor's crops. Some poor farmers had no choice but to sell their land and become landless workers or join the army of unemployed in the cities. There were spectacular successes in other places, such as the Punjab region of India, where high-yielding crops helped both the region and all of India to overcome their chronic food deficits for the first time in decades.

Anthropological Perspectives on Agricultural Development

As these processes of change were occurring in the developing world, demand arose for anthropological expertise in planning and evaluating new agricultural initiatives. By examining more and more cases of change in rural, agrarian societies, anthropologists developed a set of generalizations about successful change in rural areas. Perhaps the most widely accepted generalization from dozens of studies is that a particular development intervention must "fit" into the prevailing cultural and economic pattern if it is to be accepted and succeed. One fundamental criterion is that the intervention not demand resources that the "target" population cannot afford. This criterion is frequently ignored by planners who are unaware of the hidden costs in time, money, and other resources of the adoption of a new technology, such as a green revolution seed.

Another criterion frequently ignored in the planning process is that the expected increment in economic growth be greater than the existing level of production. Economic planners have sometimes assumed that people who do not sell labor or products on the market have no income. Subsistence production for home or local consumption is often underestimated in national production statistics, and peasants are sometimes treated as "economic zeroes." But people who are self-sufficient in food and other necessities are not zeroes, even if they do not participate in the market. Another common error is the assumption that women do not contribute to the economy of the household. Often the work done by the women, whether it be child care, food processing, hauling water, or marketing, is simply not accounted for in considering household budgets, because it has no ready cash equivalent.

As mentioned earlier, economic planners sometimes assume that all growth in production is good. Anthropologists have played a role in asking what other consequences development schemes may have in the lives of ordinary people who are their targets. The central anthropological question of development has shifted from, How can peoples' attitudes be changed? to, How do people evaluate the choices open to them, and how do they act on them? Most anthropologists agree that development schemes would be improved if there were consultation with the people who are supposed to benefit from the schemes *before* implementation.

THEORIES OF UNDERDEVELOPMENT

The beginning of Western economics is often traced to Adam Smith's book *The Wealth of Nations* (1776). This book suggested that people create wealth through the efficient functioning of markets, which, if allowed to operate without interference, would automatically produce the greatest welfare for the most people. This book is often regarded as the first great defense of capitalism and *laissez faire* economics. The wealth of nations continues to be an important topic in the second half of the 20th century.

The competition between socialist and capitalist ideologies following World War II, as well as the competition for capital and product markets, led to a tremendous focus on the developing countries, which were on the receiving end of many political and economically motivated development schemes. Not only investors and developers but also anthropologists and other social scientists turned their attention to the Third World and the complex issues involved in development. Contemporary social science has fashioned a number of theories to explain why some societies forged ahead while others remained in a state of social and economic stagnation. Two of the most comprehensive, though still not fully satisfactory, are modernization theory and dependency theory.

Modernization Theory

A number of experts writing in the 1950s and 1960s suggested that the internal organization of LDCs prevented them from building dynamic, growth-oriented societies. These experts saw non-Western people as prisoners of traditional social systems that inhibited innovation and discouraged risk taking. This approach, which defined development in terms of economic growth and looked for obstacles to growth in the social and psychological features of society, became known as **modernization theory**. Modernization theory rests on a dichotomy between "traditional" and "modern." For this reason, modernization theory is sometimes known as "dual society" theory. The theory views societies as divided into both traditional and modern sectors; change occurs when ideas diffuse from the modern sector into the traditional sector.

---

green revolution Beginning in the 1960s, a new approach to agricultural development based on the use of hybrid seeds, fertilizer, pesticides, and mechanized cultivation and harvesting.

agricultural inputs Fertilizers, pesticides, herbicides, and other products or processes that enhance crop production.

modernization theory A post–World War II approach to economic development that emphasized the diffusion of "modern" values and organizational structures from dynamic centers to stagnant peripheries.

One early proponent of the traditional-modern dichotomy was anthropologist Robert Redfield (1941), who used the terms *folk* and *urban* to describe the two sectors. According to Redfield, the folk tradition was rooted in the countryside and based on ancient tribal and peasant beliefs, especially religious beliefs. Social life was based primarily on kinship ties; social relations were generally harmonious and disagreements rare. Change was slow since the people were basically conservative and resistant to new ideas. Cities, on the other hand, were dynamic and constantly changing. Urban social life was based on contracts rather than kinship ties, and actions were justified in rational rather than sacred terms. Cities bred conflict and strife, and consequently new ideas were constantly arising.

Redfield put forward the folk-urban continuum as a set of ideal types that no real-life community fits exactly. Actual communities can be set along a scale from the folk to the urban type. Redfield conducted a series of community studies in the Yucatan (1941) in which he tried to show that the differences among the communities were based primarily on how isolated the community was from urban influences. Redfield's views are no longer widely accepted among anthropologists, because they failed to account for the complex society even of the Yucatan itself. However, Redfield was one of the first anthropologists to make the traditional-modern distinction.

Modernization theory, developed after Redfield, suggested that certain kinds of ideas were prevalent in each of the two sectors. Describing the traditional sector, with its peasants and landowners, one economist wrote (Hagen 1962, 83–84):

> The image of the world of the simple folk and elite includes a perception of uncontrollable forces around them that restrict and dominate their lives. . . . The lines of dependence extend upward to the spiritual powers to whom the members of the society appeal for protection. . . . Each individual finds his place in the authoritarian hierarchy of human relationships . . . the simple folk find satisfaction in both submissiveness and domination; their personalities as well as those of the elite are authoritarian. . . . In these societies, except for struggles within the class of the elite itself, class relationships are fixed.

In such societies people are unwilling to defy tradition and make changes. The logical conclusion is that tra-ditionalism must be removed before economic development can occur.

Another expert asserted that, for a society to progress economically, basic values must change, along with certain fundamental aspects of social organization (Hoselitz 1960):

> A change in the pattern of family organization has been observed to accompany all really far-reaching instances of economic growth. . . . It may even be argued that the abolition of certain aspects of the traditional [extended] family is necessary, because with them the demands of the new economic order could not adequately be met.

Responses to Modernization Theory. Clearly the modernization theorists had predetermined ideas about the role of values, the family, and authority in development. When some of these ideas were put to empirical tests during the 1960s and 1970s, they did not stand up very well. Case studies from India, Pakistan, Mexico, and Taiwan showed that extended families were often involved in new and innovative undertakings, involving new technologies and the assumption of considerable risk. Far from liabilities, the extended family's mutual trust, ability to pool resources, and acceptance of a single authority were valuable assets in certain kinds of activities, such as small- and medium-scale industrial development. For example, traditional patrilineal extended families in rural Taiwan were found to be extremely flexible and efficient producers of small, finely machined parts for the electronics industry (Hu 1983). These families made substantial investments in machinery and turned out precision products as independent producers under contract to central factories.

Modernization theory has also been criticized for its equation of growth with development. Many societies have undergone significant economic growth in the postwar periods, seeing per capita GNP multiplied several times. In many countries, however, such as Mexico, Brazil, Indonesia, and Nigeria, high rates of growth have been accompanied by a worsening quality of life and health for many citizens. While these countries have large cities, prosperous industrial centers, and some areas of dynamic agricultural production, they also have teeming shanty towns, grinding poverty, and malnutrition. Additionally, they are experiencing serious environmental deterioration due to overexploitation of resources and industrial pollution.

Most dramatically, while there is great wealth in these countries, it is unevenly distributed. The rich in Brazil and Nigeria live gilded lives surrounded by servants, cars, swimming pools, and many privileges, while the poor live in deep poverty. The privileged are often highly conservative, as became evident during the 1960s and 1970s, when the elites in several LDCs supported takeovers by repressive military regimes. The ethnocentric idea that economic growth automatically brings better distribution of income, greater democracy, moderate political regimes, and a better standard of living for the average person has been discredited. This is one of the reasons for the current distinction between growth and development mentioned earlier.

Psychological Variants of Modernization Theory. Closely related to modernization theory are psychological and cultural approaches that seek to identify other obstacles to economic development. In 1961 psychologist David McClelland published *The Achieving Society,* in which he suggested that human beings had a measurable need for achievement and that this need varied in intensity from one place to another. McClelland claimed that development was more likely to occur in a country where this need, which he called **N-achievement**, was high. McClelland developed a measure of N-achievement based on the narratives in children's stories. When stories depicted a high level of movement and concern for the future, McClelland coded the society as high in N-achievement. A cross-national survey showed that countries with high N-achievement scores had grown more than those with low scores. McClelland presented data from time periods *before* growth took place, so he was able to claim that high N-achievement was a sufficient condition for economic growth.

McClelland's conclusions have been widely challenged. While there is a relationship between N-achievement and economic growth, it is not certain that the relationship is causal. The conditions that permit economic growth—including the development of financial and physical infrastructure, a stable

political climate, markets for products, and the acceptance of new ideas—need to accumulate for several years before a move to sustained economic growth takes place. Thus, they could be conditions for the rise of both N-achievement and economic growth. Many factors are involved, including both internal and external influences. If a country is invaded, for example, economic growth might stop no matter how high the N-achievement of the population. Psychological theories of development have not convinced most investigators that achievement motivation and similar constructs are necessary and sufficient conditions for growth.

Another difficulty with such theories is that a wide range of personalities and attitudes can be found in most countries. Some people avoid risks at all costs and hate to deviate from their everyday routines; others welcome opportunity when it arises. Such individuals can be found in any society. When approached in this manner, the question of achievement motivation can be seen in a new light. Any measure of motivation should present a "normal distribution" (Figure 19.5) in any given society. The largest number of people should be about average in their degree of motivation, willingness to take risks, and adherence to tradition, with highly unmotivated and highly motivated people falling to either side on the bell-shaped curve. McClelland's position (see Figure 19.6) is based on the premise that achievement motivation is not normally distributed cross-culturally. It is impossible to test McClelland's hypothesis rigorously because there is no standardized, cross-culturally valid test of achievement. Even in low-achievement societies, however, there will be some risk-oriented individuals at the extreme end of the curve. It doesn't take a whole population full of entrepreneurs to bring about development. There are other factors involved, and McClelland's approach does not account for them.

Cultural Variants of Modernization Theory. From 1900 to about 1960, American anthropologists wrote frequently about the acceptance or rejection of items across cultural boundaries. The prevailing explanatory

---

N-achievement A measure of the psychological need people have for achievement.

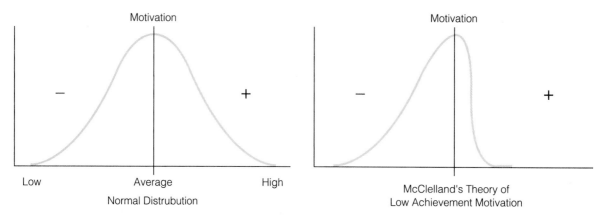

Figure 19.5 *Psychologist McClelland suggested that motivation and economic development were closely related. His theory supposes that more people worldwide have low achievement motivation than high, which causes more economically disadvantaged than developed countries. A normal distribution curve (left), however, suggests that about equal numbers of people would be less and more motivated. McClelland's theory has been widely challenged.*

model was a **cultural template** model. According to this approach, any new item of culture is evaluated in terms of the cultural expectations of the receiving society. If people find that the new item fits into their own cultural pattern, they will adopt it, sometimes with changes; if the item is incompatible, the people will reject it. Margaret Mead employed this model in *Cultural Patterns and Technical Change* (1955). She suggested that Greeks patterned experience after the

body, for example, so that things were seen as related to each other as hands to arms or knees to legs. Mead wrote, "the lineal diagram as a blueprint of action is not within the framework of Greek life; the nearest most Greeks come to a diagram is a map which is diagrammatic of something concrete" (1955, 90).

Taking Mead literally, one might wonder how the ancient Greeks produced so many great architects and planned monuments like the Acropolis in Athens with

Figure 19.6 *Why do cultures accept some imported items and reject others? In Yoyogi Park in Tokyo, for example, these Japanese teens show enthusiastic, individual responses to Euro-American rock music, even though their culture values control and group efforts.*

such symmetry, given their cultural aversion to diagrams. By the same token, it would make no sense at all for rock music to find acceptance in Japan with its stress on control and valuing the group over individual will. Yet rock music has become wildly popular in Japan (Figure 19.6). While the template model provides a plausible explanation for the acceptance or rejection of innovations, it is not really testable, because there are no fixed criteria for cultural compatibility. In fact we have few clues to why cultures accept some items and reject others. Why, for example, do Americans enjoy such specialties of French cuisine as *Boeuf Bourguignon* (beef stew with wine) and *Caneton à l'Orange* (roast duckling in orange sauce) but not horsemeat, another French favorite?

Another approach, popular in both American and British anthropology, is the functionalist or "holistic" approach. This approach stresses the integration of culture, or the interconnectedness of many different aspects of culture. According to this point of view, certain items of culture are accepted and others are rejected because of the way they fit, or do not fit, into the overall cultural matrix. Consider, for example, the resistance in the United States to the adoption of the metric system. The metric system of weight, measure, and temperature is easier to learn and use than the cumbersome English system, in which 12 inches equal 1 foot; 3 feet, 1 yard; and 5280 feet, 1 mile. Why do North Americans resist the simpler metric system? Is it pure inertia, conservatism, or something else?

According to anthropologist Richard A. Barrett (1984) the reason lies in the fact that the American industrial system, including the specifications of millions of different parts, is geared to the English system of weights and measures. He shows that industrial interests, which favored metrification in 1902, have actually lobbied against it in recent years because they have so much invested in plans, machinery, and parts. It would have been relatively easy to switch to a metric standard in the early years of industrialization; now the cost could be staggering (Barrett 1984, 111–

112). Inertia, or resistance to change, is often a function of how much is invested—financially, physically, politically, even emotionally—in the status quo and how costly it would be to change. Although this is a powerful metaphor, it may often be difficult to measure how much people have "invested" in something when the investment is measured in emotional or symbolic terms.

Limited Good. In 1965 anthropologist George Foster wrote an article formalizing an observation that many anthropologists have made informally in the field and in their writing. He noted that peasants tend to be cautious in their attitudes and resistant to social change. Most anthropologists define peasants as the rural segment of complex societies, which produces food and other commodities partly for subsistence and partly for sale. This description refers to a large segment of humankind, including most of the populations of India, China, Pakistan, Indonesia, Nigeria, and Mexico. Peasants are characteristically subordinate to other social groups, merchants, landlords, and local and regional political leaders.

Foster argued that peasants do not contribute to national economic growth and that they are inhibited from doing so by a common cognitive orientation. In other words, peasants share a world view that prevents them from participating in economic growth. Foster identified this cognitive orientation as the "image of limited good," which he defined as follows (1965, 296):

> [P]easants view their social, economic and natural universes, as one in which all of the desired things in life such as land, wealth, health, friendship and love, manliness and honor, respect and status, power and influence, security and safety *exist in finite quantity and are always in short supply.* . . . [I]n addition, *there is no way within peasant power to increase available quantities.*

As evidence, Foster gave examples showing that peasants in different parts of the world were prone to

---

cultural template The pattern of values and expectations that an individual uses as a standard of comparison for alternative life-styles.

envy, attempted to conceal wealth, and were suspicious of anything that upset the status quo. Even goods like health were seen as limited (see Box 19.1). As an example, Foster cited a peasant belief in Guatemala that blood once lost cannot be replaced. Foster also suggested that **machismo**, the Latin American code of manliness, was connected with a peasant belief that one can only be macho by denying it to others.

Because they were so suspicious and fearful that someone else would get the best of them, peasants were unable to cooperate or agree to leadership from within the community. A leader would automatically have more authority than others, hence he or she would be subject to extreme envy. Therefore peasants could be expected to avoid leadership roles. Foster wrote (1965, 302):

> [P]easants are individualistic, and it logically follows from the Image of Limited Good that each minimal social unit (often the nuclear family and, in many situations, a single individual) sees itself in perpetual, unrelenting struggle with its fellows for possession of or control over what it considers to be its share of scarce values. This is a position that calls for extreme caution and reserve, a reluctance to reveal one's true strength or position. It encourages suspicion and mutual distrust. . . . Since an individual family that makes significant economic progress . . . is seen to do so at the expense of others, such a change is seen as a threat to the stability of the community.

According to Foster, the consequence of this orientation was that peasants avoided economic progress; they would not work harder for fear of arousing suspicion or envy, and they avoided accumulating wealth so as not to upset community stability. Under the circumstances, said Foster, peasant conservatism was a rational attitude that provided the maximum of security. He concluded (1965, 310) that the

> primary task in development is [to] try to change the peasant's view of his social and economic universe, away from an Image of Limited Good toward that of expanding opportunity in an open system *so that he can feel safe* in displaying initiative. The brakes on change are less psychological than social. Show the peasant that initiative is profitable, and that it will not be met by negative sanctions, and he acquires it in short order.

Foster's theory was criticized by many anthropologists because it appeared to blame peasants for a condition over which they had no control. Some critics pointed to examples of peasant societies that were not individualistic. Other critics pointed out cases where peasants distinguished themselves from others, took leadership roles, and assumed risks. Perhaps the most serious criticism was that peasant societies are often faced with real scarcity and that this condition was largely a result of political and economic forces outside the peasant community. In other words, peasant images of limited good may be accurate reflections of the limitedness of concrete goods in the world they live in (Acheson 1972, 1974). It is paradoxical, argued Foster's critics, to expect that people who have nothing will accumulate the resources to work their way out of their situation.

Dependency Theory

The 1960s were not yet over when a resounding response to modernization theory and its psychological and cultural variants was heard. The first salvo came from Latin American social scientists who attacked the dichotomy between "traditional" and "modern" societies. They argued that development and underdevelopment were two sides of the same coin. According to these theorists, the dual societies to which modernization theorists referred were actually unified social systems tied together by relations of **dependency**. Underdevelopment in **satellite** areas is part of the process of development (capital accumulation) in the **metropolis**. Economic growth is not necessarily the product of an enlightened or progressive population; instead it may result when one group takes the opportunity to increase its wealth at the expense of other groups.

Dependency Relationships in Northeastern Brazil. To get a better understanding of the dependency approach, consider Brazil, the largest country in South America, with a rapidly growing population of 150 million people. It has vast natural resources and a developed industrial base. Brazil exports a wide variety of goods, such as coffee, sugar, soybeans, citrus concentrate, poultry, shoes, automobiles, military equipment, and airplanes.

Brazil's wealth is unevenly distributed, however. Northeastern Brazil is a predominantly agricultural region, producing sugar cane and other crops, although poverty in the rural zones has driven increasing numbers of people into cities on the coast. In the countryside and the poor urban neighborhoods, income is low, diet is poor, and infant mortality rates are among the highest in the world, a result of a combination of malnutrition and infectious disease. Southern Brazil, on the other hand, presents such a contrast to the northeast that it seems to some like a different country. Agriculture is highly productive in the south, and most of the country's industries are concentrated there. Centered around São Paulo, this area has a higher standard of living, lower infant mortality, and higher levels of educational attainment than the rest of the country (Figure 19.7). Such contrasts are common in developing countries. Dependency theory focuses on the relationship between more developed and less developed regions of the world.

Historical factors are important in establishing patterns of dependency. In the case of Brazil, the Northeast was once a wealthy region. Portuguese colonizers imported millions of African slaves to plant, harvest, and mill sugarcane to satisfy Europe's "sweet tooth." The sugar system has been described as the richest system of colonial agriculture in history. The plantation owners and others in the colonial system enjoyed lives of unparalleled luxury and power. Gradually other sugar producers in the New World began to compete with Brazil for market share. The demand for Brazilian sugar fell and the cost of production rose. By 1888, when slavery was abolished in Brazil, the northeastern sugar industry was already in decline. Meanwhile, planters in São Paulo had begun to plant cane as well and had achieved much higher productivity levels.

The sugar planters of the northeast became the dominant politicians in their region; they used their influence to consolidate their positions, tolerating no major changes or interference. They are a classic example of an entrenched regional elite who have used political means to preserve their power and suppress movements for social change. For example, the northeastern planters successfully lobbied the government to set higher prices for northeastern sugarcane than for cane produced in the south. In spite of generous government sugar subsidies, however, the wages paid to cane workers are extremely low; sometimes the workers are obliged to give free work days to the planter in exchange for housing or a small plot of land on which to grow food. With help from an authoritarian central government, planters have thwarted attempts by religious and other progressive forces to organize the workers for higher wages and better working conditions.

Today northeastern Brazil has a population of more than 40 million. The arid interior undergoes frequent droughts, which send crowds of famished migrants to coastal cities when their crops fail. Many northeasterners live in houses built of mud and sticks and lacking running water and sanitary facilities. Peasants have fatalistic attitudes and appear to be resigned to lives of deprivation and injustice (Box 19.1).

To the casual observer, the dual society model is appealing. Brazilians tend to present the Northeast as an undeveloped region trapped in traditions, while the South is portrayed as a dynamo, humming with productive activity. The situation is not so simple, however. There are large pockets of poverty in the South, and the elites of the Northeast live in comfort with a standard of living as high as anywhere in the world. More importantly, the two regions are tightly interdependent. The Northeast has supplied much of

---

machismo A code of manliness based on superiority to women, sexual prowess, and the denial of these characteristics in other men.

dependency In development, the condition of less-developed countries in which they require technology, know-how, and capital exports from the industrialized countries for economic growth to occur.

satellite The dependent, underdeveloped, nonindustrialized areas of the world in contrast to the more-developed areas that control technology and capital.

metropolis A dominant center of capitalist development (primarily in Europe, Japan, and North America), which receives inexpensive natural resources, commodities, and labor from satellite areas and exports technology, capital, commodities, and know-how.

Figure 19.7 *The Piracicaba region of São Paulo in southern Brazil (top) has many sugar cane fields, and the standard of living is much higher here than in the northeast sugar cane region. The affluence can be seen in this São Paulo neighborhood (bottom).*

the labor that has made possible the agricultural and industrial booms in the South. The Northeast is also a major market for goods produced in the South. The terms of trade are weighted in favor of the South. The Northeast receives little private investment and only a small share of public investment. Many of the businesses operating in the Northeast are subsidiaries of southern-based firms; the profits are not reinvested in the region. The South is more central to government policies than the Northeast. The Northeast is not sim-ply poorer and more "backward" than the South; it is closely linked to it. Thus, the dualist, "two Brazils" idea does not stand up well under scrutiny.

The dependency approach distinguishes between **underdeveloped areas**, as in the case of northeastern Brazil, and **undeveloped areas** as in the case of the !Kung San. Underdeveloped regions are generally the outcome of very intensive development; in a sense they are "overdeveloped," or **overspecialized** in the production of a narrow range of commodities. North-

BOX 19.1

Fatalism among the Oppressed

Religion in northeastern Brazil is a fatalistic version of Roman Catholicism: Whatever happens is God's will and one must conform to it. One asks the saints and the Virgin Mary for favors (*graças*), but they are not to blame if the favor is not granted. Peasants and plantation workers in northeastern Brazil tend to be resigned to living in continual poverty and want. While they do not seem to think in terms of "limited good," they are not optimistic about bettering their situation. A common expression goes, "All waters flow to the sea," which corresponds to the English phrase, "The rich get richer." The phrase *se Deus quiser* (God willing) is also used frequently and expresses the pervasive fatalism and resignation.

The primary strategy for betterment is not self-help but an attempt to recruit a wealthier person as a source of assistance. The strategy is played out by a continual show of humility. Peasant men remove their hats and machetes before entering a house. They speak in low voices to people of higher rank, taking care to avoid eye contact. They use terms of address derived from medieval Portuguese, which can be translated as "Your Mercy" or "Your Excellency." A dependent never finds fault with an employer or other high-status people. Outside visitors are sometimes startled at the degree of loyalty and devoted service offered by low-ranking people. It is common for a poor farmer to arrive at the home of a patron at dawn to present a few fresh hen's eggs, even though his own family is doing without.

One of the functions of ideology in highly unequal societies is to induce people to accept their station in life. In traditional Catholic society, one plays out one's life role in the expectation of some future reward. In India Hinduism has the concept of being "twice born." By accepting his or her caste position without complaint, one earns the possibility of coming back to a future life at a higher caste level.

I personally experienced the unnerving degree of fatalism among these people while I was living in a small village in the semiarid interior of northeastern Brazil. A small boy suffered an injury in an accident: His mother was trying to shoo a pig out of the house and swung a machete, hitting her son in the eye. When I learned of the accident, I asked the child's parents if they didn't want to take the boy to a doctor. They refused at first and agreed only when I offered to take the child in my jeep and to pay the doctor. We drove 125 km (78 mi) to the nearest town where an ophthalmologist could be found. The doctor prescribed medication and made a new appointment for the boy. I purchased the prescription and drove the family back to their village. For a week, I checked frequently to see that the parents were using the medication properly. Often they seemed to have "forgotten."

A day before the second doctor visit, I went around to see what plans the parents had made to arrange transportation to the doctor. I told them I had work to do and that, since it was no longer an emergency, they should go out to the road by jeep and wait for the bus to take them to the town where the doctor was. At first they refused, and only after a great deal of persuasion did they agree to make the trip on their own.

I was never sure why they resisted so strongly even though they knew their son's eyesight was at stake. I believe now that they had no confidence that they could save the boy's eyesight with their own meager efforts; if the rich foreign visitor did not take him to the doctor himself, there would be no cure. In the years since, each time I have returned to the village, the boy—now a young man—has presented me with a live chicken, grateful that he did not lose his eyesight, and his mother has come by to say, "If it weren't for Our Lord, and your help, sir, my boy wouldn't have his eye."

---

underdeveloped areas Areas that have participated in the world capitalist system through intense but narrowly based economic development characterized by low income, poverty, and dependency.

undeveloped areas In development studies, areas of the world that have never been involved in the accumulation of capital.

overspecialization The production of a narrow range of commodities, which may lead to underdevelopment.

eastern Brazil, for example, became underdeveloped as the result of a process of capital accumulation involving intensive investment, forced migration, resource exploitation, market expansion, and a highly specialized agricultural estate system. The region was left where it is today not by a lack of investment or a fatalistic world view but by the nature of the process that economist André Gunder Frank calls the development of underdevelopment (1966). An undeveloped system, by contrast, has not undergone a process of intensive investment or resource exploitation. The !Kung San are not developed by modern standards, because they have never been involved in the process of capital accumulation. They are not underdeveloped, simply undeveloped.

Dependency is a key concept in underdevelopment. The basic relationship between a developed metropolis and a dependent satellite region, like northeastern Brazil, tends to be reproduced at other levels. For example, the relationship prevailing between Brazil's northern and southern regions is similar to the relationship between Brazil and the developed countries of North America and Europe. Brazil is heavily dependent on foreign countries for investment capital and technology. While foreign investors tend to feel they have contributed a great deal to Brazil's growth, some dependency theorists argue that they have extracted more than they have contributed.

Dependency relations may also be reproduced at the local and regional levels. Dependency has social, psychological, political, and economic dimensions. The organization of production on northeastern Brazilian plantations has been compared to the feudal system in Europe, in which labor was tied to the land (as serfs on feudal manors) and could be bought and sold. While there are some similarities, the overall structure of agriculture in northeastern Brazil is not feudal but modern, rooted in capitalist commodity markets. The dependency of workers on the landlord, however, is undeniable.

Responses to Dependency Theory.   Dependency theory made an important contribution to the understanding of underdevelopment. What appears to be a lack of sustained development may be the outcome of a historical process of underdevelopment. What seem to be internal psychological or social obstacles to growth, such as peasant conservatism or resistance to change, may be the outcome of previous cycles of de-velopment. The histories of many of the world's "traditional" peoples provide evidence for this approach. Societies that appear to be rooted in the timeless past have actually undergone major transformations.

But dependency theory also leaves gaps in anthropologists' understanding of development. Some critics feel that the dependency model exaggerates the importance of the relationships between metropolitan centers of control and subordinate satellites and relieves the people of an underdeveloped region of any responsibility for their situation or for improving their lot. Dependency theory also implies that development will come about by breaking down the patterns of investment, technology transfer, and political control between the developed world and underdeveloped regions. It is not certain that this would be a sufficient condition for development. Some countries and regions have attempted to develop without the entanglement of foreign investment and export-oriented production. There have been some successes, but the number of failures is large. Tanzania, in East Africa, was one country that refused foreign investment and avoided dependence on exports. The Tanzanians found that their autonomy was worth little when it came to raising the living standards of their people. Albania, a small country in the Balkans, is another example of a failed attempt to develop autonomously. A number of experts are now concluding that, while dependency relations can be highly debilitating to a developing region, many problems are beyond the ability of developing countries to solve on their own.

World Systems Theory

At this point it might be helpful to step back and attempt to take a long view of the theories we have been discussing. Modernization theory grew out of a concern with economic growth and reconstruction in the post–World War II period. In those optimistic days modernization theorists suggested that the entire world might one day enjoy standards of living comparable to those in the United States and Europe. Although it focused on factors presumed to be obstacles to economic development, the modernization approach assumed that eventually, given the right conditions, the underdeveloped regions could pass through the same developmental process as the developed regions and become developed themselves.

Dependency theorists challenged this idea, suggesting that the conditions under which the wealthy countries developed are no longer present. They argued that the developed countries achieved development precisely by exploiting other regions, plundering their resources, and dominating their markets. If the underdeveloped countries of today were ever to develop, they would have to do so by a different route. If the two theories agreed on any point, it was that there were common or universal processes taking place at the level of the nation state.

In the mid-1970s a new approach to development rejected the premise of processes bounded by national borders. Immanuel Wallerstein, a political scientist, was one of the first to suggest that the fundamental error of earlier theories of development was to assume that separate but comparable processes of development or underdevelopment were occurring in any particular country. He suggested instead that the appearance of "parallels" was due to the fact "that a single capitalist world-economy has been developing since the 16th century and that its development has been the driving force of modern world change" (Hopkins 1982, 11). Rather than consider how the process was the same or different in Chile or Nigeria, **world systems theory** proposed to examine every individual case in relation to the central, unfolding expansion of a world capitalist system.

According to this view, questions regarding the historical role of a particular group, say, the 16th-century sugar planters of northeastern Brazil, would be asked in a new way: What is the place of this group in the "international division of labor"? The argument is that the role of this class cannot be understood in relation to its local context alone. It was part of a system whose boundaries extended well beyond the borders of any particular state. In the case of the Brazilian sugar planters, we would need to consider the Portuguese mother country; its African allies,

which supplied it with slaves; and the European sugar market.

At any given time in history the **core**, or center of capital accumulation and decision-making, is located in a different place. In the 16th century it was in Portugal and Spain, but gradually it moved to northern Europe, settling for a time in England and then migrating across the Atlantic to the United States. The periphery also shifts and expands as the world system evolves and develops. European states—particularly Britain, France, and Germany—moved to the **periphery,** or marginal areas of the system, for a time and then gained power and autonomy as their economies were revitalized and joined together in the European Community. The basic categories of world systems theory are derived from Marx: capital, production, and class. But Marx's idea of a historical process that occurs again and again in different contexts has been changed. The world systems approach postulates a single unified process; the task of understanding it is to determine how any particular set of events is related to that process.

The idea of understanding the entire world in terms of a single process with many ramifications is very appealing. In different contexts the idea of one world is brought up with increasing frequency. The oil shocks of 1973 and 1979 showed that developed countries are dependent too, in this case on the oil and other natural resources of LDCs. The idea of a global environment is also gaining currency with the debates about the **greenhouse effect**, global warming, and ozone depletion. These phenomena are jointly caused by many different regions and have consequences that are global in scope.

World systems analysis tells us that the interconnectedness of events is not a new phenomenon. It has been with us since the 16th century, when the current expansion of Europe began. It is a useful antidote to an approach that splits the world up into regions,

---

world systems theory   An approach to economic development suggesting that the world has become increasingly integrated since the 16th century in a unified world capitalist system.

core   In the world systems theory of economic development, the center of capital accumulation (in contrast with the periphery).

periphery   In world systems theory, areas of the world that have the least capital accumulation and serve the economic needs of the core.

greenhouse effect   The warming that takes place when increasing amounts of heat from the sun are trapped by carbon dioxide in the earth's atmosphere.

Figure 19.8   *The cooling tower of a nuclear power plant in Salem County, New Jersey, stands as a stark reminder of the interconnections in our contemporary world. We now have power to fuel many of our industrial projects, but are we poisoning our natural environment in the process?*

countries, or, at the most, empires. It also corrects for the sometimes narrow view of anthropologists who see the world as so many separate tribes or peoples (Fig. 19.8).

On the other hand, as anthropologist Eric Wolf observed, the world focus "omits consideration of the range and variety" of the different peoples of the world (1982, 23). Without such a consideration, the approach seems to deprive particular regional populations of their individuality and their ability to influence history. Wolf argued that the idea of a "periphery" was merely a vague "cover term" that expressed little more than the equally vague idea of a "traditional society."

Wolf attempted to combine particularistic ethnography with the sweep and power of a world systems approach. He argued that we cannot begin to understand the development and shape of non-Western populations without understanding how each one has responded to the impact of Western expansion. Unlike many anthropologists, Wolf did not treat indigenous peoples as the passive victims of Western exploitation but as creative actors responding with their own cultural and physical resources to the challenge of Western contact. Contrary to what some theories suggest, Wolf argued that the expansion of capitalism has created not one homogeneous world culture but a constantly ramifying, highly diverse set of cultures, each with a distinctive self-image and view of the world.

The stability and well-being of the world depends on the changes now taking place in the LDCs. Some writers have predicted a catastrophe of war and famine if the current gap between the rich and the poor continues to grow. Others believe that the gap is a necessary part of the growth of modern capitalism and that it will continue indefinitely until some entirely new form of organization takes its place. As we have seen, many development programs have attempted to attack underdevelopment during the second half of the 20th century. The results have often been negative for the most vulnerable parts of the population: rural producers, poor urban dwellers, and other impoverished groups. Often the planning that took place did not consider the full costs of development or how they would be distributed. On the other hand, development has sometimes succeeded, especially when there was participation by the people involved themselves. Anthropologists have much to contribute to the process of development, because they are able to observe, gauge, and predict the impact of economic change on people in LDCs.

Contemporary social science has fashioned a number of theories to explain why some societies forged ahead while others remained in a state of economic and social stagnation. Some anthropologists reject the idea of progress altogether, suggesting that such measures are merely the tools of capitalist society. Ultimately we will reach understanding only by looking simultaneously at local, regional, national, and international processes, a task that challenges anthropologists to go beyond the traditional scope of their discipline.

SUMMARY

- Much of the wide gap between the rich and poor of the world can be attributed to colonial domination, which created a structure that transferred wealth from the poor to the rich.
- Mechanisms of colonial control have evolved considerably in 500 years, from the exaction of tribute and ports of trade, to direct political control, and, more recently, to complex financial and economic institutions that maintain control without direct political intervention.
- Modernization theory emerged in the 1950s as an attempt to explain the social and psychological obstacles to development.
- Modernization theory rests on a dichotomy between "traditional" and "modern" societies. According to this theory, development, as measured by economic growth, is retarded by rigid forms of authority, extended family structures, religious beliefs, and psychological and cognitive blocks to achievement. While many studies have shown the existence of different attitudes and orientations in developing versus developed countries, it has not been clearly shown what is cause and what is effect.
- Dependency theorists argue that development and underdevelopment are two sides of the same coin.
- An underdeveloped society arises from a process of underdevelopment and should not be confused with an undeveloped society.
- Economic growth is not necessarily the product of an enlightened or progressive population; it may be the result of a group's seeing an opportunity to increase its wealth.
- Some investigators have decided that the process of development cannot be understood on a regional or national basis alone. They see all modern world change as tied in to a single "world economic system."
- Each people has responded to the expansion of Western capitalism in a different way, and the specific stories of each one must be written to avoid dissolving the people studied in broad generalizations appropriate to none of them.

GET INVOLVED

1. Select a series of films or novels that depict the colonial experience in a particular country. For example, you might choose *A Passage to India* and *Gandhi* as film representations of colonialism in India. Or you might select films and novels depicting the relation of Euro-American settlers to native Americans in North America, such as *A Man Called Horse* or *Dances with Wolves*. Review these documents carefully for clues about the structure of the colonial system. What are the economic, legal, and social aspects of the relationships? If the colonial relationship broke down, what led to its destruction?

2. Some experts believe that modern capital exports have recreated a colonial system in many LDCs, such as Korea, Mexico, Taiwan, and Brazil. Make a visit to local retailers selling clothing, electronics, and other manufactured goods with a high labor input. Examine these goods for labels showing the country where they were manufactured. If necessary, write to the retailer or supplier to learn where the items were manufactured, assembled, and finished. You will find that many of these goods were produced in foreign countries. Make a list of these countries and seek out information concerning labor and wage conditions in the processing zones where these goods were produced.

3. Make a list of the ten agricultural products most used in your household. Your list will probably include such items as coffee, sugar, tea, meat, dairy products, fruits, and vegetables. Pay a visit or write to the purchasing agent for your local grocery chain. Where are these commodities produced? What are the labor and political conditions in these areas? How much does the original producer of each product receive for the quantity you purchase in a typical week?

SUGGESTED READINGS

Bodley, John H. 1988. *Tribal peoples and development issues: A global view*. Mountain View, Calif.: Mayfield.

Foster, George M. 1965. Peasant society and the image of limited good. *American Anthropologist* 67:293–315.

Frank, A. G. 1966. The development of underdevelopment. *Monthly Review* 18:17–31.

Kottak, Conrad P. 1983. *Assault on Paradise: Social change in a Brazilian village*. New York: Random House.

Soto, Hernando de. 1989. *The other path: The invisible revolution in the Third World*. New York: Harper and Row.

Wolf, Eric. 1982. *Europe and the people without history*. Berkeley: University of California Press.

Third World and Development

Tony Barclay is president of Development Alternatives, Inc., a Washington consulting firm. He has carried out long-term field research on rural development in Kenya as well as numerous project planning, evaluation, and management assignments throughout sub-Saharan Africa.

Tony Barclay in his office at Development Alternatives, Inc.

The main practice areas of my company, Development Alternatives, Inc. (DAI), include agriculture, natural resources management, economic planning, and small enterprise development. DAI has always been exclusively an international firm, with a balance in its project portfolio between Africa, Asia, and Latin America, but since late 1989, the firm's geographic scope has expanded to include Eastern Europe and now encompasses almost 90 countries.

I joined DAI in 1977, after completing my Ph.D. in the applied anthropology program at Teachers College, Columbia University. My dissertation was based on an 18-month field study of a sugar project in western Kenya that relied on a contract farming system involving thousands of small-scale sugar cane farmers. All told, I lived in Kenya for almost seven years (1968–1970 and 1974–1977), first as a Peace Corps teacher, later as a field researcher, and then as a rural sociologist on a multicountry study of the African sugar industry funded by the U.N. Environment Program.

DAI hired me to strengthen its social science capacity at a time when the firm was beginning to expand rapidly. Founded in 1970, DAI had made its mark by producing practical, project-oriented studies and evaluations focusing on the theme of small farmer development. The firm's business in sub-Saharan Africa was growing, and it was starting to compete successfully for large-scale technical assistance contracts to undertake project implementation over periods of three to six years. This in turn attracted an increasingly diverse range of technical specialists to DAI's core consulting staff.

Initially DAI assigned me to provide consulting support to the firm's newest project, in the North Shaba region of Zaire, where an ambitious (and ultimately very successful) effort was being made to revitalize smallholder farming in an area that produced food for the urbanized mining areas around Lubumbashi. I helped the project's resident staff conduct rapid reconnaissance surveys in villages where agricultural extension, marketing, and road improvement activities were planned, and I trained them in data collection, analysis, and communication techniques. These steps laid essential groundwork for the later introduction of improved seed varieties, adaptive field trials, and village-based extension activities. Returning to the area more than a dozen times over an eight-year period, I witnessed the evolution of a project that was remarkable for its resilience in a hostile political and economic climate and for its responsiveness to the farmers' own interests.

While broadening my experience in rural Africa through consulting projects in Sudan, Botswana, Cameroon, Niger, and Burkina Faso, I gradually moved into a management role within the firm. Along with several other anthropologists who joined DAI in the late 1970s, I found satisfaction in synthesizing the work of interdisciplinary teams and in guiding such teams to produce coherent, action-oriented results. There is such breadth and diversity in the field of anthropology, and it offers so many insights on value systems and behavior, that the role of integrator and team leader in tackling development problems is one where anthropologists seem to have unique advantages.

By 1979 DAI's rapid growth had created a niche for a general manager to oversee firmwide operations in partnership with the chief executive officer, whose background is in development economics. This gave me a rare opportunity to learn and apply business skills in a collegial, intellectually stimulating environment. I was fortunate to be able to fill some obvious gaps in my training by attending an intensive Stanford Business School management course that was geared to the needs of smaller companies.

I often think my job offers an ideal combination of interesting subjects, diverse responsibilities, and talented colleagues. When I entered graduate school, I knew that I wanted to put the tools and perspectives of anthropology to work in an action-oriented setting. But my career path was open-ended, since I had no idea where I would find a means of doing this. Looking back and looking ahead, I feel exceedingly fortunate to be part of a growing organization that strives to make a difference in the development process.

Industrialism in the Third World: a scene from the Golden Lion bicycle factory in Chanzou, China.

20

URBAN AND INDUSTRIAL CULTURE

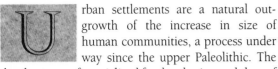

rban settlements are a natural outgrowth of the increase in size of human communities, a process under way since the upper Paleolithic. The development of specialized food gathering and then of food production made it possible for people to live together in large, densely packed settlements. Large permanent settlements provide several benefits. The populations of these settlements are able to defend themselves and their property from attack more effectively than smaller scattered groups. People can establish stable relationships in larger settlements, and a complex division of labor can arise. A potter working in a small isolated village cannot spend all her time making pots: There simply isn't enough demand. In a large permanent settlement, specialties can develop based on steady, substantial demand. As a settlement grows, the demand for goods and services gives rise to a group of specialists who share ideas and techniques with each other. People sharing ideas on topics of common interest are likely to develop new ideas, not only about technology but also about other topics, such as interacting with the supernatural, healing the sick, and governing their group. Thus an urban settlement is likely to be a center of intensive communication and innovation.

City life also imposes costs, and living with many people brings new problems. As we saw in Chapter 16, the number of potential conflicts increases at a higher rate as the number of people rises. In an urban environment with a diversity of specialties, interests, and backgrounds, each individual must adjust to a wide range of behavior. In an essay called "The Metropolis and Mental Life" (1903), the German sociologist Georg Simmel wrote that the impersonal nature of city life led people to emphasize their uniqueness to retain a sense of identity.

In a small village, people are likely to know everyone they meet. This is known as a "face-to-face" community. Face-to-face communities also exist in urban settlements—families, school groups, workmates, church groups, neighborhoods—but only as segments of a larger population. As people encounter more people whom they do not know or recognize, the level of stress may rise. Cities can be stressful in other ways too: The anonymous contacts, the noise, the fast pace of life, the danger, the rapid flow of information, the high population density are all factors contributing to stress. Cities may also pose health problems (Box 20.1).

Cities are often viewed as "unnatural" settlements. Many writers have commented on the artificiality of life in a "built environment." We have seen, however, that all peoples modify their environments in some ways. Hunters often kill animals that play a role in seed dispersal, thereby influencing plant communities. Farming can have major effects on the environment. Massive erosion caused by grain farmers in the American Midwest created a "dust bowl" in which all agriculture was nearly destroyed. Urban habitats are complex and the degree of environmental modification may be greater, but cities are natural products of human action just as much as other settlement forms. The same basic biological and social processes go on in cities as in other settlements. Every environment, rural or urban, presents a unique set of problems, opportunities, and dangers. As we will see, urban dwellers find adaptive solutions to problems in much the same fashion as tribal or peasant peoples.

WHAT IS URBAN?

Different social scientists define *urban* in different ways. One way of deciding what is town and what is countryside is by looking at population size and density. In many countries the census designates as urban any settlement with more than 10,000 inhabitants. But how are the boundaries drawn? Many rural areas with people living in separate farmhouses contain 10,000 people. Clearly some notion of **population density** should also be involved. However, there are many high-density populations that do not satisfy our intuitive sense of what an urban settlement is. There are tribal populations, such as the Chimbu of Papua New Guinea, with population densities over 450 per km^2 (Brown 1978). But tribal organization, even when tightly packed together, does not have the diversity that goes with urban life.

Neither do the Chimbu reside in **nucleated settlements**. Nucleated settlements are concentrated populations having a distinct center where ceremonial, administrative, and commercial activities take place (Figure 20.1). This is a common pattern in European and American cities with their town squares and central business districts. There are clear advantages to

Figure 20.1 *An example of a 16th century and a 20th century nucleated settlement. The model of Tenochtitlan, the Aztec capital of Mexico, shows the population settled around a ceremonial center; canals and causeways connected the center to the outlying areas. Compare it to the central district of Washington, D.C., where impressive buildings are clustered around the U.S. Capitol.*

having closely related activities concentrated in a single area. There is also, no doubt, a symbolic function to clustering the largest buildings in a central place where their combined grandeur can impress visitors with the power and authority of the ruling elite.

Nucleation is not a sufficient definition of urbanism, however. Many modern cities are becoming less dependent on a central business district. Modern telecommunications and transportation have made it possible for many activities to be coordinated in distant locations. The very idea of a central city has become questionable, especially as cities have grown too large for people to walk to the central section from nearby residential areas. City planners have found that it is difficult, sometimes impossible, to transport large numbers of people into a central city each morning for work and then home again after work. The problem is magnified when the mode of transport is the private automobile; most cities cannot accommodate large traffic flows in their central districts.

After World War II the United States and other countries underwent **suburbanization.** The preferred style of living for the middle class became the detached one-family house, a departure from the attached housing and multiple dwellings that had predominated since the turn of the century. Urban "sprawl" depended on cheap energy, because suburban housing and cars to provide transportation out to the suburbs have high fuel requirements compared to multiple dwellings or mass transit. After the 1973 and 1979 Arab oil shocks, energy prices rose dramatically. Some middle-class families moved back into the city, and many businesses and offices moved "out" into the suburbs. As a result, in many cities the city center is being abandoned. This has reached the point in some cities, such as Detroit and St. Louis, at which the urban centers are in danger of dying.

Another criterion of urbanism relates to food production. Food must be produced on the land, and farming is generally done outside of cities. There are,

---

population density The number of people per km² or mi².

nucleated settlement A settlement pattern in which there is a specialized center for ceremonial, administrative, or commercial activities.

suburbanization A settlement pattern in which residential neighborhoods (often housing a relatively privileged class) are located outside the central city.

BOX 20.1

The City and Disease

Living in a city can be hazardous to your health. Consider what it's like living in a nonurban setting. In small villages, particularly nomadic settlements, people can avoid coming into contact with disease carriers. Food is brought into the village fresh and consumed promptly. People walk outside the village to defecate or urinate. They bathe in running streams and draw fresh water from wells or streams. When houses become infested with rats or other vermin, villagers can move to a nearby site and build a new village.

Now consider the urban settlement. People live packed densely together in enclosed spaces. They can easily transmit contagious diseases to each other, especially diseases conveyed by airborne microorganisms, such as smallpox, or diseases conveyed through intimate contact, such as syphilis. Insects and rodents thrive in cities, feeding on bits of unused food and human excreta. In passing from one dwelling to another, they may become disease vectors, transmitting parasites or other germs to people.

In the city food is brought in by strangers. People may not know where it comes from or how fresh it is. The settlement may be too large for people to go outside to defecate and urinate, and clean streams for bathing are too far away. In cities these functions go on inside houses. Water is a precious commodity in the city. Even after the introduction of the aqueduct and piped water in ancient Rome, few people had access to running water. Until the advent of plumbing it was impossible to bring enough clean water into a settlement to wash dirt from the body and excrement from

the floor. As late as 1911, two-thirds of working-class homes in Manchester—the cradle of British industrialism—lacked indoor toilets. Even today, in countries like Indonesia only 43 percent of the urban households have access to safe water.

Even running water does not necessarily solve the problem of waste disposal. It is necessary to dispose of the accumulated excreta and water used for bathing or washing. Sewers and septic systems are complex and expensive. In many modern cities, raw sewage simply flows into open ditches running down the middle of the street. Sewers have been known in Europe since Roman times, but, as historian William McNeill wrote (1976, 240),

> until the 1840s a sewer was simply an elongated cesspool with an overflow at one end. The flow of water through them . . . was sluggish because water supplies were sharply limited. The new idea [which emerged in England in the 1840s] was to construct narrow sewers out of smooth ceramic pipe and pass enough water through to flush the waste matter toward some distant depository.

This plan removed sewage from the city but still did not dispose of it. The Englishman who promoted enclosed sewers also had the idea of collecting and selling the waste to farmers as fertilizer. This idea, which is now practiced in a few advanced urban sewage systems, was not put into practice in the 19th century because farmers had far cheaper sources of fertilizer, their livestock. The solution was to allow urban sewage to drain untreated into rivers, streams, and bays, a

---

however, many cities in Africa and Asia where substantial amounts of food, particularly livestock, are grown within the city limits (Figure 20.2). We also identify urbanism with trade and markets. But some cities, such as those in ancient Peru, exist without markets. Trade goes on both within and outside of cities in many societies. Urban centers are often, but not always, centers of administration.

The most durable criteria for urban settlements are social criteria. Urban settlements arise in complex, stratified societies. Urban centers do not play any single functional role; they have a combination of political, administrative, industrial, commercial, ceremonial, and military functions. Urban settlements are defined, then, as centers with a high "density of role relationships" (Southall 1973). In other words, urban centers bring together in close interaction people occupying different social strata and playing different roles. It is not simply the presence of the "butcher, the baker, the candlestick maker," the banker, the bookie, and the construction worker, but their interaction that makes a city.

common practice to this day. The result, of course, was contamination of drinking water.

The relationship between contaminated water and diseases was not understood until after 1870. Even then many people doubted that water carried disease, and improvements were delayed because of the high cost of piped water and sewer systems. In 1892 a dramatic event in Hamburg, Germany, demonstrated the value of safe water. Hamburg drew its water directly from the Elbe River. The neighboring city of Altona had a separate system that filtered its water. When a cholera epidemic struck Hamburg, people living in homes supplied with Altona water were not affected by the disease (McNeill 1976, 242).

How have urban populations maintained themselves with so many hazards to life? In fact their survival has been precarious at several points in human history. Between 1200 and 1393, China is estimated to have lost nearly 60 million people of an initial population of 123 million, largely as a result of the bubonic plague (McNeill 1976, 144). About one-third of the population of Europe died from plague between 1346 and 1350, and there were recurrent epidemics of plague in Europe until the early 18th century (McNeill 1976, 149–151). Bubonic plague is caused by a bacillus, *Pasteurella pestis,* that is transmitted by fleas carried by rodents. Cities played a part in these and other epidemics by harboring the rat hosts and facilitating transmission of diseases.

Death from infectious disease was the primary factor in population control until the 19th century. If pre-industrial cities had not been constantly replenished by newcomers from the countryside, they would have diminished instead of growing. One estimate shows that in the city of London during the 1700s, there were 6,000 more deaths than births each year.

Most industrialized societies have found ways of overcoming the hazards to health that accompany urban living. Meat and other fresh food are inspected by authorities before they are sold. The state provides running water, garbage collection, and sewer systems and controls insects and other pests. The state also provides health facilities and vaccination programs to immunize people against contagious diseases. Despite the importance of modern medical practices, however, there is evidence that sanitary measures like piped water and sewers were more effective in reducing disease and mortality than vaccines, antibiotics, and many other modern medical practices. Many modern cities still have not adopted such measures as sewage treatment, and in the LDCs, mortality from contagious disease is still very high in the cities.

Modern epidemics like the worldwide pandemic of AIDS and the recent outbreak of cholera in Peru and neighboring countries are closely related to the cultural behavior and social organization of the societies experiencing them. The urban environment is an excellent example of how human culture affects the environment, which in turn creates new conditions for the biological and social survival of the populations that inhabit cities.

Urban areas are set off from other areas not only by the style of architecture and the density of interaction but also by urban behavior itself. To speak of "urban behavior" does not mean that urbanites are essentially different from rural dwellers in some way. What is meant is that their habit of interacting with people in different roles does give them a different style of behavior. The difference between rural and urban behavior is obvious to people everywhere. The contrast may be the source of antagonism and often a special kind of humor.

URBAN CULTURE

Many sociologists and anthropologists regard city life with a built-in negative bias. Cities, they feel, are disorderly forms of social organization. They represent the breakdown of orderly human life. In Chapter 19 we saw that anthropologist Robert Redfield, who used the terms *folk* and *urban* to describe the two sectors of a society, saw a contradiction between city life on the one hand and family life, religion, and tradition on the other. Much research has been done in recent years to

Figure 20.2 *In many urban centers in Africa and Asia, food and livestock are produced and raised within city limits. These camels are being driven to a slaughterhouse along a busy street in Cairo, Egypt.*

clarify these ideas and to try to discern whether these judgments have any basis in evidence.

City Families

One of the most enduring myths in the study of urban culture is that family life invariably breaks down in urban environments. There is some evidence for this in the decreasing size of the household typical in modern cities. However, as you recall from Chapter 14, household and family are not necessarily the same unit. The decreasing size of households in cities is a result of several factors. For one, space is scarce in cities, so most of the housing is designed for small families. Living space may be so limited that a household must either limit its size or undergo a decline in its standard of living. For another, in modern cities the income-producing unit is often the individual; there is little economic advantage to maintaining a

large household, as might be the case if the family were the unit of production. One benefit of extended families is the sharing of child care and other domestic work. Modern states may assume some of this responsibility through day-care centers and schools. A third factor favoring small households in cities is that industrial and bureaucratic organizations often favor workers who can pick up and move when the occasion demands. A nuclear family with one or two wage earners is more mobile than more complex family forms. Thus, even in cities where the extended family traditionally predominates, such families tend not to reside together.

This does not mean that the extended family does not exist or is not important in an urban context. There is evidence from studies in Brazil, Mexico, Puerto Rico, India, and China that extended family organization is important in cities, even when not based on coresidence. In New Delhi, India, upper-class people use their family ties as a means for affirming and reinforcing their status. Family corporations are common as members of extended families pool their resources to operate a business. Family businesses are sometimes regarded as old-fashioned and uncompetitive. But there are many sectors in which family businesses predominate, such as restaurants in the United States or the weaving industry in Italy. Kinship ties may be a liability in such businesses as law firms, because some family members may lack the necessary skills yet feel entitled to share in the profits. On the other hand, some businesses thrive on family ties because there is a high level of trust among family members and because kin can ask greater sacrifices of each other than of nonkin.

Kinship ties are also important to lower-class people who have no capital in urban-industrial environments. Kinship ties are especially important to rural migrants who move to cities. Rural migrants to Lima, Peru; Washington, D.C.; Bombay, India; and Lagos, Nigeria, all follow similar patterns. They seek out family members who moved in earlier and rely on them for guidance, housing, food, and, most of all, jobs, until they can stand on their own feet. Extended family ties may actually be intensified in urban settings. Anthropologist Oscar Lewis, known for his studies of Tepoztlan, a Mexican rural village, traced Tepoztecos who migrated to Mexico City. He found that family life was as stable in Mexico City as in Tepoztlan and that the importance of extended family ties increased in the city (Lewis 1952).

City life can be stressful to a poor urban migrant. The poor in large cities suffer from chronic lack of cash, poor access to health care, and unemployment. Added to this are problems of crime and violence, drugs, and child care. These are familiar problems to inner-city residents in the United States. People with few other resources frequently make use of an extensive kinship network to help them out of trouble. Studies like those of anthropologist Helen Safa (1974) in the slums of San Juan, Puerto Rico, and political scientist Janice Perlman (1980) in the *favelas* of Rio de

Janeiro, Brazil, show people relying heavily on both consanguineal ("blood") and affinal (marital) kin.

Urbanites also interact with many nonkin and strangers in the course of an average day. A person's behavior is shaped by the various social settings in which he or she participates. When anthropologists sought ways of defining these webs of interaction in a precise way, they found that methods developed in the context of small-scale, kin-based societies were not adequate. At first it seemed sufficient to develop some new descriptive categories, such as the **voluntary association**, which, unlike the clan or household, was based on individual choice and mutual interest. Later anthropologists developed **network analysis** as a systematic approach to describing and analyzing the social roles, frequency (or density) of interaction, and quality of people's relationships. Network analysis does not assume the existence of particular groups but begins by gathering information on the activities and contacts of individuals. An individual may be linked to, say, five other individuals, forming a "star" (Figure 20.3). If these individuals also have links to each other, the unit formed is known as a "zone." Stars and zones have different social characteristics. Communication is likely to be more intense and efficient in a zone than in a star, because it does not depend so heavily on a single individual. Such measures make it possible to analyze "density" of social relations. Some studies suggest that the success of an individual's adaptation to the urban environment is directly related to the density of his or her personal network.

City Dwelling: Squatments

The urban **squatment**, or lower-class neighborhood constructed (often illegally) out of readily available materials by the inhabitants themselves, is a familiar sight in Bombay, India; Rio de Janeiro, Brazil; Lima,

---

voluntary association   A group formed around some mutual interest or need, such as a cooperative, neighborhood association, or congregation.

network analysis   A systematic approach to describing and analyzing social roles, frequency of interaction, and quality of human relationships.

squatment   An urban neighborhood inhabited mainly by poor people and migrants living in substandard housing, often built illegally on unused land.

Figure 20.3 *Examples of networks.
(a) A* star *showing ego at the center of
a social network; (b) a* zone *showing
a similar network with linkages between the other members. These linkages can be any sort of role relationship: casual acquaintance, fellow
church member, coworker, and so on.
Some investigators suggest that the
zone allows for greater social control,
since there is a potential for coordination and agreement among the members of ego's own network.*

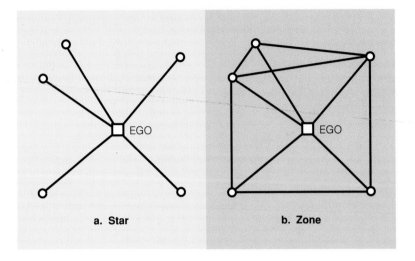

a. Star   b. Zone

Peru; Jakarta, Indonesia; Bangkok, Thailand; and
many other cities of the developing world (Figure
20.4). Squatting is not common in the developed
countries, although similar kinds of communities
arise in areas of aging, substandard housing, or slums.
Squatments, or "shantytowns," were common in the
United States during the 19th and early 20th centuries. Squatments are constructed—often by rural migrants—on unused land (steep hillsides, along sewage
canals, or on stilts over flooded areas) as close as possible to the commercial or industrial center of the city.
From these settlements people go out in search of
employment either as regular employees in businesses
or as independent craftpersons providing services
such as laundry, domestic service, child care, gardening, or construction.

The ties of interdependence that develop among
residents of these spontaneous communities are so
important to successful adaptation that disrupting
them may be devastating to the people involved. Elaborate social networks involving kinship, friendship,
sexual relations, debt, and business relations are
woven among members of these communities. For
these reasons the residents often do not regard living
in a squatment as a disadvantage and fiercely resist
attempts to relocate them. Because they live close to
the urban core, however, slum dwellers are frequently
subject to relocation as the land they occupy becomes
more valuable and in demand.

Anthropologist Peter Marris studied the results of
slum clearance in Lagos, the capital city of Nigeria.
Families in Lagos are often polygynous, living in big

households that reproduce the structure of a rural
compound. In these households a man, his wives, and
their children live under one roof. Marris carried out
twin surveys: one on a population living in central
Lagos, the other in a new suburb built to house the
people evicted by slum clearance. He asked the respondents whether they had relatives living within a
mile of their own homes. The results are shown in
Table 20.1. Commenting on the consequences of relocation, Marris wrote (1974, 333):

> Slum clearance . . . means that family groups tend to
> be disrupted. This can be especially hard for old peo-
> ple who had lived in family property and been cared
> for by relatives around them. Their relatives else-
> where are no longer so aware of their needs, and they
> themselves cannot afford the fare to go and ask them
> for help. The system of mutual support begins to
> break down. Many of the people . . . who were used
> to giving regular help to their relatives could no
> longer afford it.

Marris found that household heads in central Lagos
were far more likely to make regular contributions to
relatives than those in the relocation zone. Not only
family ties but also commercial ties were disrupted: A
shoemaker who once had a profitable business was
relocated. He told Marris, "Since I came [to the relocation area there is] not sufficient money to rent a shop
here, let alone work here. . . . If you look at the street
now, you will not see a single man. They have all gone
to Lagos, and take their shoes for repair. . . . This is
not a place, but a punishment from God" (p. 335).

Figure 20.4 *An urban squatment in Bombay, India. Squatments spring up on unused (and often undesirable) land near commercial or industrial centers, where the residents of these communities seek work. Close social and economic ties often develop among the inhabitants of squatments, which may be severely disrupted if the population is forced to move.*

Table 20.1 The Effect of Relocation on Family Proximity in Lagos, Nigeria

Lives within a Mile	Central Lagos (Percentage)	Rehousing Estate (Percentage)
Mother	44	15
Brother	54	27
Sister	37	15
Half-brother or sister	59	35

Source: Marris 1974, 332.

Women were also affected by the move. In Lagos, as in other polygynous societies, women do not depend on their husbands for daily necessities and child support. Many women support themselves and their children with income from small businesses, setting up stalls in central market places. Marris found four times as many wives earning nothing in the relocation area as in central Lagos. So relocated women lost not only family contacts and support but also business opportunities.

Urban dwellers in Lagos, as elsewhere, rely on an elaborate system of mutual support. When the state took over some prime urban real estate, it inadvertently disrupted networks that had provided an important safety net for the poor population. In some cases the state pays a price for such intervention in the form of increased crime rates, higher medical and welfare costs, and demand for subsidized housing. There are case studies with similar results in many other parts of the world. These cases suggest that spontaneously formed settlements may be highly adaptive for their residents, while planned communities are not. The dilemma of the urban squatment is familiar to planners and social scientists all over the world. Spontaneously formed communities often have poor-quality slum housing and other deficiencies, but they often meet people's needs more effectively, and far more cheaply, than structures imposed from outside.

URBANISM
AND INDUSTRIALISM

While urbanism is not tied to any particular form of production, industrialization has always brought an acceleration in the growth of urban settlements. There are many linkages between the two. First let us consider exactly what **industrialism** is. Industrial production involves the intensive use of capital and of power technology to produce goods in a standardized, efficient manner. Industrial production is organized to allow **economies of scale**, or production techniques in which efficiency increases as the number of units produced rises.

The industrial revolution began in 18th century England largely in the context of textile production. At that time cloth production went on in the cottages and workshops of independent weavers. Merchants could buy cloth in quantity only by pooling the output of several weavers, and this presented problems of variation in quality and quantity. England had made agreements with other countries that allowed the British to export cloth in exchange for wines and other goods. The British strategy was to increase domestic production and stimulate consumption abroad. As we saw in the previous chapter, the British discouraged, even prohibited, cloth production in their colonies.

The demand for loomed cloth was great. Eventually, some merchants began to shift production to factories to raise output and to take advantage of water power for looming. Waterwheels were developed that could be connected, through a set of cogwheels, to all the power equipment in the factory (Figure 20.5). The initial technology was not a breakthrough, simply an extension of known techniques. Then came a major innovation: steam power. Steam power was first used to operate the pumps that kept mines dry. Later it was harnessed to drive factory equipment, railroad locomotives, and, toward the end of the 19th century, ships. The rise of the British textile industry stimulated coal mining, iron and steel production, and many other industrial pursuits. The economies of scale obtained through the use of power technology and expansion of plant size were enormous. Europe and North America did not lag far behind England.

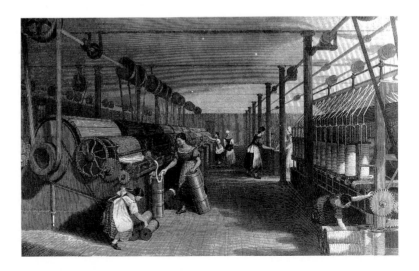

Figure 20.5 *The industrial revolution began in British textile mills such as the one depicted in this 19th-century engraving. The looms were powered by the cogwheels and belts, driven in turn by the force of the water in the waterwheel outside the mill.*

The social and economic effects of the industrial revolution were extensive. Industrial organization took people out of small workshops and homes and paid them at daily or hourly wages. Workers had little control over when or how long they worked. Industrialization meant an entirely different use of time. Early industrial workers worked 12 hours a day, seven days a week. These conditions, combined with poor diet and housing, led to serious health problems, such as tuberculosis, that ran rampant in the industrial work force.

The first industrial workers frequently were women and children, selected because they were not needed for farm work and would work for low wages. Factory owners believed they would adapt more readily to the strict demands of industrial production: obedience, adherence to schedules, and careful attention to detail. Regimentation of workers reached a high level in the early years of industrialization. Early 19th-century textile mills in Massachusetts, for example, recruited young unmarried women from farms and housed them in dormitories, where they were closely supervised in a fashion acceptable to their parents. The same pattern can be found today in clothing and electronics factories in Singapore and South Korea, where young women are recruited from rural zones and kept under strict control during both work and leisure hours (Kim 1990).

Although machines were the centerpiece of production, factory production was labor intensive: Many people were required to operate and maintain the machines, move the products around, and handle fuel and raw materials. Early industrialists saw the need for a nearby work force, and they often built housing and other amenities for workers. The housing stock of many modern cities consists largely of housing built to accommodate industrial workers, often tenements or row houses. Cities like Belfast, Northern Ireland; Brooklyn, New York; and Reading, Pennsylvania still have much of this housing intact (Figure 20.6). Most of the worker housing was drab and cheerless; com-

Figure 20.6   *This row of brownstones in Brooklyn, New York, was built in the late 19th century to house industrial workers. Ironically, what was built for the working class has become home to wealthy middle-class professionals.*

forts were few. Still, many of the workers were migrants from the rural zones where conditions were even worse.

Living in owner-built housing, workers could walk or bicycle to work. When urban centers became very large, fixed-rail streetcars, trolleys, and subways were built to carry them to and from work. Wherever industry developed, businesses and other industries arose to cater to the needs of workers. Social institutions such as hospitals, settlement houses, and worker societies also appeared, many of them partly financed by industrialists to attract, settle, and educate an industrial work force. Industrial unionism developed in the 19th century, and very gradually won better conditions for industrial workers.

---

industrialism   Economic production involving the intensive use of capital (machinery and factories) and power technology (electricity, fossil fuels, and nuclear energy) to produce goods in a standardized, efficient manner.

economies of scale   Savings in the unit cost of production as the volume of production increases.

Effects of Industrialism

Industrialism changed the very fabric of society. Independent producers seldom had the capital to compete with large factories, so small-scale producers of goods were soon forced out of business when large mills came on the scene. Factories created a demand for a large number of workers, each of whom earned the same wage for the same kind of work. To some extent, then, industrial production "homogenized" workers by reducing the differences among them while increasing the gap between workers and other social groups.

The industrial revolution created the possibility of a "mass culture" that was itself an industrial product. Objects of everyday use, such as clothing, food products, decorative objects such as pictures, and entertainment, were now mass-produced in assembly line fashion. This does not mean that people became more conformist. Many earlier social systems, such as feudal society in medieval Europe, required rigid conformity. What was different was the way in which objects and symbols were produced and consumed.

Industrialism and urbanism are so intertwined that it is sometimes difficult to sort out the effects of one from the other. Even cities that lack major industries are affected by industrialism. For example, many Third World centers like Guatemala City are now dominated by automobile traffic even though there is no automobile industry or other heavy industry in the country. It is frequently easier to consider the joint effects on social life of industrialism and urbanism than to try to determine the effects of either one alone.

Leisure Time and Industrial Society

It is widely believed that the industrial revolution created a "revolution" in leisure time. Some writers even expressed concern that there would be so much leisure that people would have to find new ways of keeping busy and finding meaning in life outside of work. Before industrialism, the idea goes, most adults who were not wealthy or sick had to spend all their time in a constant struggle for survival. With the advent of industrialism, life became easier, even for the average worker.

There is some evidence to support this idea. The average work week is getting shorter in some industrialized countries. In most industrialized countries, employees work many fewer hours than they did at the dawn of the industrial revolution. Several factors are responsible for this. Technological change increased productivity and reduced the need for labor. Labor unions and government legislation set limits on the number of hours a worker could be required to put in. And wages have risen to a point where workers can afford to limit their hours on the job.

In spite of these changes, however, the average American employee put in about as many hours of work in 1987 (an average of 41.5 hours per week) as in 1947 (about 40.5 hours per week) (U.S. Department of Labor 1989). Japanese workers spend about 41.1 hours a week on the job, Germans about 40.5, the French about 38.9 (United Nations 1986; all data for 1983). The stagnation of the length of the work week is due partly to the lack of recent gains in productivity, partly to reduction in the power of labor unions, and partly to inflation, which has put a squeeze on income. By the end of the 1970s it had become apparent that the "leisure revolution" was not a reality for most working people in the industrialized countries.

Domestic labor has been reduced by industrialism. Machines like washers, driers, gas ranges, and vacuum cleaners get some jobs done much faster and with less labor than washtubs, clotheslines, wood stoves, and brooms. Many foods are now available in ready-to-eat form, which eliminates such activities as hulling grain. However, several studies show that time spent in domestic chores has not decreased with industrialism. This may be a function of the fact that people, even workers, have many more belongings than before. In the 19th century a worker family might have lived in a few rooms and all their clothes could be stored in a single valise. Because housekeeping tasks have traditionally been considered women's work, the industrial revolution has had a different impact on women than it has on men. As women have entered the work force as wage earners, there has been some tendency for men to assume a share of housekeeping chores, but studies in different countries show that women still bear the brunt of these tasks, whether they work outside the home or not.

Industrialism and labor-saving devices had little impact on another type of work: child care. This has always been a labor-intensive activity, since there are no devices that can reduce the child's need for constant attention. Again, women bear the major brunt of this activity even when they enter the formal work force. There are several kinds of adaptations to the dilemma of child care. One has been the reduction of fertility among women in urban areas. Another has been the recruitment of persons outside the nuclear family to assist with child care. Often this role is played by a grandparent, another relative, or a hired person. A great deal of transnational migration in recent years has occurred as a function of the need for child care in families where both parents are employed outside the home. Other innovations include day-care arrangements that allow parents to work. As we pointed out in Chapter 14, there is a growing incidence of single-parent households with children in various countries, including the United States. These parents, the majority of them women, undergo particular stress in attempting to juggle family responsibilities with jobs.

The Original Leisure Class.   Anthropologist Marshall Sahlins suggested that the "original leisure class" consisted of hunter-gatherers like the !Kung San and the aborigines of Australia, because they spent only 10 to 20 hours per week in the food quest. As we saw in Chapter 11, however, when you add in time spent processing food, preparing tools, and other tasks, the average !Kung San man works about 44.5 hours per week, not very different from horticultural and other peoples. In horticultural tribal villages in central Brazil, a group of researchers found that men spent an average of 46 hours per week working, mainly in subsistence production (Gross et al. 1979). A comparable measure for peasant men in the Philippines shows a work week averaging 49.5 hours on subsistence and wage activities (Boulier 1976). Systematic data on time use in many different societies is not yet available, but the evidence on hand does *not* show a steady reduction in work time from the technologically simplest to the most complex societies on earth.

What then is the relationship between industrialism and time? Some investigators believe that the relationship is curvilinear (Johnson 1980, Munroe et al.

1983). In other words, work inputs are relatively low in simple societies with extensive subsistence strategies. Populations that become subordinate members in complex exchange systems work longer hours. Some examples are defeated peoples forced to pay tribute, renters of land, people subject to heavy taxation, small-scale agricultural producers, other participants in markets with relatively little market power, and workers in regions undergoing **primary industrialization**. In these societies—often, but not always, in LDCs—people work the longest hours.

Work time seems to decrease again in advanced industrial societies, where technological and political factors combine to reduce the time each worker has to work. Even in complex industrial societies, some workers put in many hours of work. Some of these are the least-privileged workers, who simply cannot make ends meet on their salaries; others are highly ambitious workers who are interested in earning more money and getting to the top. In complex industrial societies it is also common to find people who work two jobs or go to school while holding a job—very much the same thing as far as time is concerned.

An even greater difference between nonindustrial and industrial populations is the relative "freedom" in the use of time. The industrial worker puts in eight or nine hours on the job, beginning each workday at a specific time and regulating his or her activities by the clock. Having a higher income does not reduce the pressure of time. In fact, as economist Stefan B. Linder points out (1970), it is the wealthy who are most pressed for time, even though they could presumably afford more leisure.

Subsistence producers in egalitarian societies work as many hours, but they regulate their activities according to the weather, the season, or social needs. In central Brazilian tribal societies, for example, special ceremonies are held at irregular intervals. Several weeks of intensive activity—harvesting and processing food and preparing masks and other gear—are necessary to prepare for a ceremony. Once the ceremony is over, there is a period of relative inactivity. Men lie around in their hammocks for days on end,

---

primary industrialization   Industrialism that develops independently, without the stimulus of industrial development elsewhere.

sleeping and daydreaming. During these intervals, some men may go off hunting and gathering, others cultivate their gardens, but some relax and tell stories. After a few weeks or months, preparations begin for the next big ceremony. Women are not so lucky. As seems almost universally the case, women's work is constant while men's work is more irregular. But for both men and women the rhythm of life is not determined by clocks, calendars, or bosses.

"Time Surplus" versus "Time Famine" Societies. Anthropologist Allen Johnson compared the use of time in an industrialized society and a technologically simple society. Johnson (1978) used data collected in French towns with data he and ethnologist Orna Johnson collected among the Machiguenga, a jungle-dwelling people in Peru. To compare these two very different societies, Johnson divided time use into three broad categories: production time, consumption time, and free time (Table 20.2). Production time is defined as time spent producing, improving, or maintaining things. This includes "reproductive activities" such as child care. Consumption time includes activities that use up resources like food, money, electricity, tennis balls, or other people's time but do not yield any tangible product. This is not to say that knowledge or enjoyment are not important; they simply are not tangible. Free time is activity that neither creates values nor uses up things.

Johnson's analysis showed significant differences. French men work about 25 percent more hours than the Machiguenga men (Figure 20.7). But the differences for consumption and free time are much greater. French men's consumption time was about two-and-one-half times that of the Machiguenga men. As anyone who has ever tried to get away for a ski weekend knows, "leisure time" activities can be extremely hectic. As a result of shorter work and consumption hours, Machiguenga men have more than 50 percent more free time than their French counterparts.

Johnson suggests that a major reason for this difference is the large number of belongings that people in industrial society possess and use. For example, while most people consider listening to the stereo a form of relaxation, owning one requires us to spend time buying, assembling, and maintaining the equipment, disks, and tapes. Johnson commented on how relaxed life is in the Machiguenga village (1978, 53): "each time I return to their communities . . . I sense a definite decrease in time pressure; this is a physiological as well as a psychological sensation." Industrial societies, with their greater material productivity, their deadlines and time clocks, their elaborate transportation systems, and the importance of coordinating activities, are what Stefan Linder calls "time famine" societies. Societies like the Machiguenga have a "time surplus," or time on their hands.

Table 20.2 Time Divided into Three Categories of Activities

Production Time	Consumption Time*	Free Time*
Time on the job	Eating	Sleeping
Farming	Sports	Idle conversation
Hunting or collecting	Entertainment	Doing nothing
Food preparation	School	Visiting
Child care	Church	
Keeping house	Radio, TV, newspaper	

*The distinctions are arbitrary. It is sometimes difficult to distinguish between consumption and free time. Consumption time is generally spent using some resource in addition to time, such as a newspaper, electricity, food, or sports equipment.

Source: Johnson 1978.

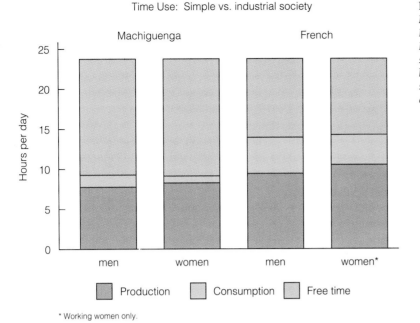

Figure 20.7 *Time use among the Machiguenga of Peru and the French. Life is more hurried and stressful in France, not so much because people spend more time at productive work, but because they spend more time consuming the goods that industrial society offers.*

Industrial Pollution

Industrialism has swollen our cities and taken away our free time. What other "benefits" will it bring? There are many answers to this question, but we focus here on a consequence of industrialism that has anthropological significance: **pollution.**

The Nature of Pollution.   Pollution is not a recent problem or an exclusive product of industrial society. Defined as contamination by harmful or obnoxious substances, pollution occurs in many kinds of societies. The Nuer people of the Sudan, for example, burn smoky fires in their tightly closed huts to keep insects away during the rainy season. Many Nuer suffer from bronchial disorders and have constant hacking coughs from inhaling so much smoke during the rainy season

(Evans-Pritchard 1940). Another example of preindustrial pollution is the mercury poisoning that occurred around the mines of Potosi, Bolivia, during the 17th and 18th centuries. The Spanish had taken over the Inca Empire and were driven by desire for precious metals. Mercury was used in the process of refining silver. Spanish colonists enslaved thousands of Indians, exposing them to mercury in mines and processing mills. Untold numbers of Quechuas and Aymaras died from exposure to the toxic metal.

Although pollution can come from natural or non-industrial sources, it is most often associated with urbanization and industrialism. Contemporary writers described early-19th-century Manchester, England, as a hell on earth (Figure 20.8). The air was heavy with smoke, chlorine, ammonia, carbon monoxide, and methane. The death rate, especially from bronchitis

pollution Contamination by substances considered harmful and obnoxious within a particular frame of reference.

Figure 20.8 *This 1866 drawing shows the pollution in England's "Black Country," near Wolverhampton, where the by-products of coal mining, iron forging, and other industries turned the air black with harmful substances.*

and pneumonia, was much higher than in nonindustrial areas. In Chicago during the 19th century, the Sanitary and Ship Canal was said to be covered with a scum of human and industrial wastes so thick that people could walk on it. The city of London has had a long history of struggle against air pollution. Smoke abatement laws were passed as early as 1273, and a man was actually executed in 1306 for burning coal. These measures did little more than retard the problem, so that by the 20th century, **smog**, a combination of smoke and fog, had again become a major factor in the health of London's residents. In 1952 an atmospheric inversion trapped pollution from coal fires in the air over London, causing an estimated 4,000 deaths.

Americans were sensitized to the problems of pollution by *The Silent Spring,* an influential book by Rachel Carson published in 1962. The book described the consequences when agricultural pesticides, particularly DDT, entered the food chain and disrupted animals' life cycles. During the 1960s, pollution became a major political issue in several industrial countries. A coalition of groups known as ecologists in France and the Green party in Germany took up the banner of a "clean environment," campaigning against unrestricted industrial growth and nuclear power. North Americans from Canada and the United States began a campaign against acid rain caused by emissions from the burning of coal in power plants and industries. Dozens of organizations such as the Sierra Club and the Audubon Society rallied around the call for a clean environment.

The politicians got the message. Attitudes changed fairly radically and sometimes very swiftly. In 1972 President Richard Nixon launched a campaign to clean up the environment in America. The Environmental Protection Agency was created to lead the fight against pollution. A new concern arose for plant and animal species in danger of extinction, and at least one project was halted—a multimillion-dollar dam in Tennessee—because it threatened a rare species, in this case a fish called the snail darter. In a recent case logging of a large area of old-growth forests in the Pacific Northwest was halted because it would destroy the habitat of another endangered species, the spotted owl. A number of major accidents in the 1970s and 1980s (including the radiation leak at Three Mile Island, Pennsylvania; the meltdown of the nuclear reactor in Chernobyl, USSR; and the death of 2,500 people from a poisonous chemical cloud released by a Union Carbide plant in Bhopal, India) added fuel to the environmental movement.

Theories about the Rise of the Environmental Movement. Given that pollution has been a recognized problem for centuries, why did Americans, Europeans, and others only recently become so concerned with the environment? Some experts suggest that people were spontaneously responding to worsening conditions. In Los Angeles, for example, the daily discharge of oxides of nitrogen nearly doubled between 1955 and the early 1970s to more than 2 million pounds per day. Nitrogen oxides are pollutants that cause lung damage and constriction of the bronchial tubes. Pollution is particularly frightening to people because it is often unseen and its effects are not immediate but cumulative. It may be more frightening than other common risks, such as traffic accidents, because the average person has no control over it.

Some psychologists have suggested that people can become desensitized to risk when they are exposed to it frequently. People who smoke or engage in hazardous occupations tend to minimize the risk inherent in these activities in their own minds. Otherwise they might become obsessed and paralyzed with fear. While this insight may apply to individual risk perception, it is not useful in explaining the rise of environmentalism, because as risks from pollution grow, the theory would predict a decline, not an increase, in environmental consciousness.

Another explanation for the rise of the environmentalist movement is that many Americans and Europeans have achieved such wealth, comfort, and control over their immediate environments that they have become more sensitive to more remote risks. This argument, heard frequently in underdeveloped countries, suggests that environmentalism is an unwanted imposition that developing nations can ill afford. Many industrial enterprises operate in underdeveloped countries under conditions that would not be permitted in more-developed countries. Installing pollution controls is expensive and increases the cost of production. Some people have even suggested that the developing countries' concern with pollution in underdeveloped countries is intended to stifle competition. But while it is probably true that the environmental movement is largely articulated by middle-class groups, it is not exclusively a middle-class, First World movement. There is no evidence that the wealthiest people or nations are the most environmentally concerned. In general, it is workers or the poor who suffer from environmental crises like the disaster at Bhopal.

Another explanation is that the risks from pollution have not changed as much as the perception of the risk. In a book called *Risk and Culture* (1982) anthropologist Mary Douglas and political scientist Aaron Wildavsky argued that there is no universal definition of risk. Douglas, an expert on pollution beliefs and taboos in non-Western societies, asserted that people define risk differently at different times and places. The authors compared Western views of pollution to those of a non-Western people, the Hima of Uganda. The Hima maintain their ethnic purity through a notion of *Iru*, a repugnance for things non-Hima. They instill a revulsion at mixing with non-Hima people, eating their food, living or working with them, or having sex with them. The Hima's pollution ideas, and the taboos that flow from them, are part of a more general belief system. To understand the Hima's fears of pollution and how they act upon them requires an understanding of the underlying social beliefs.

Douglas and Wildavsky denied that fear of pollution in the West was based on "hard" scientific evidence such as the amount of nitrogen oxide in the air. They pointed out that scientists disagree on the dangers presented by specific substances and risks and on the best measures for protection against pollution (that is, our own taboos). They demonstrated that people think about pollution in different ways depending on how they view its effects. Arguments like this force us to reconsider the environmental movement as a social movement, not simply a rational reaction to a growing problem. If people organized purely in terms of rational responses to objectively perceived risks, more organizations would combat traffic accidents than would protest air pollution because car crashes seem to claim more lives than bad air.

The question then becomes, What changes in social beliefs have occurred that have given rise to the environmental movement? Douglas and Wildavsky did not present a picture of changing American (or Western) belief systems. Rather, they based their argument on the need for certain dissident, or "fringe," groups to maintain solidarity among themselves in attacking the "establishment." Some groups have done so by building on the symbol of the environment as something "holy and pure," in danger of desecration by the unholy despoilers from government and indus-

---

smog   A combination of smoke and fog in the atmosphere.

try. According to Douglas and Wildavsky, the scientific evidence concerning pollution and its dangers functions as a kind of support for the environmentalists' underlying world view. Thus the environmental movement in the West is comparable to the Hima pollution beliefs in that ultimately both are based on irrational concepts of purity and pollution.

Critics pointed out that Douglas and Wildavsky did not analyze Western belief systems in a way that would explain the rise of the environmental movement. Their explanation was so general, it could just as easily apply to the rise of antiabortion groups in the United States or to Islamic fundamentalists in Egypt. Douglas and Wildavsky's theory would predict that the most implacable foes of pollution would be political or religious fringe groups. However, the environmental movement in the United States and other countries has moved closer and closer to the political and cultural center. Mainstream organizations like the Sierra Club and World Wildlife Fund, with millions of subscriber-members, have taken very strong positions on pollution control. This demonstrates how hard it is to understand the deeply held beliefs of one's own people. Such ideas are often so deeply rooted that we cannot easily examine them.

SUMMARY

- A great deal of the writing on urbanism is based on the premise that cities are unnatural kinds of settlements. But all human settlements follow plans reflecting the kinds of activities that go on and the ideas and intentions of the builders. From this perspective cities are no less natural than rural settlements.
- The most satisfactory anthropological definition of *urban* relates to the "density" of role relationships within a given zone. Network analysis gives anthropologists a precise tool with which to measure density.
- Contrary to many opinions, family life does not decline in cities; it may even be intensified. Families, formal institutions, and informal social networks play important roles in socializing people

and providing support. This is especially true in urban squatments in Third World cities, settlements that have often been described as "marginal" and lacking in structure.
- As cities grow and the competition for space close to the urban center becomes more intense, the poor and powerless are often displaced to the urban periphery where networks of mutual support often break down. Planned urban settlements are rarely as successful in meeting people's needs as natural and spontaneous ones.
- Cities existed long before industrialism, but the industrial revolution greatly accelerated urban growth and changed the face of modern cities, even those that have not fully industrialized.
- The early stages of industrial development in the West were very exploitative of labor.
- The development of large factories requiring strict discipline and adherence to rules and timetables may have created greater uniformity of ideas and behavior among workers. Mass production and marketing of goods also cause a reduction in cultural diversity.
- Of all the changes that people in industrial societies undergo, perhaps the most far-reaching is the loss of free time. Even leisure is spent in a hectic manner as people become caught up in a spiral of increasing work and consumption.
- One of the most unwanted products of industrialism is pollution.
- National and international movements have arisen to combat pollution and its effects on health and on the environment in general.
- Is the environmental movement a luxury of rich people in rich countries? Are these movements simply a rational response to the growing threat of pollution to human health and survival? Or did they grow out of changing cultural conceptions of purity and danger? Anthropologists ask these questions about environmentalism, but answers are not yet clear.
- We are faced with a major paradox: Industrialism has created untold wealth and the possibility for greater luxury and even higher creativity; it has also restricted personal freedom, added to the growth of poverty, increased the level of harmful pollutants, and left many people longing for the peace and simplicity of rural life.

GET INVOLVED

1. Join an organization working to improve housing in your area, such as a group helping the homeless to find shelter, groups that help build housing for low-income people with "sweat equity," or a group helping to winterize housing for senior citizens or the poor. What can you learn about the availability and quality of housing in your area? What controls housing prices in the area? What role does the state play in providing housing, making it accessible, and encouraging or discouraging the development of new housing? How fast have rents and property taxes risen over the past ten years in comparison to wages?

2. Carry out an ethnographic study of resettlement in your area. Find a group of people who have been (or are about to be) involuntarily resettled from their neighborhoods because of highway construction, urban renewal, or other developments. What provisions has the state made for them? Interview the people who will have to move. What are the costs and benefits of moving from their perspective? Will they be able to recreate their previous social structure and sources of income?

3. Join an environmental group in your area that is working to reduce a source of air, noise, or water pollution. As you work with the other members, learn how these people conceptualize pollution. Are they simply responding to an objective threat as it becomes increasingly dangerous, or is there an ideological element to their notions of purity and pollution? Are the people in the group equally concerned with all sources of pollution, or is there some particular element that motivates them?

SUGGESTED READINGS

Bourgois, Philippe. 1989. Just another night on Crack Street. *The New York Times.**

Harrison, Gail, William Rathje, and W. W. Hughes. 1975. Food waste behavior in an urban population. *The Journal of Nutrition Education.**

Johnson, Allen. 1978. In search of the affluent society. *Human Nature,* September.*

Marris, Peter. 1974. Slum clearance and family life in Lagos. Human Organization 19:123-128.

Nelson, Joan. 1979. *Access to power: Politics and the urban poor in developing nations.* Princeton, N.J.: Princeton University Press.

Spradley, James. 1972. Adaptive strategies of urban nomads: The ethnoscience of tramp culture. In *The anthropology of urban environments.* Washington, D.C.: Society for Applied Anthropology.

*This selection is anthologized in *Applying Anthropology*, 2d ed., ed. A. Podolefsky and P. J. Brown (Mountain View, Calif.: Mayfield, 1992).

ANTHROPOLOGISTS AT WORK

First Home:
Brazilians in New York City

Maxine L. Margolis is a professor of anthropology at the University of Florida in Gainesville. Her book The Moving Frontier *reports her field research on frontier agriculture in Brazil. She has also published* Mothers and Such: Views of American Women and Why They Changed *on the topic of women's roles in the United States. She is currently completing* The Invisible Minority, *a book about Brazilian immigrants in New York City.*

Maxine Margolis interviewing Dona Dalia, the owner of a rooming house where recent Brazilian immigrants in New York City find shelter, advice, employment referrals, and other services.

On a frosty Sunday morning in February I took the subway from Manhattan, where I was living, to Jackson Heights, Queens. The northwest quadrant of the borough of Queens in which Jackson Heights is located has been described as the "most diversely populated immigrant neighborhood in the world," because it has attracted such a wide range of the city's recent immigrants.

This subway ride to Jackson Heights was part of my ethnographic research on Brazilians, one of the most recent additions to the ethnic mosaic that is New York City. When I got off the train I was met by Chico, a young Brazilian from Rio de Janeiro, who had been living in New York for about 18 months. He was going to introduce me to the famous Dona Dalia (a pseudonym), the owner of a rooming house favored by Brazilians as a temporary residence

when they first arrive in New York City.

Since I had started my field research on the Brazilian community in New York City some months earlier, Dona Dalia's name had come up

over and over again in interviews with recent emigrés about their first days in the "Big Apple." I had tried to find someone who would introduce me to Dona Dalia, because I could not just show up at her front door and expect her to greet a complete stranger with open arms. I also knew that many of the Brazilians living in her establishment were undocumented aliens and that if I appeared unannounced they might suspect me of being an agent of the U.S. Immigration Service. They were undocumented because they had taken jobs in New York and stayed on after their tourist visas expired.

The boarding house was a neat, three-story, brick row house in an ethnically mixed, lower-middle-class neighborhood. Dona Dalia greeted me and offered a tour of her establishment, which was laid out to accommodate her lodgers. She led me from the sparsely furnished living room to the small kitchen. Because Dona Dalia's residents cooked for themselves, the kitchen cupboards and refrigerator were crammed with groceries carefully labeled with the names of individual boarders. A door at one end of the kitchen opened to a steep flight of stairs leading down to the basement, where the women's quarters were located. These consisted of a bedroom with two bunkbeds and a small bathroom. The men's quarters were on the second floor up another flight of stairs off the living room. Two bedrooms jammed with bunk beds housed four to six men each. Some of the beds were unmade and piled high with laundry. A man was sound asleep in a top bunk oblivious to the noise and activity that surrounded him. The place looked like a very messy college dorm room.

The greater number of beds for men than for women roughly reflected the sex ratio of boarders—70 percent men, 30 percent women—that Dona Dalia had observed since starting her business nine years earlier. Most of her residents were single, separated, or divorced. The few couples that did show up at Dona Dalia's were lodged separately: The man went upstairs to the men's quarters, and the woman went down to the basement. Dona Dalia pointed out that because she had no private facilities for couples they did not stay with her for more than a few days.

Dona Dalia collected $50 a week from each of her Brazilian lodgers and provided a number of services for them. Indeed, as I talked to Dona Dalia and some of her boarders, it became clear that her lodgings supplied far more than just shelter. Take jobs, for example, the main reason Brazilian immigrants come to New York in the first place. Dona Dalia arranged for some lodgers to get jobs as construction workers, street vendors, housekeepers, or babysitters through her contacts in New York's Brazilian community. In other cases, she advised them about where they could go to look for jobs on their own. Since it is nearly impossible to get a regular, legal job without a so-cial security card—*um social* in the lingo of New York's Brazilians—Dona Dalia arranged this too. She sometimes loaned newcomers money to buy fake social security cards and was reimbursed when they found work.

Dona Dalia was also something of an expert on U.S. immigration law and advised her boarders about how they might legalize their status by getting a "green card," the much-coveted document that turns an undocumented alien into a legal resident. And she did assorted favors for many of her boarders. While they were at work, she ran errands and made purchases for them. When she went on one of her periodic trips to Brazil, she carried letters, money, and gifts from her boarders to their families there.

In short, I discovered that Dona Dalia's boarding house was far more than a place to live. It was a combination school, counseling center, employment agency, and legal aid society that informally provided recent immigrants with most of the things they needed to know and the items they needed to have during their early days in New York. Dona Dalia's famous establishment was really a private settlement house for the Brazilian immigrants that were new to the city.

Many societies offer a range of medical choices, including Western biomedicine. Here several women and their children wait for treatment outside the Health Center, Freetown, Sierra Leone.

HEALTH, DISEASE, AND CULTURE

▲▲▲

medical anthropology unites several important themes in anthropology. It treats people both as biological organisms and as cultural beings and has both theoretical and applied aspects. It provides a window into certain cultural processes, which is invaluable for understanding cultural behavior in its widest sense. We have already referred to several aspects of medical anthropology in our discussions of the ecology of disease. For example, our discussions of malaria resistance and lactase deficiency show the role of genetic polymorphisms interacting with culture and the environment (Chapter 8). We have discussed various aspects of diet, such as the adaptation to protein scarcity (Chapters 16). We have also seen how human modification of the environment affects the incidence of disease (Chapters 8, 20).

Diseases and disease vectors are part of the environment everywhere. But cultural responses to disease are quite varied and often adaptive in the sense that they help individuals and populations reduce the incidence or severity of disease episodes. This chapter focuses on the cultural aspects of disease. It points out differences in how people recognize, categorize, and explain diseases; how they behave when they are sick; and how healing is accomplished. The chapter also looks at mental illness, an area of experience even more dependent on cultural context than physical illness. Although some forms of mental illness appear to have uniform features across cultures, which suggests a biological basis for them, others are clearly shaped by culture, and still others are unique to certain societies. This area of anthropological study is particularly revealing of the complex interplay of biology and culture.

THE CULTURAL CONSTRUCTION OF ILLNESS AND HEALTH

Illness is recognized in every society, and people everywhere respond when others become ill. But there are wide differences in how people conceive of sickness, its causes, and the proper way to heal. There are also differences in the social roles related to illness and healing. Most people learn to think about illness in culturally prescribed ways. Let us begin with a brief portrait of how people conceptualize illness in North America. An American college student was asked to write a short essay on health and sickness. Here is what he wrote:

> When the body is functioning normally, you are healthy. You stay healthy by eating well, taking vitamins, and getting enough rest. Sometimes something goes wrong and you get sick. The most common sicknesses are infections caused by germs, like colds. Another kind of sickness comes from accidents, such as when you swallow something poisonous or break a bone. Sometimes, people get sick from natural causes such as heart disease, cancer, or high blood pressure.
>
> When you get sick, you feel bad; you need to take care of yourself. You might need to stay in bed. If you are very sick, you need to see a doctor. Doctors study medicine and know all about the body so you can trust them to find out what's wrong. The doctor examines you, orders some laboratory tests, and then diagnoses your illness. After he knows what you have got, the doctor can prescribe treatment. Most sicknesses can be diagnosed and cured with proper treatment. Sometimes all you need is rest, but often you need medication, like pills or a shot. If you are seriously ill, the doctor will send you to a hospital where you lie in bed all day and let the nurses take care of you. Surgery is usually a last resort when other cures fail. Some people who get cancer or other incurable diseases go to quacks who pretend to be able to cure them, but only medical doctors have the knowledge to cure. A person has to be careful not to be taken in by superstitious beliefs.
>
> Some sicknesses are not really in the body, but in the mind. These are mental illnesses. The patient may feel bad, but there is nothing organically wrong with him, no infection, no tumor. The therapy for psychosomatic or mental illness is different. Sometimes the patient takes drugs to calm down or to feel less depressed. Psychotherapy, which is done by just talking to a doctor or psychologist, helps some patients.

Behind these views stands an explanatory model of illness based on experience, information from other people, and perhaps some knowledge of formal medicine. This particular model of illness and treatment, known as the **biomedical model,** is not shared by all Americans, but it is widespread. Let us look at some of the assumptions in this passage:

1. Health equals normal body function. Being ill is not normal.
2. One can take measures to prevent illness, but not all sickness is preventable.

3. Some diseases (infections) are caused by germs, while others have different organic causes. Accidents are another cause of illness. Mental illness has no organic cause.
4. Mild illnesses can be treated by the sick person, but serious ones require a doctor's attention.
5. Medicine is a science; doctors can determine the cause of a sickness and treat it.
6. Medicines can cure sickness by killing germs or repairing damage. Surgery is a kind of repair to the body.
7. Doctors are the only people who really understand sickness.
8. Some sicknesses are caused by the mind. People who have them require psychological, not medical, treatment.

To an anthropologist, the student's statements are neither correct nor incorrect; they are quoted to show how cultural assumptions are embedded in how people think and act in relation to sickness.

It is helpful to make a distinction between two aspects of sickness. According to Arthur Kleinman, anthropologist and physician, **disease** is a "malfunctioning of biological and/or psychological processes"; **illness** "refers to the psychosocial experience and meaning of perceived disease" (1978, 72). *Disease* is an etic term belonging to a biomedical tradition, while *illness* is an emic term that depends on the cultural context and on the individual. In the West specialists in the treatment of disease tend to focus primarily on the *disease* aspect of disorders. The afflicted persons and their families, however, usually focus on the *illness*. Kleinman points out that in certain chronic disorders, such as diabetes or asthma, "it may be difficult to distinguish the disease from the illness." A patient may have symptoms of illness even when the disease is not clinically detectable. In other cases, there may be serious illness without any detectable organic disease. A person can be totally incapacitated by an illness that has no measurable organic manifestation. On the other hand, in cases of severe heart attacks or other diseases with rapid onset, there may not be enough time for "a disease to be shaped into an illness experience" (Kleinman 1978, 74).

Modes of Perceiving Disease: Ethnodiagnosis

Societies vary in what they consider an illness. Symptoms that are considered signs of a particular disease in one place are taken as signs of some other malady in other societies. Symptoms considered important in some populations are virtually ignored in others. Illnesses common in some societies are unknown as a distinctive set of causes and symptoms in other societies. These are known as culture-bound syndromes and are discussed more fully later in this chapter.

The diagnosis of disease is subject to a high degree of ethnocentric bias. Within different traditions, varying clusters of symptoms and causes are named and diagnosed as different diseases; the study of such differences is called **ethnodiagnosis**. For example, the French believe that the liver is the cause of many physical problems. French people often say that there is something wrong with their livers when their digestion is poor or they don't feel well. Sometimes they prescribe special kinds of water, diets, or baths to improve the condition of the liver. North Americans, on the other hand, rarely refer to their livers as a cause of illness. They are much more likely to refer to the heart, lungs, or digestive system as the root cause of a malady.

Anthropologist Charles Frake (1961) observed that when a person feels sick, he or she wonders:

"Am I sick?" "What kind of disease do I have?" "What are my chances?" "What caused this disease?" "Why did it happen to me (of all people)?" . . . Every culture provides a set of significant questions, potential answers and procedures for arriving at answers. The cultural answers to these questions are concepts of illness.

---

biomedical model The explanatory model of illness that attributes disease to biological or psychological malfunctioning.

disease A biological or psychological malfunction that can cause pain, impairment, or death.

illness The psychosocial experience and meaning of perceived disease.

ethnodiagnosis The identification and description of a disease in a patient within a particular cultural framework.

In Chapter 3 we explored cultural meaning as revealed in the classification of disease by American undergraduates. In that study by Roy D'Andrade (1976) the students matched up a long list of statements about disease, symptoms, and causes, creating clusters of meaning around certain ideas. Charles Frake (1961) examined the diagnosis of disease in another society, the Subanun people of the Philippines. He showed that the Subanun first consider the cause of the disease, such as wounds, worms, or intrusive objects. Next they consider the development of the disease, such as a rash that is followed by a skin eruption. The Subanun distinguish between "internal" and "external" symptoms. In contrast to other cultural conceptions of disease, the Subanun do not see the heart as involved in internal diseases, but they frequently refer to the spleen as the location of the disease.

In examining the wide variety in beliefs about the causes of disease, anthropologist George Foster distinguished between **personalistic** and **naturalistic medical systems** (Foster and Anderson 1978). In personalistic systems, sickness is believed to be caused by an "agent" who may be a spirit, ghost, ancestor, god, or human witch. A person becomes sick as a victim of aggression. Treatment of the illness thus involves discovering who or what provoked the illness. In naturalistic medical systems, such as the one described at the beginning of this chapter, illness is explained in "impersonal, systemic terms" (Foster and Anderson 1978, 53). Naturalistic systems depend on a notion of balance or normality in the body, spirit, or social world of the sufferer. When the balance is disturbed, illness results. This may be a balance between "hot and cold," a common feature of ethnomedical beliefs in the Mediterranean and Latin America. In popular North American biomedicine, health depends on a good balance of diet, exercise, rest, and hygiene.

Medical anthropologist Donn V. Hart studied a personalistic medical system among the Samaran peasants of the Philippines (1979). The Samaran villagers believed that the causes of most serious illnesses were the actions of spirits, sorcerers (and their pets), and ancestral souls. Sickness was seen as punishment for offenses against one of these agents. The Samarans believed in "environmental spirits," capable of sending serious diseases to their victims. One such spirit, called *Tugopnon,* was an ugly being with a twisted nose and fair skin covered with spots. These environmental

spirits would not generally attack humans unless provoked, but since they were invisible, it was difficult to avoid them. For example, the villagers believed it was best not to work during the afternoon siesta because the spirits liked to nap and might retaliate if they were disturbed.

More vengeful than spirits were the souls of departed ancestors. They brought sickness to people who failed to observe certain values, such as respect for the elderly or avoidance of violence. They might punish incestuous marriages (between first cousins, for example). They had to be honored every year with rituals at harvest time; failure to perform the ritual might result in sickness. When a Samaran became sick, the question asked was, Which ancestor or spirit has the sick person offended? The treatment prescribed depended on the answer.

Thus the recognition of a sickness, the classification of the kind of sickness, and the interpretation of the sickness depend on cultural context, even in societies that accept a Western biomedical view of disease. All medical systems allow for what Western physicians call "differential diagnoses"; that is, different people may arrive at different conclusions concerning what is wrong with the patient and what should be done to heal the patient.

The Sick Role

When they are sick, most people think that how they feel and act is determined by the disease they have. Clearly disease can affect a person's outlook and behavior. As an extreme example, a person in a coma is unable to walk or talk. But being sick is not a simple response to physical disease; it involves fulfilling a culturally determined role. People in every society enact **sick roles** or behavior appropriate to an ill person. These culturally patterned ways of acting are reinforced by others. In some societies the sick role involves seclusion, while in others a sick person may be highly visible, even paraded around the village (Figure 21.1). In northeastern Brazil a man who is sick stops shaving, announcing to the world that he is ill. If one asks why, he may explain that he must not put water on his face. The sick role may involve screaming in pain or suffering in silence.

The student whose statements about illness began this chapter says that seriously ill people should go to

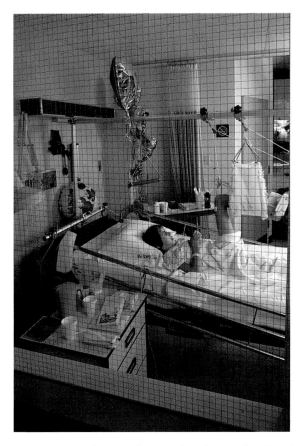 

Figure 21.1   *The sick role varies depending on the cultural context. In North America a sick person is often secluded in a hospital room, where modern medical technology can be applied (left). In Mexico a sick person may be treated in a traditional curing ceremony that includes the use of religious symbolism (right).*

the hospital for treatment. In a hospital a person is obliged to perform a certain role. Consider one patient admitted to an American hospital for tests. He did not feel sick and wanted to sit in a chair to read and talk to visitors in his hospital room. Several nurses came and ordered the patient to change into pajamas and lie in bed. Finally the doctor came in and insisted that the patient change clothes and lie in his bed. If he didn't, the doctor warned, the insurance company might not pay for the hospitalization. "If you're in the hospital," the doctor said with a faint smile, "you'd better act like you're sick."

To refer to a sick role does not deny the seriousness of the disease or the depth of suffering. The sick role is simply the conventional pattern of announcing that one is ill and signaling that one needs help. Performance of the sick role may communicate the nature and severity of the illness. In developed economies

---

personalistic medical system   A system of medical beliefs that attributes the origin of disease to an agent, such as a spirit, ghost, witch, or deceased ancestor.

naturalistic medical system   A system of medical belief that attributes the origin of disease to impersonal, systemic forces.

sick role   The behavior that is expected of a person suffering from an illness.

both medical care providers and patients carefully observe the sick role, because certain benefits can be obtained only if one plays the role properly, as shown in the example just given. Playing the sick role brings the application of medication, excused absence from work, payment of health benefits, compensation for time lost on the job, or exemption from military service. In other words, the sick role triggers performances by relatives, caregivers, and others that are culturally appropriate to the illness.

Culture-Bound Syndromes

We have already defined **culture-bound syndromes** as "folk illnesses" (Chapter 2), disorders that occur in specific cultural contexts and are recognized by the people who are afflicted by them and who treat them. There are many examples. *Susto* (literally, "fright") is an ailment we have discussed before. It affects Latin Americans from the southwestern United States to South America. The people affected are of both native and nonnative descent, rich and poor, educated and uneducated. Although recognized as a single illness, *susto* is connected with a wide variety of symptoms: *Susto* patients may complain of restlessness and loss of sleep, anxiety, loss of appetite, disinterest in dress and personal hygiene, weakness, and depression (Rubel et al. 1984). They may also suffer from fever, stomach problems, headaches, diarrhea, and chills.

In areas where *susto* is **endemic**, a person with *susto* is given special treatment. No one expects a person with *susto* to be able to work as hard as a healthy person or to accept some very stressful responsibility. Assuming a role linked to a familiar syndrome can help a person adapt by changing other people's expectations, although this need not be a deliberate strategy. *Susto*, like other illnesses, has consequences not only for the body and mind but also for the social functioning of the victim. Many investigators suggest that *susto* arises from a situation in which the ill person feels he or she cannot fulfill an expected social role. This may be so, but many people suffer frustration and anxiety over fulfillment of social roles without having *susto*. And *susto* is common among children, who might be expected to suffer less role anxiety than adults.

Taking social roles and expectations into consideration helps in the understanding of *susto* and other culture-bound syndromes, but it does not provide an explanation. An explanation would deal with the causes of the illness not simply its consequences. A satisfactory explanation, accepted by all investigators, is not yet available. Recent studies (Rubel et al. 1984) show that *susto* patients have a higher incidence of both psychological and physical disorders. They also stand a greater risk of dying than persons without *susto*. In Chapter 2, we noted Ralph Bolton's (1981) research on *susto*, which showed that it was linked both to higher levels of hostility and to hypoglycemia, a metabolic disease.

There are several other culture-bound syndromes in other parts of the world. Most of them have both psychological and physical aspects. An example is *latah*, a common illness in Southeast Asia. When startled, sufferers from *latah* often erupt involuntarily into obscene words, speaking in rapid, repetitive phrases; they may throw things, lose control over their bowels, and then suddenly return to normal. Unlike psychotics, they are aware of what they are doing but are unable to control it, and they suffer extreme embarrassment for the acts they commit during attacks. The **Windigo psychosis** is an illness that is alleged to occur among the northern Algonquian peoples of North America in which an individual becomes a cannibalistic murderer. (Cannibalism is not considered normal by northern Algonquian peoples.) As with *susto*, most of the explanations of these and other culture-bound syndromes suggest social stress as a causal factor.

Obesity, or chronic overweight, is a common culture-bound syndrome in North America. It occurs in all age and class groups but is more prevalent in some than in others. It is commonly associated with stress, with **compulsive disorders**, and sometimes with inheritance. North Americans who are obese tend to be stigmatized and suffer loss of self-esteem. In other societies people with the same physical characteristics may be complimented for their sleek looks and obvious prosperity. In northeastern Brazil, for example, being thin is not admired and is commonly thought to be the result of tuberculosis or worms.

We do not yet have full understanding of the causes of culture-bound syndromes, but as we have seen, they are linked to organic syndromes and certain outcomes, including incapacity and death. It is well established that people can die of socially induced causes, without any poison, infection, or trauma. So-called **voodoo death** is well known from Haiti and other places where people practice and believe in **sorcery**. Just how a person who has been bewitched comes to die is in dispute (Eastwell 1989, Cannon 1942), but there appears to be a pathway through the mind into the autonomic nervous system that makes voodoo death more than just a superstitious belief.

While they are diseases with specific symptoms and a definable course of development, culture-bound syndromes occur in culturally defined contexts. The study of culture-bound syndromes provides evidence that illness and disease cannot be understood apart from the social and cultural context. Nearly every disease is culture bound to some extent. Social and cultural elements are involved not only in the recognition and diagnosis of disease, but also in its causes and treatment.

Mind and Body

The Western tradition of biomedical practice stresses physical or organic aspects of disease. An extreme statement of the Western tradition is that patients with serious diseases have little hope of recovery without the intervention of medical professionals who can treat the organic cause of disease. Most disease is "self-limiting," however, and many patients recover without treatment. Self-healing is known but only partially understood from a Western biomedical point of view. Immunologists have learned, for example, that the human body has defenses that can be mobilized to combat infection. The mobilization of these defenses depends greatly on the patient's psychological state. Patients who are emotionally upset, depressed, or under stress do not recover from infections as quickly as those who are not. There is also evidence that patients who have "social support" from friends and relatives who visit them and express concern recover more rapidly than those who do not.

These observations lend support to the commonplace belief that psychological factors play a role in healing. In the United States many physicians state that a majority of their patients have symptoms that are at least partly psychological in origin. These patients may be seriously ill and in pain, yet treatment of the organic cause may have little effect. Nevertheless most doctors in the West are trained only in biomedical aspects of disease, and they pay little attention to psychological and cultural factors. Western biomedicine has yet to come to grips with the full implications of the close relationship between mind and body.

In many societies practitioners recognize social and mental factors in illness and attempt to treat those aspects. An example can be found in Taiwan (Republic of China), an island off the coast of mainland China. The Taiwanese disease category *ut siong* is related to the terms for "anxious," "grieved," "depressed," "injure," and "wound." Taiwanese doctors are familiar with the term and treat it as "real" illness. Mainland China doctors, however, trained in the classical tradition of Chinese medicine do not recognize *ut siong* as an illness, or they treat it as a mere superstition. Patients avoid mentioning *ut siong* to classically trained physicians, perhaps because they feel they will not be taken seriously (Kleinman 1978, 84–85). North American doctors who understand the social and psychological dimension of healing are said to have a good "bedside manner." They work to bolster the confidence of the patient and family in the diagnosis, prognosis, and treatment. They recognize that without this confidence the therapy will have little effect.

---

culture-bound syndrome   An illness whose diagnosis and characteristics occur within a restricted cultural range; also known as folk illness.

endemic   Prevalent in or peculiar to a local area or population.

latah   A culture-bound syndrome common in Southeast Asia involving bizarre but involuntary verbal behavior and loss of control over the bowels, followed by a sudden return to normal.

Windigo psychosis   A culture-bound syndrome found in North American native populations in which the victim is alleged to become a cannibalistic murderer.

obesity   The condition of being chronically overweight.

compulsive disorder   A condition characterized by excessive or involuntary behavior over which the afflicted person has little or no control.

voodoo death   Death caused by a magical spell.

sorcery   The use of magical spells and objects, usually to harm someone.

One aspect of this relationship is the placebo effect. A placebo is any medication or other therapy that has no known direct biological effect on the patient. A pill containing sugar is a common kind of placebo. We discussed placebos in Chapter 2 in relation to the unconscious effects that people have on each other in social research. Placebos may have powerful effects on patients who believe in their power. They have been used experimentally to treat many kinds of disease. Often they produce results equal to those obtained with "true" therapies.

Angina pectoris is a crushing pain in the chest that occurs when the heart has insufficient blood flow. For more than 100 years, angina has been treated with oral doses of nitroglycerin, which gives quick and dramatic relief. How the nitroglycerin works to relieve pain is not well understood. Some researchers (Benson and McCallie 1979) have given a placebo in place of nitroglycerin to patients suffering from angina. From 30 to 90 percent of the patients in these studies undergo significant improvement in their angina. Surgical treatments for angina were first developed in the 1950s, beginning with a relatively simple operation involving binding two shallow arteries in the chest. The surgery was considered successful because most of the patients who had it reported significant improvements in their angina. Soon after this operation became popular, however, two groups of surgeons conducted an experiment in which they performed the arterial surgery on some patients but performed "sham" operations on others, simply making incisions in the patients' chests. The patients did not know which kind of surgery had been done, nor did the cardiologists who examined them after surgery. The results showed only a small difference in the recovery rates of the real surgical patients and the sham patients (Moerman 1983, Table 21.1).

One important aspect of placebo studies is that any therapy is likely to have a placebo effect in addition to any direct organic effect. Doctors, nurses, friends, relatives, and anyone else who pays attention to the patient provide social support and may contribute to the healing process. When a sick person recovers, it may be impossible to determine how the cure took place. It could have been a spontaneous process of self-healing; it could have been a response to a biologically active therapy, such as an antibiotic; it could have come from a placebo effect; it could have been a response to social support for the patient; or it could

have been some combination of these factors. When we examine non-Western and **alternative medical systems,** we see that many of them rely heavily on nonbiological aspects of healing. They are closely tied to the belief systems and explanatory models of disease prevalent in the particular population.

Westerners often see other approaches to healing as superstitious and unscientific. We must beware of several sources of cultural bias in such beliefs. First, if one accepts that feelings and beliefs can affect the outcome of an illness episode, one cannot discount a medical system that pays attention to those feelings and beliefs. Second, there is widespread agreement, even in Western medicine, that nonrational, unscientific beliefs and feelings have a heavy influence over the outcome of disease episodes. The use of medical paraphernalia such as stethoscopes, thermometers, X-ray machines, and the special clothing worn by doctors, nurses, and other therapists have important psychological effects on patients apart from their biological use. When a doctor does not use them, patients may be uneasy and express doubt that the doctor knows what he or she is doing. Third, even when they are not scientific, alternative medical systems may rely on careful observation and discrimination of symptoms and causes in selecting therapies. Finally, nearly all Western medical practitioners who have had experience with alternative and non-Western traditions agree that these approaches can be effective in treating certain kinds of disease.

HEALING IN CULTURAL PERSPECTIVE

Treatment of disease is as culturally conditioned as recognition of it. Let us examine different kinds of treatment systems, looking at the social roles of healers as well as how they help their patients.

Shamanism

Once a person has determined that he or she is ill, the next step is often to seek treatment. In nearly every society there are specialists who heal. In simple societies there may be little or no choice of healers. The !Kung San believe that illnesses are caused by spirits

Table 21.1   Results of Real and "Sham" Surgery on Patients Suffering from Angina Pectoris

Improvement	Arterial Surgery		Sham Surgery	
	Number	Percent	Number	Percent
Substantial	43	66	10	83
Slight	22	34	1	17
Totals	65	100	11	100

Note: Results are pooled from five different studies.

Source: Moerman 1983, 160.

Figure 21.2   *Shamanistic curing is one form of healing. Here, a !Kung San shaman in a trance attempts to discover the cause of a man's illness.*

of dead ancestors who invite the living to join them. When a person becomes ill, the family may call on one or more people who are able to go into trance. While in a trance, the healer can try to identify and ward off the dead ancestor (Figure 21.2). The !Kung San say there is a substance called N/um that sits in the pit of the stomach and becomes active in the shaman during a healing dance. The rhythmic dance together with drumming and the heat of a fire cause the N/um to boil. It is this boiling energy of N/um that gives healing power to the shaman (Lee 1979, Katz 1982).

To become healers, individuals must undergo a long, difficult apprenticeship, during which they acquire the physical and psychological self-control to enter trance, heal the sick, ward off spirits, and, eventually, train new healers (see Chapter 18). !Kung shamans also learn a great deal of preventive dietary lore.

The Tapirapé of central Brazil also have a rich tradition of shamanism. All Tapirapé may occasionally meet spirits and the souls of dead people in their dreams, but only a shaman knows how to handle this experience without fear. The Tapirapé respect and need shamans to help them manage dangerous spirits, but they also fear them because they believe that illness, death, and misfortune are always caused by shamans performing sorcery. Any shaman may cross over

this divide, even against members of his own village. The most common duty of a shaman is treating the sick, usually at late night sessions. Ethnographer Charles Wagley wrote a vivid description of shamanistic curing (1943):

> A shaman comes to his patient, and squats near the patient's hammock. His first act is always to light his pipe. When the patient has a fever or is unconscious from the sight of a ghost, the principal method of treatment is by massage. The shaman blows smoke

---

angina pectoris   Severe chest pain that occurs when the heart has insufficient blood flow.

alternative medical system   A medical system that depends on a nontraditional or nonbiological belief system for its explanation and treatment of disease.

over the entire body of the patient; then he blows smoke over his own hands, spits into them, and massages the patient slowly and firmly, always towards the extremities of the body. He shows that he is removing a foreign substance by a quick movement of his hands as he reaches the end of an arm or leg.

The more frequent method of curing, however, is by the extraction of a malignant object by sucking. The shaman squats alongside the hammock of his patient and begins to "eat smoke"—swallow large gulps of tobacco smoke from his pipe. He forces the smoke with great intakes of breath deep down into his stomach; soon he becomes intoxicated and nauseated; he vomits violently and smoke spews from his stomach. He groans and clears his throat in the manner of a person gagging with nausea but unable to vomit. By sucking back what he vomits he accumulates saliva in his mouth.

In the midst of this process he stops several times to suck on the body of his patient and finally, with one awful heave, he spews all the accumulated material on the ground. He then searches in this mess for the intrusive object that has been causing the illness.

Shamans occupy an important position in Tapirapé society. As Wagley wrote, "In all life situations where chance or the unpredictable figure, the Tapirapé depend markedly upon their shamans. Thus the greatest prestige in Tapirapé culture [goes] to the shamans." Unlike the !Kung San shamans, Tapirapé shamans are paid for their services, but only if the patient recovers. The payment may be in meat, honey, or luxury goods such as beads and other ornaments, which makes shamans the wealthiest men in an otherwise egalitarian society. The payments are not sufficient, however, for Tapirapé shamans to retire from hunting and gardening. They are not full-time specialists.

How does the smoking, massaging, and retching of a Tapirapé shaman or the trance dancing of the !Kung help to cure? The performances mobilize a part of the community to support the person who is ill. They also help because the patient believes that the shaman is driving off the evil spirit or sucking out an intrusive object. These are the true causes of illness in the explanatory models of the !Kung San and Tapirapé. While they do not understand the therapy, or why it works, patients often experience relief from their symptoms after curing is performed. In shamanistic practices there is also a ready explanation for why a cure did not work. For example, a Tapirapé shaman may say that the invading spirits were stronger than

he was, or that there were too many of them. While this explanation may seem self-serving to someone who does not believe in spirits, how does it differ in form from an explanation of why a patient died after surgery in a modern Western hospital?

Medical Pluralism

In more complex societies a choice of healing systems is often available. This is known as **medical pluralism.** In pluralistic systems a patient and his or her family may consider an array of alternatives to deal with the illness that has presented itself (Figure 21.3). In Brazil, for example, a person who is feeling sick may consult a physician who is trained in Western biomedicine and has a diploma from an accredited medical school. Alternatively, the afflicted person may consult a pharmacist. Another option is a homeopathic pharmacy, where "natural" drugs are prescribed and sold. These drugs, such as a preparation of essence of celery used to treat kidney stones, are said to be compounded from organic substances. Yet another option would be to seek out a religious specialist, such as at a spiritist center or within one of the many Afro-Brazilian religious cults. At such centers the sick person can seek supernatural intervention, such as the assistance of an African *orixá* (deity), in curing an ailment.

The breadth of choice is not always apparent in North America, where biomedicine is often presented as the only valid approach. "Ask your doctor," is a common slogan, although it ignores the fact that the average person in North America cannot approach a physician with a casual inquiry. North America may be somewhat exceptional in the degree to which a single modality of healing, practiced by physicians licensed by the state, has virtually monopolized the field. Other practitioners—psychologists, nurses, chiropractors, midwives or birth assistants, and so on— are also state licensed but have secondary status and are subordinate to physicians in clinical settings like hospitals. Other kinds of healers—masseurs, nutrition therapists, and many kinds of spiritual healers— are treated as "quacks" by the medical profession.

There have been many studies of alternative curing systems in different societies, including Thailand, India, Zaire, Germany, and China. What influences people to choose one therapy over another in these

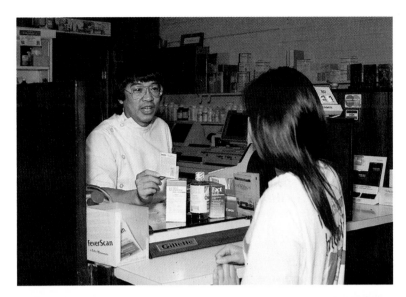

Figure 21.3 *Societies dominated by one healing system offer people fewer choices than societies characterized by medical pluralism. In the United States, a person may seek advice from a pharmacist (top), but pharmacists operate within the dominant system, Western biomedicine, and dispense medicines prescribed or recommended by licensed physicians. In Brazil, several systems exist side by side and are considered equally valid but appropriate in different situations. One choice is an Afro-Brazilian religious center (bottom), where Catholic saints and traditional African spirits are incorporated into the healing system.*

societies? In some cases different traditions offer radically different explanations for illness episodes and prescribe very different courses of treatment. However, they need not be competitive. People may simultaneously use different traditions of diagnosis and healing when they are familiar with more than one. Or they may select a particular modality of healing according to their perception of what illness they have and the difficulty or cost of obtaining treatment.

Anthropologist John M. Janzen (1978) provided a vivid account of a plural system in his book *The Quest for Therapy: Medical Pluralism in Lower Zaire*. Zaire was a colony of Belgium for 75 years. The Belgians and the missionaries had provided only as much edu-

---

medical pluralism The coexistence of a variety of medical systems within a society.

cation to the native population as was absolutely necessary for the economic functioning of the colony. At the time of independence in 1960, there was not a single Zairois trained as a physician, and 20 years later there were still fewer than 2,000 trained physicians to serve a population of over 30 million people. Many of these physicians were foreigners. Native curing traditions continued in full force alongside Western biomedicine among the Zairois, although Europeans sometimes tried to suppress native "superstitions." The Europeans saw these systems as opposed to each other, while the natives saw them as complementary alternatives.

A simplistic explanation of the persistence of native medical practices is that biomedical practitioners were too scarce or expensive for most people. Janzen pointed out, however, that even people who had full access to Western biomedicine might prefer native healing practices under some circumstances. Janzen distinguished four basic kinds of curing actively sought by the people he studied: (1) Western medicine; (2) *banganga,* or native doctors, and *bangunza,* or inspirational diviners and prophets; (3) "kinship therapy" involving relatives in diagnosis and therapeutic measures, and (4) rites of therapy and initiation.

In his analysis Janzen stressed healing within a social framework. In most studies of Western medical practice, the focus is on a single patient and the practitioner who treats him or her. In Zaire a patient was usually escorted by a group of relatives and friends to the selected practitioner. This **therapy-managing group** assumed a great deal of control, including negotiations with healers, decisions about which practitioner to visit and which therapy to adopt, and discussions about the cause of the illness and the meaning of the symptoms. Janzen wrote (1978, 9):

> A feature of therapy management in Kongo society is the collective orientation of medicine. The whole diagnostic apparatus is sensitive to the social causes of physiological affliction. African traditional medicine has been criticized by Western missionaries and colonials as superstition that victimizes individuals ostensibly to benefit the social group. But it could be equally well argued that Western medicine focuses on the individual patient and leaves the social context of his illness in pathological chaos. Kongo therapeutic attitudes, like those in many other African societies, are composed to discern the social and psychosomatic causes of illness.

Janzen presented a number of poignant case histories in his monograph to illustrate how the therapy-managing group intervened in a variety of ways on behalf of the patient, often making decisions or arrangements for the ill person. The ill person, in turn, manipulated this group and through it, practitioners, to focus attention on his or her malady (Box 21.1). In Janzen's case histories, it is remarkable how little friction or competition occurred between different kinds of practitioners. In one case, a group of relatives withdrew a seriously ill woman from the hospital against the advice of the doctors. The doctors, understanding how the system worked, did not dispute the decision, knowing it would be useless.

Social support is a secondary aspect of curing in the West; patients tend to be isolated in **dyads** with practitioners. The stress is on the doctor-patient relationship, and the doctor may view the patient's family as a nuisance. Although some physicians recognize the importance of this element, most Western physicians attach little importance to the family or other support group. An exception is when candidates are being considered for such rare and expensive therapies as heart transplants. In these cases doctors include the social support factor. Between two patients who are alike in other respects, the doctors will often select the one whose family and friends have clearly rallied around to give the patient both support and care.

Even in the West, there are some examples of nontraditional healing that form a therapy-managing group. **Alcoholics Anonymous,** one of the most effective programs known for the treatment of alcoholism, mobilizes fellow alcoholics to assist each other in recovery. One of the most important aspects of AA is the conceptualization of alcoholism as an incurable and progressive disease. This helps reduce the tendency of many alcoholics to share the broader society's view of them as moral degenerates who simply lack the will to stop drinking. The stress in AA is not on cure, as in biomedicine, but on recovery, which is seen as a continuous and lifelong process. A number of other organizations now use a similar approach in treatment of drug and tobacco addiction, compulsive gambling, and overeating. In these **12-step programs** (so called because members pass through a series of 12 steps in the process of recovery) there is explicit recognition of the spiritual dimension in recovery, another important departure from biomedicine. The participant is encouraged not to "fight" the disease but to submit to the will of a higher power.

Symbolic Manipulation in Healing

Skeptics of non-Western therapeutic styles must consider the power of the placebo effect and the importance of social support in achieving good therapeutic results. Even in cases in which standard Western biomedical therapy is applied, a cure may occur through another pathway resulting from a nonbiomedical therapy. For example, a patient with pneumonia may recover after staying in a hospital and receiving antibiotic therapy and supplemental oxygen. What cured the patient, however, might just as well be the hospital "ritual," the solicitous visits of friends and relatives, and the flowers and get well cards.

Anthropologist Kaja Finkler hypothesized that when people suffer from long-term or chronic diseases that cannot be eliminated, they are likely to obtain greater relief from symbolic manipulation than from biomedical management. Finkler studied Mexican spiritualist temples, a type of healing and worship center located in cities and towns that serve many thousands of people daily. Finkler did field research in Hidalgo State, Mexico, among a population of poor peasants and wage laborers. Those working on the land were constantly exposed to infection because of the use of untreated urban sewage water to irrigate crops. Intestinal parasites were very common, and much of the population suffered from chronic diarrhea and other diseases of the digestive system. Many people visiting the spiritualist temples for the first time had already been treated medically but had not obtained relief. Often the sufferers thought they were victimized by witchcraft and sought spiritualist help even though the spiritualists themselves rejected the idea of witchcraft (Finkler 1983).

Spiritualist curers were able to go into trance and summon spirit protectors, believed to be doctors or other gifted people who had died. Several curers sitting side-by-side received a patient, one-by-one, each

Table 21.2 Results of Spiritualist Healing: Follow-up Interviews with 107 Patients Who Visited Mexican Spiritualist Temples

Outcome	Number	Percent
Failures	38	35.5
Successes	27	25.3
Inconclusive	21	19.6
Miscellaneous	21	19.6
Total	107	100.0

Note: "Failures" are patients who sought treatment at the temple and said they followed the prescribed treatment but did not recover from the illness for which they sought treatment. "Successes" are patients who reported that they had followed the prescribed treatment and recovered from the symptoms for which they had sought treatment. "Inconclusive" refers to patients who recovered but who simultaneously sought medical treatment for their symptoms. "Miscellaneous" includes patients who did not follow the prescribed treatment and about whom it was not possible to determine results.

Source: Finkler 1983, 88.

spending about ten minutes with the patient. The first stage of healing, called a *limpia* (cleansing), involved the curer moving his or her hands up and down the patient's body while reciting a blessing. Then the patient disclosed his or her symptoms and received a treatment recommendation, which was delivered with little apparent emotion or concern for the patient. Most patients with physical symptoms were given prescriptions for teas, baths, massages, and often patent medicines. Herbs for the preparation of teas and baths were available in local pharmacies. The curers also prescribed laxatives, tonics, and vitamins that were sold over the counter in drugstores.

Finkler was able to follow up on 107 patients, inquiring about the outcome of their visit to the spiritualist temple. She did not make any medical assessment of the patients' recovery, relying on the patients' own judgments about whether they were better. Table 21.2 shows the results. The data suggest that spiritual-

---

therapy-managing group A group of relatives and friends who assist in the healing of a patient.

dyad A pair.

Alcoholics Anonymous A voluntary program of mutual assistance for alcoholics seeking to recover from their disease.

12-step program Programs modeled after Alcoholics Anonymous that recommend a series of 12 steps as a path toward recovery.

BOX 21.1

Nsimba's Story

In his study of medical pluralism in Zaire, John Janzen (1978) presented a number of case studies to illustrate his approach to African therapeutic practices. Among them was the case of Nsimba, a man in his early 20s trained as a nurse at a Swedish missionary hospital and given responsibility for a health dispensary at his home mission station, near his kinfolk. His appointment was not welcomed by an elderly African nurse who had worked in the dispensary for nearly 50 years and had attained substantial power and influence in the community. Shortly after Nsimba's arrival at the dispensary, the old nurse was retired by the mission board and Nsimba's authority was enlarged. Nsimba felt the older man's anger. He was also under pressure from relatives who felt that, since he had a paid job, he should pay for any medical fees they owed to the dispensary. Nsimba's wife had a healthy baby boy, but she suffered from frequent abdominal pain and had two miscarriages.

After a few years Nsimba developed a painful infection of the urinary tract. He was examined and diagnosed at the hospital where he had been trained. Nsimba took antibiotics, but his pain and discomfort continued. Accompanied by his father and several maternal uncles (his "therapy-managing group") Nsimba consulted a practitioner of *bangunza* who conducted a thorough inquiry into Nsimba's background. This prophet, Kuniema, uncovered an old problem, involving a dispute between Nsimba's paternal kin and Nsim-

ba's own clan. It developed that a number of Nsimba's maternal kin were suffering from various mysterious illnesses. The practitioner also mentioned a snake, and Nsimba recalled an incident in which a snake had come into his house during an attack of his illness. Nsimba believed the snake could have been sent by people—perhaps kin—who wished to do him harm. Kuniema suggested a meeting of Nsimba's paternal clan, which was held. The clan collectively asked the forgiveness of those who were suffering from illness, without acknowledging any specific acts of malice or witchcraft.

In spite of these measures, Nsimba's illness grew worse. He suffered from headaches and dizziness; he became delirious and incoherent. He took aspirin for the headaches, but it seemed only to make him worse. He requested an ambulance to take him to the mission where the doctor examined Nsimba but found no physical cause of his illness. Nsimba then consulted a local healer who applied some herbal remedies to treat *mumpompila* a disease thought to be caused by the affection of an elderly woman. After treatment Nsimba said he felt better, but he was unable to return home or to work.

Next Nismba, accompanied by his father, his mother's brother, his mother, and his sister, visited the prophet Luamba Zablon, who concluded that the entire family was sick and prescribed treatment for all of them. Luamba did not attempt to identify family mem-

---

ist healing is not always effective, although if the "successes" are combined with the "inconclusives" (patients who simultaneously got medical treatment), we see that nearly half the patients reported they recovered from their illness. Most of these patients had previously sought medical care without spiritual healing and had not experienced relief from their symptoms. Many patients, even those who did recover from their symptoms, indicated that the cleansing made them feel better.

Finkler pointed out that spiritualist therapy was most effective in treating psychosomatic symptoms, mild psychiatric disorders, simple gynecological disorders, and diseases such as diarrhea without intestinal infection. Other investigators have reported the same finding in other contexts: Nonmedical interventions are most effective where there is a significant psychological or psychosomatic component to the illness. Given the poverty, poor nutrition, and poor sanitary conditions in which the people of Finkler's study population lived, it is small wonder that they had chronic illnesses. Neither biomedical nor spiritualist treatment could affect the underlying physical causes of disease in Hidalgo. Spiritualist treatment, however, seemed more effective in reducing the psychological stress associated with illness. Finkler suggested that bers responsible for Nsimba's illness but treated them in nightly church services with hymns, Bible readings, blessings, laying on of hands, and applications of oil. Feeling better, Nsimba returned to work, only to find that a "bottle fetish" containing various items symbolic of illness had been left in his house anonymously. The bottle contained tobacco, peanuts, and a few blades of grass. The tobacco was interpreted as an intoxicant responsible for the dizziness; the peanuts—normally a sign of fertility—meant he could have no more children; and the cut grass signified that his own life would be cut off.

Now a delegation of churchmen and mission employees visited the old retired nurse who had felt jealous and angry toward Nsimba. The old nurse apologized for his ill will toward Nsimba, and the mission group assured him that they had not meant him harm by retiring him. After this Nsimba's condition improved considerably, and he returned to work part-time. He requested a transfer to another dispensary and in the meantime attended a retreat with mission personnel for a period of meditation and fellowship. Four years went by and Nsimba's transfer never came through. He was relatively free of symptoms until he was promoted to director of the dispensary, when he experienced symptoms similar to those he had had earlier. Janzen's book was written before any further developments in the case. Janzen concluded (1978, 99–100):

[T]he relation of his special professional environment to his illness appeared clear. A person of sensitive character, Nsimba had shown he could barely cope with all the incongruous expectations and duties in the several professional and kinship roles he occupied. After an initial biomedical infection, he persisted in the sick role with a series of diffuse symptoms, enjoying the support of numerous kinsmen acting as his therapy-managing group.

A Western physician might interpret Nsimba's prolonged illness as a case of malingering or hypochondriasis, yet his symptoms and his suffering were real enough. Nsimba was incapacitated, and he did not get better with conventional biomedical treatment. It is noteworthy that Nsimba was himself trained in Western biomedicine, but he apparently saw no contradiction in seeking out alternative forms of therapy for his illness. By combining a set of alternative medical practices and mobilizing the groups of relatives and nonkin focused on his illness, Nsimba found it possible to tolerate the high level of stress he felt in his work. There are many patients in Western doctors' offices whose illness experiences are also constructed from social, psychological, and physical components. By rigidly defining the therapeutic relationship as one-to-one between patient and doctor, Western biomedicine may deprive itself of a powerful weapon for combating illness.

this was so because the "cleansing" ritual of the curers symbolically purified the sufferer, ending the sick role and restoring normal physical and social function.

Finkler stressed that not everyone in her study area resorted to spiritualist healing and not all those who did were "cured." Those who did go to spiritualist temples were more often people who had experienced serious and disruptive medical problems themselves or in their families, such as the death of a family member or a life-threatening disease. Those for whom biomedicine had failed and who suffered an ongoing state of poor health were more likely to seek out and benefit from spiritualist healing. It is noteworthy that

empathy and emotional support were absent, in this curing system, but the healers manipulated symbols that had a powerful effect on some patients.

MENTAL ILLNESS

Anthropologists generally defend a strongly relativistic view of mental illness. The differences in how different societies view mental illness are perhaps greater than in the case of physical disease. The symptoms of mental illness are observed in behavior and speech, and thus the diagnosis and treatment of mental illness

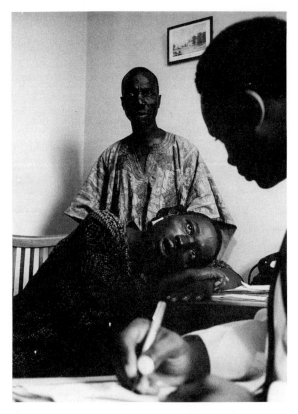

Figure 21.4 *A British-trained Nigerian psychiatrist examines a patient in the presence of a native therapist. The native therapist provides not only his own knowledge of how to treat mental illness but also important information about the patient's cultural background.*

are highly dependent on cultural context (Figure 21.4). Behavior regarded as sick or deviant in one society may not be in another. In the United States, people who hear voices speaking to them may be classified as **schizophrenics**, while other societies honor and respect people with similar experiences. For example, the shamanism practiced among the !Kung San, the Yanomamo, and the Tapirapé is based on the ability to communicate with spirits and souls that are not visible to ordinary people. These visions occur during trance, in dreams, or in drug-induced states (see Chapter 22)—all experiences considered suspect in Western societies.

Western ideas about the nature and definition of mental illness tend to be ambiguous, even contradictory. Biomedicine seeks a physiological basis for illness, but mental illness may not be assignable to any particular physiological basis. Defining an illness as

"mental" brings it under the general heading of "illness" but also stigmatizes it as nonphysical and therefore possibly not a true disease. Although many Westerners profess a clinical view of mental illness as a disorder requiring treatment, they also tend to think of mental illness in terms of "craziness," moral depravity, or even criminal behavior deserving punishment. Mental hospitals, or "insane asylums," have traditionally been the least effective kinds of treatment centers, serving more to separate persons diagnosed as mentally ill from the rest of society than to treat their illness.

Cross-Cultural Concepts of Psychosis

Robert Edgerton, a psychological anthropologist, conducted a study designed to determine the extent of cross-cultural variation in ideas about **psychosis** in four East African tribal populations, the Sebei of Uganda, the Pokot of northwest Kenya, the Kamba of south central Kenya, and the Hehe of Tanzania. The four had comparable economies and degree of Western influence. Each spoke a separate language, although there were some speakers of Swahili in all four groups. Edgerton began by finding a term in the language of each group that corresponded to the Swahili term *kichaa,* which is equivalent to the English idea of severe mental disorder or psychosis.

Some students of the subject had suggested that psychosis in Africa was strongly associated with witchcraft or sorcery. Edgerton asked a sample of adults in each society what caused *kichaa.* Many Hehe and a majority of the Kamba respondents said that witchcraft was the cause of psychosis, but only a small fraction of Pokot and Sebei believed that the two were connected. Members of the latter two groups tended to attribute psychosis to the presence of a worm in the brain.

Edgerton asked a representative sample of adults from each group to describe how psychotics behave (Table 21.3). The results show that each group recognized a diversity of symptoms, but each description tended to cluster around five major symptoms that accounted for more than half of the defining symptoms listed by respondents. At first glance, there seems to be little agreement among the four groups. Many Hehe (40 percent of those questioned) mentioned sleeping and hiding in the bush as psychotic

Table 21.3 Five Most Frequently Mentioned Symptoms of Psychosis

Kamba			Hehe			Pokot			Sebei		
Key	Number	%	Key	Number	%	Key	Number	%	Key	Number	%
1	119	20	2	183	40	4	65	16	1	65	14
3	84	14	1	57	12	3	58	14	5	58	13
5	72	12	5	41	9	8	55	13	4	53	12
11	37	6	3	38	8	6	33	8	6	53	12
4	37	6	4	21	5	9	30	7	7	43	9

Key

Rank	Behavior Described as Psychotic	Rank	Behavior Described as Psychotic	Rank	Behavior Described as Psychotic
1	Goes naked	9	Runs wildly	17	Suicide
2	Sleeps and hides in the bush	10	Wears or collects trash	18	Acts like a child
3	Murder, or attempted murder	11	Destroys property	19	Sexual misconduct
4	Talks nonsense	12	Verbal abuse	20	Climbs trees
5	Serious assault	13	Steals openly	21	Catatonic stupor
6	Shouts, screams, cries, sings	14	Eats and smears dirt	22	Hallucinations
7	Wanders aimlessly	15	Eats and smears feces	23	Compulsive actions
8	Arson	16	Injures self	24	Shaves head and bites self

Note: These are the results of asking a sample of adults from each of four East African tribal societies how a psychotic person behaves.

Source: Edgerton 1966.

behavior, while going naked was the most frequently mentioned symptom among the Kamba and the Sebei. Upon closer examination, however, the definitions of psychotic behavior are quite similar to each other. There is considerable overlap in a list of the five most commonly mentioned symptoms. Edgerton commented that the picture emerging from his survey was "quite similar to the clinical picture seen in [European-directed] mental hospitals throughout East Africa" (1966). Apparently biomedical specialists and ordinary people have similar views of what constitutes psychotic behavior. Edgerton wrote (1966):

[I]t is remarkable how alike these African conceptions of psychosis are to the Western European psychoses, particularly to the constellation of reactions known as schizophrenia. The Africans of these four tribes do not regard a single behavior as psychotic which could not be so regarded in the West.

There are some interesting differences between the kinds of symptoms viewed as psychotic in East Africa and those viewed as such in the West. Hallucinations, often a defining feature of psychosis in the West, were mentioned very rarely (less than 1 percent) in all four

schizophrenia A psychotic disorder in which the patient withdraws from reality and experiences hallucinations and other delusions or distortions of social relationships.

psychosis A general term applied to psychological disorders that cause abnormal behavior.

groups. It may seem paradoxical to Westerners that nudity should be considered psychotic behavior by these groups since most of them wear little clothing. To be naked in East Africa, however, means to expose one's genitals in public. Edgerton commented that, "Even the Pokot, whose men are typically nude, are horrified by nudity among women." Edgerton's survey revealed other differences and similarities among these four groups with respect to the management of psychotic disorders and the likelihood of recovery from psychosis.

Edgerton's work cautions us against regarding mental disease as purely culturally defined. His findings suggest that, beneath the variety of symptoms and treatment, there are cross-culturally valid categories of mental illness. This evidence combines with recent approaches to mental illness, especially schizophrenia, which seek to find a biochemical or hereditary basis for this disorder. Whatever its basis, however, there is little doubt that schizophrenia manifests itself differently under different cultural conditions, and that the management of the disease is highly variable across cultures.

Political Dimensions of Psychiatric Diagnosis and Treatment

The importance of illness in society is not limited to the fact that individuals may suffer or die from an illness. As we saw in the *susto* example, an illness may be a pivotal life crisis during which the community redefines the status of the individual. This may work to the benefit or to the detriment of the individual. We have already seen how experiences that would be defined as psychotic in some places may confer special privileges on a Tapirapé shaman. On the other hand, the epidemic of **acquired immune deficiency syndrome (AIDS)** is creating situations in which infected people are stigmatized and ostracized. For example, parents in several U.S. communities have attempted to keep children out of school who tested positive for the virus that causes the disease; in one case the home of a child with AIDS was burned down by arsonists.

Not only individuals but also the state may use medical diagnosis and treatment as a means of social control. In some cases psychiatric diagnosis and treatment are manipulated for social or political ends. There is an analogy between this and the treatment of accused witches during the Middle Ages in Europe. Certain people—mainly women—were accused of witchcraft and subjected to cruel punishment such as burning at the stake (Figure 21.5) after trials heavily stacked against the accused. Anthropologist Marvin Harris (1974) has suggested that witch-hunts created scapegoats for the civil and religious authorities, allowing them to blame misfortunes on powerless people. It was a cover-up for the mismanagement and exploitation that went on during that tumultuous period of European history. Harris cited a study showing that of 1,258 witches executed in southwestern Germany from 1562 to 1684, 82 percent were women, most of them elderly, lower-class, defenseless housewives. They were tortured and killed, Harris pointed out, not so much for what they did as for what they allegedly thought.

In some developed countries the practice of psychiatry has come under fire as a modern kind of witch-hunt. In the Soviet Union, there are allegations that the state uses the diagnosis of mental illness as a form of political repression. Psychiatric hospitals double as political prisons. Until very recently political dissidents have been confined to mental hospitals for criticizing the human rights record of the state. Some of them have been subjected to painful or abusive programs of "treatment" designed to break down their resolve.

In the West medicine is not generally a means of political repression, but some critics have argued that medical diagnosis may reflect societal biases. Men who commit certain acts are sent to jail, while women who commit the same acts are much more likely to be committed to mental institutions. The prison population of the United States is mostly men, while patients committed to mental institutions are predominantly women. This gender differential may arise from a societal tendency to think of women as less responsible for their actions, more impulsive, and therefore less culpable.

Mental Illness as Myth

Perhaps the most dramatic questions concern the matter of psychiatric diagnosis. D. L. Rosenhan, a professor of psychiatry at Stanford University, organized a small group of people with no history or signs of mental illness to pose as patients at several leading hospi-

Figure 21.5   *The witch-hunts of the 15th through the 17th centuries isolated and destroyed certain elements of the population and diverted attention from political and social problems. Some people believe that psychiatric diagnosis and treatment serve a similar function in modern societies.*

tals in the United States (Rosenhan, 1973). These "pseudopatients" were instructed to ask for help at the hospitals using the same description of symptoms. All the pseudopatients complained of hearing voices that said "empty," "hollow," and "thud." They did not elaborate further on their symptoms and otherwise spoke about their real-life backgrounds. On the basis of this performance, all but one of the eight pseudopatients were admitted to the psychiatric wards of the hospitals. Most of them were diagnosed as suffering from schizophrenia and were treated for their "disorders," usually with psychoactive drugs. They were kept in the hospital for stays ranging from 7 to 52 days.

After the experience, several of the pseudopatients told of being pushed into another world and subjected to many dehumanizing experiences. Patients were often coerced into doing what the hospital staff expected. They observed other patients being beaten or otherwise abused. Any reaction was taken as part of the patient's illness. Many kinds of behavior that

would be regarded as normal in other contexts were treated as abnormal and pathological in the hospital. For example, one pseudopatient who spent time taking notes was described by a nurse as follows: "Patient engages in writing behavior" (Rosenhan 1973, 253). The hospital staff did not interact with the patients as with normal human beings. In one incident, a pseudopatient in the day room of the ward saw a nurse, sitting behind a glass partition in full view of male patients, open her blouse to adjust her brassiere as if the patients were blind.

This brief study had the realism of participant observation in ethnography. It was sharply criticized by some for its use of deception. Nevertheless, the experiment yielded evidence that psychiatric diagnosis in U.S. hospitals is unreliable. Radically different diagnoses were made of patients complaining of the same symptoms, and a variety of different treatments was prescribed.

Rosenhan is concerned with the many thousands of mental patients confined to hospitals on the basis of

acquired immune deficiency syndrome (AIDS)   A disease, usually fatal, transmitted through blood or sexual contact, believed to be caused by a virus that disables the immune system of the body, leaving the afflicted person highly susceptible to infection.

diagnoses like those made of the pseudopatients in his study. In many cases mental patients have been locked up in mental hospitals because of possible harm they might do to themselves or others. In other cases patients have been declared "mentally incompetent" by a court at the request of relatives who seek to gain control over them or their assets. These patients were deprived of their freedom like prisoners, without being accused or tried for any crime. Mental patients may be subjected involuntarily to treatments such as **psychotherapy**, **antipsychotic drugs**, and **electroconvulsive shock.**

Thomas Szasz, a leading critic of modern psychiatric practice and the author of *The Myth of Mental Illness,* has pointed out that many aspects of the doctor-patient relationship are different when it comes to psychiatric medicine (1974). In most therapeutic relationships, the patient enters voluntarily into a relationship with the doctor to achieve a certain goal, such as the setting of a broken bone. In psychiatry, however, a doctor may decide what the patient's goals should be, how the patient should behave, and even whether the patient should be deprived of freedom. Szasz points out that if schizophrenia is really a disease, as most doctors think, it is not treated the same as other diseases. A diabetic, for example, has the right to refuse treatment, even if it brings harm to himself, but a schizophrenic does not. Szasz believes that in the United States and other developed countries there is an alliance between medicine and the state in the regulation of drugs, the determination of who may practice medicine, and the definition of therapy. He believes that physicians lay stress on schizophrenia as a disease to increase their power over people. Szasz's arguments raise troublesome questions about the social and political background of medicine.

Schizophrenia and Social Context

Another psychiatrist, Dr. Richard Warner, has asked another kind of question about schizophrenia: What accounts for differences in rates of recovery? Warner (1985) accepted the idea that schizophrenia is a cross-culturally valid disease category. Schizophrenia distorts the personality of its victims, causing them to "drop out" of society and depend on others for necessities. In developed countries most schizophrenics

never completely recover. They remain impaired and are unable to function as productive members of society. There is evidence, however, that it is possible for many schizophrenics to recover sufficiently for them to resume an independent life and hold a job.

Warner suggested that the course of schizophrenia, as with other diseases, depends on the social, economic, and political setting. Relying on large numbers of epidemiological studies, he showed that recovery rates from schizophrenia vary in different social and political contexts and at different phases of economic cycles. For example, the introduction of drugs, electroconvulsive shock, surgery, and other radical therapies in the United States during the 1930s had little effect on recovery from schizophrenia. In fact, rates of recovery declined during the Great Depression, possibly because of the high rates of unemployment and social stress. Modern antipsychotic drugs introduced in the 1950s are said to have had a major effect on recovery rates (although most specialists say they do not cure the disease but only reduce the severity of its symptoms). However, the rate of occupancy of mental hospitals (relative to the overall population) began to decline even before these drugs were introduced. The major factors contributing to the discharge of psychotic patients into the community were as much political and economic issues, such as the high cost of institutional care, as the new drugs.

Warner's findings concerning recovery rates in Third World countries are particularly interesting. A person suffering from schizophrenia in a nonindustrial setting has a better chance of recovery than in the developed countries. Warner explained this difference in terms of how schizophrenia is understood and managed in non-Western, nonindustrial societies. He suggested that schizophrenics in the Third World are not stigmatized and separated from their families and communities as they tend to be in the West. They have a better chance of returning to a productive economic role in a nonindustrial economy. Healing rituals and therapy-managing groups mobilize broad community support for the social reintegration of psychotics.

Warner suggested that knowledge gained from nonindustrial societies could be usefully employed in the management of schizophrenic disease in developed societies. He suggested a number of ways of integrating psychotics into society as productive members. While these measures will not cure schizophrenia, they could help to turn it from a highly malignant disease with a poor recovery rate into a less disabling condition with a greater likelihood of improvement (Warner 1985). Since modern Western methods of treating schizophrenia are so ineffective, ideas from other traditions deserve to be considered. This is one of many areas in which the anthropological study of medicine can yield important insights.

SUMMARY

- The study of the interaction of sociocultural and biomedical spheres is still at its beginning, but it promises to bring important new insights into disease, healing, and social behavior.
- The insights of medical anthropology include a recognition of the variation in how people think about illness, including classifications, explanatory models, and treatment.
- Personalistic models of disease always point to some factor, such as a witch or an evil spirit, external to the sufferer as the cause of illness. Naturalistic models attribute illness to an imbalance within the body or spirit of the sufferer or the sufferer's social world.
- Illness is not a simple biological event but also a social phenomenon with a culturally defined structure and roles. Certain illnesses occur only within certain cultural boundaries. Culture-bound syndromes illustrate this process.
- The sick role is learned behavior allowing for communication between a sufferer and others around him. The ill person behaves in culturally patterned ways, sensitizing people in the environment to his or her suffering.
- The healer manipulates symbols and prescribes therapy that the sufferer recognizes as powerful and effective.
- The healing process is a kind of social mobilization that typically involves more than just the healer

and the patient. Successful healing is a social and psychological process, not a purely biological matter.
- Shamanistic healing typically involves a specialist who communicates with supernatural beings to discover the cause of the illness and then manipulates powerful symbols to heal the patient.
- Complex societies typically have a variety of healing modalities from which to chose; people often use a mix of approaches.
- Because mental illness is defined in cognitive and behavioral terms, it is especially subject to cultural interpretation. Some investigators believe that the definition of mental illness is entirely culture specific, perhaps simply an extension of the beliefs and norms of the society. Other investigators suggest there are cross-culturally valid categories of mental disease.
- There is debate about the use of psychiatric diagnosis as an instrument of social or political control. Is psychiatric diagnosis a modern kind of witch-hunt? Or is it simply an inexact system of classification? Why are modern methods of therapy for schizophrenia so ineffective? The anthropological study of medicine provides an important approach to these and other questions.

GET INVOLVED

1. Become a volunteer in a local health care facility such as a nursing home, hospital, or hospice. As you interact with the patients, talk to them about what kind of social support groups they have. Do they receive visits regularly from friends or relatives? Are their relatives and friends involved by interacting with caregivers (nurses, doctors, therapists, and so on) or in making decisions about therapy? From their perspective, how important are these interventions to their comfort and recovery? How do the caregivers feel about these matters?

---

psychotherapy The treatment of nervous or mental disorders without drugs.

antipsychotic drugs Drugs that can alleviate some of the symptoms of psychotic behavior.

electroconvulsive shock A treatment in which electric shock is applied to patients with severe psychotic symptoms, depression, and other psychological disorders.

2. Make an inventory of the standard and alternative health facilities in your area, including private physicians, hospitals, physical and other special therapists, HMOs, psychologists, nutritionists, chiropractors, nurses, midwives, *curanderos,* faith healers, and health clubs. Learn what legal requirements are placed on their practices. Try to interview representative practitioners and some of their patients to learn about what choices exist from the perspective of patients. What are the circumstances under which patients seek one form of health care over another? What is the influence of economics, ethnicity, and belief systems?

3. See if you can identify any culture-bound syndromes in populations in your area. You might consider *susto,* migraine, spirit possession, liver disease, obesity, substance abuse, and others. After identifying the group within which this syndrome is common, find a way to get in contact with people who suffer from the syndrome. Remember that you must be extremely careful to respect the privacy and sensitivities of people in these circumstances. Try to get an understanding of how people in the susceptible population conceptualize the syndrome, its causes, and its cure. Collect a number of case studies of people afflicted with the syndrome. How were they diagnosed? What treatment did they seek and from whom? Was the treatment successful?

SUGGESTED READINGS

Eaton, S. Boyd, and Melvin Konner. [1985]. Ancient genes and modern health. *Anthroquest,* 1985.*

Frake, Charles. 1961. Diagnosis of disease among the Subanun of Mindanao. *American Anthropologist* 63:113–132.

Green, Edward C. 1987. The integration of modern and traditional health sectors in Swaziland. In *Anthropological Praxis,* 1987.

Levi-Strauss, Claude. 1963. The sorcerer and his magic. In *Magic, witchcraft and religion,* ed. A. C. Lehmann and J. E. Myers. Mountain View, Calif.: Mayfield, 1989.

Sheets, Payson D. 1987. Dawn of a new stone age in eye surgery. In *Archaeology: Discovering our past,* ed. Robert J. Sharer and Wendy Ashmore. Mountain View, Calif.: Mayfield.*

*This selection is anthologized in *Applying Anthropology,* 2d ed., ed. A. Podolefsky and P. J. Brown (Mountain View, Calif.: Mayfield, 1992).

Economic Shifts and Child Survival in Western Kenya

Miriam Chaiken is an assistant professor of anthropology at Indiana University of Pennsylvania and has engaged in research in Southeast Asia (principally the Philippines) and East Africa. In her work as an applied anthropologist she seeks to identify strategies for improving health and nutrition and ensuring equitable development opportunities for rural Third World communities.

Miriam Chaiken with some Kenyan friends.

UNICEF hired me to help them understand the factors that contributed to high rates of malnutrition and child mortality in western Kenya and to design a program aimed at improving the situation in a culturally appropriate manner.

I began my work in Nyanza Province, western Kenya. Although Mbita Division is located along the shore of Lake Victoria, it is prone to droughts and has poor soils. Agricultural productivity is low and crop failures frequent. Nonetheless agriculture is the primary means of livelihood for most families, and women perform most of the farm labor. Many men fish in Lake Victoria or perform wage labor in the city.

UNICEF knew from earlier surveys that Mbita was suffering from one of the highest rates of child mortality and child malnutrition in Kenya. For example, in South Nyanza District, 216 of every 1,000 children die before their second birthday, while in prosperous Central Province near Nairobi, only 85 of every 1,000 die before age two. Similarly in Nyanza Province 29 percent of children are "stunted" (too short for their age, indicating chronic nutritional stress), while in Central Province 20 percent of children were stunted (UNICEF/Central Bureau of Statistics 1983).

My research indicated that one of the problems that jeopardized the health of children was the practice of feeding babies between 6 and 18 months of age nothing other than a thin watery cereal made of maize flour and water (called *nyuka*) along with breast milk. While breast milk is nutritious and prolonged breastfeeding and commonly practiced in Mbita, these two foods in combination did not provide adequate calories, protein, or fats for the children's increasing nutritional demands. Once children were old enough to eat the foods consumed by the rest of the family, they generally began to recover from the nutritional deprivation, but they were at risk during the period before age two.

In the course of interviews, it became clear that in the past the *nyuka* was prepared differently, usually made with milk instead of water and often with the addition of cow's blood or ghee (clarified butterfat). Clearly the traditional recipe for *nyuka* would have provided a much more nutritionally appropriate food. The current way of making *nyuka* reflected the relative scarcity of milk. In the past the people of Mbita (members of the Luo ethnic group) kept large herds of cattle, and the by-products of their cattle keeping (milk, blood, ghee) were common and essential components in their diets. In the course of the 20th century, cattle keeping became much less feasible for the Luo, due to increased population density; the partitioning of land under colonial administration, which resulted in the loss of grazing lands; and the increased practice of nonagricultural economic activities. These economic shifts decreased the availability of dairy products, thus contributing to malnutrition and high mortality among Mbita children.

The task, then, was to identify other ways of improving the nutritional qualities of *nyuka*. My Kenyan counterparts and I developed a series of recipes for *Nyuka Maber* (Good Porridge), which increased the protein content of the flour used in the porridge by adding dried beans or a common and inexpensive dried fish to the grain before it was ground into flour. We suggested that mothers add a spoonful of sugar and a little cooking oil to each cup of *nyuka* before giving it to the baby, to increase the caloric content and improve the flavor of the porridge. We attempted to introduce knowledge of this recipe by conducting cooking demonstrations for women's groups; discussing it at health centers, mobile clinics, civic functions, and schools; and designing and displaying posters showing how to cook the porridge.

The new recipe for porridge fit well with existing cultural traditions. It was based on the practice of supplementing porridge, which was acceptable in traditional Luo culture; it used a common resource that was affordable by even poor families and was frequently eaten by Mbita people; and it did not require additional preparation time from the women, who were already working very hard. While the problems that confront impoverished areas like Mbita will not be easily remedied, the holistic understanding that anthropologists seek will help identify other strategies for sustainable development.

PART EIGHT

EXPRESSION IN SOCIETY

Throughout this book we have seen that human behavior is strongly dependent on a specific social and cultural context; even in the most seemingly personal realms, people act along lines set down by their society. There are rules governing how people should handle anger and aggression, whom they can marry, what their life choices and chances are going to be. Even the language they learn affects to some degree how they are going to see the world. The same is true in the expression of spiritual ideals, creative impulses, and even individual personality characteristics, areas in which we might expect to find only personal choice and private experience. Viewed from an anthropological point of view, religion, art, and personality are cultural domains that, like law or kinship, are closely tied to specific social contexts.

Part Eight is concerned with how individual impulses, aspirations, and traits are shaped and channeled by society into religious, artistic, and other forms and how these forms support and reinforce social structure. Chapter 22 looks at religion, exploring some of the elements of religious experience and several theories about the role of religion in society. Chapter 23 considers how art and artists play different roles in society and how art is related to social organization and complexity. Chapter 24 looks at the phenomenon of cultural personality, the range of personality traits selected and approved within a specific cultural context.

With these chapters, we complete the journey taken in Discovering Anthropology. It has led us down many paths and revealed many facts and ideas about humankind. Perhaps most significantly, it has shown that the range of human variation is great but not unlimited. This is because human thought and behavior are patterned along lines set down by factors over which we have little or no control—our biological and cultural inheritance. But knowledge of these limits should not be used to justify acceptance of the status quo. On the contrary, the thrust of this book has been to show the extraordinary plasticity of human thought and action. Anthropological knowledge can liberate us from fatalism and provide us with the means to understand and act on social conditions. By studying the range of possible human adaptations in both the past and the present, we gain the opportunity to make a difference in the future of humankind.

*Elements of both Christianity and in-
digenous Mayan beliefs are exhibited
in many Mayan rituals. Here a Mayan
"Sajorin" performs a ritual in
Chichicastenango, Guatemala.*

22

RELIGION AND SOCIAL STRUCTURE

▲▲▲

eligion and spirituality play a role in every society. Many people devote much of their lives to religion, and some are prepared to die for it. Many define their identity in terms of religion, especially in plural societies that encompass different religions, languages, and nationalities. Religious traditions also formulate answers to important philosophical questions, such as what knowledge is certain, what the purpose of life is, and what happens after we die. Just as they define what is true, religious traditions often brand other ideas as untrue or evil.

WHAT IS RELIGION?

Religion is a cultural domain involving ritual practice and belief in the **supernatural**. Religion selects some area of experience and defines it as **sacred** in contrast to the **profane**. In each tradition, statements about the sacred are accepted as true without any testing. Sacred knowledge is beyond question. This is why *faith* is sometimes taken as a synonym for *religion*. Science is different from religion because, in science, all statements, theories, and beliefs are subject to doubt and testing, while in religion, they are not.

This definition of religion is very broad and deliberately omits reference to features that many people assume are part of religion. For example, the definition does not refer to belief in a god or supreme being. There are many traditions that worship a single god, others that worship several gods, and still others that worship no gods at all. The Yanomamo, for example, talk about certain mythical animals, such as the jaguar, in their lore. Under the influence of hallucinogenic drugs a shaman can make contact with spirits known as *hekura*. These tiny humanlike beings can be sent on errands to cure sickness in the village or to devour the souls of enemies. No one prays to the *hekura,* nor are they all-powerful. They were not responsible for the creation of the world in the Yanomamo scheme of things.

Another common idea is that religions involve organized worship. While this is often true, many religions lack formal structure, and ritual is left up to the initiative of the individual. The !Kung San, for example, usually practice shamanism only when someone is ill. Many religions, like that of the !Kung San, lack churches or temples, priests, images of gods, or a formal **liturgy.**

Although it is a common theme, not all religions set forth a moral code that defines good and evil. While ideas about morality and ethics are present in all societies, they are not necessarily encoded in religious ideas. Neither Yanomamo nor !Kung San religious tradition has much to say about good and evil. In short, many ideas considered integral parts of Western religious traditions are missing in other traditions and vice versa.

What other features are distinctive to religious belief and practice yet still cross-culturally valid? It is helpful to distinguish between emic and etic aspects. An etic focus on religion—one framed in the observers' categories—focuses on how religion is enacted, that is, on ritual performances. Ritual behavior is distinguished from ordinary behavior because it is highly stylized, repetitive, and performed in regular cycles. Rituals are stylized in terms of body movements, colors, songs, special texts, or objects (Figure 22.1). Ritual performances vary, but certain details, such as the wine and the wafer at a Roman Catholic mass (Figure 22.2), are unchanging.

By this criterion alone, however, it would be hard to distinguish religious behavior from what goes on at football games, in courtrooms, or on the dance floor at a party. No definition of religion would be complete without reference to the *meaning* of ritual performance. The meaning of the symbolic elements of ritual cannot be ascertained through etic techniques. From the actors' (emic) point of view, ritual is distinguished by a concern with details, such as reciting a prayer properly or wearing the correct clothing. But these details may have no practical importance; they are primarily symbolic in value. In the final analysis, what distinguishes religion is that religious symbols encode meanings for its practitioners that refer to the supernatural or to unknown aspects of nature.

Religion, along with art, is often treated as **expressive culture.** The expressive side of culture is linked to artistic, emotional, and cognitive domains. It can be contrasted with the technological and economic side of culture, which is linked to production, reproduction, and exchange. Religious acts take ordinary events and ideas and add a new dimension to them. Bronislaw Malinowski, a pioneer in modern ethnographic research, saw religion as a means of making

Figure 22.1   *Religious practices typically involve the performance of rituals that link human beings with the realm of the supernatural. These Buddhist monks in prayer represent just one form such rituals can take.*

experience intelligible. He was interested in the capacity of religion to take ordinary elements of life and give them new meaning. In this view ritual is a kind of communication in which symbolic meanings are attached to certain acts, objects, and sequences.

In many traditions, everyday items can assume a special symbolic meaning. Consider the passover **seder** celebrated by Jewish families each year. At this ritual meal, people relax and make a point of reclining on pillows at the table. During the meal a service is

---

religion   A cultural domain involving ritual practice and belief in the supernatural.

supernatural   A force or existence that transcends the natural order.

sacred   Pertaining to a sphere of experience or activity that is defined as holy and treated in a reverential manner.

profane   In the ordinary or nonsacred realm of experience or activity.

liturgy   A formal, public religious ritual that is seen as a form of service to the supernatural.

expressive culture   Beliefs and behaviors—found in the domains of art, music, dance, or religion—that convey meaning and are not directly tied to production, reproduction, or exchange.

seder   The ceremonial meal and service celebrated on the first night of the Jewish festival of Passover, whose liturgy recalls the exodus of the Jews from Egypt under the leadership of Moses.

Figure 22.2 *The sacrament of the Eucharist, also known as Holy Communion, is performed in the same way in Roman Catholic churches all over the world. The church carefully prescribes and controls the details of the ritual, including the setting, the special vestments and objects, and the behaviors of both priest and communicants. Here, a priest offers a communion wafer to a worshiper in a Catholic church in Beijing.*

held following a book called the Haggadah, a prayerbook and narrative of the flight of the Israelites from Egypt. On the table are found a number of common items, such as horseradish, salt water, and a hard-boiled egg, together with traditional festive foods and wine. During the service, these familiar items acquire special meanings. For example, the horseradish, or "bitter herbs," symbolizes the bitterness of slavery, and the wine, food, and reclining are symbolic of the luxuries of freedom. The salt water represents the tears shed by the Hebrews when they were slaves in Egypt, and the egg is a reminder of sacrifice and a symbol of rebirth (Fredman 1981). Religious traditions also use uncommon or special symbols, such as rosary beads, the crucifix, or the smiling Buddha.

ELEMENTS OF RELIGION

As we have seen, religion has to be defined broadly if the definition is to accommodate beliefs and behaviors in all societies. Not all religions have a supreme being, a formal organization, or a set of moral prescriptions. In this section we consider two elements that seem to be universally present in religion: ritual practices associated with life transitions and belief in the supernatural.

Rites of Passage

Nearly all societies celebrate rituals around certain transitions of life. Ritualized events may include birth, puberty, betrothal, induction into the military, marriage, pregnancy, childbirth (for women), fatherhood (for men), retirement, death, and other "life crises." Religious ideas are superimposed on such moments, perhaps as an expression of gratitude for attaining a new stage, often as a reminder of obligations associated with a new status. When a ritual focuses primarily on a life transition, it is called a **rite of passage**. Rites of passage sanctify aspects of the new phase and certify to the community that an individual has attained a certain status. Malinowski interpreted initiation rites as follows (1948, 40):

> From a natural event, it makes a social transition; to the fact of bodily maturity it adds the vast conception of entry into manhood [or womanhood] with its duties, privileges, responsibilities, above all with its knowledge of tradition and the communion with sacred things and beings. There is thus a creative element in the rites of religious nature. The act establishes not only a social event in the life of the individual but also a spiritual metamorphosis, both associated with the biological event but transcending it in importance and significance.

Figure 22.3   *U.S. Army recruits enter a state of liminality during basic training at boot camp. Stripped of their personal identity, they are subjected to a grueling routine designed to prepare them to take on a new identity, that of American soldiers.*

Death is a rite of passage of vital concern in virtually every religious tradition. Religion interprets death to the living, explains or rationalizes its occurrence, and helps people face its inevitability. Different societies stress different transitions. Christenings, circumcisions, confirmations, first communions, Bar Mitzvahs, fraternity hazings, bridal and baby showers, weddings, and graduation ceremonies are rites of passage familiar to Westerners.

Liminality.   Anthropologist Victor Turner analyzed rituals using the idea of **liminality**, a period of ambiguity during a person's transition between one status and another (Turner 1967). Army boot camp is a good example of a liminal state. The military strips inductees of their former identity by separating them from friends and family; cutting their hair short; bathing, delousing, and marching them naked through a medical examination; and finally giving them identical uniforms (Figure 22.3). A new recruit doesn't even have medals or insignia to distinguish him from the others, because he doesn't yet belong to any unit and has no specialty or accomplishments.

In the Roman Catholic religion, the dead pass through a liminal stage. Shortly after death, the soul of a person who has not committed unpardonable sins awaits purification in a state known as **purgatory**. Purification is achieved through punishment and suffering involving searing flames. The living may assist by praying for the soul's release from purgatory.

Seclusion.   **Seclusion**, or temporary isolation from society, is a practice associated with life transitions in many societies. Seclusion symbolically removes an individual from the community, reinforcing the illusion that the old person has gone away and a new one

---

rite of passage   A ritual that focuses on the transition from one stage of life (birth, marriage, age grade membership, death) to another.

liminality   A ritual state of existence—usually temporary—between accepted social statuses, marked by ambiguity involving the suspension of some social norms.

purgatory   In Roman Catholicism, a state or place where a person's soul is purified after death through suffering before being allowed to enter heaven.

seclusion   The practice of isolating persons about to undergo a change of social status, often creating a state of liminality.

Figure 22.4 *Ritual seclusion of a Mehinaku adolescent. Among the Mehinaku, both boys and girls are secluded for months at a time behind special partitions in their homes. During seclusion, they must obey strict rules concerning diet and other activities. As in many other cultures, emergence from seclusion signifies the assumption of a new social status with new rights and responsibilities.*

has returned in his or her place. In the Mehinaku village in central Brazil, boys normally undergo seclusion for several years, starting at puberty. Ethnographer Thomas Gregor described the seclusion of one boy, Amairi. Before puberty, Amairi was a typical Mehinaku lad, adventurous, with few responsibilities, free to roam the village and the surrounding forest. At 12 he had begun a sexual affair with a girl, Uluwalu. When his father learned of this, he partitioned a small section of his house and strung Amairi's hammock inside (Figure 22.4); then he sent for Amairi and said (Gregor 1977, 226):

> "Don't you play around in here, or the Master of the Medicines will get you. Never have sexual relations with Uluwalu, unless you want to get paralyzed by the medicine spirit. Don't sleep late or go out before dusk. Make baskets and arrows; think about wrestling. Do this and you will become a champion."

During his long seclusion, Amairi underwent periodic **scarification**, scratches on his legs made with sharp dogfish teeth, to make him stronger. He was given a bland diet of manioc bread and unflavored cooked fish. Other foods were considered dangerous. Even though he had been cut off from most social contacts, he was in the constant company of the Master of the Medicine, a spirit who prescribed a potent herbal drink to him. Amairi knew that he was highly vulnerable to witchcraft during this time.

Amairi's first reaction to his seclusion was one of pride and careful attention to the rules. Later he became belligerent, even hysterical. Finally he became resigned to isolation and spent many hours asleep in his hammock or staring off into space, only intermittently working on handicrafts. Five months went by before Amairi was allowed out of seclusion during daylight hours. He spread oil on his skin, put on a feather headdress, and went out for his first wrestling match, an important ritual sport among the Mehinaku. After this event, the rigor of seclusion was relaxed, but Amairi still had to avoid being seen on his occasional outings. His diet was also changed to include small amounts of sweet porridge and food prepared with pepper and salt (Gregor 1977, 226–238). Amairi gained full freedom only after nearly three years.

The Mehinaku also prescribe seclusions, though shorter than Amairi's, for newborn children with their mothers, boys after the ear-piercing ceremony (at age 7 to 12), adolescent girls after their first menstruation, newly widowed spouses, novice shamans, and others at various transitional times (Gregor 1977). A Mehinaku might spend as much as eight years of life in seclusion. The purpose of seclusion is to protect the person against harm from witches or other sources and to allow her or him to gain strength. Withdrawal from everyday life also forces a person to think a great deal about his or her social role. The Mehinaku believe that if a person violates seclusion, he or she will not develop properly.

Seclusion, like other liminal states, provides an opportunity for learning to take place. In normal everyday life, a person occupies a certain status to which certain rules and understandings are attached. For example, a young Mehinaku boy is expected to limit his sexual adventures, but is otherwise allowed to live a carefree life of fun and games. As he grows older, he is expected to assume a role in the public life of the village, to have a voice in the men's house, to participate in wrestling matches and other ritual activities, and to assume the sexual role of an adult. During the liminal stage of seclusion, the rules of boyhood are

Figure 22.5 *The veil worn by the bride during this Hasidic wedding symbolically secludes her from the eyes of her betrothed. At the end of the ceremony, the groom removes the veil and kisses the bride, symbolically initiating the physical or sexual part of their relationship.*

suspended but the rules of manhood do not yet apply. Industriousness (in craft production) is stressed and sexual desires must be held in check during this period. The liminal stage produces an intense period of learning and reorientation in which ideas are transmitted through a symbolic medium. In the case of the Mehinaku, scarification, taboos on food, sex, and body adornment, and seclusion itself are symbolic vessels through which new ideas may be communicated. For all practical purposes, a new individual emerges at the end of seclusion.

Seclusion is also common in other societies. In the West many traditions require that a bride not see the groom on their wedding day until the moment of the ceremony. This seclusion is symbolized in many traditions by the bridal veil, which cannot be removed until near the end of the ceremony (Figure 22.5). In some European traditions the bride is literally isolated from her future husband for weeks or months before their wedding.

Ordeals. **Ordeals** are painful or humiliating experiences also involved in liminality. North American college fraternities practice "hazing," a difficult ordeal

that is said to create a sense of brotherhood among the boys who go through it together. In Brazil a middle-class girl who becomes engaged is invited by her female friends to a *cha de panela,* a kind of bridal shower. After making gifts of housewares, the guests strip the bride naked and make lewd jokes in the form of "advice" about how to behave with her future husband.

The Walbiri' aborigines of Australia circumcise boys at the first appearance of pubic hair (Meggitt 1962, 281). The boy is taken to a temporary camp, away from the main camp; from that moment on the boy is ritually isolated from contact with all women. The first major ceremony lasts all night, during which the men sing songs with important moral messages for the young. As the sun rises, the boy's mother and his father's sister are allowed briefly to weep over him, caress him, and buck up his courage. The boy is taken on a long tour of Walbiri territory, during which various items of naturalistic and supernatural interest (men's knowledge) are pointed out to him.

Upon his return another ceremony reenacts the kangaroo myth, an important charter of Walbiri society. The boy is warned never to reveal the information

---

scarification Cutting the skin for religious or beautification purposes, with the intent of leaving scars.

ordeal A rite of passage that involves the infliction of pain or discomfort.

to children or women on pain of death. For several nights running, dancing goes on in which the women weep over the boy and bid him to have courage and then are forcibly expelled from the area. Each time the women approach the boy with maternal comfort, they are driven away angrily by men. The ethnographer's description continues:

> At about one a.m. . . . the brothers rouse all the sleepers for the next stage in the ceremonies. Several of the brothers, who hold boomerangs (the male badge), stand before them and shout rhythmically as the men chant narga songs and beat the ground with their shields. The novice remains in his bed. . . . The women hold digging sticks (the female badge) and dance behind the men. . . . The boy's own mother dances with a firestick held aloft. The fire is his "life" and must burn throughout the night. The mother re-lights the stick on the next evening and finally extin-guishes it when the lad is circumcised, when he dies only to be reborn. . . .
>
> The next night, after many ritual preparations, the boy is led to a ritual bed; his chin is singed with a burning stick to encourage beard growth. The women pay him a final farewell. The boy is struck with poles and intimidated by harsh, guttural singing and dancers decorated like kangaroos. Finally, as sev-eral dancers hold the boy down, the circumciser stretches out the foreskin of his penis and slices it with a few quick strokes of a stone knife. [pp. 294, 303–304]

In these painful and terrifying moments, a boy "dies" and a man is "born." The separateness of women in the ceremony is particularly significant. A boy learns sacred lore during circumcision, which stresses his masculine identity and his distinctiveness from women.

Supernatural or Extranormal Experience

It is often noted that religion involves supernatural events, states, and beings. Not every abnormal experi-ence is a religious experience. In Western society supernatural experiences are those that are sharply distinguished from ordinary everyday consciousness. Some early theories of religion suggested that religious ideas originated in dreams, trance, or hypnotic or drugged states in which fantastic things occurred that had to be explained and rationalized in some manner.

While this theory has been rejected, supernatural events are common in most if not all religious tra-ditions. Consider the following Bible story (Exod. 3:1–6):

> Now Moses was keeping the flock of his father-in-law, Jethro . . . and he led his flock to the west side of the wilderness, and came to Horeb the mountain of God. And the angel of the Lord appeared to him in a flame of fire out of the midst of a bush; and he looked, and lo, the bush was burning, yet it was not consumed. [Then] God called to him out of the bush, "Moses, Moses! . . . I am the God of your father, the God of Abraham, the God of Isaac, and the God of Jacob." And Moses hid his face for he was afraid to look at God.

God's voice continued to speak from the middle of the burning bush, commanding Moses to lead the Israel-ites, who were enslaved by Egypt, out of slavery into "a land flowing with milk and honey." At first Moses was afraid to accept the mission that God had com-manded. Eventually, he was persuaded, and he went on to lead the Israelites out of Egypt. In this parable, something occurred beyond the boundaries of ordi-nary experience. Coming upon a burning bush, one would expect the leaves to be consumed and branches to be charred by the fire, and one hardly expects a voice to emerge from the middle of the flames. The extraordinary nature of these events gives this story its power. If God had spoken to Moses through another human being, the commands would not have seemed so compelling to Moses or to us.

At some level most religions accept the validity of extranormal or supernatural events. These may be incorporated as mythic past events retold in sacred writings, or they may constantly recur in the context of curing, divination (prophecy), and other rituals. Many religious traditions in Africa, Asia, and the Americas rely on **trance** to put worshipers or special-ists in touch with supernatural beings. One example common in North America is "speaking in tongues," which occurs when a Christian receives the holy spirit. In some traditions, extranormal experiences are induced by drugs such as alcohol, marijuana, peyote, or other **hallucinogens**. Other religions shun any use of mind-altering drugs.

In a memorable description of a drug-induced supernatural experience, ethnographer Michael J. Harner described a curing session retold by a Jivaro

Figure 22.6 *A Jivaro shaman prepares* avahuasca, *a hallucinogenic brew used to transport him into the "real" world of spirit animals and helpers. There he will gain knowledge that will help him perform his duties, including healing, in this world.*

shaman of eastern Ecuador shortly after drinking a tea made from the *Banisteriopsis caapi* vine, known to contain powerful hallucinogens (Figure 22.6).

> He had drunk, and now he softly sang. Gradually, faint lines and forms began to appear in the darkness, and the shrill music of the *tsentsak,* the spirit helpers, arose around him. The power of the drink fed them. He called, and they came. First, pangi, the anaconda, coiled about his head, transmuted into a crown of gold. Then, wampang, the giant butterfly, hovered above his shoulder and sang to him with its wings. Snakes, spiders, birds, and bats danced in the air above him. On his arms appeared a thousand eyes as his demon helpers emerged to search the night for enemies.
>
> The sound of the rushing water filled his ears, and listening to its roar, he knew he possessed the power of *Tsungi,* the first shaman. Now he could see. Now he could find the truth. He stared at the stomach of the sick man. Slowly it became transparent like a shallow mountain stream, and he saw within it, coiling and uncoiling, makanchi, the poisonous serpent, who had been sent by the enemy shaman. The real cause of the illness had been found. [Harner 1968]

Harner also details remarkable parallels in the structure and content of the vision experiences of different people scattered across South America without any direct contact with each other. Many users of *Banisteriopsis* report visions of jaguars and snakes, both of which are common throughout lowland South America and are respected and feared predators. While the commonality of the drug experiences may be due to the common environment, Harner suggests that these parallels are due in part to the nature of the drugs themselves. The drug experience certainly creates a heightened sense of anxiety and drama, which may well affect the structure and content of religious traditions.

In Mesoamerica, anthropologist Marlene Dobkin de Rios noted that ancient Mayan art is frequently decorated with motifs depicting mushrooms, frogs, and water lilies (Figure 22.7). She suggested that these items were commonly depicted because they yielded **psychotropic substances**, which may have been used by priests and shamans in ceremonial events (Dobkin de Rios 1974). This is not to say that religion is built up out of dreams, fantasies, and drug-induced visions; rather, these may be important elements in some religious traditions.

Religions vary according to the kinds of supernatural experiences they accept as authentic. The formal theology and everyday worship services of the major

---

trance An altered state of consciousness entered for the purpose of getting power or information from supernatural sources.

hallucinogens Drugs that induce visions.

psychotropic substances Drugs that induce an altered state of consciousness.

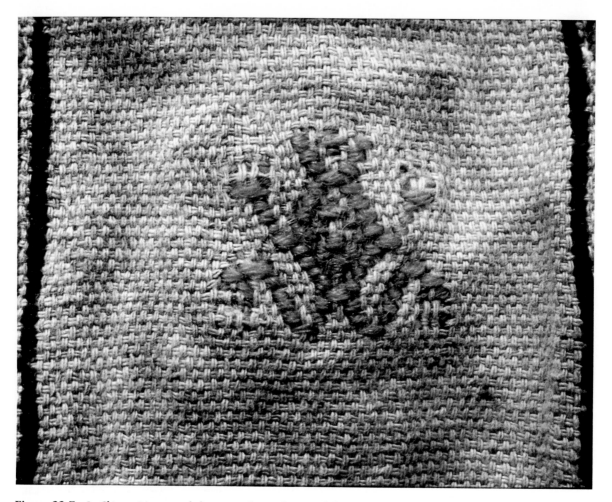

Figure 22.7 *In Chiapas Mayan mythology, a toad is said to guard the entrance to the Earthlord's cave. The actual toad, depicted here in a brocaded design, exudes a powerful hallucinogen from glands on its skin.*

Western religions (Judaic and Christian) leave little room for supernatural events, although they acknowledge that miracles occur. The most extraordinary events, such as the resurrection of Jesus Christ or the parting of the Red Sea, are thought to have occurred in the distant past. However, some modern Western religious groups regularly seek visions, engage in trance, and attempt to perform miracles such as "faith healing." Other religions, such as the shamanistic religions described here and in Chapters 18 and 21, affirm the imminence of spirits and the possibility of supernatural events.

The Origin of Religion: Psychological Approaches

Religion has been part of human experience for a very long time. How did it originate? Some theorists have attempted to explain religion in psychological terms. Sigmund Freud, the founder of psychoanalysis, proposed that religion has its roots in the helplessness people feel in the face of the powerful forces of nature. To control these feelings, people create the illusion of domination over nature by suggesting that natural events, such as storms and earthquakes, and natural objects, such as the sun and moon, are guided by humanlike intelligence. According to Freud, gods are projections of a boy's impotent rage upon discovering that his father alone has sexual rights to his mother. This image of the "primal father," present in the frightening events of nature, is the prototype for god. "Religion," wrote Freud (1928), is "an infantile obsessional neurosis." Presumably humanity would one day outgrow the need for it.

Freud's speculations about religion are heavily male-centered and based on very little valid knowledge about religion in non-Western societies. Many religions do not embody the notion of gods as do the more familiar world religions, Christianity, Islam, and Judaism. The idea that religion expresses a neurotic world view is based on Freud's personal and cultural bias. It fails to consider the complexity and subtlety of religious beliefs in technologically simple societies.

Bronislaw Malinowski also tried to explain religion in terms of human needs. Instead of basing his theory on dramas of childhood, however, he looked to what he considered to be a basic human need to understand and control the environment. Malinowski argued that **magic**, science, and religion all were present in simple societies. Magic is the manipulation of supernatural symbols to achieve specific results. Using data from his classic study of the Trobriand Islands of Melanesia, where he spent years in ethnographic research, Malinowski described the construction and use of canoes to illustrate the role of these three elements. Master canoe builders used scientific knowledge concerning buoyancy, leverage, and equilibrium (Malinowski 1948, 34). The need for magic arose only when something people depended on was beyond their knowledge and control. For example, Malinowski pointed out that magic rituals were not practiced before trips to inland lagoons, where the waters were always calm and the danger slight, but they *were* practiced before fishing trips to the open sea, where there was considerable danger. Magic, for Malinowski, came from the need to assert control over the uncontrollable, such as the weather, crop pests, and fishing luck (Box 22.1). Malinowski did not argue that magic

actually worked, but he pointed out that it did help relieve anxiety and organize the flow of work.

Religion, in Malinowski's view, consists of rituals that are performed without a particular purpose in mind, while magic is performed to achieve a particular goal. The function of religious ritual is the adaptation of people to the limitations of their existence. Other theorists have attempted to explain religion more in terms of its role in society; we consider these theories, along with the broader social context in which religion is set, in the next section.

RELIGION AND ITS SOCIAL CONTEXT

Different theorists have proposed different ways of understanding the relationship between religion and society. We consider here the theories of religion first offered by three pioneers of social science, Émile Durkheim, Karl Marx, and Max Weber.

Religion as Society Worshiping Itself: Durkheim

For more than 100 years social scientists have recognized that religion reflects and expresses social organization. Perhaps the best-known writer on religion and society was Émile Durkheim, who is regarded as the founder of modern sociology. Durkheim was fascinated with non-Western religions and wrote a great deal on the topic, including the book *The Elementary Forms of Religious Life* (1912). Like other 19th-century "comparative sociologists," Durkheim thought that society tended to evolve from a simple to a complex form. Simple societies were organized "mechanically," as many similar parts with similar functions and activities, while complex societies were organized "organically," with different parts playing different functions in a "division of labor."

To Durkheim, the simplest contemporary societies offered some insight into the origin of religion. He

---

magic   A ritual practice intended to manipulate the supernatural to achieve a specific result.

BOX 22.1

Baseball Magic

Before becoming an anthropologist, George Gmelch was a professional athlete. He found a striking illustration of Malinowski's theory of magic in American baseball (Gmelch 1971). He pointed out that in baseball there are three basic skills: hitting, pitching, and fielding. Of these, fielding is fairly reliable; fielders are successful more than 97 percent of the time. Pitching and batting, on the contrary, are highly subject to chance and random variation. Batters get hits only about a quarter of the times they are at bat. There is also considerable room for chance to affect a pitcher's success. A pitcher can turn in a great performance and still lose the game. Gmelch drew on his personal experience in baseball and also conducted interviews with players. He found that there was widespread use of magical rituals by baseball players. "One of the most popular is tagging a particular base when leaving and returning to the dugout each inning. Tagging second base on the way to the outfield is habitual with some players" (Gmelch 1971).

Gmelch cited examples of players following a variety of rituals to keep a hitting streak going. A player on a streak would eat the same foods at the same time each day, take the same route to the ball park, wear the same clothes, and carry certain good luck charms. Pitchers observed rituals religiously when they were playing well:

Dennis Grossini, former Detroit farmhand, practiced the following ritual on each pitching day for the first three months of a winning season. First, he arose from bed at exactly 10:00 A.M. . . . . At 1:00 P.M. he went to the nearest restaurant for two glasses of iced tea and a tuna fish sandwich. . . . In the clubhouse, he changed into the sweat shirt and jock he wore during his last winning game and one hour before the game, he chewed a wad of Beechnut chewing tobacco. (Gmelch 1971)

Players also observed such taboos as not allowing bats to be crossed, not stepping on chalked lines, and never, never mentioning that a no-hitter was in progress, a taboo scrupulously observed by sportscasters as well. Players were also careful to avoid numbers they considered unlucky on their uniforms and sometimes insisted on changing uniforms at midseason to get a new number if their game was not going well.

Gmelch searched in vain for examples of magic associated with fielding. He found only a single example, a shortstop who was undergoing severe difficulties with his fielding. All the many other examples of magic pertained to hitting and pitching. The magical practices associated with baseball are similar in form to those found in Trobriand fishing.

---

noted that all societies distinguish between sacred and profane realms, which are kept rigidly apart in thought and action. Durkheim paid a great deal of attention to Australian aboriginal **totems**, generally a species of plant or animal taken as the symbolic ancestor of a clan. In his view, the totem and the group it represented were one and the same: "The god of the clan, the totemic principle, can therefore be nothing else than the clan itself, personified and represented to the imagination under the visible form of the animal or vegetable which serves as totem" (Durkheim 1961, 236).

According to Durkheim, when people worship totems, idols, or gods, they are actually worshiping society itself along with its structure. The recommendations of religion are only the recommenda-

society, encoded in a religious form. Although many questions and objections to Durkheim's approach can be raised, the idea that religion is society worshiping itself has given rise to many intriguing interpretations of religion.

Patrons and Patron Saints in Brazil. In 1966 the author spent three months in a Catholic **pilgrimage** center in northeastern Brazil (Gross 1971; Figure 22.8). A pilgrimage is a ritual journey made to a sacred shrine. The core of the Brazilian pilgrimage is a ritual prayer known as the *promessa*, or "vow." When a person is in dire need of assistance yet feels helpless, he or she may direct a prayer to a particular saint such as Saint Anthony, to the Virgin Mary in one of her many forms, or to *Bom Jesus* ("Our Lord Jesus"). In the

Figure 22.8 *The pilgrimage to Bom Jesus da Lapa, undertaken by thousands of people every year in northeastern Brazil, involves seeking favors from Jesus and repaying favors previously sought. The relationship between the pilgrims and Jesus mirrors the relationship between poor clients and wealthy patrons in Brazilian society. Here, a boy leads a blind pilgrim past the line waiting to approach the altar. This pilgrim's vow was to walk on his knees from the edge of the plaza to the church.*

prayer, the pilgrim makes a vow to repay the saint if the favor is bestowed. Requests commonly involve curing the sick, settling lovers' quarrels, helping someone abstain from alcohol, or preventing an accident from happening. Pilgrims take their vows very seriously and nearly all of the tens of thousands of pilgrims who annually visit the cavern where the image of Bom Jesus is found say they came to "pay a *promessa.*" Not paying a promessa is unthinkable; in some cases people visit the shrine to pay a promessa for someone else who made a vow but was unable to repay it.

The relationship between saint and pilgrim in northeastern Brazil can be compared to social relations between people of unequal rank. These relations are often described as patron-clientage (see Chapter 18), a particularistic relationship between individuals. The patron is a controller of resources, perhaps a landowner, employer, shopkeeper, or government official. The client is a person, perhaps a peasant or urban worker, with few resources and inadequate means for securing his or her needs through the systems of justice, health care, or credit. Brazilian etiquette prescribes that the client approach a patron, hat in hand, and humbly beg for whatever he or she needs. Often patrons give credit, either by advancing wages or merchandise or by helping to finance farm equipment. This creates dependency, which holds the loyalty of the client. The patron is free to give or withhold whatever is asked and is usually not blamed or resented if he or she does not meet the client's need. Whatever is granted, however, is repayable in some form, such as household services, cheap labor, or voting the way the patron wants.

People of low rank in Brazil carefully preserve their reputations as payers of debts. Credit and debt are so

---

totem A plant, animal, or object that is viewed as the sacred representative of a kin group.

pilgrimage Ritual journey to a holy place.

important to survival and advancement that they are major themes in everyday life. Someone who does not pay off debts ceases to be creditworthy and becomes vulnerable to chance events such as disease. It is noteworthy that the promessa—the central ritual of the Brazilian pilgrimage—symbolically reinforces the importance of paying debts to powerful superiors. The pilgrimage provides an arena in which this kind of contractual relationship can be rehearsed in a sacred domain. While some Christians might feel odd describing a religious observance as a "transaction," the pilgrims to Bom Jesus da Lapa will tell anyone who asks that they have come to Lapa to "pay a debt to Bom Jesus."

Christmas in Middletown. While Durkheim's view that religion is society worshiping itself might not win universal agreement, there is little doubt that social values and religious values are intertwined in many ways. Sociologist Theodore Caplow recently revisited "Middletown," a small city in the midwestern United States which had been studied 50 years earlier by W. Lloyd Warner. One of Caplow's findings was that Christmas had been **secularized**; its religious aspects had been diminished while family aspects had been emphasized. Analyzing the Christmas-related behavior of Middletown families, Caplow and his colleagues (1982, 1983) formulated the following rules:

> The tree rule: Married couples with children of any age should put up Christmas trees in their homes. Unmarried persons with no living children should not put up Christmas trees. Unmarried parents (widowed, divorced, or adoptive) may put up trees but are not required to do so.

> The giving rule: You must give (individually or jointly) at least one Christmas gift every year to your mother, father, sons, and daughters; to the current spouses of these persons; and to your own spouse. Gifts to grandparents and grandchildren are equally obligatory if they live in your community. Christmas gifts to your brothers and sisters are not required, but if a sibling gives you a gift, you must reciprocate.

> The symbolic segregation rule: Christmas themes may be represented by religious symbols, such as the manger and the Wise Men, or by secular symbols, such as Santa, the elves, and various decorations. Never mix these two. Rudolph the Red-nosed Reindeer does not visit the Christ Child.

Caplow also detailed a series of "scaling rules" which summarized how people determined the value of a gift depending on their relationship to the recipient. The first scaling rule, for example, stated that "A spousal relationship should be more valuable than any other for both husband and wife, but the husband may set a higher value on it than the wife" (Caplow 1982).

These rules may not be the same over the entire culture area of the United States, and some people may not follow them even in Middletown. But their existence in Middletown provides evidence of the intertwining of religious and secular values, in this case kinship. Rather than suggesting that Christmas has been secularized, however, it may be more accurate to observe that kinship has been ritualized. Americans invest a great deal of time, money, and care in the selection and preparation of Christmas gifts and other Christmas rituals. Most of these revolve around the family, suggesting a great concern for family relationships even while we hear that the American family is disintegrating. Is the secularization of Christmas a form of compensation for the disintegration of the family? Or could it be the **sacralization** of values that have not diminished at all?

Secular Rituals. Ritual forms may invade even the most secular environments. Ethnologist Conrad Kottak (1978) described the McDonald's Restaurant chain as a kind of American secular temple. He pointed out the ritualistic aspects of the decor (the golden arches, reminiscent of religious architecture), the menu, and the slogans and jingles used in advertising. The repetitive stability of McDonald's menu and its slowness to change can also be compared to a religious liturgy. One never sees anyone worshiping in a McDonald's, but it is remarkable to note that most McDonald's customers scrupulously clean up their tables, as if the restaurant were a sacred place. People are less likely to litter in a McDonald's than in a public picnic ground.

The total experience of dining at McDonald's may have become a kind of secular ritual that simultaneously reaffirms American values: the innocence of childhood (alcohol is never sold at McDonald's), the joy of youth (Ronald McDonald, a clown, is the official mascot), the purity of the body (only pure Grade-A, U.S.D.A.-inspected beef is used in the hamburgers), and the sanctity of the family. McDonald's advertising slogan, "You deserve a break today," offers

Figure 22.9 *When secular objects or events are associated with religious imagery, they become more powerful and mysterious. The movie character ET was given a glowing "heart" that resembled the sacred heart of Jesus, highlighting the religious symbolism of the immensely popular film.*

support to the long-suffering mother. The familial warmth of the counter staff is stressed in their broad smiles. McDonald's contributes a share of its profits to the Ronald McDonald Foundation, which provides housing near major hospitals for the families of gravely ill children. Is McDonald's therefore a kind of religion offering ritual experiences to its customers? Perhaps it would be more accurate to say that McDonald's exploits themes and values that Americans associate with religion.

Sometimes religious motifs are borrowed from one source and applied to another medium, where they retain their power. The popular film *ET*, for example, recreates aspects of the story of Jesus Christ. ET is a gentle extraterrestrial who is accidentally abandoned by his crew after a brief probe of Earth. These creatures have glowing organs in their central body cavities, similar to pictures depicting the sacred heart of Jesus (Figure 22.9). ET encounters a kind of alter-ego in the boy Elliott (note the first and last letters of his name) who shares and understands his love. Elliott tries to mediate between the corrupt and heartless adults who search for ET. When ET is finally captured, he is symbolically crucified by bizarre space-suited cadres resembling Roman legions. ET dies, but, like Christ, he is resurrected, and, with the help of the children and kid technology, the bicycle, he escapes to make a rendezvous with his spaceship, which carries him back into the heavens from whence he came.

---

secularization   The process of limiting or reducing the realm of supernatural experience and ritual activity.

sacralization   The process of increasing the realm of supernatural experience and ritual activity or extending it to a new domain.

Religion as a Reflection of Dominant Class Ideology: Marx

Karl Marx wrote that, in class societies, religion always reflects the ideology of the dominant class. In feudal Europe, for example, religion was an integral part of the feudal system. Feudal lords (vassals) generally received rights to land from the king, who was granted the right to rule by God. Serfs, or peasants, had to work for the vassal in exchange for the right to cultivate land themselves and graze their cattle. The Christian priests of that time supported this system by endorsing the God-given rights of the nobility. They also staged rituals that reinforced the property rights of the nobility, and they preached humility and acceptance of one's station in life. The priesthood not only was identified with the nobility but also enjoyed many of the same privileges.

Feudal Europe exemplifies Marx's theory about religion and society, but many other cases are more complex. Since the Protestant Reformation in the 16th century, several competing religious ideas and practices have flourished in the West. Most of the developing countries of the world, including India, Brazil, Indonesia, and Nigeria, also have plural religions. In some cases a powerful elite espouses a single religious ideology and employs it to maintain its power. This was the case in Spain under Francisco Franco (1936–1975). Religious leaders have also used their religious identity and manipulated religious symbols to acquire power. The dramatic overthrow of the Shah of Iran and his secular regime by the Ayatollah Ruhollah Khomeini in 1979 is an example of this.

There are many other religious traditions. While they may lack the ritual elaboration and grandeur of the "great" religions, they are no less religions. Some minority religions that lack participation by the ruling classes may nevertheless reflect dominant ideologies. Some religions, called "religions of the oppressed," are practiced by downtrodden groups with little political or economic power. Some sects maintain beliefs in direct conflict with the aims of the dominant elites. One such group is the Quakers in the United States, who refuse to bear arms or fight even when their country is at war. Likewise, the Chasidim in Israel refuse to fight for the Israeli state because they believe a Jewish state can occur only after the coming of the Messiah. Even a major religion may fail to endorse the attitudes of the ruling class. The Roman Catholic bish-

ops of the United States, for example, adopted a position opposing the use of nuclear weapons in 1983 against the official position of the United States government. Religion in complex societies may not be monolithic, and it does not invariably reflect the views of the ruling class.

Religion as a Source of Social Change: Weber

Another influential theory of religion in society comes from the German sociologist Max Weber, who published *The Protestant Ethic and the Spirit of Capitalism* in 1905. Weber suggested that the Protestant Reformation helped to open the way for capitalism in Europe. His theory was based on the differences between Protestant and Catholic theology. Weber suggested that Protestantism encouraged people to save, invest, and profit. Success would be taken as a sign of divine election and salvation, ideas not present in Catholic thought. Catholics, by contrast, were exhorted to live according to God's wishes and receive their reward in the afterlife. Weber suggested that this difference helped to unleash the force of capitalism in Europe, providing religious support for investment and profit.

Weber's approach stressed the importance of religious ideas at important junctures in history. Other investigators have followed his lead, examining the role of religious thought in changing social conditions. Some writers suggest, for example, that Islamic "fundamentalism" is an important element in the recent political history of Iran, Egypt, and Saudi Arabia. The Ayatollah Khomeini was a Muslim clergyman who opposed the attempts by the monarch, Shah Reza Pahlevi to modernize Iran. From exile in France, Khomeini began to mobilize other clergymen and laypersons through sermons recorded on tape cassettes and smuggled into Iran. The Iranian clergy, seeing its power and land holdings diminish under the Shah's economic modernization program, were highly receptive to Khomeini. Khomeini preached that industrialism, sexual equality, and secularization were tools of the devil. The Ayatollah and his supporters did not hesitate to justify their political actions in religious terms. Nations perceived as enemies were characterized as "satan," while Iran's bloody war with Iraq was presented as a **jihad** or "holy war" against infidels, notwithstanding the fact that the opponents were also Muslims.

Some objections have been raised to Weber's theory of the influence of religion on society. One criticism concerns the idea that the Protestant Ethic *caused* the rise of capitalism. Weber could not prove that Protestantism influenced the rise of capitalism. Perhaps it was the rise of capitalism that paved the way for Protestantism, or possibly some other factor was crucial to the development of both institutions.

Religious Structures and Social Complexity

In spite of remarkable variation in beliefs among different religions, there are strong regularities in the structural features of religion in general. One regularity concerns the nature of religious specialist roles and how they are supported. In small-scale societies, religious specialists or shamans are usually not highly differentiated from other people, while in more complex social settings there are elaborate and specialized forms of religious leadership. There are many shamans among the !Kung San and the Yanomamo. Access to this role is not highly restricted (see Chapters 18, 21), and the rewards are not very great. You will recall that the Tapirapé shaman goes through a long apprenticeship; he is paid for his work and is slightly wealthier than the other Tapirapé. This may reflect the more elaborate social organization of the Tapirapé. But the shaman continues to farm and fish like any other man.

In the rural areas of Mesoamerica and South America, a district is commonly served by rotating religious leaders. Priests are rarely seen in these communities, so the responsibility for ritual is lodged in a rotating group of **cargueros** (see Chapter 18). The religious leadership is drawn from the community, but the positions are not permanent.

The Tewa Pueblos of Arizona have a more elaborate ritual system. It is largely aimed at controlling the weather in this arid region, where small fluctuations in rainfall can spell disaster for growing crops. The Tewa divide themselves into ordinary people and **Made People** (Ortiz 1969). The Made People are organized hierarchically and have special ceremonial duties. Because there are many of them, they do not form a small, exclusive elite. The offices they hold require them to officiate at ceremonies and to perform other duties, serving society at large. The medicine man must help all villagers who present themselves without favoritism to his own kinship group.

Shortly after the harvest the Made People are entitled to contributions of food from the ordinary people. Until this offering is made, it is improper for anyone to harvest and store food (Ortiz 1969). In this manner the Tewa established social control over the fruits of the harvest. It appears that the Made People have first pick of this food, and if there are leftovers, they go to other sacred associations (Ortiz 1969, 101). Concern with the calendar and the timing of both ritual and economic activities is a common responsibility of ritual specialists in many societies, especially the priesthood in more complex societies. In the Pueblo case, the Made People seem to enjoy certain material advantages over ordinary people.

Turning to intermediate societies like the Aztec Empire, we find a more developed role for a fully professional priesthood. Aztec priests stood just below the nobility as a sharply differentiated elite. They enjoyed many special privileges, a quality of life superior to the common people, and often a good deal of power. Priests selected many of the victims in the rites of human sacrifice for which the Aztecs are well known (see Chapters 2, 16, 17), and they personally cut out the victims' hearts with stone knives. Aztec priests were recruited from boys and girls receiving training in an academy reserved for children of the nobility (Berdan 1982, 54). The priesthood was ranked in order of devoutness with promotions at five-year intervals. Priests spent a great deal of time in service to the deity to which they had made vows. They cared for the temple and the idol, kept temple

---

jihad In Islam, a holy war waged by Muslims against non-Muslims.

cargueros Holder of an office in the civil-religious hierarchy in a Mesoamerican village.

Made People In Tewa Pueblo society, members of a social group who are arranged hierarchically and have special ceremonial duties.

fires lighted, and offered prayers and incense throughout the day and night.

Aztec priests also involved themselves in social and political affairs. They had extensive duties in the education of noble children, and they were heavily involved in warfare. Religious rites were also state rituals glorifying the state and its rulers. The priesthood used two different calendars to coordinate many events. One was a 260-day ritual calendar; the other a 365-day solar calendar. As among the Pueblos, Aztec ritual was heavily oriented toward weather—especially rainfall—as a theme (Berdan 1982, 136–137).

The role of the clergy is remarkably similar in many intermediate societies, including ancient Peru, medieval Europe, and ancient Egypt. This parallel was recognized by anthropologist Julian Steward who suggested that the "theocratic empire" was a stage in the development of the state (1949; see Chapter 17). It is easy to find evidence for a Marxian interpretation in cases like Peru under the Incas. The priesthood interpreted events in such a way as to dazzle, mystify, and intimidate the general population and fill them with dread at the slightest thought of challenging the rulers. To do so would have been to challenge the very order of the universe. In larger, more complex societies we find a tendency for religious roles to be tied up with general social and political issues. Religion assumes specific social functions that go beyond the individual village or district. Religious leaders acquire more power, prestige and, sometimes, wealth.

As the state evolved, religion diversified. Early states often imposed a state religion on all the people

Figure 22.10 *Modern religious practices take many forms, including the highly regimented cult centered on a charismatic leader. Here, the Reverend Sun Myung Moon performs a mass wedding among his followers in Madison Square Garden.*

under their domain and tolerated no others. Modern states encompass diverse models of religious belief and practice, ranging from **monotheistic religions,** such as Christianity, Islam, Buddhism, and Judaism, to shamanistic religions in which individuals practice healing, sorcery, and divination. There are religious cults that focus on charismatic leaders, some so powerful as to lead their people to their own deaths. Other cults, such as the Unification Church founded by the Reverend Sun Myung Moon or the Hare Krishna sect, recruit their members mainly from among young adults and have been highly successful in raising money to finance their activities. Such groups are characterized by a high degree of personal loyalty to a charismatic leader and a great deal of regimentation (Figure 22.10).

The power that some cult leaders hold over their followers is extraordinary. Some of these groups have successfully helped some young people to withdraw from dependency on drugs or alcohol (Galanter 1981). Some parents of members feel their children have been brainwashed by the sects' leaders. In some cases parents accompanied by professional "deprogrammers" have kidnapped their own children to wrest them away from the control of such cults. It appears that the cults' strict discipline and demand for full-time commitment provide something the members have been missing in their lives.

High Gods and Stratification

The specific content of any religious tradition depends on a number of factors, including the environment, the social functions of religion (Box 22.2), previous traditions, and neighboring traditions to those belonging to a specific population. As Durkheim observed, the content of religious ideas is also affected by social organization. Sociologist Guy Swanson (1960) made a cross-cultural comparison of religious beliefs and so-

cial organization using a sample of 50 societies from around the world. Swanson set out to test Durkheim's notion that religious beliefs are primarily influenced by the organization of the society in which they were created. Swanson first examined the phenomenon of monotheism, which he defined as a belief that a single god is the ultimate creator or director of everything, whether or not there are other lesser gods beneath the "high god."

Swanson suggested that belief in a high god would most often occur in societies where authority is divided into levels, such as a kingdom divided into districts, made up of villages composed of households. Swanson counted the levels of **sovereign groups** in each society. For example, in a simple society organized into bands or camps recognizing no higher authority, like the !Kung San, there are only two sovereign groups, the family and the camp unit. The Inca Empire, by contrast, was divided into several levels with sovereign groups ranging from the family to the local descent group, the village, the district, the province, the moiety (a dual division), and finally the central state. Table 22.1 shows Swanson's results. Of the 39 societies that could be rated for the two variables, about half were simple societies with only one or two levels of sovereignty. Of these, only 11 percent (2 out of 19) had the idea of a high god, while 91 percent (10 out of 11) of the complex societies (four or more levels of sovereignty) had the idea of a high god.

Those societies having the idea of a high god differed from each other in important respects, and their conceptions of the god itself were different. Nevertheless, Swanson's finding is consistent with the hypothesis that monotheism is related to the presence of a social hierarchy in a society (1960, 81). He further showed that societies with social classes were more likely than others to possess a belief in superior gods (1960, 96). Swanson treated other aspects of religious belief in relation to society. For example, he showed that societies having "sovereign" kinship groups other

---

monotheistic religion   A set of beliefs and practices that are centered around a belief in the existence of only one supreme deity.

sovereign group   A separate level of authority recognized in a society.

BOX 22.2

Functionalism in the Study of Religion

In many discussions of religion, statements take a functionalist form. The following is a typical functionalist statement:

Premises:
1. A certain ritual [R] is practiced regularly in society [S].
2. Societies have a need for solidarity or else they will split apart.
3. Society [S] is not splitting apart.

Conclusion:
4. Therefore, practicing [R] holds [S] together.

In this syllogism, the conclusion is invalid even if all the premises are true. It is not valid for the same reason that the following syllogism does not support its conclusion.

Premises:
1a. Vivian owns a gun that was recently fired
2a. Harry has a gunshot wound.
3a. Gunshot wounds are often fatal.
4a. Harry is dead.

Conclusion:
5a. Vivian killed Harry.

As any good detective knows, Harry could have been shot by someone else using Vivian's gun, or he could have been shot by another gun, or he could have died from other causes. More evidence is needed to assert the conclusion in (5a).

Returning to the first syllogism, let us suppose that the society [S] is the Walbiri (described on p. 1503) and the ritual is the male initiation rite. Given the energy and intensity of this ceremony, it would be hard to deny that it is important to the Walbiri. How can you demonstrate that it is the initiation rites and not something else that holds the Walbiri together? You could "test" the syllogism as a hypothesis by suppressing the Walbiri's initiation rites, but such experiments are not ethical and would not necessarily be conclusive. Having enough power over the Walbiri to prevent them from holding initiations would almost certainly involve other changes as well as outside leadership.

The "experiment" would not be sufficiently controlled to permit a clear conclusion.

There is no doubt that all societies need some kind of "glue" to hold them together. Most social scientists agree that rituals give people a common outlook and purpose, thereby enhancing social solidarity. But it is a long step from these statements to asserting that ritual and other institutions exist *because* of the need for social solidarity. Functionalist interpretations of social institutions indicate plausible relationships between cultural items but they cannot account for the presence or absence of such items. The danger of such interpretations is that one can always postulate a given need to explain any institutions, without the need for a falsifiable hypothesis. Functionalists have a way of arguing both sides of many issues. They explain some institutions as a means for reducing conflict, but when faced with evidence of conflict, they point out that societies have a need for "escape valves."

The functionalist approach, which explains social institutions in terms of the needs they fulfill, has been compared to Dr. Pangloss, a foolishly optimistic character in Voltaire's *Candide* who repeatedly asserts, "This is the best of all possible worlds." From this he concludes, "Everything that is, exists for a good reason." Because it postulates that societies are harmonious wholes with smoothly interlocking parts, functionalism is apt to fall into the Panglossian trap.

Functionalist statements are difficult to verify. For example, many people believe that the kosher dietary laws observed by orthodox Jews help maintain the solidarity of the group. In North America, however, many Jews do not observe the kosher laws yet identify closely with Judaism. One could design a test to compare the solidarity of Jews who keep kosher with that of others who do not. But how could a test measure the strength of the dietary laws and the solidarity of the group independently? A group of nonobservant Jews might also lack other features that contribute to solidarity, such as using Hebrew in religious services. The problem comes down to the difficulty of measuring social solidarity and the effects of particular customs on it. For all these reasons, functionalist interpretations of social institutions, while plausible, are seldom successful as explanations for these institutions.

Concept of a High God	Number of Sovereign Groups		
	One or Two	Three	Four or More
Present	2	7	10
Absent	17	2	1

Source: Swanson 1960, 65.

Table 22.1 Number of Sovereign Groups and the Concept of a High God

than the nuclear family (such as lineages) were more likely to believe in ancestral spirits active in human affairs.

Many other studies of individual societies demonstrate a close relationship between ideas of the supernatural and social organization among actual human groups. One should not expect religion to be a perfect mirror of society as it is presently constituted, however, for several reasons. First, there is lag. Religious beliefs may change more slowly than the underlying social matrix. Some Protestant denominations in North America now ordain both men and women as pastors, but many Christian groups, including the Roman Catholic church, have not accepted such a role for women.

Second, there is diffusion. Religious ideas may be transferred to other social groups through conquest or **missionization**. While some adaptation usually occurs, a religious idea may not be entirely compatible with the social matrix into which it has been incorporated. Third, complex societies tend to be pluralistic, encompassing diverse religious beliefs and organizational structures that may cross-cut each other. Finally, religious ideas may reflect an ideal rather than an actual state of social affairs. Some societies believe in a god who is gentle, forgiving, and charitable, while the society itself is violent, vindictive, and selfish.

Religion continues to be a central focus of inquiry in anthropology. Not only is it a convenient cultural domain for cross-cultural comparison, but also it is a fascinating area that expresses human spirituality, both reflecting social structure and values and, at times, molding them.

SUMMARY

- Many definitions of religion are too narrow to accommodate the beliefs and behavior in all societies. Not all religions have a supreme being, a formal organization, or concern themselves with morality.
- Broader definitions of religion may be based on a distinction between the sacred and the profane, between magic and religion, or between natural and supernatural events. Such distinctions are difficult to apply to some cases, although they help us think about human religion in its many manifestations.
- Some religious ideas may have their origin in dreams, trance, and hypnotic and drug states, but there is no reason to believe that these conditions provide the structure of religion itself.
- Religion transforms ordinary life experiences into more universal symbolic terms that may help prepare people for their roles in society. This is particularly true of rites of passage and the manipulation of symbols in liminal states.
- Religion cannot be separated from the social matrix. Durkheim suggested that religion could be understood as society worshiping itself. Rituals often support or reinforce social practices and may have important economic and ecological consequences as well. However, explanations in terms of function do not explain why a particular religious form assumes the shape it does.

missionization The influence that religious missionaries have over the populations with which they work.

- Religious structures are correlated with the level of social complexity in society. For example, full-time priesthoods are found only at the higher levels of complexity, while shamanism is the predominant form of religious leadership in egalitarian societies.
- Religious beliefs are also correlated with social organization. Beliefs in high gods are found mainly in societies with hierarchical social structure.
- Although the correlation between religion and society is close, the fit is not perfect. The ideas expressed by religion may be behind or ahead of their time; they may reflect social realities or social ideals.

GET INVOLVED

1. Make an inventory of the religious groups in your area. Visit as many different such groups as you can, taking care not to offend the sensibilities of anyone. Do not pretend that you are a potential convert. For each group, determine its structure, how it supports itself, and its form of religious practice, especially rituals. Does the group actively seek converts? Try to analyze the relationship between each religious practice and the larger society in which it is embedded.
2. Assemble a group of people divided equally between those who are active in the religion into which they were born and those who were recruited or converted into the religion they practice. Ask them to describe the features of the religion they practice. What appeals to the members of each group? How does participation in the group fulfill their needs?
3. Select three or four religions that are practiced in your area (other than your own), and interview persons affiliated with each one about their understanding of the supernatural. What powers outside human agency do they believe in? Do they believe in miracles, visions, divine intervention, spirit healing, life after death, black magic? Remember that you cannot carry out such an exercise without showing complete respect for the beliefs and practices of other people.

SUGGESTED READINGS

Davis, Wade. 1985. Hallucinogenic plants and their use in traditional societies. From *Cultural Survival.**

Douglas, Mary. 1979. Taboo. In *Magic, witchcraft and religion,* ed. A. Lehmann and J. Myers. Mountain View, Calif.: Mayfield.

Harner, Michael J. 1968. The sound of rushing water. *Natural History* 77 (6):28–33.

Katz, Pearl. 1981. Ritual in the operating room. From *Ethnology.**

Mendonsa, Eugene. 1976. Characteristics of Sisala diviners. In *Magic, witchcraft and religion,* ed. A. Lehmann and J. Myers. Mountain View, Calif.: Mayfield.

*This selection is anthologized in *Applying Anthropology,* 2d ed., ed. A. Podolefsky and P. J. Brown (Mountain View, Calif.: Mayfield, 1992).

Interviewing a Diviner

Alma Gottlieb teaches at the University of Illinois at Urbana-Champaign. She conducted research in 1979–1980 and again in 1985 among the Beng people of Ivory Coast. This selection is extracted from A Parallel World, *a memoir of fieldwork among the Beng that Gottlieb coauthored with her husband, Philip Graham.*

In 1979–1980 my husband and I lived in Kosangbe, a village of about 200 Beng people in Ivory Coast. While there I befriended Amenan, a young mother of six children. She knew French, and while I was learning to speak Beng, she often translated for me.

One day Amenan arranged for me to meet Lamine, the village diviner. I arrived early and we settled on a bark cloth mat. "Philip sends his regrets," I said, "his stomach hurts today."

"May God get him out of it," Amenan murmured.

Soon Lamine joined us. We exchanged greetings, and then he took out a handful of cowry shells. About an inch long, they were oval-shaped and domed on top; underneath, tiny ridges ran the length of a slit, like a mouth baring its teeth. The shells came from the Indian Ocean; they had journeyed overland carried by traders across the width of Africa.

The diviner tossed the shells on the mat to offer me a sample explanation, I assumed, of what a given pattern might mean. Instead he said, "I see your husband has a stomach ache. It's because you haven't been introduced to the Earth of your village. Give a white chicken to your Chief, and he'll sacrifice it to the Earth. Then you'll both stay healthy."

My eyes widened at this unexpected diagnosis—Lamine had been nowhere in sight when I'd told Amenan of Philip's ailment—but

Alma Gottlieb walking with her friend Amenan, who served as translator during the interview with Lamine.

Lamine continued, "Kosangbe has a lot of taboos—you may have unknowingly violated some. That chicken sacrifice will also serve as an apology to the Earth. And the Chief should tell you those taboos so you can observe them now."

What could those taboos be? But Lamine had already returned to the shells. "I see that you've spent too much money since coming here. One Friday morning, kill a white rooster, cook it in peanut sauce, and serve it with rice. Set aside a portion for you and Kouadio and let the children of your *quartier* eat the rest. After that, you won't waste money."

"Mm-hmm," I said, too astonished now to speak. Again, Lamine peered intently at the mat. "When you're getting ready to leave us, the Chief should sacrifice a white chicken to the Earth to protect you until you arrive back home."

Lamine looked up; the shells had finished speaking to him.

"Father, thank you very much," I said. "My husband and I will follow all your instructions."

Since antibiotics hadn't banished our stomach parasites, there was no harm trying a chicken. But how had Lamine deduced all his pronouncements?

"I'll show you," he said confidently and tossed the cowries again onto the mat. "Do you see that purplish shell by itself? That's a sign of good luck."

Lamine gathered the shells and tossed them again. "And these two that are stuck together, apart from the rest: If a woman can't get pregnant and isn't menstruating, it's because of twins in her family."

Amenan whispered to me, "Because the twins are bewitching her."

Lamine continued, "If she asks their forgiveness, she'll start menstruating." He tossed the shells again. "Here's one alone, with several grouped around it. The client will have a serious illness, and his family will gather round him. Then he'll recover."

It was an ingenious system: Each set of cowries represented a visual metaphor of a social dilemma. Still, the configurations of the shells thrown randomly on a mat seemed arbitrary. Later Amenan explained that this was anything but the case. "It's the bush spirits who make the cowries fall that way. That's why Lamine waters the shells each morning. It's for the spirits."

I didn't have to believe in those spirits to see their effectiveness. Lamine had a large and faithful clientele who consulted him regularly. In cases of failure, the sacrifice must have been offered on the wrong day, or the patient skipped a prescribed herbal treatment. The system was self-enclosed—much like Western medical science. Was my own faith in pills and prescriptions—which, I knew all too well, often failed to work—as rooted in belief?

Traditional masks from Taegu, Korea.

ART AND CULTURE

▲▲▲

ike religion, art is found in virtually every society. And like religion, art can be difficult to define in a way that encompasses the variation in different societies. This chapter addresses such questions as, What is art? What is the role of the artist in society? Is there a relationship between art and the social organization of a society? In seeking answers to these questions, we consider art as a form of expression in contemporary societies as well as the origins and early development of art as revealed through the archaeological record.

THE EYE OF THE BEHOLDER

Anthropologists consider **art** a form of communication within a culturally specific system of meanings. Art communicates through various media, including dance, song, instrumental music, drama, literature, painting, sculpture, and cinema. It differs from language in that it presents a highly distilled form of meaning and emotion that does not readily allow translation into equivalents. To understand this, recall from Chapter 4 that in language most statements can be put into different words without drastically altering their meaning. Artistic "statements" cannot be glossed or translated in this fashion. What would it mean, for example, to translate an ancient Greek vase into a symphony, or even into another Greek vase?

Artistic expression may be highly formal, following a strict set of rules, as in a Bach fugue, or it may be "informal," as in a jam session among rock musicians. In either case, however, there are rules or conventions that govern the expression of artistic ideas, and these rules depend on the social context in which they occur. Art may be tied in with religious ideas, political programs, or ideas about nature or history (Figure 23.1).

Within an artistic **idiom**, ideas appear on a symbolic level. Art may consist of concrete physical things, like sculpture or paintings, or more ephemeral things, like dance movements or musical sounds. Art may be permanent, like a granite statue, or fleeting, like an ad lib solo in a jazz performance. **Artists** are people who have mastered the techniques and the symbolic idiom necessary to produce art. Acquiring these techniques may require years of apprenticeship and constant practice, as in the formation of a classical

ballet dancer (Figure 23.2). Art is created by artists and "consumed" or "appreciated" by an audience. Sometimes this distinction is blurred, as in an event in which people participate by singing and dancing together. These definitions may seem to discount the inspiration, creativity, and passion of artistic creation and the thrill of appreciation that many people associate with art, but these elements may not be present in every artistic tradition.

Art and the Artist

Western definitions of art often emphasize the individual artist and creativity. The stereotypical Western artist is a loner who disregards social conventions to

Figure 23.1 *The U.S. Capitol embodies architectural ideals first expressed about 2,500 YA in the classical style of the Parthenon in Greece. Rational order, symmetrical balance, and unification of the individual parts for the greater good and beauty of the whole represent not only the classical ideal, but also the basis of democracy.*

Figure 23.2   *In Bali, Indonesia, a master teaches the Legong dance to a young student; in the United States, a teacher at the Joffrey Ballet School instructs a class of six-year-olds. In both classical traditions, training of dancers begins at an early age.*

pursue his or her creative vision. Some artists fulfill this stereotype, but others do not. During their lifetimes, some artists seem detached or alienated from their surroundings, but with hindsight we see how closely they fit in with existing traditions and the contemporary surroundings. Many Western artists, including Ludwig van Beethoven, Gustave Flaubert, Richard Wagner, Auguste Renoir, James Joyce, Jackson Pollock, Igor Stravinsky, Pablo Picasso, e e cummings, Martha Graham, Charlie Parker, Billie Holliday, Willem De Kooning, Federico Fellini, Marlon Brando, Bob Dylan, Andy Warhol, and Alvin Ailey, seemed radical and outlandish when they first came upon the scene. But it is now clear that each was on the leading edge of a developing tradition. Their works are now established and accepted; what was

radical and new when they first appeared is now a familiar part of the artistic landscape.

The idea of innovation or opposition to social conventions is not integral to the idea of art. Like Western artists during many periods in history, such as the early Middle Ages, non-Western artists are often anonymous and their individuality is little emphasized. Their works often bear no signature, and they confine themselves to working within a narrow range of styles and techniques learned from the previous generation. The Pueblo women potters studied by ethnologist Ruth Bunzel saw themselves not as inspired creators but as artisans working within a tightly bounded universe of designs passed down by their mothers (Bunzel 1929). They were not rewarded for their work; no one thought of them as special (Figure 23.3).

---

art   The creation of objects that express meaning and emotion within a culturally specific system of meanings.

idiom   The set of symbols (ideas, materials, and forms) that are used in the creation and interpretation of art.

artist   A person who has mastered the techniques and symbolism of an artistic idiom.

Figure 23.3   *Maria and Julian Martinez of the San Ildefonso Pueblo of New Mexico exhibit their work in this photograph taken about 1940. Following traditional designs, Maria shaped the pottery and Julian decorated it. Tourists found their work so beautiful that both the demand for and the value of their pots skyrocketed. Breaking from tradition, the artisans began to sign their work; now a signed Martinez pot is extremely valuable.*

The Abelam society of Papua New Guinea, on the other hand, places a high value on art and accords great prestige to skilled artists. Artists have an important role in preparing and decorating ceremonial *tambaran* cult houses used by the **patriclans**; all Abelam artists' work is done in connection with ritual events. Artists are not rewarded for innovation or departures from tradition. Ethnographer Anthony Forge (1967, 448) made the following observations:

> The Abelam artist works within fairly narrow stylistic limits sanctioned by the total society in which he lives; any work he produces cannot be shown outside the *tambaran* cult and will only be accepted for that if it satisfies the criteria of magico-religious effectiveness. A young man [who] found a growth on a tree

that resembled [a] human head, had taken it home and carved on it eyes, nose and mouth and painted it in the traditional style. When he produced it during the preparations for a ceremony . . . the organizers refused to display it or allow it in the ceremonial house; although the painting was in the correct style, the shape of the head was nothing like any of the head shapes of *tambaran* figures.

Appreciating and Understanding Art

As illustrated by the Abelam example, people in nearly every society make judgments about what is good, bad, or authentic art. In Western society art objects are traded in a specialized market, and the price of an artwork is a function of its desirability and perceived quality. Instead of priests and elders, other specialists, such as art critics, museum curators, collectors, editors, publishers, and disk jockeys, serve as gatekeepers and arbiters of taste. In complex societies, segmented by social class and ethnic groups, various forms of art typically appeal to different groups. The huge variety of art forms in a country like the United States may give the impression that any kind of art can "find its way," gaining popular acceptance. Nevertheless, even the broadest, most liberal art market sets limits that artists must observe at the risk of failing to attract an audience and sell their work.

Artworks can best be appreciated and judged by persons familiar with the genre to which they belong. A **genre** is a range of forms, techniques, and styles that define a particular tradition of art, such as French impressionist painting or "rap" music. People unfamiliar with the conventions of a particular genre are not able to judge its value reliably. Hence, an artistic tradition, much like a language, depends on both the producers of art and its consumers being bound together by mutual acceptance of a common set of symbolic meanings.

The dependence of an artistic tradition on culturally specific conventions presents a problem for cross-cultural appreciation of art. How can an audience accustomed to Western genres judge Chinese scroll painting, Japanese Koto music, carved masks from Benin in Africa, or Kwakiutl totem poles (Figure 23.4)? Each of these genres employs symbols not normally found in Western art, yet they are popular in the West.

Normally when people cross cultural boundaries they form a new set of conventions appropriate to the alien genre, but these are not the same as the conventions by which natives judge their own art. An American from Cleveland may place a Chinese temple idol in her living room and enjoy its beauty, but not from the same perspective as a Chinese visiting a temple to worship an ancestor. When they borrow ideas from other traditions, artists and audiences transform them.

Not only do artistic meanings and conventions vary from one culture to another, but also these mean-

ings and conventions change over time within cultures. Artistic change often occurs in response to social "currents." There is evidence that these currents are independent of the individuals who produce works of art. Anthropologist Alfred Kroeber demonstrated this in a study of U.S. dress styles (1940). He showed that the hemline, bodice, and other design features of women's evening dresses changed in a gradual rhythm in cycles much longer than could be explained by the impact of any influential designer. The social currents affecting cultural styles are themselves influenced by other events.

Rock music is another case in point. The United States emerged from World War II as the preeminent industrial and financial power of the West. The people who had fought in the war and pulled the country out of the Depression aspired to a comfortable, suburban life-style, but this way of life seemed very tame and limiting to their sons and daughters. Rock developed in the 1950s as a form of rebellion against blandness and conformity, drawing on both jazz and rhythm and blues and jumping across the divide between African American and white musical styles. Aimed mainly at a relatively affluent teenage set, 1950s rock was oriented to consumption and flamboyant, rebellious styles.

Later in the 1960s, the hippie movement, the civil rights movement, the development of a youth culture, the assassination of a popular young president, and the war in Vietnam contributed to the prevailing mood of rebellion. The symbol of the times became mind-expanding drugs, epitomized by the Beatles' song "Lucy in the Sky with Diamonds," with its initials LSD. But even the rebellious rockers of the 1950s and 1960s were not ready to challenge the prevailing gender stereotypes of the previous 100 years. They might have found it difficult to accept the assertive sexuality of performers like Madonna and Cindy Lauper, who became popular in the mid-1980s. Another social phenomenon, the women's movement, is at least partly responsible for the changed social perceptions that allow these women to succeed at their art.

---

patriclan A clan based on descent through the male line.

genre A range of forms, techniques, and styles that define the boundaries of a particular artistic tradition.

◀ **Figure 23.4** *Example of non-Western art forms that have gained popularity in Western culture: Japanese koto music, a bronze sculpture from Nigeria, and a Kwakiutl totem pole. Westerners may admire the artistry of these forms, but their reasons may differ from those of admirers in the artists' homelands. Artistic meanings and conventions vary considerably from culture to culture.*

WHAT IS PRIMITIVE ABOUT "PRIMITIVE ART"?

A problem occurs when the art of technologically simple societies is evaluated and judged by those in technologically advanced societies. Such art is often described as "primitive" by the critics of the more developed society; in fact, "primitive art" has been a standard label in the West for the art of tribal societies in Africa, the Pacific islands, and the Americas. The problem, as with all other uses of the word *primitive*, is that this description carries negative connotations of crudeness, childishness, and inferiority.

It is interesting to examine what Western artists identify as primitive in their own and other Western works. Igor Stravinsky's ballet score *The Rite of Spring*, for example, uses harsh dissonances, strident chords, and syncopated, irregular rhythms to create a pounding, violently percussive sound that alarmed and infuriated audiences when it was first performed in Paris in 1913 (Figure 23.5). The work portrays a "pagan ritual," in Stravinsky's terms, involving adolescent dances, games between rival tribes, and the sacrifice of a virgin. The novelty of the piece convinced many Europeans that it was based on the music of some tribal people, but it is not. Rhythms and sounds like those in *The Rite of Spring* have never been used in tribal rituals. They are entirely the product of the European music tradition and Stravinsky's creative imagination.

Figure 23.5 *Igor Stravinsky's 1913 ballet,* The Rite of Spring, *caused a riot at its opening performance. The music was unlike anything the Parisian audience had ever heard; they mistakenly assumed the pounding rhythms came from tribal music, not Stravinsky's creative imagination. This scene comes from the Joffrey Ballet's 1989 reconstruction of the ballet.*

Tim Paul
NUU-CHAH-NULTH
WOLF, 1990

Figure 23.6   *This 1990 watercolor titled "Wolf" was created by Tim Paul of the Northwest coast Nootka people. In Nootka tradition, dancers dressed as wolves and took children from the tribal longhouses into the woods to teach them tribal traditions and rituals. The artist, who grew up participating in wolf dances in his village of Zeballos on Vancouver Island, captures both wolf and child (note the abstract face in the wolf's ear) in this contemporary rendering of a traditional motif.*

Similarly, many paintings by Paul Gauguin depict Tahitian women and scenes of life in the Pacific island where Gauguin lived for many years. Some viewers believed that the bold colors and the strongly defined forms of these works, as well as the nudity and what they thought it suggested about the native morality, were typical of the "primitive" art and society of Tahiti. But again, Gauguin, although innovative, was well within his own heritage. Some art historians claim that his Tahitian works are actually derived from a classical European tradition of religious painting.

Perhaps the most famous painting in Western art with elements of "primitivism" is Picasso's *Les Demoiselles d'Avignon*. Picasso painted two of the female figures in this painting in a style suggestive of African sculpture, an art form whose power had re-

cently impressed him. Identifying the two figures as primitive, critics described them as "barbaric," "savage," and "violently dislocated." It is interesting in all these examples that Westerners define primitivism in terms of brutality, savagery, nudity, and wild emotionalism.

When we actually look at the art of tribal peoples, we find that it is not inferior to Western art in any objective sense. Tribal sculpture, masks, paintings, music, dance, and costumes do not lack subtlety, emotional depth, or any other quality we esteem in the art of complex societies (Figure 23.6). Artists from small-scale societies have produced works of great power, employing an elaborate symbolic vocabulary and displaying a high degree of **abstraction.** Labeling the art of simpler societies "primitive" is an example of ethnocentrism.

THE ORIGINS OF ART: THE "CREATIVE EXPLOSION"

Humankind began to develop an elaborate cultural repertoire long before the first art objects appeared. The first items identified as art in the archaeological record—cave paintings and sculptures—occur in the upper Paleolithic (see Chapter 7). Where was the artistic output of humans beyond 30,000 years ago? The people of the lower and middle Paleolithic may have produced song, dance, drama, and myth, but since none of these left a physical trace they cannot be shown to have existed. About 30,000 years ago, however, there was what author John Pfeiffer (1982) calls a "creative explosion." This is the earliest date of at least 200 sites, many of them caves or rock shelters in France and Spain, where thousands of paintings, carved rocks, and portable artworks suddenly intrude into the archaeological record (Figure 23.7).

The first discovery in the West of Paleolithic cave art occurred in 1879 when a young girl, Maria de Sautuola, was wandering in a cave near her home in Altamira, Spain. Maria found the ceiling of a grotto covered with images of large animals painted in vivid colors. Her father, Don Marcelino, recognized the paintings for what they were: the work of prehistoric artists. The "experts" of the time determined that the paintings were fakes; they were too sophisticated to have been done by "primitive" artists (Pfeiffer 1982, 20). Don Marcelino died before new discoveries of cave paintings in France and Spain confirmed his view that these paintings were indeed prehistoric.

Not only paintings but also carvings on stone and animal bone ("portable art") were found in great numbers. A rock shelter in France known as La Madeleine yielded the tusk of a mammoth, an animal extinct for 10,000 years, with the figure of a mammoth engraved on it. The best known portable pieces of Paleolithic art are female human forms carved from stone. Known as **Venus figurines**, they are found throughout Europe dating from 30,000 YA (Figure 23.8). There is much speculation about the meaning of these figurines; one idea is that they are "fertility symbols." However, there is no evidence that these figurines are associated with any change in the fertility status of the people who made or carried them.

Lascaux, the name of a cave in the Dordogne region of France, became a synonym for the torrent of creativity unleashed in the late Paleolithic. As at Altamira, most of the Lascaux paintings are recognizable as animals that lived in Europe during the Pleistocene. Only a few paintings show human figures. One depicts a crude stick figure of a man apparently being attacked by a bison. Curiously, many Paleolithic cave paintings were made not in large, easily accessible galleries but in small tunnels reachable only by crawling and climbing hundreds of yards in the darkness.

Why did these fine paintings and sculpture appear so late in human history? Did people lack the ability to produce them earlier on? Or was earlier art all of the sort that leaves no trace? Were these paintings casual products of people who happened to be living in the caves? Why would artists lavish their attention on inaccessible sections of dark caves? Did they not wish their work to be seen in the light of day by as many people as possible? The answers to these questions are speculative because there is so little information, but some possibilities emerge when we consider how and why this art may have emerged.

Pathways to Art: Crafts and Magic

Two trends in the development of technology during the upper Paleolithic—specialization and standardization—were probably preconditions for the develop-

---

abstraction Nonrepresentational design in art, without recognizable content.

Venus figurine A type of small statuette carved in Europe during the upper Paleolithic era with exaggerated physical characteristics such as breasts and buttocks; these figurines may have been used in fertility rituals.

Figure 23.7 *Paleolithic Europeans produced a remarkable variety of images, including cave paintings such as this one from Lascaux cave in France. They used natural pigments for paint and mixed them with a binding agent such as grease, marrow, or blood; the artists then applied the paint to the cave walls or ceilings with their fingers, wooden spatulas, and brushes made of twigs or animal hair.*

ment of art. As we saw in Chapter 7, the number and variety of tool types expanded greatly during this period. In Europe, a typical Neandertal (middle Paleolithic) site might contain 15 different tool types, while the average Cro-Magnon (upper Paleolithic) site holds 40 to 50 different types (Pfeiffer 1982, 45). Diversification of tool types suggests growth in specialization and matching of tools to specific tasks.

Furthermore, tools of a certain type closely resembled others in widely scattered sites. This suggests that tool makers were in contact with each other, exchanging information on how to make tools and adopting uniform techniques and standards of quality. These two trends together suggest the existence of a **craft community** of people who learned from each other and jointly developed their skills. Artistic production also flourishes in a community context where artists share ideas and develop a genre. Art, like crafts, requires periods of learning and practice and represents a specialized skill level. Most important, the existence of a skilled craft producer status could open a social niche for artists.

It is likely that people were technically able to make paintings and sculpture earlier in time than they appear in the archaeological record. The stone tools of the Aurignacian (about 35,000 YA) are so finely worked that we can imagine their owners being reluctant to use them for their designed purpose. It is possible that the beautifully designed Solutrean harpoons (see Figure 7.12) were in fact luxury items not intended for catching fish. It seems highly likely that specialized tool production was one path leading to the creative explosion.

Another pathway lies in the development of spiritual ideas. There is evidence of religious phenomena in the care given to the dead in Neandertal burials, dating from as early as 60,000 YA (see Chapter 7). The tools discussed above and these apparently ritual burials of some Neandertals are testimony to evolving ability and consciousness, but not yet art. Although crafts and magic may have preceded the appearance of art, they were not sufficient conditions. Spirituality refers to a focus on matters beyond the immediate problems of needs satisfaction, perhaps the supernatural. Thinking about spiritual things reflects a concern with abstract ideas, perhaps with ideals unattainable in real life. These are probably important aspects in the emergence of artistic creation.

The Emergence of Art and Social Order

What additional conditions were necessary for the appearance of art in human history? One can always suggest that human intellectual development reached a point where religion and then art became possible. But this explanation is untestable. We are better off asking, What social conditions led to the "creative explosion"? John Pfeiffer (1982) suggests that it emerged out of the strains of adaptation that occurred during the Paleolithic and that it answered the need

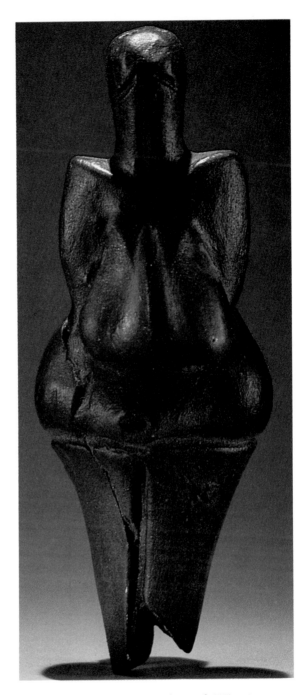

Figure 23.8 *A Venus figurine from Dolní Věstonice, Czechoslovakia, dating to about 25,000 YA.*

craft community A group of skilled art specialists who exchange information with each other, resulting in the standardization of tools, forms, and materials and the creation of an artistic genre.

for greater social control and for the formation of social consciousness. The upper Paleolithic was a period of great change. In many parts of the Old World, hunters and gatherers became more specialized within specific geographical niches. Not only new tools but also new life-styles emerged, permitting groups to survive on smaller territories, using resources more intensively, with neighbors closer by. Sedentism meant that people no longer had the option of avoiding disputes by moving off to a new location. More people lived in a single settlement for longer periods than had been the case in the average middle Paleolithic settlement. Climatic change forced populations in the northern fringes of Europe into central and southern Europe. Upper Paleolithic sites typically contained much larger populations than middle Paleolithic sites. Sites with housing for 15 to 20 people were typical in the middle Paleolithic, but upper Paleolithic sites commonly housed from 100 to 200 people.

Large, sedentary groups using resources intensively in close proximity to neighbors needed regulation. Order was needed to regulate access to resources, to settle disputes between people, and to conduct relations with neighboring groups. As ecological and social space filled up, living required more and more information. Life became less spontaneous, and it became necessary to plan and budget with smaller margins of error. Some people had to learn to manage the information necessary for successful adaptation, including technical information about house building, tool making, food storage, and plant and animal species used in subsistence; social data necessary for coordination of collective hunting and relations with neighboring groups; and information about the alternation of seasons. Some experts have suggested that cave paintings represent attempts to organize information systematically, and they have tried to read meaning into the number and arrangement of figures on cave walls. However, it is probably safer to assume that the rise of art and the need to manage larger chunks of information were two parallel and simultaneous phenomena.

What might the linkages be between the evolution of social organization and the development of art? One possible link involves the creation of symbolic emblems that abstractly define the order necessary for the smooth functioning of society. Ceremonial or ritual events repeated at regular intervals help socialize people to roles requiring strict observance of rules, such as territorial boundaries. Virtually all ritual observances involve the use of special objects and defined spaces that are designated as sacred. Today such events take place in temples, public squares, and other built spaces. The objects must have a quality that lifts them above everyday experience. Dark, inaccessible spaces, such as caves, would have served the purposes of ritual well, because they are closed environments where ritual specialists can control events and access to information by manipulating light sources.

Caves may help create liminal states in Victor Turner's sense (see Chapter 22). In such states people are unusually susceptible to new ideas, especially if they literally have to risk their lives to get to the proper viewing position. In Nerja Cave in Spain, for example, one can see 15,000-year-old paintings only by scaling a 45-foot wall to reach a small chamber. John Pfeiffer suggested (1982) that Paleolithic artists deliberately created illusions and surprises for maximum effect. The Paleolithic cave artists may have been the first to use light and dark and the feeling of danger to create sensational effects, an art that is now most evident in science fiction films like *Star Wars*. What new ideas could these specially designed environments be used to communicate? We can only speculate, but assuming a situation in which there was a need to build a stronger social organization, a secret ceremony in an unusual and inaccessible place might be the ideal spot to reinforce loyalty to a group or leader. Thus cave art may have emerged as an integral part of rituals staged for the purpose of building support for a social function.

Another linkage between social organization and art involves the creation of objects that help differentiate high-ranking people from everyone else, thus validating their status. The economic and social adjustments required by conditions during the upper Paleolithic were sufficient to activate these linkages. The art objects themselves may have been defined in such a way as to inspire awe and respect, either because of an inherent magical power attributed to them or because of the authority they represented. Virtually all authority relies on such physical symbols as altars, thrones, scepters, crowns, ceremonial robes, corner offices, fine paintings, special foods, presidential seals, palaces, and special music. All of these are typically created by artists whose work effectively supports power. The artists themselves are often supported by the wealthy and powerful.

Figure 23.9 *Body paint is an artistic means of delineating special roles in ritual performances.*

These different functions of art—socializing individuals to their roles in society and distinguishing powerful individuals from others—correspond to patterns of horizontal and vertical differentiation in society. **Horizontal differentiation** occurs when a social group is divided into distinct but roughly equal parts differentiated by symbolic emblems. These emblems may be names (e.g., Eagle or Crow), regalia (e.g., wearing feathers or body paint), or a special uniform. Dual divisions are the most common forms of horizontal elaboration. In Chapters 12 and 17, we discussed the need for new principles of organization brought by sedentism and higher local population density. In horizontal differentiation, subgroups of the local group accept special designations, forming "ceremonial corporations," activated for the performance of ritual. Artistic themes (songs, body paint, myths, and sacred paraphernalia) help distinguish these groups from each other (Figure 23.9). Perhaps artists presented ideas of symmetry, harmony, and order, leading people away from jealousy and competition. Under these circumstances, art is necessarily abstract and lacking in specific meaning. It calls attention to differences, solidifying a social order by stressing the complementarity of social roles.

Vertical differentiation, another pathway to order, is favored in larger, relatively sedentary societies. In such societies big men or chiefs use their au-

horizontal differentiation The division of a social group into distinct but roughly equal parts.

vertical differentiation The social hierarchy characteristic of ranked and stratified societies that distinguishes powerful members of society from the powerless.

thority to keep order (see Chapters 16 and 17). Here elaborate ceremonials and ritual paraphernalia play a different role in establishing order. In ranked and stratified societies, finely made garments, ornaments, and other objects are the special privilege of the leaders and rulers. The antiquity of such practices is demonstrated by the archaeological study of **grave goods**. There is evidence of ranking and stratification as far back as 20,000 to 25,000 years in the Sungir site in the Soviet Union (Pfeiffer 1982, 55). These hunter-gatherers buried highly ranked individuals with such items as ivory beads, rings, bracelets, and ceremonial tools.

In a more recent site, archaeologist Nan Rothschild (1983) found an interesting contrast. She excavated two North American hunter-gatherer burials created between 7,000 and 5,500 YA. One group on the coast of Newfoundland hunted seals and caribou from year-round base camps. The other site was on an island in Cayuga Lake, New York, occupied by a group that mainly hunted deer. The 101 burials of the latter group were relatively undifferentiated, with roughly comparable treatment of the deceased. In the Newfoundland burials, 10 of the 159 burials (5 men and 5 women) were buried with a significantly greater number and variety of grave goods.

Rothschild's interpretation was that the Newfoundland population had greater status differences because their resource base permitted sedentary camps and required greater coordination in hunting. If special honors were accorded to the high-status dead, it is likely that these people were also more privileged in life. They enjoyed special access to finely made goods as markers of their status. The honors accorded to the elites of Sungir or coastal Newfoundland is a far cry from the fabulous grave goods found in the death pits at Ur or the tombs of Egyptian pharaohs (see Chapter 17), but the principle is the same.

Thus in some cases early art works may have been a form of conspicuous consumption reinforcing the status of leaders. In Western history it has been common to find valuable artworks in the homes and workplaces of wealthy and powerful people. In fact people of great wealth often take it as an obligation to be "patrons of the arts," contributing to museums, music performances, and other high-status art activities.

There are many examples of vertical differentiation involving fine artworks from contemporary non-Western societies as well. In the tribal societies of northeastern Liberia, carved wooden masks are believed to have special powers. All initiated men know that the masks are carved by specialists for a payment, but they still believe in the masks' supernatural power. A clan leader was the keeper of an ancestral mask. Ethnographer George Harley wrote of these leaders and the masks they kept (1950, 17):

> Each was a big man in ordinary life, but a bigger man because of the secret power conferred on him through the ancestral mask of which he was the keeper. . . . In the old days [a] mask and its keepers had seen men tried and condemned to death. [The mask] had been smeared with the blood of any person executed because he had broken sacred laws. . . . [I]t had been made and consecrated by human sacrifice. During the first years of its existence it had been "kept alive" by similar sacrifice.

Through their association with sacrifice, punishment, and death the masks of northeastern Liberia acquired an aura and power of their own, independent of their owners. Village councils "consulted" the masks when making important decisions or judging criminal cases. Thus art objects can acquire symbolic "power" as a result of the social power with which they are associated.

ART STYLES AND SOCIAL ORGANIZATION

We have examined how the creation and manipulation of art reflects the power distribution in a society, but what about the content of art? Are artistic practices expressions of the social context, or do artists somehow rise above their own cultures and times? Numerous studies have shown that the content of art, even when highly abstract and **nonrepresentational**, reflects the society in which it is produced. Judith Hanna, an anthropologist specializing in dance, wrote a book comparing dance styles from different peoples around the world and showing how dance styles reflect urban or rural values and attitudes (1979). Alan Lomax, an **ethnomusicologist**, collected a vast amount of folk music and subjected it to statistical analysis. He found systematic differences in the kind of music produced by hunter-gatherers and by settled agricultural people (1962). There was an intriguing

Table 23.1 Symbolic Features of Visual Artworks Predicted by John L. Fischer's Model

| Design Elements | Type of Society | |
	Egalitarian	Hierarchical
Homogeneity	Repetitive use of similar elements	Integration of unlike elements
Use of space	Large amount of empty or irrelevant space	Little empty or irrelevant space
Symmetry	Symmetrical designs	Asymmetrical designs
Boundedness	Figures without enclosures	Enclosed figures

Source: Fischer 1961.

correlation between the size of the pitch intervals in the song styles practiced and the distance over which the group ranged. The more widely they ranged, the greater the intervals in the songs.

In another study, John L. Fischer (1961) proposed a connection between visual arts and the degree of hierarchy or stratification in society. He assumed that artists consciously or unconsciously recreate an ideal image of their society in their work. In hierarchical (vertically differentiated) societies, people are divided into those higher than and those lower than ego. In such societies the individual strives to find and maintain a secure place in the rank order. Differences in prestige exist in egalitarian (horizontally differentiated) societies, but they are not stressed. People strive to cooperate as equals and do not call attention to differences.

Fischer looked for differences in artistic designs that might reflect these social differences. He suggested, for example, that artists in egalitarian societies would create images similar to the structure of their own society, that is, with many people essentially repeating the same pattern of behavior. He proposed four indicators of variation (Table 23.1):

1. Hierarchical societies with a complex division of labor would produce correspondingly complex images.

2. Hierarchical societies would seek "to encompass the universe" (Fischer 1961), while egalitarian peoples would be content to conceive of the universe as themselves (significant objects) and everything else (empty space).

3. Egalitarian societies would produce repetitive, symmetrical designs.

4. Hierarchical societies would tend to see things as bounded or delimited, reflecting the boundaries between social statuses or classes that exist in hierarchical societies.

Fischer utilized information on art in 28 non-Western societies coded by psychologist Herbert Barry in connection with a different study. Barry had found, for example, that the drawings and designs of the Yakut, the Teton, and the Omaha (all indigenous North American tribal societies) tended to be fairly symmetrical, while those of the Balinese (of Indonesia), the Dahomeyans (of West Africa), and the Alorese (of Melanesia) tended to be asymmetrical (Figure 23.10). For information on degree of stratification or hierarchy, Fischer used codes assigned by yet another investigator. Thus the investigator's biases and expectations could not have influenced his coding.

To people accustomed to thinking that art styles are the pure products of free imagination, the results will be startling (Table 23.2). For example, of the 19

---

grave goods Objects that were buried with persons of high social status at their death.

nonrepresentational art Art that does not depict recognizable objects but focuses on abstract designs or forms.

ethnomusicologist An anthropologist specializing in cross-cultural study of musical expression.

◄ **Figure 23.10** *The complex, crowded asymmetrical Balinese painting (top) presents a striking contrast to the simple, open, and symmetrical design of the Sioux buffalo robe (bottom). Such contrasts are remarkably well correlated with social organization in Fischer's study.*

Table 23.2   Art Style Elements and Degree of Stratification in 28 Societies

	Degree of Stratification	
Art Style	Low	High
Simple design	16	1
Complex design	3	8
Space empty	12	2
Space crowded	7	7
Design symmetrical	12	2
Design asymmetrical	7	7
Unenclosed figures	12	2
Enclosed figures	7	7

Note: The probability that any of these associations is due to chance is less than 1 in 20.

Source: Fischer 1961.

egalitarian societies, 16 have relatively homogeneous designs, incorporating similar objects repetitively. Of the nine relatively stratified societies, eight of them use complex designs with different elements. In short, the data are consistent with the hypothesis that even the abstract form of artistic creations is influenced by the social structure in which the artist lives.

SUMMARY

- Artists are found in virtually every society. They produce artworks for audiences who are able to understand the symbolic meanings embedded in them.
- Art is apparently a fairly recent human product, since no traces of art can be found before about 30,000 years ago.
- Art appeared as people began to specialize and to standardize the production of utilitarian articles. It may have been a response to the growing need for social order as people settled down in denser settlements.
- Art was probably closely related to magic and ritual, as it still is in many societies.
- Art is linked to social order as a vehicle for legitimizing high rank in a hierarchical society. In addition, it can serve as a way of representing manageable social segments in relatively egalitarian societies.
- The artist is not necessarily a rebel or nonconformist as in typical Western stereotypes. Many traditions forbid an artist from straying far from a prescribed range of themes, materials, and styles. Nevertheless art styles do change over time in response to the influence of other artistic traditions and as a result of social change.

- Nearly every aspect of artistic creation is tied in some way to the social context, even the most formal and abstract aspects.

GET INVOLVED

1. Locate and attend an exhibit of "primitive art." Try to determine what the exhibitor thinks is primitive about it. Write a letter to the editor of your local paper explaining why you believe that the art may not be primitive. Try to define your terms carefully, giving examples of every concept you use. You may wish to pick out elements of the art form you are observing and show how they are used in artworks not considered primitive.

2. Organize a discussion of artists in your area, including as wide a variety as possible of professional (or dedicated amateur) artists, such as painters, commercial artists, sculptors, rock, classical, and pop musicians, dancers, writers, and poets. The only criterion should be that the art form be one with a significant audience in your area. Ask each artist to make a brief statement on what art means to her or him and how it relates to society. In the

discussion try to determine how their art relates to the social environment in terms of economics, status differences, ethnicity, the state, the formal education system, and so on.

3. Select a group of artworks, such as paintings, carvings, weavings, or songs, that have generated both aesthetic and social critiques. Compare the two forms of criticism to each other. Do social critics, anthropologists, sociologists, and so forth see the art form in the same way that "pure" art critics see it? If not, what differences exist between them?

SUGGESTED READINGS

Bunzel, Ruth. 1929. *The Pueblo potter*. New York: Columbia University Press.

Kaeppler, Adrienne L. 1978. Dance in anthropological perspective. *Annual Review of Anthropology* 7:31–49.

Lomax, Alan. 1968. *Folk song style and culture*. American Association for the Advancement of Science, Publication No. 88. Washington, D.C.: The Association.

Pfeiffer, John E. 1982. *The creative explosion: An inquiry into the origins of art and religion*. New York: Harper and Row.

Sieber, Roy. 1962. Masks as agents of social control. *African Studies Bulletin* 5 (11): 8–13.

ANTHROPOLOGISTS AT WORK

Interpreting the Image-Making of the Upper Paleolithic

Professor Conkey has been studying the prehistoric arts of the European Paleolithic for more than 20 years and has worked as an archaeologist in the U.S., Mexico, Jordan, France, and Spain. Her other major research interests include gender, social archaeology, hunter-gatherers, and material culture.

For twenty years, I have been trying to gain richer insights into the lives and works of some of the Upper Paleolithic peoples who lived in the southwestern regions of Europe, what is today southwestern France and northcoastal Spain. Although most Upper Paleolithic archaeologists study the thousands of stone tools made by these peoples, analyze their food habits from animal bones, or consider their general adaptations to the environments of the late Ice Age, I have long been convinced that the study of the images and material culture (in addition to stone tools) could be an important and provocative set of clues about the different hunter-gatherer groups who lived and who appear to have flourished in these regions for over 25,000 years. In particular, I have been trying to answer both some very specific questions about the thousands of engraved bones and antlers that have been found in striking abundance in sites of the "Magdalenian" (c. 15,000–10,000 years ago) and some general questions about image-making or "art": Why in this particular historical context, at this time and in this place, does image-making in so many media appear to flourish? What *are* the different "styles" or different systems for making various images and forms? How is the cave painting and engraving related to the other image-making activities, such as making statuettes, engraving on

Margaret Conkey kneels deep inside a cave, Le Réseau Clastres, France.

stone plaquettes, carving animals on the end of a spearthrower, or engraving geometric and figurative (usually animal) images on pieces of bone, antler, ivory? What, after all, were these people doing in the hundreds of caves in which images are still preserved? Were they really "sanctuaries," as the early interpreters thought, or were there many different uses and visitors?

Even though these may seem like relatively straightforward research questions, there are many challenging problems that must be cleared away, if possible. For one thing, the entire anthropological study of "art" has been recently called into question, if only because we have come to see how the very term *art* is one from our own cultural heritage, with its own varied and changing meanings. For us to apply this, without questioning it, to the societies we study either ethnographically or archaeologically is, in some ways, to create a kind of activity—"artistic activity"—that is not necessarily a kind of separate activity in those societies. Most ethnographically-studied societies,

in fact, do not have a category or term *art;* but this, of course, does not mean that they don't engage in dancing, singing, music, image-making, or have objects and forms that are part of both aesthetic and/or symbolic production.

When we talk about "Paleolithic art" as a single category, we have all too often just lumped together and sought a single explanation for thousands of images and media made over a period of some 25,000 or more years (about 1250 generations). What we see now is that this may be a convenient category for anthropologists, and it may serve to set off this imagery from that of later, agricultural societies of the so-called Neolithic period; but it is not helpful in terms of our really probing into the specifics of why this imagery, why in these many forms, why here and why at these times. By labeling it *art,* aren't we pre-judging what the images are all about? What we really need in archaeology, in trying to interpret what might have gone on in the past or what the images might have been about, is a grand imagination. We need to imagine a variety of possible explanations or accounts; we need to imagine multiple meanings or reasons and then see which of these many possibilities work best given our data and our abilities to make inferences from the data. And we need to recognize that just one interpretation is probably too limited. There is no reason why the painted animals on the walls of Lascaux can't be "about" many cultural issues at the same time—about hunting, about social relationships, about various metaphorical powers of different animals, or about beauty, or about technological experimentations with pigments.

Novices in a Buddhist monastery in Sikkim, India. Every family in Sikkim must send a son, exclusive of the first-born, to become initiated as a monk.

SOCIETY AND THE INDIVIDUAL

▲▲▲

hen an ethnographer returns from a field trip to a distant society, the first thing friends usually ask is, What are the people really like? The non-anthropologist is typically more interested in how ordinary people behave than in kinship, exchange networks, subsistence, or other anthropological topics. Ethnographers are besieged with questions about likes and dislikes, aggression and violence, sexual behavior, and attitudes toward work, family, and religion—in short, the personality of the typical member of the society the ethnographer has been studying.

In Chapter 1, we distinguished between anthropology and psychology in terms of the primary object of analysis. Psychologists take the behavior and inner states of individuals as their object. Anthropologists view the individual in relation to others, including ancestors, contemporaries, and descendants. When anthropologists focus on the individual, they are often interested in exploring how personality is related to culture and society. To what extent is an individual's personality the product of environmental influences and cultural expectations? To what extent do individuals share a "cultural personality"—a set of behavioral and cognitive traits that distinguish them from members of other societies? Assuming that such a pattern of personality traits exists, what forces are responsible for shaping it? These are some of the questions addressed in this chapter.

PERSONALITY AND CULTURE

A major source of cross-cultural misunderstanding is the variety of ways in which societies conceptualize the individual. Before we consider the relationship between individual personality and culture, it is well to remind ourselves that "the individual" is just as much an abstraction as "culture" and "society."

Individual Identity

In Western culture, we tend to think of each person as detached from others but sharing certain values, behaviors, and ideas, which we call "culture." It is as if each individual contains, in capsule form, the wider culture to which he or she belongs. Westerners often take the individual person as the "natural unit" of society and build scientific ideas on this notion.

In other societies, however, the individual may see himself or herself as connected—through kinship, religion, or some other way—to other people. The individual may practically disappear against a backdrop of lineages, ancestor groups, or other social units. The idea of a unique individual, while recognized, receives less emphasis. An example of such an orientation can be found among the Tzeltal-speaking Maya in the community of Tzo?ontahal in Chiapas State, Mexico, who were studied by ethnographer June Nash. Nash wrote (1970, 270):

> A fundamental understanding governing behavior in Tzo?ontahal is that people ought to do as the ancestors did. Both "knowing" and "remembering" are expressed by the same verb. . . . The behavioral corollary of this association . . . is that one should accept the word of the ancestors as a guide to behavior. The importance of obeying one's elders as the intermediaries in the transfer of ways of behaving from one generation to another is stressed in child training and is restated in the prayers uttered in ritual performances enacting the ways of the ancestors.

Because of the Western stress on the individual, we concern ourselves with such questions as, What is the relationship of an individual to culture? This question might not arise in contexts like the Maya Nash studied, because individuals do not define themselves as distinct from the rest of society.

Ethnographer Paul Bohannan made some interesting observations among the Tiv people of Nigeria when he tried his hand at wood carving. Feeling inadequate as a sculptor, he turned to making stools and chairs. To his chagrin, Bohannan found that casual bystanders would frequently pick up his piece, do some work on it, and then put it down for him or someone else to continue. Bohannan wrote (1961, 91):

> I, in Western tradition, had a feeling of complete frustration because my "creativity" and my ability were being challenged. For a few days, I tried to insist that I wanted to do the work myself, but soon had to give it up because everyone thought it silly. . . . Eventually, several of our chairs and stools [were completed]. I had a hand in all of them, but they were not my handiwork—the whole compound and half the countryside had worked on them.

Bohannan learned that Tiv artists did not work alone, each one executing each piece. Rather they worked communally. They didn't really care who the artist was who created a particular piece.

In societies with strong lineages, the individual is not so important as the lineage to which he or she belongs. Consider the Dinka of the Republic of Sudan, who were studied by Francis Deng (1972, 9):

> For a Dinka, where he comes from and where he goes to are points in the cycle of life revitalized and continued through procreation. . . . Every Dinka fears dying without a son . . . to continue his name and revitalize his influence in this world. From the time [a man] becomes of age to the time he enters the grave, the main concern is that he himself begets children to do for him what he has done for those before him.

In such a society the individual has worth and meaning primarily as part of a lineal concept. Despite these emic aspects of how the individual is defined, however, the individual still exists as a unit, and observations can be made about his or her behavior. Even where the individual seems to be submerged in the group, it is possible to identify traits that constitute an individual personality.

Personality as a Function of Culture

Personality refers to enduring qualities of individuals that distinguish them from other individuals. These may be "inner" qualities such as values and attitudes or "outer" qualities visible in behavior. It is usually assumed that the consistency of behavior is due to a fairly stable organization of forces—or "structure"—within the individual. Thus some people may be known as "bold" and others as "timid."

What is the relationship between personality and culture? Some anthropologists feel that a distinction is really not necessary. Personality variables are simply cultural variables as they apply to individuals. Since culture exists only in the minds and behavior of indi-

viduals, the way they think and act can be seen as an expression of their cultural values. Most people recognize that people from a given society tend to have a certain kind of personality. Ethnic and national stereotypes are one way of recognizing this common observation, although using them often involves overgeneralization and distortion. In Chapter 18 we examined the social aspects of these stereotypes as pertaining to ethnic groups, but we did not delve into how people actually share personality traits as members of culturally defined communities. The range of personality traits selected and approved within a particular cultural context is known as **cultural personality**.

Patterns of Culture: Ruth Benedict. In *Patterns of Culture* (1934), one of the most widely read anthropology books ever written, Ruth Benedict suggested that culture was personality "written in large letters." She wrote that each culture selects a few traits from the vast arc of potential traits, weaving them into an integrated whole. These items, or "patterns," are like master designs, or motifs, to which everything else in the society conforms. For example, "one culture hardly recognizes monetary values; another has made them fundamental in every field of behaviour" (Benedict 1934, 35).

Patterns of Culture presents ethnographic data from three different societies, the Pueblos of New Mexico, the Dobu of Melanesia, and the peoples of the Pacific Northwest of North America. Benedict systematically compared these three societies in regard to customs surrounding birth, death, puberty, and marriage. She found that the Pueblo were a "ceremonious people," holding strictly to traditional rites, deploring any emotional excess (Figure 24.1). Using terms coined by the German philosopher Friedrich Nietzsche, she referred to the Pueblos as "Apollonian," shunning emotional displays, like Apollo, the god of light and music, of Greek mythology. She pointed out that Pueblo dancing was monotonous and repetitive, not ecstatic and free. They repressed emotions like jealousy even when spouses were unfaithful, preferring a quiet divorce to a noisy quarrel. Benedict wrote (1934, 104):

---

personality An individual's unique pattern of feeling, thinking, and acting.

cultural personality The range of personality traits selected and approved within a particular cultural context.

◄ **Figure 24.1** *Ruth Benedict described members of New Mexican Pueblos as "ceremonious people." Pueblo members, such as the Tesuque Pueblo celebrating Christmas Day here, however, are far more diverse in personality than Benedict's personality type suggested.*

Whatever the psychological bent of a people . . . death is a stubbornly inescapable fact, and in Zuni [Pueblo], the Apollonian discomfort at not being able to outlaw the upheaval of death on the part of the nearest of kin is very clearly expressed in their institutions. They make as little of death as possible. Funeral rites are the simplest and least dramatic of all the rites they possess.

As reserved as the Pueblo were in the face of death, the Dobuans were, by contrast, given to aggressive excesses. Dobuans believed all deaths were caused by poison or sorcery so that no sooner did a person die than the search began to discover and punish the "murderer." In Benedict's account, the Dobuans made no attempt to repress jealousy and suspicion; rather, they made them the central focus of all behavior surrounding death and other life crises.

A third contrast was presented by the peoples of the Pacific Northwest, including the Kwakiutl. Chapter 10 described the Kwakiutl potlatch (see Figure 10.10), a feast in which the hosts humiliate the guests by heaping gifts on them in quantities too great to repay. Again following Nietzsche, Benedict chose Dionysius, the Greek god of wine and revelry, to epitomize the orgiastic expression of emotion that characterized Pacific Northwest life crises. When a highly ranked Kwakiutl died, his relatives went on a binge of destruction, killing, and suicide. Vengeance was taken against any convenient enemy to remove the "shame of death." Characterizing these people as paranoid megalomaniacs, Benedict wrote (1934, 195):

The segment of human behaviour which the Northwest Coast has marked out to institutionalize in its culture is one which is recognized as abnormal in our civilization. . . . The megalomaniac paranoid trend is a . . . danger in our society. [On the Northwest Coast it is regarded as] the essential attribute of the ideal man.

Reactions to Benedict. Benedict's approach to culture gained a wide audience, but anthropologists were

concerned at her sweeping generalizations about these three societies. Some anthropologists were uncomfortable with her use of catchwords like *Apollonian* and *Dionysian,* which do not have clear, operational definitions. Rather than evaluating her hypothesis from a neutral stance, Benedict picked and chose evidence to suit her preconception, ignoring or minimizing evidence that did not fit the picture she wanted to draw. In spite of the public success of her writings, many anthropologists responded critically. One ethnographer felt that Benedict's depiction of the Pacific Northwest people as paranoid megalomaniacs was one-sided. In her article "The Amiable Side of Kwakiutl Life," Helen Codere (1956) illustrated aspects of Pacific Northwest behavior that do not correspond to the "Dionysian" label.

Furthermore, Benedict's book seemed to suggest that the personality traits she described belonged equally to every member of each group she described. By not making allowance for varying personality types, Benedict helped perpetuate the fiction that there is no variety, deviance, or change in tribal societies. Finally, Benedict did not suggest what is responsible for the differences and similarities in personality in different societies. She sidestepped this question by quoting a Digger Indian proverb: "In the beginning God gave to every people a cup of clay, and from this cup they drank their life" (Benedict 1934; xvi). While this is an appealing statement, a cup of clay does not a scientific explanation make.

In spite of its failings, Benedict's work called attention to the importance of personality types as aspects of culture. Anthropologists, psychologists, and psychiatrists began to study "culture and personality." Some investigators searched for ways to describe and measure personality structures cross-culturally. Others looked for explanations of how personality traits are established in society. Later students of culture and personality proposed hypotheses concerning the links between personality organization and other aspects of culture, helping to fill the gap that Benedict's Digger Indian proverb left open.

Models of Personality

Since Benedict's work, anthropologists have utilized various models of personality (Barnouw 1979) to describe and analyze culture and personality variables. A

conflict model suggests that there are separate, competing forces within each individual. Perhaps the most influential is Sigmund Freud's "anatomy of the mental personality," which postulates the existence of three parts: the **id**, the lustful, appetitive part of the personality, which is driven by instinct and constantly strives for gratification; the **ego**, which mediates between the individual and the surrounding environment and helps bring desires into touch with reality; and the **superego**, the rule-oriented aspect of the personality, which is responsive to social conditioning.

Freud's model suggests that as a child develops into an adult in society, the basic forces of the personality undergo realignment, which, if successful, results in an equilibrium of these forces and a successful adjustment to life. Certain processes, like the so-called Oedipal conflict, are independent of the cultural context. Freud suggested that a young boy normally dreams of obtaining sexual gratification from his mother and feels intense rivalry with his father (see Chapter 13). As he grows older, he realizes that he cannot fulfill his fantasy, and he is forced to repress his desire to kill his father and make love to his mother. Paradoxically, it is this very repression, according to Freud, which leads to the foundation of religion, law, and morality (see Chapters 13 and 22).

Freud's model has been challenged by critics who feel that his view of the stern, authoritarian father and heavy sexual repression was a reflection more of what he saw around him in turn-of-the-century Austria than of universal human conditions. As we have seen, Freud knew almost nothing about non-Western culture and so was poorly equipped to discuss universal human tendencies. Bronislaw Malinowski used his data collected in the Trobriand Islands to challenge some of Freud's claims (Malinowski 1953).

Malinowski showed that, contrary to the Freudian pattern, "In the Trobriands there is no friction between father and son. . . . The ambivalent attitude of veneration and dislike is felt between a man and his mother's brother, while the repressed sexual attitude of incestuous temptations can be formed only toward his sister" (Malinowski 1953, 80). This may be a function of the matrilineal kinship system: Trobriand men do not support their own families; a woman and her household are supported by her brother. Since authority and inheritance are in the female line, a boy and his own father have a relaxed, friendly relationship, while relations between a boy and his mother's brother (the main authority figure) tend to be tense and strained. This would suggest that Freud's view of the Oedipus complex is culture bound. On the other hand, Malinowski implicitly acknowledged tension between Trobriander boys and their maternal uncles, similar to the Oedipus complex, so his work tends to support Freud's model.

Other models of personality do not assume the existence of antagonistic forces within the individual. A **fulfillment model** (Barnouw 1979) views personality as a set of behaviors appropriate to fulfill the requirements set by the cultural environment. Malinowski viewed culture as functioning to fulfill human needs, and cultural personality was simply an extension of that. In Malinowski's scheme, people with aggressive personalities would simply be adapting to a need for defense.

Another model, called the **consistency model** (Barnouw 1979), presumes that people behave in conformity with a mental template of correct behavior. Deviations from this template cause anxiety, so people try to behave in a manner consistent with the model. Using this model, some anthropologists have attempted to formulate the rules by which people judge their own and others' behavior. Ethnologist Ward Goodenough, for example, constructed a "duty scale" for Truk Islanders, a Micronesian people (1963). The scale was based on answers to hundreds of questions that Goodenough put to the Trukese in an eliciting framework similar to that employed by D'Andrade (see Chapter 3). Goodenough presented different social obligations in pairs and asked which one took precedence. The problem with template models is that they cannot account for deviations from cultural prescriptions or changes that occur over time.

APPROACHES TO CULTURE AND PERSONALITY

Anthropological research on culture and personality has moved well beyond the rather crude attempts by Benedict and others to characterize entire cultural traditions in terms of a few ideal types. Some experts have sought to address the question of whether certain cultural personality types occur within a given state or country. This approach is of great interest to political scientists and sociologists who are interested in voting behavior and attitudes about public policy decisions. Anthropologists, however, have been more heavily involved in developing measures of distinctive cultural personality.

National Character Studies

Perhaps the most familiar notions of cultural personality are in ideas about **national character.** This idea refers to a typical set of behavior traits or a personality structure common to the population of a certain country. The Greek historian Herodotus, writing 2,400 years ago, frequently referred to the peculiar characteristics of people from different nations as an explanation for why they behaved as they did in military campaigns, conquests, and other activities.

American Character in the 1830s: de Tocqueville. One of the best-known attempts to portray the national character of an entire country was Alexis de Tocqueville's *Democracy in America,* a French historian's account of American society in the 1830s. The book has been hailed as a masterpiece, and many of Tocqueville's predictions have come true. His work was not so much a description as a diagnosis of the effects of democracy and equality on thought and behavior. Tocqueville contrasts the "aristocratic" nations of Europe to "democratic" nations like the United States. He saw Americans as pragmatic, opti-

mistic, flexible, self-interested, and independent minded: "They owe nothing to any man, they expect nothing from any man; they acquire the habit of always considering themselves as standing alone, and they are apt to imagine that their whole destiny is in their own hands" (1945, vol. 2, 105). Paradoxically, Tocqueville also felt that democracy robbed people of true individuality, forcing them to be conformists.

Tocqueville's insights are often intuitively accurate, but it would be impossible to replicate his study because he does not report the observations on which they are based. Nor does he attempt to account for variation within American society. His work is the forerunner of studies of **political culture** in political science. However, the modern tradition takes pains to reveal the data on which conclusions were drawn, such as surveys, interviews, and analysis of election returns.

American Character in the 1950s: Riesman. Sociologist David Riesman brought the national character approach up to date with his book *The Lonely Crowd* in 1952. The study is based on specific evidence and attempts to account for regional and social variation. Using a fulfillment model, Riesman suggested that societies in different stages of development encourage different personality traits. Before entering a phase of dynamic growth, a society will encourage **tradition-directed personalities.** A society undergoing rapid growth is likely to favor **inner-directed personalities.** After growth slows and stagnation sets in,

---

conflict model A model of individual personality that assumes separate, competing forces within each person.

id According to Freud's model of personality, the lustful, appetitive part of the personality, which is driven by instinct and the desire for gratification.

ego According to Freud's model of personality, the part of the personality that mediates between the individual and the surrounding environment, bringing desires into touch with reality.

superego According to Freud's model of personality, the rule-oriented aspect of the personality, which is responsive to social conditioning.

fulfillment model A model that defines personality as a set of behaviors appropriate to fulfill the requirements set by the cultural environment.

consistency model A model that defines personality in terms of a mental template that guides people to behave in culturally acceptable ways.

national character A set of behaviors, thoughts, and feelings characteristic of the people of a country.

political culture The unique traits of political structure and process in a specific society.

tradition-directed personality According to Riesman, a personality type that accepts traditional values; encouraged by the socialization process in folk societies, which change very slowly.

inner-directed personality According to Riesman, a personality type tending toward individualistic goals, such as the accumulation of wealth or the pursuit of fame; common in societies undergoing rapid social change.

Figure 24.2 *National character studies often result in shallow, stereotypical images of a society based on insufficient evidence. Shown here is a Tai Chi class in Tiananmen Square, Beijing, and an outdoor exercise class in the United States. Chinese culture is often characterized as group oriented; on the basis of these two photos, could we say the same about American culture?*

the favored personality type is **other directed**. Riesman believed that in 1950 the United States was undergoing a transition from a period of rapid growth and change with relatively high social mobility in which individuals defined their own goals to a period of slower growth and change in which individuals were more likely to conform to the requirements set by impersonal institutions. In the phase then emerging, mobility was reduced and individuals were more dependent on others in matters of taste, direction, and goals. For Riesman the American character emerging in the 1950s was more the timid conformist than the rugged individualist.

National character studies typically rely more on insight than on careful accumulation of evidence. Because they usually try to characterize the cultural personality of people living in complex societies divided by regional, class, age, and ethnic distinctions, they often present a shallow, stereotypical picture, which, in attempting to account for all, accounts for none (Figure 24.2). Sociologists have done a great deal of survey research in some countries, in which they take careful account of variation. Often these surveys cannot be boiled down to a single uniform description.

The Study of Basic and Modal Personality

Stimulated by work like Benedict's, anthropologists have tried to approach cultural personality systematically, avoiding some of the pitfalls mentioned above. Abram Kardiner, a psychoanalyst, defined **basic personality** as the "adaptive tools of the individual which are common to every individual in the society" (1939, 237). Convinced that distinctive personality structures exist, investigators have devised or adapted tests able to measure reliably the somewhat elusive dimensions of personality. Many of these tests are known as **projective tests**. Projective tests have no right or wrong answers. They present an image or situation to the tested person as a stimulus, relying on him or her to supply the answers. The results are "scored" or analyzed by one or more experienced analysts, different from the person who administered the test. Projective tests were devised as diagnostic tools in Western societies, and there is skepticism about their validity for non-Western groups. In some cases, the tests have been translated or modified to fit the cultural context in which they are used.

One of the earliest anthropological studies of cultural personality was *The People of Alor* by Cora Du Bois (1944). In this study, Du Bois substituted a statistical concept, **modal personality**, for the idea of basic personality structure. Alor is an island in Indonesia whose people lived by planting maize, rice, and other crops. Du Bois worked in a community called Atimelang during the period of Dutch colonial control. At the time of her study there was also a growing cash economy involving pigs and the circulation of ceremonial objects. Women were the primary cultivators, while men busied themselves with financial transactions. During her 18-month stay, Du Bois collected autobiographies from several informants. She also administered Rorschach ("ink blot") tests and other projective tests to 37 Atimelangers. Psychoanalyst Abram Kardiner collaborated with Du Bois. He visited Alor briefly and analyzed the life histories and dreams Du Bois collected, while another psychoanalyst, who knew little about Alor, independently analyzed the Rorschach tests.

The two analyses were remarkably consistent. Both investigators found the Alorese to be lonely, distrustful people with little capacity for creativity and no ability to form lasting relationships. This was manifested in a high divorce rate. Many of the Alorese reported abandonment and mistreatment by parents, especially their mothers. In one autobiography, Mangma recounted that when he was a boy, his mother wanted him to weed a garden for her. When he refused, Mangma's mother tied his hands together and left him in the house. He ran away and lived with a relative for a year. Later he cleared and planted his own garden, but when he went to harvest it, his mother had taken the crop for herself. Mangma's boyhood memories include this description of practicing archery with a friend:

> When Fanmale hit the target many times, I would beat him over the head with a bow. When I hit the target many times, he would hit me over the head with a bow. We were always quarreling. Then we said we had better stop target shooting. We stopped being friends. . . . I threw out Fanmale. [Du Bois 1944, 195]

Unable to accept each other's success, their rivalry led to quarrels; rather than ending the quarrels, they ended their friendship. There were comparable stories in other autobiographies and clues to the same kind of behavior in the Rorschach responses.

Du Bois also made direct observations of behavior. She observed that babies were carried around in their

---

other-directed personality According to Riesman, a personality type that is sensitive to the moods and needs of other people and responds to external change; favored in societies that have already undergone rapid social change and have reached a relatively stable plateau.

basic personality The pattern of personality traits that is taught to members of a society from childhood.

projective test A test that examines the influence of personality on perceptions of objects and events in the external world.

modal personality The type of personality that appears most frequently in a society.

mothers' shawls until weaning. As soon as children learned to walk, however, mothers tended to leave them alone for the day with little supervision and no food. Thus the triumph of learning to walk became for the child an occasion of deprivation and loss. Children were prone to temper tantrums, especially when their mothers left for the fields in the morning. Du Bois observed that adults frequently teased and threatened children, pretending to cut off their ears or hands with knives.

Du Bois's work provided rich documentation and the means for independent corroboration of her analysis. She did not, however, overcome the **sample bias.** She interviewed and tested only a small portion of the population, and she did not draw her sample randomly. In fact Du Bois admitted that her sample was biased (1944, 191):

> The persons from whom autobiographies were secured do not represent the ideal or "type" person of Atimelang. The most successful men said they were too busy with their financial and ceremonial affairs to spend the time required for telling a life history. . . . The "ideal" women of Atimelang, of whom there were a few, were either too unassertive or too engrossed in work to come daily to my house. . . . However, the autobiographies given here do represent, on the whole, average Atimelang adults.

The assumption that there is a basic personality type shared by all members of a culture needs to be tested. Many investigators disagree with that assumption. Du Bois was more concerned with establishing a modal personality type than with accounting for the diversity of personalities among the Alorese. Du Bois helped establish cultural personality as a scientific concept, but her work left serious questions unanswered. One of the most important concerns the underlying causes of Alorese personality.

THE FORMATION OF CULTURAL PERSONALITY

It is practically a truism that personalities differ because of different experiences people have while they are growing up. Early in the development of the discipline, anthropologists began to focus on developmental stages, perhaps because of the stress laid on this by the Freudians and other schools of psychology. The basic question addressed was whether there is a universal pattern of human development—a finding that would support a biological basis for development—or whether cultural factors determine the pattern of personality development. Later anthropologists began to pose specific questions about how personality traits emerged.

Is There a Universal Pattern of Human Development?

In 1928 Margaret Mead published the influential book *Coming of Age in Samoa,* in which she suggested that adolescence is not necessarily a turbulent emotional period for Samoan girls as it is in Western societies. Her conclusions indicated that much of what Westerners considered biologically determined about female puberty was actually culture bound. More than 50 years later, anthropologist Derek Freeman challenged Mead's conclusions in a book, *Margaret Mead and Samoa* (1984). Freeman suggested that Mead had been "taken in" by her informants, who minimized the amount of conflict and turbulence in Samoan adolescence. Freeman presented his own data, which led to other conclusions. Because of differences in the time and place of data collection, it is impossible to determine whether the two accounts differ because of culture change, regional variation, or differences in fieldwork technique. In any case, it is noteworthy that Freeman's research methods were not markedly different from Mead's. Freeman concluded that Mead was so intent on demonstrating the primacy of cultural over biological variables that she ignored the universal, biologically based aspects of adolescence.

Although Freeman's critique was not decisive, many studies on female puberty do show that there are biologically programmed developmental timetables. Hormones are released that regulate growth, changes in body form and function, and moods and emotions. The exact timing and expression of these changes depends heavily on environmental factors such as diet, physical activities, and social attitudes toward these changes. Still, nearly all investigators agree that there is an important biological basis for the emotional changes that occur at puberty. Just how these interact with cultural values and expectations of children is not known (Schlegel & Barry 1986).

A recent study at Harvard University shows that the debate over "nature versus nurture" is still far from settled (AAUW 1991). The study surveyed 3,000 individuals across the United States between the ages of 9 and 15. The results show that most children entering adolescence undergo a decline in self-esteem. Among several measures, a key indicator was the teen's agreement or disagreement with the statement, "I'm happy the way I am." A good deal of the change in self-esteem is probably environmental, as children leave the relatively sheltered environment of their families, play groups, and elementary schools and enter the more competitive academic, athletic, and social worlds of middle and high schools. However, part of the difference is probably biological, a response to the hormonal changes occurring between the ages of 12 and 14. There is a striking difference between boys and girls in their responses: Boys seem to suffer less decline in self-esteem than girls (Figure 24.3). Again, this may be partly environmental, because it is well known that adult expectations and peer pressure have different effects on boys and girls. However, the size of the difference suggests that the effect, whatever it is, is very powerful.

The cultural component arises when the female group is stratified by ethnicity. Among three broad categories designated in this study, African American girls, Hispanic girls, and non-Hispanic white girls, there are striking differences. These differences are unlikely to be biologically based for reasons we have discussed in Chapter 8. Hispanic girls suffer the greatest decline in self-esteem, from 68 percent agreement with the indicator statement to 30 percent. White girls are next, dropping from 55 percent agreement to only 22 percent. African American girls, on the other hand, show only a slight drop in self-esteem with age, according to the measure used (see Figure 24.3). These data must be interpreted against a backdrop of differences in social values, experiences in the education system, and in life chances in general. The conclusions that may emerge are that biological factors probably have an important role in the decline in self-esteem as seen in the differences between boys' and girls' responses, but that cultural factors are also significant.

People continue to undergo developmental changes in biological function as well as in behavior and outlook throughout life. Recently a few anthropologists have focused on middle-aged males and females and the elderly (Brandes 1985, Brown 1982, Sokolovsky 1990). An important finding of these studies is that developmental stages occur after puberty. Little is known about the biological or hormonal changes that take place, although these probably play a role. Psychologist Daniel J. Levinson and his coworkers carried out interviews with 40 men in the northeastern United States to study life patterns. On the basis of their interviews, the investigators constructed a chart of the male life cycle (Figure 24.4). Many American men go through what is known as a **midlife crisis**. Levinson and his coworkers described this period as the midlife transition (1978, 191):

> As in all transitions, a man must come to terms with the past and prepare for the future. Three major tasks must be worked on: (1) to terminate the era of early adulthood, (2) to begin middle adulthood discarding some old elements and adding some new ones, (3) to deal with profound polarities concerning (a) youth and age, (b) destruction and creation, (c) masculine vs. feminine, (d) attachment and separateness.

One wonders whether Melanesian or central Russian men go through similar stages and attempt to resolve similar questions. A great deal remains to be learned about the transitions of adult life and how they vary cross-culturally (Brown 1982).

---

sample bias A sampling error in which the subset of a universe selected for study is not likely to be representative of the total universe.

midlife crisis In American culture, a transition period that occurs as a person passes from early adulthood into the middle adulthood, which often requires the redefinition of personal values.

Figure 24.3   *The decline in self-esteem in the transition from childhood to adolescence as measured in a 1991 study. Both cultural and biological factors play a role in the decline. Source: American Association of University Women 1991 nationwide poll of 3,000 students aged 9–15.*

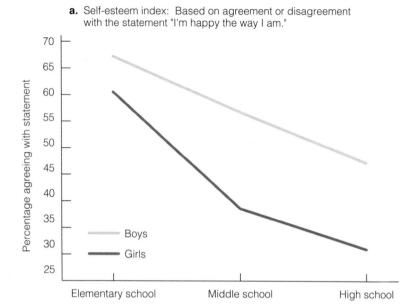

a. Self-esteem index: Based on agreement or disagreement with the statement "I'm happy the way I am."

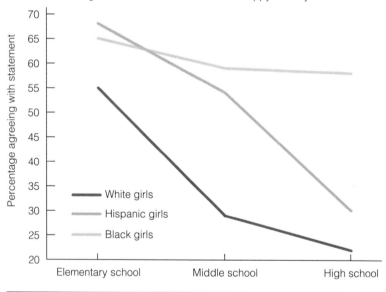

b. Self-esteem index (Girls): Based on agreement or disagreement with the statement "I'm happy the way I am."

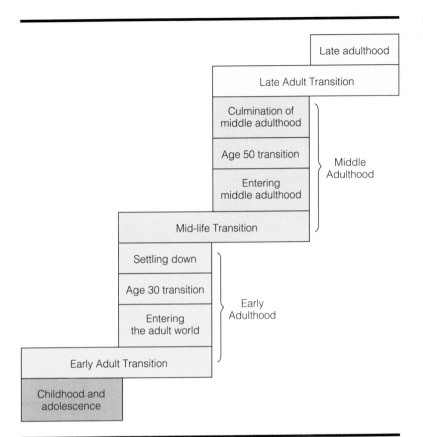

Figure 24.4 *Developmental stages in the life of U.S. males.*

The Influence of Child-Rearing Practices

Freudian theory and other psychological theories stress early childhood experiences as the foundation for personality structures. People sharing a cultural tradition often have a common set of beliefs and practices concerning how to raise a child. For example, Nancy Flowers reported (personal communication 1977) that the Xavante of central Brazil almost never punish or scold small children. They are indulgent and patient to a degree that astounds outsiders. When a Xavante boy reaches ten years of age, however, he is separated from his family and sent to live in a "bachelor's hut" (Maybury-Lewis 1967). He is considered a man only after passing through an ordeal that includes a night submerged in water and hours of standing at attention while older men threaten and kick dust on him (Figure 15.4). Could these common experiences be the cause of the Xavante male personality structure?

Child-rearing practices have attracted the most attention of all the theories of personality formation. Some early theories suggested relationships between cultural personality and a single factor in child rearing (Figure 24.5). Gorer and Rickman (1949) suggested that there was a relationship between the Russian national character and the once-common practice of "swaddling" infants in tightly wrapped clothes. Young Russians were so restricted in movement that when released they could not control themselves. Thus, the theory goes, they became a people given to long periods of brooding silence punctuated by outbursts of uncontrollable rage. This was the explanation for the Bolshevik revolution and Stalinist repression. The theory ignores the facts that children elsewhere who are tightly swaddled do not follow this pattern as adults and that many places where babies are never swaddled have experienced convulsive political movements. Attempts to establish connections between a few features of child rearing and adult personality

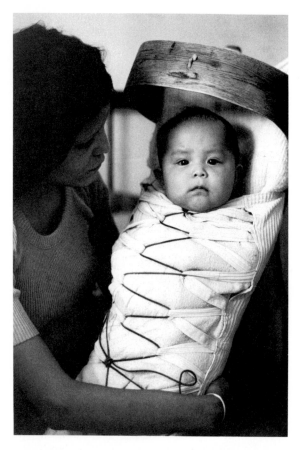

Figure 24.5 *Many Native American women traditionally kept their infants swaddled in cradleboards, which limited their infants' mobility. Attempts by some theorists to link this child-rearing practice with an adult personality characterized by uncontrollable bursts of anger have proven unsuccessful.*

structure have not been successful (Harris 1968, 445–447).

Caudill and Weinstein (1969) made detailed observations of newborn infants and their mothers in middle-class Japanese and North American homes. Although the samples were small (30 families in each group), there was a clear difference between the groups. The Japanese mothers held their babies more, trying to lull them. The American mothers stimulated their babies more, talking to them frequently. The Japanese babies were less active and quieter than the American babies. This seems consistent with adult behavior differences: The Japanese seem more disci-

plined and responsive to authority than Americans and more willing to subordinate their personal aims to those of the group. Still, one can hardly describe recent Japanese achievements in conquering world markets as passive or submissive.

The Influence of Subsistence Patterns

A pioneer study by Herbert Barry, Irvin Child, and Margaret Bacon (1959) suggested that child-rearing practices differed according to the economic system prevalent in a society. For example, in societies relying primarily on agriculture or herding,

> future food supply seems to be best assured by faithful adherence designed to maintain the good health of the herd [or crops]. Under these conditions, there [will] be a premium on obedience to the older and wiser, and on responsibility in faithful performance of the routine laid down by custom. . . . At an opposite extreme is subsistence primarily through hunting or fishing, with no means for extended storing of the catch. Here individual initiative and development of high individual skill seems to be at a premium. [Barry, Child, and Bacon 1959, 52]

Later studies bypassed child rearing as an intervening variable and sought to demonstrate a direct relationship between cultural personality and the activities of adults. One of the most sophisticated studies was done by Walter Goldschmidt and a group of collaborators during the early 1960s. Their research used an experimental model designed to distinguish between cultural influences received through traditional transmission of values and the influence of particular subsistence pursuits. The researchers selected four different East African tribal groups belonging to two major linguistic families (Table 24.1). The Sebei and Pokot speak related Kalenjin languages. The Kamba and Hehe are Bantu speakers. Goldschmidt studied two communities from each group, one depending primarily on plant cultivation, the other primarily on cattle herding (Goldschmidt 1965). Thus there were three intersecting variables in the research designs: language, ethnicity, and subsistence system.

To compare the four groups, the investigators used a battery of questionnaires and projective tests administered under controlled conditions in the native lan-

Tribe	Language	Personality Traits
Sebe	Kalenjin	Concerned with health; jealous, hostile
Pokot	Kalenjin	Concerned with cattle, beauty, sex
Kamba	Bantu	Fearful of poverty; emotionally restrained; males dominant
Hehe	Bantu	Aggressive, authoritarian, distrustful, secretive

Sources: Goldschmidt 1965, Edgerton 1965.

Table 24.1   Cultural Personality in Four East African Tribal Groups

guages. The results showed consistent personality differences among the four (see Table 24.1). These traits were not necessarily characteristic of every single member of each of these groups. They represent what statisticians call "central tendencies" in outlook and behavior as determined by the tests. Most of the traits were equally prevalent in women and men. There were some similarities based on historical connections. The two Kalenjin-speaking groups—Sebei and Pokot—were less concerned with witchcraft than the Bantu, presumably as part of their shared cultural heritage. The Kalenjin speakers desired both sons and daughters, while the Bantu speakers preferred sons. The Bantu were more focused on land and wealth than the Kalenjin, who were more likely to respect a prophet than a rich man.

Having established cultural and historical differences and similarities, the investigators turned to differences in subsistence activities. Psychological anthropologist Robert Edgerton, working with the Goldschmidt team's data, compared the herding group to the agricultural group in each of the four ethnic groups. He wanted to find out whether the kind of activities in which the people engaged had an influence on their cultural personality. By comparing pairs within groups of the same ethnic and historical background, he could control for "cultural" and historical differences.

Herding and agriculture are subsistence pursuits that involve different relationships to the habitat. The African herder is likely to work alone or with small groups of close relatives. His property is movable and he may range over a wide area, leading his flock of cattle or goats to suitable pastures, which vary as the seasons and other conditions change. He needs to be self-reliant, able to make decisions on his own, and ready to defend his flocks from predatory animals or other people. The cultivator is likely to be more sedentary, living in a more densely packed community; he or she must cooperate with a wider circle of people, often including nonrelatives. Since fields and residences occupy fixed locations, it is necessary to accommodate the needs and demands of neighbors, avoid conflict, and be willing to negotiate.

Edgerton found that there were statistically significant differences between herders and cultivators that cut across cultural and historical factors. Cultivators were more likely to consult supernatural diviners or each other before making decisions, while the herders did not. Farmers valued hard work more than the herders; cultivators were generally more hostile and suspicious than the herders. In terms of personality, "the farmers tend to be indirect, abstract, given to fantasy, more anxious, less able to deal with their emotions, and less able to control their impulses. The herders, on the contrary, are direct, open, bound to reality, and their emotions, though constricted, are under control" (Edgerton 1965, 446).

This evidence suggests that the environment and the activities by which people adapt to their environment can influence their personalities, independently of the influence of tradition. Keep in mind that these descriptive terms have been operationally defined in terms of the test instruments and do not have the same connotations they do in everyday conversation (see Chapter 2). To say that East African cultivators are more anxious than herders is not to judge their way of life negatively. The East African studies show that there are multiple influences on cultural personality, including cultural traditions, probably transmitted through child rearing and traceable to the general ecological adaptation of the group.

The Influence of Historical Factors

Immediate events and conditions may also have an effect on personality and behavior. In the Alorese case, can we be certain that the abrupt separation from the mother is the primary factor responsible for the distrustful, quarrelsome Alorese personality? Ethnographers working elsewhere in Melanesia have reported similar situations—women leaving their children and going off to work in the fields—without the same kind of personalities as the Alorese. Other factors may be responsible. Du Bois herself suggested that the high incidence of disease, such as dysentery, respiratory infections, malaria, and yaws, might be factors affecting personality development in Alor (Barnouw 1979, 123).

Another factor that Du Bois apparently did not consider was the political instability of Alorese life (Figure 24.6). In 1939 Alor was not just an isolated tribal society steeped in its own tradition. The Atimelangers shared the island of Alor with speakers of several dialects of at least eight different languages (Du Bois 1944, 14). The island was visited by the Portuguese during the age of exploration. Chinese merchants trading along the coast sparked a mercantile economy during the 19th century. Indonesian

Muslims had established themselves along the coast. Relations between them and the inland peoples were tense and distrustful. There was frequent warfare and headhunting among groups of villages. The Rajah appointed by the Dutch administration was murdered 20 years before Du Bois arrived. In reprisal the Dutch forced the Atimelangers to move their villages from traditional mountain locations into the valleys. The autobiographies contain accounts of brutal and arbitrary acts by colonial authorities. One Atimelanger told Du Bois that when he was a boy, "people were working in Likuwatang making the new trail [demanded by the Dutch to provide access]. We were moving stones when a soldier came and hit me across the neck with a thorny branch" (1944, 241). The economic situation also appears to have been highly unstable, perhaps a factor in the distrustful makeup of the Alorese personality:

> If an Atimelang plays with gusto the financial role his culture assigns him, his time will be taken up with the manipulation of . . . investments. [Because] currencies are not strictly standardized . . . there is ample play in the system for endless bargaining. In addition, debts are rarely paid except under the pressure of dunning. [Du Bois 1944, 24]

Figure 24.6   *This photo taken by Cora Du Bois in 1938 shows the Alorese elders watching the children play at lego-lego, a traditional circle dance. Their mothers' absence alone was probably not the sole cause of the distrustful personalities these children developed; economic, health, and political factors probably also contributed.*

In other words, there were many features of the political and economic environment that added to the uncertainty and distrust of life in Alor. The Alorese personality could have been an adaptation to one or more of these factors.

The cultural personality of a people may be affected by child-rearing practices, by disease patterns, by the political climate, and by the economic system. In turn, personality may have an effect on these factors. Economic life on Alor may be so turbulent because of the Alorese personalities who participate in it. The only way to sort out cause from effect in such cases is to look back in history and try to learn which events took place before others. Personality factors may well respond to historical conditions, and one would expect them to change over time as conditions change.

The Influence of Biological Factors

During the 19th century many writers suggested that there were biologically heritable differences in intelligence, inventiveness, cultural capacity, and other human qualities among different groups of people. Often these theories were used to justify colonial domination or exploitation. When anthropology emerged as an independent discipline in the early 20th century, many of the pioneers reacted strongly against this scientific racism. As part of this struggle, most anthropologists rejected biological approaches to behavior, asserting that race and culture were entirely separate categories (see Chapter 8). Eight decades later, anthropologists have begun to reconsider some hypotheses regarding biological influences on behavior.

It is well established that behavior traits can be inherited. There is evidence that biological inheritance plays a role in schizophrenia, depression, alcoholism, and obesity, the causes of which were once believed to be purely environmental. A debate is raging at this time over whether criminality is also a heritable trait. As such questions are raised, many old problems arise anew. If there is an inherited biological element in these behavior traits, what role does the environment play? The suspicion that the new theories are politically motivated is always present. For example, if the

theory that criminality is inherited were to be widely accepted, we might expect proposals for radically different approaches for treatment of criminals, more oriented to imprisonment than to rehabilitation.

Physiological Conditions. The Qolla of Peru and Bolivia are a subculture consisting of several hundred thousand Aymara and Quechua speakers living at high altitudes in the Andes range. Many ethnographers have studied the Qolla, and from their work emerges a fairly consistent picture of an aggressive, hostile, melancholy, jealous, distrustful, cruel, and vengeful personality (Table 24.2). The Qolla are heavy users of alcohol and coca (a narcotic made from the same plant used in producing cocaine). Much of their hostility is released when they are inebriated. Ralph Bolton, an ethnographer whose work on *susto* we discussed in Chapter 2, reported (1973, 229):

> The Qolla, as I have observed them, tend to swagger, especially when inebriated, and at such times they frequently indulge in monologues describing their own ferocity while laughing at the puniness of their enemies. *"Noqa q'ari kani karaho,"* they shout, gesticulating wildly in the air, as if in the face of the person being insulted. "I am a man, dammit! You, you are nothing but a dog, an ass, excrement!"

The Qolla are quick to resort to violence; Bolton's data suggests they are among the world's most homicidal people. They also engage in frequent disputes over insults real and imagined, theft, crop damages, and other affairs. While Qolla ideals refer to the need for self-defense, they do not advocate aggression for its own sake. "Instead," Bolton writes, "their moral code demands of them charity, compassion, and cooperation with all men" (1973, 339).

What explains the high level of hostility and aggression among the Qolla when their own values condemn it? Investigators have pointed to various factors, such as the harsh environment at extremely high altitudes, poor nutrition, high disease rates, high drug and alcohol use, and centuries of abuse by the Spanish and later, independent governments. But similar conditions are found elsewhere without these same effects.

Bolton suggested that the high level of aggression among the Qolla was due to a physiological condition.

Table 24.2 Personality Traits Reported by Ethnographers of the Qolla

Paredes	Forbes	Bandelier
Distrustful	Submissive	Distrustful
Pessimistic	Reflective	Submissive
Doubtful of everything	Silent	Neglectful
Expect only the bad	Cruel	Gruff
Fearful	Highly suspicious	Malicious
Noncreative impulses	Intense hate	Quarrelsome
Submissive	Distrustful	Rancorous
Hostile	Noncommunicative	Dishonest
Self-pitying		Cruel
		Pugnacious

Carter	Labarre	Romero
Anxious	Apprehensive	Reticent
Hostile	Crafty	Silent
Submissive	Treacherous	Melancholic
Utilitarian	Violent	Distrustful
Deceitful	Hostile	No imagination
Vengeful	Turbulent	Cruel
Fatalistic	Sullen	No aspirations
Miserly	Humble	Emotionally unstable
Distrustful	Melancholic	
Little appreciation for original thought	Submissive	
Unstable	Pugnacious	
Boastful	Bad humor	
	Emotionally morose	
	Jealous	
	Vindictive	

Tschopik	Squier
Anxious	Sullen
Hostile	Cruel
Irresponsible	
Submissive	
Disorderly	
Utilitarian	

Source: Bolton 1973, 228.

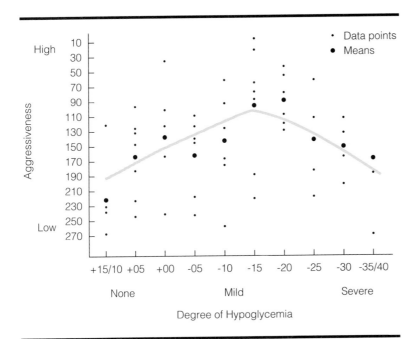

Figure 24.7 *The relationship between hypoglycemia and aggression in the Qolla population.*

Hypoglycemia is a condition of low sugar levels in the bloodstream, which is thought by some medical authorities to be related to extreme irritability and aggression as well as other symptoms ranging from headache to shock. Based on the medical literature, Bolton hypothesized a curvilinear relationship between hypoglycemia and aggression. According to this hypothesis, mildly hypoglycemic men as measured by a glucose tolerance test (GTT) would be the most aggressive; those with severe hypoglycemia would be too debilitated by other symptoms to be aggressive (Figure 24.7).

Bolton drew a sample of adult males in a particular village and administered the GTT to them. Bolton found that there was a high level of hypoglycemia in the Qolla population he tested. He also asked a set of village informants who knew them all to rank the men in the sample from most aggressive to least aggressive. There was fairly high agreement among the three in-

formants about who the most aggressive people were. Bolton then correlated the aggression rankings with the GTT results. The results were consistent with Bolton's hypothesis that mild hypoglycemia is related to aggression. Bolton did not know why so many Qolla were hypoglycemic. The condition could be congenital, or it might be related to environmental features such as diet and high altitude.

Substance Use and Abuse. There are also nonheritable biological influences on behavior. People use many substances that alter mood and behavior. These include alcohol, tobacco, caffeine, marijuana, coca, cocaine, peyote, LSD, amphetamines, tranquilizers, antidepressants, and many other prescription drugs, plus many other hallucinogens and opiates. In some cases, use of **psychoactive drugs** is part of religious behavior. We have already mentioned the ritual use of alcohol in religious fiestas in Mesoamerica (Chapters

---

hypoglycemia A medical condition caused by low blood sugar.

psychoactive drugs Drugs that have an effect on the mental states or behavior of people.

18 and 22) and the use of hallucinogens in the spirit quest of the Yanomamo (Chapter 22). Individuals who use these drugs experience and display dramatic changes in mood and behavior. The Yanomamo encounter their *hekura* spirits, while the Tzeltal Maya may simply nod off into a passive stupor.

There are two observations pertinent to this ritual use of drugs: First, use of these substances is defined as normal and natural in the cultural system of these groups. It is not defined as "substance abuse" as it would be in North America. However, the fact that the use of psychoactive substances is woven into the fabric of many cultural traditions does not mean that these substances are not dangerous to the user and others. Some cross-cultural studies suggest that alcohol use is generally a means of dealing with anxiety (Horton 1943, Bacon, Barry, and Child 1965), but the evidence is contradictory and it is difficult to define anxiety cross-culturally. In the United States, the compulsive use of alcohol is often defined as a disease. Does this mean that some aspects of normal cultural behavior are unhealthful and even dangerous? There is little doubt that this is so, and here, as elsewhere, we depart from a purely relativistic stance.

The other observation about the ritual use of drugs is that the behavior in which the individuals engage while under the influence of these drugs is not necessarily wild, unpredictable, or unacceptable to others. Although the users may "lose their senses," they are not purely "under the influence" of alcohol or drugs. Anthropologist Lola Romanucci-Ross (1986) points out that the drug or alcohol user generally follows a "script" for proper behavior while in an altered state.

These observations concerning ritual use of psychoactive substances can be extended to their use in general. The behavior of an alcohol or drug user conforms to culture-specific norms, varying from place to place. A person who gets drunk at a Christmas party in Cleveland may "lose his inhibitions" and kiss a coworker, but he is unlikely to take his clothes off, defecate in public, beat up the boss, or violate other norms no matter how drunk he may be. Drunks and people "high on drugs" are usually "under control," but it is a different kind of control and different rules apply. Thus even in altered states of consciousness, individuals express a limited range of culturally patterned behaviors and traits. Cultural personality can encompass a broad spectrum of individual differences.

SUMMARY

- *Personality* is a term referring to relatively stable features of individual thought and behavior.
- *Cultural personality* refers to the range of personality traits selected within a particular cultural context.
- Ruth Benedict's *Patterns of Culture* was one of the first systematic attempts to deal with cultural personality.
- National character studies have a long history of attempting to define the cultural personality of entire countries. These studies, like Benedict's, often make sweeping, unsupported generalizations from the individual to the group. They often fail to indicate how the particular portrait of individual personality was drawn or how typical it is of the entire population.
- Some studies have focused on the progression of stages in personality development in different cultural traditions. Some societies put more stress on particular transitions than others through rites of passage or other special treatment.
- A debate has developed in anthropology and psychology over the universality of certain important transitions, such as the turbulent transition to puberty for adolescent girls. In their zeal to affirm the cultural construction of personality, some anthropologists may have understated the significance of certain sharp divides in human development.
- Many studies have attempted to explain the basic causes of personality differences and similarities. The most common approach has been a Freudian psychological approach, which presumes that all individuals pass through certain stages and that there is a specific interplay between basic personality forces. Some investigators have challenged the universality of these stages for all societies, but there is evidence for Freudian conflicts even in non-Western societies.
- Most investigators point to child-rearing practices as the primary influence on adult personality structure. There is reason to believe that other factors are important, such as the political and economic environment and certain heritable biological features.

GET INVOLVED

1. Make a list of 20 to 30 personality traits (or get one from a standardized psychological profile test). Design a questionnaire in which you identify each of the major social, ethnic, or national groups in your area and include the list of personality traits identified by numbers or letters. Administer the questionnaire to at least 100 people, asking the respondents to list the five traits that best apply to each ethnic group listed on the questionnaire. The respondents should not identify themselves, but they should check off their own nationality. Tabulate the results, showing the overall results. If you have enough responses, you can use the results to compare the "self-image" of people from groups to the image that members of other groups have of them. Hold a discussion on the results, including people who filled out the questionnaire. Focus on whether the results reflect stereotypes that people have of other groups or actual group personality differences.

2. Hold a group discussion among people living in your area from different social and ethnic backgrounds. Inquire about variations in child-rearing customs, such as freedom of movement allowed to infants, toilet training, feeding schedules, reactions to crying and whining, punishments used, and tolerance of children in adult groups. What connections can you draw between these child-rearing customs and the typical personality of adults in each culture?

3. Do cultural personality traits change over time? Pick a society for which a literature exists over an extended period, such as the Germans, the Vietnamese, the Cheyenne, or the Porteños (natives of Buenos Aires). Can you detect a change in reports of typical personality over time? Is such change a function of the subjectivity of reporting or can you link it to changes in conditions over time? Are there aspects of personality that remain stable over time?

SUGGESTED READINGS

Benedict, Ruth. 1934. *Patterns of culture.* New York: Mentor.

Henry, Jules. 1963. American schoolrooms: Learning the nightmare. From *Columbia University Forum.**

Ochs, Elinor. 1988. *Culture and language development.* Cambridge: Cambridge University Press.

Shostak, Marjorie. 1978. Memories of a !Kung girlhood. *Human Nature* 80 (June): 82–88.

Sorenson, E. Richard. 1977. Growing up as a Fore. *Smithsonian,* May.*

*This section is anthologized in *Applying Anthropology,* 2d ed., ed. A. Podolefsky and P. J. Brown (Mountain View, Calif.: Mayfield, 1992).

Sioux Nationalism

As a junior in college, Robert Daniels helped form a student group that sent volunteers to several western reservations. He went to Pine Ridge Reservation in South Dakota, home of the Oglala Sioux, or Lakota, and ran a summer recreation program for a few dozen kids. In 1963, he returned to Pine Ridge as a graduate student in anthropology to study the multiple, and often contradictory, social and cultural identities that mark reservation life. Now a professor of anthropology at the University of North Carolina, he felt compelled to return to Pine Ridge Reservation in December 1990 to attend the commemorative ceremonies marking the 100th anniversary of the Massacre of Big Foot's band of Lakota by the 7th Cavalry at Wounded Knee.

Robert Daniels in front of a poster for KILI, a Lakota-language radio station operating on several reservations in the Dakotas.

Thirty years ago, as an undergraduate who had switched majors from mathematics to anthropology, I jumped at the chance to spend the summer doing voluntary work on an Indian reservation. I was sent to Pine Ridge, South Dakota, home of the Oglala, the largest subdivision of the Lakota or Western Sioux. There I was shocked by the pervasive problems faced in American society by those who choose to maintain their Lakota identity but deeply heartened by the insight and creativity with which they nevertheless do so.

The Oglala are the people of Red Cloud and Crazy Horse, Black Elk and Lame Deer, the Little Bighorn and Wounded Knee, the subject of innumerable films (*A Man Called Horse, Dances with Wolves*). It is a difficult heritage to bear, being the worldwide icon of "Indianness," descendants of the quintessential romantic figures in the American past yet at every turn labeled "survivors," "a remnant population," and "the great losers" in our national history.

During my first week I was taken to a church encampment 14 miles from the agency. I borrowed a blanket and slept on the cold ground, sweated in the dusty midday heat, chewed my way through boiled buffalo and fried bread, and listened to Protestant hymns sung in Lakota for hours on end. Most disorienting, however, was the fact that we were camped at Wounded Knee, just a few hundred yards from the site of the last (1890), most infamous massacre of native Americans by the U.S. Army. Initially the site struck me as a place of tragedy and shame, but I began to understand from my hosts that Wounded Knee is a consecrated place and that their presence was a statement of continuity and faith kept with the Lakota buried there in the mass grave.

I returned two summers later, now a graduate student, equipped with an old station wagon with a sleeping bag in the back. After a few weeks I met a wonderful family who were deeply involved in Lakota music and dance. As I accompanied them on and off the reservation, I found myself caught up in the complexities of expressive culture in many emotionally and socially charged situations. I remember, in particular, the powwow at Wounded Knee on July 4th. I had not expected the Lakota to celebrate anything relating to the federal government. What I found was *Sioux nationalism.* The term refers not to the Sioux Nation (although that is a significant focus of identity and political discussion on the reservation) but to patriotism for the American nation, Lakota style. Every dance starts and ends with the Sioux national anthem. This anthem to the American flag is not a translation of "The Star Spangled Banner" but a Lakota melody. Written in 1955, the words can be translated approximately as, "The flag of the President will stand forever. Underneath it the people will continue to flourish. For this purpose have I done this." The song is intended to portray a soldier preparing to meet his death in defense of

This photograph, taken around 1900, shows two Oglala men dressed for a dance; note the unusual adornment on the man on the left.

the United States. As was explained to me repeatedly, "It's not one particular soldier, but *all* soldiers."

If the dance is outdoors, the anthem accompanies the raising and lowering of the American flag. In the early 1960s the flags used were those given by the Veterans Administration to the next of kin of Lakota men who had lost their lives in World War II and the Korean War. In 1969 I attended a giveaway and re-presentation of a flag in honor of a young man killed in Vietnam.

It may seem utterly illogical that the Oglala would honor the American flag and the U.S. Army on the very ground where the 7th Calvary gunned down defenseless families, where one of the infant survivors, found clinging to her dead mother, was wearing a bonnet with an American flag beaded on it. But logic about such things can be small minded and crippling. The Lakota overcome tragedies of the past by refusing to accept a definition of self based on ill will. They set aside frustrations by focusing on current sacrifices and contributions rather than past victimizations. The anthem transforms the warrior past from a psychological liability to an asset in dealing with the present. The contradictions imposed by the larger society are turned back against it.

I once heard Ben Black Elk greet tourists who had stopped to watch a group of Oglala dancing in full regalia just outside Custer State Park. He picked up the microphone and said, "Welcome to America. We hope you like it. We hope you'll stay a long time!" You must admit it's a fresh perspective on an old problem.

THE SIOUX NATIONAL ANTHEM

Tunkashila	yanpi	ta	wapaha	kin	han
Grandfather (i.e. The President's	our	his	eagle feather staff flag)	the	
Owihanke	shni		he najin	kte	lo
End	without		stands	will	
Iyoklatetan	han	oyate	kin	han	wicicage	kta
Underneath		people	the		flourish	will
Ca	lecamu		welo		
Therefore	I do this				

The Flag of the United States will stand forever.
Underneath it the people will flourish.
Therefore I do this.

627

REFERENCES

▲▲▲

Abrahams, Roger D. 1962. Playing the dozens. *Journal of American Folklore* 75:209–220.

————. 1970. *Deep down in the jungle.* Chicago: Aldine de Gruyter.

————. 1974. Black talking on the streets. In *Explorations in the ethnography of speaking,* ed. R. Bauman and J. Sherzer, 240–262. New York: Cambridge University Press.

Acheson, James. 1972. Limited good or limited goods? *American Anthropologist* 74:1152–1169.

————. 1974. Reply to Foster. *American Anthropologist* 76:57–62.

Adams, Robert McC. 1966. *The Evolution of urban society: Early Mesopotamia and prehispanic Mexico.* Chicago: Aldine de Gruyter.

Aguilar, Francisco de. 1963. The chronicle of Fray Francisco de Aguilar. In *The conquistadores,* ed. Patricia de Fuentes, 134–164. New York: Orion.

American Association of University Women. 1991. Shortchanging girls, shortchanging America. Washington, D.C.: AAUW.

Arcury, Thomas A. 1984. Household composition and economic change in a rural community, 1900–1980. *American Ethnologist* 11 (4): 677–698.

Ardrey, Robert. 1976. *The hunting hypothesis.* New York: Atheneum.

Arens, William. 1979. *The man-eating myth.* London: Oxford University Press.

Bacon, Margaret, Herbert Barry, and Irving Child, eds. 1965. A cross-cultural study of drinking. *Quarterly Studies on Alcohol* Supplement 3.

Barlett, Peggy F., and Peter J. Brown. 1985. Agricultural development and the quality of life. In *Applying anthropology. See* Podolefsky and Brown 1992.

Barnouw, Victor. 1979. *Culture and personality.* 3d ed. Homewood, Ill.: Dorsey.

Barrett, Richard A. 1984. *Culture and conduct.* Belmont, Calif.: Wadsworth.

Barry, Herbert, Irvin Child, and Margaret Bacon. 1959. Relation of child training to subsistence economy. *American Anthropologist* 61:51–63.

Barth, Fredrik. 1969. *Ethnic groups and boundaries.* Boston: Little, Brown.

Barton, Roy F. 1919. Ifugao law. *University of California Publications in American Archaeology and Ethnology* 15 (1): 1–186.

Bascom, William. 1969. *The Yoruba of southwestern Nigeria.* New York: Holt, Rinehart and Winston.

————. 1984. The forms of folklore. In *Sacred narrative,* ed. Alan Dundes, 5–29. Berkeley: University of California Press.

Basso, Keith H. 1973. To give up on words. In *Language and social context,* ed. Pier Paolo Giglioli, 67–86. Baltimore: Penguin.

————. 1986. *The Cibecue Apache.* New York: Holt, Rinehart and Winston.

Beattie, John. 1960. *Bunyoro.* New York: Holt, Rinehart and Winston.

Benedict, Ruth. 1934. *Patterns of culture.* New York: Mentor.

Benson, Herbert, and David P. McCallie. 1979. Angina pectoris and the placebo effect. *New England Journal of Medicine* 300 (25): 1424–1429.

Berdan, Frances F. 1982. *The Aztecs of Central Mexico.* New York: Holt, Rinehart and Winston.

Berlin, Brent, and Paul Kay. 1969. *Basic color terms.* Berkeley: University of California Press.

Berreman, Gerald D. 1960. Caste in India and the United States. *American Journal of Sociology* 66:120–127.

————. 1962. Behind many masks. Society for Applied Anthropology Monograph no. 4.

Bickerton, Derek. 1983. Creole languages. *Scientific American* 249 (1): 116–122.

Binford, Lewis R., and C. K. Ho. 1985. Taphonomy at a distance:

Zhoukoudian, the cave home of Beijing Man. *Current Anthropology* 26:413–443.

———. 1981. *Bones.* New York: Academic Press.

Binford, Lewis R. 1983. *In pursuit of the past.* New York: Thames and Hudson.

Birdwhistle, R. L. 1970. *Kinesics and context.* Philadelphia: University of Pennsylvania Press.

Blinderman, Charles. 1986. *The Piltdown inquest.* Buffalo, N.Y.: Prometheus.

Bodley, John H. 1988. *Tribal peoples and development issues.* Mountain View, Calif.: Mayfield.

Bohannan, Laura. 1966. Shakespeare in the bush. In *Applying anthropology. See* Podolefsky and Brown 1992.

Bohannan, Paul. 1961. Artist and critic in an African society. In *The artist in tribal society,* ed. Marian Smith, 85–94. New York: The Free Press.

Bolton, Ralph. 1973. Aggression and hypoglycemia among the Qolla. *Ethnology* 12 (3): 227–258.

———. 1981. Susto, hostility and hypoglycemia. *Ethnology* 20 (4): 261–276.

———. 1984. The hypoglycemia-aggression hypothesis. *Current Anthropology* 25 (1): 1–53.

Borgerhoff-Mulder, Monique. 1988. Kipsigis bridewealth payments. In *Human Reproductive Behavior,* ed. L. Betzig, M. Borgerhoff-Mulder, and P. Turke, 65–82. Cambridge: Cambridge University Press.

Boserup, Ester. 1965. *The conditions of agricultural growth.* Chicago: Aldine de Gruyter.

Boulier, B. I. 1976. *Children and household economic activity in Laguna, Philippines.* Quezon City, Philippines: Institute for Economic Development.

Bourgois, Philippe. 1989. Just another night on Crack Street. In *Applying anthropology. See* Podolefsky and Brown 1992.

Brain, C. K., and Andrew Sillen. 1988. Evidence from the Swartkrans cave for the earliest use of fire. *Nature* 336:464–466.

Brandes, Stanley. 1985. *Forty: The age and the symbol.* Knoxville: University of Tennessee Press.

Briggs, Jean L. 1970. Kapluna daughter. In *Women in the field,* ed. Peggy Gold. Chicago: Aldine de Gruyter.

Brockway, Lucile H. 1979. *Science and colonial expansion.* New York: Academic Press.

Brown, Judith K. 1982. Cross-cultural perspectives on middle-aged women. *Current Anthropology* 23:143–156.

Brown, Judith K., and Virginia Kerns, eds. 1985. *In her prime.* South Hadley, Mass.: Bergin and Garvey.

Brown, Paula. 1978. *Highland peoples of New Guinea.* New York: Cambridge University Press.

Brundtland Commission. 1987. *Our common future.* Oxford: Oxford University Press.

Buikstra, Jane. 1985. Demography, diet, and health. In *Techniques for the analysis of prehistoric diet,* ed. R. I. Gilbert and J. H. Mielke, 359–422. New York: Academic Press.

Bunn, Henry T., and Ellen M. Kroll. 1986. Systematic butchery by Plio/Pleistocene hominids at Olduvai Gorge, Tanzania. *Current Anthropology* 27 (5): 431–452.

Bunzel, Ruth. 1929. *The Pueblo potter.* New York: Columbia University Press.

Burling, Robbins. 1964. Componential analysis. *American Anthropologist* 66:20–28.

Butzer, Karl W. 1982. *Archeology at human ecology.* Cambridge: Cambridge University Press.

Campbell, Bernard G. ed. 1985. *Humankind emerging.* 4th ed. Boston: Little, Brown.

Cancian, Frank. 1965. *Economics and prestige in a Maya community.* Stanford: Stanford University Press.

Cannon, Walter B. 1942. Voodoo death. *American Anthropologist* 44:169–181.

Caplow, Theodore, Howard M. Bahr, and Bruce A. Chadwick. 1982. *Middletown families.* Minneapolis: University of Minnesota Press.

———. 1983. *All faithful people.* Minneapolis: University of Minnesota Press.

Carneiro, Robert L. 1970a. A theory of the origin of the state. *Science* 169:733–738.

———. 1970b. Scale analysis, evolutionary sequences and the rating of cultures. In *A handbook of method in cultural anthropology,* ed. Raoul Naroll and Ronald Cohen, 834–871. Garden City, N.Y.: Natural History Press.

———. 1987. Cross-currents in the theory of state formation. *American Ethnologist* 14:756–770.

Carroll, Lewis. 1872. Jabberwocky. In *Through the looking glass.* London: Macmillan.

Carson, Rachel. 1962. *The silent spring.* Boston: Houghton Mifflin.

Cartmill, Matt, David Pilbeam, and Glynn Isaac. 1986. One hundred years of paleoanthropology. *American Scientist* 74:410–420.

Caudill, William, and Helen Weinstein. 1969. Maternal care and infant behavior in Japan and America. *Psychiatry* 29:244–266.

Chagnon, Napoleon A. 1966. *Yanomamo warfare, social organization and marriage alliances.* Ann Arbor, Mich.: University Microfilms.

———. 1974. *Studying the Yanomamo.* New York: Holt, Rinehart and Winston.

———. 1983. *Yanomamo: The Fierce People.* 3d ed. New York: Holt, Rinehart and Winston.

Chagnon, Napoleon A., and Timothy Ashe. 1970. *The feast.* Watertown, Mass.: Documentary Educational Resources.

Childe, V. Gordon. 1951. *Man makes himself.* New York: New American Library.

Chomsky, Noam. 1957. *Syntactic structures.* The Hague: Mouton.

Ciochon, Russell L., and John Fleagle, eds. 1987. *Primate evolution and human origins.* New York: Aldine de Gruyter.

Codere, Helen. 1956. The amiable side of Kwakiutl life. *American Anthropologist* 58:334–351.

Cohen, Mark N. 1977. *The food crisis in prehistory.* New Haven: Yale University Press.

Cowgill, George. 1975a. Population pressure as a non-explanation. In *Population studies in archaeology and biological anthropology,* ed. A. C. Swedlund, 127–131. Washington, D.C.: Society of American Archaeology.

———. 1975b. On causes and consequences of ancient and modern population changes. *American Anthropologist* 77:505–525.

Crocker, William H. 1967. The Canela messianic movement. In *Atlas do sympósio sobre a biota Amazónica* 2 (Antropologia): 69–83.

Crosby, Alfred W. 1972. *The Colombian exchange.* Westport, Conn.: Greenwood.

Dahlberg, F., ed. 1981. *Woman the gatherer.* New Haven: Yale University Press.

D'Andrade, Roy G. 1976. A propositional analysis of U.S. American beliefs about illness. In *Meaning in anthropology,* ed. K. H. Basso and H. A. Selby. Albuquerque: University of New Mexico Press.

Darwin, Charles. 1859. *On the origin of species.* London: J. Murray.

Davis, Wade. 1985. Hallucinogenic plants and their use in traditional societies. In *Applying anthropology. See* Podolefsky and Brown 1992.

Dawkins, Richard. 1976. *The selfish gene.* New York: Oxford University Press.

Deng, Francis M. 1972. *The Dinka of the Sudan.* Prospect, Ill.: Waveland.

Dentan, Robert K. 1968. *The Semai.* New York: Holt, Rinehart and Winston.

Diamond, Jared. 1987. The worst mistake in the history of the human race. In *Applying anthropology. See* Podolefsky and Brown 1992.

Diamond, Norma. 1969. *K'un Shen: A Taiwan village.* New York: Holt, Rinehart and Winston.

Divale, William, and Marvin Harris. 1976. Population, warfare and the male supremacist complex. *American Anthropologist* 78:521–538.

Dobkin de Rios, Marlene. 1974. The influence of psychotropic flora and fauna on Maya religion. *Current Anthropology* 15 (2): 147–164.

Dobyns, H. F., P. L. Doughty, and H. D. Laswell, eds. 1971. *Peasants, power and applied social change.* Beverly Hills, Calif.: Sage.

Dollard, John. 1937. Caste and class in a southern town. New York: Anchor Books.

Dornstreich, Mark D., and G. E. B. Morren. 1974. Does New Guinea cannibalism have nutritional value? *Human Ecology* 2 (1): 1–12.

Douglas, Mary. 1989. Taboo. In *Magic, witchcraft, and religion. See* Lehmann and Myers 1989.

———. 1966. *Purity and danger.* London: Routledge & Kegan Paul.

Douglas, Mary, and A. Wildavski. 1982. *Risk and culture.* Berkeley: University of California Press.

Du Bois, Cora. 1944. *The people of Alor.* 2 vols. New York: Harper.

Durkheim, Émile. 1961. *The elementary forms of the religious life.* New York: The Free Press.

Eastwell, Harry D. 1989. Voodoo death and the mechanism for dispatch of the dying in East Arnhem, Australia. In *Magic, witchcraft and religion. See* Lehmann and Myers 1989.

Eaton, S. Boyd, and Melvin Konner. 1985. Ancient genes and modern health. In *Applying anthropology. See* Podolefsky and Brown 1992.

Eckert, Penelope. 1989. *Jocks and burnouts.* New York: Teacher's College Press.

Edgerton, Robert B. 1965. Cultural vs ecological factors in the expression of values, attitudes, and personality characteristics. *American Anthropologist* 67:442–447.

———. 1966. Conceptions of psychosis in four East African societies. *American Anthropologist* 68:408–425.

Elder, Joseph W. 1968. Cultural and social factors in agricultural development. In *Development and change in traditional agriculture.* Asian Studies Center Occasional Paper, South Asia Series, No. 7. East Lansing: Michigan State University Press.

Eldredge, N., and I. Tattersall. 1982. *The myths of human evolution.* New York: Columbia University Press.

Elgin, Suzette H. 1979. *What is linguistics?* Englewood Cliffs, N.J.: Prentice-Hall.

Ember, Carol R. 1983. The relative decline in women's contribution to agriculture with intensification. *American Anthropologist* 85:285–304.

Ember, Carol R., Melvin Ember, and Burton Pasternak. 1974. On the development of unilineal descent. *Journal of Anthropological Research* 30:69–94.

Ember, Melvin. 1975. On the origin and extension of the incest taboo. *Behavior Science Research* 10:249–281.

Ember, Melvin, and Carol R. Ember. 1971. The conditions favoring matrilocal versus patrilocal residence. *American Anthropologist* 73:571–594.

———. 1979. Male-female bonding: A cross-species study of mammals and birds. *Behavior Science Research* 14:37–56.

———. n.d. Resource unpredictability, mistrust, and war. *Journal of Conflict Resolution.* In press.

Estioko-Griffin, Agnes. 1986. Daughters of the forest. *Natural History* 95 (5): 36–43.

Evans-Pritchard, E. E. 1940. *The Nuer.* New York: Oxford University Press.

Fagan, Brian M. 1987. *The great journey.* London: Thames and Hudson.

Falk, Dean. 1975. Comparative anatomy of the larynx in man and the chimpanzee. *American Journal of Physical Anthropology* 43:123–132.

Feifer, George. 1964. Justice in Moscow. In *Law and warfare,* ed. P. Bohannan, 93–113. Garden City, N.Y.: Natural History Press.

Fernea, Elizabeth W., and Robert A. Fernea. 1979. A look behind the veil. *Human Nature,* 2 (1).

Fine, Benjamin. 1975. *The stranglehold of the I.Q.* Garden City, N.Y.: Doubleday.

Finkler, Kaja. 1983. Studying outcomes of Mexican spiritualist therapy. In *The anthropology of medicine, See* Romanucci-Ross, Moerman, and Tancredi 1983.

Fischer, John. 1961. Art styles as cultural cognitive maps. *American Anthropologist* 63:80.

Food and Agriculture Organization. 1963. *FAO production yearbook,* Vol. 36. Rome: FAO.

Forge, Anthony. 1967. The Abelam artist. In *Man in adaptation,* ed. Y. Cohen, 438–450. Chicago: Aldine de Gruyter.

Foster, George M. 1965. Peasant society and the image of limited good. *American Anthropologist* 67 (2): 293–315.

Foster, George M., and Barbara G. Anderson. 1978. *Medical anthropology.* New York: Wiley.

Fox, Robin. 1983. *Kinship and marriage.* Cambridge: Cambridge University Press.

Frake, Charles. 1961. The diagnosis of disease among the Subanun of Mindanao. *American Anthropologist* 63:113–132.

Frank, André G. 1966. The development of underdevelopment. *Monthly Review* 18:17–31.

Fraser, Thomas M., Jr. 1966. *Fisherman of South Thailand.* New York: Holt, Rinehart and Winston.

Fredman, Ruth Gruber. 1981. *The Passover seder.* Philadelphia: University of Pennsylvania Press.

Freeman, Derek. 1984. *Margaret Mead and Samoa.* Cambridge, Harvard University Press.

Freeman, James M. 1979. *Untouchable*. Stanford: Stanford University Press.

Freud, Sigmund. 1928. *The future of an illusion*. London: Hogarth Press.

Friedl, Ernestine. 1978. Society and sex roles. In *Applying anthropology*. See Podolefsky and Brown 1992.

Frisancho, A. R. 1970. Developmental responses to high altitude hypoxia. *American Journal of Physical Anthropology* 32:401–407.

————. 1979. *Human adaptation*. 2d ed. St. Louis, Mo.: Mosby.

Furst, Peter T. 1978. Spirulina. *Human Nature* 1 (3): 60–65.

Gal, Susan. 1987. Code-switching and consciousness in the European periphery. *American Ethnologist* 14:637–654.

Galanter, Marc. 1981. Overview: Charismatic religious sects and psychiatry. Mimeo.

Gardner, B. T., and R. A. Gardner. 1971. Two way communication with an infant chimpanzee. In *Behavior of non-human primates*, Vol. 4, ed. A. M. Schrier and F. Stollnitz, 117–184. New York: Academic Press.

Gargett, Robert H. 1989. Grave shortcomings. *Current Anthropology* 30 (2): 157–190.

Gartlan, J. S. 1968. Structure and function in primate society. *Folia Primatologica* 8 (2): 89–120.

Gaulin, Stephen J. C., and R. W. FitzGerald. 1986. Sex differences in spatial ability. *American Naturalist* 127:74–88.

Geertz, Clifford. 1972. Deep play. *Daedalus* 101:1–37.

Gibbons, Ann. 1991. Deja vu all over again. *Science* 251:1561–1562.

Gibbs, James L. 1963. The Kpelle moot. In *Applying anthropology*. See Podolefsky and Brown 1992.

Gleason, H. A. 1955. *Workbook in descriptive linguistics*. New York: Holt, Rinehart and Winston.

————. 1961. *An introduction to descriptive linguistics*. Rev. ed. New York: Holt, Rinehart and Winston.

Gmelch, George. 1971. Baseball magic. *Transaction* 8 (8): 39–41, 54.

Goldberg, Steven. 1973. *The inevitability of patriarchy*. New York: Morrow.

Goldschmidt, Walter. 1965. Variation and adaptability of culture. *American Anthropologist* 67:400–447.

Goldstein, Melvyn C. 1987. When brothers share a wife. In *Applying anthropology*. See Podolefsky and Brown 1992.

Goodall, Jane. 1971. *In the shadow of man*. Boston: Houghton Mifflin.

Goodenough, Ward. 1963. Some applications of Guttman scale analysis to ethnography and culture theory. *Southwestern Journal of Anthropology* 19:235–250.

Goodman, Alan H., and George J. Armelagos. 1985. Death and disease at Dr. Dickson's mounds. In *Applying anthropology. See* Podolefsky and Brown 1992.

Gordon, Diana R. 1984. Equal protection, unequal justice. In *Minority report,* ed. L. W. Dunbar. New York: Pantheon.

Gorer, Geoffrey, and J. Rickman. 1949. *The people of Great Russia*. London: Cresset.

Gough, E. Kathleen. 1959. The Nayars and the definition of marriage. *Journal of the Royal Anthropological Institute* 89:23–34.

Gould, Stephen Jay. 1981. *The mismeasure of man*. New York: Norton.

————. 1983. What, if anything, is a zebra? In *Hen's teeth and horse's toes*. New York: Norton.

————. 1987. Bushes all the way down. *Natural History* 98 (2): 20–28.

Green, Edward C. 1987. The integration of modern and traditional health sectors in Swaziland. In *Applying anthropology. See* Podolefsky and Brown 1992.

Gregor, Thomas. 1977. *Mehinaku*. Chicago: University of Chicago Press.

————. 1985. *Anxious pleasures*. Chicago: University of Chicago Press.

Greuel, P. J. 1971. The leopard-skin chief. *American Anthropologist* 73:1115–1120.

Gross, Daniel R. 1971. Ritual and conformity. *Ethnology* 10 (1): 129–148.

————. 1975. Protein capture and cultural development in the Amazon basin. *American Anthropologist* 77:526–549.

————. 1984. Time allocation. *Annual Review of Anthropology* 13:519–558.

Gross, Daniel R., and Barbara A. Underwood. 1971. Technological change and caloric costs. *American Anthropologist* 73:725–740.

Gross, Daniel R., George Eiten, Nancy M. Flowers, Maria Francisca Leoi, Madeline Ritter, and Dennis Werner. 1979. Ecology and acculturation among native peoples of Brazil. *Science* 206:1043–1050.

Hage, Per, and Wick R. Miller. 1976. 'Eagle' = 'bird'. *American Ethnologist* 3 (3): 481–488.

Hagen, Everett. 1962. *On the theory of social change*. Homewood, Ill.: Dorsey.

Haley, Alex. 1976. *Roots*. Garden City, N.Y.: Doubleday.

Hall, Edward T. 1959. Space speaks. In *Applying anthropology. See* Podolefsky and Brown 1992.

Hanna, Judith. 1979. *To dance is human*. Austin: University of Texas Press.

Harley, George. 1950. *Masks as agents of social control in northeast Liberia*. Cambridge, Mass.: The Peabody Museum.

Harlow, Harry F. 1959. Love in infant monkeys. *Scientific American* 200:68–74.

Harner, Michael J. 1968. The sound of rushing water. *Natural History* 77 (6): 28–33, 60–61.

————. 1977a. The ecological basis for Aztec sacrifice. *American Ethnologist* 4:117–135.

————. 1977b. The enigma of Aztec sacrifice. *Natural History* 86 (4): 46–51.

Harris, Marvin. 1964. *Patterns of race in the Americas*. New York: Walker.

————. 1968. *The rise of anthropological theory*. New York: Crowell.

————. 1974. *Cows, pigs, wars and witches*. New York: Random House.

————. 1981. *America now*. New York: Simon and Schuster.

————. 1984. Animal capture and Yanomamo warfare. *Journal of Anthropological Research* 40:183–201.

————. 1985. *Good to eat*. New York: Simon and Schuster.

Harrison, Gail G., William L. Rathje, and Wilson W. Hughes. 1975. Food waste behavior in an urban population. In *Applying anthropology. See* Podolefsky and Brown 1992.

Hart, Donn V. 1979. Disease etiologies of Samaran Filipino peasants. In *Cultural and curing,* ed. P. Morley and R. Wallis, 57–98. Pittsburgh: University of Pittsburgh Press.

Hassan, Fekri. 1981. *Demographic anthropology*. New York: Academic.

Heider, Karl G. 1979. *Grand Valley Dani*. New York: Holt, Rinehart and Winston.

Helmer, John, and Neil A. Eddington, eds. 1973. *Urbanman*. New York: Free Press.

Henry, Jules. 1963. American schoolrooms: Learning the nightmare. In *Applying anthropology. See* Podolefsky and Brown 1992.

Herdt, Gilbert. 1981. *Guardians of the flutes*. New York: McGraw-Hill.

Hockett, Charles. 1960. The origin of speech. *Scientific American* 203:89–96.

Hoebel, E. Adamson. 1954. *The law of primitive man*. Cambridge: Harvard University Press.

———. 1960. *The Cheyennes*. New York: Holt, Rinehart and Winston.

———. 1967. Song duels among the Eskimo. In *Law and warfare,* ed. P. Bohannan, 255–262. Garden City, N.Y.: Natural History.

Hoffman, Mark S. 1991. *The world almanac and book of facts*. New York: Pharos Books.

Hole, Frank, K. V. Flannery, and J. Neeley. 1969. *Prehistoric and human ecology of the Deh Luran Plain*. Memoirs of the University of Michigan Museum of Anthropology, No. 1. Ann Arbor: University of Michigan Press.

Holloway, Ralph. 1974. The casts of fossil hominid brains. *Scientific American* 231 (1): 106–115.

Holmberg, Allen R. 1960. Changing community attitudes and values in Peru. In *Social change and Latin America today*. New York: Harper.

Hopkins, Terence K. 1982. *World-systems analysis*. Beverly Hills, Calif.: Sage.

Horton, D. 1943. The functions of alcohol in primitive societies. *Quarterly Journal of Studies of Alcohol* 4:199–320.

Hoselitz, Bert. 1960. *Sociological aspects of economic growth*. Glencoe: Free Press.

Howell, Nancy. 1979. *Demography of the Dobe !Kung*. New York: Academic Press.

Hu, Tai-Li. 1983. My mother-in-law's village. Ph.D. diss., City University of New York.

Itani, Jun'ichiro. 1961. The society of Japanese monkeys. *Japan Quarterly* 8:421–438.

Janus, Christopher G., and W. Brashler. 1975. *The search for Peking Man*. New York: Macmillan.

Janzen, John M. 1978. *The quest for therapy*. Berkeley: University of California Press.

Joans, Barbara. 1984. Problems in Pocatello. In *Applying anthropology. See* Podolefsky and Brown 1992.

Johanson, Donald, and Maitland A. Edey. 1981. Lucy. In *Applying anthropology. See* Podolefsky and Brown 1992.

Johnson, Allen W. 1971. *Sharecroppers of the Sertão*. Stanford: Stanford University Press.

———. 1975. Time allocation in a Machiguenga community. *Ethnology* 14 (3): 301.

———. 1978. In search of the affluent society. In *Applying anthropology. See* Podolefsky and Brown 1992.

———. 1980. Comment on "Does labor time increase with industrialization?" *Current Anthropology* 21:292.

Johnson, Gregory A. 1978. Information sources and the development of decision-making organizations. In *Archaeology as a social science,* ed. C. L. Redman. New York: Academic Press.

Jolly, Clifford. 1970. The seed eaters. *Man* 5:5–26.

Joyce, Christopher, and Eric Stover. 1991. *Witnesses from the grave*. Boston: Little, Brown.

Kaeppler, Adrienne L. 1978. Dance in anthropological perspective. *Annual Review of Anthropology* 7:31–49.

Kardiner, Abram. 1939. *The individual and his society*. New York: Columbia University Press.

Katz, Pearl. 1981. Ritual in the operating room. In *Applying anthropology. See* Podolefsky and Brown 1992.

Katz, Richard. 1982. *Boiling energy*. Cambridge: Harvard University Press.

Katz, S. H., 1975. Traditional maize processing in the New World. *Science* 186:765–773.

Kempton, Willett. 1987a. Two theories of home heat control. In *Cultural models in language and thought,* ed. D. Holland and N. Quinn. New York: Cambridge University Press.

———. 1987b. Variation in folk models and consequent behavior. *American Behavioral Scientist* 31:203–218.

Kertzer, David L. 1988. Flaming crosses and body snatchers. In *Applying anthropology. See* Podolefsky and Brown 1992.

Kim, Seung Kyung. 1990. Capitalism, patriarchy and autonomy. Ph.D. diss., City University of New York.

Kleinman, Arthur. 1978. Three faces of culture-bound syndromes. *Culture, Medicine and Psychiatry* 3:153–166.

Kochman, Thomas, 1970. Toward an ethnography of black American speech behavior. In *Afro-American anthropology,* ed. J. Szwed and N. Whitten, 145–162. New York: The Free Press.

Kohl, Philip. 1974. Seeds of upheaval. Ph.D. diss., Harvard University.

Kolenda, Pauline Mahar. 1963. Toward a model of the Hindu Jajmani system. *Human Organization* 22:11–31.

Konner, Melvin. 1982. *The tangled wing*. New York: Harper.

Kottak, Conrad P. 1978. McDonald's as myth, symbol and ritual. In *Anthropology*. New York: Random House.

———. 1980. *The past in the present*. Ann Arbor: University of Michigan Press.

———. 1982. Anthropological analysis of mass enculturation. In *Researching American culture,* ed. C. P. Kottak, 48–74. Ann Arbor: University of Michigan Press.

———. 1983. *Assault on paradise*. New York: Random House.

———. 1985. Swimming in cross-cultural currents. In *Applying anthropology. See* Podolefsky and Brown 1992.

Kramer, Carol. 1979. *Ethnoarchaeology*. New York: Columbia University Press.

Kroeber, Alfred L. 1917. The superorganic. In *The nature of culture,* 22–51. Chicago: University of Chicago Press, 1952.

———. 1919. Order and changes in fashion. In *The nature of culture,* 332–336. Chicago: University of Chicago Press, 1952.

Kroeber, Alfred L., and Jane Patterson. 1940. Three centuries of women's dress fashions. In *The nature of culture,* 358–372. Chicago: University of Chicago Press, 1952.

Kung, Lydia. 1983. *Factory women in Taiwan*. Ann Arbor: UMI Research Press.

Labov, William. 1972. The social stratification of (r) in New York City department stores. In *Sociolinguistic patterns*. Philadelphia: University of Pennsylvania Press.

———. 1973. Some features of the English of black Americans. In *Varieties of present day English,* ed. R. W. Bailey and J. L. Robinson. New York: Macmillan.

Lamberg-Karlovsky, Carl. 1970. Excavations at Tepe Yahya, Iran:

1967–1969. *American School of Prehistoric Research Bulletin,* No. 27. Peabody Museum, Harvard University.

Lansing, J. Stephen. 1987. Balinese "water temples" and the management of irrigation. *American Anthropologist* 89 (2): 326–341.

Leach, Edmund. 1970. *Claude Lévi-Strauss.* New York: Viking.

Leacock, Eleanor. 1978. Women's status in egalitarian society. *Current Anthropology* 19:247–275.

Lee, Richard B. 1969. Eating Christmas in the Kalahari. In *Applying anthropology. See* Podolefsky and Brown 1992.

———. 1979. *The !Kung San.* Cambridge: Cambridge University Press.

———. 1984. *The Dobe !Kung.* New York: Holt, Rinehart and Winston.

Lees, Susan H., and Daniel Bates. 1974. The origins of specialized nomadic pastoralism. *American Antiquity* 39:187–193.

Lehmann, Arthur C., and James E. Myers, eds. 1989. *Magic, witchcraft, and religion.* 2d ed. Mountain View, Calif.: Mayfield.

Lessa, William A. 1966. *Ulithi.* New York: Holt, Rinehart and Winston.

Lessa, William A., and E. Z. Vogt. 1979. *Reader in comparative religion.* 4th ed. New York: Harper & Row.

Lett, James. 1987. *The human enterprise.* Boulder, Colo.: Westview.

Lévi-Strauss, Claude. 1963. The sorcerer and his magic. In *Magic, witchcraft, and religion. See* Lehmann and Myers 1989.

———. 1965. *Tristes tropiques.* New York: Atheneum.

———. 1976. The story of Asdiwal. In *Structural anthropology,* vol. 2, 146–197. Chicago: University of Chicago Press.

Levinson, Daniel J., C. N. Darrow, E. B. Klein, et al. 1978. *The seasons of a man's life.* New York: Knopf.

Lewin, Roger. 1982. Thread of life. Washington, D.C.: Smithsonian.

———. 1983. Were Lucy's feet made for walking? *Science* 220:700–702.

———. 1984a. DNA reveals surprises in human family tree. *Science* 226:1179–1182.

———. 1984b. *Human evolution.* San Francisco: W. H. Freeman.

———. 1987. *Bones of contention.* New York: Simon and Schuster.

———. 1988. Trees from genes and tongues. *Science* 242:514.

Lewis, Oscar. 1952. Urbanization without breakdown. *Scientific Monthly* 75 (1): 31–41.

Lewontin, R. C., S. Rose, and L. J. Kamin. 1984. *Not in our genes.* New York: Random House.

Lieberman, Philip. 1975. *On the origins of language.* New York: Macmillan.

Lieberman, Phillip, and E. S. Crelin. 1971. On the speech of Neanderthal. *Linguistic Inquiry* 2:203–222.

Lindenbaum, Shirley. 1979. *Kuru sorcery.* Mountain View, Calif.: Mayfield.

Linder, Stefan. 1970. *The harried leisure class.* New York: Columbia University Press.

Loewe, Frederick, and Alan J. Lerner. 1956. My fair lady. New York: Coward-McCann.

Lomax, Alan. 1962. Song structure and social structure. *Ethnology* 1:425–451.

———. 1968. *Folk song style and culture.* American Association for the Advancement of Science, Publication No. 88. Washington, D.C.

Lorenz, Konrad. 1966. *On aggression.* New York: Harcourt, Brace, and World.

Lovejoy, C. Owen. 1981. The origin of man. *Science* 211:341–350.

———. 1988. Evolution of human walking. *Scientific American* (November): 118–125.

Maccoby, Eleanor E. 1973. Sex in the social order. *Science* 182:469–471.

Malefijt, Annemarie de Waal. 1968. *Religion and culture.* New York: Macmillan.

Malinowski, Bronislaw. 1922. *Argonauts of the western Pacific.* London: Routledge.

———. 1948. *Magic, science and religion and other essays.* New York: Doubleday.

———. [1927] 1953. *Sex and repression in savage society.* London: Kegan Paul.

Maraini, Fosco. 1979. The persistence of the ideographic script in the Far East. In *Language and society,* ed. W. C. McCormack and S. A. Wurm, 579–587.

Marcus, Joyce. 1976. The origins of mesoamerican writing. *Annual Review of Anthropology* 5:35–68.

Margolis, Maxine L. 1984. *Mothers and such.* Berkeley: University of California Press.

Marriott, McKim. 1968. Caste ranking of food transactions. *Structure and change in Indian society,* ed. M. B. Singer and B. S. Cohn, 133–171. New York: Wenner-Gren.

Marris, Peter. 1960. Slum clearance and family life in Lagos. *Human Organization* 19:123–128.

Martin, Joann. 1990. Motherhood and power. *American Anthropologist* 17:470–490.

Marx, Jean L. 1989. The cystic fibrosis gene is found. *Science* 245:923–925.

Maybury-Lewis, David. 1967. *Akwe-Shavante society.* Oxford: Clarendon Press.

McClelland, David C. 1961. *The achieving society.* Princeton: Van Nostrand.

McDermott, Jeanne. 1986. Face to face. *Smithsonian* 16 (3): 113–123.

McNeill, William H. 1976. *Plagues and peoples.* Garden City, N.Y.: Doubleday.

Mead, Margaret. 1928. *Coming of age in Samoa.* New York: Morrow.

———. 1935. *Sex and temperament in three primitive societies.* New York: Dell.

———. 1955. *Cultural patterns and technical change.* New York: Mentor.

———. 1970. The art and technology of fieldwork. In *A handbook of method in cultural anthropology,* ed. R. Naroll and R. Cohen, 248–265. New York: Columbia University Press.

Meggit, Mervyn J. 1962. *Desert people.* Sydney, Australia: Angus and Robertson.

Mencher, J. P. 1980. On being untouchable in India. In *Beyond the myths of culture,* ed. E. B. Ross. New York: Academic Press.

Mendonsa, Eugene. 1976. Characteristics of Sisala diviners. In *Magic, witchcraft, and religion. See* Lehmann and Myers 1989.

Miller, Barbara D. 1981. *The endangered sex.* Ithaca, N.Y.: Cornell University Press.

Miner, Horace. 1956. Body ritual among the Nacirema. In *Applying anthropology. See* Podolefsky and Brown 1992.

Moerman, Daniel E. 1983. Physiology and symbols. In *The anthropology of medicine. See* Romanucci-Ross, Moerman, and Tancredi 1983.

Molnar, Stephen. 1983. *Human variation.* 2d ed. Englewood Cliffs, N.J.: Prentice-Hall.

Monaghan, John. 1990. Reciprocity, redistribution, and the transaction of value in the mesoamerican fiesta. *American anthropologist* 17:758–774.

Munroe, R. H., R. L. Munroe, C. Michelson, A. Koel, R. Bolton, C. Bolton. 1983. Time allocation in four societies. *Ethnology* 22 (4): 355–370.

Murdock, George Peter. 1967. *Ethnographic atlas*. Pittsburgh: University of Pittsburgh Press.

Murphy, Robert F. 1959. Social structure and sex antagonism. *Southwestern Journal of Anthropology* 15:84–98.

Murphy, Yolanda, and Robert F. Murphy. 1985. *Women of the forest*. 2d ed. New York: Columbia University Press.

Murray, Gerald F. 1987. The domestication of wood in Haiti. In *Applying anthropology. See* Podolefsky and Brown 1992.

Myers, Robert J. 1972. *Celebrations*. Garden City, N.Y.: Doubleday.

Naroll, Raoul, and Ronald Cohen. 1970. *A handbook of method in cultural anthropology*. New York: Columbia University Press.

Nash, Jeffrey. 1977. Decoding the runner's appearance. In *Conformity and Conflict*. Boston: Little, Brown.

Nash, June. 1970. *In the eyes of the ancestors*. Prospect Heights, Ill.: Waveland.

Neel, J. V. 1970. Lessons from a primitive people. *Science* 170:815–822.

Nelson, Joan. 1979. *Access to power*. Princeton, N.J.: Princeton University Press.

Netting, Robert McC., M. Priscilla Stone, and Glenn Stone. 1989. Koyfar cash cropping. *Human Ecology* 17:299–319.

Newman, Philip L. 1965. *Knowing the Gururumba*. New York: Holt, Rinehart and Winston.

Nissen, Hans J. 1970. Grabung der quadraten K/L XII in Uruk Warka. *Baghdader Mittielungen* 5:102–191.

Oberg, Kalervo. 1955. Types of social structure among the lowland tribes of South and Central America. *American Anthropologist* 57:472–487.

Ochs, Elinor. 1988. *Culture and language development*. Cambridge: Cambridge University Press.

Odum, Eugene. 1983. *Basic ecology*. Philadelphia: Saunders.

Ortiz, Alfonso. 1969. *The Tewa world*. Chicago: Chicago University Press.

Ortiz de Montellano, Bernard R. 1978. Aztec cannibalism. *Science* 200:611–617.

Ortner, Sherry B. 1973. On key symbols. *American Anthropologist* 75:1338–1346.

Ortner, Sherry B., and Harriet Whitehead. 1981. *Sexual meanings*. New York: Cambridge University Press.

Parker, Hilda, and Seymour Parker. 1986. Father-daughter sexual abuse. *American Journal of Orthopsychiatry* 56d:531–549.

Partridge, William L., and Elizabeth M. Eddy. 1987. *Applied anthropology in America*. New York: Columbia University Press.

Pastron, Allen G. 1988. Opportunities in cultural resource management. In *Applying anthropology. See* Podolefsky and Brown 1992.

Perlman, Janice. 1980. *The myth of marginality*. Berkeley: University of California Press.

Petersen, Glenn. 1982. *One man cannot rule a thousand*. Ann Arbor: University of Michigan Press.

Pfeiffer, John E. 1977. *The emergence of society*. New York: McGraw-Hill.

———. 1982. *The creative explosion*. New York: Harper & Row.

Piddocke, Stuart. 1965. The potlatch system of the southern Kwakiutl. *Southwest Journal of Anthropology* 21:244–264.

Pilbeam, David. 1984. The descent of hominoids and hominids. *Scientific American* 250 (3): 84–96.

Pimentel, D., et al. 1973. Food production and the energy crisis. *Science* 182:443–449.

Plattner, Stuart, ed. 1989. *Economic anthropology*. Stanford: Stanford University Press.

Podolefsky, A. 1984. Contemporary warfare in the New Guinea highlands. In *Applying anthropology. See* Podolefsky and Brown 1992.

Podolefsky, A., and P. J. Brown, eds. 1992. *Applying anthropology*. 2d ed. Mountain View, Calif.: Mayfield.

Pool, Robert. 1988. Was Newton wrong? *Science*. 241:789–790.

Pospisil, Leopold. 1963. *The Kapauku Papuans of West New Guinea*. New York: Holt, Rinehart and Winston.

Powdermaker, Hortense. 1966. *Stranger and friend*. New York: Norton.

Premack, David. 1971. Language in chimpanzee? *Science* 172:808–822.

Radcliffe-Brown, A. R. 1924. The mother's brother in South Africa. In *Structure and function in primitive society,* 15–31. New York: The Free Press, 1952.

Ramirez, J. Martin, and Bobbie Sullivan. 1987. The Basque conflict. In *Ethnic conflict,* ed. J. Boucher, D. Landis, and K. A. Arnold. Newbury Park, Calif.: Sage.

Rappaport, Roy A. 1968. *Pigs for the ancestors*. New Haven: Yale University Press.

Redfield, Robert. 1941. *The folk culture of the Yucatan*. Chicago: University of Chicago Press.

———. 1967. Primitive law. In *Studies in the anthropology of conflict,* ed. Paul Bohannan, 3–24. Garden City, N.Y.: Natural History Press.

Reichel-Dolmatoff, Gerardo. 1971. *Amazonian cosmos*. Chicago: Chicago University Press.

Rensberger, Boyce. 1981. Racial odyssey. In *Applying anthropology. See* Podolefsky and Brown 1992.

Richardson, Miles. 1990. The myth teller. In *Cry lonesome and other accounts of the anthropologist's project,* 7–32. Albany: State University of New York Press.

Riesenberg, Saul. 1968. *The native polity of Ponape*. Washington, D.C.: Smithsonian Institution Press.

Riesman, David, Nathan Glazer, and Reuel Denney. 1950. *The lonely crowd*. New Haven: Yale University Press.

Robarchek, Clayton A., and Robert Knox Dentan. 1987. Blood drunkenness and the bloodthirsty Semai. *American Anthropologist* 89 (2): 356–365.

Romanucci-Ross, Lola. 1983. Folk medicine and metaphor in the context of modernization. In *The anthropology of medicine. See* Romanucci-Ross, Moerman, and Tancredi 1983.

———. 1986. *Conflict, violence and morality in a Mexican village*. Chicago: University of Chicago Press.

Romanucci-Ross, Lola, D. E. Moerman, and L. R. Tancredi, eds. 1983. *The anthropology of medicine*. Westport, Conn.: Greenwood.

Root-Bernstein, Robert, and Donald McEachern. 1982. Teaching theories. In *Applying anthropology. See* Podolefsky and Brown 1992.

Rosenhan, D. L. 1973. On being sane in insane places. *Science* 179:250–258.

Rothschild, Nan. 1983. The recognition of leadership in egalitarian societies. In *The development of political organization,* ed. E. Tooker, 165–182. Washington, D.C.: American Ethnological Society.

Rowell, Thelma. 1972. *The social behavior of monkeys.* Baltimore: Penguin.

Rubel, Arthur J., C. W. O'Nell, and R. Collado-Ardon. 1984. *Susto.* Berkeley: University of California Press.

Rubin, Joan. 1968. *National bilingualism in Paraguay.* The Hague: Mouton.

Rumbaugh, D. M., ed. 1977. Language learning by a chimpanzee. New York: Academic Press.

Safa, Helen. 1974. *The urban poor of Puerto Rico.* New York: Holt, Rinehart and Winston.

Sahlins, Marshall D. 1961. The segmentary lineage. *American Anthropologist* 63 (2): 332–345.

———. 1963. Poor man, rich man, big man, chief. *Society and History* 5:285–303.

———. 1972. *Stone age economics.* Chicago: Aldine de Gruyter.

———. 1978. Culture as protein and profit. *New York Review of Books* 25:45–53.

Schlegel, Alice, and Herbert Barry III. 1986. The cultural consequences of female contribution to subsistence. *American Anthropologist* 88 (1): 142–150.

Schneider, David. 1968. *American kinship.* Chicago: University of Chicago Press.

Seeger, Anthony. 1985. *Nature and society in central Brazil.* Cambridge: Harvard University Press.

Service, Elman. 1975. *Origins of the state and civilization.* New York: Norton.

Shapiro, Harry L. 1974. *Peking Man.* New York: Simon and Schuster.

Sharp, Lauriston. 1952. Steel axes for stone-age Australians. *Human Organization* 2:17–22.

Sheets, Payson D. 1987. Dawn of a new stone age in eye surgery. In *Applying anthropology. See* Podolefsky and Brown 1992.

Shepardson, Mary. 1963. Navaho ways in government. *American Anthropologist* 65 (3), part 2.

Shepher, Joseph. 1983. *Incest: A biosocial view.* New York: Academic Press.

Shostak, Marjorie. 1978. Memories of a !Kung girlhood. *Human Nature* 80 (June) 82–88.

———. 1981. *Nisa.* Cambridge: Harvard University Press.

Shoumatoff, Alex. 1985. *The mountain of names.* New York: Simon and Schuster.

Sieber, Roy. 1962. Masks as agents of social control. *African Studies Bulletin* 5 (11): 8–13.

Silberbauer, George. 1981. *Hunter and habitat in the central Kalahari Desert.* Cambridge: Cambridge University Press.

Simmel, Georg. 1903. The metropolis and mental life. In *On individuality and social forms,* ed. D. N. Levine, 324–339. Chicago: University of Chicago Press.

Simons, Elwyn. 1989. Human origins. *Science* 245:1343–1350.

Skelton, Randall R., H. M. McHenry, and G. M. Drawhorn. 1986. Phylogenetic analysis of early hominids. *Current Anthropology* 27 (1): 21–44.

Skinner, B. F. 1957. *Verbal behavior.* New York: Appleton-Century-Crofts.

Slobin, D. I. 1982. Universal and particular in the acquisition of language. In *Language acquisition,* ed. L. Gleitman, 128–170. Cambridge: Cambridge University Press.

Smith, Adam. [1776] 1985. *The wealth of nations.* New York: McGraw-Hill.

Smith, Mary F. 1954. *Baba of Karo.* London: Faber.

Smuts, Barbara. 1991. What are friends for? In *Applying anthropology. See* Podolefsky and Brown 1992.

Snow, Clyde C., and James L. Luke. 1970. The Oklahoma City child disappearances. In *Applying anthropology. See* Podolefsky and Brown 1992.

Sokolovsky, Jay, ed. 1990. *Cultural context of aging.* Westport, Conn.: Greenwood.

Solecki, Ralph. 1971. *Shanidar.* New York: Knopf.

Sorenson, Arthur. 1967. Multilingualism in the northwest Amazon. *American Anthropologist* 69:670–684.

Sorenson, E. Richard. 1977. Growing up as a Fore. *Smithsonian,* May, 106–115.

Soto, Hernando de. 1989. *The other path.* New York: Harper & Row.

Southall, Aidan. 1960. Homicide and suicide among the Alur. In *African homicide and suicide,* ed. P. Bohannan, 214–219. Princeton, N.J.: Princeton University Press.

———. 1973. The density of role relationships as a universal index of urbanization. In *Urban anthropology,* ed. A. Southall. New York: Oxford University Press.

Spiro, Melford E. 1958. *Children of kibbutz.* Cambridge: Harvard University Press.

Spradley, James P. 1971. Beating the drunk charge. In *Conformity and conflict,* ed. J. P. Spradley and D. W. McCurdy. Boston: Little, Brown.

———. 1972. Adaptive stategies of urban nomads. In *The anthropology of urban environments.* Washington, D.C.: Society for Applied Anthropology.

Steward, Julian H. 1949. Development of complex societies. In *Theory of culture change,* 178–209. Urbana: University of Illinois Press.

Strenio, Andrew J. 1981. *The testing trap.* New York: Rawson, Wade.

Stringer, C. B., and P. Andrews. 1988. Genetic and fossil evidence for the origin of modern humans. *Science* 239:1263–1268.

Swanson, Guy. 1960. *The birth of the gods.* Ann Arbor: University of Michigan Press.

Swift, E. M. 1988. No yen to play in Japan. Sports Illustrated, 20 March.

Szasz, Thomas. 1974. *The myth of mental illness.* New York: Harper & Row.

Talmon, Yonina. 1964. Mate selection in collective settlements. *American Sociological Review* 29:491–508.

Tanner, N. M. 1981. *On becoming human.* New York: Cambridge University Press.

Taussig, Michael. 1977. The genesis of capitalism amongst South American peasantry. *Comparative Studies in Society and History* 19:130–155.

———. 1980. *The devil and commodity fetishism in Latin America.* Chapel Hill: University of North Carolina Press.

Terrace, Herbert. 1979. *Nim.* New York: Knopf.

Thomas, R. Brooke. 1973. *Human adaptation to a high Andean energy flow system.* University Park: Pennsylvania State University.

Tierney, John, Lynda Wright, and Karen Springen. 1988. The search for Adam and Eve. In *Applying anthropology. See* Podolefsky and Brown 1992.

Tobias, Phillip V. 1983. Recent advances in the evolution of hominids with especial reference to brain and speech. *Pontifical Academy of Sciences Scripta Varia* 50:85–140.

Tocqueville, Alexis de. 1945. *Democracy in America.* Trans. H. Reeves, ed. F. Bowen. 2 vols. New York: Vintage.

Tonkinson, Robert. 1978. *The Mardudjara aborigines.* New York: Holt, Rinehart and Winston.

Toth, Nicholas. 1985. Archaeological evidence for preferential right-handedness in the lower and middle Pleistocene and its possible implications. *Journal of Human Evolution* 14:607–614.

Trager, Lillian. 1987. Living abroad: Cross-cultural training for families. In *Applying anthropology. See* Podolefsky and Brown 1992.

Trigger, Bruce G. 1969. *The Huron.* New York: Holt, Rinehart and Winston.

Trinkaus, Erik. 1983. *The Shanidar Neandertals.* New York: Academic Press.

Turner, Christy G. II. 1987. The first Americans. *Natural History* 1:6–10.

Turner, Victor. 1967. *The forest of symbols.* Ithaca, N.Y.: Cornell University Press.

———. 1973. Symbols in African ritual. *Science* 179:100–105.

Tylor, Edward B. 1871. *Primitive culture.* London: J. Murray.

———. 1889. On a method of investigating the development of institutions. *Journal of the Royal Anthropological Institute of Great Britain and Ireland* 18:245–272.

Uchendu, V. C. 1965. *The Igbo of southeast Nigeria.* New York: Holt, Rinehart and Winston.

United Nations. 1986. *United Nations statistical yearbook 1983.* New York: United Nations.

United States Department of Labor. 1989. *Handbook for labor and statistics.* Washington, D.C.: Government Printing Office.

Vayda, Andrew P. 1961. A reexamination of Northwest Coast economic systems. *Transactions of the New York Academy of Sciences,* Series II, 23:618–624.

Villa, Paola. 1983. *Terra Amata and the middle Pleistocene archaeological record of Southern France.* Berkeley: University of California Press.

Von Däniken, Erik. 1969. *Chariots of the gods.* New York: Putnam.

Wagley, Charles. 1943. Tapirapé shamanism. *Boletim do Museu Nacional (Antropologia)* 3:61–92.

———. 1968. The concept of social race in the Americas. In *The Latin American tradition.* New York: Columbia University Press.

———. 1977. *Welcome of tears.* New York: Oxford University Press.

Walker, Alan C. 1981. Dietary hypotheses and human evolution. *Philosophical Transcripts of the Royal Society of Britain and Ireland* 292:890–904.

Warner, Richard. 1985. *Recovery from schizophrenia.* London: Routledge & Kegan Paul.

Warner, W. L., J. O. Low, P. S. Lunt, and L. Strole. 1963. *Yankee city.* Abridged ed. New Haven: Yale University Press.

Washington Post, 1984. Wife burning rising in India. 22 September, A10.

Weatherford, J. McIver. 1981. *Tribes on the hill.* New York: Rawson, Wade.

Weber, Max. [1905] 1958. *The Protestant ethic and the spirit of capitalism.* New York: Scribner's.

Werner, Dennis W. 1982. Leadership inheritance and acculturation among the Mekranoti of central Brazil. *Human Organization* 41 (4): 342–345.

———. 1984. *Amazon journey.* New York: Simon and Schuster.

White, Martin King. 1978. *The status of women in preindustrial societies.* Princeton, N.J.: Princeton University Press.

Whorf, Benjamin L. [1936] 1967. The punctual and segmentative aspects of verbs in Hopi. In *Language, thought and reality.* Cambridge: MIT Press.

Wilson, Edward O. 1978. *On human nature.* New York: Bantam.

———. 1984. Snakes and psyche. *Omni* 7 (12): 38.

Witherspoon, Gary. 1980. Language in culture and culture in language. *International Journal of American Linguistics* 46:1–15.

Wittfogel, Karl. 1938. Die theorie die orientalischen gesellschaft. *Zeitschrift für Social Forschung* 7:90–122.

———. 1957. *Oriental despotism.* New Haven: Yale University Press.

Wolf, Arthur P. 1966. Childhood association, sexual attraction and the incest taboo. *American Anthropologist* 68 (4): 883–898.

Wolf, Eric R. 1982. *Europe and the people without history.* Berkeley: University of California Press.

Wolpoff, Milford H. 1980. *Paleoanthropology.* New York: Knopf.

Wolpoff, Milford H., J. N. Spuhler, F. H. Smith, J. Radovic, and G. Pope. 1988. Modern human origins. *Science* 241:772–773.

World Bank. 1990a. *World Bank atlas 1990.* New York: Oxford University Press.

———. 1990b. *World development report 1991.* New York: Oxford University Press.

Worsley, Peter M. 1959. Cargo cults. In *Magic, witchcraft, and religion. See* Lehmann and Myers 1989.

Wright, H. T., and G. A. Johnson. 1975. Population, exchange, and early state formation in southwestern Iran. *American Anthropologist* 77 (2): 267–289.

Zihlman, Adrienne L. 1978. Women in evolution. *Signs* 4:4–20.

———. 1982. *The human evolution coloring book.* New York: Barnes and Noble.

Zubrow, Ezra. 1975. *Prehistoric carrying capacity.* Menlo Park, Calif.: Benjamin-Cummings.

INDEX

CREDITS